新编现代英语语法

Modern English Grammar (Newly Edited)

顾　问　杨元兴
主　编　江沈巨
副主编　高俊丽　蔡炳成　李万豫
　　　　樊永松　胡桢文　朱光成
　　　　朱栋华
审　订　杨元兴

苏州大学出版社

图书在版编目(CIP)数据

新编现代英语语法/江沈巨主编. —苏州：苏州大学出版社，2015.12
ISBN 978-7-5672-1597-9

Ⅰ.①新… Ⅱ.①江… Ⅲ.①英语-语法-高等学校-教材 Ⅳ.①H314

中国版本图书馆CIP数据核字(2015)第294758号

书　　名：	新编现代英语语法
作　　者：	江沈巨　主编
责任编辑：	汤定军
策　　划：	汤定军
装帧设计：	刘　俊
出版发行：	苏州大学出版社(Soochow University Press)
社　　址：	苏州市十梓街1号　邮编：215006
印　　装：	苏州恒久印务有限公司
网　　址：	www.sudapress.com
E - mail：	tangdingjun@suda.edu.cn
邮购热线：	0512-67480030
销售热线：	0512-65225020
开　　本：	787mm×1092mm　1/16　印张：32　字数：968千
版　　次：	2015年12月第1版
印　　次：	2015年12月第1次印装
书　　号：	ISBN 978-7-5672-1597-9
定　　价：	69.80元

凡购本社图书发现印装错误，请与本社联系调换。服务热线：0512-65225020

《新编现代英语语法》编委会

顾　　问	杨元兴
主　　编	江沈巨
副 主 编	高俊丽　蔡炳成　李万豫　樊永松
	胡桢文　朱光成　朱栋华
审　　订	杨元兴
编　　委	（以姓氏笔画为序）
	九　鼎　孔沛琳　元　兴　李万豫
	在　娜　任文莺　朱光成　朱栋华
	江沈巨　杨丽莎　杨　萁　吴文静
	张　莹　陈　彦　罗　欣　赵　诚
	赵明盈　赵雯娟　爱　国　高俊丽
	雪　莲　蔡炳成　蔡艳蕾　樊永松
	胡桢文
策　　划	汤定军
责任编辑	汤定军
封面设计	刘　俊
责任校对	周　敏
责任印制	何桂林

前　言

21世纪的世界已不再是以前的世界了,它已缩小成了"地球村"。中国在走向世界,中国人很多年前就掀起了学习外语的热潮,尤其出现了学习英语的热潮。人们常说,英语是世界"普通话",掌握了英语,就像长了一对翅膀,可以飞向世界。因此,中国要走向世界,要与世界接轨,英语非但不能"走开",而且必须要不断加强,那种"不学ABC,照样干革命"的极左思潮绝不能再来。

在全球化背景下,语言已成为国家综合国力的重要组成部分,也与国家的安全密切相关,重视和加强外语教育能促进改革开放的深入发展。毋庸置疑,外语在促进国际交流、科技进步、经济和国防建设、文化艺术的交流等方面能起到不可估量的推动作用。有关部门应该高瞻远瞩,把握好外语教育的大方向。

要学好英语,一定要掌握它的语音、词汇、语法,注重听、说、读、写能力的培养,而掌握语法是学好英语的一个重要环节。英语,同这个世界一样,也在不断地变化,为此,我们编写的语法书和其他一切有关英语语言方面的书籍都要力求"现代",不能落伍,要及时反映出这种不断变化着的语言新现象。因此,我们这本《新编现代英语语法》也力求做到"现代",除了讲解一些基本语法内容外,还力图反映出现代英语语言和语法研究的新内容,为读者解决一些英语学习上碰到的疑惑。

《新编现代英语语法》立足于现代英语语言发展的基础,把英语语法中的主要内容列为论述对象,系统地加以阐述,力求讲得有理、说得详细,以语言事实为依据,以权威著作为佐证,让读者从本书里学到一些英语语法方面的新东西,获取一般语法书上难以找到的新知识。

《新编现代英语语法》共30章。由于语言的基本单位是句子,所以我们撰写本书的出发点是以句子为主线,在强调句法的前提下深化词法的介绍和讨论。在撰写时,我们遵循"新"、"实"、"透"原则:突出一个"新"字,即写法新、内容新;落实一个"实"字,即力求实用,学用结合;贯穿一个"透"字,即所讲之点,尽量透彻。在谈到形容词时带出定语从句;讲到副词时引出副词从句;说到数词时延伸出了含数词表达的一些问题;在讲完"介词"之后,详细论述了现代英语句法研究的新动向——移位句,即虚拟移位、右移位和左移位;在词类的叙述方面讲得全面、深入、细致,接受了旧体例语法书不常见的"限定词";动词的时、体上,采用"二时六体"的新观点,另辟了英语中表示将来意思的新内容;在非谓语动词的叙述上仍把动名词从v-ing分词中分开,目的是把现在分词和动名词讲得透一些。在处理词汇、句子的论述上,做到词法之中有句法、句法之中有词法,做到了句法、词法的巧妙结合。特别要提到的是,《新编现代英语语法》尽量囊括了现代英语语言研究的新资料,像英语中移位现象、对短语句定义的更正等;还沿用了不少杨元兴先生在 *A Complete Collection of English Sentence*

Patterns（上海外语教育出版社，2007）和 English Sentence Pattern and Syntax（北京语言大学出版社，2012）里面论述到的许多新观点、新结论，由此证实了《新编现代英语语法》是一部体现了现代英语语言研究的新著作。

《新编现代英语语法》的特色是：体例独特，内容新颖，取舍得当，论证权威，语言通俗。每章后面均配上内容精当的练习，便于读者自测，利于教师检查。为减轻读者负担，电子版练习和参考答案挂在出版社网站，供读者免费下载。

《新编现代英语语法》实为大中学校学生的好老师、教师的好帮手、英语自学者的好朋友、雅思和托福应试者的好向导、语言研究者的好参谋。

《新编现代英语语法》由杨元兴谋篇，江沈巨组织书稿，并完成了三万余字的送审稿。江沈巨还编写了相当部分的书稿，练习基本也由他完成。参加《新编现代英语语法》编写者为来自全国数十个大中学校的一线教师及部分博士生导师和语法专家，他们分别来自上海外国语大学、北京大学、南京大学、武汉大学、四川大学、苏州大学、苏州科技大学、苏州科技大学天平学院、江苏理工大学、河南新乡学院、苏州工业园区职业技术学院、苏州旅游与财经高等职业技术学校等院校和一些国内著名中学。全书初稿出来后，由江沈巨、高俊丽、蔡炳成、李万豫、樊永松、胡桢文、朱光成、朱栋华等分头统稿，尔后江沈巨跟九鼎先生一起，耗时四年多，对全书章节进行全面修整、提炼，对整体内容进行增删补缺；与此同时，杨元兴先生又添写了好些新章节，插入了许多新内容，斧正了一些章节，并对全书内容逐章审读，最后完成了《新编现代英语语法》的定稿工作。

《新编现代英语语法》的问世，是我们有关各方精诚合作的结果，也是我们对外语教学的又一个小小的贡献。

最后，我们对美国语言学家 E. W. Gilman 的指导，对张月祥、汤定军教授的精心指点，对九鼎先生四年多为《新编现代英语语法》的诞生所付出的心血，对苏州大学出版社的大力支持，一一表示衷心的感谢！

由于时间仓促、水平有限，本书定有不少未尽之处，还请专家、读者批评指正。

杨元兴　江沈巨
2015 年 3 月于苏州伊顿小镇

目　录

第1章　词、词组、句子、句子成分 ·· 1
　1.1　词、词组 ·· 1
　1.2　句子 ·· 3
　1.3　句子成分 ·· 5

第2章　主动词、助动词和情态动词 ·· 14
　2.1　主动词 ·· 14
　2.2　助动词 ·· 30
　2.3　情态动词 ·· 34

第3章　动词的时、体和将来意思表达法 ·· 45
　3.1　时、体概述 ·· 45
　3.2　时、体的分类 ·· 45
　3.3　将来意思表示法 ·· 57

第4章　动词的语态 ·· 60
　4.1　语态概述 ·· 60
　4.2　被动句与主动句的关系及被动句的时体 ·· 60
　4.3　"be + 过去分词"的两种结构 ·· 61
　4.4　使用被动句的原因 ·· 62
　4.5　主动句与被动句的转换 ·· 63
　4.6　主动句转换成被动句的注意点 ·· 67
　4.7　行为被动语态和状态被动语态 ·· 67
　4.8　被动语态中 by 短语和 with 短语 ·· 69
　4.9　双重被动句 ·· 71
　4.10　"get + 过去分词"构成的被动句 ·· 72
　4.11　"不及物动词 + 介词"构成的被动句 ·· 75
　4.12　结构主动，意思被动 ·· 75
　4.13　结构被动，意思主动 ·· 76

第5章　动词不定式 ·· 78
　5.1　动词不定式概述 ·· 78
　5.2　动词不定式形式表 ·· 78
　5.3　动词不定式的句法功能 ·· 78
　5.4　动词不定式的时态和语态 ·· 90
　5.5　不定式被动语态的句法功能和主动、被动语态的选用 ······························ 92
　5.6　动词不定式的否定式 ·· 93

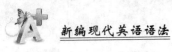

  5.7 动词不定式的逻辑主语 ………………………………………………… 94
  5.8 分裂不定式 ……………………………………………………………… 94
  5.9 动词不定式不带 to 的情况 ……………………………………………… 95
第 6 章 现在分词和过去分词 ……………………………………………………… 99
  6.1 现在分词 ………………………………………………………………… 99
  6.2 过去分词 ………………………………………………………………… 109
第 7 章 动名词 …………………………………………………………………… 119
  7.1 动名词概述 ……………………………………………………………… 119
  7.2 动名词的形式 …………………………………………………………… 119
  7.3 名词性质的动名词 ……………………………………………………… 119
  7.4 动名词的动词性质 ……………………………………………………… 124
  7.5 动名词的时、体、态 …………………………………………………… 125
  7.6 动名词的否定式 ………………………………………………………… 127
  7.7 动名词的复合结构 ……………………………………………………… 127
第 8 章 宾语(从句)、引语 ……………………………………………………… 129
  8.1 宾语 ……………………………………………………………………… 129
  8.2 宾语从句 ………………………………………………………………… 130
  8.3 引语 ……………………………………………………………………… 133
第 9 章 名词和名词性从句 ……………………………………………………… 138
  9.1 名词 ……………………………………………………………………… 138
  9.2 名词性从句 ……………………………………………………………… 168
第 10 章 代词 …………………………………………………………………… 173
  10.1 人称代词 ……………………………………………………………… 173
  10.2 物主代词 ……………………………………………………………… 174
  10.3 反身代词 ……………………………………………………………… 175
  10.4 相互代词 ……………………………………………………………… 177
  10.5 指示代词 ……………………………………………………………… 177
  10.6 疑问代词 ……………………………………………………………… 178
  10.7 关系代词 ……………………………………………………………… 180
  10.8 不定代词 ……………………………………………………………… 181
第 11 章 数词 …………………………………………………………………… 185
  11.1 数词的分类 …………………………………………………………… 185
  11.2 基数词 ………………………………………………………………… 185
  11.3 序数词 ………………………………………………………………… 186
  11.4 数词的具体用法 ……………………………………………………… 188
  11.5 分数词 ………………………………………………………………… 189
  11.6 小数 …………………………………………………………………… 189
  11.7 百分数 ………………………………………………………………… 189
  11.8 成数 …………………………………………………………………… 190
  11.9 表示约数的五种方法 ………………………………………………… 190
  11.10 表示"年代"、"公元"的方法 ……………………………………… 191
  11.11 用英语数词编号 …………………………………………………… 192

11.12	数学计算和公式表示	192
11.13	日期表示和读法	193
11.14	钟点的表示	193
11.15	"度"表示法	193
11.16	dozen, score, hundred, thousand, million 的用法	194
11.17	数词用法上的几个易错点	195
11.18	英语中表达汉语"量词"的方法	196

第12章 限定词(一) …………………………………………………… 199
12.1　限定词的定义 …………………………………………………… 199
12.2　限定词的范围 …………………………………………………… 199
12.3　限定词的搭配 …………………………………………………… 200

第13章 限定词(二)——冠词 …………………………………………… 207
13.1　冠词的分类 ……………………………………………………… 207
13.2　冠词的用法 ……………………………………………………… 207
13.3　冠词的位置 ……………………………………………………… 209
13.4　不定冠词 a/an 与 one 的异同 ………………………………… 210
13.5　冠词的省略、重复等 …………………………………………… 211

第14章 连词和感叹词 …………………………………………………… 213
14.1　连词 ……………………………………………………………… 213
14.2　感叹词 …………………………………………………………… 216

第15章 介词 ……………………………………………………………… 219
15.1　介词概述 ………………………………………………………… 219
15.2　介词的分类 ……………………………………………………… 219
15.3　表示否定意义的介词 …………………………………………… 223
15.4　介词词组的句法功能 …………………………………………… 224
15.5　介词的双词性和多词性 ………………………………………… 224
15.6　介词后的宾语 …………………………………………………… 225
15.7　与动词搭配组成短语动词的介词 ……………………………… 226
15.8　介词的省略 ……………………………………………………… 227
15.9　介词的后置及介词与其宾语的分离 …………………………… 228

第16章 句子移位 ………………………………………………………… 229
16.1　移位概述 ………………………………………………………… 229
16.2　移位的分类 ……………………………………………………… 229

第17章 语气、虚拟语气 ………………………………………………… 241
17.1　语气 ……………………………………………………………… 241
17.2　虚拟语气 ………………………………………………………… 241

第18章 句子的倒装 ……………………………………………………… 252
18.1　句子倒装概述 …………………………………………………… 252
18.2　倒装的需要 ……………………………………………………… 252

第19章 句子的强调 ……………………………………………………… 260
19.1　语音强调 ………………………………………………………… 260
19.2　词汇强调 ………………………………………………………… 262

| 19.3 | 句法强调 | 267 |
| 19.4 | 修辞强调 | 272 |

第20章 陈述句 274

| 20.1 | 陈述句的概述 | 274 |
| 20.2 | 陈述句的七个句型 | 274 |

第21章 疑问句 287

21.1	疑问句概述	287
21.2	一般疑问句	287
21.3	特殊疑问句	293
21.4	选择疑问句	302
21.5	附加疑问句	304
21.6	陈述疑问句	313
21.7	回响疑问句	313
21.8	修辞疑问句	314

第22章 祈使句 316

22.1	祈使句概述	316
22.2	祈使句的主语	316
22.3	祈使句谓语动词的特点	318
22.4	祈使句与词汇意义的关系	320
22.5	祈使句的强调式	322
22.6	祈使句的否定式	323
22.7	祈使句与状语	325
22.8	祈使句的表达形式	327
22.9	let 祈使句	329
22.10	无动词祈使句	333

第23章 感叹句 334

| 23.1 | 感叹句的分类 | 334 |
| 23.2 | 感叹句型的转换 | 338 |

第24章 形容词、形容词(定语)从句 339

24.1	形容词的定义	339
24.2	形容词的分类	339
24.3	描绘性形容词和限定性形容词	342
24.4	形容词的前缀与后缀	343
24.5	-ing 形容词与 -ed 形容词的区别	346
24.6	形容词的排序	346
24.7	形容词的大小写问题	347
24.8	"the + 形容词"表示某类人	347
24.9	形容词的比较等级	348
24.10	形容词的句法功能	352
24.11	形容词(定语)从句	355
24.12	简单句式定语句	355
24.13	复合句式定语句	355

第25章 副词、副词(状语)从句 360
- 25.1 副词 360
- 25.2 状语从句 363

第26章 否定句 440
- 26.1 否定句概述 440
- 26.2 词汇类否定句 440
- 26.3 结构类否定句 443
- 26.4 否定范围 444
- 26.5 多余否定(赘言否定) 448
- 26.6 含蓄否定 448
- 26.7 如何加强否定的语气 449
- 26.8 两种转移否定 450

第27章 句子的省略 452
- 27.1 句子的省略概述 452
- 27.2 省略的类型 452
- 27.3 省略在具体句中的体现 453

第28章 句子的替代 466
- 28.1 句子的替代概述 466
- 28.2 替代与省略的区别 466
- 28.3 名词性替代 466
- 28.4 副词性替代 468
- 28.5 动词性替代 470
- 28.6 从句性替代 472

第29章 单词句和短语句 476
- 29.1 单词句和短语句概述 476
- 29.2 使用单词句和短语句的语境和好处 476
- 29.3 单词句和短语句的分类 476
- 29.4 单词句和短语句与省略的关系 479
- 29.5 单词句和短语句的句法功能 480
- 29.6 关于单词句、短语句的一些说明 482

第30章 主语与谓语的一致 483
- 30.1 主语与谓语一致的原则 483
- 30.2 主语与谓语一致的形式 483

第1章 词、词组、句子、句子成分

1.1 词、词组

词是音、形、义和语法特点四者的统一体。如 book，它的音是/buk/，它的义是"书"，它的形(或叫外壳)是 b-o-o-k 四个字母，它的语法特点是在句中可作主语(The book is on the table.)、作宾语(He gave me a book.)等。

要注意的是，词不等于词汇。词用 word 表示，词汇是 vocabulary，它们之间是个体与总体之间的关系。因此，一般来说词的总和构成语言的词汇。英语的词汇大约有一百多万个。这些词汇由本族语词汇(Native Words)和外来词汇(Borrowed Words)两大类构成。当然，本族语词汇是英语中的核心词汇，它们在语言中使用得最多，是生活中最必需的、意义最明确的、生命力最强的基本词汇的总和。这些基本词汇有名词方面的词，像表示季节的词 spring, summer, autumn, winter, 像表示人体部位的词 arm, head, foot, hand, 像表示动作方面的词 go, come, run, work。基本词汇还有助动词、介词、连词、代词、数词等。虽然基本词汇在英语中所占的比率不大，但它们的使用频率却非常高，特别在口语中。然而，英语中很多词是外来词，人们常说英语是世界上外来词汇最多的语言之一。在整个英语语言发展过程中，有些外来词汇已看不出其来自何种语言，如 chalk, school, street, cup, wine, kettle, sickle, mountain 等词来自拉丁语，cake, call, crop, crave, egg, husband, ill, kind, knife, law, skill, take 等来自丹麦语。以上这些词不借助词源词典是不可能知道的，因为它们在形式上与英语词汇已分不出彼此了。

英语的词类有好多种。它们是：

名词(Noun)：room, Beijing, London, sun, air, flour
代词(Pronoun)：you, she, they, somebody, one, which
形容词(Adjective)：small, big, happy, beautiful
副词(Adverb)：quickly, very, now, fast
数词(Numeral)：one, three, second, fortieth
介词(Preposition)：in, at, without, except
连词(Conjunction)：and, but, when, although
感叹词(Interjection)：ah, oh, phew, ugh
动词(Verb)：work, say, get, research
助动词(Auxiliary Verb)：can, do, may, shall, would
限定词(Determiner) a, an, the, this, that, such, every

词要构成词组才能出现在句子中。词所构成的词组有名词词组和动词词组两大类，这些词组构成句子的主语和谓语。

每个名词词组有其中心词，中心词可以是单个名词(Single-Word Noun)，如(a) pencil, woman, mountain；也可以是复合名词(Compound Noun)，如(a) door-handle, television screen。名词中心词的修饰词可以是限定词、形容词或形容词词组，还可以是名词或名词词组、介词词组、非限定动词词组，还有其他主谓结构。限定词在修饰名词中心词中有着最特殊的重要地位，这是因为限定词的取舍和选择决定于中心词的性质，如可数还是不可数，是单数还是复数。根据中心词的性质，有时前面必须有限定词，有时又可不用,有时却又是可用或者不用。这种名词中心词与限定词使用有一种固定的搭配关系,因此限定词的使用与否不可随意变动。

(1) 名词中心词修饰语的位置

名词中心词修饰语的位置有两种:前置和后置。限定词修饰名词中心词时均前置,但 enough 除外。其他修饰语有的要前置,有的要后置,有的既可前置也可后置。

① 前置

限定词、形容词作名词中心词的修饰语时前置,如:*a* book,*these* books,*little* water,*a funny* story,*new* machines,*black* tea,*a very attentive* boy。

② 后置

名词中心词后置的情况有三种:修饰-body,-one,-thing 结尾的复合不定代词时,形容词后置;介词短语作名词中心词的定语时后置;受到结构的限制,形容词只能后置。

I have something *important* to tell you. 我有重要的事情要告诉你。
Nobody *else* but Mary went there. 是玛丽而不是别人去那儿。
Is there anything *interesting* in the story? 故事里有有趣的东西吗?
Any man *brave enough* can do the work. 有足够勇气的男子都能干那工作。
She speaks with an accent *more Russian than English*. 她说带有俄语口音的英语。

③ 既可前置,也可后置

有些形容词作名词中心词定语时可以前置,也可以后置;有时前置或后置意思一样,有时则有别。

A. 意思相同

Mr. Smith can tell us a *much funnier* story than that.
= Mr. Smith can tell us a story *much funnier* than that. 史密斯先生能给我们讲比那个有趣得多的故事。

B. 意思有别

The *present* situation concerns all the students *present*. 现在的情况关系到在场的每个学生。

显然,第一个 present 与第二个 present 的意思完全不同,The present situation = The situation now;而后面的 students present = those who are here。

(2) 动词词组

动词词组是以动词为中心词的词组。在动词采取其限定形式时叫限定动词词组,在采取其非限定形式时叫非限定动词词组。动词还可采取简单形式和复杂形式,或叫简单动词词组和复杂动词词组。

① 简单限定动词词组

简单限定动词词组只有一个主动词,或外加宾语或补语。

The moon *rose*. 月亮已升起。
His boat *sank*. 他的船沉了。
Her husband *is a teacher*. 她丈夫是一位老师。(含补语)
We *saw nothing*. 我什么也没看见。(含宾语)
I *saw her out*. 我看见她出去了。(含宾语补语)

② 复杂限定动词词组

复杂限定动词词组指由助动词加上一个主动词或带有宾语或补语的动词词组。

His boat *may sink*. 他的船可能要沉。
The situation *is changing*. 形势在变化。

The delegation *has left*. 代表团走了。
He *had bought a new house*. 他已买了幢新房。
What did you *see*? 你看见了什么？

③ 简单非限定动词词组

简单非限定动词词组，是指在一个简单句中，除了谓语动词外，还有一些非限定动词，这些非限定动词在句中作某些句法功能。

I heard Mary *singing in the garden*. 我听见玛丽在花园里唱歌。（v-ing 动词形式作宾语补足语）
To kill time, she plays cards every day. 为了打发时间,她每天打牌。（动词不定式形式作目的状语）

④ 复杂非限定动词词组

复杂非限定动词词组是指那种以两个动词结构形式出现的非限定动词。

Having finished her homework, Rose went to bed. 罗丝做完了作业上床睡觉。（完成式复杂非限定动词词组 having finished her homework 在句中作时间状语，其逻辑主语是 Rose）
Having been taken to a beautiful park, the little girl got excited. 那个小女孩被带到一座美丽的花园,她非常兴奋。（完成被动式复杂非限定动词词组 Having been taken to a beautiful park 在句中作原因状语，其逻辑主语是 the little girl）

简单或复杂非限定动词词组在句中可作主语、宾语、补语、状语及名词修饰语，关于那部分内容，可参见"非谓语动词"有关章节。

1.2 句子

英语的句子就其结构划分有简单句、并列句和复合句。

(1) 简单句

简单句的基本句型有以下七种：

A. 主语 + 谓语动词（不及物动词）(SV)
B. 主语 + 谓语动词 + 补语（SVC）
C. 主语 + 谓语动词（不及物动词）+ 状语（SVA）
D. 主语 + 谓语动词（及物动词）+ 宾语（SVO）
E. 主语 + 谓语动词（及物动词）+ 宾语 + 宾语补足语（SVOC）
F. 主语 + 谓语动词（及物动词）+ 宾语 + 状语（SVOA）
G. 主语 + 谓语动词（及物动词）+ 间接宾语 + 直接宾语（SVoO）

(2) 简单句分述

① SV 句型

这种句型中的谓语动词不带状语,也不带宾语,有时仅两个词。当然,像这样的句子后如带上状语,那意思会更清楚。

Iron rusts. 铁生锈。
Iron rusts easily. 铁容易生锈。
Iron rusts easily in wet weather. 铁在潮湿天气里容易生锈。

② SVC 句型

这种结构就是"主语 + 连系动词 + 表语"结构。里面的谓语动词是 be，即 is, am, are, was, were 及其他的各种形式的连系动词。有时,谓语动词也可以是像 seem, look, become, appear 等特殊连系动词。

Her hair is yellow. 她的头发是黄的。
His wish is to become a scientist. 他的愿望是成为一名科学家。
Lunch is at twelvet o'clock. 中餐12点开饭。
Most young people are in good health. 多数年轻人身体健康。
His plan sounds perfect. 他们的计划听起来极好。
My work then was raising pigs. 我那时的工作是养猪。

③ SVA 句型

在这种句型中谓语动词是不及物动词,但它们后面要带状语,不然句子意思不完整。

Iron rusts easily (in wet weather). 铁(在潮湿天气里)容易生锈。
We have lunch at eleven. 我们11点吃中饭。
Who swept the floor this morning? 今天早上谁扫的地?
The Greens are staying in the Holiday Inn. 格林一家住在假日酒店。
She has been singing for an hour. 她已唱了一小时歌了。

④ SVO 句型

这种句型中的谓语动词后面只跟一个宾语,所以这种动词也叫单宾语及物动词(Monotransitive Verb)。此种句型可以不跟状语,意思是完整的。

We'll do our best. 我们会尽力的。
She is writing a letter. 她在写信。
Who is reading the novel? 谁在看那部小说?
The villagers have been looking for the lost child the whole night. 村民们一整夜都在找那丢失的孩子。
We haven't finished our work. 我们还没完成我们的工作。
He didn't open the door (for me). 他没(为我)打开门。(此句如带了状语 for me,则属 SVOA)

⑤ SVOC 句型

在这个句型中,谓语动词仅限于某些带复杂宾语(Complex Object)的及物动词(Complex Transitive Verb)。我们也常把复合宾语称作宾语和宾语补足语。要注意的是,宾语与宾语补足语之间存在着逻辑上的主谓关系。

She treats the boy as her own. 她把那男孩当作亲生的。
Mary turned all the lights on. 玛丽把所有的灯全开了。
He has proved her wrong. 他已证实她错了。
We encouraged them to air their views. 我们鼓励他们提出自己的看法。

有一点要说明的是,所谓的"单宾语及物动词"、"双宾语及物动词"和"复杂宾语及物动词"也是相对的,它们有很多交叉现象,像 I found a novel. I found him a novel. I found the novel very interesting. 三句中的动词 find 就是这种情况。

⑥ SVOA 句型

很明显,这个句型是在"句型 SVO"后面加上状语而成。

He met your brother in the Green Park today. 他今天在绿色公园碰到了你弟弟。
Who laid the laptop on the desk? 谁把笔记本电脑放在那办公桌上的?
She can't help crying at a sad movie. 她看了忧伤的电影禁不住要哭。

⑦ SVoO 句型

在这种句型中的谓语动词也是及物动词,也叫双宾语及物动词(Ditransitive Verb)。句型中的第一个小写 o 代表间接宾语(Indirect Object),第二个大写 O 代表直接宾语(Direct Object)。

Bob passed me an apple. 鲍勃递给了我一个苹果。

Mrs. White bought me a pair of shoes. 怀特太太给我买了双鞋。

Bring him some water, please. 请给他拿点水来。

She told her teacher everything. 她告诉了她老师一切(事情)。

Note：间接宾语在直接宾语之前,但有时也可将间接宾语置后,这时原间接宾语前必须加上 to,for 等介词。因此,我们可以把 We must buy her some clothes 改为 We must buy some clothes for her,可把 She told her teacher everything 改为 She told everything to her teacher。

1.3 句子成分

英语句子的成分有主语(Subject)、谓语(Predicate)、表语(Predictive)、宾语(Object)、补语(Complement)、定语(Attribute)、状语(Adverbial)、同位语(Appositive)、独立成分(Independent Element)等。

(1) 句子成分的定义

① 主语

主语相当于句子的主题,它指明这个句子讲的是什么。可作主语的词语有名词、代词、动词不定式、v-ing(动名词)、it、数词、从句等。

Air can lift up the plane. 空气能托起飞机。(名词)

He is good at learning language. 他擅长学习语言。(代词)

To see one time is better than to hear a hundred times. 百闻不如一见。(动词不定式)

Reading in bed is a bad habit. 躺在床上看书是个坏习惯。(动名词)

56% of Chinese college students write blogs. 中国56%的大学生写博客。(数词)

It's not easy to master a foreign language. 掌握一门外语并不容易。(it作形式主语)

Who will be chairman of our club is not announced. 谁将是我们俱乐部的主任还没宣布。(从句)

② 谓语

谓语说明主语的情况,提供新的信息。它们常由限定动词充当。谓语有简单谓语和复合谓语,谓语动词必须有人称、时态、语态和语气的变化。

A. 简单谓语

由一个动词或一个动词短语构成,其中包括各种时态、语态、语气和疑问式、否定式、强调式等。

Do you speak Russian? 你讲俄语吗?(现在时疑问句)

Very seldom *does she eat* any breakfast. 她很少吃早餐。(现在时倒装句)

They *are working* hard. 他们在努力工作。(现在进行体)

Don't make any noise. 别作声。(现在时否定式祈使句)

Everybody *laughed*. 大家都笑了。(过去时)

She *did see* you in the park last night. 她昨晚的确看见你在公园里。(过去时强调句)

B. 复合谓语

a. 情态动词+不定式

You *may go* there this afternoon. 你今天下午可去那里。(现在时表示将来动作)

We *shan't be coming* back today. 我们今天不回来。(将来进行体)

We *must have been playing* tennis in the park when you phoned. 你打电话来时我们一定是在公园里打网

球。(将来完成进行体)

　　b. 半助动词 + 不定式

We *have to do* something for them. 我们必须为他们做点事。

We *are going to have* a meeting this afternoon. 今天下午我们要开会。

They *are sure to have eaten* everything up. 他们一定把东西全吃完了。

　　c. 连系动词 + 表语

The station *is a mile away*. 车站离这里一英里。

The box *feels strong*. 这箱子感觉很结实。

The milk *went bad*. 牛奶坏了。

C. 说明动作的谓语

The bus *stopped* suddenly. 公交车突然停了。(过去时)

Who *has turned* on the radio? 谁打开了收音机？(现在完成体)

D. 说明状态的谓语

These classrooms *are clean*. 这些教室干净。(现在时)

He *seemed angry*. 他似乎生气了。(过去时)

③ 表语

表语是连系动词后说明主语"是什么"或"怎么样"的成分。可作表语的词语有：名词(短语)、代词、形容词、数词、动词不定式、过去分词、副词、复合结构、从句、v-ing 分词(动名词)等。

A. 名词、代词、从句等作表语

He is *a great thinker*. 他是个伟大的思想家。(名词)

That man was *I/me*. 那是我。(代词)

This is *mine*, that is *yours*. 这是我的，那是你的。(名词性物主代词)

The picture is *very beautiful*. 这幅画真漂亮。(形容词)

She is *seventy-four*. 她 74 岁了。(数词)

Her wish is *to become a doctor*. 她的愿望是做个医生。(动词不定式)

This glass is *broken*. 这只杯子破了。(过去分词)

Is anything *up*? 发生事情没有？(副词)

The war is *over*. 战争结束了。(副词)

That's *what I hope*. 那是我所希望的。(从句)

B. v-ing 形式作表语

关于 v-ing 形式作表语有两种情况：一是名词性质的 v-ing 分词作表语；二是形容词性质的 v-ing 分词作表语。

　　a. 名词性质的 v-ing 形式作表语

用 v-ing 形式作表语是表示句子主语的内容，其前不可用 very 修饰。这种 v-ing 形式除了起名词的作用外，它也有动词的性质，既可带宾语，有时还可带状语，这就叫动名词。

The only thing that interests him is *dancing*. 他的唯一感兴趣的事是跳舞。

What he has got in his mind is *bringing* the meeting to a successful conclusion. 他一心所想的是使会议获得成功。(带宾语和状语)

Another *goal* was ending the chaos in the country. 另一目标是结束国家的混乱状态。(带宾语和状语)

　　b. 形容词性 v-ing 形式作表语

这类分词作表语表示主语的特征和属性，而且其前可用 very 之类的副词修饰。

The story is *very moving*. 故事很感人。

I think it's *a bit embarrassing*. 我认为这有点让人为难。
This book is *more interesting* than that one. 这本书比那本有趣。

c. v-ing 形式作表语时的体态

v-ing 形式作表语时常用一般体主动语态,很少用被动语态和完成体,但复合结构除外。

This year's sales are *encouraging*. 今年的销售额令人鼓舞。
The sport Pascal like best is *canoeing down a mountain stream*. 帕斯克尔最喜欢的运动是划独木舟沿山溪顺流而下。
Their way of fighting the "disease" was *producing their dictionary*. 他们与这种"语言疾病"斗争的方法是拿出他们的字典。
The only reason for selling it is *the owner's getting a new car*. 卖掉它的唯一原因是卖主有了一辆新汽车了。
All she wanted was *her son being given the job*. 她只希望这工作能给她儿子。
The thought that he couldn't get rid of was *his having made the mistake himself*. 他无法摆脱的想法就是他自己犯了那个错误。
This is *John Smith speaking*. (电话用语)我是约翰·史密斯。(复合结构)
That's *what I hope*. 那是我所希望的。(从句)
Your coat is *where you left it*. 你的外衣还在你(自己)放的地方。(从句)
The students remained *puzzled*. 学生们依然迷惑不解。(过去分词)
Ralph is *delighted* with the recent news. 最近的消息使拉尔夫很高兴。(过去分词)

④ 宾语

及物动词后的宾语是动词的行为、动作的对象,介词后的宾语是介词涉及的对象。宾语还可分双宾语、形容词宾语、复合宾语、介词宾语等。

A. 直接宾语

直接宾语(Direct Object)表示直接对象、结果、内容、工具等。直接宾语可分为一般直接宾语和特殊直接宾语两种。

a. 一般直接宾语

一般直接宾语就是及物动词后带上一个宾语,这种宾语有名词、代词、数词(短语)、动词不定式(短语)、从句、it 等充当。

● 名词等作宾语

I'll do *some shopping*. 我要去买些东西。(名词作宾语)
Do you know *him*? 你认识他吗?(代词作宾语)
I have read *three of these letters*. 我看了其中的三封信。(数词作宾语)
She wants *to go to Italy*. 她想去意大利。(动词不定式作宾语)
Do you like *to go for a walk with us after supper*? 晚饭后跟我们一起去走走吗?(动词不定式短语作宾语)
I wonder *whether/if they will arrive on time*. 我不知道他们能否准时到。(从句作宾语)

● it 作宾语

it 作宾语的情况稍复杂,它可作实义宾语、先行宾语、习语中动词的宾语、名词转化成动词后的宾语等。

* 作实义宾语

it 作实义宾语时,是指前面出现过的名词或短语。

She threw the ball to me and I caught *it*. 她把球扔给我,我把它接住了。(宾语 it 指前面出现过的 the ball)
If I can pass the final examination in Maths, I call *it* good luck. 如果我能通过数学期末考试,我称之为运

气好。(宾语 it 指 If I can pass the final examination in maths 这个从句所指的那件事)

* 作先行宾语

某些动词(如 consider, deem, find, think 等)后接复合宾语时,宾语如是不定式短语、v-ing 形式短语和从句,要用 it 作先行宾语,而把真正的宾语置于宾语补足语的后面。

He thought *it* polite *to answer her letter.* 他认为给她回信是合乎礼貌的。

You will find *it* a great pleasure *talking to her.* 你会发现和她谈话很愉快。

I made *it* quite clear to you *that I was not coming.* 我向你清楚地表示过我不来。

* 作习语中动词的宾语

英语中有一些习语常用 it 作动词或介词的宾语,这时 it 没有实际词汇意义。

I don't think this car will *make it* to the top of the hill. 我认为这辆老爷车开不到山顶。(句中 make it 作"成功"讲)

Go it while you are young. 年轻时要拼命干。(go it 意为"拼命干")

* 作名词转化成动词后的宾语

英语中有极少几个名词可以转化成动词,这时也常用 it 作它们的宾语,这时的 it 也没实际词汇意义。

In that old town we *cabbed it.* 在那古镇,我们乘到了马车。

Shall we *tram it* or *bus it*? 我们乘电车还是坐公共汽车?

b. 特殊直接宾语

英语里有一种特殊的直接宾语叫同源宾语(Cognate Object),它表示和动词相同、相近或相似的意思。同源宾语多数用在某些不及物动词之后,它实际上是一种习惯用法,所以不是任何动词后都可跟同源宾语的。

I slept *a peaceful sleep* last night. 昨晚我睡了个安静觉。

Rose dreamed *a wonderful dream* last night. 罗丝昨天晚上做了奇妙的梦。

He shouted *his loudest shout.* 他声嘶力竭地叫喊。

Note: 如同源宾语前有形容词最高级或含最高级意义的词修饰时,其后的同源宾语可以省去。

B. 关于双宾语及其前面的动词

双宾语是指间接宾语和直接宾语。间接宾语通常指人,直接宾语指物,一般间接宾语在前、直接宾语在后。英语中有 accord, allow, answer, ask, assign, award, build, bring, buy, call, catch, cause, charge, choose, cook, cost, cut, deal, deny, do, envy, fetch, find, fine, fix, forgive, get, give, owe, pass, pay, post 等不多的动词可带双宾语。

a. 间接宾语

间接宾语(Indirect Object)是双宾语及物动词(Ditransitive Verb)后表示动作接受者的部分,通常由名词或代词及其短语来担任。

Mary gave *him* a book. 玛丽给了他一本书。

I'll give *you* something to eat. 我会给你一些东西吃。

They promised *me* that everything would be ready by noon. 他们答应我中午前一切都会准备好的。

b. 双直接宾语

有少量动词(如 answer, ask, envy, forgive, own, pay, teach, telephone, tell, write 等)后接的间接宾语和直接宾语可看作双直接宾语,因为两个宾语中省去任何一个,句子意思依然完整。

Mr. Green writes *me a letter* every week. 怀特先生每周写一封信给我。

Mr. Green writes *a letter* every week. 怀特先生每周写一封信。

Mr. Green writes *me* every week. 怀特先生每周给我写信。

c. 形容词宾语

形容词宾语,是指那些意思不完整的形容词,后面需要加宾语,即形容词宾语(Adjective Object),进行补充,组成形容词短语,在句中充当一定的成分。可带形容词宾语的情况有两种:一种是形容词 worth 后接宾语;还有一种是某些形容词与介词搭配后变成形容词短语,后面跟宾语。

- 形容词 worth 后接宾语

worth 是表语形容词,意思是"值得……",它后面必须要跟宾语后意思才完整。它的宾语常由名词、代词、v-ing 形式、从句等担任。

The Industrial Exhibition is well worth *a visit*. 这个工业展览会很值得参观。(名词)

How much is the old picture worth? 那幅古画值多少钱?(名词)

Your old car isn't worth *repairing*. 你的那辆旧车不值得修了。(v-ing 形式)

This book is worth *what I paid for it*. 这本书值得上我为它花的钱。(从句)

- 形容词短语后的宾语

有些形容词与介词搭配后变成形容词短语,这时它们后面跟宾语。这些形容词短语主要有 afraid of, aware of, certain of, clear about, concerned about, confident of 等。

Are you *aware* of *the time*? 你知道是什么时间了?

Most boys are *fond of football*. 大多数男孩喜欢足球。

His team is *thirsty for success*. 他的球队渴望成功。

Note:be worthy 后可接:of + 名词或相当于名词的词; to be + 过去分词; being + 过去分词; of being + 过去分词。

Robert is worthy *of confidence*. 罗伯特是个可以信赖的人。

This book is worthy *to be studied* carefully. 这本书值得仔细学习一下。

This work is worthy *being done*. 这工作值得做。

This film is worthy *of being seen*. 这电影值得看。

以上句子中的 to be studied 不可改作 to study …, being done 不可改作 doing, of being done 不可改作 of doing。

上面那些形容词短语中,有些形容词也可直接作表语,但它们的意思有所不同。

She *is sick of* summer. 她讨厌夏天。(句中的 is sick of = doesn't like)

She is *sick*. 她病了。(此处 sick = ill)

d. 复合宾语

复合宾语由宾语和宾语补足语组成。复合宾语的两个组成部分之间在逻辑上有主语和谓语的关系。宾语补足语可由名词、代词、形容词、动词不定式、v-ing 形式(现在分词)、过去分词、副词、介词短语等担任。

We considered her *a cold-hearted woman*. 我们认为她是个冷漠的女人。(名词)

What do you call it in English? 这用英语怎么说?(疑问代词)

Leave the door *open*, please. 请把门开着。(形容词)

Did you see him *go out*? 你有没有看见他走出去?(动词不定式)

Note:有些动词(如 see, hear, observe, notice, watch, look at, listen to 等)后面的动词不定式宾语补足语要省去不定式符号 to,但在被动结构中不省。

I saw him *going out just now*. 我看见他走出去的。(现在分词)

She found the door *closed*. 她发现门关着。(过去分词)

At night we can see all the lights *on*. 晚上我们看见灯全开着。(副词)

We found everything *in good order*. 我们发现一切井井有条。(介词短语)

C. 介词宾语

介词不能单独使用,后面必须带宾语后构成介词短语。可作介词的宾语大致有名词、代词、数词及其短语、不定式短语及 wh-词引导的动词不定式,介词 but, in, rather than 等后可接以 that 引导的从句作介词的宾语。

I'm going to *the post office*. 我上邮局去。

Peter stood behind *me*. 彼得站在我后面。

I'll be back by *eleven*. 我11点回来。

What do you like to do besides *swim*? 除了游泳,你还喜欢什么?

You may dance with *whomever you like*. 你想跟谁跳舞就跟谁跳。

What can we get in *here*? 我们在这里能弄到什么? (副词 here 作介词 in 的宾语)

⑤ 定语

定语是一种修饰名词或代词及其短语的成分。定语常由限定词、数词、名词、动词不定式、现在分词、过去分词、介词短语、副词、从句等担任。

A. 关于定语的例解

a pencil, *the* book, *my* brother, *Tom's* transistor, *every* student, *whose* umbrella（限定词作定语）

four teachers, *one or two* days, *ten to twelve* feet（数词作定语）

a *flower* garden, an *exercise* book, the *foreign language* department（名词作定语）

I have many books *to read*.（动词不定式作定语）

a *swimming* pool 一个游泳池（动名词）, a *sleeping* car 一节卧车车厢（动名词作定语）

a *sleeping* child 一个睡着的孩子, a *running* dog 一只奔跑着的狗（现在分词作定语）

Is this the book *bought* last month? 这是上个月买的书吗?（过去分词作定语）

He is a teacher *of English*. (= He is an English teacher.)（介词短语作定语）

The village *nearby* is his home town.（副词作定语）

She has made an *out and out* mistake.（副词短语作定语）

Do you know the man *who is speaking*?（从句作定语）

B. 定语的排序

一般情况下,单词作定语放在被修饰词前,词组、短语作定语常置后。定语可以表示大小、长短、形状、新旧、好坏、颜色、式样等,具体的顺序是:

a. 限制性—描绘性—分类性

a wonderful thing, a lecture to be held the day after tomorrow

a small wooden table, 不说 *a wooden small table

a famous Chinese writer, 不说 *a Chinese famous writer

b. 与名词关系不密切的在后

a beautiful large green carpet

a small round old gray table

⑥ 状语

状语用于修饰动词、形容词、副词,有时也可修饰短语和句子。状语可由副词、介词短语、动词不定式（短语）、wh- + 现在分词、过去分词（短语）、形容词、名词短语、从句等构成。

He was *badly* ill. 他病得厉害。（副词作状语）

I'll be back *in a few minutes*. 我几分钟后回来。（介词短语作状语）

They stopped *to have a rest*. 他们停下来休息。（动词不定式作目的状语）

Mind your steps *when getting off the bus*. 下车时小心脚下。（wh- + 现在分词作状语）

Seen from the top of the hill, the city looks very beautiful. 从山顶上看,这城市真漂亮。（过去分词短语作状语）

They all rushed over, *anxious to know what had happened*. 他们冲过来,急切地想知道发生了什么。（形容词短语作状语）

The sports meet will be held on Monday, *rain or shine*. 不管晴天还是下雨,运动会将于星期一举行。(名词短语作状语)

I'll tell you *when he comes*. 他来了我会告诉你。(时间状语从句作状语)

⑦ 同位语

同位语是补充说明或进一步解释句中的一个词或短语,或一个句子的特殊成分,并与这词语充当同一个句子成分。同位语可分两大类:一类是词语的同位语,另一类是句子的同位语。

A. 词语同位语

词语同位语中常见的有名词、代词的同位语,还有数词、动词不定式和复合结构作同位语。

My friend *Peter* got the first prize. 我的朋友彼得得了第一名。(名词 Peter 是名词 friend 的同位语)

We are *both* from the south. 我们俩都是南方人。(代词 both 是 we 的同位语)

She painted the house *herself*. 她自己漆的房子。(反身代词 herself 是 she 的同位语)

We *two* are from Nanjing, and they *three* are from Shanghai. 我们两个是南京人,他们三个是上海人。(数词 two 是 we 的同位语,three 是 they 的同位语)

She has a desire *to learn English well*. 她有个欲望——学好英语。(动词不定式 to learn English well 是名词 desire 的同位语)

The hall has two doors, *one leading to the kitchen, the other to the street*. 这大厅的两扇门中,一扇通向厨房,一扇通向街道。(复合结构 one leading to the kitchen, the other to the street 是 two doors 的同位语。)

This machine weighs a ton *or 1,000 kilograms*. 那机器有一吨重,或1000千克。(or 引出的 1,000 kilograms 是前面 a ton 的同位语)

The young lady is *more than pretty*, that is, *beautiful*. 那年轻女士不止漂亮,而是很美。(形容词 beautiful 是前面形容词 pretty 的同位语)

She always writes so—*clearly and neatly*. 她写字总是这样,既清楚又整齐。(副词 clearly and neatly 是副词 so 的同位语)

She is good at *English*, especially *at English grammar*. 她擅长英语,特别是英语语法。(介词短语 at English grammar 是介词短语 at English 的同位语)

Playing football, *his only interest in life*, has brought him many friends. 踢足球,他一生中的唯一爱好,使他认识了许多朋友。(句中的 his only interest in life 是作主语的非限定动词短语 Playing football 的同位语)

She bought five books that day, *such as a Chinese-English Dictionary, an English-Chinese Dictionary, a dictionary of English Verbs*, etc. 她买了五本书,如汉英辞典、英汉辞典、英语动词词典等。(such as 后的 a Chinese-English dictionary, an English-Chinese Dictionary, a dictionary of English Verbs 是 five books 的同位语。)

He knows three languages, *namely* (viz.) *Chinese, English and French*. 他懂三种语言,即汉语、英语和法语。(namely 引出的 Chinese, English and French 是 three languages 的同位语)

Note:上面倒数第二句的 such as 后只要略举几例,不必举全,与此相同的还有 for example/instance;而倒数第一句中 namely 后要把前面所说数字举全,与 namely (viz.)相似的还有 that is (to say) 等用来表示解释,或叫换种说法。

B. 简单句的同位语

简单句的同位语就是指后面的同位语是前面那句简单句的同位语,当然这同位语不是一个句子。

Miss Green sat there dozing off in a deck-chair, *a bit of luxury for her*. 格林小姐坐在帆布躺椅上打盹,这对她来说是一种难得的享受。(句中的名词短语 a bit of luxury for him 是前面句子的同位语)

The leaves are falling from the trees, *a sign that summer is over*. 树叶在从树上落下,这是秋天要到来的迹象。(句中的 a sign 是前面句子的同位语,that summer is over 是定语从句,修饰 a sign)

C. 从句的同位语

复合句中的从句也可以有同位语。这些同位语有时是词语,有时也可能是从句。

She told me *that she had been a teacher of English*, *a fact which I had not known before*. 她告诉我她以前做过英语老师,这事我以前不知道。

Robert put it *where there was light*, in other words, *where everybody could see it*. 罗伯特把它放在有光的地方,换句话说,就是大家看得见的地方。

上面两句的同位语不同,例句 1 中 a fact 是前面宾语从句 that she had been a teacher of English 的同位语,a fact 后的 which I had not known before 是 a fact 的定语从句;而例句 2 中的从句 where everybody could see it 是 where there was light 的同位语。

D. 同位语从句

有些名词(如 idea, conclusion, feeling, question, doubt 等)后常有名词性从句作其同位语。

I have no idea *what he said at the meeting*. 我不知道他在会上说了什么。

She has a feeling *that her team is going to win*. 她有个感觉她的队要赢了。

They came to the conclusion *that the work could be done well*. 他们得出结论——那工作可以做好。

⑧ 独立成分

独立成分就是指那些与主语、谓语不发生结构上关系的成分。它们在句中的位置比较灵活。英语中的独立成分有三种,即感叹语、称呼语和插入语。

A. 感叹语独立成分

感叹语(Interjection)表示喜、怒、哀、乐等各种不同的感情或情绪。因为它没有一定的实义,所以在句中不构成任何句子成分,但它与全句有关联,不能脱离句子而存在。

Ah! So you are back now! 啊! 你回来了! (感叹词感叹语)

Oh! You are too late already! 唉! 你已经太迟了! (感叹词感叹语)

Help! *Help*! 救命! 救命! (名词 help 转化为感叹语)

Fire! 失火了! (名词 fire 转化成感叹语)

Dear! I've lost my watch! 哎呀,我把手表丢了! (形容词转化为感叹语)

Oh dear! Why should you so dull! 天哪! 你怎么这样笨! (短语感叹语)

I'm supposed to be on a diet, but *hang it*, I will have a piece of cake! 我得节食,但该死,我总是要吃一片面包的! (动宾结构感叹语)

B. 呼唤语独立成分

Mary, what are you doing there? 玛丽,你在那里干什么? (呼唤语感叹语)

And you, *my friends*, will have to work harder. 你们,我的朋友们,干活必须要卖力些。(呼唤语作感叹语)

What, do you really mean it? 什么,你真是这个意思吗? (疑问代词 what 转化为感叹语)

My, what a downpour! 哎呀,好大的雨呀! (形容词性物指代词转化为感叹语)

Behave yourself, *you*! 你,你要规矩些! (人称代词转化为感叹语)

Wonderful/Great! We can go to visit the Greta Wall! 妙极(太好)了! 我们可以去游览长城了! (形容词转化为感叹语)

Come, tell me all about it. 喂,把这件事全告诉我吧。(动词 come 转化为感叹语)

Say! What a watermelon! 唷! 多大的西瓜! (动词 say 转化为感叹语)

Well, it can't be helped. 嗯,只好如此了。(副词 well 转化为感叹语)

Why, even a child knows that! 哎呀,这连小孩子都知道呀! (副词 why 转化为感叹语)

C. 插入语独立成分

插入语(Parenthesis)也是独立成分。它用来插入句中表示说话人的看法、态度、总结或附加解释。

Frankly, I don't trust Mr. Wang. 坦率地说，我不信任王先生。(副词作插入语)

Wonderful, Shenzhou VI with two Chinese spacemen has succeeded in traveling into space. 太好了，装载着两名中国宇航员的神舟六号已成功地进行了太空旅行。(副词作插入语)

Most of all, we should make a careful plan first. 最重要的是，我们得先制订一个细致的计划。(形容词作插入语)

She is, *on the whole*, a hardworking student. 她，总的说来，是个勤奋的学生。(介词短语作插入语)

第2章　主动词、助动词和情态动词

英语中动词的分类涉及很多语法问题和语义问题，而动词分类又必须从不同的角度来进行。我们把动词分为三种：主动词、助动词和情态动词（也有语法书把情态动词归入助动词）。主动词也叫普通动词或实义动词（Notional Verb），它表示句子主语的动作或状态。这三种动词中，主动词非常复杂，相比之下助动词、情态动词比较简单。

2.1 主动词

所谓主动词（Main Verb）和助动词（Auxiliary），是指动词在构成动词词组中所起的作用而言，实际上这些都要在具体句子中才能体现出来。动词词组是以主动词为中心的词组。在肯定的陈述句中，主动词可以单独组成动词词组，有时要增加补语、宾语或状语。有时动词词组只有一个主动词，有时是一个主动词加上一个或一个以上的助动词组成，有时又会有两个或以上主动词（叫并列或多个谓语）加上助动词。

The sun *rises*. 太阳升起。（一个主动词）
She *worked hard*. 她卖力地工作。（一个主动词 + 一个状语）
She *doesn't work hard*. 她工作不卖力。（一个主动词 + 一个助动词[否定式] + 状语）
Does she *work hard*? 她工作卖力吗？（一个助动词 + 一个主动词 + 一个状语）
The ship *will sink*. 那船将沉没。（一个主动词和一个助动词）
The boat *is sinking*. 那小船在下沉。（一个主动词和一个助动词）
The boat *has been sinking*. 那小船已在下沉着。（一个主动词和两个助动词）
I *will get up* at six tomorrow and *catch* the first bus to Wumen Village. 我明天六点起床，然后赶头班公共车去吴门村。（一个助动词，两个主动词）

及物动词（Transitive Verb）、不及物动词（Intransitive Verb）和连系动词（Linking verb），这三个主动词就其名称而言，及物动词和不及物动词的区分就看后面是否带宾语，而连系动词就是本身有词汇意义，但又不能单独构成谓语，它必须组成系表结构，连系动词起着联系的作用。

(1) 及物动词

及物动词可分单宾语及物动词和双宾语及物动词两种。

① 单宾语及物动词

单宾语及物动词后面只带一个宾语。
She *like English*. 她喜欢英语。
Her father *caught a big fish*. 她父亲捉到一条大鱼。
Mary *loves music*. 玛丽喜爱音乐。
He *played basketball* in the morning. 他上午打篮球了。
John *bought an air-conditioner* from a shop online last week. 约翰上周从一个网上商店买了一台空调。

及物动词后面的宾语必须由具有名词性质的单词、短语或者从句来担当，包含名词、代词、不定式、动名词、名词短语或名词性从句。

A. 名词、名词短语和名词性从句作宾语

a. 名词作宾语

I bought *a skirt*. 我买了一条短裙。

He wrote *a letter*. 他写了一封信。

She adopted *a boy*. 她收养了一个男孩。

b. 名词短语作宾语

He bought *a pen and a notebook*. 他买了一支钢笔和一个笔记本。

She met *the boy with brown hair* again. 她又遇到了那个长棕色头发的男孩。

He saw *a group of people* just now. 刚刚他看到一群人。

c. 名词性从句作宾语

在复合句中,当谓语的宾语是一个从句时,这个从句就叫作宾语从句(Object Clause)。宾语从句是名词性从句的一种,具有名词的功能,在主句中担任宾语。

I noticed *that someone was peeping at me*. 我注意到有人偷窥我。

I wonder *what you are thing about*. 我不知道你在想什么。

He didn't know *whether he should invite her to dinner or not*. 他不知道是否应该邀请她吃饭。

B. 代词作宾语

I didn't see *her*. 我没有看见她。

Let's discuss *it*. 让我们讨论它吧。

I miss *you*. 我想你。

C. 不定式作宾语

I want *to see you*. 我想见你。

He planned *to study abroad*. 他计划去国外学习。

He pretended *to know it*. 他假装知道。

Note:有些及物动词习惯上只能用不定式作宾语。这类及物动词有:afford, agree, aim, appear, arrange, ask, beg, care, choose, claim, constent, decide, decline, demand, desire, determine, expect, fail, fear, happen, help, hesitate, hope, manage, offer, plan, prepare, proceed, pretend, promise, refuse, resolve, seem, swear, trouble, threaten, wish 等。

We decided *to go there*. 我们决定去那里。

He refused *to attend the meeting*. 他拒绝去参加会议。

I promised *to buy him a bicycle*. 我答应给他买一辆自行车。

D. 动名词作宾语

The little girl practices *playing the piano* every day. 这小女孩每天都练习弹钢琴。

I love *singing*. 我爱唱歌。

Would you mind *closing the door*? 你介意关上门吗?

a. 有些及物动词习惯上只用动名词作宾语。这类及物动词有:acknowledge, advise, admit, allow, antipate, avoid, appreciate, bar, complete, confess, consider, defend, defer, delay, deny, dislike, enjoy, envy, escape, excuse, fancy, favour, finish, forbid, forgive, hinder, imagine, include, involve, keep, mention, mind, miss, pardon, permit, postpone, practice, quit, recall, recommend, report, resist, resume, risk, suggest, tolerate, understand 等。

She avoided *seeing him again*. 她避免再见到他。

I considered *traveling abroad*. 我考虑去国外旅游。

He denied *smoking in this room*. 他否认在这个房间抽过烟。

b. 有些动词后面既可以用动名词又可用不定式作宾语,意思不变。这类及物动词有:attempt, begin,

commence, continue, intend, start 等。

He attempted *picking an apple* from the tree. (= He attempted *to pick an apple* from the tree.) 他试图摘树上的苹果。

He began *learning English*. (= He began *to learn English*.) 他开始学习英语。

She intended *buying a new car*. (= She intended *to buy a new car*.) 她打算买一辆新车。

c. 如果及物动词后面的宾语表示"认识"或"了解"的意思，那么只能用不定式作宾语。因为动名词表示进行，而"认识"或"了解"只是短暂性的动词。

Jane began understanding him. （误）

Jane began *to understand him*. （正）珍开始了解他。

John started realizing his mistake. （误）

John started *to realize his mistake*. （正）约翰开始意识到他的错误。

d. 有些动词后面既可以用动名词又可用不定式作宾语，但是意思有所不同。

● like, love, hate, prefer 等及物动词后接动名词作宾语时，通常表示一般性或习惯性的动作，而后接不定式作宾语时则多表示一次性或具体动作。但在现代英语中，人们越来越不加区别地使用。

I hate *swimming* in the river. 我讨厌在河里游泳。（指通常情况）

I hate *to swim* in the river today. 我今天不想在河里游泳。（指今天不想）

She loved *playing the violin*. 她喜爱拉小提琴。（指通常情况）

She loved *to play the violin* when he came to see her. 当他来看她时她喜欢拉小提琴。（指具体情况）

● forget, remember, regret 等及物动词后接动名词作宾语时，通常动名词（非谓语动词）表示的动作发生在及物动词（谓语动词）表示的动作之前。而及物动词后接不定式作宾语时，通常不定式短语（非谓语动词）表示的动作发生在及物动词（谓语动词）表示的动作之后。

I remember *mailing the letter*. 我记得把这封信寄出了。（已经寄出）

I remember *to mail the letter*. 我记得要把这封信寄出。（还未寄出）

I forgot *buying you this book*. 我忘记已经给你买了这本书。（买过了，但忘记了）

I forgot *to buy you this book*. 我忘记给你买这本书了。（忘记买了）

● 动词 stop、短语动词 go on 等后接动名词和不定式作宾语时，表示的意思不同。动词后接动名词时表示停止或继续做某事。动词后接不定式时表示一种目的，停止或继续的目的是为了做另外一件事。

He stopped *talking about it*. 他停止谈论这件事。（不再谈论）

He stopped *to talk about it*. 他停下来，（开始）谈论这件事。（停下正在做的事情，目的是要谈论）

He went on *repairing his car*. 他继续修理汽车。（他不间断地做同一件事）

He went on *to repair his car*. 他继续修理汽车。（做完一件事后，接着做另一件事）

● try, propose, mean 等后面接动名词和不定式的意思也不大相同。

I tried *losing weight* last month. 上个月我尝试着减肥。（试试看）

I tried *to lose weight* last month. 上个月我努力减肥。（试图，努力）

He proposes *waiting* till the rain stops. 他建议等雨停下来。（建议）

He proposes *to wait* till the rain stops. 他想等雨停下来。（想，意欲）

This event means *starting a business campaign*. 此事件意味着开始了一场商业运动。（意味）

I didn't mean *to hurt you*. 我不想伤害你。（想，意欲）

● want, need, require 等后面接动名词，表示被动意义，如后接动词不定式一定用被动式。

These chairs need *repairing*. 这些椅子需要修理。（被修理，表示被动）

The flowers want *watering*. 这些花需要浇水了。（被浇水，表示被动）

② 双宾语及物动词（S + V + Oi + Od）

双宾语及物动词就是后面带两个宾语（Object），一个为直接宾语（Direct Object），另一个为间接宾语

(Indirect Object)。间接宾语紧跟动词,直接宾语跟在间接宾语之后。一般来讲,直接宾语为人,间接宾语为物。可跟双宾语的动词有许多,如 bring, buy, give, hand, leave, lend, offer, sell, send, show, tell, teach, write 等。

I asked *him a question*. 我问了他一个问题。

My brother will give *me a bicycle*. 我哥哥将送我一辆自行车。

He brought his *mother a bouquet of flowers*. 他带给他母亲一束花。

A. 双宾语的顺序

在"及物动词+双宾语"句型中,要注意两个宾语的顺序。

a. 直接宾语为人称代词、间接宾语为名词时,直接宾语必须在前。

He will give his brother them. (误)

He will give them to his brother. (正)他将要把它们给他的哥哥。

b. 直接宾语与间接宾语都为人称代词时,直接宾语在前较常见。

He will give her it. (少见)

He will give it to her. (常见)他会把这个给她。

B. 有些带双宾语的动词可以用 S+V+Od+Prep.+Oi 句型代替

像上面的例句 He brought his mother a bouquet of flowers,也可以表达为:He brought a bouquet of flowers to his mother. 两个句子意思大致相同。第一句强调的是带给动作的对象是他的母亲,第二节强调的是带给动作的内容是花束。

a. S+V+Od+Prep.+Oi 句型中,当表示"给予"的意思时,介词要用 to。这类动词有:bring, give, hand, lend, offer, pass, promise, sell, send, show, teach, tell, write 等。

She lent me 50 Pounds last Sunday. (= She lent 50 Pounds to me last Sunday.) 上个周日她借给我 50 英镑。

I told you the story. (= I told the story to you.) 我给你讲了这个故事。

He teaches me French. (= He teaches French to me.) 他教我法语。

b. S+V+Od+Prep.+Oi 句型中,当表示"代劳"或"为……"的意思时,介词要用 for。这类动词有:buy, leave, make, order, sing 等。

Jenny sang us a song. (= Jenny sang a song for us.) 珍妮为我们唱了一首歌。

I bought her a pen. (= I bought a pen for her.) 我为她买了一支笔。

Her father made her a toy. (= Her father made a toy for her.) 她父亲为她做了一个玩具。

c. S+V+Od+Prep.+Oi 句型中,当表示"从……中"的意思时,介词要用 of。这类动词有 ask 等。

May I ask you a favor? (= May I ask a favor of you?) 我可以请你帮个忙吗?

d. 有些动词后面所带的间接宾语和直接宾语之间要有介词。

• 动词+人(间接宾语)+of+物(直接宾语)

这类动词的句型跟上面的 S+V+Od+of+Oi 不同。上面的是"动词+物(直接宾语)+of+人(间接宾语)"。这类动词有:accuse, cheat, cure, deprive, inform, notify, persuade, remind, relieve, rid, rob, suspect, warn 等。

The gangster *robbed* me *of* my handbag. 这个歹徒抢了我的手袋。

They *accused* him *of* a crime. 他们控告他犯罪。

They *informed* me *of* their decision. 他们通知了我他们的决定。

Note:这类动词后面的直接宾语和间接宾语顺序不能颠倒。

• 动词+人(间接宾语)+with+物(直接宾语)

这类动词有:furnish, provide, present, supply 等。它们都具有"提供"的意思。

They *provided* me *with* all I needed. 他们提供给我所有我需要的东西。

Those people *furnished* the hotel *with* fake paintings. 那些人给这家酒店提供假画。

The supermarket *supplied* the restaurant *with* fruit. 这个超市给这家饭店提供水果。

Note：这类动词后面的两个宾语位置可以颠倒，但是相应的介词发生了变化。

They *provided* me with all I needed. (= They *provided* all I needed for me.) 他们提供我所有需要的东西。

Those people *furnished* the hotel with fake paintings. (= Those people *furnished* fake paintings to the hotel.) 那些人把假画提供给这家旅馆。

The supermarket *supplied* the restaurant with fruit. (= The supermarket *supplied* fruit to the restaurant.) 超市把水果供应给这家饭店。

C. 动词 + 物（直接宾语）+ to + 人（间接宾语）

这类动词有：explain, introduce, propose, recommend, express 等。

John *explained* the reason to his manager. 约翰向经理解释原因。

She *introduced* her boss to me. 她把她的老板介绍给我。

He *recommended* this good method to his colleagues. 他向同事推荐这个好方法。

Note：这类动词后面的两个宾语的顺序理论上可以颠倒，并且相应的介词不变，但是这种用法较少。

John *explained* to his manager the reason. 约翰向他的经理解释原因。

She *introduced* to me her boss. 她把她的老板介绍给我。

He *recommended* to his colleagues this good method. 他向同事推荐这个好方法。

但是不可以把上面的句子变成下列句式：

John *explained* his manager the reason. 约翰向他的经理解释原因。

D. 及物动词 + 宾语 + 补足语（句型为 S + V + O + OC）

及物动词后面除了需要跟宾语之外，有时候也需要跟宾语补足语。宾语补足语是补充说明宾语的成分，通常置于宾语之后。宾语和宾语补足语合在一起构成复合宾语。

当然，很多动词实际上既可以作及物动词，又可以作不及物动词。比如 sing 这个词，既可以说 He sings a song(他唱歌)，又可以说 He is singing(他在歌唱)。

有些动词虽然是及物动词，后面带有宾语，但是意思表达不够完整，需要有补足语对宾语加以补充说明。这个补足语通常放在宾语后面，叫作及物动词的宾语和宾语补足语，又叫及物动词的复合宾语。

a. 可作宾语补足语的词语

宾语补足语通常由名词短语、形容词短语、副词短语、介词短语以及非谓语动词短语充当。

People call him *little Jack*. 人们叫他小杰克。(名词短语 little Jack 作宾语补足语)

I found this book *very interesting*. 我发现这本书很有趣。(形容词短语 very interesting 作宾语补足语)

The boy should put the toys *away*. 这个男孩应该把玩具收拾好。(副词 away 作宾语补足语)

He found himself *in trouble*. 他发现自己身陷困境。(介词短语 in trouble 作宾语补足语)

She heard someone *screaming*. 她听到有人尖叫。(非谓语动词［现在分词］screaming 作宾语补足语)

b. 可带宾语补足语的动词

● 表示感官的动词：see, hear, feel, watch, notice, observe 等。

He *watched* the girls dancing. 他观看女孩们跳舞。

I *noticed* a man following me. 我注意到一个男人跟踪我。

I *saw* Jenny dance. 我看到珍妮跳舞。

● 表示使役的动词：make, have, get 等。

He *made* her happy. 他让她很高兴。

The vicar *had* the tree cut down. 牧师让人把树砍掉了。

I want to *get* things done quickly. 我想快点把事情做完。

- 表示"使……保持某种状态"的动词：keep, leave 等。

You must *keep* the children away from the fire. 你必须使孩子们远离火。

I *left* the light on last night. 昨晚我把灯开着。

- 表示"命名"、"任命"、"指定"的动词：name, call, elect, appoint, assign 等。

They *named* the baby George. 他们给婴儿取名乔治。

All the children *called* her Mum. 所有的孩子都叫她妈妈。

We *elected* him teamleader. 我们选他当队长。

Note：如果补足语是表示职位的名词，通常该名词前省略冠词。

- 表示"认为，视为"的动词：believe, consider, find, think, regard 等。

We *found* this book difficult. 我们发现这本书很难。

I *consider* you my good friend. 我把你当作好朋友。

I *regard* him as a great artist. 我把他看作是伟大的艺术家。

E. 反身及物动词

反身及物动词（Reflexive Verb）必须用反身代词作宾语。这类词数量不多。

These boys are expected to *behave themselves*. 这些男孩应该守规矩。

He *absented himself* from work. 他没有来上班。

She *availed herself of* every opportunity to learn French. 她抓住每个机会学习法语。

a. 反身及物动词的结构

这样的结构是"反身动词＋反身代词＋介词结构"。其中的介词有 in, of, on, to, with 及其他一些介词。

- 介词 in

clothe oneself in 穿，dress oneself in 穿，engage oneself in 从事，lose oneself in 专心于

- 介词 of

avail oneself of 利用，think oneself of 考虑，deliver oneself of 说出，rid oneself of 除去

- 介词 on

pride oneself on 以……骄傲，revenge oneself on 报仇，seat oneself on/in 坐

- 介词 to

abandon oneself to 沉湎于，accustom oneself to 习惯于，adapt oneself to 适用于，addict oneself to 沉湎于，address oneself to 忙于，confine oneself to 局限于，dedicate oneself to 献身于，devote oneself to 专心于、献身于，engage oneself to 和……订婚，give oneself to 专心于，resign oneself to 委身，服从

- 介词 with

amuse oneself with/by 以……自娱，burden oneself with 使负担，busy oneself with/about/at/in 忙于，familiarize oneself with 精通，occupy oneself with 忙于

- 其他介词

absent oneself from 缺席，distinguish oneself by 因……扬名，present oneself at/for 出席

b. "反身动词＋反身代词＋介词短语"结构的替代结构

这一结构通常可以用"be＋反身动词的过去分词＋介词结构"来表示，介词基本不变。

He dressed himself in a black suit. （＝ He was dressed in a black suit.）他身穿一套黑西装。（介词不变）

She devoted herself to the educational career. （＝ She was devoted to the education career.）她献身于教育事业。（介词不变）

He distinguished himself by his versatility. （＝ He was distinguished for his versatility.）他因多才多艺而闻名。（介词有变）

③ 限定动词和非限定动词

英语中的限定动词(Finite Verb)和非限定动词(Non-Finite Verb)的区别在句中才能体现出来。一般动词在词典或词汇表中都以"原形"(base form)形式出现。事实上,有些动词可以是限定动词,但同时也以非限定形式出现,有的动词却不具有这种特点。

限定动词和非限定动词的最明显的区别在于:前者在句中有"时"(tense)的标记,而后者没"时"的标记。

有些动词在句中出现时有五种形式,这五种形式也叫"语法形式"。

原形	现在时	过去时	不定式	v-ing 形式	v-ed 形式
look	looks	looked	to look	looking	looked
eat	eats	ate	to eat	eating	eaten
work	works	worked	to work	working	worked
sit	sits	sat	to sit	sitting	sat

英语中的基本助动词和情态助动词只有个别的词有以上五种形式。

原形	现在时	过去时	不定式	v-ing 形式	v-ed 形式
be	is/am/are	was/were	to be	being	been
have	has	had	to have	having	had
do	does/do	did	to do	doing	done
can		could			
may		might			
will		would			
dare					
need					
must					
		ought to			
		used to			

④ 规则动词和不规则动词

A. 规则动词

英语中的规则动词就是它们的过去式和过去分词均在原形动词词尾加-ed,如 listen→listened, listened; walk→walked, walked; stop→stopped, stopped。英语中的绝大多数动词是规则动词,即使现在新增的动词多数也是规则动词。

B. 不规则动词

不规则动词就是它们的过去式和过去分词并不在词尾加-ed,而是有它们独特的形式。不规则动词在英语中只占少数,大概 200 个左右。为便于记忆,我们把不规则动词分为三大类:①三个形式都相同;②两种形式相同;③三种形式都不相同。

现在所展示出来的三表选自杨元兴先生所著的《学生英语短语动词词典》(广西教育出版社,1994)的附录 I 中的部分内容。

a. 三种形式都相同

不定式	过去式	过去分词	汉语
bet	bet/betted	bet/betted	打赌
broadcast	broadcast/broadcasted	broadcast/broadcasted	广播

续表

不定式	过去式	过去分词	汉语
burst	burst	burst	爆炸,破裂
cast	cast	cast	抛,投
cost	cost	cost	花费,价值为
cut	cut	cut	切
hit	hit	hit	击
hurt	hurt	hurt	伤害
knit	knit/knitted	knit/knitted	编结
let	let	let	让
overset	overset	overset	搅乱,打翻
put	put	put	放,置
reset	reset	reset	重放,重新安排
rid	rid/ridded	rid/ridded	免除;解除
set	set	set	安放,竖立
shut	shut	shut	关
slit	slit	slit	切开,撕开
split	split	split	劈开
spread	spread	spread	传布
thrust	thrust	thrust	捅,戳
undercut	undercut	undercut	从下部切开
underlet	underlet	underlet	廉价出租
unset	unset	unset	使移动,使松动
upset	upset	upset	弄翻,打乱

b. 两种形式相同

不定式	过去时	过去分词	汉语
abide	abode(abided)	abode(abided)	居住
awake	awoke	awoke(awaked)	醒悟
beat	beat	beaten	击打
become	became	become	变成
bend	bent	bent	使弯曲
bind	bound	bound	捆、绑,装订(书)
bite	bit	bit	咬
breed	bred	bred	饲养
bring	brought	brought	带来
build	built	built	建造
burn	burnt	burnt	燃烧
buy	bought	bought	买
catch	caught	caught	捉住
cling	clung	clung	黏着;坚守;坚持

续表

不定式	过去时	过去分词	汉语
come	came	come	来
deal	dealt	dealt	处理
dig	dug	dug	挖掘
dream	dreamt/dreamed	dreamt/dreamed	做梦
dwell	dwelt	dwelt	居;住;住宿
feed	fed	fed	饲养
feel	felt	felt	感到
fight	fought	fought	战斗
find	found	found	发现,找到
flee	fled	fled	逃走
fling	flung	flung	投;掷;摔
forget	forgot	forgot (forgotten)	忘记
get	got	got	得到
grind	ground	ground	磨碎(成粉)
hang	hung	hung	挂
have	had	had	有
hear	heard	heard	听见
hold	held	held	抓住
keep	kept	kept	遵守
kneel	knelt	knelt	跪下
lay	laid	laid	置放,下蛋
lead	led	led	领导,引导
lean	leant (leaned)	leant (leaned)	倾斜,靠
leap	leapt (leaped)	leapt (leaped)	跳,跃
learn	learnt (learned)	learnt (learned)	学会
leave	left	left	离开
lend	lent	lent	借出
light	lit (lighted)	lit (lighted)	点燃
lose	lost	lost	失去
make	made	made	制造,使
mean	meant	meant	意思是
meet	met	met	遇见
melt	melted	melted (melten)	融化
overcome	overcame	overcome	克服
pay	paid	paid	付
read	read [red]	read [red]	读
rebuild	rebuilt	rebuilt	重建

续表

不定式	过去时	过去分词	汉语
retell	retold	retold	复述
say	said	said	说
seek	sought	sought	寻觅;求得
sell	sold	sold	出售
send	sent	sent	送,派
sew	sewed	sewn（sewed）	缝纫
shine	shone	shone	照耀
shoot	shot	shot	射击
sing	sang（sung）	sung	唱歌
sink	sank（sunk）	sunk（sunken）	沉下
sit	sat	sat	坐
sleep	slept	slept	睡
slide	slid	slid	使滑动
smell	smelt	smelt	嗅出
speed	sped	sped	加速
spell	spelt/spelled	spelt/spelled	拼写
spend	spent	spent	花费;度过
spin	spun	spun	纺
spit	spat	spat	唾吐
spoil	spoilt（spoiled）	spoilt（spoiled）	损伤
stand	stood	stood	站
stave	staved（stove）	staved（stove）	凿孔;敲破
stick	stuck	stuck	附着;坚持
strike	struck	struck（stricken）	敲打,击
string	strung	strung	扎上
sweep	swept	swept	打扫
teach	taught	taught	教
tell	told	told	告诉
think	thought	thought	想
unbend	unbent	unbent	使变直
unbuild	unbuilt	unbuilt	毁灭
underbuy	underbought	underbought	以便宜之价格买进
underfeed	underfed	underfed	不给足量食物
unsay	unsaid	unsaid	取消(前言)
uphold	upheld	upheld	举起,支持
weep	wept	wept	哭泣
win	won	won	赢

续表

不定式	过去时	过去分词	汉语
wind	winded/wound	winded/wound	弯曲;前进
wring	wrung	wrung	拧;绞

c. 三种形式都不同

不定式	过去时	过去分词	汉语
arise	arose	arisen	起来;上升
awake	awoke	awaked/awaken	使醒;唤醒;起床
be (is, am)	was	been	是
be (are)	were	been	是
bear	bore	born, borne	忍受,出生
begin	bgan	bgun	开始
befall	befell	befallen	降临;发生
bid	bade/bid	bidden/bid	命令;嘱咐
blow	blew	blown	吹
break	broke	broken	打破
choose	chose	chosen	选择
do	did	done	做
draw	drew	drawn	拉,牵
drink	drank	drunk	喝,饮
drive	drove	driven	驾驶
eat	ate	eaten	吃
fall	fell	fallen	落下
fly	flew	flown	飞
forbid	forbade	forbidden	禁止
forgive	forgave	forgiven	宽恕
freeze	froze	frozen	冰冻
give	gave	given	给
go	went	gone	去
grow	grew	grown	生长
hide	hid	hidden	躲藏
know	knew	known	知道
lie	lay	lain	躺
mistake	mistook	mistaken	误解
overthrow	overthrew	overthrown	推翻;击败
ride	rode	ridden	乘,骑
ring	rang	rung	打铃
rise	rose	risen	升起

续表

不定式	过去时	过去分词	汉语
see	saw	seen	看见；领会
shake	skook	shaken	摇
show	showed	shown	显示
sing	sang	sung	唱歌
sow	sowed	sown/sowed	播种
speak	spoke	spoken	说话
spring	sprang	sprung	跳跃
steal	stole	stolen	偷窃
swear	swore	sworn	宣誓
swim	swam	swum	游泳
take	took	taken	拿，取
tear	tore	torn	撕，扯
tread	trod	trodden	踩，踏
underdo	underdid	underdone	不尽全力做
undergo	underwent	undergone	遭受；忍受
underwrite	underwrote	underwritten	签名于下
undo	undid	undone	解开，解决
unfreeze	unfroze	unfrozen	（因旱暖）提早融雪
wake	woke	waked/waken	醒，唤醒
wear	wore	worn	穿，戴
weave	wove	woven/wove	织（布）
withdraw	withdrew	withdrawn	收回；撤销
write	wrote	written	写

(2) 不及物动词

① 不及物动词概述

不及物动词(Intransitive Verb)，顾名思义，就是后面不能带宾语的动词，也就是说不需要宾语就能表达出完整的意思。

Something *happened*. 有事情发生了。

He *left*. 他离开了。

This great moment *came* at last. 这一伟大的时刻终于到来了。

② 不及物动词的用法

A. 主语＋不及物动词（句型为SV）

a. 这类词可以单独存在，之后不需加任何词类意思就很完整。

Time *flies*. 时光飞去。

The wolf *died*. 这匹狼死了。

That thief *escaped*. 那个小偷逃走了。

b. 不及物动词之后可以接副词、介词短语、状语从句等来修饰该动词。

Time flies *quickly*. 时光很快飞去。(副词 quickly 修饰 flies)
The wolf died *near the fox's cave*. 狼死在狐狸洞穴附近。(介词短语 near the fox's cave 修饰 died)
That thief escaped *when the police came here*. 当警察到达的时候那个小偷逃走了。(状语从句 when the police came here 修饰 escaped)

c. 有些动词可作及物动词，又可作不及物动词。有些动词，当它们后带宾语时是及物动词，不带宾语就是不及物动词。

{ Man can *speak*. 人会说话。(speak 作不及物动词，没有宾语)
{ I can *speak* English. 我会说英语。(speak 作及物动词，English 作 speak 的宾语)

{ The little boy *hid* behind a big tree. 这个小男孩藏在一棵大树后面。(hid 作不及物动词，没有宾语)
{ He *hid* the gun in the bush. 他把枪藏在灌木丛中。(hid 作及物动词，the gun 作 hid 的宾语)

Note：有些明显的不及物动词有时也可以作及物动词。

{ He *walked* away. 他走开了。(walked 作不及物动词，意思为"行走")
{ He *walked* his dog every evening. 他每天傍晚遛狗。(walked 作及物动词，意思为"遛……，带着……溜达"，his dog 作 walked 的宾语)

{ The bird *flied* away. 鸟飞走了。(flied 作不及物动词，意思为"飞行")
{ The children *flied* kites in the park. 孩子们在公园里放风筝。(flied 作及物动词，意思为"放飞"，kites 作 flied 的宾语)

d. 有些不及物动词 + 介词 = 及物动词

He *thought of* traveling abroad. (= He *considered* traveling abroad.) 他考虑去国外旅游。
She *called on* her old friend yesterday. (= She *visited* her old friend yesterday.) 她昨天拜访了她的老朋友。

e. 有些及物动词常作不及物动词，此时表示被动意义，这时主语通常是物。
The toys *sold out* in several hours. 这些玩具在几个小时之内就卖完了。

B. 不及物动词与同源宾语

有些不及物动词后面接与其意思相同的名词时，可作及物动词。因为此动词与宾语为同一语源，所以我们把动词称为同源动词（Cognate Verb），把动词的宾语则称为同源宾语（Cognate Object）。

He *is living a happy life* in the countryside. 他在乡村过着幸福的生活。
Betty *dreamed a wonderful dream* last night. 贝蒂昨晚做了一个奇妙的梦。
He *laughed a hearty laugh*. 他开心地大笑。
His mother *sighed a big sigh*. 他妈妈大大地叹了一口气。

（3）连系动词

① 连系动词概述

系动词（Link Verb）就是连接主语和表语，表示谓语关系的动词。有些专家把系动词归入不及物动词范畴内。但是本书认为，与不及物动词可以独立担当谓语不同，系动词不能独立担当谓语。它后面必须接有表语，构成系表结构，用以说明主语的状态、性质、特征等情况。表语也可以被看成是一种主语补足语。

此类动词的句型为"主语 + 系动词 + 表语"（S + V + P）。

He *is* ill today. 他今天生病了。
He *looks* unhappy. 他看起来不高兴。
It *becomes* warmer and warmer. 天气变得越来越暖和。

② 连系动词的种类

A. 状态系动词

这是最基本的系动词，只有 be 一词，用来表示状态，可以翻译成"是"，或不翻译。

第 2 章　主动词、助动词和情态动词

Her father *is* a teacher. 她父亲是一位老师。

He *is* happy today. 他今天很高兴。

His name *is* John Smith. 他的名字是约翰·史密斯。

B. 感官系动词

像 look（看起来），sound（听起来），smell（闻起来），taste（尝起来），feel（摸起来）等表示感觉、知觉的词。这些动词后面的表语不能是名词，必须是形容词。

Our boss *looked* upset. 我们老板看起来很难过。

That *sounds* reasonable. 那听起来很合理。

The roses *smell* sweet. 这些玫瑰闻起来很香甜。

The fish *tastes* terrible. 这鱼尝起来味道很糟糕。

The cloth *feels* soft and smooth. 这布料摸起来既柔软又光滑。

Note： 这些词后面还常跟 like 介词短语或者连词 as if 引导的表语从句。

He *looks* like a big boss. 他看起来像一个大老板。

She *looked as* if she had been a Hollywood star. 她看起来像好莱坞明星。

C. 表象系动词

appear, seem 表示"似乎，看起来像"。

This old man *appeared* badly hurt. 这个老人似乎受了重伤。

The machine doesn't *seem* to work well. 这台机器似乎不好用。

D. 持续系动词

keep, rest, remain, stay, lie, stand 等用来表示主语继续或保持某种状态。

He always *kept* silent in her presence. 有她在场时他总保持沉默。

This matter *rests* a mystery. 此事仍是一个谜。

The situation *remains* unchanged. 形势仍然未变。

Nothing *stays* the same for long. 任何事都不会长久不变。

During the winter the seeds *lie* dormant in the soil. 冬天种子在土壤中休眠。

The government *stands* ready to take action. 政府准备采取行动。

E. 终止系动词

prove 和 turn out 表示主语已终止动作，表示"证实"、"变成"的意思。

The rumor *proved* false. 这谣言证实有假。

His plan *turned out* a success. 他的计划终于成功了。

F. 变化连系动词

become, get, come, go, fall, turn, grow, run 表示"渐渐变成"。

Our country *is becoming* stronger and stronger. 我们国家变得越来越强大了。

It *is getting* very common. 这个变得非常普遍。

This envelope *has come* unstuck. 这封信开了。

The children *went* wild with excitement. 孩子们欣喜若狂。

The baby soon *fell* asleep. 这个婴儿很快睡着了。

The girl *turned* blue with cold. 那女孩冻得脸色发青。

He *grew* rich little by little. 他渐渐变得富有。

Time *is running* out. 时间不多了。

Notes： a. become 和 get 主要指一个人暂时性的身心变化或永久性的自然变化，还可用于指天气的变化和事物发展的趋势。

Because of this role she played in the play, she *became* famous overnight. 由于她在戏里扮演的角色，她一

夜成名了。
He *got angry* at hearing the bad news. 听到这个坏消息他很生气。
It's *getting warmer and warmer*. 天气变得越来越暖了。
This small town *became very beautiful*. 这个小镇变得很美丽。

b. come 和 go 表示事物状态的变化。come 常用于"好"的变化，go 则常用于"坏"的变化。
Her wish *came true*. 她的愿望实现了。
Everything *came right*. 一切顺利。
The machine *has gone wrong*. 这台机器坏了。
Fish soon *goes* bad in hot weather. 大热天鱼很快会坏。

c. come 和 go 的主语一般为物，但是当表语是 mad, crazy, blind, deaf, lame 等或表示颜色时，常用人作主语。
He *went mad* in the end. 最后他疯了。
This old woman *went blind*. 这个老太太眼睛瞎了。
The boy *went deaf* because of illness. 这个男孩由于生病变聋了。
This man *went blue* with fear. 这个人吓得脸色发青。

d. turn 常接与颜色或情绪有关的形容词。
Her face *turned pale* when somebody told her about that. 当有人告诉她那事时，她的脸色变得苍白。
The leaves are *turning green*. 树叶正渐渐变绿。
John's face *turned red* when he heard that. 当他听说这个时他的脸变得通红。

e. fall 用作连系动词只限于和少数形容词或名词搭配。
He *fell asleep* when he was reading. 他读书时睡着了。
Jim suddenly *fell ill* yesterday. 吉姆昨天突然病了。
The kid *fell silent* at last. 这个孩子终于静了下来。
She *fell prey to* fears. 她遭受着恐惧的折磨。
Lots of people *fell victims to* fascism. 许多人成了法西斯的受害人。

f. grow 表示人和事物特征的静态形容词，也接表示天气的形容词，侧重逐渐变成。run 后接 short, dry, low, deep 等形容词，主语多为可以流动、能够消耗的东西。
The man *grew fatter and fatter*. 这个男人变得越来越胖。
Their money was *running short*. 他们的钱快用光了。
Her tears *ran dry*. 她的眼泪流干了。
Still waters *run deep*. 静水流深。

（4）单词动词和短语动词

所谓单词动词（Single-Word Verb）就是一个词形式的动词，而短语动词（Phrasal Verb）就是由两个或两个以上的词所组成的动词。

① 单词动词

英语中多数动词为单词动词。
I *saw* a bird flying in the sky. 我看见一只鸟在天空中飞翔。
What did you *do* last night? 你昨晚干什么了？

② 短语动词

这里，我们把由两个或两个以上的词所组成的动词统称短语动词。现代英语语法认为，那些"动词+副词/介词/名词/形容词"结构的动词形式都可称为短语动词。杨元兴先生在《21世纪英语短语动词四用指南》(南京大学出版社,2008)中把"v.＋adv, v.＋prep., v.＋adv.＋prep., v.＋adj., v.＋n., v.＋n.＋prep. phr., 甚至 v.＋v."等结构全列为短语动词一类中去,这是现代英语的一种新反映。

Jim has *admitted to* breaking the window. 吉姆已承认打破了窗子。(v.＋prep.)

I always *get up* early in the morning. 我每天总是一早就起床。(v.＋adv.)

I'm *looking forward to* some warmer weather after this bitter winter. 严冬过后,我盼望着天气会暖和一些。(v.＋adv.＋prep.)

Take off your jacket if you *get hot*. 你若热,就脱掉外衣。(v.＋adj.)

We all *make mistakes* occasionally. 我们偶尔都会犯错误。(v.＋n.)

In the days before eletric calculators all children had to *learn their tables by heart*. 在没有电子计算机的时代,孩子们都得记住乘法表。(v.＋n.＋prep. phr.)

Where did you *lay hold of* this Chinese medicine? 你从哪里得到这种中草药的?(v＋n.＋prep.)

You'll have to *make do* with cold meat for dinner. 你只好凑合着吃冷肉当晚餐了。(v.＋v.)

(5) 动态动词和静态动词

从词汇意义上讲,英语动词可分为动态动词(Action Verb)和静态动词(State Verb),动态动词和静态动词也叫动作动词和状态动词。

① 动态动词

动态动词是表示运动状态的动词,它们可分为表示持续动作的动词、表示短暂动作的动词、表示状态改变和位置移动的动词三类。

A. 表示持续动作的动词

表示持续动作的动词主要有 eat, drink, fly, play, read, talk, walk, work, rain, run, snow 等。

We will *eat* meat for Lunch. 我们中饭吃肉。

He *is writing* a novel. 他在写一部小说。

Her mother *works* in a hospital. 她的母亲在一家医院工作。

It *rained* yesterday, and it began to *snow* at nine this morning. 昨天下了雨,今天上午九点又开始下雪了。

B. 表示短暂动作的动词

英语中有些动态动词所表示的动作比较短暂。它们是 close (a book/a window), open (one's eyes, a letter), hit, jump, knock (at/on the door), put (the books in order), take out 等。

Open all the windows, please. We are hot. 把窗子全打开。我们热呢。

A young man *jumped* into the river to save the drowning boy. 一个青年人跳入河中去救那落水小孩。

C. 表示状态改变、位置移动的动词

像 get, become, grow, turn, change, arrive, reach, leave 等动词,它们本身明显就有状态变化和位置移动的意思。

Autumn is in. The leaves of the trees *are turning* yellow. 秋天到了,树叶在变黄。

They *will leave* Nanjing for Beijing tomorrow morning. 他们明天早上将离开南京去北京。

② 静态动词

静态动词是与动态动词相比之下是相对静止状态的动词。这些动词大致有四类:A. be 和 have; B. 有与 be 和 have 类似意义的动词; C. 表示心理或情感状态的动词; D. 一些感觉动词。

A. be 和 have

其词义"是"、"有",这就很明显地表示出了"静"的意思。

Professor Li *is* an expert in English Grammar. 李教授是英语语法方面的专家。

He *has* a daughter who is teaching in a primary school. 他有个女儿,她在一所小学任教。

B. 有与 be 和 have 类似意义的动词

这些类似动词有 concern, compare, contain, cost, equal, exist, hold, interest, involve, fit, lack, matter, measure, owe, possess, resemble, weigh, apply to, belong to, consist of, depend on, deserve, differ from, stand for 等。

Don't *concern* yourself about what she says. 别管她说什么。

Life is often *compared* to voyage. 人生常被比作航海。

This coat *fit* me well. 这外套我穿正合适。

2.2 助动词

(1) 助动词概述

顾名思义,助动词(Auxiliary Verb),就是帮助实义动词的词类。它本身并无词义,只是置于实义动词前面,协助实义动词构成各种时态、语态、语气、疑问、否定结构等。一般说来,英语的助动词有 5 个:be, do, have, shall 和 will。

The baby *is* called little Johnny. 这个婴儿被叫作小强尼。(句中的助动词 is 与实义动词 call 构成 is called, 表示被动语态)

He *will* go to New York tomorrow morning. 他明天上午将要去纽约。(助动词 will 与实义动词 go 一起表示将来时态)

I *did* tell him about it that day. 我那天的确告诉他这个事情了。(助动词 did 置于实义动词 tell 前,表示强调语气)

Do you like a banana? 你喜欢香蕉吗?(助动词 do 与实义动词 like 构成 do … like, 其形式为现在时一般疑问句)

I *didn't* want to see the film. 我不想去看那部电电影。(助动词 did 的否定形式 didn't 与实义动词 want 构成过去时否定式)

(2) 助动词分述

① 助动词 be

A. 助动词 be 的形式

		肯定式	否定式
原形		be	
现在式	第一人称单数	am/'m	am not/'m not
现在式	第三人称单数	is/'s	is not/isn't/'s not
现在式	第二人称单复数和第一、三人称复数	are/'re	are not/aren't/'re not
过去式	第一、三人称单数	was	was not//wasn't
过去式	第二人称单复数和第一、三人称复数	were	were not/weren't
现在分词		being	not being
过去分词		been	not been

B. 助动词 be 的用法

a. 由"助动词 be + 动词现在分词"构成各种进行体

I *am listening to* music. 我在听音乐。(现在进行体)
He *is not painting* now. 他现在不在画画。(现在进行体)
I *was walking* in the street when he ran into me. 当他遇到我时我正在大街上走。(过去进行体)
They *were drinking* tea in the lounge just now. 刚才他们在休息室喝茶。(过去进行体)
I *shall/will be working* this weekend. 这个周末我将要工作。(将来进行时)
They *will be arriving* at ten o'clock. 他们将于10点钟到达。(将来进行时)
I told him that I *should/would be coming* to see him the next day. 我告诉他我第二天就去看他。(过去将来进行时)
She said that she *would be setting off* the next morning. 她说她第二天上午出发。(过去将来进行体)

b. 由"助动词 be + 动词过去分词"构成各种被动语态

I *am called* little Prince by them. 我被他们称为小王子。(一般现在时的被动语态)
He *is loved* by everyone. 他为大家所爱戴。(一般现在时的被动语态)
I *was accompanied* home by him last night. 昨晚我由他陪伴回家。(一般过去时的被动语态)
The dog *was fed* just now. 狗刚才已经喂食了。(一般过去时的被动语态)
I *shall be given* one more chance to try tomorrow. 明天我将会再被给予一次机会尝试。(一般将来时的被动语态)
The activities *will be organized* by the government agency. 这些活动将由政府部门组织。(一般将来时的被动语态)
My boss told me that I *should be sent* abroad the next year. 我的老板告诉我，我将在第二年被派往国外。(过去将来时的被动语态)
The post office claimed that a new set of stamps *would be issued* by the end of this year. 邮局声明一套新的邮票将于今年年底发行。(过去将来时的被动语态)

② **助动词 do**

A．助动词 do 的形式

		肯定式	否定式
	原形	do	do not/don't
现在式	第三人称单数	does	does not/doesn't
	第一、二人称单数，所有人称复数	do	do not/don't
	过去式	did	did not/didn't

B．助动词 do 的用法

a. 由"助动词 do + not + 动词原形"构成一般现在时和一般过去时的否定形式

I *don't like* playing basketball. 我不喜欢打篮球。(一般现在时的否定形式)
It *doesn't matter*. 不要紧。(一般现在时的否定形式)
He *didn't attend* the meeting yesterday. 他昨天没有去开会。(一般过去时的否定形式)
They *did not receive* good education when they were children. 他们小时候没有接受良好的教育。(一般过去时的否定形式)

b. 由助动词 do 构成一般现在时和一般过去时的疑问结构

Do you *know* he is coming? 你知道他要来吗？(一般现在时的一般疑问句结构)
Did you *go* to see him last week? 你上周去看他了吗？(一般过去时的一般疑问句结构)
What *do* you *like*? 你喜欢什么？(一般现在时的特殊疑问句结构)
How *did* you *sleep* last night? 你昨晚睡得怎样？(一般过去时的特殊疑问句结构)

He *doesn't like* watching TV, *does* he? 他不喜欢看电视,对吗?（一般现在时的附加疑问句结构）
She told you about it, *didn't* she? 她告诉你这件事了,不是吗?（一般过去时的附加疑问句结构）
Don't you *go* there to meet her? 你不去那儿接她吗?（一般现在时的否定疑问句结构）
Why *didn't* you *get* your things ready last night? 为什么你昨晚不把东西准备好呢?（一般过去时的否定疑问句结构）

c. 助动词 do 用于替代,以避免句中动词的重复
I hate that sort of advertisement. So *do* I. 我讨厌那种广告。我也是。（do 代替 hate）
I'm sorry, but I don't think I know you. In fact you *do*. 很抱歉,我想我不认识你。事实上你是认识我的。（do 代替 know）

d. 助动词 do 用于强调
Do tell me where he is! 一定要告诉我他在哪里。（助动词 do 强调动词 tell）
He *does love* the dishes in that restaurant. 他的确很喜欢那家餐馆的菜肴。（助动词 does 强调动词 love）
She *did come* to see you yesterday. 她的确昨天来看你了。（助动词 did 强调动词 come）

③ 助动词 have

A. 助动词 have 的形式

		肯定式	否定式
现在式	原形	have/'ve	have not/haven't/'ve not
	第三人称单数	has/'s	has not/hasn't/'s not
	第一、二人称单数以及所有人称复数	have/'ve	have not/haven't/'ve not
过去式		had/'d	had not/hadn't/'d not
现在分词		having	not having
过去分词		had	

B. 助动词 have 的用法
由"助动词 have + 动词过去分词"构成各种完成体
Have you *finished* your work? 你完成你的工作了吗?（现在完成体）
He *has gone* to Paris. 他去巴黎了。（现在完成体）
I *hadn't waited* long before he came. 我没等多久他就来了。（过去完成体）
They didn't explain *what had* happened. 他们没有解释发生了什么事情。（过去完成体）
They *will have lived* here for twenty years by next month. 到下个月他们住在这里将有二十年了。（将来完成体）
By tomorrow afternoon the weather *will have cleared up*. 到明天下午天气将会放晴。（将来完成体）
Since then they *have been working* on it. 从那时起,他们就一直在忙这件事。（现在完成进行体）
What *have* you *been doing* since we met last time? 自从上次我们见面以来你一直在做什么?（现在完成进行体）
He told me that he *had been working* since last Sunday. 他告诉我说自从上周日以来他一直在工作。（过去完成进行体）
We *had been looking* for him for several months before we found him. 我们在找到他之前已经找寻了好几个月了。（过去完成进行体）
Next October I *shall/will have been working* here for ten years. 到明年十月,我就在这里工作十年了。（将来完成进行体）
It *will have been raining* a whole month if it does not stop raining tomorrow. 假如明天雨还不停,那就下了整

整一个月了。（将来完成进行体）

③ 助动词 shall 和 will

A. 助动词 shall 和 will 的形式

我们可以把助动词 shall 和 will 看成是同一个助动词，只是根据不同人称所表现出的不同形式。它们的具体形式如下：

	时态	肯定式	否定式
第一人称单复数 shall	将来时	shall/'ll	shall not/shan't
第一人称单复数 should	过去将来时	should/'d	should not/shouldn't/'d not
第二、三人称单复数 will	将来时	will/'ll	will not/won't
第二、三人称单复数 would	过去将来时	would/'d	would not/wouldn't/'d not

B. 助动词 shall 和 will 的用法

a. shall 用于各种将来时态的第一人称

I *shall meet* you at the railway station tomorrow. 明天我将到火车站接你。（一般将来时）

We *shall be going* to Germany next month. 下个月我们就要去德国。（将来进行时）

We *shall have received* a reply by this time tomorrow. 明天这个时候，我们将会得到一个答复。（将来完成体）

Next week I *shall have been staying* here for two years. 到下周我就待在这里满两年了。（将来完成进行体）

b. should 用于各种过去将来时态的第一人称

I thought that I *should miss* the train, but in fact I fortunately caught it on time. 我原以为我会赶不上火车，但是事实上我幸运地及时赶上了。（过去将来时）

I told him that I *should be coming* to see him the next day. 我告诉他我第二天就去看他。（过去将来进行体）

The tour guide told us that we *should have arrived* there before dark. 导游告诉我没说我们会在天黑之前到达。（过去将来完成体）

I wrote to him that by the end of the week I *should have been staying* with Rose for one month. 我写信对他说，到这个周末我就跟罗丝待了一个月了。（过去将来完成进行体）

c. will 用于各种将来时态的第二、三人称

Captain Charles Alison *will sail* from Portsmouth tomorrow. 查尔斯·埃里森船长明天就要从朴次茅斯起航了。（一般将来时）

Will you *be washing* your car tomorrow? 明天你将洗你的汽车吗？（将来进行体）

They *will have finished* this bridge in a year's time. 他们将于一年后完成这座桥。（将来完成体）

It *will have been raining* a whole month if it does not stop raining tomorrow. 假如明天雨还不停，那就下了整整一个月了。（将来完成进行体）

d. would 用于各种过去将来时态的第二、三人称

She told me that Mr. Jones *would see* me the next day. 她告诉我琼斯先生第二天要见我。（过去将来时）

She said that she *would be setting off* the next morning. 她说她第二天上午出发。（过去将来进行体）

He said that they *would have cleaned and landscaped* Central Park by the end of July. 他说他们在七月底将清理干净中央公园并加以美化。（过去将来完成体）

Catherine told me that by the end of September they *would have been living* in the small village for a month. 凯瑟琳告诉我，到九月底他们将在这个小村庄居住一个月了。（过去将来完成进行体）

Note: 现代英语中第一人称往往用 will 代替 shall，用 would 代替 should。

2.3 情态动词

(1) 情态动词概述

情态动词(Modal Verb),也叫情态助动词。它本身具有一定的情态意义,与动词一起表达说话人的情感、意志、观点(请求、意愿、推测、命令或怀疑)等意思。情态动词后接动词原形,一起构成谓语动词短语。

情态动词主要有 can (could), may (might), must, have to, will (would), shall (should), ought to, used to, dare, need 等。它们没有人称和数的变化,只有原形和过去式两种形式(must 只有一种形式)。大多数情态动词具有多个意义,如 can 既可以表示能力又可以表示可能,还可以表示允许,need 既可以作实义动词又可以作情态动词。

有些语法专家把情态动词归为助动词一类。它跟助动词的共同之处是:两者都不能独立担当谓语,而是需要与实义动词一起表达说话人的意思。它跟助动词的不同在于它更多地倾向于表达说话人的情感和意愿,而助动词主要协助动词完成时态、语态等方面的表达。

Can you play piano? 你会弹钢琴吗?

I *must* go now. 我必须要走了。

May I use your cell phone, please? 我可以借用一下你的手机吗?

How *dare* you talk to your teacher in this way? 你怎么敢跟你老师这样说话?

You *ought to* go to see your grandparents. 你应该去看你的祖父母。

You *needn't* do that. 你不必那么做。

I *used to* get up at six o'clock every morning. 我过去每天都6点起床。

(2) 情态动词分述

① 情态动词 can 和 could

A. 情态动词 can 和 could 的形式

	肯定式	否定式
现在式	can	cannot/can't
过去式	could	could not/couldn't

B. 情态动词 can 和 could 的用法

a. 表示能力 此时常译为"能够"、"能"、"会"。can 既可以指现在,也可以指将来。could 指过去。在表示能力时,可以用 be able to 的相应形式或时态来代替。

She *can* take care of herself. (= She *is able to* take care of herself.) 她能照顾她自己。

I *can* see you tomorrow. (= I'll *be able to* see you tomorrow.) 我明天能见你。

He *couldn't* understand her. (= He *wasn't able to* understand her.) 他不能理解她。

She *could* cook when she was only ten years old. (= She *was able to* cook when she was only ten years old.) 她10岁的时候就会做饭了。

Note: could 表示过去的能力,常用于过去一般性的能力。当表明过去一个动作经过努力已经成功地完成的时候,我们常用 was/were able to,而不用 could。此时 was/were able to 意为 managed to,可以用后者来替代。

He *was able to* go to London yesterday and he enjoyed himself very much. (= He *managed to* go to London yesterday and he enjoyed himself very much.) 他昨天去了伦敦,并且玩得非常高兴。

b. **表示许可**　此时用于肯定句或否定句,常译为"可以"或"能"。can 既可以指现在,也可以指将来。could 则指过去。

You *can* keep it if you like. 如果你喜欢你可以保存下来。

You *can't* smoke here. 你不能在这里抽烟。

You *can* go home tomorrow. 你明天可以回家。

He said that I *could* use his computer. 他说我可以用他的电脑。

c. **表示请求**　此时用于疑问句,常译为"可以"或"能"。此时 can 和 could 可以互换,但是 could 更为委婉客气。

Can/Could I use your telephone, please? 我能用你的电话吗?

Can/Could you drive me to the station tomorrow morning? 明天上午你能开车送我到车站吗?

Can/Could I have two tickets, please? 我能买两张票吗?

Note：肯定回答时,常用"Certainly","Sure"或"Yes, I can";否定回答时,常用"No, I'm afraid not"或"No, you can't"。回答时不可用 could。

d. **表示推测或可能性**　此时表达了说话人对内容的不确定性。这种推测分对现在情况、将来情况的推测和对过去情况的推测三种。

• can 和 could 都表示对现在或将来的推测,两者都可以用于肯定句、否定句和疑问句。但在肯定句中 could 比 can 较为常用,且比 can 语气较为委婉,含义更不确定。

She *can/could* be wrong. 她可能错了。

Can/Could he really be ill? 他真的会生病吗?

It *cannot/could* not be Tony. He is doing his homework at home. 不可能是托尼。他正在家写作业。

• 当表示对过去的推测时,应在 can 或 could 之后接 have done 形式。can 多用于疑问句和否定句,极少用于肯定句。could have done 形式除了表示对过去事物的推测之外,还表示过去能做某事,但事实上并未做,有遗憾、惋惜之意。这一形式为虚拟语气结构。

Can/Could he *have done* that? 他会这么做吗?(表示推测)

He *can't/couldn't have completed* his job. 他不可能已经完成了工作。(表示推测)

She *could have finished* her job. 她可能已经完成工作。(表示推测)

If I had worked hard, I *could have passed* the examination. 如果我努力学习的话,我就能够通过考试了。(表示虚拟)

He *could have told* me, but he didn't mention it at all. 他本来可以告诉我的,但是他根本就没提。(表示虚拟)

• 当表示对过去事物的肯定推测时,通常用 must have done 或 may have done。must have done 意为一定做过某事,而 may have done 则表示或许做过某事。

② 情态动词 may 和 might

A. **情态动词 may 和 might 的形式**

	肯定式	否定式
现在式	may	may not
过去式	might	might not/mightn't

B. **情态动词 may 和 might 的用法**

a. **表示许可**　此时用于肯定句和否定句,常译为"可以"。may 既可以指现在,也可以指将来。might 指过去。

You *may* take whatever you want. 你想要什么就可以拿什么。

You *may* drive my car tomorrow. 你明天可以开我的车。

Pets *may* not be taken into this restaurant. 宠物不可以被带到这个饭店。

She said I *might* find him in his parents' house. 她说我可以在他父母家找到他。

He told me that I *might* smoke in the room. 他告诉我可以在房间里吸烟。

b. 表示请求　此时常用于疑问句,可译为"可以"。此时 may 和 might 可以互换,但是 might 更为委婉客气,语气更有礼貌。回答下面句子时,肯定回答为 Yes, please 或 Of course, you may。否定回答为 No, you may not。不用 No, you might not。但在现代英语中,回答 May I …? 问题时,常常回答 No, you mustn't 或 No, you can't。

—*May/Might* I ask you a question? 我可以问你一个问题吗?
—Yes, please. Go ahead. 可以啊,请问。

—*May/Might* I come and see you? 我可以来看你吗?
—Yes, you may. 可以。

—*May/Might* I have a little whisky? 我可以喝一点威士忌吗?
—No, you can't. 不,你不能。

Note：表示许可或请求时,上述句子中的 may/could 可以由 can/could 代替。may 和 can 区别不大。can 较口语化,最常用,最不正式。could 比 can 较客气委婉。may 比 can/could 较正式,更客气,更恭敬。而 might 最犹豫、最客气,也最不常用。

c. 表示推测、可能性　此时暗含说话人对说话内容的不确定,具体情况是：

• may 和 might 都表示对现在或将来的推测,只用于肯定句和否定句。在肯定句中,may 比 might 可能性要大一些,即 might 比 may 更不确定。

It *may/might* rain this afternoon. 下午可能下雨。

He *may/might* be ill. 他可能生病了。

The play *may/might* begin at any moment. 戏剧可能马上就要开演了。

• 当表示对过去的推测时,有两种表达方式：一种为"might + 动词原形"结构,放在宾语从句中,并且主句中的谓语为一般过去时；另一种为"may/might + have done"结构。

I thought that it *might rain*. 我当时认为或许会下雨。

He *may/might have noticed* his wife's strange behavior. 可能他已经注意到他妻子奇怪的举止。

She *may/might have telephoned* last night, but I'm not sure. 或许她昨晚打过电话,但是我不确定。

d. 用于虚拟语气　此时说话者常常表达祝愿、假设,或者表达遗憾、责备等感情。像这种情况有三种：

• 表达祈愿虚拟语气：may + 主语 + 动词原形

May our friendship last forever! 愿我们的友谊地久天长!

May you have a happy life! 祝你生活幸福!

• 表示陈述内容与现在事实相反或将来不可能发生的事情：might + 动词原形

If you didn't mind, we *might go* there. 如果你不介意,我们可能就去那儿了。(表示事实上你反对,因此我们不会去那里)

If he tried hard, he *might succeed*. 如果他努力的话,他或许能成功。(表示事实上他不努力,他也不会成功)

• 表示陈述内容与过去事实相反：might + have + 动词分词

If I had been there, I *might have helped* it. 如果我当时在那里,或许我能帮忙。(表示当时我不在那里,也没有帮忙)

If he had had money, he *might have bought* a car. 如果他有钱,或许他已经买车。(表示当时他没有钱,也没有买车)

③ 情态动词 must 和 have to

A. 情态动词 must 和 have to 的形式

must 只有一种形式，后面接动词原形，而 have to 则具有 have 的各种形态。

		肯定式		否定式	
	原形	must	have to	mustn't	don't have to
现在式	第三人称单数	must	has to	mustn't	doesn't have to
	第一、二人称单数以及所有人称复数	must	have to	mustn't	don't have to
过去式			had to		didn't have to
现在分词			having to		
过去分词					

B. 情态动词 must 的用法

must 表示义务，常译为"必须"或"一定要"，表示主观上的必须或个人意志，后接动词原形，表示现在和将来的状况。如果表示过去，用 had to 代替。

a. 用于肯定句

You *must* come back now. 你必须现在回来。

We *must* obey the traffic law. 我们必须遵守交通规则。

You *must* finish the work before dark. 你一定要在天黑之前完成工作。

b. 用于疑问句　肯定回答为 Yes, you must，表示必须要做某事；否定回答为 No, you needn't，表示不必做某事。否定回答不可用 No, you mustn't。

　　{ —*Must* I do it myself? 我一定要亲自做这件事吗？
　　 —No, you *needn't*. 不，你不必。

　　{ —*Must* he appear in court tomorrow? 明天他必须要出庭吗？
　　 —Yes, he *must*. 是的，他必须。

c. must 的否定形式表示禁止

You *must not* enter this office. 你不能进入这个办公室。

They *must not* leave this city during this time. 这个期间他们不得离开这座城市。

You *mustn't* smoke in the hospital. 不许在医院里吸烟。

d. must 表示建议　此时强调说话人强烈的决心或对他人的劝告。

This road is very busy. You *must* drive slowly. 这条路很繁忙。你得慢些开车。

You *must* be careful. The dog bites. 你必须要小心。这条狗咬人。

e. must 表示推测　此时常译为"一定"，只用于肯定句，暗含说话人确信极有可能。此种推测可分三个时间概念，即对现在、过去和将来三种时间上的推测。

● 对现在状况的推测　此时用 must do 或 must be doing 结构。

It's already one o'clock. You *must be* hungry now. 已经一点钟了，你一定饿了。

His mother is coming to see him. He *must be* very happy. 他妈妈来看他了。他一定很高兴。

They *must be having* a good time now. 他们现在一定玩得很开心。

The final examination is coming near, so they *must be working* hard these days. 期末考试就要到了，所以他们这些天一定很用功。

● 对过去状况的推测　此时用 must have done 结构。

The ground is wet. It *must have rained* last night. 地面是湿的。昨晚一定下雨了。

My bag is missing. I *must have left* it in my office. 我的包不见了。我一定落在办公室了。

- 对将来状况的推测　此时用 must be doing 结构。

According to the weather report, it *must be raining* tomorrow. 根据天气预报,明天一定会下雨。

They will take the 10:05 train, so they *must be arriving* at 5 pm. 他们将乘10:05的火车,所以他们一定会在下午5点钟到。

　　f. must 用于虚拟语气中　must 用于虚拟语气句中其结构是 must have done,表示与过去事实相反。

If you had set out earlier, you *must have caught* the train. 如果你早点出发,你一定能赶上那趟火车。

If you had come here yesterday, you *must have seen* him. 如果你昨天来这里,你一定就见到他了。

C. 情态动词 have to 的用法

　　a. have to 表示义务　此时常译为"必须"或"不得不"。暗含动作的执行者有勉强或被迫之意。后接动词原形,用于肯定句、否定句或疑问句。可以表示过去、现在及将来的时间。

I *had to* stay up late every night during those days. 在那些日子我不得不熬夜。

Do you *have to* stay up so late? 你非得要睡得这么晚吗?

The child will *have to* finish his homework on his own. 这个孩子必须得独立完成作业。

You don't *have to* do so. 你不必这么做。

　　b. have to 表示建议　此时强调说话人强烈的决心或对他人的劝告。

You *have to* make friends with the local people. 你得跟当地人交朋友。

If you want to improve your oral English, you *have to* practice a lot. 如果你想提高英语口语,你得多多练习。

　　c. have to 的替代表达　在口语中,常用 have got to 代替 have to,用 has got to 代替 has to,它们的意思完全等同。

　　④ 情态动词 will 和 would

will 和 would 既可作助动词,又可作情态动词。有些人认为,作为情态动词,will 表示现在和将来,而 would 表示过去,但这种看法并不完全正确。其实它们有相似的地方,也有各自固定的用法。

A. 情态动词 will 和 would 的形式

	肯定式	否定式
现在式	will/'ll	will not/won't
过去式	would/'d	would not/wouldn't/'d not

B. 情态动词 will 和 would 的用法

　　a. 表示意愿和决心　will 可指现在和将来,would 常用于间接引语,指过去的将来。

I *won't* accept his present. It is too expensive. 我不会接受他的礼物。太贵了。

—*Will* you marry him? —Yes, I *will*. —你愿意嫁给他吗? —我愿意。

He asked me if I *would* go to Shanghai together with him. 他问我是否愿意跟他一起去上海。

He said that he *wouldn't* say that to her. 他说他不会对她说这样的话。

　　b. 表示习惯或反复发生的动作　此时用于肯定句,will 表示现在状况,而 would 则表示过去习惯的动作。

Every morning he *will* read newspapers before breakfast. 每天早上他都会在早餐前读报纸。

He *will* have his own way. 他总是想怎样就怎样。

I *would* walk to work. 我过去走路去上班。

Would he always be like this? 他总是这个样子吗?

　　c. 表示请求或征询对方意见　此时用于疑问句,would 并不表示过去,它与 will 含义相同,只是比 will 更委婉客气。

Will you forgive me, please? 请你原谅我好吗?

Will you buy me a bicycle? 你会给我买辆自行车吗?

Would you tell me the way to the railway station? 请你告诉我去火车站的路好吗?

Would you please give me a bigger one? 你能给我那个大一点的吗?

d. 表示推测　这可指现在或将来,用于第二人称和第三人称。will do 或 will be doing 表示对目前情况的推测,而 will/would have done 表示对过去的动作或状况的推测。

This *will* be the article you are looking for. 这可能就是你找的文章吧。

It *would* be about ten when he left home. 他离开家的时候可能是 10 点钟。

He *will have arrived* by now. 现在他可能已经到了吧。

I guess he *would have finished* the task by now. 我猜他现在可能已经完成任务了。

e. would 用于虚拟语气　此时表示说话人的愿望等情感,具体分为:

● 用于 wish 之后的从句

I wish the snowstorm *would* stop for a moment. 我希望暴雪停一会儿。

I wish they *would* leave now. 我希望他们现在就离开。

● 用于虚拟语气中的主句

If I were you, I *would* tell him the truth. 如果我是你,我会告诉他实情。(表示与现在事实相反)

If he went away tomorrow, I *would* go with him. 如果他明天离开,我就跟他一起走。(表示将来不可能发生的事)

If you had worked hard, you *would* have passed the examination. 如果你努力的话,你就通过了考试。(表示与过去事实相反)

f. would 的常用短语

would like 意为"想要"、"愿意",语气委婉客气,省略形式为 'd like。

Would you *like* to have a drink with me? 你想跟我喝一杯吗?

Would you *like* her to be your assistant? 你愿意她做你的助手吗?

I'd like to know what you're thingking about. 我想了解你们在想什么。

Note:like 和 would like 意思不同,前者是一般性的喜欢,而后者意为"想要"。do you like 和 would you like 意思也不同,前者问对方的喜好,后者表示款待对方。

He *likes* playing football. 他喜欢踢足球。

I'd like to play football this afternoon. 我下午要去踢足球。

—*Do* you *like* reading books? —Yes, I do. —你喜好读书吗? —是的,我喜欢。

—*Would* you *like* some coffee? —Yes, please. —你想喝点咖啡吗? —好的,请拿来。

g. would rather 和 would sooner　这两结构意思相同,意为"宁可"、"宁愿",表示选择之意。省略形式为 'd rather 或 'd sooner。后面常与 than 连用,构成 "would rather/sooner + 动词原形……than + 动词原形……",表示"宁可……而不愿……"。

I *would rather* go to work *than* do nothing at home. 我宁愿去工作也不愿在家里无所事事。

I *would sooner* not go together with you. 我宁可不跟你一起去。

Would you *rather* stay here than go anywhere else? 你宁可待在这里也不愿去其他任何地方吗?

Which *would* you *rather* have, water or beer? 你想要什么,水还是啤酒?

h. would rather + that 从句　常译为"我多么希望",表达的是虚拟语气,意为与事实相反。

I *would rather* (that) I were a singer. 我多么希望我是一名歌手。(与现在事实相反)

I *would rather* (that) I had finished my homework yesterday. 我多么希望我昨天就完成作业了。(与过去事实相反)

i. Would you mind doing …? 和 Would you mind if …? 从句　这两句意为"您介不介意……?"。

Would you mind my coming with you? 您介意我跟您一起来吗?

Would you mind if you opened the window for me? 您介意帮我把窗户打开吗?

Note：if 从句中的谓语动词用一般过去时,以便与 would 一致。此种表达比 Do you mind …? 语气要委婉客气。

⑤ 情态动词 shall 和 should

就像 will 和 would 一样,人们习惯上也把 shall 和 should 当成一个词的两种形式：shall 表示现在和将来,should 表示过去。但是作为情态动词,这两个词各自逐渐拥有自己的用法,表达不同的意思。

A. 情态动词 shall 和 should 的形式

	肯定式	否定式
原形 shall	shall/'ll	shall not/shan't
原形 should	should/'d	should not/shouldn't/'d not

B. 情态动词 shall 的用法

a. 表示征询对方意见　此时用于第一、三人称的疑问句, shall = would you like … to/do you want … to。

Shall I fetch this file for you? 要不要我为你去取这个文件?

= *Would you like* me to fetch this file for you?

= *Do you want* me to fetch this file for you?

Shall he prepare for the conference? 要不要他为大会做准备?

= *Would you like* him to prepare for the conference?

= *Do you want* him to prepare for the conference?

Note：下面的附加疑问句用 shall we 表示反问。

Let's go to the theatre, *shall we*? 我们去看戏,好吗?

b. 表示向对方承诺　此时用于第二、三人称的肯定句或否定句。

You *shall* get your money. 你一定会拿到你的钱的。

He *shall* have my reply next week. 他一定会在下周得到我的答复。

c. 表示命令、威胁对方　此时用于第二人称陈述句,而 you shall = you must。

You *shall* never treat your mother in this way. (= You *must* never treat your mother in this way.) 你不能这样对待你的母亲。

You *shall* obey the law. (= You *must* obey the law.) 你必须要遵守法律。

d. 用在正式法律条文中,此时所有人称一律用 shall。

In consideration of the foregoing, Party B shall, for itself and its legal representatives, promise to pay Party A the sum of 1,000,000 (one million) dollars in manner as follows. 鉴于上述内容,乙方及其法人代表,承诺以下列方式支付甲方款项 1000000 美元整(壹百万美元整)。

Party A shall expend the value of the payments already received by Party A on the building. 甲方须将所收款项用于本建筑。

C. 情态动词 should 的用法

a. 表示义务　意为"应该",可用于各种句式,指过去、现在和将来。指过去时,常用 should have done 形式表达过去应完成但未完成的动作。

I *should* go now. 我现在应该走了。(表示现在)

You *shouldn't* read books in the sun. 你不应该在阳光下读书。(表示现在)

He *should* go to visit his grandmather tomorrow. 他应该明天去看望他祖母。(表示将来)

You *should have told* me the truth earlier. 你应该早点告诉我真相。(表示过去,事实上并未告诉我,虚拟

语气)

I should have finished my paper. 我应该做完我的论文。(表示过去,事实上并未完成,虚拟语气)

b. 表示推测　此时意为有很大可能。

The work is not difficult. She *should* finish it on time. 这工作并不难。她应该会准时完成。

The money *should* be enough because I won't stay there for a long time. 钱应该够了,因为我在那里不会待很长时间。

c. 用于间接引语　此时主句中谓语动词是一般过去时。

I said, "I *shall* be back in thirty minutes." 我说:"我会在三十分钟后回来。"(直接引语)

I said that I *should* be back in thirty minutes. 我说我会在三十分钟后回来。(间接引语)

d. 用于虚拟语气　should 用于虚拟语气时有下面几种情况:

● should have done 结构　在情态动词 should 的用法中已经介绍过。这个结构也常常用在含有 if 从句的复合句中,表示与过去事实相反。

If you had worked harder, you *should have succeeded* in the final examination. 如果你再努力一些,你就会在最后考试中成功。(与过去事实相反)

If you had come here last time, everyone *should have been* glad. 如果上次你来了,大家都会很高兴。(与过去事实相反)

● "it is adj./n. + that + 主语 + should + do/have done"结构　此结构表达了说话人的主观意见、感情色彩等。作表语的名词或形容词有:a pity, good, important, imperative, natural, necessary, proper, regrettable, right, strange, surprising, wonderful 等。should 可以省略。

It is not proper that one *should* speak loudly in public. 在公共场所大声喧哗是不对的。

It is strange that he *should* do like this. 他这样做真是奇怪。

● 用表达建议、要求、命令等意志的动词后　若有 that 引导的宾语从句,从句中使用 should, should 可以省略。这些动词有:ask, command, demand, desire, insist, order, propose, recommend, require, request, suggest 等。

He *suggested* that we *should* set off at once. 他建议我们立即动身。

I *insist* that they *should* pay me the money. 我坚持他们付我钱。

● 用于 lest 和 for fear 之后　此时意为"以免"、"唯恐"。

I got up early *lest* I *should* arrive late. 我起床很早,以免迟到。

Be careful *lest* you *should* fall from the ladder. 小心点,以防你从梯子上摔下来。

He worked hard *for fear* that he *should* fail. 他很努力地工作唯恐失败。

Put on the coat *for fear* that you *should* catch the cold. 穿上外套,以免你感冒。

⑥ 情态动词 ought to

A．情态动词 ought to 只有一种形式

肯定式	否定式
ought to	ought not to/oughtn't to

B．情态动词 ought to 的用法

表示义务、责任、劝告等　此时意为"应该",可用于各种句式。

a. ought to 通常指将来

You *ought to* visit your grandparents tomorrow. 你明天应该拜访你的祖父母。

He *ought not to* do that. 他不应该做那事。

Ought I *to* tell him about it? 我应该把这个告诉他吗?

b. ought to 指现在的状况时有两种结构:ought to 接静态动词;ought to 接 be doing 结构,以强调正在

进行的状况。

You *ought to* be kind to others. 你应该待人友善。

You *ought to* be in class now. 你现在应该在上课。

He *ought to* be working in the office. 他现在应该正在办公室工作。

This is what I *ought to* be doing. 这是我应该做的事情。

c. ought to 也可指过去的状况 这种情况下常指应该完成却未完成的动作,有时带有遗憾、责备等感情色彩。

He *ought to* have finished his college education. 他本应该已经完成了大学学业。

You *ought not to* have told him about this. 你不应该告诉他这个。

d. 表示推测 此时暗指有很大可能性,语气比 must 稍弱。

He studies hard, so he *ought to* succeed in the English examination. 他学习很努力,所以英语考试应该会成功。

It has been long since I saw him last time. He *ought to* grow taller. 自从上次看到他很长时间了。他应该长高了。

Note:一般情况下,ought to 和 should 含义相同,但是 ought to 比 should 语气要强烈,更强调义务的意义。

⑦ 情态动词 used to

A. 情态动词 used to 的形式

肯定式	否定式
used to	used not to/usedn't to/didn't use to

B. 情态动词 used to 的用法

a. used to + 动词原形 此结构表示过去存在的习惯或状态,常译为"过去曾经"、"以前经常",暗指现在已经不存在。

I *used to* play piano every day. 我过去每天弹钢琴。

This is the house where I *used to* live. 这是我以前住的房子。

Notes:would 和 used to 的区别:

● used to 强调过去习惯做某事,现在没有此习惯,而 would 只单纯表达过去习惯。

● would 常跟 every day, often, frequently 等时间副词连用,而 used to 不必。

● would 有时可以替代 used to,但是当表示过去的状态时只能用 used to,而不用 would。

b. used to 结构的疑问句形式

—*Used* he *to* go to gamble money every weekend? 以前他每个周末都去赌钱吗?(较少用)
—No, he *used not/usedn't*. 不,他没有。

—*Did* you *use to* have a big dog? 你以前有一只大狗吗?(较常用)
—Yes, I did. 是的,我有。

—She *used to* be very fat, *didn't she/usedn't she*?
—Yes, she did/she used.

c. used to 结构的否定句形式

He *used not to/usedn't to* drink. (= He *didn't use to* drink.) 他过去不喝酒。

d. 与 used to 易混淆的结构

● be/get used to sth/doing sth 此结构意思是"习惯于/变得习惯于……",这个结构的主语往往是人。to 是介词,后面接名词或动名词。

I'm *used to getting up* early. 我习惯于早起。

He has *got used to* the Chinese food. 他已经习惯了中式餐。
- be used to do 被用来做…… 此结构是被动语态，主语往往是物。

This knife *was used to* cut meat. 这把刀用来切割肉类。

This room *is used to* store shoes. 这个房间用来储存鞋子。

⑧ 情态动词 dare

dare 既可作情态动词，又可作实义动词。它的情态动词用法如下：

A．用于疑问句，此时表示"敢于"、"有勇气"等。

　　Dare you swim across the river? 你敢游过这条河吗？（情态动词）

＝*Do you dare* to swim across the river?（实义动词）

　　Dare he ask you such a question? 他敢问你这样的问题吗？（情态动词）

＝*Does he dare* to ask you such a question?（实义动词）

　　You *daren't* go out at night, *dare* you? 你不敢晚上出去，对吧？（情态动词，肯定回答：Yes, I dare.；否定回答：No, I daren't.）

＝You *don't dare* (*to*) go out at night, *do* you?（实义动词，肯定回答：Yes, I do.；否定回答：No, I don't.）

B．用于否定句，意为"不敢"，若 dare 为实义动词，其后面的 to 可省略。

　　I *daren't* stay outside when it is thundering. 打雷的时候我不敢待在外面。（情态动词）

＝I *don't dare* (*to*) stay outside when it is thundering.（实义动词）

　　She *daren't* drive a truck. 她不敢开卡车。（情态动词）

＝She *doesn't dare* (*to*) drive a truck.（实义动词）

C．How dare …? 表示生气、愤怒及谴责。

　　How dare you behave like that? 你竟敢如此放肆？

　　How dare he say that to me? 他怎么敢对我说这种话？

D．I dare say … 表示"我想"、"我敢说"。

　　I *dare say* he will like you. 我敢说他会喜欢你的。

　　I *dare say* she hates this sort of thing. 我想她不喜欢这类事情。

⑨ 情态动词 need

need 和 dare 一样，既可作情态动词，又可作实义动词。作情态动词用法如下：

A．用于肯定句

need 用于肯定句时大多为实义动词，作情态动词时常用于疑问句和否定句，但是当肯定句中含有否定或疑问之意时，仍可用情态动词 need。

　　I *need* your survey report. 我需要你的调查报告。（实义动词）

　　You *need* to make an appointment with my manager. 你需要跟我的经理预约。（实义动词）

　　He *doesn't need* to worry. 他不必担心。（实义动词）

　　I *hardly need* say how much I love it. 不必说我有多爱它。（情态动词）

　　I wonder if you *need* do it. 我不知道你是否需要做那个。（情态动词）

　　All you *need* do is keep silent. 你所需要做的只是保持沉默。（情态动词）

B．用于疑问句

表示"必须"、"必要"、"需要"等。

　　Need you go to Shanghai tomorrow? 你明天必须去上海吗？（情态动词）

＝Do you *need to* go to Shanghai tomorrow?（实义动词）

　　She *need not* go, *need* she? 她不需要去，对吗？（情态动词）

＝She *doesn't need* to go, *does* she?（实义动词）

Note：need 和 must 用于疑问句时都表示是否有必要之意。用 need 提问时往往希望得到否定答复，主观色彩较浓，所以有疑问词的疑问句多用 must。针对 need 或 must 疑问句，肯定回答为"Yes，主语 + must"，否定回答为"No，主语 + needn't"。

——*Need* I learn how to drive a car? 我需要学习开车吗？（情态动词）

—— = I *needn't* learn how to drive a car, *need* I? 我不必学习开车，对吗？

——Yes, you must. 是，你必须要。

——No, you needn't. 不，你不必。

C. 用于否定句

表示"不必"、"不需要"，缩写形式为 needn't。

　　He *needn't* come here. 他不必来这里。（情态动词）

　　= He *doesn't need* to come here. （实义动词）

Note：needn't 和 don't have to 都有"不必"之意，但是 needn't 具有主观感情色彩，而 don't have to 较客观。

You *needn't* go to work today. 你今天不必去上班。（主观愿望）

You *don't have to* go to work today. 你今天不必去上班。（客观事实）

D. 情态动词 need 表示过去的用法

　　a. need + do：这一形式和表示现在和将来一样。

He asked me if I *need* leave at once. 他问我是否我需要立刻离开。

She told him that he *need* not work so hard. 她告诉他不需要那么卖力地工作。

　　b. needn't have done：这一结构表示过去不必完成但已完成的动作。

She had too many toys. You *needn't* have bought them to her. 她有太多的玩具。你没有必要给她买这些。（已经买了）

The teacher told me that I *needn't* have done all the exercises. 老师告诉我没有必要把所有练习都做了。（已经做了）

第3章　动词的时、体及将来意思表达法

3.1　时、体概述

时态是一种用于动词的语法概念,用以表示各种时间概念和动作方面的形式。时态和时间是两个不同的概念。时间是泛指,是全人类共有的概念,无论哪个名族,使用哪种语言,所有的时间概念都是共同的。而时态是一个语法范畴,用来表示不同时间的动作及动作完成的情况,这里的时间都是相对的时间。在不同语言中具有不同的时态,这里主要讨论的是英语中的时态。英语中的时态不仅种类多、区别细,且用法也很广。

现代英语语法研究认为,英语动词的"时"有两种:现在时(Present Tense)和过去时(Past Tense)。

Water boils at 100℃. 水在摄氏100度沸腾。(现在时)

One today is worth two tomorrow. 一个今天抵得上两个明天。(现在时)

It was in 1960 that he was born. 他出生于1960年。(过去时)

He worked from 5 am to 12 pm that day. 他那天从早上5点一直工作到晚上12点。(过去时)

时态中的"体"指的是动作方面,共分为四种:一般、完成、进行和完成进行。它们都各有其特点。

- 一般方面:用以叙述一个单纯的事实,时间可以不具体。有些动词的一般方面常表示动作已完成或为习惯动作。
- 完成方面:表示一个动作已完成的事实。它包含两个时间,动作发生在前一时间,而说话人的兴趣在后一时间,即该动作对后一时间的影响。
- 进行方面:表示一个动作在某一时间段内进行。此时,说话人的兴趣不在于动作何时发生,而在于动作在他所关心的时间点正在进行。进行方面往往呈现出一种场景,描写性强,具有画面感,形象生动。
- 完成进行方面:它兼具完成和进行两个方面的特点,跨越两个时间,但两者往往相聚不远,表示动作从前一时间持续到后一时间,没有间断。

3.2　时、体的分类

根据"时"和"体"的组合,可将时、体分为二时六体。

体 时	一般	完成	进行	完成进行
现在	现在时	现在完成体	现在进行体	现在完成进行体
过去	过去时	过去完成体	过去进行体	过去完成进行体

(1) 现在时

一般现在时是英语时态中最为常见的时态之一。句中的谓语动词常用来表示习惯性或反复发生的动作。但也有些动作表示言行并进、瞬间即逝的动作,如实况解说、操作演示以及在时间、条件状语从句中也可表示将来的含义。

① 现在时的形式

一般现在时的构成如下：

肯定式	否定式	疑问式
I work.	I do not work.	Do I work?
You work.	You do not work.	Do you work?
He (She, It) works.	He (She, It) does not work.	Does he (she, it) work?
We work.	We do not work.	Do we work?
You work.	You do not work.	Do you work?
They work.	They do not work.	Do they work?

② 现在时的用法

A. 表示习惯性、反复发生的动作以及人或事的一般特征

I go to work every day. 我每天上班。

He is always busy with his farm work. 他总是忙于他的农活。

Tom gets up at 7 o'clock every morning. 汤姆每天早晨7点起床。

They always make fun of him. 他们总是捉弄他。

Barking dogs seldom bite. 吠犬不咬人。

Make hay while the sun shines. 趁热打铁。

They never take a taxi. 他们从来不乘出租车。

Don't ever be late again! 别再迟到了！

The Winter Olympics are usually held two years before the Summer Olympics. 冬季奥运会通常是在夏季奥运会之前两年举行。

Note：表示这种用法时，一般现在时常与表示频度的副词及副词短语连用，常见的有：always, often, usually, sometimes, frequently, generally, never, hardly, seldom, rarely, daily, monthly, yearly, five times a week, twice a year, ever 等。

B. 表示客观真理或科学事实

Spring follows winter. 冬天之后是春天。

Time and tide wait for no man. 岁月不待人。

Where there is a will, there is a way. 有志者，事竟成。

The sun rises in the east. 太阳从东方升起。

The earth moves round the sun. 地球绕着太阳转。

Light travels faster than sound. 光速比声速快。

Practice makes perfect. 熟能生巧。

Knowledge is power. 知识就是力量。

There are seven days in a week. 一个星期有七天。

C. 表示现在

表示现在就是说话时刻发生的动作或存在的状态，这一时刻往往是短暂的。

What time is it now? 现在几点了？

My watch says half past ten. 我的表是十点半。

Are you busy? 你忙吗？

What's Nanjing like now? 南京现在情况如何？

They take no money with them. 他们身上没带钱。

The patient is much better now. 病人现在好多了。

He wears a tall hat and carries an umbrella. 他戴着一顶高帽子,拿着一把伞。

I am in the middle of this great forest in South America. 我现在在南美洲这个大森林的中部。

Now, look, I open the door. 你瞧,我现在来开门。

Here he comes! 他来了!

D. 表示将来计划,即最近的将来

I'm off. 我要走了。

I leave tomorrow. 我明天离开。

The film begins in a minute. 电影马上开始放映。

What happens next? 接着会发生什么?

When do they return from their honeymoon? 他们度蜜月什么时候回来?

I read my paper tomorrow. 我明天要宣读我的论文。

Tomorrow is Sunday. 明天是星期天。

When's dinner? 晚饭什么时候开始?

The future is bright. 未来是光明的。

When does the meeting take place? 会议什么时候开始?

Note: 一般现在时表示将来意思时,常与表示转移的动词连用,如:go, come, fall, arrive, leave, start, begin, sail, meet, stay, return 等,并且与时间状语连用。这些动词表示从一处到另一处或从静到动、从动到静的过渡。

E. 常用于各种从句中

一般现在时常用于各种从句中,表示将来。

Once you get there, you'll love it. 你一到那里,就会喜欢那里的。

I will tell them after you leave. 你离开后我就告诉他们。

Next time I'll do as he says. 下次我会按照他所说的去做。

The state government will give $10,000 to any one who brings him to justice. 州政府悬赏10000美元给将此犯捉拿归案的人。

I'll give you anything you ask for. 你要什么我都会给你。

Anyone that comes will be warmly welcomed. 任何人来都会受到热情欢迎。

His success will depend upon how he starts the plan. 他的成功取决于他如何开始他的计划。

I will keep silent even though everyone asks me about it. 即使所有人都问我,我都会保持沉默。

We'll go on a picnic if it is fine on the weekend. 如果周末是晴天,我们将会去野餐。

When Mary comes across a new word, she always looks it up in the dictionary. 每当玛丽遇到新单词,她都会查字典。

F. 表示过去

一般现在时表示过去既可表示很近的过去,又可表示很远的过去,表达这种意思时,常与 tell, say, write, think, forget 等词连用。

He tells me that you will go to Beijing next week. 他告诉我你下周要去北京。

Do you forget what I say? 你忘了我说的话了吗?

It is long, long ago. 那是很久很久以前的事了。

The year is 1986. 那年是1986年。

He is long dead. 他早已去世了。

He leaves a wife and two children. 他身后有一妻两子。

You break my heart. 你让我心碎了。

What wind blows you here. （是）什么风把你吹来了。

G．用于新闻标题或文学作品中

这表示客观事实。

President Resigns. 总统辞职了。

Meat Prices Rise Again. 肉价又涨了。

The article describes social problems. 这篇文章描述的是社会问题。

Algerian Troops fire on Anti-Government Rioters. 阿尔及利亚部队向反政府武装开火。

Fifty Are Killed in an Aircraft Crash. 50人在飞机失事中遇难。

We reach the moon. 我们登上了月球。

Avalanches kill 15 in Italian villages. 意大利村庄15人死于滑坡。

China's ace spiker Lang Ping (left) rises high in a game against the U.S. 中国优秀主攻手郎平（左）在与美国队的比赛中高高跳起扣球。

Chaucer writes that love is blind. 乔叟写到爱情是盲目的。

Darwin thinks that natural selection is the chief factor in the development of species. 达尔文认为自然淘汰是物种发展中的主要因素。

(2) 过去时

一般过去时由动词的过去式构成，常与表示过去的时间状语连用，表示过去某一时刻发生的动作或存在的状态，也可表示过去连续或反复发生的动作或习惯。

① 过去时的形式

一般过去时的构成如下：

肯定式	否定式	疑问式
I worked.	I did not work.	Did I work?
You worked.	You did not work.	Did you work?
He (She, It) worked.	He (She, It) did not work.	Did he (she, it) work?
We worked.	We did not work.	Did we work?
You worked.	You did not work.	Did you work?
They worked.	They did not work.	Did they work?

② 过去时的用法

A．表示过去经常发生的动作或存在的状态

一般过去时经常表示过去某一时刻发生的动作或存在的状态，常与过去的时间状语连用，如 yesterday, last night, last month, on Sunday, the other day 等。

He visited China last April. 他于去年4月访问了中国。

They went out just now. 他们刚出去。

I stayed with my husband in Nanjing last summer. 去年夏天我和丈夫待在南京。

They had a baby last month. 他们上个月生了个小孩。

Tom suddenly fell ill yesterday. 昨天汤姆突然生病了。

We suffered a lot those days. 那些年我们受了很多苦。

He was born in 1900. 他生于1900年。

Where were you yesterday afternoon? 昨天下午你去哪里了？
Did you sleep well last night? 昨晚你睡得好吗？
On Friday 16th October, 1987, a hurricane struck the southeast of England. 1987年10月16日，星期五，一场飓风袭击了英格兰东南部。

Notes：a. 过去时也可以表示过去某一段时间发生的动作或存在的状态，可与由 for, during, since 等引导的时间状语连用。

We stayed in the garden for a long time. 我们在花园待了很长时间。
Last May, I spent two weeks in London. 去年5月，我在伦敦待了两周。
She became silent since then. 从那以后她就变得沉默了。
He lived in Florida until he was eighteen. 他一直住在佛罗里达直到18岁。
During the night, I heard someone scream. 晚上我听到有人在尖叫。
He never smoked. 他以前从不抽烟。

在一定的上下文中，时间状语也可省略。

About 700 people died in the earthquake and the fires. 大约700人死于地震和火灾。
Einstein led a simple life in the USA. 爱因斯坦在美国过着简朴的生活。

b. 时间状语也可以由从句担任，从句中也用一般过去时，表示过去发生的动作或存在的状态。

As soon as he received the telegram, he drove to the station. 他一收到电报，就开车去了车站。
When you were out last night, a friend came to visit you. 你昨晚出去时，一个朋友来拜访你。
They worked long hours for several weeks before everything returned to normal. 他们在几周里工作很长时间才使一切恢复正常。
Were there any telephone message for me while I was away? 我外出时有我的电话吗？

B. 表示过去反复发生的或习惯性的动作

一般过去时表示过去反复发生的或习惯性的动作，常与表示频率的词连用，如 always, often, usually, sometimes, never, every day, now and then 等，但是这种用法是以过去的时间为前提的。

Last year, I went to the theatre every day. 去年，我每天都去剧院。
While she was in London, she called on us every day. 当她在伦敦时，每天都来拜访我们。
John seldom wrote to me. 约翰很少写信给我。
He used to drink coffee at night. 以前他常在晚上喝咖啡。
China is not what she was. 中国不再是过去的样子了。
The couple lived in Suzhou years ago. 几年前，那对夫妇住在苏州。
Jack was often late for school. 杰克经常上学迟到。
When she was a little girl, she was very shy. 还是小女孩时，她就很害羞。
You were always a pretty girl. 你总是这么漂亮。
She was usually dressed in black. 她总是穿着黑衣服。

C. 表示现在时间和将来意思

一般过去时在特定的句型中常表示现在时间和将来意思。

a. 表示婉转

hope, think, want, wonder 等动词的过去时表示现在时间的婉转语气。

What did you want? 你要买点什么？（比 What do you want? 更婉转）
I hoped you could give me some help. 我希望你能给我一些帮助。（比 I hope you can give me some help. 更婉转）
Could you give me a favour? 你能帮我个忙吗？（比 Can you give me a favour? 更婉转）

b. 表示想象

在 It's (high) time that …, I wish …, I'd rather … 等句型中的过去时都表示将来的意思,是一种想象。

It's time we went home. 我们该回家了。

I wish I were in Beijing. 但愿我在北京。

{ —Shall I open the window? 我把窗户打开好吗?
  —I'd rather you didn't. 我宁愿你别开。

I'd rather they came tomorrow. 我宁愿他们明天来。

还有像下面的那些虚拟句:

If only Dad were home! 如果爸爸在家就好了!

Even though he were here, he would not help us. 即使他在,也不会帮我们。

D. 一般过去时的特殊用法

You asked for it! 是你自找的!(表示责备)

I told you so. 我早就告诉过你。(言下之意:你就是不听,表示埋怨)

He deserved it. 他活该。(表示幸灾乐祸)

(3) 现在进行体

现在进行体表示现阶段或说话时正在进行的动作及行为,由 be 动词和动词的现在分词构成。

① 现在进行体的形式

现在进行体的构成如下:

肯定式	否定式	疑问式
I am working.	I am not working.	Am I working?
You are working.	You are not working.	Are you working?
He (She, It) is working.	He (She, It) is not working.	Is he (she, it) working?
We are working.	We are not working.	Are we working?
You are working.	You are not working.	Are you working?
They are working.	They are not working.	Are they working?

② 现在进行体的用法

A. 表示现阶段正在进行的动作

就是说话时刻正在进行的动作,通常与表示现阶段的时间状语连用,如 now, at present, today, this week, this month, this term, this year 等。

He is writing a novel now. 他目前在写一部小说。

The house is being built these days. 最近房子正在建造。

Don't worry. I'm feeling better now. 别担心,我现在好多了。

They are painting the house at present. 目前,他们正在粉刷房子。

He is working abroad this year. 今年他在国外工作。

在特定的上下文中,时间状语也可省略不用。

We are having English class. 我们在上英语课。

I'm sitting on a bench near the river with my friend. 我和朋友坐在河边的长凳上。

Please keep quiet. The students are taking an exam in the next room. 请安静,学生们在隔壁教室考试。

He is losing his hair. 他正脱发。

They are considering whether to continue with the experiment. 他们在考虑要不要继续试验。

B．表示按计划或已安排好要做的事

现在进行体表示按计划或已安排好要做的事,常含有"意图"、"安排"或"打算"的含义,并与表示将来的时间状语连用。但这一用法只适用于 go, come, leave, start, arrive, return, spend, sail, meet, fly 等表示位置的移动或变化动词,这类动词也叫动作动词。

The guest is leaving by train tonight. 客人今晚坐火车走。

They are coming tomorrow. 他们明天来。

I am changing my room. 我要换房间了。

What are they doing after school today? 今天放学后他们准备干什么?

Betty is going on a holiday at the weekend. 周末贝蒂要去度假。

C．表示经常性、重复性或习惯性的动作

现在进行体表示经常性、重复性或习惯性的动作,此时必须与表示频度的副词连用,如 only, merely, simply, really, fast, rapidly, steadily, forever, all the time, always, constantly, continually, repeatedly, again 等。该用法带有一定的感情色彩,可表示惊奇、不满、厌烦、埋怨、赞赏等情绪。

She is always complaining. 她总是在抱怨。

The little boy is always making trouble. 小男孩一直不停闯祸。

Jane is forever losing things. 珍妮总是丢三落四。

You are always finding fault with me. 你总是挑我的毛病。

It's always raining in London. 伦敦总是下雨。

D．用在状语从句中

这种用法指在时间状语或条件状语从句中表示将来正在进行的动作。

Look out when you are crossing the street. 过马路时要当心。

Don't wake him up if he is still sleeping at 7 tomorrow morning. 明早7点如果他还在睡觉,别叫醒他。

If you say that once more, I'm leaving. 如果你再这么说,我就要走了。

E．表示补充说明

在下面两种情况下,现在进行体作补充说明用。

a. 在不少情况下,表示正在进行的动作的汉语句子中并没有"正在"这样的字眼,但译为英语时必须用进行时态。

It's raining heavily. 下大雨了。

How is everything going? 事情进展如何?

b. 有些动词通常不能用进行体。不能用进行体的动词有:

• 表示感觉或感情的词,如 hear, see, smell, taste, feel, seem, notice, hate, love, like, want, wish, refuse, prefer, forgive 等。

• 表示存在或所属的词,如 exist, stay, remain, obtain, have, own, form, contain, belong to 等。

• 表示认识或理解的词,如 understand, know, remember, forget, believe, think, doubt 等。

(4) 过去进行体

过去进行体表示过去某段时间或某一时刻正在发生或进行的行为或动作,由 be 动词的过去式和动词的现在分词构成。

① 过去进行体的形式

过去进行体的构成如下:

肯定式	否定式	疑问式
I was working.	I was not working.	Was I working?
You were working.	You were not working.	Were you working?
He (She, It) was working.	He (She, It) was not working.	Was he (she, it) working?
We were working.	We were not working.	Were we working?
You were working.	You were not working.	Were you working?
They were working.	They were not working.	Were they working?

② 过去进行体的用法

过去进行体表示过去某时正在进行的动作,经常与时间状语连用。它可用在简单句中,也可用于复合句中,用在复合句中时常出现在主句中。

What were you doing at nine last night? 昨晚9点你在做什么?

We were having dinner when they came. 他们来的时候,我们正在吃饭。

The boy was doing his homework when his father came back from work. 当他爸爸下班时,小男孩正在做作业。

A. 表示过去某段时间内持续的动作

过去进行体表示过去某段时间内发生的持续的动作。

Carlos was staying at home all last week. 上周整整一周卡洛斯都在家待着。

They were building a dam last spring. 去年春天他们一直在修一个水坝。

B. 表示与过去某个动作同时发生的动作

过去进行体表示与过去某个动作同时发生的动作。

I was reading while she was writing. 我在读书,她在写字。

C. 有时用于主句时,其后的when从句动作表示意外

有时过去进行体用于主句,位于其后的when引导的从句表示意外发生的情况。

I was walking in the street when it began to rain. 我正在街上走着,突然下起了雨。

D. 表示过去将来的动作

过去进行体表示过去将来的动作常用来表示过去的打算,仅限于come, go, leave, depart, start 等一些动作动词。

He didn't know whether she was coming. 他不知道她是否会来。

The delegation was departing three days later. 代表团打算三天后动身。

(5) 现在完成体

现在完成体是英语动词完成体的一种。该体态表示过去已完成的动作对现在产生或本应该产生的后果。其与情态动词连用,表示一个过去的动作或一个猜想已发生的动作。其与不同的时间状语搭配可表示动作发生的次数或持续的状态。

① 现在完成体的形式

现在完成体的构成如下:

肯定式	否定式	疑问式
I have worked.	I have not worked.	Have I worked?
You have worked.	You have not worked.	Have you worked?
He (She, It) has worked.	He (She, It) has not worked.	Has he (she, it) worked?
We have worked.	We have not worked.	Have we worked?
You have worked.	You have not worked.	Have you worked?
They have worked.	They have not worked.	Have they worked?

② 现在完成体的用法

A．表示结果

现在完成体表示结果，句中的动作虽然发生在过去，但对现在有影响。现在完成体跨越两个体间，一为过去，一为现在。

I have been to Shanghai for many times. 我去过上海很多次了。

Mary has already gone to America. 玛丽已经去美国了。

He has lost his bag. 他的包丢了。

I have learned English for many years. 我学习英语很多年了。

He has been a writer all his life. 他一生都从事写作。

China has won the prize. 中国获奖了。

I have been offered a scholarship by the University. 我得到了大学的奖学金。

The past has vanished like smoke. 往事如烟。

Note：现在完成体表示最近发生的动作，此体常与 just, recently, already, yet, still, at last, finally, almost 等副词连用。

What good movies have you watched recently? 你最近看了什么好电影？

I still haven't passed my driving test. 我还没通过驾驶考试。

At last he has done it. 最后他成功了。

The plan hasn't been finally approved. 该计划还未最后通过。

We have almost finished the experiment. 我们几乎完成了这个实验。

B．表示持续的动作

现在完成体表示持续的动作，即过去体间发生的动作，一直持续到现在（可能还要继续下去），因此多与持续性动词如 live, learn, study, wait, teach 等连用。体间状语常用 since 加一个过去的体间点，用 for 加一段体间，用 by 加一个现在体间。

Great as Newton was, many of his ideas _____ today and are being modified by the work of scientists of our time.

A) are to challenge 　　C) have been challenged
B) may be challenged 　　D) are challenging

全句的意思是"虽然牛顿是个伟大的人物，但他的许多见解直到今天还在受到挑战，并且被现代科学家的工作所修正。" challenge 是及物动词，在本句中应当是被动语态；其动作延续到今天，所以要用现在完成体态。可见答案是 C) have been challenged。A) are to challenge 和 D) are challenging 都是主动语态，不可能是答案。B) may be challenged 虽然是被动语态，但意思与全句内容不合，所以不对。C) 表示发生在过去，但对现在仍有影响的动作或情况。通常用点动词，如 arrive, begin, find, give, lose 等。

John has broken his left leg. 约翰摔断了左腿。

Notes：a. 现在完成体是联系过去和现在的纽带。现在完成体和过去时的区别在于：现在完成体强调动作的动态，或受动态的影响，是动态的结果，对现在有影响；过去时只表示过去的某个具体时间里发生的动作，与现在没有联系。

He worked in that hospital for 8 years. 他曾经在那家医院工作了 8 年。（这只是讲述一个过去的事实，他现在已经不在那家医院了。）

He has worked in that hospital for 8 years. 他已经在那家医院里工作了 8 年。（表示他从过去开始工作，一直工作到现在，现在仍在那家医院工作。）

b. 因为含有 for 加一段体间或 since 加一个体间点这样的体间状语的完成体有动态和延续性的特点，所以不能使用终端动词或瞬间动词。

My sister has been married for 5 years. 我的姐姐已经结婚5年了。(过去分词作表语,表示状态,可以延续)
My sister has married. Don't disturb her. 我的姐姐已结婚了。别打扰她。(终端动词)
I have learned French for two years. 我学习法语已经两年了。
I haven't met her since last year. 自从去年起,我就没见过她。
He has lived here for a long time. 他住在这儿已经很久了。
I have taught them not to judge other people by their appearance. 我教过他们不要以貌取人。
They have been very active in protecting the environment. 他们一直积极保护环境。
The old man has lived here for more than twenty years. 老人已在此住了二十多年了。

c. 现在完成体也可以和表示现在的体间状语如 now, always, often, today, lately, frequently, regularly, sometimes, this morning, this week, this month, this year 等连用。

I have been busy today. 我今天很忙。
I've told you a dozen times. 我已告诉你很多次了。
I have often thought about this. 我经常思考这个问题。
She has attended classes regularly. 她总是准时上课。
It has rained every day this week. 本周每天下雨。

C. 现在完成体还可用于下列特殊结构中

a. 在"this is the first/second/third ... time that ..."或在"It is the best(worst, most interesting)+名词+that"后面跟现在完成体。

This is my first time that I have visited China. 这是我第一次访华。
This is the most interesting film I have ever seen. 这是我看过的最有趣的电影。
That is the only book that he has written. 这是他唯一写过的一本书。
This is the second time that the products of our company have been shown in the International Exhibition. 这是我公司产品第二次参加国际展览会。

b. 在句型"It is/has been ... since ..."中所使用的两种体态都正确。

It is/has been 10 years since I last saw him. 从我上次见到他以来已经10年了。

c. 用在"no sooner than","hardly/scarcely ... when","before","prior to"等结构中,主句要求完成体。

I haven't met that professor prior to today. 以前我从未见过那位教授。

(6) 现在完成进行体

现在完成进行体表示从过去某一时间开始一直延续到现在的动作。这一动作可能刚刚开始,也可能仍在继续,并可能延续到将来。基本结构为"have/has + been + doing"。

① 现在完成进行体的形式

现在完成进行体的构成如下:

肯定式	否定式	疑问式
I have been working.	I have not been working.	Have I been working?
You have been working.	You have not been working.	Have you been working?
He (She, It) has been working.	He (She, It) has not been working.	Has he (she, it) been working?
We have been working.	We have not been working.	Have we been working?
You have been working.	You have not been working.	Have you been working?
They have been working.	They have not been working.	Have they been working?

② 现在完成进行体的用法

A. 表示从过去一直持续到现在的动作

现在完成进行体表示从过去一直持续到现在的动作或刚刚结束的动作。

I've been writing letters all this morning. 我写了一上午信。（动作不再继续）

O'Neil is ill. He's been lying in the bed for three weeks. 奥尼尔生病了，已卧床3个星期了。（动作会继续下去）

B. 现在完成进行体表示从过去到现在的重复性动作

现在完成进行体所表示的动作并不是一直在进行的动作，而是断断续续地反复发生的动作。

What have you been doing all this time? 你一直都在干什么来着？（动作可能继续下去）

That reporter has been contributing articles to this magazine all these years. 这些年那个记者一直为这家杂志撰稿。（断断续续地反复发生的动作）

(7) 过去完成体

过去完成体表示在过去的某个时间或动作以前已经发生的动作或已经存在的状态，即过去完成体的动作发生在"过去的过去"，句中有明显的参照动作或时间状语，这种时态从来不孤立使用。

① 过去完成体的形式

过去完成体的构成如下：

肯定式	否定式	疑问式
I had worked.	I had not worked.	Had I worked?
You had worked.	You had not worked.	Had you worked?
He (She, It) had worked.	He (She, It) had not worked.	Had he (she, it) worked?
We had worked.	We had not worked.	Had we worked?
You had worked.	You had not worked.	Had you worked?
They had worked.	They had not worked.	Had they worked?

② 过去完成体的用法

A. 表示过去某时间之前结束的动作或状态

When he got there, the train had already left. 他到了那儿时火车已经离开了。

Ina realized she had made a mistake. 艾娜意识到她犯了个错误。

There had been 25 parks in our city up till 2000. 截止到2000年，我市共有25个公园。

By the end of last term we had finished the book. 上学期结束时，我们已完成了此书。

They finished earlier than we had expected. 他们完成得比我们期待得要快。

B. 与 when 等引导的从句连用

过去完成体与 when 等引导的从句连用。常与过去完成体连用的句型有：had + just/barely/hardly/scarcely + done … when …, no sooner … than …，表示"刚……就……"、"不等……就……"的固定句型。其中主句用过去完成体，从句用一般过去体。

No sooner had we left the house than it began to rain. 我们刚离开家就开始下雨了。

I had not gone much farther before I caught them up. 我没有走多远就赶上他们了。

I had hardly finished my work when he came to see me. 我刚完成工作他就来看我了。

I had no sooner got into the room than it began to snow. 我刚走进房间天就开始下起雪来了。

No sooner had I arrived home than the telephone rang. 我刚到家电话就响了。（注意主谓倒装）

C. 表示持续到过去某时间之前的动作或状态

过去完成体表示持续到过去某时间之前的动作或状态。

We had finished the work by nine o'clock yesterday. 昨晚 9 点前我们已完成了工作。

The company had completed the project by the end of 1999. 到 1999 年年底公司已完成了那个项目。

D. 表示"第几次做某事"

此时主句用过去时,从句用过去完成体。

That was the second time that she had seen her grandfather. 这是她第二次见到她的爷爷。

It was 3 years since we had parted. 我们分别已经三年了。

E. 某些动作动词的过去完成体表示未实现的愿望、打算和意图

这些动词主要有 hope, expect, think, intend, mean, want, suppose 等。

I had hoped that I could do the job. 我本希望能得到这份工作。

I had intended to see you but I was too busy. 我本打算来看你,但我太忙了。

F. 典型题例

例 1:Until then, his family _____ from him for six months.

A) didn't hear   C) hasn't heard
B) hasn't been hearing D) hadn't heard

全句的意思是:"到那时为止,他家里已经有六个月没得到他的消息了。"由此可以看出,谓语动词的动作延续到过去的某一时刻才完成,因此谓语要用过去完成体。答案是 D)。其他选项中:A) didn't hear,因为一般过去时只表示过去发生的事情或存在的状态,所以不能与时间状语 for six months 连用。B) hasn't been hearing,现在完成进行体表示过去某时刻继续到现在或现在还在进行的动作,与题意不符。C) hasn't heard,现在完成体表示从过去某一时刻到现在为止发生的动作。而题中的 then 只表示过去的某一时刻,不能表示现在时间。

Note:"过去的过去"这种逻辑关系常通过上下文体现出来,而不一定受某个时间状语的限制。

例 2:There had been someone in our room just now, because I noticed a burning cigarette end on the floor when we opened the front door. 刚才有人在我们的房间里,因为我们打开前门进来时,我注意到地板上有一支仍在燃烧的香烟。

分析:虽然时间状语是 just now,似乎应该使用一般过去时,但是"在房间里"这个状态是在"开门"和"注意"这两个过去的动作之前就存在的,所以应该用过去完成体。

(8) 过去完成进行体

过去完成进行体主要表示持续到过去某时之前的动作。

① 过去完成进行体的形式

过去完成进行体的构成如下:

肯定式	否定式	疑问式
I had been working.	I had not been working.	Had I been working?
You had been working.	You had not been working.	Had you been working?
He (She, It) had been working.	He (She, It) had not been working.	Had he (she, it) been working?
We had been working.	We had not been working.	Had we been working?
You had been working.	You had not been working.	Had you been working?
They had been working.	They had not been working.	Had they been working?

② 过去完成进行体的用法

过去完成通行体主要表示持续到过去某时之前的动作。

I had been looking for it for days before I found it. 这个东西,我找了好多天才找着。

The telephone had been ringing for three minutes before it was answered. 电话铃响了三分钟才有人接。

He was tired. He'd been working all day. 他累了。他工作了一整天。

After he'd been lecturing for half an hour, Professor Brown had a drink of water. 布朗教授讲了半小时课之后才喝了一点水。

3.3 将来意思表示法

(1) 用"shall/will + 动词原形"表示将来意思

用"shall/willl + 动词原形"表示将来意思时,其中 shall 用于第一人称,will 用于第二人称和第三人称。但是现在,尤其在美国,不管什么人称,都用 will,只在客气的问句中用 shall。

① shall/will 的形式

一般将来时的构成如下:

肯定式	否定式	疑问式
I shall work.	I shall not work.	Shall I work?
You will work.	You will not work.	Will you work?
He (She, It) will work.	He (She, It) will not work.	Will he (she, it) work?
We shall work.	We shall not work.	Shall we work?
You will work.	You will not work.	Will you work?
They will work.	They will not work.	Will they work?

② "shall/will + 动词"表示将来意思的具体用法

A. 表示单纯的将来事实

此时经常与表示将来的时间状语连用,如 tomorrow, soon, later, next time, in … minute, next week (month, year)等。

I *shall be* 20 years old *next year*. 明年我就 20 岁了。

I'*ll start tomorrow*. 我明天出发。

You'*ll be* all right *soon*. 你很快就会好起来的。

I'*ll tell* you everything *next time*. 下次我把一切都告诉你。

How long *will you be staying* in Paris? 你在巴黎待多久?

Next year will be the centenary of this firm. 明年是这家公司的一百周年。

The doctor *will be* with you *in a few minutes*. 医生马上就来。

They *will finish* the hospital *next month*. 下个月医院就将完工。

B. 与表示将来的时间状语连用

将来意思还经常与 by, until, from, after, before, up to 表示将来某个时间以前或以后的时间状语连用。

I'*ll be* back *by three*. 我会在 3 点前回来。

The bridge *will be finished by 2020*. 此桥在 2020 年前完工。

I *shall stay* in Paris *until next week*. 我会在巴黎待到下周。
We *won't arrive* home *until midnight*. 我们半夜才会回家。
We *shall have* leisure *after next Wednesday*. 下周三后我们有空。

C. 与表示频率的时间状语连用

将来意思也经常和表示频率的时间状语 always, often, ever, never, eventually 等连用,表示一种承诺或决心。

I *will always respect* my parents. 我会一直尊重我的父母。
I *shall remain* in love with you all my life. 我会爱你一生一世。
I'*ll never break* my promise. 我从来不会背弃诺言。
None of us *will ever reveal* this secret to anyone else. 我们谁都不会泄露这个秘密。

D. 表示最近的将来

将来意思也可与表示现在的时间状语连用,表示最近的将来,如 now, today, tonight 等。

I *shall do* it *now*. 我马上就做。
There *will be* no rain *today*. 今天不会下雨。
Mary *will probably phone* us *this evening*. 玛丽今晚很可能打电话给我们。

E. 与现在时表示将来意思的从句连用

复合句中的时间状语也可以由从句担任,但从句中则用一般现在时表示将来意思。

When I *have* time, I'*ll go*. 我有时间就会去。
I *shall stay* here until my business *is concluded*. 我会待在这直到事情办好。
I'*ll ask* him as soon as he *comes*. 他一来我就问他。
We *shall go* unless it *rains*. 除非下雨,我们一定去。
No matter how much it *costs*, I *will take* it. 无论多少钱,我都要买下。

在一定的上下文中,时间状语可以省略。

I know you *will like* it. 我就知道你会喜欢。
Go ahead. I'*ll catch up*. 往前走。我会赶上的。

F. 其他表示将来意思的形式

a. be going to 表示说话人的意图或打算

We *are going to* visit London this fall. 今年秋天我们要去伦敦。
He *is going to* get better. 他会好起来的。
They *are going to* move to their new house soon. 他们很快就要搬新家了。
Look out! The ice *is going to* crack. 小心!冰要开裂了。
Are you *going to* have a walk after supper? 晚饭后你想去散步吗?

b. be to do 表示计划或安排要做的事

The German Prime Minister *is to visit* China. 德国总理即将访华。
John and Mary *are to be married* in May. 约翰和玛丽打算在5月结婚。
We *are to discuss* the report next week. 我们计划下周讨论这份报告。
The worst *is yet to come*. 最坏的还没来呢。
Such problems *are to be avoided*. 今后要避免这类问题。

c. be about to 表示即将(正要)做某事

The meeting *is about to* begin. 会议马上就开。
He *is about to* break down. 他快要崩溃了。
It seems that the clouds *are about to* disperse. 乌云似乎就要消散了。
Autumn harvest *is about to* start. 秋收就要开始了。

d. 现在进行体可表示按计划或安排即将发生的动作,所用动词一般表示位置的变化或移动,此类动词包括:join, play, eat, take, wear, move, do, leave。

She *is giving* a concert next month. 下个月她要举办演奏会。

We *are leaving for* Beijing after the performance. 演出结束后我们要去北京。

We *are moving* to a new hotel this evening. 今晚我们要搬到一个新的酒店。

G. 用 be, go 等动词的现在时表示将来

用动词 be, begin, go, leave, open, return 等动词的一般现在时表示按规定、安排要发生的动作。

Today *is* Sunday, and tomorrow *is* Monday. 今天星期天,明天是星期一。

The train *leaves* at 8 am. 火车早晨 8 点出发。

The delegation *arrives in* Nanjing this afternoon. 代表团下午抵达南京。

The plane *takes off* at 5 pm. 飞机下午 5 点起飞。

The film *begins in* a few minutes. 电影几分钟后开始。

第4章 动词的语态

4.1 语态概述

语态(Voice)是动词的一种形式,用以说明主语与谓语动词之间的关系。英语的语态是通过动词形式的变化体现出来的。英语中有两种语态:主动语态(Active Voice)和被动语态(Passive Voice)。主动语态表示主语是动作的执行者。被动语态表示主语是动作的承受者,即行为动作的对象。人们一般所说的被动语态好像就指"be + 过去分词"型,其中的 be 动词必须与句子主语在人称和数上保持一致。实际上还有一种"get + 过去分词"的被动语态。

4.2 被动句与主动句的关系及被动句的时体

(1) 被动句与主动句的关系

主动句的主语是动作的执行者,被动句的主语是动作的承受者。主被动句关系和演变如下图:

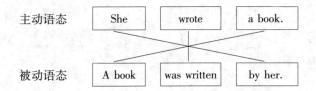

(2) 被动句的时体

被动句的基本结构是"主语 + be + 过去分词"。其中的 be 动词必须与句子主语在人称和数上保持一致。一般来说,被动语态除了现在完成进行体和过去完成进行体外,都有相应的时、体,也有表示将来意思的被动语态。但"be + 过去分词"既可构成被动语态,也可构成复合谓语,要注意区别。

① **一般现在时:am/is/are + 过去分词**

Lost time *is never found* again. 光阴一去不复返。

Time *cannot be added* to a person's life, but it *can be made* more valuable by avoiding waste. 时间不能加进一个人的生命里,可珍惜光阴可以使生命变得更有价值。

② **一般过去时:was/were + 过去分词**

Bob *was seen* to take away the dictionary. 有人看见巴勃拿走了那本词典。

The 29th Olympic Games *was held* in Beijing from August 8, 2008 to August 24, 2008. 第29届世界奥林匹克运动会于2008年8月8日至8月24日在北京举行。

③ **现在进行体:am/is/are being + 过去分词**

Solar energy *is being used* in every possible way. 目前太阳能在尽可能地被加以利用。

These new tractors *are being sent* to our hometown. 这些新拖拉机正在运往我家乡。

④ 过去进行体：was/were being + 过去分词

His new car *was being driven* badly. 他的新车开得很差。

The plan *was being discussed* this time yesterday. 昨天这个时候正在讨论那计划。

⑤ 现在完成体：have/has been + 过去分词

Bumper harvest *have been reaped* for years. 连续几年获得了大丰收。

The English Grammar written by Robert *has been translated* into many foreign languages. 罗伯特写的《英语语法》已经译成了许多国家的文字。

⑥ 过去完成体：had been + 过去分词

By 4 pm the article *had been typed* by my daughter. 到下午4点，那篇文章已由我女儿打好了。

The auditorium opposite our school *had been built* in 2013. 我们学校对面的大礼堂是2013年建的。

⑦ 表示一般将来：shall/will be + 过去分词

His new book *will be published* by the end of this month. 他的新书将于这月月底出版。

A lecture on English-American literature *will be given* by Professor Ling this afternoon. 今天下午由林教授做英美文学讲座。

⑧ 表示过去将来：should/would be + 过去分词

Our monitor said that our proposal *would be considered* with great care. 我们班长说我们的建议将会被慎重考虑。

She asked if she *would be invited* to the party. 她问是否邀请她参加晚会。

⑨ 表示将来完成：shall/will have been + 过去分词

By the end of this year the book *Mankind will have been finished*. 到今年年底,《人类》这本书将已写成。

Before they return the meeting *will have been ended*. 在他们回来前，会议将已结束。

⑩ 表示过去将来完成：should/would have been + 过去分词

Alice told me that preparations *would have been finish*ed by ten o'clock. 爱丽丝告诉我，准备工作到10点时将已完成。

Our English teacher said that Lesson Ten *would have been copied* in exercise-books five times by five. 我们英语老师说到5点钟要把第十课的课文在练习本上抄写完五遍。

4.3 "be+过去分词"的两种结构

从结构上看，"be+过去分词"有两种形式：一种是被动语态；另一种是系表结构，也叫复合谓语。"be+过去分词"是被动语态结构，一般后可加上 by 短语（施动者），而系表结构后不可加施动者 by 短语。"be+过去分词"是系表结构的话，其中-ed 分词往往是形容词。

其实，-ed 形容词大多由原来的及物动词转化而来，现在的词典都把它们视作形容词。-ed 形容词有：accomplished, accustomed, amused, amazed, astonished, closed, completed, complicated, confined, confused, connected, covered, crowded, decided, dedicated, delighted, devoted, deserted, disappointed, discouraged, distinguished, dressed, exhausted, experienced, faded, fatigued, finished, frightened, illustrated, inexperienced, injured, interested, known, killed, learned, lined, loaded, married, mispronounced, paved, painted, pleased, posted, puzzled, qualified, recovered, reserved, satisfied, saved, soaked, surprised, surrounded, tinged, tired, translated, typed, undressed, unloaded, worried 等。

事实上，-ed 形容词作表语用极为普遍，此种用法表示主语所处的状态。

I am *astonished* that she didn't come. 她没来，使我感到惊异。

They were *delighted* at the news that you were successful. 他们听到你成功的消息极为高兴。

She was somewhat *amazed* to hear his answer. 听到他的回答后，她感到有点惊异。

Wendy became very *confused* and forgot what she wanted to say. 温迪被弄得极为糊涂，忘了要说什么。

4.4 使用被动句的原因

使用被动句的原因很多，或许是对动作的承受者更为关心，或许侧重动作行为者，或许是动作执行者难以明确或不必或不便说出，或许是说话者本身就是动作行为者，或许是双方都知道动作执行者而无须说出，或许是出于行文需要。

(1) 对动作的承受者更为关心或侧重时

The novel *was written* by a very good friend of mine whom we are going to visit this afternoon. 这部小说是我的一个要好的朋友写的，他就是我们今天下午要去拜访的人。

The tree in front of the church *was struck* by lightning. 教堂前的那棵树为雷电所击。

(2) 动作执行者不必说出或难以明确时

Bread *is made* from flour. 面包是用面粉做的。

The room *had been cleaned*. 房间已被打扫过。

The flight *was cancelled* due to the frog. 班机因雾停航。

(3) 说话者本身是行为者时

在这种情况下是为了表示礼貌和措辞婉转，或者不愿把自己说出来时，可用被动句来表达。

You *have been told* many times that it is not easy to be a real editor-in-chief. （我）说过多少次要做个真正的主编是不容易的。

Everybody *is expected* to abide by the following principles and regulations. （我）希望大家遵守下述原则和规定。

(4) 双方都知道或从特定的上下文中可知谁是动作的执行者时

Mr. White *was elected* leader of the team. 怀特先生被选为他们的队长。

I told him that my master had dismissed me. No reason had assigned, no objection *had been made* to my conduct. 我告诉他，我的主人已解雇了我。可是，没说明理由，也没对我的行为提出异议。

(5) 在着重事物时

After a hole *was made* in a cord, a narrow glass tube *was inserted* and the cord *was inserted* into the neck of a bottle filled with colored water. On doing this, some of the water rose in the tube. The level of the colored water in tube *was marked*. 在软木塞上打孔后，插进一根细玻璃管，再把软木塞插进装满颜色水的瓶颈里。这样做时，试管里的颜色水就上升，标明了试管中水的水平。

在上面的短文中，出现的都是被动句，这是因为科技文章中着重事物、物质的过程，而不太注意动作的行为者，所以人们常用被动语态来组句行文。

(6) 在新闻报道中

A young lady and her baby (*were*) *killed* in the bed-room in our city yesterday night. 昨晚,我市一年轻女士和她的婴儿在卧室被杀。

A taxi-driver *is alleged* to have kicked an old man in the stomach. 据说出租车司机踢了一个老人的腹部。

上面的新闻之所以这样写,是因为人们对新闻报道的首要关注点是"事",而不是做事的人,因此作者会着重写出"事情",不提及行为者,即使要提及,也就在文章的后面一笔带过了事。

(7) 在书刊的前言、内容提要和戏剧、电影的场景画面中

The book which *is being written is designed* for those who are the beginners in learning English. 这本正在写的书是为初学英语的人撰写的。

The enemy's main blockhouse. In the distance are green bean-fields. On the blockhouse tower on the right *can be seen* the back of a Japanese sentry; on the low wall to the left *is written* "Enforce Order". 日寇中心炮楼。远处豆苗正绿;近处铁丝网密布;右侧的炮楼上可见日寇哨兵的背影;左则墙上涂有"强化治安"的字样。

The materials in *English Sentence Patterns and Syntax* by Beijing Language and Culture University Press *are introduced* progressively and systematically. And in each chapter abundant exercises *are provided*. 在北京语言大学出版社出版的《新编英语句型句法全解》一书中,那些材料得到了循序渐进而又系统的介绍,每章后都提供了大量的练习。

从上面三句中可见,例句 1 是作者向人说起他写的那本书,其读者对象是英语初学者;例句 2 显然是一个剧本或电影中的场面和画面,在电影、戏剧的场面和画面中用被动句更能体现其客观性和形象性;例句 3 是所写书的一点说明。对于这些内容的表达常用被动句,为的是避免过多地提及作者自己。

(8) 出于行文需要时

为了使上下文更好地衔接,有时用被动语态可达到很好的效果。在这种情况下,前面分句或句子是主动语态,后面分句或句子是被动语态。

Our director *began* to speak, and *was listened to* attentively by the actors. 导演开始讲话,演员们都专心地听着。

Mr. Green *raised* a new proposal, which *was warmly supported* by the people who were present at the meeting. 格林先生提出了一个新建议,该建议得到了与会人士的热情支持。

4.5 主动句与被动句的转换

主动句包含着各种结构的句子,主动句与被动句的转换情况各不相同。

(1) S + V + O

Everybody likes the film. 大家都喜欢那部电影。(主动句)
→ The film is liked by everybody. (被动句)
Bruce writes a letter every week. 布鲁斯每周写一封信。(主动句)
→ A letter is written by Bruce every week. (被动句)

(2) S + V + o + O

这种句型中,谓语带了两个宾语,小 o 代表间接宾语,常指"人",大 O 代表直接宾语,常指"物"。这种

句子的特点就是其标志动词(除 last, cost 外)后略去直接宾语后句子就不成立。这种句子变成被动语态时,可把其中一个宾语作动词的主语,另一个宾语保留在原处,叫作保留宾语(Retained Object)。

She gave me a book. 她给了我一本书。

→ I was given a book.

A book was given (to) me.

Her father bought her a new bike. 她父亲给她买了一辆新自行车。

→ She was bought a new bike.

→ A new bike was bought for her.

像 give, buy 可带间接宾语和直接宾语的动词有:grant, leave, lend, pass, pay, promise, read, return, show, send, teach, throw, write 等;do, cook, fetch, find, get, make, order, paint, play, save, spare, reserve, sing 等。第二组动词后面带的直接宾语变为被动句的主语后,原来的间接宾语前加介语 for,而且介词 for 不能省略。

His father bought him a computer. 他父亲给他买了一部电脑。

→ A computer was bought *for* him (by his father).

Tom fetch her an apple. 汤姆去给她拿了只苹果来。

→ An apple was fetched *for* her.

(3) S+V+O+O

此句型中的两个 O 是表示两个双直接宾语,这种句子与上面的不同,它略去其中的一个直接宾语后句子还成立。但要注意,含双直接宾语的句子变为被动句时,一般只能把表示人的直接宾语变为被动句的主语,在极个别情况下也有把表示物的直接宾语变为被动句的主语的,但不能在表示人的直接宾语前加上介词 to 或 for。

He forgave her her rudeness. 他原谅她的鲁莽。

→ She was forgiven her rudeness.

We struck the enemy a heavy blow. 我们给敌人以重创。

→ The enemy was struck a heavy blow.

能够带双直接宾语的动词不多,它们是 ask, answer, catch(打,击), envy, excuse, forgive, hit, lead, pardon, strike, take(带领)等。

(4) S+V+O+Oc

凡含有复合宾语的句子变为被动句时,须将主动句中的宾语变成被动句的主语,原宾语补足语保留在原处不变,不过此时它已是主语补足语了。

He calls me *Beloved Na Na*. 他一直叫我可爱娜娜。

→ I am called *Beloved Na Na*. (名词宾语补足语不变)

I have kept her *waiting long*. 我让她等了好久。

→ She has been kept *waiting long*. (现在分词宾语补足语不变)

I heard the song *The East Is Red* sung everywhere. 我听到到处有人在唱《东方红》这支歌。

→ The song *The East Is Red* was heard sung everywhere. (过去分词宾语补足语不变)

We advised the boy *not to play all day long*. 我们叫那孩子不要整天玩耍。

→ The boy was advised *not to play all day long*. (动词不定式否定式宾语补足语不变)

She asked me *to post the letter for her*. 她要我给她寄掉那封信。

→ I was asked *to post the letter for her*. (动词不定式短语宾语补语不变)

My brother painted the house *white*. 我弟弟把房子漆成白色。

→ The house was painted *white*. (形容词宾语补足语不变)

I saw her *out*. 我看见她出去了。

→ She was seen *out*. (副词宾语补足语不变)

She often mistakes me *for my younger brother*. 她常常把我误认为我的弟弟。

→ I am often mistaken *for my younger brother*. (原介词短语宾语补足语不变)

要注意的是,有些动词(如 make, see, hear, watch, notice, observe, perceive 等)后的动词不定式在主动句中是不带 to 的,但被动句中要恢复 to。

I heard Viv *say good-bye* to her parents. 我听见维维向她父母道别。

→ Viv was heard *to say good-bye* to her parents. (原动词不定式短语宾语补足语 say good-bye 恢复成 to say good-bye)

Who saw him *repair the machine*? 谁看见他修理机器了?

→ By whom was he seen to repair the machine? (原动词不定式宾语补足语 repair 恢复成 to repair)

但动词 let 后面可以不带 to。

The boy was let (to) go out to play. 允许这男孩出去玩。

(5) S + V + that Clause

含有宾语从句的主动句变为被动句时有以下三种情况:

① it 作被动句的形式主语

以 it 作被动句的形式主语时,be 动词的形式应根据原句的时态而选用不同的 be,如 is/am/are/was/were/will be/have been/had been,原主动句的谓语动词变为过去分词,后面的宾语从句不变。

Her mother said (that) she was much better. 她母亲说她好多了。

→ It was said that she was much better.

She asked if/whether they were leaving for Beijing. 她问他们是否要去北京。

→ It was asked if/whether they were leaving for Beijing.

They haven't decided when they will have the meeting. 他们还没决定在什么时候开会。

→ It hasn't been decided when they will have the meeting.

② 把宾语从句的主语变作被动句的主语

对含有 that 所引导的宾语从句变为被动句的另一种方法,就是把宾语从句的主语变作被动句的主语,原主句中的谓语动词则变为被动句的过去分词,而宾语从句的谓语动词变作动词不定式短语,特别要注意的是,这动词不定式短语的时态要与原来宾语从句的时态相一致。

I believe that they are doing *her best*. 我相信他们在尽力干。

→ They are believed *to be doing* their best.

Her parents expected that *she should become* a teacher. 她父母亲希望她成为教师。

→ She was expected (by her parents) *to become* a teacher.

③ 以 wh-词引出的宾语从句只能直接作被动句的主语

要注意是,含有 what, whatever, whoever 等词引出的宾语从句不可采用含有 it 形式的被动句,也不把宾语从句的主语变作被动句的主语,而是要直接用从句作被动句的主语。

Chairman of the club will announce tomorrow what are to be put on the agenda. 俱乐部的主席明天将宣布什么将列入议程。

→ What are to be put on the agenda will be announced tomorrow.

We must keep whatever was said here secret. 我们这里所说的不管什么话都要保密。

→ Whatever was said here must be kept secret.

(6) S + Phrasal V + O

在短语动词作谓语动词的主动句中,有的短语动词是双词短语动词,有的是三词短语动词。双词短语动词要把它们看成一个不可分割的及物动词;三词短语动词又是另一种情况。

① V + Prep.

"动词+介词"的短语动词变为被动句时,把"动词+介词"看成一个整体及物动词。

A middle-aged woman *looks after* her two children. 一位中年妇女照料她的两个小孩。

→ The two children are *looked after* by a middle-aged woman.

I have never *heard of* such things. 我从没听说过这种事情。

→ Such things have never been *heard of*.

Note:"动词+介词"可能是短语动词,也可能不是短语动词。是短语动词的,那就可变为被动语态,不是短语动词的就不可变为被动语态。

② V + Adv.

"动词+副词"的短语动词变为被动句时,也把其看作一个整体。

Toby has *left out* two words in the last sentence of his article. 托比在他文章的最后一句中漏了两个词。

→ Two words were *left out* in the last sentence in his article.

We have *put off* the Class Meeting till next Monday. 我们把班会推迟到下星期一。

→ The Class Meeting has been *put off* till next Monday.

③ V + N + Prep.

"动词+名词+介词"型的三词短语动词不少,这类短语动词变为被动语态时有两种方法:一是把三词动词当成一个"整体"对待,把这整体中的介词后的宾语作为被动句的主语;另一种把三词动词作为"松散结构"对待,把三词动词中间的名词作为被动句的主语。

A. 以"整体"对待

They *paid* much *attention to* what I had said at the meeting. 他们对我会上讲的话很在意。

→ What I had said at the meeting was *paid* much *attention to* by them.

His arrival *put an end to* our conversation. 他的到来终止了我们的谈话。

→ Our conversation was *put to an end* by his arrival.

B. 以"松散结构"对待

You must make full use of your time. 你们必须充分利用你们的时间。

→ Full use of your time must be made.

The manager couldn't find any fault with Bob. 经理找不出巴勃什么岔子。

→ No fault could be found with Bob.

像上面那样的三词短语动词常见的有:catch hold of, keep pace with, make use of, make mention of, pay attention to, put an end to, lay stress on, lose sight of, lose touch with, set fire to, take care of, take notice of 等。

(7) S + V [动词+副词+介词] + O

这种三词短语动词变为被动句时把它们作为一个整体看。

Mary's mother *looked down upon* her boy-friend. 玛丽的母亲看不起她的那个男朋友。

→ Mary's boy-friend was *looked down upon* by her mother.

They have long *done away with* this practice. 他们很久以来就放弃了这种做法。

→ This practice has been long *done away with* by them.

(8) S + V + to-infinitive (as object) + O

在含动词不定式复合谓语的主动句变为被动句时,只要把动词不定式后的宾语变为被动句的主语,同时要把原不定式变为被动式。

Their grandsons used to sing the song "I Love Tiananmen in Peking." 他们的孙儿们以前常常唱《我爱北京天安门》。

→ *I Love Tiananman in Pekimg* is used to be sung (by their grandsons).

We are to discuss the plan this Saturday. 我们打算本周六讨论那个计划。

→ The plan is to be discussed this Saturday.

He is going to finish the novel next week. 他下星期将完成那部小说。

→ The novel is going to be finished next week.

We have to tell her the truth. 我们得把实话告诉她。

→ She has to be told the truth.

Note:在含动词不定式复合谓语后有间接宾语和直接宾语时,变为被动句时可把其中的任何一个宾语变为被动句的主语。

They are sure to give us a warm welcome. 他们一定会热烈欢迎我们的。

→ We are sure to be given a warm welcome.

→ A warm welcome is sure to be given (to) us.

4.6　主动句转换成被动句的注意点

(1) 主动句必须是 S + V + O

这种句型中的动词必须是及物动词,其后还要有宾语。

I like her novel. 我喜欢她的小说。

→ Her novel is liked by me.

(2) 有些主动句不可变为被动句

有些主动句中,表示状态的及物动词后跟的是反身代词、相互代词及含义上不可分割的固定词组作宾语时,就没有相应的被动句。

I *have* a nice house to live in. 我有一所好房子居住。

The property *has changed* hands recently. 这财产最近已易主。

How could they *see* each other in the fog? 在雾中他们怎能看清对方呢?

The new leader *lacks* experience. 那个新领导缺乏经验。

(3) 有些被动句也没有相应的主动句

Rose was born on August 8, 2008. 罗丝出生于2008年8月8日。

A chance like that is not to be sneezed at. 那样的机会不能被忽视。(此句不可说成:We are not to sneeze at a chance like that.)

4.7　行为被动语态和状态被动语态

"be + 过去分词"被动语态有行为被动语态和状态被动语态之分。行为被动语态所表示的是动作,其主语是动作的承受者,而状态被动语态却说明主语的特点或所处的状态。可是,这样界定还是比较含糊,我们要对它们作具体的分析才能区别出这两种被动语态。

(1) 看能否带 by 短语

区别是行为被动语态还是状态被动语态,看能不能带 by 短语(行为者)是一个相当重要的原则。这是因为从行为被动语态的定义上讲,它是表示动作行为的,而能带表示动作行为的 by 短语就肯定了动作的行为者。绝大多数的"be + 过去分词"的结构是行为被动语态。

The windows of the room *were opened by me.* 这房间窗子是我打开的。(行为被动语态)

The windows of the room *are* now *opened.* 这房间的窗子现在开着。(状态被动语态,不可添加 by 短语)

但也要注意,并非有了 by 短语就是行为被动语态。

The old man *was surrounded by her grandchildren.* 那老头被他的孙儿们围住。(by 短语是动作的发出者,当然是行为被动语态)

Guilin *is surrounded by hills and mountains.* 桂林被大大小小的群山所围。(by 短语并非发出动作而触及句子的主语,所以是状态被动语态)

"be + 过去分词"后的 by 短语还可能表示或兼示原因、方式,这时也属状态被动语态。

No. 110 Road *was held up by a traffic accident.* 110 号大路由于交通事故被封闭。

The tree *is known by its fruit.* 看到果子就知道是什么树。

(2) 从时、体、态上判别

从时、体、态上来看,状态被动语态通常只用于一般现在时和一般过去时,而行为被动语态可有十种时、体、态。

The book *is closed.* 书合着(没翻开)。

The sentence *was* neatly *written* on the blackboard. 这句子很整齐地写在黑板上。

(3) 从状语上区分

"be + 过去分词"是动态被动语态还是静态被动语态,可从它们是否是现在时或将来时进行判定,其状语也能告诉我们。

① 如是反复性的或习惯性的状语,那就是行为被动语态,不然就是状态被动语态。

Our desks and chairs *are painted every year.* 我们的办公桌和椅子每年漆一次。(状语 every year 表示反复性,句子就是行为被动语态)

My desk *is newly painted.* 我的办公桌是新漆的。(状语 newly 表示状态性,因此句子是状态被告动语态)

The post office on our street *is usually opened* at 8:30 am. 我们街上的邮电局通常上午8:30开门。(状语 usually 表示反复或习惯性,此句是行为被动语态)

② 当"be + 过去分词"结构是过去时,有时间、地点、目的或方式状语时,那句子常是行为被动语态;没有时间状语时,可根据上下文而定。

The article *was written last week.* 这篇论文是上星期写的。

All the windows *were widely opened.* 所有的窗子都大开着。

A book *was written* by David in praise of the workers and peasants in new China. 戴维写了一本书以赞颂新中国的工农大众。

The door of the hall *was shut* when I passed by at eight, but I don't know when it *was shut.* 当我8点钟经过那里时礼堂门关着,但我不知道(门)是什么时候关上的。

上述前三句分别有时间、方式和目的状语,当然是动态被动语态;第四个句子中第一个 was shut 反映了我 7 点钟经过时门开着这个状态,而第二个 was shut 表示的是门在什么时候被某人关上的动作,因此是行为被动语态。

③ 在 "be + 过去分词" 的过去时结构中,如过去分词是持续性动词,表示动作正在进行时,即使没有状语,多数也是行为被动语态。

The sick woman *was carried* to a near hospital. 那个病妇正在被送往附近的一家医院。

These children *were* well *looked after* in nursery. 这些小孩在幼儿园受到很好的照料。

4.8 被动语态中 by 短语和 with 短语

被动语态中行为者常是 by 短语,然而表示行为者还有 with,to 等引导的短语。

(1) by 短语

by 短语的使用与否比较复杂,很难进行全面的归纳。

① 要用 by 短语的情况

A. 如被动句主语在主动句中是被强调的成分,那么变为被动句时应该加 by 短语。

The students themselves planned, designed and made the new robot. 学生们自己计划、设计和制造了这台新机器人。

→ The new robot was planned, designed and made *by the students themselves*.

Even the children can read this kind of novel. 就连小孩子也能看懂这种小说。

→ This kind of novel can be read even *by children*.

B. 省去了 by 短语后句子意思不完整或含糊不清时。

Barry played the part of the old engineer in the play. 巴里在剧中扮演那个老工程师。

→The part of the old engineer in the play was played *by Barry*.

C. 由疑问代词作主语的主动句变为被动句时,by 短语不能省去。介词 by 可以置于句末,或与疑问代词一起置于句首。

Who made the cake? 谁做了这蛋糕?

→ *Who* was the cake made *by*?

Who won the first prize in the competition? 谁获得了比赛的头奖?

→ *By whom* was the first prize won in the competition?

D. 在特别强调动作是谁做的被动句中,必需加 by 短语。

ABC Bank in Suzhou granted us a loan. 苏州农业银行给我们贷了一笔款。

→ We were granted a loan *by ABC Bank in Suzhou*.

E. 在英译有"由……"、"为……所为"的意思的汉语句子时,所译的英语被动句要加上 by 短语。

《人类的故事》那本书是由一个名叫亨德里克·威廉·房龙(1882—1944)的人写的。

→ The book named *The Story of Mankind* is written *by a* man named Hendrik Willem Van Loon (1882—1944).

这个计划将由一个特别委员会讨论。

→The plan will be examined *by a special committee*.

她由她的叔叔抚养大的。

→ She was brought up *by her uncle*.

② 可省去 by 短语的情况

A. 说语者把焦点从主动句中主语转移到宾语时，转换成的被动句后的 by 短语常被省去。

No one has used that computer for ten years. 那电脑已十年没人用了。

→ That computer hasn't been used for ten years.

William had finished the book in 2007. 威廉在 2007 年写完了那本书。

→ The book had been finished in 2007.

B. 有复合宾语的主动句变为被动句时，后面不带 by 短语。

I heard them sing in the next room. 我听见他们在隔壁房间唱歌。

→ They were heard to sing in the next room.

C. 当有双宾语的主动句变为被动句时，常省去 by 短语。

Aunt Li gave the little boy a big apple. 李阿姨给了那小男孩一只大苹果。

→ The little boy was given a big apple.

→ A big apple was given (to) the little boy.

My uncle bought her an English-Chinese dictionary. 我叔叔给她买了一本英汉词典。

→ She was bought an English-Chinese dictionary.

→ An English-Chinese dictionary was bought for her.

D. 在把"S＋V＋宾语＋状语"的句型转换成被动句时，by 短语常被省去。

They set up a football team named *Panda Football Team* in 2010. 他们在 2010 年成立了一个名叫熊猫足球队的队。

→ A football team named *Panda Football Team* was set up in 2010.

His aunt brought him up in the countryside. 他的婶婶在农村里把他抚养大的。

→ He was brought up in the countryside.

E. 有宾语从句的主动句变为被动句时，后面不带 by 短语。

We believe you will regret doing so. 我们相信你这样做会后悔的。

→ It is believed you will regret doing so.

→ You are believed to regret doing so.

F. 当原主动句的主语是有生命时，by 短语可省；原主动句的主语是无生命时，变为被告动句后就不省 by 短语。

Vera didn't follow my advice. 维拉没听我的劝告。

→ My advice wasn't followed. （省 by 短语）

Somebody followed her. 有人跟在她后面。

→ She was followed. （省 by 短语）

Relief followed amazement. 惊奇了一阵之后,心里便轻松下来。

→ Amazement was followed by relief. （不省 by 短语）

(2) with 短语

一般人很少听到介词 with 引出的短语也可表示被动句中动作的执行者。这种用法主要用于借喻场合和某些固定词组。

① 借喻场合

借喻场合是指精神、思想方面的抽象概念表达。

Daisy, she was seized *with a fever*. 戴西，她发烧了。

Al, he was suddenly struck *with an idea*. 阿尔,他突然想出了个主意。

② 固定词组

后接 with 短语的固定词组主要有 be crowded with, be packed with, be lined with, be thronged with, be filled with 等。其中，介词 with 的宾语如是有生命的东西或人时，那这个宾语既是动作的执行者，又是动作的承受者。在这种情况下，with 不能被 by 所代替。

The square *was lined with* hundreds of people. 广场上排着成百上千的人。

The auditorium *was packed with* students. 礼堂里挤满了学生。

上面两句均为被动语态。如果 with 后的宾语是表示事物的名称，没有触及主语的动作，只表示了由于某种动作的结果，那就是状态被动语态。

Most of the streets in the town *are lined with* trees on both sides. 镇上多数街道的两旁都种着树。

Three main roads *were covered with* water. 三条大道被水淹没。

（3）to 引出的短语行为者及 to 被 by 替换后的意思

① 介词 to 引出被动句的行为者

在一些固定词组里，to 可以引出行为者短语，这些词组常是 born to, known to, married to, unknown to 等。

Was she *born to a worker's family*? 她出身于工人家庭吗？

His elder brother has been *married to Rose*. 他的哥哥与罗丝结了婚。

He is *known to us* all for his excellent work. 我们大家都知道他工作很出色。

② to 被 by 替换后的意思

以介词 to 引出的短语表示行为者，以 by 替换时，表示方式。

A man is known *by the company* he keeps. 通过了解他交的朋友就知道他的为人。（by 引导的短语变成了方式状语）

4.9　双重被动句

双重被动句指的是句子的主语是谓语动词的承受者，同时又是动词不定式的行为对象，这样的句子结构叫双重被动句（Double Passive Sentence），如 No question on the subject *is required to be discussed*.（关于那个论题的问题无须讨论。）

（1）双重被动句的结构由来

双重被动句源于"V+不定式（宾语）+宾语"、"V+宾语+被动动词不定式"和"V+含被动语态的宾语从句"三种结构。

① 由"V+不定式（宾语）+宾语"变来

这结构变为被动句有两种方法：变为双重被动句，就是把动词不定式的宾语变作被动句的主语，原来主动句的谓语变为被动式，把原来的动词不定式变为被动动词不定式；变为一般被动句。

We attempted to form a studying plan. 我们试图制订一个学习计划。

→ A studying plan *was attempted to be formed*.（双重被动句）

Anna hoped to gain still greater progress. 安娜希望获得更大的进步。

→ Still greater progress *were hoped to be gained*.（双重被动句）

Jim attempted to form a studying plan. 吉姆试图制订个学习计划。

→ It *was attempted*（by Jim）to form a studying plan.（一般被动句）

Dora hoped to gain still greater progress. 多拉希望获得更大的进步。

→ It *was hoped*（by her）to gain still greater progress.（一般被动语态）

② 由"V + 宾语 + 被动动词不定式"变来

这种结构的主动句变为被动句时,是将主动句中的宾语变为被动句的主语,原主动句的谓语动词变为被动结构,原来的被动动词不定式保留不变。

The director ordered the document to *be typed out* at once. 董事长命令立刻把文件打印出来。

→ The document *was ordered* to *be typed out* at once.

I believed him to be interested in English. 我相信他对英语会感兴趣。

→ He *was believed* to be interested in English.

显然,上述主动句中的动词不定式均是宾语补足语。可带"宾语 + 动词不定式"作宾语补足语的动词主要有:advise, allow, announce, desire, enable, expect, intend, mean, permit, wish 等。还要提一下的是,其中一些表示爱好、偏爱、意志意思的动词,它们过去分词前的 to be 在主动句和被动句中均可省去。

The head ordered the letters (to be) sent. 头儿命令把信寄出去。

→ The letters *was ordered* (to be) sent.

His two daughters want the story (to be) told again. 他的两个女儿要求把这故事重讲一遍。

→ The story *was wanted* (to be) told again.

③ 由"V + 含被动语态的宾语从句"变来

这种句子变为双重被动句时,就是把宾语从句的主语变作被动句的主语,从句中的谓语动词被动结构变为不定式被动结构。

They never expected that the sports meet should be put off. 他们从来没想到运动会要延期举行。

→ The sports meet *was* never *expected* to *be put off*.

They proposed that he should be praised for his fine work. 他们建议因他工作出色应受到表扬。

→ He *was proposed* (by them) to *be praised* for his fine work.

4.10 "get + 过去分词"构成的被动句

一般说起被动语态,似乎就指"be + 过去分词"的被动语态。然而,我们对现代英语口语和非正式文体中常使用的"get + 过去分词"结构的被动语态注意不多。

(1) "get + 过去分词"示例

Adam often *gets punished* in school. 亚当在学校常受到惩罚。

John *will be getting whipped*. 约翰将要受到鞭打。

You'*ll soon get accustomed* to the change of climate. 你很快就会习惯气候的变化。

Did your letter *get answered*? 你收到回信了吧?

(2) "get + 过去分词"和"be + 过去分词"的比较

① 表示动作(结果)还是表示状态

"get + 过去分词"的被动语态常表示动作(的结果),较少表示状态;"be + 过去分词"既可表示动作,又可表示状态。

Mr. White *got hurt* on his way to the company. 怀特先生在去公司的路上受了伤。

How did your glasses *get broken*? 你的眼镜怎么打破了?

The police say that the woman *was shot* when they found her, but they don't know when she *was shot*. 警察说当他们找到那女人时,发觉已毙命,但不知道她在什么时候被击毙的。

上例中的"get + 过去分词"被动结构表示动作是明显的,而且表示出的是动作的结果。而上例第 3 句中的两个 was shot 分别表示毙命的状态和动作(被谁击毙的),但这样解说似乎比较含糊。如要明晰地表示动作,应把第二个 was shot 改成 got shot,那就清楚了。

② 渐进动作还是一般动作

"get + 过去分词"表示动作逐渐变化的过程,"be + 过去分词"仅表示一般的动作。

The more she heard, the more she *get excited*. 她真是越听越激动。

The front door *was closed* by his son. 前门被他儿子关上了。

③ 明晰表示动作用"get + 过去分词"

如果要明晰地表示动作,那就用"get + 过去分词"替代"be + 过去分词"。

At that time Dustin was not yet married, but he *got married* in 2011. 那时候达斯廷还没结婚,2011 年才结婚。

④ 时态使用上有别

从时态使用上来看,"get + 过去分词"可用于将来进行体和完成进行体,而"be + 过去分词"不可用于这些体态。

The poor Carl *will be getting whipped*. 那可怜的卡尔将受鞭打。

⑤ "get + 过去分词"后一般不带 by 短语

"get + 过去分词"被动语态后一般不带表示动作执行者的介词短语,如不能说 The little girl got given an apple by her mother, 但偶尔也说 The naughty boy got punished *by his father*。

⑥ 可用助动词 do 对"get + 过去分词"进行强调

"get + 过去分词"被动结构可加助动词 do 表示强调。当然,在一般现在时和一般过去时的疑问句中也必须加助动词,此是基本语法规则,这是因 get 是行为动词。"be + 过去分词"被动语态不可用 do 对其进行强调。

The naughty boy wondered if he *did get sent* home. 那调皮男孩不知道他是否真的要被送回家。

Flora *did get prepared* to accept the new task. 弗洛拉确实做好了接受那新任务的准备。

Did Colin's letter *get answered*? 科林收到回信了吗?

⑦ 不适宜用"get + 过去分词"代替"be + 过去分词"的情况

从表层结构来看,"get + 过去分词"结构后不带表示动作执行者的 by 短语,但偶尔也有带的。

The naughty boy *got punished* yesterday *by his father*. 那个调皮男孩昨天受到他父亲的惩罚。

Little Tom *got struck by a brick*. 小汤姆被砖头砸中了。

但这样界定是不够的,我们必须通过深层结构分析才能看出"be + 过去分词"结构能否换成"get + 过去分词"结构。下列情况的"be + 过去分词"结构不宜换成"get + 过去分词"结构。

A. 含有双宾语结构的句子变为被动语态时,间接宾语和直接宾语均可作为被动句的主语,但这种句子的被动句不可用"get + 过去分词"替代。

Rose teaches us Chinese every day. 罗丝每天教我们汉语。

→ We are taught Chinese every day.

不可说成:* We get taught Chinese every day.

→ Chinese is taught us every day.

不可说:* Chinese get taught us every day.

B. 一些感官动词(如 hear, see, listen to, look at, watch)作主动句谓语的句子在变作被动句时不可用"get + 过去分词"结构替代。

Who saw her typing in the office? 谁看见她在办公室打字?

→ Who was she seen typing in the office by?

不可换成：* Who got she seen typing in the office by?

I found that all the seats were occupied. 我发现所有的位子都有人坐了。

→ All the seats were found (to be) occupied.

不可换成：* All the seats got found (to be) occupied.

C. "V+名词+介词短语"结构的被动句不可用"get+过去分词"替代。这种句子变为"be+过去分词"句时，动词宾语或介词宾语作为被动句的主语。但这样的被动句也不能用"get+过去分语"形式的被动句替代。

Our head often find fault with Tom. 我们的头常找汤姆的岔子。

→ Fault is often found with Tom.

不可变为：* Fault often gets found with Tom.

→Tom is often found fault with.

不可变为：* Tom often gets found fault with.

D. 在"V+宾语从句"的句型中常用it作被动句的形式主语，be动词根据原句的时态而选用is/am/are/was/were/will be/have been/had been，原主动句的谓语动词变为过去分词，后面的宾语从句不变。也可以把宾语从句的主语作被动句的主语，其他部分作相应变化。像这种情况的被动句也不可用"get+过去分词"形式的被动句替代。

Doctor Li said (that) she was much better. 李医生说她好多了。

→It was said that she was much better.

不能变为：* It got said that she was much better.

→She was said to be much better.

不可变为：* She got said to be much better.

⑧ 用"get+过去分词"被动语态的情况

A. 在不知道动作执行者或没有动作执行者时因为"get+过去分词"被动语态后一般不带by短语的动作执行者，所以用这样的结构正好符合这样的要求。

Robert's new car *got bogged down* in the mud. 罗伯特的新车陷进了泥潭。

His cap *got caught* on a nail. 他的帽子给钉子挂住了。

Ten of them *got wounded* in the battle. 他们中十个人在战斗中负了伤。

B. 在表达由一种状态变为另一种状态时，因为"get+过去分词"被动语态包含渐进的意思，而"be+过去分词"被动语态不含此义。

I *got acquainted* with Rose five years ago. 我是五年前开始与罗丝相识的。

When we heat a boiler of water, the water at the bottom of the boiler *gets warmed* first and spreads. 当我们给锅炉的水加热时，首先是锅底的水变热，然后扩散。

C. "get+过去分词"被动语态可以替换"使役动词 have/make+名词/代词+过去分词"被动语态，但"be+过去分词"一般不能。

His father had a bad tooth pulled out last week. 他父亲上星期请医生拔了一颗坏牙。

→A bad tooth *got pulled out* last week.

We made our work done properly. 我们把工作做得很恰当。

→Our work *got done* properly.

在"get+名词/代词+过去分词"转换成"get+过去分词"结构后，句意有所不同。

They get their house painted every year. 他们每年漆一次房子。

Their house *gets painted* every year. 他们的房子每年上次漆。

We got the enemy beaten. 我们把敌人打败了。

The enemy *got beaten.* 敌人被打败了。

很明显,上例第一、三句表示的是自己或请别人做某事,或者表示经历;而第二、四句所表示的是句子主语是行为的对象。

D. "get + 表示'产生……状态'、'引起……感情'的过去分词"可构成被动语态。

The manager *got annoyed* when Jim arrived late again. 吉姆又迟到了,经理很生气。

Why did Mary get so excited over the news? 玛丽为什么听到那消息如此兴奋?

4.11 "不及物动词+介词"构成的被动句

一般说来,只有及物动词和相当于及物动词的短语动词可转变为被动语态,但是有些不及物动词后面跟介词后也可以构成被动语态。

The babies *are taken good care of* by the teachers. 孩子们由老师照料得很好。

The plan *was approved of.* 这个计划得到赞同。

4.12 结构主动,意思被动

(1) 肯定句中某些谓语的动词与某些副词连用时表示被动

一些副词(如 easily, badly, well 等)与谓语动词连用时,主动形式表示被动意思。这些谓语动词常是 burn, clean, cut, drive, eat, increase, iron, lock, photograph, play, read, saw, sell, shut, sleep, wash, wear 等不及物动词。

Nylon washes well. 尼龙好洗。

Her brother always photographs badly. 她弟弟总拍不好照。

The sofa bed sleeps much better than the old wood one. 那沙发床比木头床睡起来舒服些。

(2) 某些不及物动词直接使用时表示被动

一些表示事物本质属性的不及物动词(begin, blow, close, fasten, fill, miscarry, open, wear, wind up 等)可直接使用,以主动形式表示被动意思。

The letter miscarried. 信投错地址了。

Her hat blew off. 她的帽子吹掉了。

The cloth has worn thin. 这布烊掉了。

The question deserves considering. 这问题值得考虑。

(3) 主动形式的动名词表示被动意义

在英语中,有些动词或介词结构要求用动名词作其宾语。这时,句子的主语与动名词表示的动作之间的关系是被动的。

① 一些特定动词后动名词宾语表示被动意义,这些特定动词是 need, want, deserve, bear, require, merit(值得), stand, repay 等。

Your shirt *needs washing*, as it is too dirty. 你的衬衣太脏,要洗了。

His fine qualities *required praising.* 他的优秀品质值得赞扬。

This book will *repay reading and reading.* 这本书值得一读再读。

His language won't *bear repeating.* 他的话不堪重复。

These new books *want numbering.* 这些新书需要编号。

② 在某些介词后的动名词也以主动形式表示被动意义,这些介词主要有 above, beyond, under, past, far from, in need of 等。

This question is *above mentioning*. 这个问题不必提了。
The boiler is *under reparing*. 这锅炉正在修理。

(4)"系动词+形容词表语"的主动形式表示被动意义

这些系动词主要有:feel, seem, taste, smell, sound, look, prove 等。
Stone *feels rough*, but glass smooth. 石头摸起来粗糙,而玻璃有光滑之感。
Their conclusion certainly *sounded reasonable*. 他们的结论听起来当然有道理。
Honey *tastes sweet*. 蜜尝起来很甜。
"(be)+worth(形容词)+v-ing"结构中,v-ing 也是主动结构表示被动意义。
The film is *worth seeing*. 那部电影值得一看。

(5)"不及物动词+形容词"主动结构表示被动意义

这些不及物动词有:blow, drink, eat, smoke, cut, wash, wear 等。
The window *blew open*. 窗被吹开了。
The soup *drinks delicious*, but rather hot. 这汤喝起来味道很好,就是太烫。
The beef *cuts tender*. 这牛肉切起来很嫩。

(6)有些"be+v-ing"结构表示被动意义

某些动词的 v-ing 形式与前面的 be 动词所组成的主动结构表示被动意义。这些动词有:cook, bake, haul, play, work out, owe, fill, bind, publish, copy, build, finish, milk, show, fire 等。
The rice *is cooking*. 米饭在煮着。
This game *is constantly playing*. 这种游戏现在常玩。
This kind of plan *is working out* successfully. 这种计划在成功地制订着。
These cows *are milking*. 这些奶牛正在挤奶。

4.13 结构被动,意思主动

英语中也有好多句子就其形式是被动的,但意思却是主动的,如 She was lost in the woods.(她在林中迷了路。)The boy was tempted to go on.(那男孩想继续干下去。)有时,"be+过去分词"表示动作完成后主语所处的状态,也就是状态被动句,常含有主动意义。

(1)"be+'使引起……感情'的过去分词"形式的被动句

Rose *was very pleased* to spend her holiday with you in Nanjing. 罗丝很高兴与你一起在南京度过了假期。
He *is determined* to get there on foot. 他决心步行上那儿去。
She *is prepared* to finish the work before noon. 她准备中午前完成那工作。
We *were worried* about her safety. 我们担心她的安全。

(2)"be+原带反身代词动词的过去分词"形式的被动句

We *were stretched out* on the lawn. (=We stretched ourselves out on the lawn.) 我们直躺在草地上。
They *were habituated* to getting up early. (=They habituated themselves to getting up early.) 他们习惯于早起了。

（3）"be +'表示运动、终止、变化等意义的不及物动词的'过去分词"形式的被动句

The enemy *was run away*. 敌军逃跑了。
Her daughter *is grown up*. 她的女儿长大了。
He *is finished with* it. 他做完了这件事。

（4）表示意向、决心、智力、体力等意思的过去分词与 be 连用时表示主动意思

这些过去分词主要有：determined, inclined（相信）, set（决心）, resolved（决心）, opposed, prepared, experienced, tired, exhausted（疲倦）等。

We *were determined* to win the game. 我们下定决心赢得比赛。
I *am inclined* to believe what you have said. 我倾向于相信你说的话。
She *is prepared* to write a book *On the Importance of Mastering a Foreign Language*. 她准备写一本《论掌握一门外语的重要性》的书。
Mr. Green *is experienced i*n teaching English grammar. 格林先生教英语语法有经验。

（5）表示感情色彩的过去分词与 be 动词连用时表示主动意思

有些过去分词（如 amazed, annoyed, astonished, attached, convinced, delighted, depressed, disgusted, excited, fascinated, frightened, shocked, satisfied, started, upset 等）是表示感情色彩的，它们与 be 动词连用表示主动意思。

He *is amazed* by what you have told me. 他听了你给我说的话感到惊奇。
He *was greatly annoyed* to learn that the train would be delayed. 他听说火车将晚点大为恼火。
We *were astonish*ed that he was not an Englishman. 我们很惊讶，他不是英国人。
She *was greatly attached to* her profession. 她非常热爱她的专业。

第 5 章　动词不定式

5.1　动词不定式概述

动词不定式是非谓语动词,是动词的一种非限定形式。动词不定式在句中能起名词、形容词、副词等作用,其否定形式是"not + 不定式"。动词不定式在句中可用作主语、复合谓语、宾语、表语、宾语补足语、定语、状语;动词不定式有比较复杂的时态和语态的变化,而且其本身也可以带宾语、状语等。

He tried *to work out* the problem in five minutes. 他试图在五分钟之内算出这道题。(作宾语)
To see is *to believe*. 眼见为实。(作主语和表语)
I'm sorry *to have kept* you waiting. 对不起,让你久等了。(完成式)
Tom is glad *to have been given* a chance to visit Beijing. 汤姆很高兴有机会访问北京。(完成被动式)
You must try your every effort *to do* the work well. 你必须尽你最大的努力做好这工作。(动词不定式本身带宾语)

5.2　动词不定式形式表

形式	主动语态	被动语态	否定式
一般式	to do	to be done	not to do/not to be done
进行式	to be doing	/	not to be doing
完成式	to have done	to have been done	not to have done/not to have been done
完成进行式	to have been doing	/	not to have been doing

5.3　动词不定式的句法功能

(1) 作主语

动词不定式(短语)作主语时,一般表示具体的、个别的、一次性的或具有将来意味的动作,谓语动词通常用单数。常见的句型有下列四种:

① 直接作主语

To stop the work now seems impossible. 现在把这工作停下来似乎已不可能。
To lean out of the window is dangerous. 把头伸出窗外是危险的。
To master a foreign language requires painstaking effort. 掌握一门外语需要下苦功夫。

② 以 it 作先行主语

在更多情况下采用 it 作先行主语,而把不定式真正主语放到句子末尾,这样可避免头重脚轻的现象。常见的这类句型有下面六种:

A．It＋be＋形容词＋不定式

It is difficult *to learn a foreign language*. 学外语很难。

It's still possible *to catch the train*. 还有可能赶上火车。

It's essential *to revise the plan*. 修改计划是至关重要的。

B．It＋动词＋宾语＋不定式

It requires patience *to be a teacher*. 当老师要有耐心。

It took me three years *to save up for a car*. 我用了三年时间才省出钱买辆小汽车。

It does you a lot of good *to swim in the sea*. 在大海里游泳对你有好处。

C．It＋动词＋宾语＋宾补＋不定式

It makes me sick *to think about it*. 一想到它我就恶心。

It made her laugh *to hear these jokes*. 听到这些笑话让她笑起来。

It keeps me fit/healthy *to go jogging* every evening. 每天晚上慢跑锻炼使我身体健康。

D．It＋be＋名词＋不定式

It's our duty *to obey the law*. 遵守法律是我们的责任。

It's a great honor *to hear you speak so highly of me*. 听到你这么夸奖我真是莫大的荣幸。

It is a pity *to waste a lot of time and much money*. 浪费许多时间和金钱是很遗憾的。

E．It＋be＋介词短语＋不定式

It's beyond me *to work out this problem*. 要算出这道题我力所不及。

It is not within my power *to answer the question*. 回答该问题不属我的职责范围。

It's against my principles *to do such a thing*. 做这样的事是违反我的原则的。

F．It＋be＋形容词＋for/of sb．＋不定式

When will it be *convenient for me to call*? 我何时去拜访方便呢?

It was nasty *of Jim to behave* like that. 吉姆那样做事真是太卑劣了。

It was very thoughtful *of her to come to see me* when I was ill. 承蒙她在我生病时来看我,我很感激。

③ what/when/where/which/who/how＋不定式(短语)

How to solve the problem is very important. 如何解决这个问题是非常重要的。

Where to find the source of water is still unknown. 在什么地方能找到水源仍是个未知数。

What to do next remains undecided. 下一步干什么未定。

④ "for there to be＋名词"结构

本结构可位于句首作主语,也可用 it 作形式主语,for there to be 作真正主语。

It's a great pity *for there to be much trouble* in the company. 公司里矛盾多实在是件不幸之事。

It's impossible *for there to be any more apples*. 不可能有更多的苹果了。

For there to be a mistake in a computer's arithmetic is impossible. 计算机在计算上出错是不可能的。

For there to be so few people in the street was unusual. 大街上行人如此少实在罕见。

Notes：A. 不定式直接作主语时,在很多情况下都可用动名词代之。

To read/Reading good books makes me happy. 读好书使我快乐。

To swim/Swimming is an interesting sport. 游泳是一项有趣的运动。

但是,如果作主语的不定式表示较强的对比或某些具体情况,通常不用动名词替代。

To respect others is to be respected. 尊重别人就是尊重自己。

To finish this job in one day is impossible. 要在一天之内完成这项工作是不可能的。

B. 如果作主语的不定式短语是"及物动词＋宾语",则可以把这个宾语移至句首成为主语,而把不定式移至句尾。

To build the museum took the workers two years. 建造这个博物馆花了工人们两年的时间。

The museum took the workers two years to build. (the museum 是 build 的逻辑宾语)

To deal with the matter is hard. 处理这件事很难。

The matter is hard to deal with. (the matter 是 deal with 的逻辑宾语)

C. "It + be + 形容词 + of sb + 不定式"句型与"It + be + 形容词 + for sb + 不定式"句型的区别：

a. 表示人物性格特征的形容词常同 of 搭配，构成"It + be + 形容词 + of sb + 不定式"句型，常见的这类形容词有 brave, careful, careless, clever, considerate, cruel, foolish, good, honest, kind, nice, rash, rude, stupid, silly, thoughtful, wise, generous, nasty, greedy, selfish, lazy, polite, modest, wrong, unkind, impolite, unwise 等。这是一个带有感情色彩的不定式结构，这类形容词同 of 后的名词或代词关系密切，在意义上存在着主表关系。

It was very *thoughtful of* her to come to see me when I was ill. (= She was thoughtful to come to see me when I was ill.) 承蒙她在我生病时来看我,我很感激。

It was *nasty of* Jim to behave like that. (= Jim was nasty to behave like that.) 吉姆那样做事真是太卑劣了。

这一结构均可改成"主语 + be + 形容词 + 不定式"，但已无感情色彩可言。在口语中，这种结构可由 how 引出，表示强烈的感叹。句中 it is, it was 常被省略。

How thoughtful (it was) of her to come to see me when I was ill!

How generous (it is) of Lewis to lend me the big sum of money!

b. 表示事物性质的形容词常同 for 搭配，构成"It + be + 形容词 + for sb + 不定式"句型，常见的表示难易、舒适、方便的形容词有 easy, heavy, necessary, possible, important, difficult, hard, convenient, pleasant, impossible, tough 等。这类形容词同 for 后的名词或代词关系不密切，没有意义上的主表关系，但却与句中的不定式结构有意义上的主表关系。

It is *hard for* him to get rid of his bad habits. 他要摆脱陋习是困难的。

≠ He is hard to get rid of his bad habits.

= For him to get rid of his bad habits is hard.

It is *easy for* me to see through her tricks. 我识破她的诡计很容易。

≠ I am easy to see through her tricks.

= For me to see through her tricks is easy.

D. 两种不定式逻辑主语的表意

在"It + be + 形容词 + for sb + 不定式"句型中，不定式的逻辑主语既可以是人，也可以是表示无生命的事物。试比较：

It is *foolish of her* to buy the picture. 她真傻买了那幅画。

It is *foolish for her* to buy the picture. 她买了那幅画真傻（是傻瓜行为）。

第一句强调的是当事人"她"的性格特征，意为 She is foolish to buy the picture；第二句强调的是"买画行为"的性质，意为 For her to buy the picture is foolish。

(2) 动词不定式(短语)作复合谓语的一部分

动词不定式作复合谓语一部分时有下列五种结构形式：

① **不带 to 的不定式和某些助动词构成复合谓语。**

Shall I *help* you? 要不要我帮你？

I *should think* so. 我想是这样的。

② **不带 to 的不定式和情态动词构成复合谓语。**

You *must keep* this in mind. 你必须记住这一点。

She *might not like* the idea. 她可能不赞成这个想法。

③ **不定式和某些动词构成复合谓语。**

He *happened to live* in the same area. 他碰巧住在同一个地区。

How did Tom *get to know* all this? 这一切汤姆是怎么知道的?

④ **不定式和某些形容词构成复合谓语。**

She *is certain to return*. 她一定会回来的。

Joe was *apt to become* excited. 乔很容易激动。

⑤ **不定式和某些被动结构构成复合谓语。**

You *are expected to speak* at the meeting. 大家期待你在会上发言。

Lei *is known to have fallen in love with her sweetheart* at first sight. 大家都知道,蕾对她心爱的人一见钟情。

(3) 动词不定式(短语)作表语

① 动词不定式(短语)作表语

主语是以 aim, ambition, duty, hope, idea, intention, mistake, plan, purpose, task, suggestion, goal, wish, step 等为中心词的名词词组,或以 what 引导的名词性从句作主语,后面的不定式则说明主语的内容。

Mary's task is *to set the table*. 玛丽的任务是摆桌子。

My only wish is *to do something for the public*. 我唯一的愿望是为公众做些事。

The purpose of education is *to develop a fine personality in children*. 教育的目的是发展儿童完美的品格。

Our plan is *to complete the building in two years*. 我们的计划是两年内完成那座大楼。

What I would suggest now is *to start work at once*. 现在我要建议的是立刻开始工作。

如果句子的主语和表语都是表动作的词,通常两者都用不定式动名词。

To see is *to believe*. /Seeing is believing. 眼见为实。

To teach is *to learn*. /Teaching is learning. 教也是学。

有时候,作主语的不定式相当于一个条件从句。

To love others is *to be loved*. (=If you love others, you will be loved by others.) 爱人即爱己。

To see her is *to love her*. (=If one sees her, one will love her.) 见了她就会爱上她。

② "what/which/when/where/who/how + 不定式(短语)"结构作表语

The problem is *where to buy such a dictionary*. 问题是在哪能买到这样一本字典。

The question is *when to hold the meeting*. 问题是何时开会。

The difficulty is *how to operate the machine*. 困难是如何操作这台机器。

③ 少数不及物动词后的不定式作表语

这类不及物动词是 be, seem, appear, prove, turn out, look, remain, happen 等。

A. "be +不定式"结构用来表示"预定"、"义务/责任"、"命运"、"可能性"、"命令"、"禁止"等意思。

Jane and Tom *are to meet* at the school gate at 1:30 pm. 简和汤姆约定下午1:30在学校门口见面。(预定)

One *is to struggle* for one's living. 人要为自己的生存奋斗。(义务/责任)

He *was never to see* his wife and children again. 他命中注定再也见不到自己的妻子和儿女了。(命运)

This kind of grass *is to be seen* everywhere. 这种草哪儿都能见到。(可能性)

You *are to come* when I call. 我叫你时,你必须来。(命令)

Children *are not to smoke*. 儿童不准吸烟。(禁止)

B. "seem, appear, prove, turn out + 不定式"结构中的 to be 可以省略,意思不变。也可以用"It + 动词 + that 从句"的句型替代。

He *seems* (*to be*) *ill.* (= It seems that he is ill.)他似乎生病了。

She *appears* (*to be*) *very young.* (= It appears that she is very young.)她看起来很年轻。

④ **不定式作表语时,有时可用主动形式表示被动意义**

这类常见的不定式动词主要有 blame, let, do, see, find out, observe 等。

She *is to blame.* (= She is to be blamed.)她应该受到责备。

The house *is to let.* (= The house is to be let.)该房屋出租。

Something *is still to find out.* (= Something is still to be found out.)有些东西还有待查明。

⑤ **不定式作表语用于被动态时含情态意义**

不定式作表语用于被动态时相当于 can(could), should, ought to, must 等。

The rules and regulations *are to be observed.* 这些规章制度必须遵守。(must)

Lei *is to be rewarded.* 蕾应受奖励。(should)

She *is nowhere to be found.* 哪儿也找不到她。(can't be)

These fine dictionaries *are not to be sold.* 这些好字典不应卖掉。(ought not to be)

Notes：A. 不定式结构作表语时通常带 to,但如果主语部分有实义动词 do(可以是限定动词形式,也可以是非限定动词形式),此时 to 可以省略。

All you have to do is *listen.* 你只要听着就行了。

What she wanted to do was *start the work at once.* 她打算立刻开始工作。

The only thing I can do is *wait and see.* 唯一我能做的是等着瞧。

All I did was *empty the bottle.* 我所做的是把瓶子倒空。

B. "be + 不定式"用于第一人称疑问句时,表示征求意见。

What *am* I *to do* if I have no money? (= What should I do if …)如果没有钱,我该怎么办呢?

C. 不定式(短语)作表语也可由先行词 it 来构成,但此时的不定式短语已充当主语了。

Mary's task is *to set the table.* (= *It* is Mary's task *to set the table.*)玛丽的任务是摆桌子。

My only wish is *to do something for the public.* (= *It* is my only wish *to do something for the public.*)我唯一的愿望是为公众做些事。

(4) 动词不定式(短语)作宾语

不定式(短语)作宾语时,一般表示特殊的、具体的事宜,还指一次性的行为。其句型可有如下几种:

① **不定式(短语)直接作及物动词的宾语**

常见的及物动词有：afford, agree, arrange, appear, ask, attempt, bear, beg, begin, care, choose, claim, consent, continue, commence, dare, decide, decline, demand, deserve, desire, determine, expect, fail, fear, forget, guarantee, happen, help, hesitate, hope, intend, learn, long, manage, mean, need, offer, plan, pledge, petition, plot, pray, prepare, pretend, promise, refuse, resolve, seek, swear, tend, threaten, undertake, venture, volunteer, vow, want, wish 等。

I can't afford *to live in a detached house.* 我住不起独门独院的房子。

Lei volunteers *to be photographed by her lover.* 蕾愿意让她心爱的人拍照。

Barry longs *to meet her lover again.* 白利渴望再次与她相爱的人见面。

Notes：A. believe, consider, feel, find, judge, make, regard … as, suppose, think 等动词后如果是不定式作宾语,且补足语是形容词或名词,此时常用先行词 it 作形式宾语,而把真实宾语不定式后移。

I don't think *it* necessary *for you to go on with the experiment.* 我认为你们没有必要继续这项实验。

We consider *it* our duty *to do so*. 我们认为这样做是我们的责任。

Tom considers *it* a pity *to be kept in the house in fine weather*. 汤姆认为好天气时老待在屋里是件令人遗憾的事。

Mr. Jiang makes *it* a rule *to walk five kilometers every evening*. 江先生规定自己每晚走五公里路。

B. 有些动词如(expect, hope, intend, mean, plan, think, want 等)的过去完成式和不定式连用时表示过去未曾实现的希望、意图或打算。

I *had intended* to write to her. 我本打算给她写信的。

They *had meant* to finished the work in a year. 他们本想在一年内完成这工作的。

② "what/which/when/where/who/how/whether + 不定式(短语)"结构作宾语

常跟"疑问词/连接词 + 不定式(短语)"作宾语的动词有 ask, consider, decide, discover, explain, find out, forget, inquire, know, learn, remember, see, settle, show, tell, think, understand, wonder, discuss 等。

She doesn't know *what to do next*. 她不知道下一步该干什么。

Henry learned *how to swim last summer*. 亨利去年夏天学会了游泳。

Xiao Li found out *where to buy fruit cheaply*. 小李打听出在哪儿买水果便宜。

Mary wondered *whether to laugh or to cry*. 玛丽感到啼笑皆非。

有些双宾语及物动词也能用"疑问词 + 不定式(短语)"作直接宾语。

Please inform *me where to get the tickets*. 请告知我在哪儿能买到这些票。

Could you *tell me how to operate the machine*? 你能告诉我怎样操作这台机器吗？

I advised *you which to buy*. 我建议你买哪个。

③ **不定式(短语)作介词宾语**

"what/which/when/where/who/how/whether + 不定式(短语)"结构作介词宾语。

Mr. Wang gave some advice *on how to learn a foreign language*. 王先生给了一些如何学习外语的建议。

Then there is the problem *of what courses to offer*. 接着就是开些什么课程的问题。

They were worried *about whether to turn left or right*. 他们为该向左拐还是向右拐而发愁。

此外,英语中有少数几个介词(如 besides, but, except, save, than 等)后面可以跟不定式(短语)作宾语。上述几个介词均表示"除……之外"的意义。

The enemy had no choice *but to lay down their arms*. 敌人只能放下武器。

He did nothing *but play games*. 他除了玩游戏外,什么都不做。

I think nothing *except to be a doctor*. 我一心想成为一名医生。

He did everything *except clean the floor*. 除了拖地板外,他什么都干。

Tom did nothing on this ship *save entertain his guest*. 在这条船上,汤姆除了招待客人之外什么都不干。

I promised to lend some money to her *besides pay/paying her back*. 除了还她钱以外,我还答应借给她一些钱。(注意:此句中的 besides 表示完成了两个动作,即 lend 和 pay 这两个动作)

She had no choice *than to wait for the doctor* to arrive. 她只能等医生的到来。

Note:不定式结构作介语 but, except, save 的宾语时,如果主语部分有实义动词 do,此时 to 可以省略。besides 和 than 后的不定式可带 to,也可以省略 to,但 besides 后多跟动名词或名词。

④ **不定式(短语)作形容词的宾语**

动词不定式也可以用来作某些形容词的宾语。但有些语法学家认为此时的不定式是用作修饰形容词的状语。这些常用的形容词有:anxious, able, afraid, determined, eager, free, glad, pleased, sure, sorry, willing 等。

I am sorry *to have kept you waiting*. (= I am sorry because I have kept you waiting.) 对不起,让你等了。

Li Na is pleased *to see her sweetheart*. (= Li Na is pleased because she has seen her sweetheart.) 见到她的心上人,李娜很高兴。

Robert was delighted *for Mary to come and stay*. (= Robert was delighted because Mary had come to stay.) 玛丽过来住,罗伯特非常高兴。

(5) 动词不定式(短语)作宾语补足语

能用不定式(短语)作宾语补足语的动词有以下几类:

① 许多动词可跟一个由"名词/代词 + 不定式"构成的复合宾语,常见的这类动词有:advice, allow, ask, beg, bribe, cause, challenge, command, compel, convince, direct, enable, encourage, expect, forbid, force, induce, instruct, invite, help, hate, hire, inspire, intend, lead, oblige, order, permit, persuade, press, recommend, remind, request, require, teach, tell, tempt, train, urge, want, warn, wish 等。

George asked her not *to leave the country*. 乔治叫她不要出境。
Her English teacher advices her *to buy a better dictionary*. 她的英语老师建议她买本好一点的词典。
I beg her *to forgive me*. 我恳求她宽恕我。

Notes: A. know 和 find 意为 see, hear 时,也可接不带 to 的不定式(多用于过去式或完成式)。
I have never *known* (= seen) Jane *lose* her temper. 我从未见过简发脾气。
I *found* (= saw) the work *do* well. 我看到工作做得很好。

B. demand, hope, suggest 等动词后面不能接动词不定式作宾语补足语。
He hoped Li Hua *to lend him a hand*. (误)
He hoped *that Li Hua would lend him a hand*. (正) 他希望李华能帮他一把。
I suggested her *not to go there alone*. (误)
I suggested *that she should not go there alone*. (正) 我建议她不要单独去那里。

C. 动词 help 后的不定式 to 可以省去,也可以保留。
He helps the little girl (*to*) *finish her homework every day*. 他每天帮助这个小女孩完成家庭作业。

② 少数感官动词和使役动词可跟一个由"名词/代词 + 不带 to 的不定式"构成的复合宾语,常见的这类动词有:feel, hear, listen to, look at, notice, observe, see, watch 及 have, let, make 等。

I heard Jane *lock the door*. 我听见简锁门了。
Henry watched the children *skip rope*. 亨利看孩子们跳绳。
Did you see anyone *enter the house*? 你看见什么人进屋了吗?
Tom felt something *crawl up his arm*. 汤姆感到有东西顺着他的手臂往上爬。
You must have someone *repair the computer*. 你必须叫人来修理这台电脑。
She made him *move the car*. 她让他把车移动一下。
I won't let Xiaoming *do it*. 我不让小明做这事。

如果这类句子变为被动结构时,不定式前需加 to。
Jane was heard *to lock the door*. 有人听到简把门锁上了。
The children were watched *to skip rope*. 人们在观看孩子们跳绳。

③ 有些表示心理状态的动词可跟由 to be 不定式短语充当的宾语补足语,这类表示心理状态的动词有:consider, declare, esteem, guess, feel (= think), find (= consider), imagine, judge, know, prove, believe, suppose, think, understand, show, discover 等。

We consider him (*to be*) *a good officer*. 我们认为他是个好官员。
I found her (*to be*) *dishonest*. 我认为她不诚实。
They had proved Mary (*to be*) *wrong*. 他们已证明玛丽是错的。

The accused declared himself (*to be*) *innocent*. 被告宣称他是无辜的。

I know this *to be a fact*. 我知道这是个事实。

I judged him *to have been a gambler*. 我判断他曾是个赌徒。

I should guess her *to be around forty years old*. 我猜想她大约 40 岁。

She esteems herself *to be lucky*. 她自认为是幸运的。

在上述动词中，consider, declare, find, prove, think 等动词后的 to be 往往可以省略。

Note：这类表示心理状态动词后的不定式有时可以是完成式或进行式，但此时的不定式就不是 to be 了。

We considered Keith *to have acted disgracefully*. 我们认为基思的表现很可耻。

They believed George *to be hiding somewhere*. 他们认为乔治躲在什么地方。

④ 有些短语动词后可跟动词不定式短语作宾语补语像这类短语动词主要有：shout to, appeal to, call on, plead with, count on, rely on, depend on, care for, long for, arrange for, ask for, prepare for, provide for, vote for, wait for, wish for 等。

I will arrange for you *to come*. 我将安排你来。(句中 you 充当不定式 to come 的逻辑主语)

Joe asked for the designs *to be ready by Friday*. 乔要求周五前完成设计。

Anne can't wait for us *to finish talking*. 安妮不能等我们把话谈完。

I am counting on Dirk *to help me through*. 我指望德克帮我渡过难关。

She shouted to Joe *to come over*. 她喊乔过去。

(6) 动词不定式(短语)作定语

① 动词不定式与其所修饰的词之间的关系

不定式与其所修饰的词之间的关系往往是动宾关系，如果该不定式是不及物动词或者该不定式本身有宾语，其后应有必要的介词。

I want water *to drink*. 我要水喝。

Joe is a pleasant fellow *to work with*. 乔是个很好共事的人。

Anne bought a bookshelf *to put her books on*. 安妮买了一个书架放书。

Ivan offered me a cup of coffee *to refresh my spirit with*. 伊凡给我端来一杯咖啡，让我提提神。

Notes：A. 不定式所修饰的名词可以是及物动词的宾语，也可以是双宾动词的宾语。

I *want someone* to talk to. 我想找个人交谈。(someone 是及物动词 want 的宾语)

Please *give me a book* to read. 请给我一本书看。(a book 是双宾语动词 give 的直接宾语)

B. 如果不定式所修饰的名词或代词是不定式动作的地点、工具、时间、方式等，不定式后面须加相应的介词。这种带介词的不定式作定语可以转换成"介词+关系代词"引导的不定式作定语。

Jane is looking for a room *to live in*. (= Jane is looking for a room *in which to live*.) 简在寻找一间房子住。(地点)

George needs a pen *to write with*. (= George needs a pen *with which to write*.) 乔治需要一支笔写字。(工具)

Xiaoming only had long nights *in which to study*. 小明只有漫漫长夜可用来学习。(时间)

That's the only way (*in which*) *to overcome the difficulties*. 那是战胜困难的唯一方法。(方式)

Note：如果不定式所修饰的名词是 time, place 或 way，那么不定式后面的介词可以省去。

Henry had no place to live (in). 亨利没有居住的地方。

I have only a short time to decide (in). 我只有很少的时间来做决定。

That's no way to talk (in). 不应这样谈话。

② 作定语的不定式可以表示情态意义

作定语用的不定式可以表示情态意义,此时相当于一个含有情态意义的定语从句。

You have no friend to depend on (= whom you *can* depend on). 你没有可以依靠的朋友。
Jane brought a nurse to take care of her mother(= who *may* take care of her mother). 简带来一位护士,照顾她母亲。
Joe left me a lot of problems to solve(= which I *must* solve). 乔给我留下一大堆问题去解决。
He has his parents to consider(= whom he *should* consider). 他还应该考虑他的双亲。
Lei is a woman to be trusted(= who *can* be trusted). 蕾是个可以信赖的女士。
It is a sign never to be forgotten(= that we *will* never forget). 那景象永远也忘不了。

③ 有些名词后常跟不定式作定语

这类名词有 time, way, right, reason, effort, ambition, chance, opportunity 等。

It's *time* to go to bed. 该睡觉了。
There is no *reason* to doubt her words. 没有理由怀疑她的话。
Thank you for giving me the *chance* to make the speech. 谢谢你给我发言的机会。
Anne has a burning *ambition* to become famous. 安妮一心想成名。

④ 某些动词和形容词派生出来的名词后也可用不定式作定语

这类常见的名词有 ability, agreement, anxiety, attempt, claim, decision, determination, need, plan, promise, readiness, tendency, obligation, inclination, eagerness, impatience, wish, willingness, failure, efusal 等。

We made a *decision* to put off the meeting until next week. (= We *decided* to put off ...)我们决定将会议推迟到下星期。
He persisted in his *refusal* to go home. (= He *refused* to go home.) 他坚持不肯回家。
Keith's *anxiety* to succeed led him to work hard. (= Keith was *anxious* to succeed.) 基思迫切想成功,这促使他努力工作。
Lei's *ability* to analyse the problem really surprises her darling. (Lei is *able* to analyse the problem.) 蕾分析这个问题的能力真叫她心爱的人吃惊。

⑤ 被某些特定的词修饰的名词后或以它们为中心词的,常用不定式作定语

被 only, the first, the second, the last, the next, the best 等特定词所修饰的名词,或由这些词直接充当中心词,其后常用不定式作定语。

Li Ming will have to be *the next* person to go. 李明必定是下一个要走的人。
Practice is *the only* way to learn a language. 练习是学习语言的唯一方法。
Jim is *the first* to bear hardships, *the last* to enjoy comforts. 吉姆是个吃苦在先、享受在后的人。
George would be *the last* to agree to the plan. 乔治决不会同意这项计划。

⑥ 主动/被动不定式作定语的情况

用不定式作定语时,有时用主动式或被动式均可,有时只能用主动不定式,有时却又只能用被动不定式。

A. 有时用主动不定式和用被动不定式作定语,意思相同。 如果我们把着重点放在人们的义务,那么用主动式和被动式均可。

There's a lot of *work to do/to be done*. 有许多工作要做。
The people *to interview/to be interviewed* are in Room 101. 要接受面试的人在101房间。

B. 如果我们所想到更多的是完成动作的那个人,则用主动式较常见。

I've got much work *to do*. 我有好多工作要做。

I've sent *Jane* a form *to fill in*. 我寄给简一份表格让她填。

C. 如果我们所想的更多的是某个动作，或那个动作的承受者，则用被动式更常见。

The carpets to be washed are in the garage. 要清洗的地毯在车库里。

Jane's desk is covered with *forms to be filled in*. 简的书桌上铺满了要填写的表格。

D. 有时用主动不定式和被动不定式作定语的意思是截然不同的。

There are many beautiful birds *to see* (＝ worth seeing) in the park. 公园里有许多漂亮的鸟值得一看。

There are many beautiful birds *to be seen* (＝ that can be seen) in the park. 公园里可以看到许多漂亮的鸟。

I'm bored—there's nothing *to do*. (＝ I have nothing to do now.) 我感到无聊——没有什么事可做。

There's nothing *to be done* (＝ There's no way of putting it right)—I'll have to replace a broken chair with a new one. 没有办法——我只好用新椅子更换破了的椅子。

（7）动词不定式（短语）作状语

动词不定式修饰动词或形容词时，一般放在被修饰的动词或形容词之后。它们在句中可表示目的、原因、结果、条件、方式、程度等。

① 不定式（短语）作目的状语

一般来说，动词不定式作目的状语时，不定式位于句首比在后面更为正式，语气更重些。

To master a foreign language, one must work hard at it. 要掌握好一门外语，就要对它下功夫。

Henry went to America *to learn English*. 亨利去美国学英语。

A friend of mine came *to see me* last week. 上周有个朋友来看我。

A. "in order to ＋动词原形" 与 "so as to ＋动词原形" 强调目的。

为了强调目的，我们常用"in order to ＋动词原形"和"so as to ＋动词原形"来表达；但应注意 in order to 置于句首或句中均可，而 so as to 不能置于句首。

Jane reads *China Daily* every day *in order to/so as to improve her English*. 简每天读《中国日报》以便能提高她的英语水平.

In order to catch the train, Joe started out early. 为了能赶上火车，乔早早就出发了。

Note：so as to 不同于 so … as to，前者是目的状语，相当于 in order to，表示"以便"，而后者是结果状语，so 后面跟形容词或副词，表示"到这种程度以致……"。so as to 前面可用逗号，而 so … as to 则不可。试比较：

The test questions are kept secret, *so as to* prevent cheating. 考题保密，以防作弊。（目的）

Ruth was *so* naive *as to* believe his words. 露丝竟天真地相信了他的话。（结果）

B. 几个特殊动词后的不定式作目的的状语。

在美国英语中，在动词 come, go, run 后可接不带 to 的动词不定式作目的状语。

She will go *tell* him about it. 她去告诉他此事。

Come *see* a film with me this evening. 今晚来和我一起看电影。

Run *help* that little girl over there. 快跑去帮助那边的那个小女孩。

C. for there to be 也可作目的状语。

For there to be no mistake, all of us must check the results got from the experiment. 为了不出错误，我们大家必须检查实验结果。

② 不定式（短语）作原因状语

不定式作原因状语主要有两种句型：一是位于表示感情的不及物动词之后，说明发出动作的原因；二是位于形容词和过去分词之后，用于说明形容词和过去分词。

A. 位于表示感情的不及物动词之后，说明动词发出动作的原因。
Mrs. Green *rejoices to hear* that her daughter will come to see her. (= Mrs. Green rejoices *because she has heard that* …) 听说她的女儿要来看她，格林太太很高兴。
Tom *trembled to think* of those days. 汤姆想到那些岁月就不寒而栗。
B. 位于形容词和过去分词之后，说明形容词和过去分词。
不定式位于形容词和过去分词之后作原因状语主要有下面几种情况：
a. be + 表示情绪的形容词和过去分词 + 不定式
常用的这类形容词有：angry, content, furious, glad, happy, impatient, mad, proud, sorry, wild, thankful, amazed, ashamed, astonished, bored, delighted, disappointed, displeased, dissatisfied, excited, horrified, overjoyed, pleased, shocked, surprised, thrilled, grieved, worried, annoyed, relieved, puzzled 等。
I'm very sorry *to give you so much trouble*. (= I'm very sorry *because I have given you so much trouble*.) 实在对不起，我给你带来这么多麻烦。
He was *disappointed to find* that all the tickets were sold out. 发现票已全部售完他很失望。
We shall be very *happy to cooperate* with you in the project. 在此项目中与你们合作，我们非常高兴。
b. be + 表示运气好坏的形容词 + 不定式
常用的这类形容词有：lucky, unlucky, fortunate, unfortunate 等。
George was *lucky to find* such a good job. (= George was lucky *because he had found such a good job*.) 乔治很幸运找到这样好的工作。
Gray was *fortunate to escape* being injured. 格蕾很幸运未受伤。

③ "be + 表示方式的形容词和过去分词 + 不定式" 作方式状语
常用的这类词有：slow, quick, prompt, willing, ready, prone, reluctant, sure, able, apt, certain, keen, fit, free, liable, unable, hesitant, welcome, due, eager, worthy, fated, inclined, prepared, determined, qualified, unqualified 等。这些表示意愿、能力、倾向、企图、快慢、适宜、可能性、心理状态、个人态度等形容词或过去分词后接的不定式常作方式状语。
He is *prompt to act*. (= He is *prompt in acting*.) (= He acted *promptly*.) 他行动迅速。
I'm *sure to win*. (= I will surely win.) 我一定会赢。
The water is *fit for us to drink*. 这水适合我们喝。
Jack is *hesitant to accept* her proposal. 杰克犹豫不决地接受了她的建议。
Anne is *eager to learn music*. 安妮渴望学习音乐。
Lei seems *willing to try* again. 蕾似乎愿意再尝试一次。
He is *likely to go back* on his words. 他可能要食言。
He was *determined to teach* her a lesson. 他决心给她一个教训。
Li Na is *anxious for me to go* there again. 李娜渴望我再去那里。

④ 不定式(短语)作条件状语
不定式(短语)有时也可以表示条件，可置于句首或句尾，这要视句子内容、结构而定。
To be successful (= If one wants to be successful), one must do one's best. 要想成功，就要竭尽全力。
How can you catch the train *to start* so late (= if you start so late)? 要是这么晚才动身，你怎么能够赶得上火车？
You will regret one day *for your son to marry* her (= if your son marries her). 要是你儿子同她结婚的话，有一天你会后悔的。
Ruth should have been sorry *to have missed* the chance (= if she had missed the chance). 要是失去那个机会的话，露丝会很难过的。

⑤ 不定式(短语)作结果状语

不定式(短语)表示结果常见于下列几种情况：

A. 不定式作结果状语时往往仅限于 learn, see, hear, to be told, make, deserve 等几个具有终止含义的动词，常表示未预料到的结果，这种不定式结构前面有时带有 only。

What have I said *to make* you so angry? 我说了什么话使你这样生气？
She returned home *to learn* her daughter had gone to Beijing. 她回家后才知道她女儿已去了北京。
Anne hurried to the post office *only to find* it was closed. 安妮匆忙赶往邮局，结果已经关门了。
What has she done *to deserve* this severe criticism? 她做了什么，遭到如此严厉的批评？

B. "so ... as to ..." 结构表示结果。

She was *so* careless *as to* leave her car unlocked. 她如此粗心大意，车门都没锁就走了。
Jane's mother worried *so* much about Jane's safety *as to* be unable to sleep all night. 简的母亲非常担心简的安全，以致整夜不能入睡。

C. "such (...) as to" 结构表示结果。

Gray is not *such* a fool *as to* believe that. 格蕾不是个傻瓜，不会相信那一套。（句中 such 是形容词，修饰后面的名词 a fool）
Henry's progress was *such as to* surprise his parents. 亨利的进步很大，让他的父母亲都感到惊奇。（句中 such = so great，充当形容词，不定式 as to 修饰前面的形容词 such）

D. "enough to ..." 结构表示结果。

She is old *enough to* understand what I said. 她已经足够大，应该能明白我在说什么。
Would you be good *enough to* close the door? 可否劳驾您关门？

E. "too ... to ..." 结构表示否定的结果。

She is *too* young *to* understand what I said. 她年纪尚小，不能明白我在说什么。
Tom was *too* tired *to* walk any farther. 汤姆太疲倦了不能再继续走了。

Notes：a. "too ... to ..."结构有时可以与 not enough to 结构替换使用。

The road is *too* narrow for two cars *to* pass. (＝The road is *not* wide *enough* for two cars *to* pass.) 这条路太窄，两辆汽车开不了。

b. 某些形容词在"too ... to ..."结构中没有否定的含义，此时的 too 相当于 very, extremely, exceedingly, 表示肯定。too 后面的形容词往往是表示"乐意"、"高兴"、"容易"、"渴望"等意义的词，这类形容词有 anxious, apt, delighted, eager, easy, glad, kind, pleased, ready, surprised, willing 等, too 前还经常有 all, but, only, never, not 等副词修饰。

One is *never/not too* old to learn. 活到老，学到老。
I'm *only too* pleased to help you. 我非常愿意帮助你。
We are *but too* glad to meet you. 我们很高兴遇到你。
She is *too eager* to know the result of the test. 她急于想知道考试成绩。
Beginners are *too apt* to overlook such grammatical errors. 初学者很容易忽视这些语法错误。

⑥ 不定式(短语)作句子状语

有些不定式短语可用来修饰整个句子，故可称作句子状语(Sentence Adverbial)。它们常用来表明说话人的态度，在句中作独立成分。常见的独立不定式有下面一些：

to be honest 老实说   to return to my subject 言归正传
to be plain with sb. 坦白地说 to change the subject 换一个话题
to be frank with sb. 坦白地说 to use his own words 用他自己的话说
to be brief 简言之   to say nothing of 姑且不讲

to be exact 精确地说	not to speak of 更不用说
to be sure 当然/的确	to conclude 总之
to tell you the truth 实话跟你说	to start with/to begin with 首先
to speak frankly/sincerely 坦白地说	to sum up 概括地说
to put it straight/plainly 直率地说	(It is) strange to say 说来奇怪
to put it in another way 换句话说	(It is) curious to mention 说来奇怪
to cut a long story short 长话短说	(I'm) sorry to say 说来很难过
to bring the story short 长话短说	not to mention 更不用说
to cut the matter short 长话短说	let alone 更不用说
to make matters worse 更糟的是	

这些短语大都置于句首,偶尔置于句中或句尾,而且须用逗号与其他句子成分隔开。

To put it in another way, she was sweet-tempered. 换句话说,她脾气非常好。

To be honest, I just don't like her. 说实话,我就是不喜欢她。

Strange to say, her hair turned white during the night. 说来奇怪,她的头发一夜之间变白了。

To make a long story short, Keith's project ended in a failure. 长话短说,基思的计划失败了。

Imperialism is, *to tell the truth*, digging its own grave. 说句实话,帝国主义在给自己挖坟墓。

She's a nice person, *to be sure*. 毫无疑问,她是一个好人。

⑦ **不定式独立结构作伴随状语**

不定式独立结构作伴随状语时,通常位于句末,用以说明主句动作后将要发生的事,作伴随或解释说明状语。

They divided the work, *Henry to wash* the vegetables and *Anne to cook* the meal. 他们分配工作:亨利洗蔬菜,安妮烧饭。

Here are the first four volumes, *the fifth one to come out* next year. 这是前四卷,第五卷将于明年出版。

5.4 动词不定式的时态和语态

动词不定式本身不表示"时"的特征,它的时间关系必须借助于句中的谓语动词来体现。

Gray seems to be enjoying herself. (= It *seems* that Gray *is enjoying* herself.) 格蕾似乎玩得很痛快。

Gray seemed to be enjoying herself. (= It *seemed* that Gray *was enjoying* herself.) 格蕾当时似乎玩得很痛快。

Mike is sorry to have troubled me. (= Mike *is sorry* that he *has troubled* me.) (= Mike *is sorry* that he *troubled* me.) 迈克打搅了我,感觉对不起。

Martin was very pleased to have seen me. (= Martin *was very pleased* that she *had seen* me.) 马丁当时很高兴地见到了我。(= 马丁当时很高兴,因为她见到了我。)

(1) 动词不定式进行体

动词不定式进行体表示动作的延续,其动作与句子谓语动词动作同时发生;它们的句法作用与动词不定式一般式相同:作主语、复合谓语、宾语、表语、状语、宾语补足语、主语补足语等。

It's a delightful experience *to be touring the lake district*. 在湖区旅游是一段愉快的经历。(主语)

John happened *to be traveling in that area*. 约翰恰好在那个地区旅游。(复合谓语)

She really hopes *to be working with me*. 她的确希望和我在一起工作。(宾语)

Mary's wish is *to be studying Chinese in China*. 玛丽的愿望是能到中国学中文。(表语)

My son is happy *to be earning his own living*. 我的儿子很高兴能自食其力。(原因状语)

They found the ice *to be melting*. 他们发现冰在融化。（宾补）
The thief is thought *to be hiding in the woods*. 人们认为小偷躲藏在林子里。（主语补语）

① 表示延续一段时间的动作。
You're lucky *to be living in such a nice place*. 你真幸运住在这么漂亮的地方。

② 表示谓语动词的动作发生时正在进行中的动作，这两个动作几乎是同时发生的。
They seemed *to be discussing something important*. 他们似乎在讨论重要的事情。

③ 在谓语动词之后的动词不定式进行体表示将来的动作。
The old man seems *to be dying*. 这老人似乎快要死了。

（2）动词不定式完成体

动词不定式完成体可表示较早发生的动作或较早可能发生的动作。它还可作复合谓语、主语、宾语、表语、状语、定语、宾语补足语、主语补足语等；与某些动词连用时表示过去未曾实现的希望、意图或打算。

① 表示较早发生的动作。
The man was relieved *to have survived the accident*. 那名男子为在事故中幸免于难而感到宽慰。

② 表示较早可能发生的动作。
She seemed *to have left her umbrella behind*. 她似乎把雨伞掉落下来。

③ 在句中可作复合谓语、主语、宾语、表语、状语、定语、宾语补足语、主语补足语等。
Gray *is supposed to have heard of the matter*. 格蕾应该已听说此事。（复合谓语）
It's a mistake *to have come here*. 来了这里是个错误。（主语）
Sophia remembers *to have told her lover about it*. 索菲娅记得告诉过她的恋人这件事。（宾语）
Sophia's sweetheart felt ashamed *to have done such a thing*. 索菲娅心爱的人做了这样的事感到很愧疚。（原因状语）
It was one of the good books *to have appeared on the subject*. 这是该科目中已出版的好书之一。（定语）
We found the snow *to have melted*. 我们发现雪已融化了。（宾语补足语）
John was believed *to have discussed the problem with*. 据信约翰曾和布鲁斯讨论过这个问题。（主语补足语）

④ 有些动词（如 expect, hope, intend, mean, plan, think, want, wish 等）与"过去式＋不定式的完成体"连用时，表示过去未曾实现的希望、意图或打算。
Jane hoped to have passed the examination. 简本希望通过那次考试的。
I intended to have written to her. 我本打算给她写信的。

（3）动词不定式完成进行体

动词不定式完成进行体所表示的动作在谓语动词所表示的动作之前一直在进行，强调动作的连续性，在句中可作主语、主语补足语、宾语、状语、复合谓语等。

It's a great pleasure *to have been staying with Peter*. 和彼得待在一起有很大的乐趣。（主语）
She is said *to have been doing* this work for twenty years. 据说她干这工作已二十年了。（主语补语）
Xiaoli pretended *to have been studying*. 小李假装一直在学习。（宾语）
Jane is sorry *to have been troubling me* all the time. 简一直在麻烦我,感觉对不起。（原因状语）
He appears *to have been waiting* a long time. 他似乎已等了好长时间了。（复合谓语）

5.5 不定式被动语态的句法功能和主动、被动语态的选用

动词不定式被动语态同主动语态一样，在句中可作主语、主语补足语、宾语、宾语补足语、表语、定语、状语和复合谓语。如果逻辑主语是动作的执行者，不定式用主动式；如果逻辑主语是动作的承受者，不定式用被动式。试比较：

The mother asked *me to clean the room*. 母亲叫我打扫房间。（主动式）
The mother asked *the room to be cleaned*. 母亲要求把房间清扫一下。（被动式）

(1) 动词不定式一般式被动语态的用法

It's a great honor *to be invited to Gray's birthday*. 被邀请参加格蕾的生日聚会十分荣幸。（主语）
Tom is said *to be sent to work* in his hometown. (= It is said that Tom will be sent to work …) 据说汤姆将被派往他的家乡工作。（主语补足语）
I wish *to be sent to work* in my hometown. 我希望被派往我的家乡工作。（宾语）
He doesn't expect the book *to be so well written*. 他没料到该书会写得如此好。（宾语补足语）
They are *to be married* soon. 他们很快要结婚了。（表语）
Anne was the first one *to be asked to speak*. 安妮是第一个被邀请发言的人。（定语）
Joe has to shout *to be heard*. 乔大声呼叫以便能被听得见。（状语）
The parcel *has to be sent* by air mail. 这个包裹得寄航空。（复合谓语）

(2) 动词不定式完成式被动语态的用法

It was his good fortune *to have been invited to Gray's birthday*. 他很幸运已被邀请参加格蕾的生日聚会。（主语）
The book is said *to have been so well received*. 据说该书已如此受欢迎。（主语补语）
Rod expects *to have been sent to work* in my hometown by the end of the month. 罗德期待本月底能被派往我的家乡工作。（宾语）
He doesn't expect the book *to have been so well received*. 他没料到该书已如此受欢迎。（宾语补语）
The burglar is *to have been dealt with by the law*. 这个强盗已被绳之以法。（表语）
This camera is the first of its kind *to have been sold here*. 这里销售的这类相机中，这是第一台。（定语）
John was very happy *to have been admitted into the club*. 约翰很高兴已被批准加入俱乐部。（状语）
The machine *seems to have been damaged*. 这台机器似乎已被损坏。（复合谓语）

(3) 动词不定式主动语态表示被动意义

动词不定式主动语态表示被动意义的表达情况大致有以下七种：

① 在"名词/代词 + be + easy（difficult, hard, fit 等）+ 不定式"结构中

尽管句中主语是动作的承受者，不定式在意义上是被动的，形式上却是主动的。其实，可看成是省略了不定式的逻辑主语 for you, for me, for us 等。

The book is *easy* (for me) *to read*. 这本书（我）很容易读懂。
The water was not *fit* (for you) *to drink*. 这水（你）不宜喝。

② 不定式在句中作定语时

虽然不定式同其所修饰的名词有动宾关系，也要用主动形式，因为句中的主语是不定式动作的执行者。
Jane has a large family *to support*. (= Jane supports a large family.) 简有一大家子人要养活。

I have an essay to write this evening. (= I will write an essay this evening.) 我今晚有篇论文要写。

③ 在 there be 句型中

当不定式在句中作定语时，尽管不定式同其所修饰的名词有动宾关系，也要用主动形式，因为此时可看成是省略了不定式的逻辑主语 for you, for me, for us 等。

There is a lot of work (*for me*) *to do*. 有许多工作(我)要做。

There are two letters (*for you*) *to write* this evening. 今晚有两封信(你)要写。

④ 在 too … to 和 enough to 结构中

在 too … to 和 enough to 结构中，用的是主动不定式态表示被动意义。偶尔也可用被动态，但主动态更为常见。

The English-Chinese dictionary is cheap *enough to buy*. 这本英汉词典很便宜就买到了。

The water is *too* hot *to drink*. 水热得没法喝。

⑤ to blame, to let, to do 作表语时

I am *to blame*. 这是我的过错。

This house is *to let*. 此屋出租。

Much/A great deal of work remains *to do*. 还有许多事要做。

What is *to do* tomorrow？明天要做些什么？

⑥ 不定式在句中作定语时

如果句中的间接宾语是不定式动作的执行者，且直接宾语又是不定式动作的承受者，那不定式要用主动式表示被动的意思。

I will give *you* some books *to read* on the way. 我给你几本书在路上看。(you 是 to read 动作的执行者, books 是 to read 动作的承受者)

Mary will find *me* something *to eat*. 玛丽来给我找点东西吃。(me 是 to eat 的逻辑主语, something 是 to eat 的宾语)

⑦ 不定式与 worth 连用时

不定式与 worth 连用时，那不定式要用主动式来表示被动的意思。

The film is *worth* going *to see*. 这部电影值得一看。

The new English-Chinese dictionary is *worth* going *to buy*. 这本新英汉词典值得去买。

5.6 动词不定式的否定式

动词不定式的否定形式是"not to + 动词原形"，它同肯定式一样，在句中可作主语、复合谓语、主语补足语、宾语、宾词补足语、表语、定语、状语。

It made me disappointed *not to find* Rod there. 没发现罗德在那使我感到很失望。(主语)

She *oughtn't to be told* about it. 不应该把此事告诉她。(复合谓语)

She is believed *not to be living in Suzhou*. 据信她现在不住在苏州。(主语补语)

The two lovers pretended *not to have met before*. 两个恋人假装以前未见过面。(宾语)

The teacher warned him *not to do it again*. 老师警告他别再做这件事了。(宾语补足语)

These books are *not to be sold*. 这些书不应卖掉。(表语)

The naughty boy made a promise *not to do it again*. 那调皮鬼许下不再做这件事的诺言。(定语)

Sophia was very unhappy *not to have been admitted into the university*. 未被大学录取，索菲娅感到很难过。(状语)

5.7 动词不定式的逻辑主语

每个不定式都有其逻辑主语,它可能是句子的主语或宾语。

Jane had a lot of letters *write*. (Jane 是句中的主语,同时也是 to write 的逻辑主语)

Anne will give *me* something *to read*. (me 是句中的宾语,同时也是 to read 的逻辑主语)

当句中没有适当的词可作不定式的逻辑主语时,可以借助"for + 名词或代词 + 不定式"结构来表示不定式的逻辑主语。这种不定式结构在句中可作主语、宾语、表语、定语和状语。

It's necessary *for us to learn* a foreign language. (句中 for us 是 to learn 的逻辑主语)

(1) 作主语

① for ... to ... 结构

It won't be easy *for you to find* a good job. 你想找一份好工作不容易。

It will take a lot of hard work *for John to pass* the examination. 约翰要想通过考试必须付出很大努力。

② of ... to ... 结构

It's nice *of you to invite* me to your party. 你真好,想到邀请我来参加聚会。

= You are very nice to invite me to your party.

= How nice (it is) of you to invite me to your party!

(2) 作宾语

① 主语 + 谓语 + it + 宾语补足语 + for ... to 结构(宾语)

I think it better *for you to see* the doctor. 我想你最好看一下医生。

② 主语 + 谓语 + 间接宾语 + for ... to 结构(直接宾语)

I promised Mike *for my son to meet* him at the railway station. 我答应迈克让我儿子去火车站接他。

(3) 作表语

The simplest thing is *for you to resign* at once. 最简单的办法是你马上辞职。

(4) 作定语

It's time *for Lei to reconsider* her decision. 现在是蕾重新考虑她的决定的时候了。

(5) 作状语

Keith stood aside *for me to pass*. 基思站到一边让我过去。(目的状语)

Mr Wang is anxious *for his students to pass* the entrance examination. 王老师渴望他的学生们能通过入学考试。(原因状语)

The text is *too long for the students to learn* by heart. 课文太长,学生们背不下来。(结果状语)

The reference book is *easy enough for pupils to read*. 这本参考书很容易,小学生们能看懂。(程度状语)

5.8 分裂不定式

不定式通常是不可拆开的,但有时为了避免句意不清,可在中间加一副词,构成"to + 副词 + 动词"结构,这就是所谓的分裂不定式(Split Infinitive)。

Our object is *to further cement* friendly relationship between the countries. 我们的目的是进一步加强两国之间的友谊。

Tom began *to slowly get up* off the floor. 汤姆开始慢慢地从地板上站起来。

A successful businessman should be able *to readily accommodate* to the changing economic conditions. 一个成功的商人应该能很快地适应变化的经济情况。

Henry was too ill *to really carry out* his duty. 亨利病得太重,不能切实履行他的职责。

构成分裂不定式的词一般放在小品词 to 与动词原形之间,但在不定式进行式、完成式和被动语态中,所插入的副词应放在第一个助动词或 be 之后。

I'm sorry to have *always* kept you waiting. 很抱歉,我总是让你等久了。

They seemed to be *really* discussing something important. 他们似乎确实在讨论重要的事情。

Note:如果不定式短语有两个助动词,那么该副词应放在第二个助动词之后。

His two English grammar books published before seemed to have been *so well* received. 他以前出版的两本英语语法书似乎很受欢迎。

试比较下面句子的差异:

Her lover *silently prepared* to accompany Lei. 为了陪伴蕾,她的恋人在默默地做准备。

Her lover prepared *to silently accompany* Lei. 她的恋人准备默默地陪伴蕾。(分裂不定式)

I *remembered clearly* to have told her about it. 我清楚地记得告诉过她这件事。

I remembered *to have clearly told* her about it. 我记得曾清楚地告诉过她这件事。(分裂不定式)

5.9　动词不定式不带 to 的情况

通常情况下,我们在动词不定式前要用 to。

He wants *to go* with me. 他想跟我一起去。

It's very kind of you *to say* so. 你这样说很友善。

但在某些情况下,to 可用可不用;而在另一些情况下,则一定不能用,这就是所谓的不带 to 的动词不定式(Bare Infinitive)。不带 to 的动词不定式 常见于下列几种情况:

(1) 在情态助动词之后

在情态动词 will, shall, would, should, can, could, may, might, must 等之后,要使用不带 to 的动词不定式。

Nothing *will go* wrong. 没有事情会出错。

She *could have phoned* me. 她本来可以打电话给我的。

I *must go* now. 我一定得走了。

(2) 在 why (not) 之后

这种结构的肯定式表示不满或委婉的批评,否定式则表示建议或提出问题。

Why worry about such trifles? 为何为琐事烦心?

You're looking tired. *Why not take* a holiday? 你看上去很疲倦。怎么不休假呢?

Note:why not 之后可以接名词、名词短语或动名词短语。

Why not a cup of tea? 为什么不要一杯茶呢?

Why not taking a holiday? 怎么不休假呢?

(3) 在 make, have, let 等动词之后

使役动词 make, have, let 等可以接宾语和不带 to 的不定式。
The official *made Gray fill out* a form. 那名官员要格蕾填写一份表格。
Anne *lets her children stay up* very late. 安妮让孩子们待到很晚才睡。
Jane will *have the porter bring up* her bags. 简叫行李员把她的包带上来。
但在被动形式中,动词不定式要带 to。
Gray *was made to fill out* a form.

(4) 在 see, hear, watch 等感官动词之后

在感官动词 see, hear, watch, look at, listen to, notice, observe, feel 等后可以接宾语和不带 to 的不定式。
I *heard someone knock* on the door. 我听见有人敲门。
Tom *saw the men leave* the building. 汤姆看见那些人离开大楼。
Henry *felt someone pat* him on the shoulder. 亨利感到有人轻轻地拍了拍他的肩膀。
Notes：① 在被动形式中,动词不定式要带 to。
The men *were seen to leave* the building. 有人看见那些人离开大楼。
② 当 know 意为 see, hear 时,也可接不带 to 的不定式(多用于完成式或过去式)。例如：
I *have never known* (= seen) Mike's lover lose her temper. 我从未见过迈克的爱人发脾气。
I *have never known* (= heard) Joe tell lies. 我从未听说过乔撒谎。
当 know 用于一般式,其后只跟 to be。
I *know* this *to be* a fact. 我知道这是事实。
③ 当感官动词 see, feel 意为 know 时,并以 to be 为其宾语补足语,此时不可不用 to。
We *felt* the plan *to be impossible*. 我们觉得这个计划不可行。
I *see* this *to be* a fact. 我知道这是事实。

(5) 在 had better, would rather / would sooner, rather than 等结构之后

在 would rather / would sooner / had rather / had sooner ... than(与其……不如), had better(最好), had best(最好), rather than/sooner than(而不……), rather ... than(宁愿……而不)等结构后用不带 to 的不定式。
We *would rather / would sooner / had rather / had sooner die* than surrender. 我们宁死也不投降。
I didn't enjoy the show. I'd *rather have stayed* at home. 我不喜欢这个演出。早知道我宁愿待在家里。
John decided to accept the offer *rather than take/taking* his case to court. 约翰决定接受这个提议而不是把案子提交法院。
Note：在否定句中,not 放在 had better, would rather 后,而在否定疑问句中,not 放在 had 和 would 后。
We'd *better not* be late. 我们最好不要迟到。
Had I *not* better do it tomorrow? 明天我最好不做那件事吗?

(6) 在 be 动词之后

当动词不定式作表语说明句中动词 do 的具体内容时,作表语的不定式不带 to,有时也可带 to。
The only thing she can do is (*to*) *apologize*. 她唯一能做的就是道歉。
What the police did was (*to*) *charge into the crowd*. 警方所做的就是冲入人群。

(7) 在介词 except, besides, but, save, than 后

当句中有实义动词时，其后边作介词宾语的不定式不带 to。

John does everything *except cook*. 约翰除了烧饭什么都做。
Jane has done nothing *but grumble* all day. 简除了整天发牢骚什么事都没做。
I can not do anything *than wait and see*. 我只能等着瞧。
Henry will do anything *save lend* Mary money. 亨利决不借钱给玛丽。
Did he do anything *besides hit* you? 除了打你之外，他还有没有什么别的举动？

Note：如果句中没有实义动词时，其后边作介词宾语的不定式则要带 to。

She had no choice *but to bear* it and wait. 她没有别的选择，只好忍耐和等待。
There is nothing to do *but* (*to*) *give up* the plan. 没有别的办法，只好放弃该计划。(but 前的 do 不是作实意动词的，而是不定式作定语，故不定式可带 to)

(8) 在 cannot but do sth 等结构后

在 cannot but do sth, cannot help but do sth, cannot choose but do sth（=cannot help doing sth）中，but 后跟的不定式不带 to，表示"不得不"的意思。

I cannot *but think* so. 我不得不这么想。
= I cannot help *but think* so.
= I cannot choose *but think* so.
= I *cannot help thinking* so.（英式英语）

(9) 在一些固定搭配中不用 to

类似的固定搭配有 make believe（假装），let slip（错过），let go（释放），let fall（掉落），go hang（听其自然），make do（设法应付），hear tell/say/speak/talk（听说）。

Gray *made believe* that she was innocent. 格蕾假装她是无辜的。
Don't *let slip* such a good opportunity. 不要错过这样一个好机会。
I *hear say* that there will be a meeting this evening. 我听说今晚有个会议。
Joe has often *heard tell* of such things. 乔时常听说起这类事情。

Note：在 hear tell/say/speak/talk 固定搭配中，其实在 hear 后省略了 people，someone 等词语。故上述例句可改成：

I hear *people* say that there will be a meeting this evening. 我听人说今晚有个会议。
Joe has often heard *someone* tell of such things. 乔时常听人说起这类事情。

(10) 在动词 go, come, run 后

go，come，run 作为命令句，其后可接不带 to 的不定式充当目的状语，表示命令、建议或请求，常见于美式英语。

Go tell the young lady. 你要去告诉那位小姐。
= You'll *go to tell* the young lady.
= You'll *go and tell* the young lady.
Come have supper with us. 请你来和我们共进晚餐。
= Will you *come to have* supper with us?
= Will you *come and have* supper with us?
Run get me a computer. 你快跑去给我找台电脑来。

= You can *run to get* me a computer.
= You can *run and get* me a computer.

Note：上述谓语动词后的不带 to 的动词不定式前面也可理解为省去了连词 and,不过此时后面的动词与前面的谓语动词是并列谓语,不能与省略 to 的动词不定式混为一谈。

(11) 在 and, or, as, like 等连接词后

如果有两个动词不定式结构由 and, or, as, like 等连在一起,第二个动词不带 to。

John didn't know whether to stand *or sit*. 约翰不知道是站着还是坐下。

It's quite necessary for you to read more *and have* more practice. 你多读、多练是十分必要的。

Why don't you do something useful *like take* a walk? 你为什么不做点有益的事,比如散散步？

It's as important to master morphology *as master* syntax. 掌握词法与掌握句法一样重要。

(12) 在动词 help 后

如果 help 的主语参与宾语的动作,其后常用不带 to 的不定式;如果 help 的主语不参与宾语的动作,其后的不定式可带 to,也可不带 to。

Gray will *help* me *solve* it. 格蕾会帮助我解决此事。

The mastery of foreign language *helps* me (*to*) *acquire* modern scientific knowledge. 掌握外语有助于我获取现代科学知识。

第6章 现在分词和过去分词

6.1 现在分词

分词有现在分词(Present Participle)和过去分词(Past Participle)。通常现在分词表示主动意义,是正在进行的动作,是一种动态。现在分词既有动词性质,有时态和语态的变化,并可带上自己的宾语、状语等,又有形容词性质。现在分词的否定式是在现在分词前加 not。现在分词在句中可用作表语、定语、补语、状语等。过去分词表示被动意义,是已完成的动作。过去分词也有动词的特征,可有自己的逻辑主语、宾语和状语,又有形容词和副词的特征。其句法作用是作表语、定语、宾语补语、主语补语、状语等。

(1) 现在分词的形式

时态 \ 语态	主动式		被动式	
	肯定式	否定式	肯定式	否定式
一般式	doing	not doing	being done	not being done
完成式	having done	not having done	having been done	not having been done

(2) 现在分词的句法功能

现在分词可作表语、定语、宾语补足语、主语补足语、状语等。

① 作表语

可以作表语的现在分词常用有表示情绪的词、表示状态和品质的词,这些词就如杨元兴先生在《新编英语句型句法全解》里称作为形容词性质的现在分词,这种现在分词的特征是可以接受 very 之类副词的修饰,还可有比较等级。现在分词作表语时,它的主语可以是 that 从句。

A. 表示情绪的词作表语

She was *very amusing*. 她很有趣。

The book was *rather boring*. 那本书相当枯燥乏味。

The flowers look *even more charming* after the rain. 雨后那些花看上去更加艳丽迷人。

B. 一些表示状态、品质的现在分词作表语

The ticket is *missing*. 那张票不见了。

They are always *very obliging*. 他们总是乐于助人。

The difference was *most striking*. 差别很明显。

C. that 名词从句作主语时,现在分词可作其表语

现在分词的主语还可以是 that 引导的名词性从句,但这种情况一般由 it 作先行主语,当然主语也有不是 it 的情况。如前面的形容词是表示意向的,那 that 从句中谓语常用"should + 动词原形"。这种结构表示喜悦、讨厌、惊奇、不安等情绪。

It is *annoying* that the meeting should be put off. 会议延期了,使人扫兴。

It is *disconcerting* that he should be absent. 他不在场,使别人都感到为难。

It is *perplexing* that they should make such a plan. 他们竟然制订了这样一个计划。

这种形容词性质的现在分词还有:alarming, annoying, boring, charming, confusing, comforting, disgusting, distressing, disappointing, discouraging, disturbing, encouraging, exciting, fascinating, frightening, interesting, inviting, missing, misleading, obliging, pleasing, puzzling, pressing, promising, refreshing, striking, shocking, surprising, touching, thrilling, tempting, vexing 等。

D. 关于现在分词和动名词作表语的问题

现在分词和动名词(也叫名词性质的现在分词)都可以作表语,但分词作表语时保持了它的形容词特征,对主语加以描述,动名词作表语时则表示一个行为动作。

The day was so *charming*. 天气真是好极了。(分词 charming 具有形容词的特征)

His hobby is *collecting stamps*. 他的爱好是集邮。(动名词 collecting 表示行为)

E. 不及物动词的现在分词不能用作表语

一些不及物动词的现在分词不能用作表语,却能用作定语。

the *existing* conditions 现有条件　　　　the *remaining* days 剩下的岁月

a *booming* town 日渐繁荣的城市　　　　the *lasting* peace 持久的和平

the *ruling* class 统治阶级　　　　　　the *ageing* population 日益老化的人口

the *developing* countries 发展中国家　　the *living* things 有生命的东西

② 作定语

现在分词作名词修饰语可分为前置修饰语和后置修饰语两种。

A. 单个现在分词作定语

单个分词作定语一般放在被修饰语之前。上节提到的那些充当表语的现在分词几乎都可以用作定语用。

That's a *frightening* thought. 那是个可怕的想法。

She is a *promising* new writer. 她是一位很有希望的新作家。

I found her a *charming* person. 我发现她是一个讨人喜欢的人。

A *barking* dog seldom bites. 吠犬不咬人。

She opened the letter with *trembling* hands. 她用颤抖的手拆开那封信。

It is dangerous to swim in *running* water. 在急流中游泳很危险。

B. 作前置定语的现在分词来源

作前置定语的现在分词可以是源自及物动词,但更多的是来自不及物动词。作前置定语的及物动词的现在分词,其意义上的宾语可以是人,也可以是物。

a. 意义上的宾语为人

a *puzzling* problem 困扰人的问题(=a problem that puzzles someone)

a *moving* film 一部感人的电影(=a film that moves people)

a *fascinating* girl 迷人的女孩(=a girl that fascinates people)

misleading advertisements 误导的广告(=advertisements that mislead people)

b. 意义上的宾语为物

the *arresting* scenery 吸引人的景色(=the scenery that arrests one's attention)

a *forgiving* smile 宽恕的微笑(=a smile that shows forgiveness)

a *knowing* person 知道内情的人(=a person who knows the secret)

an *understanding* man 善解人意的人(=a man who understands other's feelings)

c. 复合形容词

- 由"名词+现在分词"构成的复合形容词相当于定语从句中动宾关系。

peace-loving peoples 爱好和平的民族 (= peoples who love peace)

English-speaking peoples 说英语的民族 (= peoples who speak English)

- 由"形容词+现在分词"构成的复合形容词,相当于定语从句中谓语与补语的关系。

a *good-looking* girl 一个漂亮姑娘 (= a girl who looks good)

a *sweet-smelling* rose 一朵气味芬芳的玫瑰 (= a rose that smells sweet)

- 由"副词+现在分词"构成的复合形容词,相当于定语从句中谓语与状语的关系。

the *well-meaning* advice 善意的忠告 (= the advice that means well)

a *hard-working* man 一位勤奋的男人 (= a man who works hard)

C. 现在分词作定语与动名词作定语的比较

现在分词与其所修饰的名词在逻辑上具有主谓关系;动名词则表示其修饰的名词的用途,二者在逻辑上无主谓关系。

a *sleeping* child 熟睡的孩子 (= a child that is sleeping) (现在分词)

a *sleeping* car 卧车 (= a car used for sleeping) (动名词)

a *running* stream 奔流的小溪 (= a stream that is running) (现在分词)

running shoes 跑步用的鞋 (= shoes used for running) (动名词)

D. 在下列情况下,现在分词(短语)作后置修饰语

a. 表示对比或强调时

There she saw a lot of people *coming and going*. 她在那里看见许多人来来往往。

There are people *crying* and people *laughing*. 有人哭,有人笑。

b. 被修饰词前面有形容词最高级或代词(all, one, those, something, someone 等)时

He is the greatest poet *living*. 他是在世的最伟大的诗人。

Those *remaining* had to face all kinds of difficulties. 留下来的人必须面对各种困难。

Most of the people *singing* were women. 唱歌的人中,大部分是妇女。

Let me tell you something *interesting*. 让我告诉你一些有趣的事情。

c. 在固定结构或习惯说法中

They wandered in the hills for seven days *running*. 他们一连7天在山中漫游。

That is nothing *doing*. 不行。

He died in the year *following*. 他在第二年去世了。

I will not write to her for the time *being*. 暂时我不打算给她写信。

d. 在现在分词短语的作用接近一个定语从句时

We are brothers *sharing* (= who shares) *weal and woe*. 我们是患难与共的兄弟。

We plan to build a highway *leading* (= which leads) *into the mountains*. 我们计划修一条公路通往山区。

Who is the girl *talking* (= who is talking) *to Tom*? 和汤姆交谈的女孩是谁?

He was woken up by a bell *ringing* (= which was ringing). 他被铃声惊醒。

A young lady *writing* (= who writes) *novels* came to us yesterday. 一位写小说的年轻女士昨天来向我们做报告。

Do you know the number of people *coming* (= who will come) *to the party*? 你知道来参加晚会的人数吗?

Note:在把现在分词短语改为定语从句时,从句谓语可以是一个一般时态的动词,也可以是一个进行时态的动词;有时从句谓语所表示的时间与句中谓语所表示的时间不相同,尤其当现在分词表示经常或瞬间动作的时候。现在分词的完成式往往不能作后置修饰语。

Do you know anybody *having lost* a watch? 你知道有谁丢了一块表吗? (误)

Do you know anybody *who's lost* a watch? 你知道有谁丢了一块表吗?

③ 作宾语补足语

在两类动词后面，可用现在分词（短语）作宾语补足语。这两类动词中，一类是感觉、感官动词，另一类是使役、致使动词。此时的现在分词表示正在进行的主动意义。

A．在感觉、感官动词后

这类动词有 see, hear, feel, smell, watch, find, notice, observe, look at, listen to 等。

I found those students *studying very hard*. 我发现那些学生学习很认真。

I didn't notice her *leaving*. 我没注意到她离开。

Listen to the birds *singing*. 听鸟儿在歌唱。

As he spoke, he observed everybody *looking at him curiously*. 他讲话时，他观察到每个人好奇地看着他。

I heard someone *knocking at the door*. 我听见有人在敲门。

We've been watching the boys *swimming*. 我们一直在观看男孩们游泳。

I felt someone *patting me on the shoulder*. 我感觉有人轻拍我的肩膀。

B．在使役、致使动词后

这类动词有 have, set, keep, get, catch, leave, start 等。

The smoke started her *coughing*. 吸烟使她咳嗽不止。

I'm sorry to have kept you *waiting*. 对不起，我让你久等了。

They caught him *doing evil*. 他们当场抓住他在做坏事。

The joke set them all *laughing*. 这个笑料使他们所有的人开怀大笑。

His remarks left me *wondering about his real purpose*. 他的话使我怀疑他的真正目的。

Notes：a. have 表示"允许"时，后接现在分词或不带 to 的不定式均可，此时的 have 常用于否定结构。

I won't have you *doing that again*. 我不允许你再这样做。

I won't have you *do that again*. 我不许你再做那件事。

b. set 后的宾语补足语通常是现在分词，不用过去分词。

Her words set me *thinking deeply*. 她的话让我深思。

His action set her *wondering*. 他的行为使她疑惑不解。

C．"as＋v-ing 分词"作宾语补足语问题

在某些谓语动词后作宾语补足语的现在分词前有时可加 as，这时的现在分词就如杨元兴先生在《新编英语句型句法全解》中所说的叫"名词性现在分词"，这类动词有：regard, describe, accept, think of, quote, consider, show, picture, see 等。

We *regarded* the contract *as having been rescinded*. 我们认为合同已被废除。

They *described* the boy *as (being) very clever*. 他们把这个男孩子描述得很聪明。

I *considered* this sentence pattern *as (being) useful*. 我认为这种句型是有用的。

Note：as 后所带的 v-ing 分词到底是现在分词还是动名词，取决于 as 的词性，我们认为这里的 as 作介词比较恰当，那其后的 v-ing 也就是传统语法讲的动名词。对于这个问题，在刘重德的《as 的用法研究》和杨元兴的《谈谈 as 引出的宾语补足语》(《中国外语》)上均有详述。从现代语言角度讲，把这种 v-ing 分词看作名词性现在分词比较确切，这种观点已获得了广泛共识。

分词与不定式作宾语补足语的区别在感觉动词和感官动词后面，用分词作宾语补足语，也可用不带 to 的不定式宾语补足语，其区别是：分词作宾语补足语表示动作正在进行，尚未完成，只表示动作过程的一部分，而不定式宾语补足语则表示动作已完成、表示动作的全过程；有时，现在分词表示重复性动作，不定式表示一次性动作。

I saw her *go upstairs*. 我看见她上楼去了。（全过程）

I saw her *going upstairs*. 我看见她上楼的。（过程的一部分）

I saw a soldier *get on the train* and disappeared. 我看见一个士兵上了火车,消失了。(全过程)
I saw a soldier *getting on the train*. 我看见一个士兵在上火车。(过程的一部分)
She heard the door *slamming*. 她听见门在砰砰作响。(重复性动作)
She heard the door *slam*. 她听见门"砰"的一声关上了。(一次性动作,已完成)
Xiaolei felt the tears *rolling down her cheeks*. 小蕾感到眼泪不断地流了下来。(重复性动作)
Xiaolei felt the tears *roll down her cheeks*. 小蕾感到眼泪流了下来。(一次性动作,已完成)

④ 作主语补足语

上述感觉、感官动词如果转换为被动语态,原来作宾语补足语的现在分词短语则变为主语补足语,说明主语的动作或状态。

I heard her singing that song again. 我再次听见她唱那首歌。
She was heard *singing that song again*. 再次听见她唱那首歌。
We often saw Mary reading late at night. 我们经常看见玛丽读书到深夜。
Mary was often seen *reading late at night*. 经常看见玛丽读书到深夜。
They will keep the machine running for two days. 他们将使这台机器连续运转两天。
The machine will be kept *running for two days*. 这台机器将连续运转两天。

⑤ 作状语

现在分词(短语)作状语时表示的动作是主语动作的一部分,与谓语表示的动作或状态是同时或几乎同时发生的,有时先于谓语动词的动作。现在分词(短语)可以作时间、原因、方式、条件、结果、目的、让步等状语,一般要用逗号同其他成分隔开,如在分词短语前加上相应的连词时,可表示强调。

少数现在分词可作副词用,以加深形容词的程度或状态,表示"极度"、"非常"、"很",其程度比 very 稍强。

It was *freezing/biting/piercing/perishing* cold yesterday. 昨天寒冷刺骨。
There have been several *boiling/burning/scalding/scorching* hot days this month. 这个月来有几天非常热。

A. 作时间状语

现在分词作时间状语用时相当于 when 或 while 引导的从句。

Hearing the news (= When they heard the news), they immediately set off for Shanghai. 听到这个消息,他们立即出发到上海去了。
Doing morning exercise in the park (= While I was doing …), I met a friend of my father's. 在公园晨练时,我碰到了我父亲的一个朋友。

Notes: a. 作时间状语的分词短语也可放在主语后或句尾,放在句尾时最强调。

Having written an important letter, I listened to the music for a while. 写完一封重要的信之后,我听了一会儿音乐。
I, *having written an important letter*, listened to the music for a while. (最不强调)
I listened to the music for a while, *having written an important letter*. (最强调)

b. 如果分词表示的动作紧接着谓语动作之后发生,分词短语应放在句尾。

She sat down, *listening to their talk*. 她坐了下来,听他们谈话。

c. 如果分词表示的动作先发生,谓语动词动作紧接着就发生,分词短语应放在句首。

They stepped aside, *seeing a car coming*. (误)
Seeing a car coming, they stepped aside. (正) 看见一辆车开了过来,他们就站到一边。

B. 作原因状语

现在分词作原因状语时相当于 as, since, because 引导的从句,往往放在句子的前半部分。

Living in the country (= As I was living …), I could make friends with the villagers. 由于我住在农村,所以

我可与村民交朋友。

Not knowing how to solve the problem (＝Since I didn't know how …), I asked the teacher. 不知道如何解这道题,我请教了老师。

C. 作方式、伴随状语

作方式或伴随状语用时,由于没有相应的连词,因此在进行句型转换时只能改写成并列句。

She stood at the window *watching the sunset* (＝and watched the sunset). 她站在窗前看日落。

He walked down the hill, *singing softly to himself* (＝and sang softly to himself). 他从小山上走下来,一路哼着曲儿。

Note:有些语法学家认为,英语中有些动词如 go, come, sit, stand 等都可以看作是 be 动词的变体,其后的现在分词可被认为是主语补足语(表语),但我们认为作为方式、伴随状语更能被接受。

We sat *telling* stories to the children. 我们坐着给孩子们讲故事。

The boy came *running* to meet me. 那个男孩跑过来迎接我。

作方式、伴随状语的还有:stand talking, lie reading, sit listening to, come crying, come singing, come shouting 等。

D. 作条件状语

当现在分词作条件状语用时,相当于 if, unless 等引导的从句。

Exercising every morning (＝If you exercise …), you will improve your health. 如果你每天坚持晨练,你的健康就会好转。

Paying by credit card (＝Unless you are paying by …), please pay in cash. 除非你用信用卡付款,否则请付现金。

E. 作结果状语

现在分词作结果状语用时,相当于 so that, which 引导的结果从句。

They opened fire, *killing one of our patrolmen* (＝so that they killed …). 他们开枪打死了我们一个巡逻兵。

The snow lasted a week, *resulting in a serious traffic confusion in the whole area* (＝which resulted in …). 雪下了一星期,造成整个地区严重的交通混乱。

F. 作目的状语

现在分词作目的状语用时,相当于 in order that, in order to 引导的目的从句或表示目的的不定式。

It would be nice to go *boating*. (＝It would be nice to go in order that we may/might boat 或 in order to boat.) 去划船真好。

How nice it would be to go *shopping*! (＝How nice it would be to go in order that we may/can shop!) 去购物多好啊!

下列这些动词后的 v-ing 分词结构均可看作目的状语:go climbing/fishing/unting/riding/sailing/skating/skiing/swimming/walking/shooting/bathing/hiking/picnicking/drinking/golfing/sporting。

G. 作让步状语

现在分词作让步状语时,相当于 though, even if 等引导的从句。

Sitting near the fire (＝Though I sat …), I still felt cold. 坐在火边上,我还觉得冷。

Admiting what she has said (＝Even if I admit …), I still think that she hasn't tried her best. 尽管承认她所说的话,但我仍然认为她没有尽最大努力。

Note:"being＋形容词、名词、介词短语"表示时间、原因、伴随情况等,可放在主语前(最自然)、主语后(较文气),也可放在句尾。这些用法中的 being 常可省略。

(*Being*) *Weary and worried*, Jim slept the whole day. 吉姆忧心忡忡,疲惫不堪,睡了一整天。

Jim, (*being*) *weary and worried*, slept the whole day.

Jim slept the whole day, (*being*) *weary and worried*.

(3) 现在分词的完成体

现在分词完成体所表示的动作发生在谓语动词动作之前,作时间和原因状语用,表示时间时常置于句首,表示原因时置于句首、句末均可。

Having sent the children to bed (=When she had sent …),she began to study. 安排孩子睡觉后,她开始学习。(时间)

Having done the first part of the research (=After/When we had done …),we were divided into two groups. 第一部分的研究完成之后,我们就分成了两个小组。(时间)

Having studied hard (=Since he had studied …),he got high marks in the test. 由于学习努力,他在考试中得了高分。(原因)

I was unable to accept your invitation,*having promised to accompany my mother to the concert* (=because I had promised …). 我因已答应陪我母亲赴音乐会而不能接受你的邀请。(原因)

Notes: ① 当句中谓语动词所表示的动作和现在分词所表示的动作在时间上不一致时,不能用现在分词一般式。

Who is the person *breaking the glass*? 打碎玻璃杯的那个人是谁?(误)
Who is the person *that broke the glass*? 打碎玻璃杯的那个人是谁?(正)
Finishing his work, he went out to play. 完成了工作后,他出去玩耍了。(误)
Having finishing his work,he went out to play. 完成了工作后,他出去玩耍了。(正)

② 非谓语形式的 there being/there having been 结构可用作状语,表示原因。

There being nothing to do (=As there was nothing …),they went home. 由于没事可做,他们便回家了。

There having been no news about her for a long time (=As there had been …),they thought that she was dead. 由于很长时间都没有她的音讯,他们以为她死了。

(4) 现在分词的被动语态

现在分词的被动语态有一般式被动语态和完成式被动语态两种。

① 现在分词的一般式被动语态

在表示一个被动动作时,如果这个动作是现在正在进行的,或与句中谓语动词所表示的动作同时发生,就可以用现在分词一般式被动语态来表示。分词一般式被动语态在句中作定语、状语、宾语补足语。

A. 作定语

The house *being built* (=that is being built) is a big project. 正在施工的那幢楼是一项很大的工程。

The equipment *being improved by the research group* (=which is being improved …) will be tested tomorrow. 研究小组正在改进的设备将于明天测试。

B. 作状语

Being surrounded (=As the enemy troops were being surrounded),the enemy troops were forced to surrender. 敌军正被包围,结果被迫投降。(原因)

While being turned into water (=While ice is being turned …),ice—a solid,takes in much heat. 冰是一种固体,被变成水时吸收大量的热。(时间)

C. 作宾语补足语

Did you see the boy *being questioned* (=who was being questioned) *by the police*? 你看见那男孩受到警察审问了吗?

When he came to,he found himself *being looked after* (=that/who was being looked after) *by a girl*. 醒来时,他发现一个女孩正在照顾他。

② 现在分词的完成式被动语态

现在分词完成式被动语态强调分词所表示的动作发生在谓语动作之前。现在分词的完成式被动语态在句中可作状语、定语。

A. 作状语

Having been warned about typhoon (＝When/after the fishermen had been warned about …), the fishmen sailed for the nearest harbour. 听到台风警报,渔民们便驾船向最近的港口驶去。(时间)

Having been given such a good book (＝As we have been given …), we should read it very carefully. 给了我们这么好的一本书,我们应该非常仔细地阅读。(原因)

Oil drilling, *although having been continuously improved* (＝although it has been continuously improved), is still a complicated process. 石油钻探,虽然经过不断改进,仍然是个复杂的规程。(让步)

B. 作定语

Tube making is a kind of technology *having been studied* (＝which has been studied) *by many scientific workers*. 管子的制作是经许多科学工作者研究出来的一种技术。

(5) 现在分词的否定式

现在分词的否定式由"not＋现在分词"构成,在句中主要作状语。

Not having a telephone (＝Since I do not have a telephone), I shall have to write to him. 没有电话,我得写信给他。(一般式的否定式,表示原因)

Not having heard from her son for a long time (＝Since the mother had not heard from …), the mother worried a great deal. 很长时间没有她儿子的消息,母亲非常担忧。(完成式的否定式,表示原因)

Not being seen by any one (＝While he was not seen …), he escaped. 他趁无人看见时逃跑了。(一般式被动语态的否定式,表示时间)

Not having been trained for a long time (＝Since we have not been trained …), we do not know how to operate the complicated system. 由于未经过长时间的培训,我们不懂得如何操作这种复杂的系统。(完成式被动语态的否定式,表示原因)

(6) 现在分词的独立结构

现在分词有时可以在其前用名词或代词来表明分词的动作由谁执行,此系现在分词的逻辑主语,这种结构称为独立结构(Absolute Construction)。它们在句中作状语,表示时间、原因、条件、方式和伴随等,其位置于句首或句末均可。比较下面两句:

Being ill in bed (＝Since I am ill), I cannot go to school. 我因为卧病在床不能去上学。(分词短语作原因状语)

Mother being ill in bed (＝Since mother is ill in bed), I connot go to school. 因为母亲卧病在床,我不能去上学。(独立结构作原因状语)

① 作时间状语

The experiment being over (＝When the experiment was over), we put the instrument back in place. 试验结束后,我们把仪器放回原处。

The dark clouds having dispersed (＝After/When the dark clouds had dispersed), the sun shone again. 乌云已散去,太阳又普照大地了。

② 作原因状语

The river having risen in the night (＝As the river had risen …), the crossing was impossible. 夜里河水上涨,渡河不可能了。

All the tickets having been sold out (= As all the tickets had been sold out), they went away disappointed. 票已售完,他们失望地走了。

③ 作条件状语

We're playing golf this afternoon—*weather permitting* (= if the weather permits). 要是天气允许,我们今天下午去打高尔夫球。

I'll take you home, *your daughter having not come* (= if your daughter has not come).

④ 作方式或伴随状语

现在分词独立结构作方式或伴随状语时,通常后位。由于没有相应的连词,作方式或伴随状语时无法用状语从句替换,但可以改写成并列句。

She walked along the path, *her daughter following close behind* (= and her daughter followed close behind). 她沿着小路走,其女儿紧跟在后面。

She watered the flowers, *her husband feeding the birds* (= and her husband fed the birds). 她浇花,丈夫喂鸟。

(7) with/without 型分词独立结构

有时,独立结构中的逻辑主语前可以加介词 with 或 without,这种带介词的 with/without 的分词独立结构在句中常作方式、伴随、时间、条件、原因、让步等状语,有时也有作定语的情况。

The old man sat reading, *with his dog sleeping beside him* (= and his dog was sleeping …). 老人坐着看书,他的狗在他的旁边睡觉。(方式或伴随)

Without the temperature falling rapidly (= When the temperature did not fall rapidly), they could go with the test. 温度不急剧下降时,他们能继续试验了。(时间)

She wants to do that *without them knowing* (= if they do not know) she helped. 在他们不知道是她帮忙的情况下,她愿意办此事。(条件)

With the tall boy sitting in front of me (= Since the tall boy sits …), I can't see the words on the blackboard. 由于那高个的男生坐在我前边,我看不见黑板上的字。(原因)

An object may be hot *without the motion in it being visible* (= although the motion in it isn't visible). 一个物体,即使其内部运动不可见,仍可能是热的。(让步)

We went into a waiting room *with a fan spinning overhead* (= whose fan was spinning overhead). 我们走进一个候诊室,头上有个电扇运转着。(定语)

Note:这种结构中除用分词外,还可以用不定式、形容词、介词短语、副词、名词等,它们在句中主要作状语,表示方式、伴随、原因等,有时也有作同位语的情况。

She knew that *with him to help her* (= since he would help her), she could and would succeed. 她知道,有他帮忙,她能够而且一定会成功。(原因)

The stranger stared at me *with his eyes wide open* (= and his eyes were wide open). 那陌生人睁大眼睛盯着我。(表方式或伴随)

They are sure to win the victory *with so many people behind them* (= because so many people are behind them). 有这么多人支持,他们肯定能赢得胜利。(原因)

Last night he was so tired that he fell asleep *with the lamp on* (= and the lamp was on). 昨晚他太累了,亮着灯就睡着了。(方式或伴随)

She used to sit reading in the evening *with her cat, her only companion*. 她总是坐着看书,猫是她唯一的同伴。(同位语)

(8) 现在分词(短语)作句子状语

有时,现在分词(短语)用来表示说话人对所说的话的一种态度,它们已变成固定词组,可以看作一种句子的独立成分(Independent Element),这些独立成分意义上的主语表示泛指的 we, one, you。此时,这种意义上的主语可以省略。

Generally speaking (= If we speak generally), the climate in Kunming is mild all the year round. 一般说来,昆明的气候常年温和。

Judging by his testimonials (= If we judge by his testimonials), I think he will suit the post. 从他的推荐信看,我认为他适合这项工作。

类似的固定词组还有:

strictly speaking 严格地说	broadly speaking 广义地说
personally speaking 就我个人来说	properly speaking 正确地说
roughly speaking 大概说	comparatively speaking 比较地说
frankly speaking 坦白地说	calculating roughly 大致算来
honestly speaking 诚实地说	politically speaking 从政治方面说
biologically speaking 从生物学角度说	talking of 说到
speaking of 谈到	judging from 从……上看/来判断
theoretically speaking 从理论上讲	allowing for 考虑到

(9) 无依着现在分词结构

我们知道,现在分词短语相当于状语从句,其逻辑主语通常就是主句的主语。比较下面两句:

Looking up at the sky, she saw the moon shining bright and clear. 仰望天空,她看见月亮皎洁、明亮。(现在分词短语作时间状语)

主句中的主语是 she,因此 Looking up at the sky = When/As she was looking/looked up at the sky, she saw the moon … 如果分词短语的逻辑主语不是主句的主语,这样的分词短语就是无依着现在分词结构(Unattached Present Participle Construction)。不少语法书也称之为悬垂分词结构(Dangling Participle Construction)。

Looking up at the sky, the moon shone bright and clear. 仰望天空,月亮皎洁、明亮。(无依着现在分词)

显然,主句的主语 the moon 不可能是现在分词短语 Looking up at the sky 的逻辑主语,故该分词短语也就悬垂无依着了,被看作不符合语法规则,是不可取的。上述病句可用两种方法加以改正:

一是把分词短语扩展成状语从句,主句结构不变:When/As she was looking/looked up at the sky, the moon shone bright and clear.

二是保留分词短语,改变主句的主语,使之能成为分词短语的逻辑主语,并做其他相应变化:Looking up at the sky, she saw the moon shining bright and clear.

但是也有例外,有时分词短语在句中找不到自己的逻辑主语,而是依着在不应该依着的词语上,这就是"无依着现在分词结构"。在不引起歧义或语义混乱的情况下,"无依着分词"是可以接受的。在下列情况下会出现"无依着分词"现象:

① 当分词的逻辑主语未明确列出,但从上下文中可理解其逻辑主语是 we, you, one 等泛指人的词语时,"无依着分词"是可以接受的。

When carrying a gun (= When you carry …), it should never be pointed at anyone. 持枪时,千万不要枪口对人。

Dining in this restaurant (= When one dines …), a jacket and tie are required. 在该饭店用餐时,要求着西装、打领带。

② 在科技英语中,由于科技语体通常避免使用人称主语,所以常出现"无依着分词"。

Using the electric energy (= When we use …), it is necessary to change its form. (我们)使用电能时必须改变其形式。

Installing a boiler (= When you install …), the floor space which is available is very important. 安装锅炉时,设备可利用的面积是非常重要的。

③ 分词的逻辑主语是主句的其他成分或通过上下文体现出来时,"无依着分词"也是可以接受的。

Walking or sleeping (= Whether I walked or slept), this subject was always in *my* mind. 不论(我)是走路或是睡觉,我总是在想着这个问题。

Getting down from the bus (= When I was getting down …), *my* ankle was sprained. (我)从公共汽车上下来时,我的脚踝扭伤了。

Sitting in the chair (= When I was sitting …), an idea suddenly occurred to *me*. (我)坐在椅子上时,我突然想起一个主意。

Being French (= Although she is French), it's surprising that *she*'s such a terrible cook. (她)虽然是法国人,但令人感到惊奇的是,她的厨艺很糟糕。

Having so little time (= Since I had …), there was not much that *I* could do. 由于(我)时间很少,我能做的事情很有限。

在英语中虽然"无依着分词"可被接受,但为了避免引起分歧或语义混淆,英语学习者应尽量避免使用这种结构,特别是英语初学者更不要去模仿。

6.2 过去分词

(1) 过去分词概说

通常过去分词表示被动意义、已完成的动作。过去分词既有动词的特征,有自己的逻辑主语、宾语和状语,又有形容词和副词的特征。过去分词在句中可作表语、定语、宾语补语、主语补语、状语等。

(2) 过去分词的句法功能

① 作表语

过去分词作表语时往往表示主语的状态或状况。

Never touch an electric wire when it is *broken*. 绝不要碰断了的电线。

He's *gone*. 他走了。

It looks *decayed*. 它看上去已经腐败了。

The mountain was *covered with* snow all the year round. 山上终年积雪。

I became *acquainted with* some of them. 我和他们中间一些人熟悉起来。

常见的能作表语的过去分词有:accustomed, ccomplished, amazed, amused, astonished, broken, burst, bored, closed, completed, confused, complicated, contented, covered, crowded, charmed, decided, dedicated, delighted, devoted, disappointed, discouraged, done, dressed, drunk, exhausted, experienced, faded, frightened, gone, hurt, finished, illustrated, injured, interested, killed, known, loaded, learned, lost, married, overgrown, painted, prepared, pleased, puzzled, posted, qualified, recovered, reserved, satisfied, saved, shut, spent, surrounded, surprised, translated, tired, undressed, unknown, upset, won, wounded, worried 等。

大多数过去分词前是不能和程度副词连用的,但少数过去分词(如 annoyed, amazed, amused, astonished, bored, confused, crowded, charmed, disappointed, discouraged, encouraged, excited, faded, frightened, interested, known, mistaken, troubled, tired, puzzled, pleased, upset, worried 等)词典中已收作完全形容词。完全形容词一般可用程度副词 very, very much, rather, too 等修饰。尚未形容

词化的过去分词,如 changed, drawn 等,一般用 much 修饰。

They were *very/very much/rather upset* when they parted. 分手时,他们心里很难过。

She is *very much opposed to* your going abroad for further study. 她非常反对你去国外深造。

Notes：a. 过去分词是动词被动式的组成部分时,前面可以用 much 或 very much 修饰但不能用 very。

He is *very much/much admired* by his students. 他的学生十分钦佩他。（正确）

He is very admired by his students. （错误）

That's Alice unless I'm *very much/much mistaken*. 那人就是艾丽斯,除非我完全搞错了。（正确）

That's Alice unless I'm very mistaken mistaken. （错误）

He's *well known* in the art world. 他在艺术界是位知名人士。（正确）

He's very known in the art world. （错误）

very, very much 和 much 都可以与 amused 连用。

I was *very amused/very much amused/much amused* by Miranda's performance. 我看了米兰达的表演,感到非常开心。

b. 可用过去分词作表语的系动词除 be 外,常见的还有 appear, become, feel, get, grow, remain, seem 等,后跟过去分词作表语,表示主语的状态。

He appeared *well prepared* for the TV debate. 对电视辩论会他似乎准备很充分。

The battery became *exhausted after long use*. 长久使用后,电池耗尽了。

She could not help feeling *depressed*. 她禁不住感到很沮丧。

c. 有些过去分词作表语时,经常与某些特定的介词连用。

He was *alarmed at* what he had just heard. 对刚刚听到的消息他很惊慌。

The house is *surrounded with* trees. 房子的周围都是树。

She was *puzzled about* it. 她对此困惑不解。

She is *very qualified for* the post. 她很胜任该职位。

He is *lost in* thought. 他陷入沉思。

He looks *ashamed of* these wild statements. 他对这些轻率的言论感到脸红。

His large business is *based on* good service. 他的巨大企业是以优良的服务为基础的。

He was *accustomed to* hard work. 他习惯于艰苦的工作。

A. 少数不及物动词的过去分词作表语

有少数不及物动词,如 go, come, fade, set 等,它们的过去分词也能作表语,表示动作的完成。

His job was *gone*. 他的工作丢了。

The sun is *set*; let's go home. 太阳已下山,我们回家吧!

The curtains are *faded*. 窗帘褪色了。

B. 过去分词用作表语及其有关问题

过去分词用作主语补足语时,后可接 that 从句和不定式短语。那些过去分词主要有 amazed, amused, annoyed, astonished, determined, disappointed, frightened, inclined, pleased, puzzled, satisfied, shocked, surprised 等。

We were *surprised that he came*. 他来了,我们感到惊讶。

I was *amazed that he should speak English so fluently*. 他的英语讲得如此流利,我很惊讶。

I feel *rather inclined to go*. 我非常想去。

I'm *puzzled what to do next*. 我不知道下一步怎么办好。

Note：过去分词作表语（或叫主语补足语,这时的过去分词已是形容词）,后跟 that 从句,这种 that 从句起何种句法作用,语法界有以下几种观点：

a. that 从句与前面的过去分词一起看作主语补足语。较早的中外语法书多持这种观点。

b. that 从句在这类结构中起原因状语作用，要注意的是此时的形容词应是表示心境和情绪的形容词，如 I'm sorry (that) I broke your glasses，(相当于 I'm sorry *because* I broke your glasses) We were surprised that he came. (在意义上就相当于 We were surprised because he came.)。

c. 现代英语语法研究称"be + 形容词 + that 从句"的结构中，that 从句称作宾语从句，或叫形容词宾语从句(Object Clause of Adjective)。

C. "be + 过去分词（形容词性）"结构（简称系表结构）与被动语态的比较

过去分词用作表语时，相当于形容词，表示状态；过去分词用于被动语态时则表示动作，句子主语为动作的对象。系表结构中 be 只有一般和完成时态；而被动语态可以有多种时态。

The shop is closed now. 商店现在已经关门了。(系表结构)

It is usually closed at 5:30. 它通常 5:30 关门。(被动结构)

The teapot is broken. 茶壶破了。(系表结构)

It was broken by my brother. 它是我弟弟打破的。(被动结构)

He is injured in the leg. 他腿部有伤。(系表结构)

He had been injured during the war. 他是在战争中受的伤。(被动结构)

D. 用作形容词的过去分词与现在分词的比较

interesting, boring, exciting 等用来描述引起这些感觉的事或人。在张道真所著的《英语语法大全》第 92 页上，这些形容词被称为"激起情绪"的形容词(Adjectives of Exciting)，和这些形容词连用的名词多指物，较少指人。interested, bored, excited 等形容词则用来说明人们的感觉，被称为"感到情绪"的形容词(Adjectives of Feeling)，与这些形容词连用的名词多指人（或指有情绪的动物），而不指物。上述这两种形容词不仅用在名词前作定语，还可作表语等。

I was very interested in the lesson. 我对这堂课很感兴趣。(正确)

I was very interesting in the lesson. (错误)

The lesson was really interesting. 这堂课确实很有意思。(正确)

The lesson was really interested. (错误)

I don't enjoy the party because I was bored. 我不喜欢这次聚会，因为我厌烦了。(正确)

I don't enjoy the party because I was boring. (错误)

It was a terrible boring party. 这是一次极其乏味的聚会。(正确)

The children always get excited when Granny comes. 奶奶来的时候，小孩子们总是很兴奋。(正确)

The children always get exciting when Granny comes. (错误)

Granny takes the children to exciting places. 奶奶带着孩子们去令人兴奋的地方。(正确)

His explanations make me very confusing. (错误)

His explanations make me very confused. 他的解释把我弄得很糊涂。(正确)

③ 作定语

过去分词（短语）作定语时，相当于被动语态的定语从句。及物动词的过去分词表示被动的或已完成的意义，被修饰的名词是分词行为的承受者。而不及物动词的过去分词通常表示已完成的动作，但表示主动意义，被修饰的名词是分词动作的执行者。

A．作前置定语

a. 及物动词的过去分词作前置定语时表示被动的意思，作形容词用的过去分词可改成动词为被动的定语从句。

Lost time (= Time which is lost) is lost forever. 失去的时间永远失去了。

I received a letter *written* (= which was written) *in English*. 我收到一封用英语写的信。

b. 有些不及物动词的过去分词作前置定语时，表示主动的意思或完成的状态，作形容词用的过去分词可改成动词为主动的定语从句。

The ground is covered with the *fallen* leaves. (= The ground is covered with the leaves which have fallen.) 地上覆盖着落叶。

She wore a *faded* coat. (= She wore a coat whose color had faded.) 她穿了一件褪了色的外套。

Notes: • 大多数及物动词的现在分词和过去分词有主动和被动之分。

a *criticizing* speech = a speech which criticizes sb/sth 一个批评性的发言

a *criticized* speech = a speech which was criticized 一个遭到批评的发言

• 不及物动词的现在分词和过去分词有进行体和完成体之分。

boiling water = water that is boiling 正在沸腾的水

boiled water = water that has boiled 烧开过的水

falling leaves = leaves that are falling 正在飘落的树叶

fallen leaves = leaves that have fallen 已经落在地上的树叶

a *drowning* man = a man who is drowning 快淹死的人

a *drowned* man = a man who has drowned 已经淹死的人

• 有些过去分词作前置定语时,既可表示主动意义,也可表示被动意义。

a *threatened* foe = a foe that threatens us 构成威胁的敌人

threatened species = species that are threatened 有灭绝危险的物种

a *surprised* look = a look that shows surprise 惊奇的表情

a *surprised* boy = a boy that is surprised 受惊吓的男孩

c. 由"副词+过去分词"形成的复合形容词作前置定语,其关系相当于定语从句的谓语与状语的关系。

a *beautifully-dressed* woman = a woman who dresses beautifully 衣着华丽的女人

a *well-behaved* child = a child who behaves well 循规蹈矩的孩子

a *much-praised* man = a man who is praised much 倍受称赞的人

d. 由"形容词+过去分词"构成的复合形容词作前置定语,其关系相当于定语从句的谓语与补语关系。

a *ready-made* dress = a dress which is made ready 现成的衣服

a *high-born* child = a child who was born high 出身高贵的孩子

green-painted houses = houses which are painted green 漆成绿色的房子

e. 由"名词+过去分词"构成的复合形容词作前置定语,其关系相当于定语从句的主谓关系。

hand-made shoes = shoes made by hand 手工做的鞋

a *heart-broken* woman = a woman whose heart is broken 伤心的妇人

f. 由"形容词或名词+拟拟分词"构成的复合形容词作前置定语,其关系相当于定语从句的动宾关系。所谓拟拟分词,是指在名词词尾加-ed,它们可与其他一些词构成复合形容词,意思为"具有……"。

a *one-eyed* general = a general who has one eye 独眼将军

a *three-legged* table = a table that has three legs 三条腿的桌子

a *noble-minded* man = a man who has noble mind 思想高尚的人

B. 作后置定语

a. 表示对比或强调时,须作后置定语。

Money *lent* is money *spent*. 钱借出去就等于花掉的了。(重点在 lent 和 spent)

Lent money is *spent* money. 借出去的钱就等于花掉的钱。(重点在 money)

b. 如果被修饰词前面有形容词最高级,或是代词(all, one, those, something, someone 等)时,作后置定语。

Among those *invited* were some ladies. 被邀请的人当中有些是女士。

c. 有时跟在名词后的可能是一个单一的过去分词,而不是短语,这时它是后置定语。

They didn't allow us to make the alterations *suggested*. 他们不允许我们做提出的修改。

The designers decided to change the materials *used*. 设计者决定改变所用的材料。

The man *concerned* was her husband. 有关者即是她的丈夫。

She likes all the courses *offered*. 她对所开的课程都很喜欢。

How much time is there *left*? 还剩下多少时间?

d. 过去分词短语作后置定语时,其作用相当于一个定语从句。

What's the language *spoken* (= that is spoken) *in that country*? 那个国家讲的是什么语言?

I know the girl *employed* (= who is employed) *by this company*. 我认识受雇于这家公司的那个女孩。

The play *put on* (which was put on) *by the teachers* was a big success. 老师们表演的戏很成功。

e. 作定语的过去分词短语常指已经完成的动作,若要表示现在正在进行的动作,就要用过去分词的进行形式(being +过去分词结构)。

The matter *being discussed* (= which is being discussed) is of vital importance. 正在讨论的那个问题很重要。

I knew nothing about the experiment *being conducted* (= which was being conducted) *there*. 我对在那里进行的试验一无所知。

Note: 比较前、后置定语的不同含义:

the method *adopted* 采取的办法　　　the people *involved* 有关人士
an *adopted* child 养子　　　　　　　the *involved* explanation 复杂的解释
the authorities *concerned* 有关当局　the cars *used* 所用的车子
a *concerned* expression 忧虑的神情　the *used* cars 用的(旧)车子

③ 作宾语补足语

过去分词(短语)一般只在三类动词后作宾语补足语:感觉、感官动词;使役、致使动词;表示"希望"、"要求"等意义的动词。这种用法中的现在分词表示正在进行的主动意义,过去分词则表示已经完成的被动意义。

A. consider, expect, feel, find, observe, think, hear, see, watch, notice, smell, listen to, look at 等表示感觉和心理状态的动词

He heard his name *called*. 他听见有人叫他的名字。

She saw the thief *caught by policemen*. 她看见那个小偷被警察抓住了。

He felt a great weight *taken off his mind*. 他感到心头如释重负。

B. catch, have, make, get, start, leave, keep, help 等表示使役、致使的动词

He kept the horse *tied to a tree*. 他把马一直拴在一棵树上。

He could make himself *understood*. 他能让别人明白他的意思。

He left the door *firmly fastened*. 他把门关得严严的。

You ought to get your article *published*. 你应把你的文章发表出去。

Many youngsters have their hair *colored*. 许多年轻人把头发染了色。

Notes: a. have 后接过去分词短语作宾语补语时有几种意义:

I had a new bookcase *made*. 我让人做了一个新书橱。(致使)

She had her arm *broken in an accident*. 在那次事故中她的胳膊被摔断了。(遭受)

I will not have my house *turned into a hotel*. 我不允许把我的房子变成旅馆。(允许)

I'll have my first novel *written by this time next year*. 明年这时我的第一部小说就全部写好了。(主语的行为)

b. make 后的宾语补语只能用过去分词,不能用现在分词。

The writer made himself *known by the novel*. 这位作家通过小说使自己出名。

On these questions, we have made our views *understood*. 关于这些问题，我们已经讲明了我们的观点。

C. like, want, wish, order 等表示"希望"、"要求"意义的动词

We want the work (to be) *finished by Monday*. 我们要求该工作在星期一之前完成。

I won't like such questions (to be) *discussed at the meeting*. 我不喜欢在会议上讨论这样的问题。

The viewers wish the serial film (to be) *continued*. 观众希望这部连续剧能继续。

Note：在这一类动词后的宾语补足语，其不定式的被动语态"to be"往往被省略，就成了过去分词结构。

④ 作主语补足语

find, discover, leave, keep, see, make 等少数动词可变为被动式，原来作宾语补足语的过去分词短语就成了主语补足语，说明主语所处的状态。

A lot of old newspapers are kept *locked away there*. 许多旧报纸一直锁在那里没动。

The painting was found (to be) *spoiled by vandals*. 人们发现那幅画已被破坏成性的狂人毁坏。

Our views have to be made *known to them all*. 我们的观点必须让他们全部了解。

⑤ 作状语

过去分词作状语时，其表示的动作是句子主语承受的动作，它们之间的关系是被动关系。过去分词作状语时可表示时间、原因、条件、方式、伴随、让步等。

A. 作时间状语

此时相当于时间状语从句，多表示先于谓语的被动行为，有时为了突出时间或不引起歧义，可在过去分词前加 when, while, once, until, till, as soon as 等。

Seen from the plane (= When the islands are seen …), the islands are extremely beautiful. 从飞机上看，那些岛屿非常美。

Once published (= Once the book is published), the book caused a stir. 这书一出版就引起了轰动。

The girl is very shy, and never speaks *until spoken to* (= until she was spoken to). 这女孩怕羞，别人不跟她讲话，她从不说。

B. 作原因状语

此时相当于原因状语从句，多表示一个先于谓语的被动行为，其前通常不用连词。

Deeply shocked (= Because I was deeply shocked), I was unable to speak. 我大为吃惊，话都说不出来了。

He was almost asleep, *worn out by the strain* (= since he was worn out …). 他精疲力竭，差一点睡着了。

This book, *written in simple English* (= because it is written in simple …), is suitable for beginners. 这本书，由于使用简单英语写作，适合初学者。

C. 作条件状语

此时相当于条件状语从句，多表示一个先于谓语的被动行为，其前通常可用连词 if, unless 等引导。

United (= If we are united), we stand; *divided* (= if we are divided), we fall. 团结则存，分裂则亡。

We won't come *unless invited* (unless we are invited). 除非受到邀请，否则我们是不会来的。

Driven carefully (= If the car was driven …), the car should last a long time. 这辆车子如果驾驶得细心，应该能用很长时间。

D. 作方式或伴随状语

过去分词（短语）作方式或伴随状语时一般后置，用来说明主要动作。多数表示一个与谓语动词同时发生的被动行为，由于没有相应的连词，所以无法用状语从句替换，但可以改写成并列句。

The two men strode along, *helped by a torch* (= and they were helped …). 那两个人打着手电筒大步走着。

The teacher stood there, *surrounded by many students* (= and he was surrounded by …). 老师站在那里，身边围着许多学生。

He came back, *utterly exhausted* (= and he was utterly ...). 他回来时精疲力竭。

比较下面两句中分词所表示的不同含义：

Not seen by anyone, Tom left the house. (= Tom was not seen by anyone when he left the house.) 汤姆离开屋子，没被人看见。（伴随状语）

Not seen by anyone, Tom stole the money. (= As he was not seen by anyone, Tom stole the money.) 由于没被人看见，汤姆偷了钱。（原因状语）

E. 作让步状语

过去分词作让步状语时相当于让步状语从句，此时一般前置，多表示一个先于谓语的被动行为，其前通常可用连词 though, although, even if/though, whether ... or 等引导。

Though warned of danger (= Though he was warned of ...), he still went skating on the thin ice. 尽管警告有危险，他仍然在薄冰上滑冰。

Her spirits, *though crushed* (= though it was crushed), was not broken. 她的精神，虽然受到挫折，但并没有崩溃。

Even if invited (= Even if she is invited), she won't go. 即使请她，她也不会去。

（3）过去分词的被动语态

在表示一个被动动作时，如果这个动作是现在正在进行的，或与句中谓语动词所表示的动作同时发生，就可以用现在分词一般式被动语态来表示。过去分词一般式被动语态则通常表示一个先于谓语的被动行为，在句中可作定语、状语、宾语补足语等。

① 作宾语补足语

She saw the wounded man *being carried* into the hospital. 她看见那位受伤的男人正被抬进医院。（动作正在进行）

She saw the wounded man *carried* into the hospital. 她看见那位受伤的男人被抬进医院了。（动作已完成）

He found himself *being followed* by a wolf. 他发现自己正被一条狼跟着。（动作正在进行）

He found himself *followed* by a wolf. 他发现自己被一条狼跟着了。（动作已完成）

② 作定语

The house *built* (= that was built) is a big project. 施工的那幢房子是一项很大的工程。

The play *put on* (= which was put on) *by the first year students* was very good. 一年级学生演的那个剧很好。

③ 作状语

Surrounded (= As the enemy troops were surrounded), the enemy troops were forced to surrender. 敌军被包围了，结果被迫投降。

When turned on (= When the radio is turned on), the radio still does not work. 打开之后，收音机仍然没有声音。

（4）过去分词的否定式

过去分词的否定式是在过去分词前加 not 而成，在句中主要作状语。

Not given careful consideration (= Since the work is not given ...), the work can not be easily completed. 由于考虑不周，这工作不易完成。

Not driven carefully (= If the car is not driven carefully), the car can not last a long time. 这辆车如果驾驶得不细心，不可能用很长时间。

（5）过去分词独立结构

过去分词有时可以在其前用名词或代词来表明分词的动作由谁执行，即分词的逻辑主语。但这些名词或代词不是句子的主语,这种结构称为独立结构(Absolute Construction)。它在句中作状语,表示时间、原因、条件、方式、伴随、结果等,其位置在句首或句末均可。

① 作时间状语

All our savings gone (= After all our savings was gone),we began looking for jobs. 积蓄都用光了之后,我们开始找工作。

Her tea finished (= When her tea was finished),she went on with her work. 喝过茶,她继续工作。

② 作原因状语

Their strength exhausted (= Because their strength was exhausted),they sank down one by one. 他们筋疲力尽,一个接一个地倒下了。

His leg badly hurt (= Since his leg was badly hurt),he had to stay in bed. 他腿受重伤,只能卧床。

③ 作条件状语

He will come *if asked* (= if he is asked). 若受到邀请,他会来的。

Given good health (= If I am given good health),I hope to finish the work this year. 如果身体好,我希望今年完成这份工作。

④ 作方式、伴随状语

He sat silently,*eyes closed* (= and eyes were closed). 他静静地坐着,双目紧闭。

Mr. Lei walked along the street,*lost in thought* (= and he was lost in thought). 雷先生漫步街头,沉浸在思索中。

⑤ 作结果状语

It rained and rained,*many houses washed out* (= so that many houses were washed out). 雨不断地下,许多房屋被雨水冲走。

They went to work early,*the task finished ahead of time* (= so that the task was finished ahead of time). 他们早早地去工作,任务被提前完成了。

(6) "with/without + 名词/(宾格)代词 + 过去分词"的独立结构

与现在分词独立结构一样,过去分词独立结构中的逻辑主语前有时也可以加 with 或 without,在这种结构中,过去分词多表示一个先于谓语动词或与谓语动词同时发生的被动行为。在句中作方式、伴随、时间、条件、原因状语等。

The girl listened,*with her head bent slightly forward* (= and her head was bent slightly forward). 姑娘听着,头稍稍探向前。(伴随)

They travelled together for two days *without a single word spoken* (= and no word was spoken). 他们一起旅游了两天,一句话也没说过。(方式)

They filed downstairs *with the job finished* (= when the job was finished). 活干完后,他们鱼贯而行地下楼去了。(时间)

With no reason given (= If no reason was given),such inquiry was impermissible. 不说明理由,这种查询是不允许的。(条件)

Without any grain left in the house (= Since there wasn't any grain left in the house),he had to go begging. 家里没有一粒粮,他只好出去乞讨。(原因)

(7) 现在分词(短语)与过去分词(短语)的比较

现在分词(短语)与过去分词(短语)的区别主要表现在语态和时间上。在语态上,现在分词(除被动式外)表示主动意思,过去分词表示被动意思。在时间上,现在分词表示动作正在进行,过去分词则表示动作的完成。

① **在语态上**

The audience was *bored*. 观众们都感觉烦了。(被动)
The play was *boring*. 这戏令人厌烦。(主动)
The workers soon became *tired*. 工人们很快就感到累了。(被动)
The work was *tiring*. 这工作挺累人的。(主动)

② **在时间上**

the *rising* sun 正在升起的太阳　　　　a *moving* story 令人感动的故事
the *risen* sun 升起了的太阳　　　　　a *moved* audience 受感动的观众
boiling water 沸腾着的水　　　　　　the *changing* world 变化着的世界
boiled water 煮沸了的水　　　　　　the *changed* world 已经起变化的世界
fading flowers 正在凋谢的花　　　　*developing* countries 发展中国家
faded flowers 凋谢了的花　　　　　*developed* countries 发达国家
exciting news 令人振奋的消息　　　a *boring* speech 令人乏味的演讲
an *excited* audience 感觉兴奋的观众　a *bored* traveler 感觉厌倦的旅行

A. 过去分词作前置定语既可以表示已完成的被动动作,也可以表示已完成的主动动作。不管是及物动词还是不及物动词,凡是"已经完成了的"主动动作或被动动作,作前置定语时一律用过去分词,而不用现在分词的被动式,原则上语态服从时态。

主动动作(已完成)　　　　　　　　　　被动动作(已完成)
an *escaped* prisoner 逃犯　　　　　　*smoken* fish 熏鱼
a *retired* general 退休的将军　　　　*armed* forces 武装部队
departed relatives 离去的亲人　　　　*canned* food 罐头食品
a *moved* audience 受感动的观众(正)　a *broken* car 一辆破汽车(正)
a *being moved* audience(误)　　　　a *being broken* car(误)

B. 有些作前置定语的过去分词只表示主动意义,没有"已完成"这种含义,这些过去分词已经成为完全形容词。

a *practiced* man = a man skilled through practice　技术娴熟的人
a *professed* friend = a man who professed to be a friend　一个自称是朋友的人
a *contented* man = a man who contents himself with what he has　一个知足的人
an *experienced* woman = a woman who has the right kind of experience　有经验的女人
the *cultivated* people = the people having good education and manners　有修养的人

C. 有些作前置定语的过去分词不表示动作的完成与否,只表示被动这一概念。

a *man-made* satellite 人造卫星　　　a *guided* missile 导弹
a *so-called* professor 所谓的教授　　the *interested* party 有利害关系的一方

(8) 无依着过去分词结构

如前所述,当过去分词短语在句中作状语且不带有自己的逻辑主语时,通常句子的主语就是过去分词的逻辑主语。

Exhausted, the children fell asleep at once. 孩子们由于过度疲劳立即就入睡了。(the children 是 exhausted 的逻辑主语)

但是也有例外,有时过去分词短语在句中找不到自己的逻辑主语,而是依着在不应该依着的词语上,这就是"无依着过去分词结构"。我们认为,只要在一定的上下文中不引起歧义或语义混乱的情况下,"无依着分词"是可以接受的。在下列情况下会出现"无依着分词"现象：

① 当过去分词的逻辑主语未明确列出，但从上下文中可理解其逻辑主语是 we，you，one 等泛指人的词语时，"无依着分词"是可以接受的。

Caught in a traffic jam (= If you are caught …)，it is easy to lose patience. 如遇上交通拥挤，就容易着急。

When depressed (= When one is depressed)，a new hat will make a woman feel happier. 感到沮丧时，一顶新帽子会使女人感到快乐。

② 过去分词的逻辑主语是主句的其他成分或通过上下文体现出来时，"无依着分词"也是可以接受的。

Painted white (= Since the house was painted …)，we like *the house* better.（由于房子）被漆成了白色，我们更喜欢它了。

Tied to a post (= When the boat was tied to …)，the sea was tossing *the boat* up and down.（船）被拴在一根桩上时，海浪打得船不停地上下颠簸摇摆。

Pinned to the door by a knife (Since the notice was pinned …)，the man saw *a notice*.（由于一张通告）被一把刀子钉在门上，那人看见了一张通告。

③ 另外，在报刊和科技英语中，由于报刊、科技语体通常避免使用人称主语，所以也会出现一些"无依着过去分词"，但比"无依着现在分词"出现得要少些。

Hated and persecuted by all (= Since they were hated and persecuted …)，the reader feels sympathy for *them*.（由于他们）被大家痛恨和困扰，那位读者同情他们。

第 7 章　动 名 词

7.1　动名词概述

动名词(Gerund)也是动词的一种非限定形式,由动词原形加-ing 构成,与现在分词同形。动名词兼有动词和名词的特征和作用,其名词特征表现在可作主语、宾语、表语、同位语、定语、宾语补足语等,其动词特征表现在可以带宾语、状语等。

7.2　动名词的形式

形式	主动式	被动式	否定式
一般式	doing	being done	not doing/not being done
完成式	having done	having been done	not having done/not having been done

7.3　名词性质的动名词

动名词的名词性质就是指动名词起名词一样的作用,在句中可起名词一样的句法功能。

(1) 作主语

Eating too much makes one fat. 吃太多会使人发胖。
Saying is easier than doing. 说比做容易。
Being late is an unforgivable sin here. 迟到在这里是一种不可原谅的严重过错。
Being lost can be a terrifying experience. 迷路有时会很可怕。

① 用 it 作先行主语,真主语动名词置后
有时可用先行词 it 作形式主语,而把动名词主语放到句子后面。充当表语的名词和形容词通常是:use, pity, bore, good, time, fun, hard, funny, nice, odd, worth, difficult, worthwhile, interesting, tiring, better, foolish, enjoyable, pointless, crazy, terrible 等。
It is no use *crying over spilt milk*. 覆水难收。
It's a wonder *meeting you here*. 在这里碰到你真是奇迹。
It's pointless *arguing about it*. 争辩这事没意义。
It's tiring *sitting there from morning till night*. 从早到晚坐在那里很累人。

② there is + no + 动名词
这结构相当于 it is impossible to do sth. ,表示"没法……"。
There is no *persuading her*. 没法劝说她。
There is no *hiding of evil* but not to do it. 要人不知,除非己莫为。

(2) 作表语

Her hobby is *singing*. 她的爱好是唱歌。
Her regret is *having done so much for him and being abandoned by him*. 她遗憾的是,曾为他奉献了那么多,而却被他抛弃了。
His trouble is *having tried every means and being still poor*. 他的麻烦是,一切办法都试过了,却依然贫穷。
I'm *for doing nothing* till the police arrive. 我主张在警察到来之前不要采取任何行动。

(3) 作宾语

① 直接作及物动词的宾语

有很多动词后面跟动名词(短语)作宾语。
Viv avoids *giving her any personal information*. 维维拒绝告诉她的任何个人情况。
He denied *taking the key*. 他否认拿了那把钥匙。
I hate *lying and cheating*. 我讨厌撒谎欺骗。
He has given up *playing football*. 他现在不踢足球了。

像 avoid, deny, hate, give up 等的动词还有 admit, anticipate, allow, acknowledge, approve, bar, ban, complete, consider, confirm, delay, detest, despise, enjoy, escape, excuse, envision, ensure, encourage, fancy, finish, forgive, favour, facilitate, foresee, guarantee, hinder, imagine, involve, imply, keep, justify, loathe, mind, miss, omit, overlook, pardon, postpone, permit, practise, prevent, propose, picture, predict, prohibit, recall, resent, recollect, resist, reject, risk, recommend, stand, suggest, shrink, substantiate, shun, visualize 以及大量的动介型结构短语动词,如 feel like, give up, leave off, look forward to, object to, put off 等。

但在 advise, allow, permit, recommend 后,如果提到有关的人,可用动词不定式。
He advised *me to leave* right now. 他劝我马上就离开。
They don't allow *us to park* here. 他们不许我们在这里停车。

A. 有些及物动词可跟动名词也可跟动词不定式作宾语,但动名词作宾语表示一般的、习惯的、抽象的、经常性的行为;不定式表示特殊的、具体的、一次性的行为。常用的这类动词有:

a. 表示"喜爱"、"厌恶"、"恐惧"之类的词 like, love, prefer, dislike, dread, fear, hate, loathe 等
I'd hate *to leave/leaving you* like that. 我真不愿意这样离开你。
They preferred *to watch/watching TV*. 他们喜欢看电视。
She loves *to have/having lots of children round her*. 她喜欢周围有许多孩子。

b. 表示"容忍"之类的词 bear, endure, stand 等
He can't bear *to be/being criticized*. 他忍受不了别人的批评。
I can't stand *to be/being kept waiting*. 我忍受不了让我久等。

c. 表示"继续"、"开始"、"停止"、"打算"之类的词 continue, start, begin, cease, intend 等
The band began *to play/playing*. 乐队开始演奏。
They ceased *to talk/talking* and I began reading. 他们停止了交谈,我开始看书。
She intended *to come/coming back soon*. 她打算不久就回来。

但有时有点细微的差别,在 begin, start, cease 后,不定式表示情况发生了变化,而动名词则表示有意识地开始或停止。
Suddenly it started *to snow*. 天突然下起雪来。
Mike began *to cry*. 迈克哭了起来。

The matter has ceased *to be a mystery to her*. 这事对她不再是个谜。

Then little boy started *singing*. 那小男孩开始唱歌。

She began *making preparations for the final examination*. 她开始做期末考试的准备。

They have ceased *making cars*. 他们已停止生产轿车。

Note：如果 begin, start 用于进行时态时，其后不宜再用动名词，以避免-ing 形式的重复。

He is beginning to see his mistakes. 他开始认识到自己的错误。

It's starting to rain. 天开始下起雨来。

B. 有些及物动词可以用动名词作宾语，也可以用不定式作宾语，但两者意思不同。这类词主要有 chance, can't help, go on, forget, learn, leave off, mean, propose, regret, remember, stop, try, dread 等。试比较：

Should we chance *getting home* before it snows? 我们该不该碰碰运气看下雪前能否到家？（chance doing sth 表示碰碰运气、冒险试试）

We chanced *to be out* when he called. 他来拜访时，碰巧我们不在家。（chance to do sth 表示碰巧做某事）

I can't help *laughing*. 我不禁笑了起来。（can't help doing sth 表示禁不住做某事）

I can't help *to clean the place up*. 我不能帮助打扫这地方。（can't help to do sth 表示不能帮助做某事）

They went on *talking*. 他们继续谈着。（go on doing sth 表示继续原来所做的事）

They went on *to talk about other matters*. 他们接着又谈别的事情。（不定式是目的状语，表示接着做另一件事）

I forget *telling her about it* (= that I told her). 我忘记了此事已经告诉过她。（动名词表示过去的动作，事情已做过，但忘了）

I forget *to tell her about it*. 我忘记将此事告诉她。（不定式表示将来的动作，事情还没做）

He has learned *swimming*. 他学过游泳。（learn doing sth 表示学习做某事，不一定学会）

He has learned *to swim*. 他已学会游泳。（learn to do sth 表示学会做某事）

She has left off *working*. 她停止了工作。（leave off doing sth 表示停止做某事）

That day she left off *to work earlier than usual*. 那天她离家去上班比平时早。（leave off to do sth 表示离开某地去做某事，不定式充当目的状语）

His words mean *refusing us*. 他的话意味着拒绝我们。（mean doing sth 表示意味着）

I meant *to call on you*. But I was so busy. 我打算/本想去拜访你。但是我太忙了。（mean to do sth 表示打算/本想做某事）

She proposes *catching the early train*. 她建议赶早班火车。（propose doing sth 表示建议做某事）

She proposes *to catch the early train*. 她打算/要去赶早班火车。（propose to do sth 表示打算/要做某事）

I regret *missing the film*. 我懊悔没有看上那部电影。（动名词 missing 指过去）

I regret *to say* that I can't come. 我很抱歉，不能来了。（不定式 to say 指现在）

I remember *locking the door*. 我记得把门锁上了。（locking 表示已完成的动作）

Remember *to lock the door*. 记住要锁门。（to lock 表示未完成的动作）

He stopped *smoking* last week. 他上星期戒了烟。（stop doing sth 表示停止做某事，smoking 充当 stopped 的宾语）

He stopped *to smoke*. 他停下来吸烟。（stop to do sth 表示停下正做的事以便做另一事，不定式 to smoke 充当目的状语）

Try *knocking at the back door* if nobody hears you at the front door. 前门如没人答应，就敲后门试试看。（try doing sth 表示试试某种做法是否行得通）

Try *to get some sleep*. 设法去睡一会儿吧。（try to do sth 表示努力/设法去做某事）

I dread *to think* what might happen to you all alone in the big city. 我不敢想象你一个人在大城市里会发生

什么事情。(dread to do sth 表示不敢想象做某事)

I always *dreaded being asked questions* by my teacher in class. 我总是害怕在课堂上被我的老师提问。(dread doing sth 表示使人害怕做某事)

② 作介词宾语

A. 有许多"动词+介词"构成的短语动词后可以跟动名词作介词宾语。

He insisted on *writing at once*. 他坚持马上就写。

True happiness consists in *being contented with oneself*. 真正的幸福在于知足。

Robbie couldn't keep from *laughing*. 罗比禁不住笑了起来。

常见的这类短语动词有:go on, get through, insist on, persist in, keep on, think of, care for, give up, put off, dream of, feel like, aim at, set about, succeed in, abstain from, apologize for, believe in, worry about, take to, refrain from, complain about, resort to, object to, look forward to, pay attention to 等。

B. 有不少"be+形容词+介词"的结构后也常可用动名词作介词宾语。

I was afraid of *making them uneasy*. 我怕使他们感到不安。

She is desirous of *winning the match*. 她渴望赢这场比赛。

She is awfully good at *looking after people*. 她很会照顾人。

He was not accustomed to *associating with such people*. 他不习惯于和这类人来往。

常见的这类短语形容词有:be aware of, be apprehensive of, be apologetic for, be confident of, be equal to, be exact in, be fond of, be guilty of, be fearful of, be hopeful of, be awkward at, be intent on, be suitable for, be unconscious of, be right in, be wrong in, be desirous of, be interested in, be afraid of, be keen on, be angry about, be excited at, be surprised at, be responsible for, be tired of, be accustomed to, be capable of, be used to, be sick of, be fed up with 等。

C. 在 How about, What about 后也常用动名词作介词宾语。

How about *coming with us to the club*? 和我们一道去俱乐部如何?

How about *going for a walk after supper*? 晚饭后去散步怎么样?

What about *having a glass of beer*? 来杯啤酒如何?

Note:动名词作介词宾语时,有时介词可以省去,特别是在美语中。

Do you have any difficulty (in) understanding spoken English? 在理解英语口语方面你有困难吗?

What's the use (of) *talking with him*? 跟他谈有什么用?

She is late (in) *coming*. 她来迟了。

Tom is busy (in) *writing a report*. 汤姆正忙于写报告。

We lost no time (in) *carrying out the plan*. 我们抓紧时间执行这个计划。

He made a living (by) *selling newspapers*. 他以卖报为生。

We must prevent the trouble (from) *spreading*. 我们必须防止麻烦变大。

I am through (with) *asking questions*. 我要问的问题问完了。

They took turns (at) *playing host*. 他们轮流做东。

③ it 作形式宾语,动名词作真宾语

当动名词(短语)作宾语且后跟宾语补足语时,要用 it 作形式宾语,将作宾语的动名词(短语)移至宾语补足语之后。

I think it useless *learning a theory without practice*. 我认为学习理论而不实践是没有用的。

We took it our duty *helping her to pass her English examination*. 我们认为帮她通过英语考试是我们的义务。

(4) 作宾语补足语

在很少数情况下动名词才用作宾语补足语,只是此时的动名词相当于名词。
We term it *walking on two legs*. 我们称这为"两条腿走路"。
People call that *killing two birds with one stone*. 人们称那为一箭双雕。

(5) 作同位语

This is my recreation, *reading novels*. 这就是我的娱乐——看小说。
I krow this is his only hobby, *making model airplanes*. 我知道这是他的唯一爱好——做模型飞机。

(6) 作定语

动名词作前置定语时,说明它所修饰的名词的用处及与之有关的动作,只能单独使用,不能带宾语或状语。

The *turning* speed of the new machine is much higher than that of the old one. 这台新机器的转速比那台旧的快得多。
Their *working* plan will be made next week. 他们的工作计划将于下周制订出来。

动名词作定语修饰名词,两者结合即构成复合名词。这类复合名词很多,常见的有:

sleeping bag 睡袋	dining car 餐车
running track 跑道	sleeping pill 安眠药片
waiting room 候车室	parking lot 停车场
singing competition 歌咏比赛	swimming pool 游泳池
cooking oil 食用油	flying suit 飞行服
hearing aid 助听器	dressing table 梳妆台
watering can 洒水壶	drinking water 饮用水
operating room 手术室	driving licence 驾驶证
walking stick 手杖	racing car 赛车
reading room 阅览室	milking machine 挤奶器
washing machine 洗衣机	opening speech 开幕词
dancing hall 舞厅	reading material 阅读材料
building material 建筑材料	diving board 跳板
closing speech 闭幕词	working hours 工作时间

动名词作定语则表示其修饰的名词性质,二者在逻辑上无主谓关系,而现在分词与其所修饰的名词在逻辑上具有主谓关系。

动名词作后置定语时,必须与其前边的介词一起构成短语作定语。这时的动名词可以带有自己的宾语。这种介词短语是一种名词性定语,表示抽象概念,并不强调动作,而且时间概念也不强。

His method *of organizing the work* is commendable. 他组织这项工作的办法值得称赞。
She hasn't much experience *in running factories*. 她没有多少管理工厂的经验。
She couldn't invent a reason *for not going*. 她编造不出不去的理由。
I had the chance *of visiting Beijing*. 我有机会访问北京。
He had no intention *of defending himself*. 他无心为自己辩护。
It's a device *for opening bottles*. 这是一种开瓶装置。

这类介词短语作定语修饰的名词,常见的有:way (of), art (of), chance (of), opportunity (of), hope (of), process (of), possibility (of), importance (of), necessity (of), intention (of), honour (of), means (of), right (of), surprise (at), astonishment (at), excuse (for), apology (for), plan (for), experience (in), skill (in), practice (of), choice (of), custom(of), objection (of), aptitude (for), reason (of), time (for), desire (of), patience (in)等。

这类名词可以接"介词+动名词",也可以接动词不定式,意义上没有区别。

reason of doing sth	capacity of doing sth
reason to do sth	capacity to do sth
time for doing sth	mood of doing sth
time to do sth	mood to do sth
patience in doing sth	way of doing sth
patience to do sth	way to do sth
desire of doing sth	freedom in doing sth
desire to do sth	freedom to do sth
objection of doing sth	necessity of doing sth
objection to do sth	necessity to do sth
chance of doing sth	choice of doing sth
chance to do sth	choice to do sth
honour of doing sth	claim of doing sth
honour to do sth	claim to do sth

Notes：A. 在名词 refusal, promise, effort, desire, attempt, ability, ambition, resolution, tendency, determination, failure 等后不可接"of+动名词",但可以接不定式结构。

He was filled with ambition to become famous. 他一心想成名。（正确）

He was filled with ambition of becoming famous. （错误）

They showed a desire to improve relations. 他们表现出改善关系的愿望。（正确）

They showed a desire of improving relations. （错误）

B. 但在名词 purpose, method, idea, habit 等后只能接"of+动名词",不可接不定式结构。

I have the habit of resting after lunch. 我有午饭后休息一下的习惯。（正确）

I have the habit to rest after lunch. （错误）

He came to Beijing for the purpose of seeing his family. 他来北京是为了探亲。（正确）

He came to Beijing for the purpose to see his family. （错误）

7.4 动名词的动词性质

所谓的动名词的动词性质是有限的。它可带宾语,可有表语和状语,但不可直接作句子的谓语。

(1) 后面可接宾语

After *reading the novel* I went to bed. 看完小说,我上床睡觉了。

Most of the children like *playing baseball*. 大多数小孩喜欢打棒球。

At the meeting he stressed the importance of *defeating their competitors*. 会上他强调了击败竞争对手的重要性。

She was grateful for *my attending her graduation*. 她感谢我来参加她的毕业典礼。

(2) 后面可接表语

He dreamed of *becoming a doctor*. 他梦想当一名医生。

Being idle is the cause of his failure. 懒惰是他失败的原因。

Instead of *becoming cheerful*, he became rather sad. 他没变得快乐，反而更加忧愁。

(3) 动名词(短语)可带状语

Getting up early is considered a good habit. 早起被认为是一种好习惯。
Would you mind *speaking more slowly*? 你是否可以说得慢一点？
I enjoyed *swimming in the lake*. 我喜欢在湖里游泳。

此外，动名词的动词特征还表现在它的语态和时态变化上。

Respecting others means *being respected*. 尊重他人就是尊重自己。(被动式)
She was not sure of *having done anything wrong*. 她不敢肯定是否做过什么错事。(完成式)

Note：虽然动名词本身不能作状语，但放在介词后就可以起到状语作用，表示时间、原因、目的、让步、方式、否定等。

On learning that Tom had passed his examination, I rang him up. 获悉汤姆通过考试，我立即给他打了个电话。(时间状语)
He had not bought a new suit *since coming to Oxford*. 来牛津之后他没买过一件新衣服。(时间状语)
The little girl was praised *for doing her homework well*. 那个小女孩因作业做得好而受到表扬。(原因状语)
He was charged *with assaulting a policeman*. 他被控袭击警察。(原因状语)
She dissuaded me *from buying it*. 她劝我不要买那东西。(目的状语)
We went to town *for sightseeing*. 我们进城去游览。(目的状语)
Without waiting for any reply, he left the room. 他不等答复就离开了房间。(方式状语)
He earned his living *by writing novels*. 他以写小说谋生。(方式状语)
With all his boasting, Henry achieved very little. 尽管亨利大吹大擂，但他取得的进步很小。(让步状语)
In spite of his having lied to me, I fell for his story. 尽管他对我说了谎，我还听信他的故事。(让步状语)
Instead of going to New York, we got off at Boston. 我们没去纽约，而是在波士顿下了车。(否定状语)
She once did it *without being caught*. 有一次她干了这事，却没有被发现。(否定状语)
I took great pleasure *in helping her*. 我把帮助她当作最大的乐趣。(范围状语)
I congratulated her *on winning the competition*. 我祝贺她赢得比赛。(范围状语)

7.5 动名词的时、体、态

(1) 动名词的一般式

动名词的一般式从属于句中谓语动词的时态，它所表示的动作与谓语动词所表示的动作同时发生或在其后发生或在之前发生。

I am interested in *collecting stamps*. 我对集邮感兴趣。(同时)
She is proud of *being beautiful*. 她以自己的美丽为荣。(同时)
I have no doubt of *her passing the exam*. 我相信她会通过考试。(以后)
Her success will depend on *her working harder and being assisted by friends*. 她的成功取决于自身更努力和朋友们的帮助。(以后)

在有些明确表示时间的动词和介词 after, on, upon, for 之后，常用一般式代替完成式，表示动名词动作发生在谓语动作之前。

Thank you *for giving us so much help*. 感谢你给了我们这么多的帮助。(之前)
On finding that the engine was working badly, the pilot was obliged to land. 飞机驾驶员一发现引擎不灵就被迫降落。(之前)

(2) 动名词完成式

动名词完成式所表示的动作皆发生在谓语动词所表示的动作之前,可作谓语动词的宾语,也可作介词的宾语。

I could not recall *having heard anyone say that before*. 我不记得以前听人说过这话。
Allan repented *having shot the bird*. 阿伦悔不该射死那只鸟。
I accused her of *having broken her word*. 我指责她不守信用。
After *having had some practice*, he decided to try again. 经过一番练习,他决定再试一次。

Note: 由于有时动名词的一般式与完成式均可表发生在谓语动词前的动作,故两者往往意思相同。但前者显然比较简洁。例如,I remember locking the door. (我记得把门锁上了)显然较 I remember having locked the door. 简洁。

(3) 动名词一般式用于被动式

当动名词的逻辑主语是行为的承受者时,用动名词的被动式。同动名词的一般式一样,动名词一般式被动式所表示的动作与谓语动词所表示的动作同时发生或在其后发生或在之前发生。

He hates *being interrupted*. 他不愿意被人打断。(同时)
I remembered *being taken to Paris* as a child. 我记得小时候曾被带到巴黎。(之前)
He hopes to get out without *being seen next time*. 他希望下次不被人看见溜出来。(以后)

(4) 动名词完成式用于被动式

动名词完成式被动式所表示的动作皆发生在谓语动词所表示的动作之前,可作谓语动词的宾语,也可作介词的宾语。

I don't mind *having been written like this*. 我不介意被描写成这样。
I remember *having been told* that she was the best student in class. 我记得曾有人告诉我她是班里最好的学生。

Notes: ①在 want, need, require, deserve, merit, bear/stand, be past/beyond, be worth, demand 等之后的动名词,其主动形式表示被动意义,意义与动词不定式被动式一样。

My car *wants repairing* (= to be repaired). 我的车需要修理。
My son's room *needs white washing* (= to be white washed). 我儿子的房间需要粉刷。
The trees *require trimming* (= to be trimmed). 树木需要修剪。
Such hardships *are beyond/past bearing* (= being borne). 这样的苦是不堪忍受的。
His language won't *bear repeating* (= to be repeated). 他的用语不宜/不堪重复。
The book *is worth reading* (= is worthy to be read/worthy of being read). 这本书值得看。
The little boy *deserves/merits praising* (= to be praised). 这小男孩应该受到表扬。
That matter *demands looking into* (= to be looked into). 那件事需要调查。

② stand, bear, be past 后亦可用动名词被动式。

His language won't *bear being repeated*. 他的用语不宜/不堪重复。
She can't s*tand being teased* with questions. 她不能容忍别人用问题来取笑她。
The watch *is past being repaired*. 这块表已经无法修了。

③ 如果存在一个与-ing 形式意思相同的名词,通常要选用名词。

Tom deserved punishment (= to be punished). 汤姆应该受到处罚。(正确)
Tom deserved punishing. (错误)

7.6　动名词的否定式

动名词的否定式由 not 或 never 加动名词(被动态)构成。

Trying without success is better than *not trying at all*. 尝试没有成功也比不尝试好。
Jane hated herself for *not having worked hard*. 简悔恨自己没有用功。
He was nervous from *having never before spoken in public*. 他由于从未做过公开演讲而感到紧张。
She feels sorry for *not being admitted into the university*. 她为未被大学录取而感到难过。
He was angry about *not having been invited*. 他因没有受到邀请而生气。
He prided himself on *having never been beaten in chess*. 他为弈棋上从未被击败而自豪。

7.7　动名词的复合结构

一般情况下,动名词的逻辑主语为谓语动词的主语。如果动名词动作的发出者不是谓语动词的主语时,则需要有自己的逻辑主语。这种物主代词/代词宾格或名词所有格/名词通格加动名词就构成了动名词的复合结构。这种结构在句中可作主语、表语、宾语、介词宾语。动名词复合结构使用的一般规则如下:

(1) 逻辑主语是有生命的名词,作主语时,必须用名词或代词所有格;用 it 作形式主语时,动名词的逻辑主句通常用所有格,有时也可以用主格形式。作宾语/介宾时,逻辑主语可用所有格,也可用名词通格或代词宾格。

The student's knowing English well helps him in learning French. 这位学生通晓英语对他学法语很有帮助。(主语)
His leaving is a great loss. 他的离开是一个很大的损失。(主语)
It's no good *your talking with* your parents like that. 你那样跟你父母讲话没有好处。(形式主语)
It's hardly possible *we starting* so early. 我们这次早出发几乎是不可能的。(形式主语)
Do you mind *my (me) smoking* here? 你介意我在这里抽烟吗?(宾语)
He can not permit *his daughter and son being insulted*. 他不许他女儿和儿子受到侮辱。(宾语)
They insist on *Mary's (Mary) going* there with them. 他们坚持要玛丽跟他们一起去那儿。(介词宾语)
I am astonished at *Jane (Jane's) suddenly becoming* rich. 我对简突然富起来感到吃惊。(介词宾语)

(2) 逻辑主语是无生命名词或抽象概念名词时,只用通格。

Do you hear *the rain pattering* on the roof? 你听见雨点打在屋顶上了吗?(无生命)
He is opposed to the idea of *money being* everything. 他反对金钱万能的观点。(无生命)

(3) 逻辑主语是以 s 结尾的名词或是一个以上名词构成的词组,只用通格。

It was quite unexpected *the students finishing* the exam so soon. 学生们这么快就答完考卷,十分出乎意料。(s 结尾)
He can not permit *his daughter and son being insulted*. 他不许他女儿和儿子受到侮辱。(名词词组)

(4) 逻辑主语是数词、指示代词或不定代词 this, that, somebody, someone, nobody, none, anybody, anyone 时,只用通格。

In spite of *the four telling* the same story, I couldn't believe it. 尽管有四个人在讲述同一个故事,我仍然不相信。(数词)
She was woken up by *somebody shouting* outside. 她被外面喊叫的人吵醒了。(不定代词)
I couldn't imagine *that being* possible. 我无法想象那是可能的。(指示代词)

(5) 动名词复合结构作表语时,其逻辑主语通常用名词所有格或物主代词。

Our sole worry is *Li Ming's relying too much on himself*. 我们唯一担心的就是李明太自信了。(表语)

The reason why I have made much progress is *my having been helped by my friends*. 我取得很大进步的原因是我得到了我朋友们的帮助。(表语)

Notes：① 动名词作宾语/介宾时，其逻辑主语可用所有格，也可用名词通格或代词宾格；而现在分词作宾补时，其逻辑主语只能用宾格或名词通格，不能用所有格。

I saw *him wearing* a red shirt. 我看见他穿着红衬衫。(wearing 是现在分词，him 不可变为 his)

I dislike *him/his wearing* a red shirt. 我讨厌他穿着红衬衫。(wearing 是动名词，其逻辑主语用 him 或 his 均可。)

② 动名词的逻辑主语充当介词 with 的宾语时，其逻辑主语用通格。

He felt lonely with his wife being dead. 由于他妻子已故，他感觉孤独。

③ 动名词复合结构作主语时，如果作逻辑主语的物主代词带有 all，both 作同位语，这时的名词或代词所有格可用主格形式。

He and his younger brother both being sick makes hard work for the rest of the family. 他和他弟弟都病了，这可忙坏了家里其他人。

第8章 宾语(从句)、引语

8.1 宾语

宾语(Object)是及物动词等后表示补充说明的部分;介词后也可带宾语,形容词和形容词短语后也可带宾语。宾语主要由名词及其等同语及其他一些词语担任。

直接宾语是及物动词后表示动作的直接对象或结果的词语。更具体地说,它表示下面一些意义:

(1) 表示动作所及的对象

He like *English*. 他喜欢英语。
What did you do? 你干什么工作?

(2) 表示动作使役的对象

The young lady is walking *the dog*. (= The young lady is leading the dog for a walk.) 那年轻女士在蹓狗。
He stood *the child* on his knees. 他使小孩站在他两膝腿上。(= He made the child stand on his knees.)
The man ran *his horse* up and down. 那个男士让他的马跑来跑去了一会儿。

(3) 表示动作的目的

Mr. Green nodded *his agreement*. 格林先生点头同意。
Rose kissed *good-bye*, then drove off. 罗丝吻别后开车走了。

(4) 表示动作的结果

Professor Chen has written *twelve books*. 陈教授已写了十二本书了。
My wife and I had built *a beautiful house* ourselves. 我和我妻子自己动手建了一个漂亮房子。

(5) 表示事件

The Committee had *an important meeting* yesterday. 委员会昨天开了个重要会议。
Miss Li and Mrs. White are having *an argument*. 李小姐跟怀特太太在争吵。

(6) 表示动作的内容

What did you see in the park? 你在公园里看到了什么?
She asked *some questions* at the meeting. 她在会上问了些问题。

(7) 表示动作的处所

The captain walked *the deck*. 船长走过甲板。
Peter swam *the river* easily. 彼得不费劲地游过了那条河。
Note:第一句中的 walk 作及物动词用,意为"走过,行过",而后面的 deck 是地点名词。同样,第二句中的 swim 也是及物动词,作"游泳,游过"讲,后面的 river 当然是处所名词。

(8) 表示动作的终及

We are determined to climb *the peak of science and technology*. 我们决心攀登科技顶峰。

Finally Mr. Yangs reached *the Golden Summit of Mount Emei* on the morning of July 21, 1992. 杨先生一家终于在 1992 年的清晨登上了峨眉山的金顶。

(9) 表示与动作有关的人或物

We should respect the *grey hairs*. (= We should respect the people with grey hairs) 我们应当尊敬长者。

Can you read *Mark Twin*? 你能看懂马克·吐温所写的书吗?(Can you read Mark Twin's works?)

(10) 表示实施动作的工具

He is smoking *a pipe*. 他在抽烟斗。

Mr. White stuck *an awl* through the leather. 怀特先生用钻子钻皮革。

(11) 表示动作的执行者

The hotel sleeps 500 people. 那家旅馆可住 500 人。

The hall will seat 1,000 people. 那礼堂能坐 1,000 人。

(12) 表示动作的量度

Mr. Green could not sleep *a wink* that night. 格林先生那晚失眠。

The house costs *more than one million dollars*. 这房子价值一百多万美元。

8.2 宾语从句

(1) 连接宾语从句的连词

连接宾语从句的连词有单纯连词、连接代词、连接限定词和连接副词。

① 用单纯连词连接

这些从属连词有 that, whether (... or), if, but (that), lest 等,that 在口语中常省去。

I thought (that) you could speak French. 我以为你能讲法语。

You must decide whether you are going or staying. 你必须决定是走还是留下。

Rose asked if Henry was working hard. 罗丝问亨利工作是否卖力。

I don't doubt but (that) he is an honest man. 我不怀疑他是个诚实的人。

Jim fears lest Mary (should) decide to leave him. 吉姆害怕唯恐玛丽决定离开他。

Notes: A. 连词 that, whether (... or) 和 lest 还可以引出形容词宾语从句。

He is hopeful *that* she will go there at once. 他满怀希望她会马上去那里。

I'm not sure whether John wrote the article, or Tom. 我不能肯定是约翰写了那篇文章,还是汤姆写的。

She is afraid lest/that the gold watch should be stolen. 她担心那块金表被盗。

B. whether 和 that 还可连接少数几个介词的宾语从句。

Mr. White has no special fault except (that) he smokes too much. 怀特先生除抽烟太多外别无其他特别的缺点。

It all depends on *whether* Peter will support us. 这全取决于彼得是否支持我们。

C. 连词 whether 和 if 均可引出宾语从句,意思上没区别,但 if 更常用。要注意的是,whether 后可加 or not, if 后不可以,但 whether/if … or not 又是可以的。

She asked me *whether/if* I had time that afternoon. 她问我那天下午是否有空。

I wonder *whether/if* she knows we are here. 我不知道她是否知道我们在这里。

Mrs. Green didn't say whether or not she would go there with you. 格林太太没说她是否跟你一起上那儿去。（句中的 whether 不可换用 if）

Mrs Green didn't say whether/if she would go there with you or not.

D. whether/if 宾语从句可转换成"whether + to do sth"短语,但不能转换成"if + to do sth"短语。

I don't say if (whether) I shall stay here another week. (= I don't say whether to stay here another week) 我没说是否在这儿再待一星期。（正确）

I don't say if to stay here another week. （错误）

② 用连接副词连接

用来连接宾语从句的副词有 how, when, where, why 等。连接副词可以连接动词后的宾语从句,也是可连接介词后的宾语从句和形容词宾语从句。

A. 连接动词后的宾语从句

I'll tell you *why* most of us choose to learn English. 我要告诉你为什么我们多数人决定学英语。

Tell me *when* you'll be back. 告诉我你什么时候回来。

Who knows where he has been these days? 谁知道他这些天上哪儿了?

Let the old worker tell you *how* the new machine had been made by them. 让那位老工人告诉你们这部新机器怎样被他们造出来的。

B. 连接介词宾语从句和形容词宾语从句

We were astonished *at how* old his wife looked. 看到他妻子这样老相我们感到惊讶。

I'm not sure *when* he will get there. 我不好肯定他什么时候到达那里。

C. 用连接代词连接

这些连接代词有 what, which, who(m)等。它们既可连接及物动词后的宾语从句,也可连接介词和形容词后面的宾语从句。

a. 连接及物动词后的宾语从句

I don't care *what* you said at the party. 我不介意你在晚会说的话。

Tom and Jim are twins and most of us can't tell *which* is which. 汤姆和吉姆是双胞胎,我们中大多数人分不清谁是谁。

b. 连接介词和形容词后的宾语从句

Jim will gave the apple to *whoever* wants to eat it. 吉姆要把这苹果给任何想吃的人。

Li Na gave a description of *what* she had seen. 李娜把她所见到的做了描述。

I'm not certain *which* is right and *which* is wrong. 我弄不清哪个对哪个错。

D. 用连接限定词连接

这些连接限定词有 what, which, whose 等。

Tom asked his mother *what* clothes he should wear. 汤姆问他母亲他该穿什么衣服。

I wonder *whose* hat it is. 我不知道这是谁的帽子。

I know which side I should be on. 我知道我该站在那一边。

(2) 不可接 that 从句的动词

ask, refuse, let, like, cause, force, condemn, admire, celebrate, entreat（恳求）, dislike, loathe

（厌恶），overlook（忽视），love，help，take（认为），forgive，behold（看到），bid（命令），hate，hear，see，want 等后不可接 that 引导的宾语从句，但上述某些词可用 it 或 the fact 作为媒介，后跟 that 从句。

He overlooked the fact that he had made another mistake. 他忽视了自己已经犯了另外一个错误。（正确）

He overlooked that he had made another mistake. （错误）

I take it that you should rewrite the paper. 我认为你应该重写论文。（正确）

I take that you should rewrite the paper. （错误）

I admire their winning the match. 我羡慕他们赢得了比赛。（正确）（可接动名词）

I admire that they won the match. （错误）

I want him to come at once. 我想要他立刻来。（正确）（可接宾语＋不定式）

I want that he comes at once. （错误）

（3）不可以 that 从句作直接宾语的动词

有些动词不可以 that 从句作直接宾语，不用于"动词＋间接宾语＋that 从句"结构。常见的有：envy，order，accuse，refuse，impress，forgive，blame，denounce（指责），advise，congratulate 等。

She forgave him for breaking his promise（＝his breaking）. 她原谅他没有信守承诺。（正确）

She forgave him that he had broken his promise. （错误）

He impressed the manager as honest man（＝with his honesty）. 他给经理留下了诚实的印象。（正确）

He impressed the manager that he was an honest man. （错误）

I envy her speaking English so well. 我羡慕她英语讲得好。（正确）

I envy her that she speaks English so well. （错误）

Excuse me for coming late. 对不起，我来迟了。（正确）

Excuse me coming late. （正确）

Excuse me that I come late. （错误）

（4）宾语从句的转换

有些宾语从句可以转换成短语，所表达的意思不变。

① 转换成复合宾语

I noticed that someone was standing at the gate. 我注意到有人站在门口。

→I noticed someone standing at the gate.

I think it is necessary to call him at once. 我认为有必要马上打电话给他。

→I think it necessary to call him at once.

② 转换成"wh-＋不定式"短语

由 wh-词引出的宾语从句常可转换成这些词引导的不定式短语。

She doesn't know whether she should accept or refuse. 她不知道她该接受还是拒绝。

→She doesn't know whether to accept or refuse.

Mary doesn't know what she should do next. 玛丽不知道下一步该干什么。

→Mary doesn't know what to do next.

She can't decide which button she should press. 她决定不了该按哪个键。

→She can't decide which button to press.

③ 转换成 v-ing 分词短语

其分词就是原宾语从句中的谓语动词的原形分词形式。

I cannot recall I said it. 我记不得我说过这话。

→I cannot recall saying it.

Jean denied that he had been there. 琼否认去过那里。

→Jean denied having been there.

We remember that we heard Professor Li spoke on that subject. 我们记得我们听到李教授讲过那个课题。

→ We remember having heard Professor Li spoke on that subject.

④ 转换成其他结构

有时,通过改谓语动词为不及物动词或以同义动词替代原动词等手段,把动词宾语从句和形容词宾语从句转换成其他结构。

She insisted that I should stay there for another week. 她坚持我再在那里面待一个星期。

→ She insisted on me/my staying there for another week.

Peter wished that he would visit London again. 彼得想再游览伦敦。

→ Peter expressed his wish to visit London again.

You may be sure that he is honest. 你可能认为他是诚实的。

→ You may be sure of his honest.

Li Zaina is confident that she will get a copy written by Professor Ma himself. 李在娜确信能得到一本毛教授本人写的拷贝。

→ Li Zaina is confident of getting a copy written by Professor Ma himself.

(5) 宾语从句与主句的时体问题

① 主句现在时或将来时,宾语从句可用任何时态

She says she hates being laughed at. 她说她恨人家取笑她。

I say each of you will be given a hat tomorrow. 我说你们明天每人会有顶帽子。

He will repeat what he said yesterday. 他将把他昨天说的话重复一次。

② 主句过去时,宾语从句要用过去时范畴时态

My uncle told me he would be there soon. 我伯伯告诉过我他很快要到那儿了。

Mary said she had seen the film last week. 玛丽说她上星期看过那部电影了。

③ 如果宾语从句表达的是客观真理或不能改变的客观事实,那也可用在主句是过去的句子里。

Rose's mother told her the earth *is* round. 罗丝的母亲告诉她地球是圆的。

Our teacher said that the Yellow River *is* the second longest river in China. 我们老师说黄河是中国第二条最长的河流。

Did he say that the train *leaves* at 15:30? 你是说火车将于 15:30 开出吗?

8.3 引语

我们在引述某人的话时,一般采取两种形式:一种是直接把他的话表达出来,这些话要用引号括出来,这叫直接引语(Direct Speech);另一种是间接地把说话人的话表达出来,即说话人用自己的话把原说话人的话说出来,这时就不用引号,这种表达叫间接引语(Indirect Speech)。这种间接引语和直接引语,除部分祈使句间接引语外,基本上属主句和宾语从句一类内容。不论那类句子,直接引语变为间接引语时都涉及时、体形式、人称代词、限定词、表示时间或地点的词语以及语序等要做相应调整变化方面的问题。

(1) 词语变化

	在直接引语中	在间接引语中
指示代词	this	that
	these	those
表示时间的词语	now	then
	today	that day
	this week (month, etc.)	that week (month, etc.)
	yesterday	the day before
	last week (month, etc.)	the week (month, etc.) before
	three days (a year, etc.) ago	three days (a year, etc.) before
	tomorrow	the next (following) day
	next week (month, etc.)	the next (following) week (month, etc.)
地点副词	here	there
动词	come	go
	say to me (him, etc.)	tell me (him, etc.)

(2) 陈述句的间接引语

陈述句由直接引语变作间接引语时,如引述动词(Reporting Verb)是现在时形式,那间接引语中的时、体形式不变更。

He says to me, "I live in Shanghai." →He tells me that he lives in Shanghai.

如引述动词是过去时形式,那间接引语中的动词的时、体就要作相应的变化。

Jim said, "I am going to Nanjing to see my father." →Jim told me that he was going to Nanjing to see his father.

① 时间推移到过去

现在时→过去时;现在进行体→过去进行体;现在完成体→过去完成体;将来时间→过去将来时间……

Yi Lan said, "I'm in Harbin *now*." 于兰说,"我现在在哈尔滨。"

→ Yi Lan said that she was in Harbin *then*.

Jean said, "I *have finished* my composition." 琼说,"我写完了我的作文。"

→ Jean said she *had finished* her composition.

Father said, "The meat will go off (变质) if you don't cook it today." 父亲说,"如果你今天不把肉烧了,它就要变质。"

→ Father said the meat would go off if I didn't cook it that day.

② 引述句保持现在时

当引述句是科学真理、客观事实和现在习惯动作以及格言时,尽管引述动词是过去时,引述句里动词仍用现在时。

Little Robert said, "Two plus two *is* four." 小罗伯特说:"2+2=4。"

→ Little Robert said two plus two *is* four.

Jim said,"Life holds many surprises."吉姆说:"人生包含着许多意想不到的事情。"

→ Jim said (that) life holds many surprises.

③ 引述句保持虚拟式

当引述句中动词是虚拟式时,变间接引语时保持虚拟式。

"I suggest the exhibition *be put off* till *next month*." Mr.White said. 怀特先生说:"我建议展览会延期到下个月。"

→ Mr. White suggested the exhibition *be put off* till *the next month*.

④ 引述句保持原时态

当引述句中的谓语动词的动作或状态在引述时仍在进行或存在着,此时要保持原来的动词时态。

Tom said,"I'm fifty."汤姆说:"我 50 岁了。"

→ Tom said he is fifty.

The boss of the inn said,"Our inn has two hundred rooms."旅馆的老板说:"我们旅馆有200间房间。"

→ The boss of the inn said his inn has 200 rooms.

⑤ 关于 must do sth, had better do sth

A. 情态动词 must

因为情态动词 must 没有过去式,所以引述句的 must 在间接引语中保持 must 不变。

"It must be pretty late, I really must leave now." Chang Ming said. 张明说:"真的很迟了,我现在必须走了。"

→Chang Ming said it must be pretty late and he really must leave then.

有时也可用 had to 代替 must。

Lao Yang said,"My car doesn't work and I must walk to work."老杨说:"我的车子坏了,必须步行上班。"

→Lao Yang said his car didn't work and he must/had to walk to work.

B. 半助动词 had better

当引述句中的谓语动词前有半助动词 had better 时,变为间接引语时保持原状不变。

Jim said, "You'd better ask your teacher for help."吉姆说:"你最好去请求老师帮忙。"

→Jim said I had better ask my teacher for help.

⑥ 过去时推移到过去的过去

A. 过去时变过去完成体;过去进行体变为过去完成进会行时

当引述句中的谓语动词是过去时时,变间接引语为过去完成体;过去完成体变成过去完成进行体。

Mother said,"I didn't recognize Rose."母亲说:"我没有认出罗丝来。"

→Mother said she hadn't recognized Rose.

Mary said,"I was joking with Rose."玛丽说:"我在跟罗丝开玩笑。"

→Mary said she had been joking with Rose.

B. 保持过去时和过去完成(进行)时

当过去的过去已经很明显,或所转述的是强调事实本身,过去时或过去完成(进行)时可以不变。

Li Ming said,"I saw you in the park yesterday."李明说:"我昨天在公园里看见你的。"

→Li Ming said he saw me in the park the day before.

John said,"We hadn't returned to the library when Mary came."约翰说:"当玛丽来的时候我们还没回到图书馆。"

→John said they hadn't returned to the library when Mary came.

C. 不改变一般过去时或过去进行体

当直接引语中用的是想象中一般过去时或过去进行体,变为间接引语时一般过去时和过去进行体不变动。

Rose said,"It's time we *went* to bed."罗丝说:"我们该上床睡觉了。"
→Rose said it was time they *went* to bed.
William said,"I wish I *knew* French."威廉说:"但愿我懂法语。"
William said he wished he *knew* French.

D．时间状语从句中的一般过去时和过去进行体可以不变

Linda said,"When I *was* in Suzhou I often *went* to the Big Public Park to have a cup of tea in the morning."琳达说:"我在苏州时早上常去大公园喝茶。"
→Linda said she often *went* to the Big Public Park to have a cup of tea in the morning when she *was* in Suzhou.

(4) 疑问句的间接引语

对疑问句的引述,除了要注意上述所提到的那些变化规则外,还要注意到各类疑问句的不同要求及它们的词序变化,有时还要添加主句。

① 真疑问句的引述

A．一般疑问句、附加疑问句和选择疑问句的引述

这三类疑问句的引述有所不同,引述一般疑问句和附加疑问句时通常用 whether 或 if,引述选择疑问句时通常只用 whether …。

"Does he still depend on his parents?""他还在依靠父母?"
→I wondered whether/if he still depended on hid parents.(添主句)
"They live in groups, don't they?""他们群居,是不是?"
→She asked if/whether they lived in groups.
"Is this book written by you or her?""这本书是你写的还是她写的?"
→I asked him whether that book was written by him or her.

B．引述特殊疑问句时用原句中的 wh-词引出

She asked the boy,"What's your name?"她问那男孩:"你叫什么名字?"
→She asked the boy what his name was.
"Why are you standing at the gate?""你干吗站在门口?"
→He asked why I was standing at the gate.
"When did you arrive?""你什么时候到的?"
→She asked when I had arrived?

② 伪疑问句的引述

伪疑问句是指那些虽表面上看来是疑问句,实际上并非是提出问题,而只是表示请求、建议、提议、劝告等意思。引述这种疑问句时要借助其他表达手段来表示相同的交际功能。

A．表示请求、劝告时常用"ask/advise/want, etc. +object +infinitive"结构

"Would you post the letter for me?""能把这封信给我寄掉吗?"
→ He asked me to post the letter for him.
"Why don't you give her a hand? She was your close friend.""你怎么不帮帮她? 她曾是你的好朋友。"
→ He advised me to give her a hand and he mentioned that she had been my close friend.

B．表示建议时常用"suggest +v-ing 分词"结构,Why not …? How about …? 之类的结构也用此种表示引述

"Shall we get there by plane?""我们乘飞机去那儿吧?"

→ He suggested getting there by plane. / He suggested that they should get there by plane.

"Why didn't you return home yesterday?" "你怎么昨天没回家呀？"

He suggested that I should return home the day before.

"Why not start at once?" "干吗不马上动身呢？"

→He suggested starting at once.

C．表示提议时常用"offer＋infinitive"结构

"Shall I e-mail the article to you?" "要不要我把那篇文章 e-mail 给你？"

→ He offered to e-mail the article to me.

(4) 祈使句和感叹句的引述法

① 祈使句的引述

祈使句的引述可分三种情况。

A．一般祈使句

一般祈使句引述时多用"v．＋object＋infinitive"结构，这些表示祈使的动词有 ask, advise, beg, remind, tell, urge 等。

Ask the children there to be quiet. 叫那边的小孩保持安静。

→He told *me to ask the boy* there to be quiet.

Take care of the dog. 照料好那只狗。

→She *wanted me to take care of* the dog.

B．表示命令的祈使句

引述表示命令的祈使句时，可用"v．＋that clause"，而从句中常是"be＋to-infinitive"。

"Don't drive too fast." "车别开得太快。"

→He told me that I wasn't to drive too fast.

C．表示劝告、建议的祈使句

引述此种祈使句时可用"suggest/say＋that clause"或"suggest＋v-ing 形式"结构。

"Let's have a walk after supper." "我们晚饭后去散步。"

→He suggested that we should have a walk after supper. 或 He suggested having a walk after supper.

D．表示提议的祈使句

引述表示提议的祈使句时，也可用"offer＋infinitive"结构。

"Let me make supper for you." "我给你们做晚饭。"

→ He offered to make supper for us.

② 感叹句的引述

A．用 how, what, that 作为引述句的引导词

"How pretty she is!" "她多么漂亮！"

→ He said how pretty she is.

"What a lovely house!" "多么漂亮的房子啊！"

→He remarked what a lovely house it was. 或 He remarked that it was a lovely house.

B．根据原句意思改写成与原句意思相当的陈述句

"How terrible his handwriting is!" "他的书法太糟了！"

→ He commended on his terrible handwriting.

"How kind of you!" "你真好！"

→ He praised my kindness. 或 He acknowledged my kindness.

第9章　名词和名词性从句

9.1 名词

(1) 名词的分类

从结构上讲,名词可分"单一名词"(Single-Word Noun)和"合成名词"(Compound Noun);从表义上分,有普通名词(Common Noun)与专有名词(Proper Noun)两类。

① 单一名词

单一名词指一个词构成的名词,如:group,people,book,girl,hair,table,water,difficulty。英语中的大部分名词是单一名词。

② 合成名词

合成名词指由两个词或者更多个单词合成的名词。合成名词可分成两类:一类从形式分,另一类按词义分。

A. 从形式上划分的合成名词

a. 写成一个词的合成名词

常用的有:goldsmith,boyfriend,seaside,spaceship,typewriter,headmaster,warehouse,warhead,friendship,greenhouse,homework,breakdown(失败),lookout(注意),breakup(破裂),income(收入),uprising(起义)等。

b. 带连字符的合成名词

用连字符连起来的合成名词为数不少,如:night-club,arm-chair,reading-room。有些词可以构成许多名词。例如,fire 可构成 fire-alarm(火警),fire-bomb(燃烧弹),fire-engine(消防车),fire-escape(太平梯),fire-fighter(消防员),fire-power(火力),fire-practice(消防演习)。

c. 不带连字符的合成名词

有些合成名词从形式上看是两个单一的词,从意义上讲是一个合成名词,只是中间没有连字符连接,这些词常见的有:fire brigade(消防队),fire extinguisher(灭火器),fire station(消防站),music lessons(音乐课),water pump(水泵),horror film(恐怖电影),zip code(邮政编码),cotton goods(棉织品)。

d. 其他一些合成名词的书写情况及结构

• 两个词语构成的合成名词常连写。常见的这些词有:teacup(茶杯),housewife(家庭主妇),lawsuit(诉讼),bookmark(书签),bookworm(书呆子),bookstall(书报摊),bookstore(书店)。

• 也有两个短词组成的合成词不连写的情况。这些常见的词有:busstop(公共汽车站),tea break(饮茶休息时间),tealeaf(茶叶),teatable(茶几),tea party(茶会)。

• 有些"动词或动名词+其他词"构成的合成名词不用连字符号,makeup(化妆),setup(结构),tryout(试用)。

• 由"self+其他词"构成的词不连写。这些词有:selfrespect(自尊心),selfcontrol(自我控制),selfdefence(自卫),selfinterest(自私的考虑),selfconfidence(自信)。

e. 由三个词构成的合成名词带连字符,如:son-in-law(女婿),mother-in-law(婆婆,岳母),editor-in-chief(主编),commander-in-chief(总司令),hide-and-seek(捉迷藏),man-of-war(军舰)。

- 有些完全被接受为合成名词,这些词可连写或中间加连字符,有的可分开写。
  * 连写或加连词符号:sunbathing(日光浴),sunglasses,sunrise,battle-cry(口号)。
  * 不用连字符而分开写:writing materials(书写材料),working class(工人阶级),working atmosphere(工作环境),working age(工龄)。

B. 按照"词义和结构"划分的合成名词

a. 形容词 + 名词
a black list(黑名单),a black sheep(败家子),a green house(温室),a heavy weight(重量级拳击手),a white lie(无害的谎言),old hand(老手),red tape(繁文缛节)

b. 动名词 + 名词
a running mate(竞选伙伴),a skating-rink(溜冰场),a walking-stick(手杖),baking powder(发酵粉),drinking water(饮用水),sleeping-pill(安眠药)

c. 名词 + 动名词
book-keeping(簿记),daydreaming(白日梦),handwriting(书法),horse-riding(骑马),sunshine(日光浴),weightlifting(举重)

d. 名词 + 名词
a car key(车钥匙),an aircraft(航空母舰),an air-conditioner(空调机),air raid(空袭),airport shuttle(机场班车),bank account(银行账户)

e. 其他合成名词
- hotchpotch(US hodgepodge,大杂烩),handy-panky(阴谋诡计),hocus-pocus(无聊言行),jiggery-pokery(欺骗行为),argy-bargy(大声争吵)
- turnover(营业额),breakthrough(突破),get·together(联欢会),Breakup(关系破裂),show-off(卖弄)
- income(收入),outcome(结果),downfall(垮台),outbreak(爆发),by product(副产品),out-patient(门诊病人),forget·me·not(勿忘我植物),touch·me·not(凤仙花),good-for-nothing(不中用的人),go·between(媒人,中间人),merry-go-round(旋转木马),bride·to·be(未来新娘),comrade·in·arms(战友),looker·on(旁观者),nouveau riches(暴发户),stay-at-home(不爱出门的人)

③ 普通名词和专有名词
按照表义来讲,名词可分普通名词和专有名词两大类。

A. 普通名词

普通名词可以分为四类:个体名词、集体名词、物质名词和抽象名词。

a. 个体名词
个体名词(Individual Noun)指人或物的个体,能与不定冠词连用并能够计数的名词,如:two tractors(两台拖拉机),three umbrellas(三把伞),several students(几个学生),many essays(许多篇小品文)。

- 指个体而存在的人或事物
She has *three brothers*. 她有三个哥哥。
There are *hundreds of* parks in the city. 这座城市有数以百计的公园。
Most offices have *computers*. 多数办公室里都有电脑。

- 指抽象的东西
He's been here for *a month*. 他在这里待了一个月了。

He gave her *an account* of his progress. 他向她讲述了他的进展情况。

The affair remained *a complete mystery*. 这件事整个还是个谜。

I had *a dream* last night. 昨晚我做了一个梦。

b. 集体名词

集体名词(Collective Noun)是一群人或物的总称,如:police(警察),furniture(家具),government(政府),poetry(诗歌)。

- 集体名词的界定和说明

集体名词表示由若干个体组成的集合体的总称。一般集体名词本身虽然只有单数形式,但其后所跟的谓语动词既有单形也有复形。从意义上理解,用单形谓语的集体名词强调一个集合整体,用复形谓语的则暗含集合体内每个成员体的意义。到底用单形还是复形,有时则取决于话语者的习惯。一般来说,在英国英语中常用复形谓语,而美国英语则习惯用单形动词作谓语。下面是一些集体名词单复形谓语动词的搭配例解:

We wanted to reach beyond the audience who *lived* in the area and who *were* acquainted with the New England Free Press. 我们不想局限于居住在本地并了解新英格兰自由出版社的那些读者。

The youth of today *is/are* trying to adapt itself/themselves to rapidly changing circumstances. 当代的青年们正努力使自己适应日新月异的环境。

A wise manager will never feel that his *staff is* complete without at least one woman as a member of it. 高明的经理都认为,他的工作人员要配齐的话,至少需要一位女性在中间。

All my staff *are* trained nurses. 我所有的护士都是训练有素的。

He does not think that *profession does not have* a high character. 他并不认为那种职业中没有一个品德高尚者。

The whole *profession fight* tooth and nail against it. 同行全体人员都极力反对。

Note:有个别的集体名词本身也有复数形式,因此可以把它们看成已转化为复数个体名词。

For the TV variety *shows* it is a matter of greatest importance that they should cater for the taste of the audiences. 对于电视文艺晚会来说至关重要的是它们要迎合不同观众的口味。

The peoples of the world *build* cultures adapted to their peculiar needs. 全世界各民族都建立了适应自己独特需要的文化。

Several youths and girls *are* standing at the street corner. 几个小伙子和姑娘站在街拐角处。(此处 youth 不是"青年"的总称,而是"男青年"之意,即为可数的个体名词)

- 一些常见的集体名词及其使用情况

* 单数集体名词可单、复数看待

对于单数集体名词,有时单数看待,有时又复数看待,也就是说把其作为整个一体看,就看作单数,否则就看作复数。

The public *was* unlikely to support it. 公众支持它的可能性不大。

The enemy *has* suffered heavy losses. 敌人受到重大损失。

The enemy *were* attacking the town. 敌军正在攻打该城。

The government *is* discussing the proposal. 政府在讨论这一提议。

The government *are* discussing the proposal. 政府(人员)正在讨论这个建议。

The audience *enjoys* every minute of the performance. 观众自始至终欣赏这次演出。

The audience *are* dressed in a variety of ways. 观众有形形色色的穿着。

The Committee of Public Safety *is* to deal with this mater. 公共安全委员会将处理此事。

The committee *are* of the opinion that the time is inopportune. 委员会认为时机尚不适宜。

* 单数集体名词后,单、复数动词兼用

The press *was* (*were*) not allowed to attend the trail. 不允许新闻界旁听审判。
The jury *is* (*are*) about to announce the winners. 评委会将宣布优胜者名单。
The youth of today *is* (*are*) better off than we used to be. 今天的青年比我们过去处境好。
The teaching staff of this college *is* (*are*) excellent. 这所大学的教师都是出类拔萃的。
The public *has* (*have*) a right to know what's in the report. 公众有权知道这篇报道的内容。
The local council *are* (*is*) in charge of repairing roads. 当地政府会负责道路的维修工作。

* 少数集体名词后，动词用单数

The play's cast *was* given a standing ovation. 对这个剧组的成员大家起立鼓掌。
Our company *is* sending him to work in Boston. 我们公司派他到波士顿工作。
The entire community *is* behind the appeal. 整个社区都支持这项呼吁。

* 一些集体名词后，动词用复数

The police *have* caught the murder. 警方已经抓到了杀人犯。
The crew *are* paid to do all the work on the ship. 船员被雇佣在船上工作。

* 关于"集体名词＋of 短语"问题

有时，集体名词后可以跟一个由 of 引起的短语，这个短语用以说明、描述、修饰前面的集体名词。

a brood of chicks 一群小鸡　　　　　a group of tourists 一批游人
a bunch of flowers 一束花　　　　　a herd of cattle 一群牛
a clump of trees 一个树丛　　　　　a pride of lions 一群狮子
a company of journalists 一群新闻记者　a team of visitors 一队参观者
a flock of sheep 一群羊　　　　　　a troupe of acrobats 一批杂技演员
a gang of criminals 一群罪犯　　　　an army of volunteers 一队志愿人员

c. 物质名词

物质名词（Material Noun）是指那些不能分为个体的物质，通常不能与不定冠词连用，它们本身不能计数，如：water（水），steel（钢），coal（煤），cotton（棉花），sugar（糖）。

物质名词表示无法分为个体的实物名词，一般情况下均为不可数，以单数形式出现，后也就跟单数谓语动词，但有时又可以复数形式出现，这时的物质名已向个体意义转化，表现出与原来完全不同的词义。

● 一些物质名词的例解

就如上面所说，物质名词是无法分为个体的实物名词，所以它们后面的谓语动词就用单数形式。

Now we eat fewer carbohydrates (sugars and starches)and more *is* refined, like cane sugar. 我们现在摄入的碳水化合物（糖类和淀粉类）种类少了，而且精加工过的多了，如蔗糖。（此处复形物质名词表示不同的种类个体，而谓语 is 则表示仍把其整体看成不可数的物质）
Peter broke his waters on a Sunday. 彼得出生在一个星期天。[此处 waters 转义为"（分娩时的）羊水"]
Children played joyfully on the sands. 孩子们在沙滩上快乐地玩耍。（此处 sands 与 waters 用法相似。表示大片的沙）
The sands of his life are numbered. 他的岁月已屈指可数。（此处的 sands 转化为可数，引申义为"岁月，寿命"）

● 物质名词与单位词

表示物质名词的量通常可以用单位词与物质名词（Unit Noun）一起组成短语表示、但某些表示饮料、食物的物质名词可用复数代替单位词。

May I serve two cakes for you? 我给你拿两块蛋糕来好吗？
Would you get us two gin and tonics, please? 请给我们拿两杯杜松子酒好吗？
May I have two sugars for my coffee? 我可以在咖啡里放两块糖吗？

● 物质名词的特殊用法

一般来说,物质名词是不可数的,所以它们没有复数形式,但有时也可用作可数名词,此时,其前有时直接加不定冠词,表示"一份"、"一杯"等,有时其前有不定冠词加量词。

* 表示"一份"、"一杯"等意思

I'll mix *a salad*. 我去拌一盘生菜。

A chocolate ice-cream for me. 给我一份巧克力冰淇淋。

A *dozen beers*, please. 请来一打啤酒。

* 有时表示"一种"的意思

有时用作可数名词的物质名词表示"一种"。

It was *a special tea* which tasted of orange blossoms. 这是一种特别的茶,有橘子花味。

They produce *a large range of cheeses*. 他们生产各式各样的干酪。

* 物质名词的复数形式表示特定意思

The ship was in European *waters*. 船在欧洲水域航行。

We often played on the *sands* when we were young. 我们年幼时常常在沙滩上玩耍。

The *rains* are very long in South. 南方的雨季特别漫长。

* 物质名词表示数量的方法

对物质名词进行数量表示,其前可加"a ... of"的方法进行,不过此时的"a ..."后的英语名词是因后面的物质名词不同而习惯上用不同的词,在译作汉语时也要选择相应的量词,如:a ball of wool(一团毛线),a bar of chocolate(一块巧克力)。

a kilo of salt 一公斤盐	*a length* of cloth 一段布料
a bottle of brandy 一瓶白兰地	*a loaf* of bread 一块面包
a cake of soap 一块肥皂	*a lump* of sugar 一块砖糖
a can of beer 一罐啤酒	*a pinch* of sugar 一小撮白糖
a cube of ice 一块冰	*a sheet* of paper 一张纸
a cup of tea 一杯茶	*a slice* of cake 一片蛋糕
a grain of sand 一粒沙子	*a stretch* of water 一片水域
a jar of jam 一罐果酱	*a tube* of toothpaste 一管牙膏

* 物质名词个体化

少数物质名词也可作为个体名词用,这就是物质名词个体化,那样也就变为可数了。

用作物质名词

He was chopping *wood*. 他在砍柴。

Oil and *water* will not mixed. 油与水不能混合。

Children like to play with *sand*. 孩子们爱玩沙子。

用作个体名词

They entered *a wood*. 他们走进一个树林。

She has begun a portrait in *oils*. 她开始画一张油画画像。

The children are playing on the *sands*. 孩子们在沙滩上玩。

d. 抽象名词

抽象名词(Abstract Noun)表示人或物的品质、状态等抽象概念,通常不能与不定冠词连用,它们也不能计数,如:friendship(友谊), happiness(幸福), progress(进步), courage(勇气)。

抽象名词主要指一些抽象概念的名称,它们一般是不可数的,没有复数形式,前面也不能加冠词 a, an。

• 抽象名词的含义

抽象名词表示一切抽象概念,如性质、行为、状态、感情等,所以可说其含义较广,而且用法也比较复杂,除多数为不可数之外,有时又可作可数用,有时又两者兼而有之,不过两者兼有时词义就有所变化。因此,当抽象名词成为可数时,其意义转化后还含有表示抽象事物的种类、具体的行为等个体概念,其复数形式已增加了原单数形式没有的新义。

We have to deal with the existing medical *system* and fight whenever possible for improvements and changes. 我们必须考虑现存的医疗制度并尽可能为实现某些改善和新的变化而奋斗。

We publish this book so as to support those women and men working for *change*. 我们出版这本书是为了支持那些为变革而努力的女士和男士。

We can describe only what *life* has been for us. 我们只能描述生活对于我们自己意味着什么。

Those were the days when girls' *lives* centered around finding a man and then woman's *lives* around husband and children. 在那个时代里女孩子们的生活中心是找到一个男人,而后女人们的生活重点则围绕着丈夫和孩子们转。

We know each other well—our *weaknesses* as well as our *strengths*. 我们彼此熟知各自的弱点和长处。

It was the first time we had looked critically, and with strength, at the existing *institutions* serving us. 这时我们第一次用审视的并且带有一定力度的目光观察我们所享用的现存制度。

We have comforted each other the *best* we could through four parents' *deaths* and the *illnesses* of several others. 我们在思维小组成员的父母去世及其他几位父母生病的时候曾尽力地互相安慰。

There is a fourth reason why *knowledge* has generated so much new *energy*. 知识为什么产生了如此大的新能量还有第四种原因。

We are freed of some of these preoccupations and can start to use our untapped *energies*. 我们摆脱了某些先入之见,能够开始利用我们尚未发挥出的全部精力。

All these can cause *frustration*, *anxiety*, *anger and fear*. 这些都有可能导致挫折感、焦虑、愤怒和恐惧。

This thriving resort town has retained its village *charm*. 这座繁荣的游览城市还保留着乡村风光的魅力。

But Europe held forth the *charms* of storied and poetical association. 然而在传奇和诗意的联想方面,欧洲却具有其特殊的魅力。

He is out of *touch* with reality. 他脱离现实。

My mother belongs to that sort of women who would bear *hardship* without complaint. 我妈妈是那种可以毫无怨言地忍受苦难的女性。

Students of English often encounter *difficulty* with profession titles. 学英语的学生在使用职衔称呼方面常遇到困难。

Sometimes *difficulties* and *hardships* can bring out one's best qualities. 有时各种磨难能使人发挥其最优秀的品质。

- 抽象名词表示单数

一般来说,抽象名词以单数看待,其前基本不加任何冠词,但有时加定冠词,那就表示特定的含义。

Knowledge is power. (谚语)知识就是力量。

What *fun* they had! 他们玩得多开心!

We had *justice* on our side. 正义在我们这一边。

Too much *violence* was shown on television. 电视上暴力出现得太多。

I did not have *the courage* to tell you. 我没有勇气告诉你。

We enjoyed *the beauty* of nature. 我们欣赏大自然的美。

He works hard for *the welfare* of the poor. 他为穷人的福利努力工作。

有些抽象名词可加不定冠词,表示"一种";其前不加 a 或 an,表示抽象。

He is in immeasurable *joy*. 他沉浸在极大的欢乐之中。

He has no real feeling for *beauty*. 他没有真正的美感。

He is held in *affection*. 他极为大家爱戴。

The story stirred her *sympathy*. 这故事激起了她的同情心。

What *a joy* to have you with us! 有你和我们在一起真令人高兴!

That new car is *an absolute beauty*. 那辆新车漂亮极了。

He had *a warm affection* for them. 他对母亲有一种温馨的感情。

He had *a nature sympathy* for them. 他对他们有一种自然的同情。

We have *a great respect* for the professor. 我们很尊重教授。

There is *a beauty* in simplicity. 朴实之中有一种美。

After *a brief peace*, war broke out again. 经过一段短暂的和平时期,战争又爆发了。

- 抽象名词表数、量的方法

不可数的抽象名词同物质名词一样,经常需要搭配某种单位词表示量;某些复数形式的抽象名词,表面上看是可数的,但一般不能用数词直接修饰(含义为 a kind of 的 a/an 除外)来表示,而需要用"数词+kind of"等方法来进行修饰。

These *three kinds of change* have affected nearly every chapter in the book. 这三种变化几乎影响了本书的各个章节。(此处 change 的词义偏重抽象的概念。)

We have been meeting once a week for 12 years and have become *a kind of family* to one another. 我们12年来一直每周聚会一次,彼此已成为某种意义上的家庭成员。(此处 family 为抽象的概念。)

These *four kinds of pressures* have interwined and worked together on college students. 这四种压力互相关联,共同作用于大学生们身上。

These are the *three kinds of influences* all urban women are subject to. 这就是所有城市妇女共同承受的三种影响。(注意在以上两句中,我们不能直接说 four pressures 或 three influences)

- 抽象名词具体化

有些抽象名词也可用作个体名词,代表具体的东西,这就叫抽象名词具体化,这样它们当然也可有复数形式,其前也可有不定冠词。

* 用作抽象名词

What are the principles of *democracy*? 什么是民主的原则?

It's beyond my *power* to help you. 我没有能力帮助你。

Religion meant more and more to her. 宗教对她越来越重要。

* 用作个体名词

A true *democracy* allows free speech. 真正的民主国家允许有自由言论。

The great *powers* held an international conference. 这些大国开了一次国际会议。

There are many *religions* in the world. 世界上有许多宗教信仰。

上述四类词中,第一类个体名词和第二类集体名词是可以用数来数的,也叫可数名词(Countable Noun);三、四类物质名词和抽象名词是无法以数计算的,也叫不可数名词(Uncountable Noun)。

B. 专有名词

专有名词表示特定的或者独一无二的人或物,如人名、地名、机关、组织的名称等。

a. 专有名词的特点

专有名词最明显的特点是:如是一个词的专有名词,那不管在什么地方都得大写;如是两个或两个以上词组成的专有名词,不管在什么地方,每个词的第一个字母也都要大写。

Asia 亚洲	Shakespeare 莎士比亚
New York 纽约	Tian An Men Square 天安门广场
Uncle Tom 汤姆大叔	Uncle Sam 山姆大叔

b. 专有名词与定冠词

- 不带定冠词的情况

* 一般的人名前通常不带定冠词,如:Edward(爱德华),Will(威尔),President Bush(布什总统)。
* 一般地名前不带定冠词,如:West Lake(西湖),Taihe Lake(太湖)。
* 与国家相关的人的名词前不带定冠词,如:American(美国人),Chinese(中国人),Japanese(日本人),Russian(俄国人)。
* 某些抽象事物组成的名称前不带定冠词,如:Buddhism(佛教;佛法),English, Geneva(日内瓦)。
* 月份、周日及节日名词前不带定冠词。
* 书名、电影及诗歌名词前不带定冠词。如:Gone With the Wind(飘), Ode to the West Wind(西风颂),(la)Marseillaise(马赛曲), A Tale of Two Cities(双城记)。
* 家庭人员的称呼前不带定冠词。如:Mum, Mother, Dad, Father, Auntie, Uncle Tom。

● 带定冠词的情况

* 河流、海洋、群岛、海峡等名称前带定冠词,如:the Nile(尼罗河), the Philippines(菲律宾群岛), the Pacific(太平洋)。
* 某些由普通名词组成的专有名词前带定冠词。

● 名词的跨类、可数与不可数的变化等现象

以上所讲的名词分类并不是绝对的。有些名词,特别是某些常用的名词,在不同的句子或不同的上下文中可以属于不同的类别。

He is the owner of three *businesses*. 他是三个商号的老板。

We won't do much *business* with him. 我们不愿意和他做生意。

There is no *school* tomorrow. 明天停课。

There is *a school* nearby. 附近有一所学校。

There are three *rooms* in this flat. 这一套间有三间房间。

There is much *room* for improvement. 大有改进的空间。

I picked up *a stone* and threw it into the pond. 我捡起一块石头,把它丢进池塘。

All the houses are built of *stone*. 所有的房子都是石头建造的。

I'm going to buy *an iron*. 我打算去买一个熨斗。

The tool is made of *iron*. 这工具是铁制的。

第一句中 businesses 是个体名词,可数;而第二句中 business 为抽象名词,不可数。第三句中 school 为个体名词,可数;而第四句中 school 则为抽象名词,不可数。room 在第五句中为个体名词,而在第六句中则为抽象名。stone 在第七句中为个体名词,而在第八句中为物质名词。iron 在第九句中为个体名词,而在第十句中则为物质名词。由此可见,英语的名词究竟属于何种类别,则往往要在一定的句子或上下文中才能判定。

(2) 名词的可数与不可数

在实际语言表达中,如何用准可数名词与不可数名词是个基本技能和起码的要求。可数名词的情况比较简单,不少个体名词,如桌子、椅子、书、笔、人等在汉语和在英语中都是可数名词;但也有不少名词在汉语概念中是可数名词,而在英语中却是不可数的。

① 不可数和可数

A. 不可数实例

Our firm supplies kitchen *equipment*. 我们公司提供厨房设备。

The book contains much useful *information*. 这本书包含许多有用的知识。

No *news* is good *news*. (谚语)没有消息就是好消息。

They examined all *baggage* at the airport. 他们在机场检查了所有行李。

B. 变为可数的途径

如要把上面那些不可数的名词变为可数,表示"一件"这类概念,就得在前面加"a+有关名词+of"这种定语来实施。

a (an) piece (article) of furniture 一件家具　　a piece of fossil 一块化石
a piece of advice 一条忠告　　　　　　　　　an article of clothing 一件衣裳
a piece of news 一条消息　　　　　　　　　　a piece of equipment 一件设备
a piece of facial tissue 一张面巾纸

a. 在抽象名词和物质名词前加"a+有关名词+of"

a ray of sunshine 一缕阳光　　　　a slice of bacon 一片腊肉
a burst of applause 一片掌声　　　 a large sum of money 一大笔钱
a fit of anger 一顿脾气　　　　　　a cut (piece) of meat 一块肉
an atom of sympathy 一点点同情　　a small quantity of sugar 少量白糖
a stroke of good luck 一阵好运气　 a large amount of material 大量材料
a suit of clothes 一套衣裳　　　　　an expanse of water 一片水
a slip of paper 一张纸条　　　　　　a glass of water 一杯水
a shower of criticism 一阵批评　　　a stretch of land 一片土地
a length of cloth 一段布　　　　　　a portion of food 一份饭菜

b. "a+有关名词+of"表示形态

"a+有关名词+of"作定语,不仅能表示数量,有时也能表示形态。

a bar of gold 一根金条　　　　　　a grain of rice 一粒米
a blade of grass 一根草　　　　　　a lump of coal 一块煤
a bowl of soup 一碗汤　　　　　　 a stick of chalk 一根粉笔
a can of orange juice 一罐橘汁　　　a stick of charcoal 一根木炭
a cartoon of cigarette 一条香烟　　　a truck-load of coal 一卡车煤
a cube of ice 一方块冰

c. "a+有关名词+of"与可数名词连用

"a+有关名词+of"还可与可数的复数个体名词连用。

a bag of cashew nuts 一包腰果　　　a package of sweets 一大包糖果
a basket of apples 一篮苹果　　　　a packet of cigarettes 一包烟
a bunch of flowers 一束花　　　　　a packet of envelopes 一沓信封
a handful of peanuts 一把花生　　　a pair of shoes 一双鞋
a host of difficulties 好些困难　　　 a pair of spectacles 一副眼镜
a pack of hounds 一群猎狗　　　　 a series of attempts 一系列的尝试
a pack of lies 一大堆谎言　　　　　a set of gardening tools 一套园艺工具
a pack of wolves 一群狼　　　　　　a swarm of letters 一大批信件

d. 物质名词和抽象名词兼作个体名词

很多物质名词和抽象名词都可以兼作可数名词和不可数名词,但意思不同。

- 物质名词(不可数):copper(铜),gold(金子),paper(纸),wood(木头)
  个体名词(可数):a copper(铜币),a gold(金牌),a paper(报纸,证件,论文),a wood(树林)
- 抽象名词(不可数):authority(权威),democracy(民主),pleasure(高兴) power(力量)
  个体名词(可数):an authority(权威人士),a democracy(民主国家),a pleasure(使人感到愉快的事),a power(大国)
- 抽象名词个体化的另一种方法

抽象名词有时可表示具体的东西，这时它就可加 a(n)，甚至有复数形式。

＊抽象名词（不可数）

Light travels faster than *sound*. 光比声的速度快。

We enjoyed the *beauty* of nature. 我们欣赏大自然的美。

I'm sorry to give you so much *trouble*. 真对不起，给你添了这么多麻烦。

＊表示具体的东西（可数）

The *lights* are on. 灯都开了。

She is a *beauty*. 她是一个美人。

His son is a great *trouble* to him. 他儿子给他造成很大麻烦。

② 具体名词抽象化

有些具体名词有时也可抽象化，表示抽象概念。

A．具体名词（可数）

I want a double room with *a view*. 我要一间能看到风景的双人房间。

They are building *a new school*. 他们在盖一所新学校。

Is there *a church* round here? 这一带有教堂吗？

Butterflies flattered among *the flowers*. 蝴蝶在花间飞舞。

B．表示抽象东西（不可数）

There is not so much *room* for these books. 没有这么大的地方来放这些书。

School begins at 8 o'clock. 8点钟开始上课。

Grandpa never went *church*. 爷爷从来不做礼拜。

The roses are in *flower*. 玫瑰开花了。

③ 一些"对词"

英语中有不少对词，它们的意思相近，但一个是可数，另一个却是不可数。

A．可数名词

a pome 一首诗　　　　　a machine 一台机器　　　　a laugh 一阵笑声

a garment 一件衣裳　　　a bag（a case）一件行李　　a loaf 一块面包

B．不可数名词

poetry（总称）诗歌　　　machinery（总称）机器　　　laughter 笑声

bread 面包　　　　　　　clothing（总称）衣裳

(3) 名词的数

名词的"数"（Number）也是个语法范畴。它是区别名词单复数的屈折变化形式。可数名词有单数（Singular Number）和复数（Plural Number）两种形式；有时，其他名词，如物质名词、抽象名词，由于某种情况变化而也有单数和复数的变化。

可数名词通常就是名词的原形（Base Form）；复数名词有两种，即规则复数（Regular Plural）和不规则复数（Irregular Plural）。规则复数是在原形的词尾加-s 或-es，或把结尾 y 变为 i，再加-es 等构成；凡不是通过加-s/或-es 构成的复数便是不规则复数。

① 规则名词复数的构成

A．在词尾直接加-s

大部分可数名词，包括以不发音的元音字母 e 结尾的名词，通常在词尾直接加-s 构成复数。

tool→ tools 工具　　　　bath→ baths 浴室　　　　room→rooms 房间

side→ sides 边　　　　　sea→ seas 海　　　　　　worker→workers 工人

B．在词尾加-es

以-s,-x,-z,-sh,-ch结尾的名词,加-es变为复数。

gas→ gases 气体 　　　　　　class→ classes 班级
box→ boxes 箱子 　　　　　　buzz→ buzzes 嗡嗡声
church→ churches 教堂　　　 bush→ bushes 灌木林

C．变y为i,然后再加-es

以"辅音字母＋y"结尾的名词,变y为i,然后再加-e。

city→ cities 城市 　　　　　　spy→ spies 间谍
lady→ ladies 贵妇人 　　　　　factory→ factories 工厂

D．以"元音字母＋y"结尾的名词,直接在词尾加s

ray→rays 射线 　　　　　　　play→ plays 戏剧
toy→ toys 玩具 　　　　　　　boy→ boys 男孩

E．以"辅音字母＋o"结尾的名词,有直接加-s的情况,也有加-es的情况

以"辅音字母＋o"结尾的名词,一般加-es,也有只加-s的情况,还有既可加-es,也可加-s的情况。

a. 只在词尾加-s

photo→ photos 照片 　　　　　memo→ memos 备忘录
kilo→ kilos 千克 　　　　　　　piano→ pianos 钢琴

b. 加-es

potato→ potatoes 土豆 　　　　echo→ echoes 回声
hero→ heroes 英雄 　　　　　　torpedo→ torpedoes 鱼雷

c. 有的既可加-s,也可加-es

motto→ mottos/mottoes 箴言 　　cargo→ cargos/cargoes 货物
buffalo→ buffalos/buffaloes 水牛　volcano→ volcanos/volcanoes 火山

F．以"元音字母＋o"（包括以-oo）结尾的名词,加-s

radio→ -radios 收音机 　　　　　embryo→ -embryos 胚胎
bamboo→ bamboos 竹子 　　　　zoo→ zoos 动物园

G．以f或fe结尾的名词,变f为v,再加-es或-s

leaf→ leaves 叶子 　　　　　　wolf→ wolves 狼
Knife→ knives 小刀 　　　　　　wife→ wives 妻

Notes：a. 但也有以f结尾的名词可直接加-s变为复数。

roof→ roofs 屋顶 　　　　　　　chief→ chiefs 首领
gulf→ gulfs 海湾 　　　　　　　belief→ beliefs 信仰

b. 还有少数以f结尾的名词可按以上两种方法变为复数。

scarf→ scarves/scarfs 披巾 　　　dwarf→ dwarves/dwarfs 矮人
hoof→ hooves/hoofs 蹄子 　　　handkerchief→ handkerchieves/handkerchiefs 手帕

② 不规则复数的构成

A．普通英语名词的不规则复数的构成

a. 通过内部元音变换构成

foot→feet 足;尺 　　　　　　　mouse→mice 老鼠
louse→lice 虱子 　　　　　　　goose→geese 鹅
man→men 男人 　　　　　　　tooth→teeth 牙

b. 通过加-en变为复数(包括内部元音也略有变化)

child→children 孩子　　　　　　　　　ox→oxen 牛
brother→brethren 兄弟（只用于庄严场合）
c. 有些名词的单复数同形
像 sheep（羊），aircraft（飞机），species（物种），deer（鹿），means（方法），barracks（营房），fish（鱼），series（系列），steelworks（钢厂），Chinese（中国人）等比较常见。
He is as timid as a *sheep*. 他像绵羊一样怯懦。
We are grazing the *sheep* in the next field. 我们在旁边的地里放羊。
The speed of this *aircraft* is very high. 这架飞机的速度非常快。
All *aircraft* must fuel before flight. 所有飞机飞行前都必须加油。
The dog roused a *deer* from the bushes. 狗惊起了丛林中的一只鹿。
Male *deer* usually have horns on their heads. 公鹿头上通常有角。
My *goldfish* has died. 我的金鱼死了。
The fisher drew in the net and found two *goldfish* in it. 渔夫收了网，发现有两条金鱼在里面。
常见的单复数同形的名词还有：
- 某些动物的名称

bison（野牛）	deer	grouse（松鸡）
cod（鳕鱼）	fish	goldfish
halibut（大比目鱼）	mullet（胭脂鱼）	salmon（鲑鱼）
moose（麋）	reindeer（驯鹿）	sheep（绵羊）
shellfish（贝壳动物）	trout（鳟鱼）	whitebait（银鱼）

- craft 及 craft 构成的词

hovercraft（气垫船），spacecraft（宇宙飞船）
- 表示某国人的名词

I'm proud I am a *Chinese*. 我骄傲我是中国人。
The *Chinese* eat with chopsticks. 中国人用筷子吃饭。
His wife is a *Vietnamese*. 他的妻子是越南人。
The *Vietnamese* are noted for their cookery. 越南人因其烹调而出名。
It was invented by a *Swiss*. 这是一位瑞士人发明的。
The *Swiss* did not take their fate lying down. 瑞士人并不甘心接受被征服的命运。
Note：不能说 an English，要说 an Englishman。有些词则要加-s，如 Scots。
- 还有一些其他单复同形的名词

This rare bird has become an endangered *species*. 这种珍禽已成为濒临灭绝的物种。
There are over 200 *species* of fish. 有两百多个品种的鱼。
The quickest *means* of travel is by plane. 最快的交通工具是飞机。
Radio and television are important *means* of communication. 无线电和电视是重要的通信手段。
She's *offspring* of a scientist and a musician. 她是一位科学家和一位音乐家的女儿。
How do parents pass genes on to their *offspring*? 父母是怎样把基因遗传给自己的子女的？
- 特殊情况的词

fruit 通常作总称或集体名词，没有复数形式。
I like *fruit* and vegetables. 我喜欢水果和蔬菜。
This pudding has two pounds of fresh *fruit* in it. 这个布丁里有两磅鲜果。

在表示某种水果时可有复数形式。

The potato is a vegetable, not a *fruit*. 马铃薯是一种蔬菜,不是一种水果。

The country exports tropical *fruits*. 该国出口热带水果。

用于抽象或比喻时也可有复数形式。

They enjoy the *fruits* of their hard labor. 他们享受自己辛勤努力的成果。

hair 通常作单数,是头发或动物毛发的总称。

She was slender and had long dark *hair*. 她身体苗条,有一头长长的黑发。

He had a few grey *hairs*. 他有几根灰白色的头发。

fish 通常单复数同形。

He caught a big (several) *fish*. 他捕了一条大鱼(几条鱼)。

但 fish 也可有复数形式 fishes,表示"几条鱼"或"几种鱼"。

We caught three little *fishes*. 我们捕到了三条小鱼。

There were *fishes* of many hues and sizes. 有各种色泽和大小的鱼。

有一些名词有两种复数形式。

The *herring*(s) usually lives (live) in large shoals. 鲱鱼通常生活在大的浅水区。

Zebra(s) is (are) (a) more difficult prey. 斑马是一种比较难捕获的猎物。

一些带-s 词尾的词通常用作单数。

The accident took place at a *crossroads*. 事故就发生在一个十字路口。

The business cycle is a *series* of peaks and troughs. 商业周期就是淡旺期交替。

B. 外来词的复数形式

a. 一些外来词的复数形式

stratum→strata 阶层　　　analysis→analyses 分析　　　thesis→theses 论文

criterion→criteria 标准　　phenomenon→phenomena 现象　medium→media 媒体

basis→bases 基础　　　　crisis→crises 危机　　　　　curriculum→curricula 课程

bacterium→bacteria 细菌

b. penny 的两种复数形式

pennies 指硬币:I only have a few pennies with me. 我身上只有几个便士。

pence 指钱数多少:Tomatoes are 30 pence a pound. 西红柿30便士一磅。

c. 两种复数形式

另外一些外来词则有两种复数形式:原来的复数形式和英语化的复数形式。

单数形式	原来的复数形式	英语化的复数形式
sanatorium	sanataria	sanatoriums 疗养院
formula	formulae	formulas 公式
antenna	antennae	antennas 天线
index	indices	indexes 索引
appendix	appendices	appendixes 附录
cactus	cacti	cactuses 仙人掌

d. 以加-s 或-es 方式构成复数形式

还有少数外来词已完全英语化,以加-s 或-es 方式构成复数形式。

genius→geniuses 天才　　　album→albums 相册,影集　　　apparatus→apparatuses 仪器

③ 复合名词的复数的构成

复合名词(Compound Noun)指由两个或者两个以上简单词(Simple Word)构成的名词,其复数形式的构成有如下几种情况:

A. 把主体词变复数

son-in-law→ sons-in-law 女婿
man-of-war→ men-of-war 军舰
looker-on→ lookers-on 旁观者
runner-up→ runners-up 亚军

B. 把所组成的两个词都变成复数

某些由 man,woman 构成的合成词,其两部分都要变作复数。

a man student→ men students 男学生
manservant→ menservants 男仆
但:policeman→ policemen 男警察
　　houseboy→ houseboys 家仆;僮仆
a woman doctor→ women doctors 女医生
woman-doctor→ women-doctors 女医生
policewoman→ policewomen 女警察
chorus girl→ chorus girls 女家仆;女僮仆

C. 把最后一个组成词变复数

air-raid→ air-raids 空袭
toothpick→ toothpicks 牙签
lay-by→ lay-bys 停车场
boy-friend→ boy-friends 男朋友
grown-up→ grown-ups 成年人
touch-me-not→ touch-me-nots 凤仙花

④ 某些物质名词和抽象名词后带-s 后的意义

有些物质名词和抽象名词后也可带-s,不过这些词这样变化后,它们的意义就不同了。

air 空气→ airs 微风;摆架子
brain 脑子→ brains 脑力,智能
food 食品→ foods 各类食品
green 绿色→ greens 青菜
look 看→ looks 容貌
ruin 毁坏→ ruins 废墟,遗迹
sand 沙→ sands 沙滩
water 水→ waters 水域
authority 权威→ authorities 当局
damage 损坏→ damages 损害赔偿费
glass 玻璃杯→ glasses 玻璃,玻璃杯,眼镜
iron 铁→ irons 熨斗,镣铐
manner 方式→ manners 礼貌
regard 尊敬→ regards 问候
time 时间→ times 时代
work 工作→ works 著作,工厂

⑤ 不可数名词的计数

我们都知道,不可数名词没有单复数的区别,因而也不可能就其本身来计数,如果要计数的话,就得使用"单位词"(Unit Noun)来协助。

A. 用通用单位词计数

有一些单位词,如 piece,bit,item,article 等,其搭配能力较强,因此可称为"通用"单位词,这些通用单位词可用来对不可数名词计数。

a piece of meat 一块肉
a bit of advice 一点意见
an item of news 一则新闻
an article of furniture 一件家具
a piece of paper 一张纸
a few bits of wood 少量木片
two items of programme 两个节目
several articles of clothing 几件衣服

B. 用个数的单位词计数

我们也常用以形状表示个数的单位词计数。

a bar of chocolate 一条巧克力
an ear of corn 一根玉米
a tube of toothpaste 一支牙膏
a cake of soap 一块肥皂
a head of cabbage 一颗卷心菜
two heads of cattle 两头牛

C. 用度量的单位词计数

every inch of land 每寸土地　　　　　five yards of cloth 五码布
three ounces of gold 三两黄金　　　　an acre of land 一英亩土地
a bowl of rice 一碗饭　　　　　　　　two spoonfuls of cough mixture 两调羹咳嗽药水
several truckloads of steel 几卡车钢材

D. 用动态的单位词计数

a fit of coughing 一阵咳嗽　　　　　a peal of applause 一阵掌声
a flash of lightning 电光一闪　　　　a display of force 一次炫耀武力

⑥ **其他一些词的复数形式**

A. 年份的复数形式

在数字年份的后面加-s 或 's
the 1670s（1670's）17 世纪 70 年代

B. 缩写词、首字母缩写词等的复数

a. 缩略词是由一个词删去首部或尾部而成的，如 tele（vision），ad（vertisement），Mr.（先生），Dr.（博士/医生），Prof.（教授），kg（千克），ft（英尺）等；有少量缩略词是由一个词删去首尾两部分而成的，如 flu（influence）（流感），frig/fridge（refrigerator）（冰箱）等。

b. 首字母缩略词由一个词组中的各主要词的第一个字母组成，如 WHO（the World Health Organization）（世界卫生组织），BBC（British Broadcasting Corporation）。

c. 拼词是由两个词的各一部分或全部拼缀而成的，如 telecast（=television + broadcast）（电视广播），motel（=motor + hotel）（汽车游客旅馆），mobot（=mobile + robot）（遥控活动机器人）。

d. 以下几类词的复数形式，除表示度量衡的一些缩写词往往不加-s 外，一般都以加-s 或 s 构成，如 VIP（very important person）→ VIPs/VIP's（要人），MP（member of parliament）→ MP's/MPs（国会议员），yr.（year）→ yrs（年），hr.（hour）→ hrs（小时），No.（number）→ Nos（数字/号码），motel（汽车旅客旅馆）→ motels，demo（demonstration）→ demos（示威游行/示范产品）。

e. 在缩写词后加-s 或 s（小写），如 VIPs 或 VIP's（Very Important Persons，贵宾们），MPs 或 MP's（Members of Parliament，国会议员们）。

⑦ **英语字母的复数**

英语字母的复数是在字母后加 's。
Mind your b's and d's. 注意你的 b 和 d 的写法。
'Banana' has three a's and two n's. banana 一词中有三个 a 和两个 n。

⑧ **有两种复数形式的词**

The herring(s) usually lives (live) in large shoals. 鲱鱼通常生活在大的浅水区。
Zebra(s) is (are)(a) more difficult prey. 斑马是一种比较难捕获的猎物。

⑨ **通常用于复数形式的词**

此类词大约有三种：A. 表示由两部分构成的东西；B. 有些以-ing 结尾的词；C. 还有其他一些情况。

A. binoculars 双筒望远镜　　　braces 背带　　　　　　briefs 三角裤
　　compasses 两脚规　　　　　cords 灯芯绒裤　　　　ear-phones 耳机
　　glasses spectacles 眼镜　　jeans 工装裤　　　　　knickers 短衬裤
　　nail-clippers 指甲刀　　　　overalls 工装裤　　　　pants 裤子
　　pliers 钳子　　　　　　　　pyjamas 睡衣裤　　　　scales 天平
　　scissors 剪刀　　　　　　　shorts 短裤　　　　　　slacks 便装

specs 眼镜　　　　　　sunglasses 太阳镜　　　　tights 紧身衣
tongs 钳子　　　　　　trousers 裤子　　　　　　trunks 游泳裤
underpants 内裤

B. belongings 所有物　　clippings 绞下的东西　　doings 行为
earnings 挣的钱　　　　findings 调查结果　　　　savings 储蓄
shavings 刨花　　　　　sweepings 扫拢的垃圾　　surroundings 环境
tidings 消息　　　　　　winnings 赢的钱　　　　　writings 作品

C. amends 补偿　　　　annals 编年史　　　　　archives 档案室
armed forces（陆海空）三军　arms 武器　　　　　arrears 欠账
ashes 灰烬　　　　　　assets 资产　　　　　　bowels 肠
brains 头脑　　　　　　clothes 衣服　　　　　　congratulations 祝贺
contents 目录　　　　　dominoes 骨牌　　　　　dregs 渣滓
dues 应交的费　　　　　effects 个人用品　　　　fireworks 烟火
goods 货物　　　　　　greens 青菜　　　　　　guts 胆量
living-quarters 住宅区　oil-colours 油画　　　　outskirts 城郊
particulars 细节　　　　remains 残余　　　　　riches 财富
stairs 楼梯　　　　　　statistics 统计资料　　　thanks 感谢
tropics 热带　　　　　　valuables 珍贵物品

⑩ 不是复数形式的以-s 结尾的名词

A．某些疾病名称

bends 潜水病　　　　　diabetes 糖尿病　　　　　measles 麻疹
mumps 腮腺炎　　　　　rabies 狂犬病　　　　　　rickets 佝偻病
shingles 带状疱疹　　　syphilis 梅毒

B．某些学科名称的词

acoustics 光学　　　　　acrobatics 杂技　　　　　aerodynamics 空气动力学
aeronautics 航空学　　　athletics 体育运动　　　　economics 经济学
electronics 电子学　　　genetics 遗传学　　　　　linguistics 语言学
logistics 后勤学　　　　mathematics 数学　　　　mechanics 机械力学
obstetrics 产科学　　　　physics 物理学　　　　　politics 政治
statistics 统计学　　　　modynamics 热力学

C．一些活动名称的词

billiards 台球，弹子　　　cards 打纸牌　　　　　　darts 掷镖游戏
draughts 国际跳棋　　　skittles 撞柱游戏

Note：有些名词用于某个特定意思时，通常用复数形式。

the authorities 当局　　　see the sights 观光　　　the odds 机会
the waters of the river 滚滚江水　　Chinese waters 中国水域
go with the pictures 去看电影　　customs 海关
accept their terms 接受他们的条件　　put on airs 摆架子
judge a person by his looks 以貌取人　　personal effects 个人用品
in high spirits 情绪高昂　　natural resources 自然资源
hold talks 举行会谈　　consider her feelings 考虑她的感情
make matters worse 使情况恶化　　working conditions 工作条件

watch his movements 监视他的活动
serve refreshments 用点心招待
have good manners 很礼貌
break off diplomatic 断绝外交关系
travel expenses 路费
show your papers 把证件拿出来
strengthen the defence 加强防御工事
internal affairs 内部事务

⑪ 形态特殊名词的单复数变化及其词义

这里所说的形态特殊的名词的单复数变化及其词义是指：以-s 结尾的普通名词；以-s 结尾的专有名词；以-s 结尾的表示疾病的名词；以-ics 结尾的学科名词；由两部分构成的物体的名称词等。

A．以-s 结尾的普通名词

普通名词中有一些特殊的以-s 结尾的词，与它们连用的谓语动词常用单数形式，如果单复数形式都有，那么词义可能有所变化。

What's the *odds*? 那又有什么不同？（此处 odds 意为"不同"）

The *odds* are ten to one that our football team will win the game. 我们的足球队十有八九会赢得这场比赛。（此处 odds 意为"机会"）

The *remains* of the meals were/was thrown away. 剩饭菜被倒掉了。（此处 remains 意为"剩余物"）

His *remains* were cremated. 他的遗体被火化了。（这里的 remains 意为"遗体"）

B．以-s 结尾的专有名词连用的谓语动词

与以-s 结尾的专有名词连用的谓语动词一般采取单数形式，它们包括组织名称、报纸杂志名、戏剧作品名、地名等；表示国名和组织机构名以及山脉、湖泊、大陆名的复数专有名词，当被看作整体时动词用单数，而当强调其组成的若干部分时，动词复数。

The United Nations comprises most of the countries of the world. 联合国由世界上大多数国家组成。

The United Nations have proclaimed the fundamental rights of all men and women without distinction. 联合国中各政府都已宣布无论男女都同样享有基本权利。

How many *times* have you been there? 你去过那里几次？（这里的 times 是"次数"）

Times Square is near our office building. 时代广场靠近我们的办公大楼。（此处 times 是"时代"的意思）

C．以-s 结尾表示疾病名称的词后的谓语动词

与以-s 结尾表示疾病名称的词连用的谓语动词一般用单数，在非正式用语有时可用复数。极个别的词，如 measles，作疾病的名称时是单数意义，而作"疾病引起的红斑点"解时要以复数对待。

Measles takes a long time to get over. 麻疹需要很长时间才能痊愈。

The *measles* begin to turn pale on the face. 脸上的斑点开始转淡。

D．以-s 结尾的游戏与运动名称词的"数"

以-s 结尾的游戏与运动名称词一般取单数义，个别的如 cards 习惯取复数义。

E．以-ics 结尾的学科名词的"数"

以-ics 结尾的名词，当它们取学科名称、技术名词等意义时，动词常取复数形；同样，当它们前面有物主代词或 the, such 等词修饰时，词义也转化为具体意义，动词也常取复数形式。

Acoustics deals with sound. 声学是研究各种声音的学问。

The *acoustics* of the hall are faulty. 这个大厅的音响效果不好。

Analytics is my favourite study. 分析学是我最喜欢的学科。

His *analytics* are above criticism. 他的分析方法没什么可挑剔的。

Classics is now taking a back seat. 古典文学现在处于次要地位了。

What are his *classics* like? 他的古典学课学得怎么样？

Linguistics is my specialized line. 语言学是我的专业。

Such *linguistics* are much sought after. 这种语言学现在很吃香。

F. 由两部分构成的物体的名称词的"数"

compasses,glasses,jeans,scissors 等词通常取复数义,但如果前面用单位词 a pair of 修饰,则后面的谓语动词与不定冠词一致,取单数义。

⑫ 一些转化名词的数

有些由原是形容词、分词转化来的名词,它们的数的形式与一般名词的数形式稍有不同,要加以注意。

A. the＋形容词

有些表示人的特征、状态、条件的形容词,如果和定冠词连用,就转化为泛指一类或一群人的名词,它们虽本身无复数形式,但含有复数意义,须跟复数谓语动词。

The innocent are often deceived by *the unscrupulous*. 天真无邪往往为无耻小人所欺骗。

The blind are taught trades to fit them for work in the world. 盲人接受各种专业训练,以便在世上能胜任自己的工作。

B. 表示人或事物特点的形容词转化来的名词有单复数

有些表示人或事物特点的形容词其本身即可转化为可数名词使用,有单复数变化,并要求谓语动词与其一致。

They are more or less the *regular* of this place. 他们多少可以算是这里的常客。

I'd like to have some *earlies*. 我要吃点时鲜蔬菜。

Men are great *sillies*. 人是大傻瓜。

C. "the＋-ch 或-sh 结尾的表示民族意思的形容词" 名词

有些以-ch 或-sh 结尾的表示民族意思的形容词和定冠词连用,转化为表示整个民族的复数意义的名词,如 the English,the British,the Spanish,the Dutch,the French,the Danish 等。如果要表示个人,那就需要在这类词后面加上-man,-woman 等。

The English often drink beer in pubs. 英国人经常在酒馆里喝啤酒。

The Welsh are well known for their singing. 威尔士人以歌唱著称。

D. "the＋-s 或-se 结尾表示民族的形容词" 名词

有些以-s 或-se 结尾表示民族的形容词加定冠词后,除上述用法外也可以和不定冠词或数词连用表示个人,但要注意表示复数具体个人时词尾无复数形式变化。这类词有 Chinese,Vietnamese,Japanese,Portuguese 等。

The two *Japanese* were making for the same interviewee,government spokesman Mr. Gallagher. 那两个日本人冲向同一个被采访者——政府发言人盖乐尔先生。

The *Portuguese* often peeps down at the street from behind his window curtains. 那个葡萄牙人经常从他的窗帘后面向下面的大街张望。

E. 形容词名词化后转化为抽象名词的数

上述两类由形容词名词化后转化为抽象名词,后面须跟单数谓语动词。

The *good* in him outweighs the *bad*. 他的优点多于缺点。

The *latest* is that he is going to run for election. 最新消息说,他打算参加竞选。

⑬ 由分词转化来的名词的数

这类词的单复数意义的选择应根据具体的上下文来定夺。

A. 名词化的过去分词一般没复数

名词化的过去分词一般没有复数形式,往往指特定的个人,作单数名词用。

The *deserted* comes to realize finally that he has been cut off from happiness. 那个被遗弃的人终于渐渐明白:他已与幸福无缘了。

The *accused* was sentenced to death by the court. 法庭宣判被告死刑。

B. 有时名词化的过去分词作复数用

The dispossessed are demanding their rights. 被剥夺权力者在要求他们的权利。

⑭ 由动名词转化来的名词的数

名词化的动名词，有些习惯用复数形式，有些则没有复数形式，有些单复数同形，有些则有单复数两种用法。它们中有些是固定用法，要设法记住。

All her *savings* were drawn out from the bank and contributed to the public cause. 她的所有积蓄都从银行里取出来捐给了公益事业。(savings 只有复数形式，跟复数动词)

It's a *living*. 这是混饭吃的工作。(living 为可数名词，但一般只用单数形式，尤其在习语 make a living 中)

In the Indo-European family, English has the largest number of *borrowings* from other language. 在印欧语系中，英语使用的外来借用词可谓最多。(borrowing 为可数名词，单复数形式都有)

Where is the *doings* to open this with? 打开这个东西的那玩意儿在哪儿？(doings 作"不知名的东西"解时单复数同形)

Are there going to be some big doings around here tomorrow night? 明晚这儿有什么盛大的社交活动吧？(doing 作"社交活动"或"种种事情"、"行为举止"解时只有复数形式及意义)

He often quotes the *sayings* of Albert Einstein. 他常引用爱因斯坦的话。(saying 为可数名词)

Hang all the *washing* out to dry. 把洗好的衣服都拿出去晾。(washing 只有单形，不可数)

This case of juvenile offence was caused by an inadequate family *upbringing*. 这宗少年犯罪案是缺乏家庭教育造成的。(upbringing 为不可数名词，但可以由不定冠词及形容词修饰)

It's not my *liking* to go walking on a cold day. 我不喜欢在大冷天出去散步。(liking 的用法同 upbringing)

(4) 名词的格

英语名词的格(Case)，也是一种语法范畴，它是用于表示名词(或代词)与句子中其他词之间意义关系的一种形式。名词的格有通格(Common Case)和所有格或属格(Possessive Case)两种。

① 通格

通格就是不用"'s"来表示的那些名词形式。当名词作句子的主语、宾语、补语等时，都用无词形变化的形式，这就是通格形式。

Suzhou is a beautiful city. 苏州是个美丽的城市。(作主语)

The capital of China is *Beijing*. 中国的首都是北京。[作补语(表语)]

She likes *apples* very much. 她非常喜欢苹果。(作宾语)

② 所有格表示的范围和构成方法

所有格一般是在名词后加"'s"构成，它主要用于表示有生命的人或高级动物的名词，但也有用于非生命的名词；就是"'s"所有格也并非只是简单地在名词后加"'s"构成，因为名词的形式和组成并不相同，所以它们构成所有格也不完全相同；表示所有格，还可用介词 of 短语表示，所有格它们的意思都是"……的"。

A. 所有格的构成形式

名词所有格的构成形式有两种：一是在名词后加"'s"，另一种是在名词后以介词 of 短语表示，它们的意思都是"……的"。不过这两种形式在使用时有时有区别，有时没区别。

a. -'s 所有格

● 英语中许多名词，主要是指有生命的名词，可以在词尾加"'s"表示所有关系。

Tim's father is the editor-in-chief of the book, *An Outline of Modern English Grammar.* 蒂姆的父亲是《现代英语语法纲要》那本书的主编。

He's my *husband's* classmate. 他是我丈夫的同学。

● 如原词已有复数词尾-s，则只加" ' "。

the workers' reading-room 工人阅览室　　　　a scientists' rest-home 科学家疗养院
the professors' living quarters 教授住宅区　　the hens' eggs 母鸡蛋
the horses' tails 马尾巴　　　　　　　　　　the students' grades 学生级别
my friends' luggage 我朋友们的行李

- 如果原复数词不带-s 词尾,那要加"'s"。

children's magazines 儿童杂志　　the Working People's Palace of Culture 劳动人民文化宫

- 以-s 结尾的专有名词的所有格

以-s 结尾的专有名词构成所有格时其后仍然加"'s",或只加"'",但读音都是/iz/。

St Thomas's (St Thomas') Hospital 圣托马斯医院　　Engels' (Engels's) childhood 恩格斯的童年
Jones' (Jones's) plays 琼斯的剧本　　　　　　　　Dickens' (Dickens's) novels 狄更斯小说
Engles' (Engels's) works 恩格斯著作　　　　　　　Burns' (Burns's) poems 彭斯的诗歌

- 合成名词的所有格

合成名词的所有格还是在词尾加"'s"。

the editor-in-chief's office 总编室　　　my father-in-law's business 我岳父的商号
editors-in-chief's office 总编室　　　　his brothers-in-law's business 他的姐夫们的商号

- 并列名词的所有格
* 共有与否

并列名词所有格的构成依语义而定:如果一件东西为两人共有,只在后一个名词词尾加-s';如果不是共有,而是分属各人所有,则在每个并列名词之后各加-'s。

Ellen and Mary's room 爱伦和玛丽合住的房间(共有)
Ellen's and Mary's room/Ellen's room and Mary's room 爱伦的房间和玛丽的房间(各有)

* 看作整体

还有一些并列名词通常作为一个整体看待,这种名词词组只在最后加-'s 构成属格。

an hour and a half's talk 一个半小时的谈话　　a cat and dog's life 吵吵闹闹的生活

- 带后置修饰短语的所有格

带后置修饰短语名词词组时,仅在词组的末尾加-'s 构成所有格。

somebody else's problem 别人的问题
the Duke of Normandy's property 诺曼底公爵的财产
the Government of Britain's policy 英国政府的政策

- 表示时间、地点、度量、天体名称等名词的所有格

上面提到的那些名词所有格多数属有生命的名词,也涉及一些无生命名词的所有格。另外,某些表示时间、地点、度量、天体名称的名词也可以有所有格。

today's newspaper 今日的报纸　　　　an hour's drive 一小时的车程
the world's population 世界的人口　　Shanghai's industry 上海的工业
five ton's capacity 五吨的容量　　　　a pound's weight 一磅的重量
the moon's orbit 月球的轨道　　　　　the sun's energy 太阳能

- 某些成语中的所有格

within a *stone's* throw 一箭之遥　　　at *one's* wit's end 智穷之计
a *bird's* eye view 鸟瞰　　　　　　　a *hair's* breath 间不容发
for friendship's sake 为了友谊　　　　at one's wit's end 黔驴技穷
out of harm's way 不要受损害　　　　to one's heart's content 尽情地
in our mind's eye 在我们心目中　　　(keep) at arm's length 保持距离
the earth's surface 地球表面　　　　　for goodness' sake 看在上帝分上

to get one's money's worth 物有所值　　　　　a stone's throw 一箭之遥

③ of 所有格

of 所有格多用于无生命的东西或名词化的词。像 the subject of the sentence（句子的主语），the foot of the mountain（山脚），the livelihood of the poor（穷人的生计），the mystery of the unknown（未知事物的神秘性）等就很典型。

而在报刊文章的标题或提要中多用-'s 所有格，以使文字简洁。
The P. L. O. Head's Ultimate Crisis 巴解组织领导人的最后危机（标题文字）
To the White House's dismay, he's using it. 令白宫惊恐不安的是,他正在使用这种权利。（提要文字）

但当需要连用两个所有格时,最好把两种结合起来（起码要避免连用-'s 所有格），根据句子的侧重点、念起来是否顺口等原则处理。

④ -'s 所有格与 of 所有格的关系

人们常说,-s 所有格常用于有生命的人、动物之类的名词,of-所有格常用于无生命的东西的名词,其实也不然,它们有时是可以替换使用的。前面说到的那些 's 所有格一般都可以用 of-所有格替代；然而,也不能把 's 所有格与 of-所有格完全画等号。

A．'s 所有格一般可以用 of 所有格替代

Mr. Smith's passport = the passport of Mr. Smith. 斯密斯先生的护照
students' books ≠ the books of the students 学生们的书
the visitors' arrival = the arrival of the visitors 旅客们的到来

B．有些 's 所有格不可用 of 所有格替代

children's clothes ≠ the clothes of the children 孩子们的衣服
women's magazines the magazines of the women 妇女杂志

其实,第一句的 children's clothes = the clothes for the children, 第二句中的 women's magazines = the magazines for the women。

⑤ 双重所有格

双重所有格（Double Genitive）就是把"'s"形式和"of"用在一起。它们更具体的形式 有两种：一种是"不定冠词+n+of+n's"形式，另一种是"指示代词（this/that/these/those）+ n. + of +n's"。要特别注意的是,这两种形式中都不能以定冠词 the 开头,结尾的 's 所有格必须是人称名词或人称代词,而且所指的对象必须明确。

A．第一种双重所有格

第一种双重所有格"不定冠词+n. + of +n's"通常指第一个 n 中的一部分或一个,含义稍有些模糊,日常用语中习惯这样用。它与单纯的 of 所有格区别在于：强调的重点不同,比如在下面这小段对话中,双重所有格和 of 所有格就表现出了意义上微妙差别。

W：Who told you that? 谁跟你这么说的？
M：A friend of your husband's. 你丈夫的一位朋友。（意为"你丈夫的朋友中的一个"）
M：If he says such things, he is not a friend of my husband. 他如果这么说,那他就不是我丈夫的朋友。（强调"我丈夫的朋友"）

另外,当所有格所修饰比较特殊的名词（如 portrait, picture, painting, photograph, stature, criticism, opinion, judgement, condemnation 等）时,使用双重所有格或使用 of-所有格句子的意义大不相同。

The only thing that impressed him at Mrs. Brown's was a portrait *of a young lady* which was hung on the hall. 布朗太太家里唯一给他留下深刻印象的是挂在大厅墙上的一幅年轻女性的肖像。（此处 of 所有格表示属性,即"一个年轻女性的肖像"）

Now the whole town was talking about a portrait *of this young lady collector's* which was stolen a few days before. 现在全镇人都在议论几天前被盗的这个年轻女收藏家所收藏的一幅肖像。（此处双重所有格表示所有关系，即"这个年轻女收藏家所收藏的一幅肖像"）

The whole speech was regarded as a condemnation *of modern warfare*. 整篇讲话被看成是对现代战争的谴责。（of 所有格表示动宾关系，即"对现代战争的谴责"）

He had prepared himself for a condemnation *of his family's*. 他已准备好了应付来自家人的谴责。（双重属格表示来源关系，即"来自他家里人的谴责"）

B．第二种双重所有格

第二种双重所有格"指示代词（this/that/these/those）+ n. + of + n's"这种形式往往含有表示说话人的喜爱、赞赏、抱怨、厌恶等感情色彩，我们在翻译或朗读此类句子时一定要反映出这样意思，表达出那种情感、语气来。

That little brother of John's broke my window glass again! 约翰的那个宝贝弟弟又把我的窗玻璃打碎了！（嗔怪、抱怨的语气。）

If only you had come with me and seen those wonderful performances of the children's. 你真应该跟我一起去看看那些孩子们的精彩表演！（赞叹的语气）

⑥ 名词所有格的深层意义

名词属格通常是表示"所有"关系，以上所举诸多例句子多属此类型；但除此之外，名词所有格对于所修饰的名词还可表示其他语义关系，如主谓关系、动宾关系、用途关系、来源关系、同位关系等。

A．表示所有关系

这是所有格最主要的用法。

Mr. Smith's passport has been visaed. 史密斯先生的护照已经被签证了。

Here the gravity of the earth is neglected. 这里地球的引力被忽略不计。

B．表示主谓关系

his father's departure 相当于 His father departed.

Helen's arrival 相当于 Helen arrived.

C．表示主动关系

前面名词表示后面动作的执行者。

He was pleased by the King's praise. 国王对他的赞扬使他很高兴。

The scientist's invention earned him a medal. 那科学家的发明让他获得了一枚奖章。

D．表示动宾关系

前面名词表示动作的承受者。

the prisoner's release 相当于 Somebody released the prisoner.

Hery's murder 相当于 Somebody murdered Henry.

The play ends with Hamlet's murder. 剧本以哈姆雷特被害结束。

The film star's admirers crowded round him. 这位电影明星被他的崇拜者围住了。

E．表示用途关系

children's clothes 相当于 clothes for children

women's magazines 相当于 magazines for women

F．表示来源关系

Newton's law 相当于 the law formulated by Newton

my mother's letter 相当于 a letter from my mother

G．表示同位关系

在当代英语中一般只用 of 所有格表示。

the pleasure *of meeting you* 相当于 Meeting you is a pleasure.

H. 表示属性关系

It was not until 1897 that the first women's college in the U. S. was founded. 直到1897年美国第一所女子学院才建立。(属性关系：a college for women)

an absence of ten days 缺席10天(属性关系：The absence lasted ten days)

I. 表示其他一些关系

有时名词所有格的后面可以不带名词,这种情况主要用于表示住所、商店、诊所、教堂、宫殿等公共场所的意思。

He stayed at the *Patterson's*. 他住在帕特逊家。

He lives opposite the *tobacconist's*. 他住在烟草店对面。

I had a decaying tooth extracted at the *dentist's*. 我在牙医诊所把一颗龋齿给拔了。

You can see *St Paul's* from Fleet Street. 从舰队街你能瞧见圣保罗大教堂。

He was received at *St James'*. 他在圣詹姆斯宫受到接见。

⑦ 's 所有格与 of 所有格的"专用"和"兼用"

在英语里,这两种所有格有时有它们的专用情况,有时却又能兼用。

A. 所有格的专用情况

a. 必须用 's 所有格和常用 's 所有格的情况

● 表示类别或属性时,必须用。

a doctor's degree 医生的级别(不能说成 the degree of a doctor)

men's shoes 男鞋(不能说成 the shoes of men)

children's stories 儿童故事(不能说成 the stories of the children)

● 当被修饰词有同位语时,必须用。

Bob bought the book at Brown's, the bookseller's. 巴勃那本书在布朗店买的,那个书店。(The bookseller's 不能说成 the shop of the bookseller)

● 表示度量时,必须用 's 所有格。

five years' schooling 五年的学校教育(不说 schooling of five years)

● 表示住宅、店铺、教堂、学校等处所时,必须用 's 所有格。

She met at her *aunt's*（home）. 她在她叔叔家遇到我的。

Can you tell me where nearest the *tailor's*（shop）is? 你能告诉我最近的缝纫店在哪吗?

Have you ever been to *St Paul's*（Cathedral）? 你去过圣保罗大教堂吗?

b. 要用 of 所有格的情况

● 表示同位、部分、描绘时。

the city *of Dublin*（= the city Dublin）都柏林市

the front *of the hall*（= the front part of the hall）礼堂前部分

a woman *of courage*（= a courageous woman）一个勇敢的妇人

● 名词化的形容词/分词

表示名词化的形容词或名词化的分词的"所有",要用 of 所有格。

ambitions of *the young* 青年人的抱负(不可说 the young's ambitions)

the demands of *the wounded*（受）伤(人)员(的)通知(不可说 the wounded's demands)

B. 's 所有格与 of 所有格的兼用

● 表示人、人类整体以及社会、政治组织的名词

Chairman Mao's works = the works of Chairman Mao 毛主席的著作

Newton's laws = the laws of Newton 牛顿定律

the peasants' farm tools = the farm tools of the peasants 农民的农具

the majority's opinion = the opinion of the majority 多数人的信念

the Senates' committee = the committee of the senates 参议院委员会

- 表示某些无生命东西的名词

某些无生命东西的名词,可兼用's 所有格和 of 所有格。

China's foreign policy = the foreign policy of China 中国的外交政策

Asia's future = the future of Asia 亚洲的前途

the book's title = the title of the book 书的标题

the game's law = the law of the game 游戏规则

- 表示较高动物的名词

a dog's tail = the tail of a dog 狗尾巴

the lion's mane = the mane of the lion 狮子的鬃毛

a panda's life = the life of a panda 熊猫的生命

⑧ 名词所有格的用法

名词所有格除了用于表示人的名词外,还可用于高级或少量低级动物的名词,也可用于无生命东西、时间、国家、机关名词及一些车船、用具等名词。

A. 用于表示人的名词，即"（某人）的"

Mr. Brown's house 布朗先生的房子,

my daughter's favourite dish 我女儿最喜欢的菜

This is one of Vinci's works. 这是达·芬奇的作品之一。

Did you visit St Paul's Cathedral? 你有没有去看圣保罗大教堂？

a man's hospital 男性医院　　　　　　the women's lavatory 女厕所

Archimedes' Principle 阿基米德原理　　a men's club 男子俱乐部

a judge's uniform 法官制服　　　　　gentlemen's wear 男装

St Thomas' Park 圣托马斯公园

B. 用于一些表示高级动物的名称或少量表示低级动物的名称

The donkey moved at a snail's pace. 驴以蜗牛的速度慢慢行进。

It's made from mare's ,cow's or ewe's milk. 它是由马奶、牛奶或羊奶做的。

C. 用于表示一些无生命东西的名词

a. 表示时间的名词

It was a summer's evening. 这是一个夏天的夜晚。

We have two week's vacation for Spring Festival. 春节我们有两周的假。

He agreed without a moment's hesitation. 他毫不犹豫地同意了。

After that they had a good night's sleep. 之后他们好好睡了一夜。

b. 表示某些集体的名词

There was a raid on the Democratic Party's Headquarters. 有人袭击了民主党的总部。

You must obey the majority's view. 你必须服从多数人的意见。

c. 表示国家、城市的名词

It's the city's biggest supermarket. 它是这座城市最大的超市。

It was the first time I had left England's shore. 这是我第一次离开英国海港。

It's the country's biggest lake. 它是这个国家最大的湖泊。

d. 机构组织等的名词

We sat in the station's waiting-room until evening. 我们在车站候车室等到晚上。
Jones studies at Harvard's Department of linguistics. 琼斯在哈佛大学语言系学习。
the European Economic Community's exports 欧洲经济共同体的出口额

e. 表示车、船、用具等的名词

The plane's engine is in a good condition. 这架飞机发动机状态良好。
You can predict a computer's behavior. 你可以预见一台电脑的性能。
The car's design is unique. 这辆车的设计很独特。

⑨ 's 所有格后名词的省略

在一些情况下，'s 所有格后名词可以省略。

A．一般 's 所有格后名词的省略

在 's 所有格所修饰的名词在上文已经出现过时可省略。

His memory is like an elephant's. 他的记忆力太迟钝了。(= an elephant's memory，直译：他的记性差得像一头大象。)
I don't think this is my fault, but nobody's. 这不是我的错；谁也没有错。(= nobody's fault)

B．表示住所后 's 所有格的名词可省略

The murder happened just at the Johnsons. 凶杀案正是在 Johnson 家发生的。
Those pictures evoked my memory of happy children at my grandparents. 那些相片唤起我对在祖父母家度过的快乐童年的回忆。

C．以名人的名字命名的公共建筑物后的名词可省略

一些以名人的名字命名的公共建筑物后的名词习惯上总是省略的。

St Paul's (Cathedral) 圣保罗大教堂   St Jame's (palace) 圣詹姆士宫

D．一些营业场所后的名词可省略

the barber's 理发店，the grocer's 杂货店，(BrE) the chemist's/(ArE) the druggist's 药店，Johnson's 约翰逊商店

E．所有格所修饰的名词如果刚刚提过，可以省略

This is not my umbrella, but Jim's. 这不是我的伞，是吉姆的。
Her love, like Jennie's, was sincere. 她的爱情，和珍妮的爱情一样，是真挚的。
"Whose coat is this?" "It's my mother's." "这是谁的大衣?" "是我妈妈的。"

(5) 名词的性

英语名词的性(Gender)有四个：阳性(Masculine Gender)，表示男人或雄性动物；阴性(Feminine Gender)，表示女人或雌性动物；通性(Common Gender)，表示男女性或雌雄性通用；中性(Neuter Gender)，表示无生命、无性别的事物或抽象的概念。

① 一些常见名词的阳性、阴性对照表

阳性	阴性
actor 演员	actress 女演员
bridegroom 新郎	bride 新娘
chairman 男主席	chairwoman 女主席
count 伯爵	countess 女伯爵, 伯爵夫人

续表

阳性	阴性
emperor 皇帝	empress 女皇帝,皇后
gentleman 先生	lady 女士
god 神	goddess 女神
headmaster 中学校长	headmistress 中学女校长
heir 继承人	heiress 女继承人
hero 英雄	heroine 女英雄
host 主人(对客人而言)	hostess 女主人
king 国王	queen 女王,王后
lad 少年	lass 少女
landlord 男房东	landlady 女房东,女地主
manager 经理	manageress 女经理
masseur 男按摩师	masseuse 女按摩师
master 主人(对仆人而言)	mistress 女主人
monk 和尚	nun 女尼
nephew 侄儿	niece 侄女
poet 诗人	poetess 女诗人
policeman 警察	policewoman 女警察
priest 男教士	priestess 女教士
prince 王子	princess 公主
salesman 售货员	saleswoman 女售货员
shepherd 牧羊人	shepherdess 女牧羊人
sir 先生	madam 夫人
steward(轮船、飞机上的)招待	stewardess 女招待
usher(电影院的)带座员	usheress 女带座员
waiter 餐馆服务员	waitress 女服务员
widower 鳏夫	widow 寡妇
wizard 男巫	witch 女巫

② 一些动物名词的阳性和相对应的阴性

阳性	阴性
lion 狮子	lioness 母狮子
tiger 老虎	tigress 母老虎
bull 公牛	cow 母牛
stallion 公马	mare 母马

续表

阳性	阴性
ram 公羊	ewe 母羊
cock, rooster 公鸡	hen 母鸡
drake 公鸭	duck 母鸭
leopard 公豹	leopardess 母豹
dog 公狗	bitch 母狗
fox 狐狸	vixen 母狐狸
gander 公鹅	goose 母鹅
boar 公野猪	sow 母(野)猪
stag 公鹿	doe 母鹿

③ 一些个体名词的阳性、阴性及通性对应表

阳性	阴性	通性
father	mother	parent
man	woman	person
son	daughter	child
boy	girl	child
king	queen	monarch/sovereign/ruler
cock/rooster	hen	fowl, chicken
stallion	mare	horse
gentleman	lady	
monk	nun	
uncle	aunt	

④ 阳性名词加上词尾变化(或词缀)构成对应的阴性名词

在很多欧洲语言中,词的词尾变化是性的一种表示方法。现代英语中为一小部分词保留了这种方法,其中大部分是从其他欧洲语言中借来的词,少部分为古英语的残留痕迹。这类词只能特别记忆,因为在现代英语中阴性后缀(如-ess)是不能随意加在所有阳性名词上的。

阳性	阴性
boy friend	girl friend
male student	female student
man servant	woman servant
congressman	congresswoman
landlord	landlady
he-wolf	she-wolf

由于社会历史和观念的变迁,像上表中这种性的表达方式越来越普遍,很多职业和社会地位以前是由男性所垄断的,所以表现在词汇上没有必要加上性别修饰词,因为"通性"即有"男性"之含义。随着越来越

多的女性参与社会竞争,进入各种职业和拥有某种地位,通性名词上的性别修饰词从"不需要"演变为"需要"变更,所以有些职业的名称词在指女性时就加上阴性修饰词。某些历史上为女性垄断的职业名称则反之。

阳性	阴性	通性
writer	woman writer	writer
doctor	woman/female doctor	doctor
engineer	female engineer	engineer
male nurse	nurse	nurse

(6) 代词与名词在"性"上的一致

英语代词中只有第三人称单数有性的区别,所以代词与名词在"性"上的一致主要指 代词 he/she/it 及它们的宾格和所有格与其所指名词在"性"上的一致。

① 代词 he/she 指称相应的阳性和阴性单数名词

通常第三人称单数代词是依照所指名词在一般意义上的性来决定的:阳性人称代词用 he 指称;阴性人称名词用 she 指称;通性人称名词依实际情况确定用 he 或 she 指代;当指人的集体名词取单数意义时,应按名词的实际情况确定选用 he 或 she;表示动物的词或无生命、抽象事物的中性名词一般用 it 指称。

② 第三人称单数代词带感情色彩用法

第三人称单数代词还有许多带感情色彩的用法。通性人称名词 baby 和 infant,一般用 it 指称;但孩子的父母或与其有感情联系的人总是会用 he 或 she 来指明其性别的。

表示动物或无生命、抽象事物的词,如果用 he 或 she 来指称,也就往往含有感情色彩,如国名或地区名如果仅作地理名称解,则用不带感情色彩的 it;如果视为政治、经济、文化、民族单位,则用阴性代词 she 指称,这同汉语文化中"祖国母亲"、"母亲河"或用"她"来指称祖国、故乡等概念是同样道理。

Greece has an area of about 131,000 sq km. *It* is scantily peopled. 希腊面积大约131,000平方公里,人口稀少。

在文学文体中,某些大自然现象或抽象事物常被带感情色彩地人格化,如 sun, death, love 等常被视为阳性,而 moon, earth, spring, autumn, peace 等被视为阴性。这往往与古典神话中代表这些事物的神的性别形象有关。读者如果掌握一些希腊、罗马的古典神话知识,处理此类问题就会得心应手了。

Love begins playing his old tricks every spring. 爱神每年春天就开始玩起了他的旧把戏。

The clouds were driving over the moon at their giddiest speed and wholly obscuring her. 云层飞速地飘向月亮并且全遮住了她。

人们对于自己所喜爱的或有感情关系的动物或无生命物也会用 he 或 she 来指称。这种用法范围之广,例子之多,可谓举不胜举。

③ 泛指意义的单数通性人称名词的指称

泛指意义的单数通性人称名词的代词指称是一个特别需要注意的问题。传统上,如果通性人称名词在意义上不强调性别区别,则一律采用阳性第三人称单数代词指称。

If such a person passes for a Christian, he is guilty of obtaining respect under false pretenses. 就算这种人被大家误认为是基督徒,他也犯了用欺骗换取尊敬之罪。

近几年来,受女权运动思潮的影响,很多人对这种"以偏概全"概念代表两性全体的思维表达方式有所保留,于是让人们开始习惯于同时使用阴、阳代词来指称单数通性名词。

A teacher knows his or her students only in relation to the course. 教师只有通过课业来了解学生。

但这种谨慎的做法如果上下文中多次出现也会显得累赘。我们可以考虑几种变通的手段：一是以复数通性名词代替单数来表示泛指意义，则代词指称可以用性别含混的 they, their 等，如：When teachers get more and more effort from their classes, the student who is doing normal work can be perceived as not doing well.（当老师们班上有越来越多的学生给自己加码时，那个维持正常工作量的学生就会被认为是不努力的）。二是概念措辞，避免使用代词，如：When a customer calls, ask him or her to leave his or her phone number. → When a customer calls, be sure to ask for a phone number.（如果有顾客打电话来，一定要留下（他的）电话号码）。

用通性名词表示泛指概念是当代英语发展趋势，它避免了被斥为含有性别歧视色彩的用法，如大家都熟知的以 man/men 代表"人类"之义，现在多用 person, human 等词代替。同样，用新造对应于阳性词的阴性词来表示女性也是女权意识的一个体现，如相对于 chairman, 有 chairwoman 来指"女性主席"。但由于上文提到过的"两种性别修饰词的使用并不平衡"的现象，"通性词＋性别标志"的构词法有时还是难免会造成心理敏感，所以在表达泛指意义时，使用通性名词（如 chairman）还属上策。

（7）名词的句法功能

名词（词组）可作句子的主语、表语、宾语、同位语、呼语状语、状语等。

① 作主语

Psychology and *economics* are social sciences. 心理学和经济学是社会科学。

Where there is *a will*, there is *a way*.（谚语）有志者，事竟成。

② 作表语

History is her *major*. 历史是她的主修课。

Smoking is my only *weakness*. 抽烟是我唯一的缺点。

③ 作宾语

They agreed to fax us *their plans* tomorrow. 他们同意明天把计划传真给我们。

She gave her child *a first-rate* education. 她给了她孩子一流的教育。

④ 作定语

She studies at *an evening* school. 她上夜校。

He bought me *a diamond* necklace. 他给我买了一个钻石项链。

⑤ 作同位语

You *boys* sit on this side. 你们男孩坐这边。

This is our chairman, *Mr. Smith*. 这是我们的主席史密斯先生。

⑥ 作呼语

Be quiet, *children*! 安静点，孩子们！

Come in, *Mr. Brown*. 请进，布朗先生。

⑦ 作状语

名词（短语）作状语，与其他句法功能相比，要复杂些。名词（短语）作状语较常见的有表示时间、重量、长、宽度、比率、方式、让步、程度、地点等，有时它们前面经常含有数量词相伴。

Wait *an hour*, please. 请等一小时。（表示时间）

She'll be back *Saturday*. 她周六回来。（表示时间）

They went out of fashion *years* ago. 它们几年前就过时了。（表示时间）

She was falling *head* down when a tree on the cliff stopped her. 她头朝下跌落时悬崖上的一棵树挡住了她。

(表示方式)

They will come *rain or shine*. 不论晴天还是下雨,他们都回来。(表示让步)

He loves his job *heart and soul*. 他全身心地热爱他的工作。(表示程度)

The bridge is *five miles* long. 这座桥长五英里。(表示长度)

Mr. Green is a man who is *city* born and *city* bred. 格林先生是个生在城市,长在城市的人。(表示地点)

There are few Professors who were *Harvard* educated in our college. 我们学院的教授没几个曾受教于哈佛大学。(表示地点)

⑧ 作介词宾语

He majored in anthropology at *Cambridge*. 他在剑桥大学主修人类学。

She has made outstanding contribution to *architecture*. 她对建筑学做出了突出的贡献。

⑨ 构成复合宾语

They gave him *some money*. 他们给了她一些钱。

He painted the table *a brighter color*. 他把桌子漆成了更鲜亮的颜色。

A. 单数、不可数名词作定语

一般情况下,名词作定语常用单数,有时也用不可数名词作定语。

body temperature 体温	box-office value 票房价值	piano lessons 钢琴课
seat belt 座带	eye drops 眼药水	song and dance troupe 歌舞团
horror film 恐怖电影	time zone 时区	identity card 身份证
tomato sauce 西红柿汁	import duty 进口税	trade union 工会
income tax 所得税	trade deficit 贸易逆差	inquiry office 问事处
water pipe 水管	news broadcast 新闻广播	welcome speech 欢迎辞
orange juice 橘汁	weather station 气象站	paper money 纸币
weather forecast 天气预报	brain concussion 脑震荡	cotton goods 棉织品
fire brigade 消防队	emergency department 急诊部	power plant 发电厂
press conference 记者招待会		

B. 复数名词作定语

虽然在绝大多数情况下作定语的名词都用单数形式,但有时也有用名词的复数形式作定语的。

honours student 优等生	arms depot 军火库
arts degree 文科学位	grants committee 补助金委员会
communication satellite 通信卫星	careers guide 就业指导
sports meet 运动会	customs officer 海关人员
parks department 园林部(局)	examinations board 考试委员会
two-thirds majority 三分之二多数	entertainments guide 娱乐指南
courses committee 课程委员会	commodities fair 商品交易会
saving bank 储蓄银行	customs house 海关大楼

C. 名词作定语和形容词作定语的比较

有不少名词前面既可以用名词作定语,也可用形容词作定语,它们之间的区别主要在意思上。

用名词作定语	用形容词作定语
gold reserve 黄金储备	golden sheen 金色光泽
silver coins 银币	silvery metal 银白色的金属
heart trouble 心脏病	hearty welcome 热情的欢迎

续表

用名词作定语	用形容词作定语
art circle 艺术界	artistic family 有艺术修养的家庭
stone bridge 石头桥	stony heart 铁石心肠
snow mountain 雪山	snowy hair 雪白的头发
rain drops 雨滴	rainy night 雨夜
rose garden 玫瑰园	rosy cheeks 红红的脸颊
colour film 彩色电影	colourful flags 彩旗
mountain village 山村	mountainous region 山区
history teacher 历史老师	historical standpoint 历史观点
geography lesson 地理课	geographical terms 地理名词
peace talks 和谈	peaceful construction 和平建设
youth delegation 青年代表团	youthful appearance 年轻的模样
production plan 生产计划	productive worker 劳动能手

如果有派生的形容词,需要弄清它的确切意思。如果根本没有形容词,在很多情况下可用名词作定语,或与之构成合成词。

bus stop 公共汽车站　　plane station 机场　　railway ticket 火车票
taxi driver 出租车司机　　car park 停车场　　hair style 发式
face cream 面霜　　tooth ache 牙疼

9.2　名词性从句

在句子中起名词作用的各种从句,称为名词性从句(Noun Clause)。名词性从句实际上是名词的扩大,它们在句中就是起名词的作用。因为名词在句中可作主语、表语、宾语、同位语、宾语补足语等,所以名词性从句在句中也能作那些句子成分。这五种从句与主句间一般不用逗号分开。

名词从句包含主语从句、表语从句、宾语从句及同位语从句,这是一般语法书上的观点;其实,宾语补足语从句也属此类从句。

(1) 主语从句

主语从句是指那些由连词引导,在句中作主语的从句。

① 引导主语从句的连词

A. 单纯连词 that, whether, whether … or

That she is still alive is a consolation. 她还活着是一种安慰。
Whether it will do us harm or good remains to be seen. 对我们是好是坏还要拭目以待。
Notes: a. 以 that 引导的主语从句中,that 没有实际意义,它只起引导作用,却又不可省略。但如果上面第一句换成 It is a consolation (that) he is still alive,那 that 可省,特别在口语中。
b. whether 引导主语从句可以放在句首,但 if 不能引导主语从句。
Whether she comes or not makes no difference. 她来不来都没有关系。(正确)
If she comes or not makes no difference. (错误)

B. 连接代词 who, whom, whoever, whomever, what, which, whichever

Whoever breaks the law deserves a fine. 无论是谁违反纪律都要受到惩罚。

What seems easy to some people seems difficult to other people. 对有些人来说似乎简单的事情对另一些人来说可能是困难的。

C. 连接限定词 whose, what, which

Whose fault it is remains a mystery. 这是谁的过失还是个秘密。

Whichever horse comes in first wins. 无论哪匹马先到就赢。

D. 连接副词 when, where, why, how

When the sports meeting will be held has not been announced. 运动会什么时候召开还没宣布。

Where he went was London. 他去的地方是伦敦。

② it 形式主语先行，主语从句后置的情况

A. 当主语从句较长时

为了使句子显得平衡，我们常用"It be ... that/whether/how"句型，而把主语从句置后。在非正式文体中，that 往往省略。

It is a pity (that) Li Hua doesn't know French. 李华不懂法语是件憾事。

It was not known whether there was gold left in the mine. 矿石里是否还有金子尚不清楚。

It's not my business how Mary chooses to live. 玛丽选择什么样的生活与我无关。

B. 当主句谓语动词是被动语态时

It was admitted that she danced well. 她舞跳得好得到大家认可。

It is not yet settled whether we are going to Beijing next week. 我们下周是否去北京还没决定下来。

It has not been decided that the show shall not be open on Monday. 展览在不在周一展出还未决定。

C. 当主句是疑问句或感叹句时

Is it true that he has been injured in an accident? 他在事故中受伤了是不是真的？

How is it you don't like peaches? 你怎么不喜欢桃子？

How strange it is the dogs are so quiet today! 狗狗今天这么安静真奇怪啊！

D. 当主句的谓语动词是 appear, come, happen, matter, look, occur, seem, strike 等时

It appears that Jane was very hard up. 简显得手头很紧。

It seems that only Tom knew what had happened. 好像只有汤姆知道发生了什么。

E. 在突出主句的表语时

It's a pity (that) he didn't join the party. 他没有参加聚会真可惜。

It's still unknown whether she is coming or not. 她来不来还不知道。

It's a mystery to her how it all happened. 事情怎样发生的对她来说是个秘密。

F. 在分裂句中

It was he who had been right. 对的是他(不是别人)。

It was yesterday that the unfortunate incident occurred. 就在昨天不幸事故发生了。

G. 当主语从句以连词 if/whether, but (that), as if/though 引导时

It was not clear to me if/whether Wu Na likes the present. 吴娜是否喜欢这礼物我尚不清楚。

It is not impossible that such a day may come. 这样的一天到来不是不可能的。

It seems as if Henry is the first to come. 看来亨利是第一个来。

③ 主语从句必须前置的情况

当主语从句由强式词"wh- +ever"引导时，必须置于句首。

Whoever goes will be welcome. 谁去都受欢迎。

Whatever I have is at your service. 我的东西你随便用。

Whichever you want is yours. 你想要什么就拿去好了。

④ 主语从句的句型转换

A. 主语从句→不定式

It is strange that they are together. 他们在一起真奇怪。

→It is strange for them to be together.

It is stupid that one should be so conceited. 如此骄傲是愚蠢的。

→It is stupid to be conceited.

B. 主语从句→v-ing 分词短语

It surprised her greatly that you should drive a car to Chicago in your condition. 以你的情况驾车上芝加哥极大地惊扰了我。

→Your driving a car to Chicago in your condition disturbs me greatly.

It made things all the worse that Bob was discharged by the manager. 鲍勃被经理解雇使事情变得更糟。

→Bob's being discharged by the manger made things all the worse.

C. wh-词引出的主语从句 → wh-＋动词不定式短语

Who(m) she should turn to is what she wants to know. 该请谁帮忙是她想知道的。

→Who to turn to is what she want to know.

D. 下列含先行主语 it 的主语从句与上述主语从句的转换方式有所不同

It's certain that we'll forget the key. 我们会忘记那把钥匙的。

→ We're certain to forget the key.

It seems that she has made a mistake. 她似乎犯了个错误。

→She seems to have made a mistake.

It is known that he is a coward. 大家都知道他是个懦夫。

→He is known to be a coward.

It is said that you are working in some factory. 据说你在某个工厂工作。

→ You are said to be working in some factory.

(2) 表语从句

表语从句(Predicative Clause)作句子的表语,置于主句中的连系动词之后。

① 引导表语从句的连词

A. 单纯连词 that (在口语中, that 可以省去), whether, as, like as if/though, because, lest

The reason was (that) you were afraid. 理由是你害怕。

My attitude is that students should not cheat in examinations. 我的态度是学生考试不应该作弊。

His first question was whether Rose had arrived. 他的第一个问题是罗丝是否到了。

The reasons are as (what) follows. 理由如下。

John looks like he will get the job. 约翰看来好像会得到那工作。

It is like she remembered the matter. 她好像记得那事。

The reason I am here is because I wish to lend a hand. 我之所以到这儿来是因为我希望能帮上忙。

Lei was in mortal fear lest (=that) he should see her. 蕾非常害怕他会看见她。

B. 连接代词 who (m), what, which, as

She is not who she was thought to be. 她已不是人们想象中的她。

This is what he wants to know. 这就是他想知的。

The question is which of you should go. 问题是你们中谁该去。

Things are not always as they seem to be. 事物不是总像表面上那样的。

What Tom wants to know is what you said at the meeting. 汤姆想知道的是你们在会上说了些什么。

C. 连接限定词 whose, what, which

The problem is whose name should be put foremost. 问题是谁的名字排在最前面。

I asked him what clothes I should wear. 我问他我该穿什么衣服。

The question is which restaurant I should go to. 问题是我该上哪家餐馆。

D. 连接副词 when, where, why, how

This is where we found it. 这就是我们找到它的地方。

What we want to know is how she will get there. 我们想知道的是她将如何到那里。

② 表语从句转换成短语的情况

A. that 引导的表语从句转换成动词不定式短语

Our plan is that we shall finish the work in two weeks.

→ Our plan is to finish the work in two weeks.

What she wants is that you will talk to Mr. Green.

→What she wants is for you to talk to Mr. Green.

B. 以 wh-引导的表语从句转换成动词不定式短语

The question is what we should do next.

→ The question is what to do next.

What I want to know is where we shall begin.

→What I want to know is where to begin.

C. 有时表语从句可以转换成 v-ing 形式短语

The greatest trouble was that we did not know all the details.

→The greatest trouble was our not knowing all the details.

What trouble me was that Helen was leaving for New Zealand.

→What trouble me was Helen's leaving for New Zealand.

(3) 同位语从句

同位语从句用于对名词做进一步解释,说明名词的具体内容。能接同位语从句的名词有：belief(相信), hope(希望), idea(想法), doubt(怀疑), news(消息), rumour(传闻), conclusion(结论), evidence(证据), suggestion(建议), problem(问题), order(命令), answer(回答), decision(决定), discovery(发现), explanation(解释), information(消息), knowledge(知识), law(法律), opinion(观点), possibility(可能性), principle(原则), truth(真理), promise(许诺), report(报告), thought(思想), statement(声明), rule(规定), certainty(肯定), probability(可能), likelihood(可能)。同位语从句一般由 that 引导,但也可以用关系代词(what, which, who)、关系副词(when, where, why, how)或 whether (if)引导。

The news that we are invited to the conference is very encouraging. 我们被邀请去参加会议的消息令人鼓舞。

Einstein came to the conclusion that the maximum speed possible in the universe is that of light. 爱因斯坦得出的结论是,宇宙中的最大速度是光速。

There arose the question where we could get the loan. 这样就产生了一问题：我们到哪里弄贷款。

Nobody can explain the mystery why he suddenly disappeared. 没有人能解开他突然消失了这个谜。

I have no idea what has happened to him. 我不知道他发生了什么事。

There is some doubt (as to) whether he will come. 有点怀疑他是否会来。
He has a feeling that his team is going to win. 他有个感觉他的队要赢了。
There is no doubt that (=but) he is the guilty one. 毫无疑问，他是个罪犯。
Your original question, why he did not report it to the police earlier, has not yet been answered. 你最先的问题，他为什么不早些报告警察，还没有回答呢。

(4) 宾语补足语从句

宾语补足语可以由名词、形容词、副词、动词不定式、分词、介词短语等担任，一般语法书上都这样阐述。然而宾语补足语也可由从句充当，却被忽视了。作宾语补足语的从句除了具有宾语补足语的特点之外，它不能用 that，而必须由 what 引出。

His education has made him what he is. 他的教育已使他成为现在这个样子。
You may call the new tool what you like. 你要怎么称呼这个新工具就怎么称呼它好了。
——What has made China what she is today? 是什么使得中国成为今天这样？
——It is Reforming and Opening-up. 是改革开放。

(5) 关于 what 引导名词从句的词性

what 既可以是疑问代词，也可以是关系代词，其区别是：what 从句的谓语动词含怀疑、询问、不肯定的意义时，what 为疑问代词；反之，指具体的事件，表示肯定意义时，what 就是关系代词。比较：

I don't know what he is writing. 我不知道他在写什么。（疑问代词）
I know what he meant. 我知道他的意思。（关系代词）
What is happening outside is not known. 不知道外面在发生什么事。（疑问代词）
What is happening outside does not concern us. 外面发生的事与我们无关。（关系代词）
The question is what she told her son befor she died. 问题是她临死之前告诉了她儿子什么。（疑问代词）
The decision is what she told her son before she died. 她做的决定就是她临死之前告诉她儿子。（关系代词）

第10章 代 词

10.1 人称代词

人称代词(Personal Pronoun)表示人称范畴以及它们的屈折变化形式,指"你"、"我"、"她"、"他"、"它"、"我们"、"你们"、"他们"等。

(1) 人称代词形式

人称代词有三种人称和两个数,它们的人称、性、数与格如下表:

人称	单数		复数	
	主格	宾格	主格	宾格
第一人称	I 我	me 我	we 我们	us 我们
第二人称	you 你	you 你	you 你们	you 你们
第三人称	he 他	him 他	they 他们	them 他们
	she 她	her 她	they 她们	them 她们
	it 它	it 它	they 它们	them 它们

(2) 人称代词的句法功能

① 作主语

She lost her wallet in the park. 她在公园里丢了她的钱包。

I hesitated a moment, and then sat down beside her. 我犹豫了一会儿,然后在她身边坐下来。

We both started as we saw each other. 我们两人一见面,都吃了一惊。

② 作宾语

人称代词宾格在句中作直接宾语、间接宾语与介词宾语。

I don't know *her*. 我不认识她。(直接宾语)

If you see Jim, give *him* my regards. 如果你见到吉姆,请代我问候他。(间接宾语)

Notes: a. 两个人称代词分别用作间接宾语和直接宾语时,间接宾语前应加 to,并置于直接宾语之后。

I gave *it* to *him*. 我把这个给了他。(而不说 I gave him it.)

b. 如其中一个为其他代词,则可采用间接宾语在前、直接宾语在后的形式。

I gave *him* some. 我给了他一些。

③ 作表语

Open the door, please. It's *me*. 请开门,是我。

It's *I* who did it. 是我做的。

上面最后一句中,表语用的主格,这是后面跟有 who 或 that 引导的从句。但 It is her that we are talking with. (我们是跟她在交谈) 用宾格,这是因为 her 是从句里 with 的宾语。

人称代词的用法上还要注意以下一些问题：

① 人称代词单独使用时，一般不用主格而用宾格。

—I'd like to go back in here. —*Me*, too. —我想回到这里来。—我也想。

—Will anyone go with him? —Not *me*. —有人愿和他一同去吗？—那不会是我。

② as，than 作介词用时，其后接宾格，作连词时用主格。

人称代词用于 as 和 than 之后，如果 as 和 than 用作介词，也往往用宾格，作连词用时就用主格。

He's younger than *me*. 他比我年轻。

Edward is as good a student as *him*. 爱德华和他一样是个好学生。

She's as old as *I* am. 她与我同岁。

You're taller than *she* is. 你比她高。

③ 在感叹疑问句中，人称代词宾格可用作主语，起强调作用。

Me get caught? 我会被逮住？

Him go to the States! 他怎会去美国！

④ we 和 you 可用作同位语结构的第一部分。

We girls often go to the movies together. 我们女孩子经常一起去看电影。

He asked *you* boys to be quiet. 他要你们男孩子安静些。

⑤ 有时，we，you，they 可用来泛指一般人。

We/You have to be cautious under such circumstances. 在这种情况下大家应特别小心。

We/You should keep calm even when *we/you* are in danger. 即使在危险时刻也要保持冷静。

They don't allow us to talk here. 这儿不准说话。

⑥ 以 we 代替 I。

为使口气显得谦虚一些，在文章、书的前言里，还有做报告时，人们常以 we 替代 I。

In this book *we'll* give you something new that you cannot find in any other English grammar books. 在这本书里我们将提供给你一些任何其他语法书里找不到的新东西。

⑦ 英语中的"先人后己"现象。

英语里，谁都知道"I"总是大写的，但在并列主语中，"I"总在最后。

Mary, Rose and *I* went to visit Suzhou in May. 玛丽、罗丝和我五月份去游览了苏州。

⑧ 代词 it 也指人。

it 主要指刚提到的事物，以避免重复，但 it 也可以指动物或婴儿(未知性别的婴儿或孩子)，在口语和电话中也指"人"。

They watched the train until *it* disappeared in the distance. 他们观察那列火车直到它消失在远处。

The baby has been crying from the morning. What's wrong with *it*? 那小孩从早晨起一直哭。它怎么了？(介词宾语)

—Is this your dog? —No, *it* isn't. —这是你的狗吗？—不是的。

Look at the bird. *It* always comes to my window. 瞧只鸟，它总是飞到我的窗前来。

It was Peter who lent me the money. 是彼得借钱给我的。

Ann (on the phone): Who is *it*/*that*? 安(打电话)：谁啊？

Bill: *It's* me. 比尔：是我。

10.2 物主代词

物主代词是表示所有关系的代词。物主代词有形容性物主代词和名词性物主代词两种。

(1) 物主代词的形式

数	人称	形容词性物主代词	名词性物主代词
单数	第一人称	my	mine
	第二人称	your	yours
	第三人称	his	his
		her	hers
		its	its
复数	第一人称	our	ours
	第二人称	your	yours
	第三人称	their	theirs

(2) 物主代词的句法功能

① 作定语

作定语用的只是形容词性物主代词，与 own 搭配起来表示强调。

My computer has been updated. 我的电脑已经升级了。
She turned away *her* eyes. 她把目光移开。
Their ideals have changed. 他们的理想变了。
I saw it with *my own* eyes. 那是我亲眼所见。
Mind *your own* business. 不要管闲事。

② 作主语、宾语和表语

名词性物主代词才能作主语、宾语和表语。

Hers is a pretty colorless life. 她的生活是一种相当平淡的生活。（主语）
This is your coat. *Mine* is in the room. 这是你的外衣。我的在房间里。（主语）
She would shut herself up in her room, Julio in *his*. 她常把自己关在房间里，朱利奥也是一样。（宾语）
My pen is broken. Please lend me *yours*. 我的钢笔坏了，请把你的借给我。（宾语）
—Whose book is this? 这是谁的书？
—It's *mine*. 是我的。（表语）
I knew that the house was *hers*. 我知道那房子是她的。（表语）

③ "of + 名词性物主代词"的用法

名词性物主代词有时也可以与 of 连用，构成双重属格。

A. 表示部分概念

He is a friend *of mine*. 他是我的一个朋友。

B. 表示感情色彩，多含贬义或讽刺

Is it the new car *of yours* that broke down on the way to Jiangning yesterday? 难道这就是你那辆去江宁半路上抛锚的新车子？（意为质量不好）
Look at that big nose *of his*! 看他那大鼻子！（有贬义）

10.3 反身代词

反身代词(Reflexive Pronoun)是一种表示反射或强调的代词。通过反身代词指代主语，使施动者把动作形式上反射到施动者自己。因此,反身代词与它所指代的名词或代词形成互指关系,在人称、性、数上得保持一致。

(1) 反身代词的形式

人称	单数	复数
第一人称	myself 我自己	ourselves 我们自己
第二人称	yourself 你自己	yourselves 你们自己
第三人称	himself 他自己 herself 她自己 itself 它自己	themselves 他们/她们/它们自己

(2) 反身代词的句法功能

I want to build *myself* a country house. 我想给自己建一座乡间别墅。(宾语)

He is always thinking of *himself*. 他总是想着他自己。(宾语)

They quarreled among *themselves*. 他们之间发生了争吵。(宾语)

Bob is not quite *himself* today. 鲍勃今天感到不适。(表语)

Be *yourself*, please. 请自然一点。(表语)

The representatives of the strikers wanted to see the boss *himself*. 罢工工人的代表想要见老板本人。(同位语)

I fixed the windows *myself*. 我自己装的窗户。(同位语)

反身代词在使用中还要注意以下一些问题:

① 与某些动词连用表示某种特定意义

Help *yourself* to some fruit. 请吃点水果。

He shaves *himself* once a day. 他一天刮一次脸。

Why did you absent *yourself* from school yesterday? 你昨天为何没去上学?

② 反身代词用于某些固定习语中

- by oneself 独自干,单干

He said he wanted to go out to have a walk *by himself*. 他说他想独自出去散步。

I managed to do it *by myself*. 我是自己做成这件事的。

This is a machine that works *by itself*. 这是一台自动化的机器。

- for oneself 替自己,为自己;自己

We'll have to judge *for ourselves*. 我们得自己来判断。

He demanded the right to decide *for himself*. 他要求得到自己做决定的权力。

- of oneself 自动地

The enemy will not perish *of himself*. 敌人不会自行消灭的。

- between ourselves 勿与外人道私下说的话

All this is *between ourselves*. 这些都不能告诉别人。

Between ourselves, Mr. Black has gone abroad. 不要和外人讲,布莱克先生已出国了。

- among themselves ……之间

They had a heated discussion *among themselves*. 他们之间进行了热烈的讨论。

- in oneself 本性;自身

He is not bad *in himself*. 他本质不坏。

This is a good idea *in itself*. 这主意本身不错。

10.4 相互代词

相互代词是表示相互关系的代词。它所指代的名词或代词必须是复数形式，each other 通常只用于两个人，one another 用于三人以上。

(1) 相互代词形式

宾格	属格
each other 相互	each other's 相互的
one another 相互	one another's 相互的

(2) 相互代词的句法功能

① 作宾语

I help him, he helps me and we help *each other*. 我帮他，他帮我，我们互相帮助。
We did not know *each other* before. 我们以前互不认识。
They have been separated from *one another* for a long time. 他们分开很久了。

② 作定语

They looked into *each other's* eyes for a silent moment. 他们彼此一时相对无言。
The two old men often call *each other's* nickname when they meet. 这两个老人见面时常常互相喊绰号。

③ 补充汉译英时的意义

有时在汉语中没有"相互"、"彼此"的词，而在译成英语时却要使用相互代词作补充。

他们现在不常见面。They don't often see *each other* now.
你们常通信吗？Do you often write to *one another*?
他们以前就认识。They have known *each other* before.

10.5 指示代词

指示代词是用来指示或标识人或事物的代词，与定冠词和人称代词一样，都具有指定的含义。它们所指的对象取决于说话者和听话者共同熟悉的语境。指示代词有 this, that, these, those 及 such 五个。

(1) 指示代词形式

	单数	复数
近指	this（student）这个（学生）	these（students）这些（学生）
远指	that（student）那个（学生）	those（students）那些（学生）

(2) 指示代词的句法功能

① 作主语、宾语、表语、定语、状语等

Are *these* your books? 这些是你的书吗？（主语）
This is my first visit to America. 这是我第一次到美国来。（主语）

Who's *that* speaking? 请问是哪位？（打电话用）（主语）
I will keep *this* in mind. 我会记住这一点的。（宾语）
You can choose one from *these*. 你可以从这些里面选一个。（宾语）
My idea is *this*. 这就是我的想法。（表语）
Oh, it's not *that*. 噢, 问题不在那儿。（表语）
Do you know *that* man? 你认识那个人吗？（定语）
These flowers are very beautiful. 这些花非常漂亮。（定语）
He said he didn't want *that* much. 他说他不需要那么多。（状语）
The book is about *this* thick. 那本书大约有这么厚。（状语）

② this, these 指近；that, those 指远

具体地说，指示代词 this 和 these 指时间与空间上较近的事物，that 和 those 指时间与空间上较远的事物。

This building was built last year, *that* one was built many years ago. 这栋大楼是去年建的, 那栋是很多年前建的。（指空间）

Those stars are too far away to be seen with naked eyes. 那些星星离得太远, 肉眼看不见。（指空间）

During the whole of *this* time, Scrooge had acted like a man out of his wits. 在整个这段时间, 斯克鲁吉像是失魂落魄似的。（指时间）

That stormy night, the witness was killed in the hospital. 那个暴风雨之夜, 证人在医院里被杀了。（指时间）

③ that 和 those 指代前面提到过的事物；this 和 these 指代随后要讲的事物

That view point is proved to be wrong, and *this* is what people are thinking correct now. 那个观点被证明是错误的，下面才是人们认为正确的观点。（that 指前，this 指后）

Those are the problems we should solve. 这些就是我们应该解决的问题。（those 指前）

Written on the placard are *these* words: we want peace. 牌子上写着这样一些字:我们要和平。（these 指后）

④ those 作定语从句的先行词

Those who were present at the meeting were all celebrities. 出席会议的都是名流。

Those who are able to work were given jobs. 能工作的人都给分配了工作。

⑤ such 在句中作主语、宾语、表语、定语等

Such is life. 生活就是这样。（主语）

Such often occurred in the past. 这种事情过去经常发生。（主语）

Take from the drawer *such* as you need. 从抽屉里拿你需要的东西吧。（宾语）

Just before Christmas they wanted help with trees and *such*. 正是在圣诞节前他们需要帮手来布置圣诞树之类的东西。（宾语）

The waves were *such* as I never saw before. 这样的海浪, 我从未见过。（表语）

The foreign visitors said they had never seen *such* plants before. 外宾说他们以前从未见过这类植物。（定语）

Note：当名词后有限制性定语时，名词前不用 this 或 that 表示"这个"或"那个"，要用 the。

May I have a look at *the* skirt you bought yesterday? 我能不能看一下你昨天买的裙子？（skirt 后有定语从句 you bought yesterday, 其前要用 the。）

What do you think of *the* proposals put forward by Mr. Wang? 你觉得王先生提的建议怎么样？（proposals 后有过去分词短语 put forward by Mr. Wang 作定语，其前要用 the）

10.6 疑问代词

疑问代词引导的疑问句为特殊疑问句。它们一般都在疑问句句首，并在从句中作某一句子成分（如主

语、宾语、表语等)。

(1) 疑问代词形式

疑问代词有 who(谁,主格),whom(谁,宾格),whose(谁的,属格),what(什么),which(哪个,哪些)等。其中 who,whom,whose 只能指人,what 和 which 可指人或物。它们可具有单数概念或复数概念。

(2) 疑问代词的句法功能

① who 的功能

who 的意思是"谁",是主格,通常作主语。

Who is that woman? 那个妇女是谁?

Who are those people? 那些人是谁?

who 在口语中可代替 whom 作宾语

Who did you ask about it? 关于那件事你问过谁了?

② whom 的功能

whom 的意思是"谁",是宾格,在句中作宾语,常用于书面语中。

Whom do you want to see? 你想见谁?

Whom do you talk about? 你们在谈论谁?(whom 作介词 about 的宾语)

③ whose 的功能

whose 的意思是"谁的",是属格,具有名词和形容词的性质。

Whose book is this? 这是谁的书?(形容词性)

Whose is this book? 这书是谁的?(名词性)

whose 可在句中作如下成分:

作主语:*Whose* is better? 谁的更好?

作表语:*Whose* are these pencils? 这些铅笔是谁的?

作宾语:*Whose* are you going to borrow? 你打算借谁的?

作定语:*Whose* umbrella is this? 这是谁的伞?

④ what 的功能

what 的意思是"什么",具有名词和形容词的性质。

What are you doing? 你在做什么?(名词性)

What sport do you like best? 你最喜欢的运动是什么?(形容词性)

what 可在句中作如下成分:

作主语:*What's* happening? 发生了什么事?

作表语:*What* is your mother? 你母亲是干什么工作的?

作宾语:*What* do you mean? 你是什么意思?

What did you talk to him about? 你和他说了什么?(介词宾语)

作定语:*What* color do you like? 你喜欢什么颜色?

⑤ which 的功能

which 的意思是"哪个",在句中可作主语、表语、宾语、定语等。

作主语:*This* is my bag. Which is yours? 这是我的书包,哪个是你的?

作表语:*Which* is your favorite subject? 你最喜欢哪个科目?

I can't tell *which* is which because they are so alike. 我分辨不出谁是谁,因为他们太像了。

作宾语：*Which* do you like best? 你最喜欢哪一个？
作定语：*Which* glasses do you want? 你想要哪些杯子？
　　　　Which platform does the London train leave? 去伦敦的火车从哪个站台开出？

⑥ who, what 和 which 后可加 ever 来加强语气

Whatever are you thinking about? 你到底在想些什么？
Whoever are you looking for? 你到底在找谁？
Whichever do you prefer? 你究竟要哪个？

10.7　关系代词

关系代词是用作引导定语从句的关联词。它们在从句中可作主语、表语、宾语、定语等，另一方面它们又代表主句中为定语从句所修饰的那个名词或代词（通称为先行词）。关系代词有 who, whose, whom, that, which, as 等。

（1）关系代词句的用法

关系代词既代表主句中所修饰的（先行）词语，又在其所引导的从句中承担一个成分，如主语、宾语、表语、定语等。

This is the man *who* saved your son. 这就是救了你儿子的那个人。(who 在从句中作主语，先行词是 man)

The man *whom* I met yesterday is Jim. 我昨天见到的那个人是吉姆。(whom 在从句中作宾语，它的先行词是 man)

A child *whose* parents are dead is an orphan. 失去父母的孩子是孤儿。(whose 在从句中作定语，它的先行词是 child)

He wants a room *whose* window looks out over the sea. 他想要个窗户面临大海的房间。(whose 在从句中作定语，它的先行词是 room)

① who, whom 和 whose 的用法

A. who 和 whom 代表人，在从句中作主语时用 who, 作宾语时用 whom。但若 whom 作介词宾语且介词放在其前时，不能省略；如介词位于句末时，可以省略。whose 代表某人（物）的，在从句中作定语。

The man *who* insists upon seeing with perfect clearness before he decides, never decides. 坚持看清楚一切后才做决定的人永远也做不了决定。(who 作主语)

He is a man (*whom*) everybody respects. 他是一个人人都尊敬的人。(whom 作宾语，可以省略)

He is a man from *whom* we all should learn. 他是我们大家都应该学习的人。(whom 作介词宾语且介词位于其前，不能省略)（此句也可以是：He is a man (whom) we should all learn from.）

The people *whose* houses were damaged will be compensated. 房子被损坏了的人将给予补偿。

B. Who, whom 和 whose 可用于非限制性定语从句中，代表某人（物）或某人（物）的，此时不能用 that。

My sister, *who* is a nurse, came home for a few days. 我姐姐回家住了几天，她是个护士。

② which 的用法

A. which 代表物，在从句中可作主语或宾语，作宾语时可以省略，但作介词宾语且介词位于其前时不能省略。

The book *which* helps you most are those *which* make you think most. 最能使你获益的书是那些最能让你深思的书。（作主语）

This is a factor *which* we must not neglect. 这是一个我们绝不能忽略的因素。(作宾语,可省略)
Where is the book from *which* you quoted this sentence? 你引用这句话的那本书在哪儿?(作介词宾语且介词位于其前时,不能省略)

B. which 可用于非限制性定语从句中,代表物。

The desk, *which* I bought second-hand, is made of oak. 我买的这张书桌是用橡木做的,它是二手货。

③ that 的用法

that 可以代表事(物)也可代表人,在从句中可以作主语或宾语,作宾语时可省略,但不能用于非限制性定语从句中。代表人时 who 比 that 用得多些,代表物时 that 比 which 用得多些。如

The letter *that* came this morning is from my mother. 今天早晨收到的那封信是我母亲寄来的。(that 代表物,在从句中作主语)

Those students *that* failed the exam will have to take it again. 考试不及格的学生必须补考。(that 代表人,在从句中作主语)

Have you forgotten about the money (*that*) I lent you last week? 你忘了上星期我借给你钱的事了吗?(that 代表物,在从句中作宾语,可省略)

All the people (*that*) I invited have agreed to come. 所有我邀请了的人都同意来。(that 代表人,在从句中作宾语,可省略)

The hotel (*that*) we stayed at was both cheap and comfortable. 我们住的那家旅馆既便宜又舒服。(that 代表物,在从句中作介词宾语,可省略)

10.8 不定代词

不指明代替任何特定名词或形容词的代词叫不定代词。不定代词表示各种程度和各种类型的不定意义。他们在逻辑意义上是数量词,具有整体性或局部的意义。不定代词可分为普通不定代词、个体代词和数量代词。

(1) some, any

some 多用于肯定句,修饰复数可数名词和不可数名词,作"一些"解。它还可修饰单数可数名词,作"某一"解。

H-5 avian influenza first broke out in *some* Asian countries. H-5 型禽流感首先在亚洲爆发。
Some people are early risers. 有些人起得很早。

any 通常用于否定句、疑问句或条件句,修饰单数或复数可数名词以及不可数名词。any 还可以用于肯定句,作"任何的"解。

If there are *any* new magazines in the library, take *some* for me. 图书馆如果来了新杂志,替我借几本。
Are there *any* stamps in the drawer? 抽屉里有邮票吗?
Is there *any* money with you? 你身上带钱了吗?
You can come here *any* time. 你什么时候来都行。
You can get it at *any* shop. 你可以在任何一家商店买到它。

(2) either, both, all

① either 表示"两者中的任何一个"

Either of the brothers is selfish. 两兄弟都非常自私。
Either will do. 两个都行。

② both 两个都(修饰可数名词,统指两者)

Tom and Jack *both* made some progress. 汤姆和杰克两个都有所进步。
Both of them should make concessions. 他们双方都应做出让步。

③ all 全部的,所有的

此词指两个以上的人或物,修饰可数名词和不可数名词。
All the students contributed to the fund. 所有的学生都为基金会捐了款。
All of the money has been spent. 钱都花完了。
We are *all* for you. 我们都支持你。
Say *all* you know and say it without reserve. 知无不言,言无不尽。

(3) no, neither, none

① no 不

此词可修饰单数和复数可数名词以及不可数名词。
Time and tide wait for *no* man. 时不我待。
There are *no* clouds in the sky. 天上没有云。
I have *no* money for such things. 我没钱买这些东西。

② neither 两者中哪个都不

Neither answer is correct. 两个答案都不对。
Neither of the two countries is satisfied with the result of the talk. 两个国家都不满意会谈的结果。

③ none 没有一个人(或东西)

它既可指可数名词(其所指范围是两个以上的人或物),又可指不可数名词。
All of the trees were cut down, and *none* were left. 所有的树都被砍了,一棵也不剩。
None of the students failed the examination. 没有一个学生考试不及格。
None of this money is his. 这笔钱没有一点儿是他的。

(4) few, a few, little, a little

① few, a few

few 的意思是"没有几个",a few 的意思是"少数"、"几个",都用以修饰可数名词;a few 表示肯定意义,few 表示否定意义。
The problem is so difficult that *few* people can solve it. 这个问题太难了,几乎没人能做出来。
Only *a few* people can solve this problem. 只有几个人能解决这个问题。
Few of them want to go. 他们中几乎没有人想去。
A few of them want to go. 他们中有几个人想去。

② little, a little

little 表示"没有多少",a little 表示"少量",都修饰不可数名词;a little 表示肯定意义,little 表示否定意义。
There is *little* rainfall this spring. 今年春季雨水很少。
Although it did not rain for the whole month, there is *a little* water in the pond. 虽然整整一个月没下雨了,但池塘里还有一点水。

(5) many, much, most

① many 的意思"许多",用以修饰可数名词

Many of the problems have been solved. 大部分问题已经解决了。
Many workers think that the situation will change soon. 很多人认为局势会很快改变。

② much 的意思是"许多",用以修饰不可数名词

Much of the money has been spent. 这笔钱的大部分已经被花掉了。
They have finished *much* of the work. 他们已经完成了大部分的工作。

(6) another, other, the other, others, the others

① another 指同类中多个东西中的"另一个",其意思也作 one more 讲

This watch doesn't work, I must get *another* one. 这块表坏了,我该另买一块了。
He went back to work too soon, and was laid up for *another* three months. 他回去上班过早,结果又病倒三个月。

Note：other 与物主限定词连用也可指余下的另一个或全部。
Use your *other* hand. 用你的另一只手。
Mary is older than me but my *other* sisters are younger. 玛丽比我大,其余的都是我妹妹。

② other 单独使用时指"其他的"、"另外的人或物"

There must be some *other* reason for him refusing to help. 他不予帮助一定另有原因。
I saw Tom with some *other* fellow students. 我看见汤姆和其他一些同学在一起。

③ the other (one/ones) 指同类中余下的另一个或另一些

I'll have to use our duplicate key. I lost *the other* one. 我不得不用我们的备用钥匙了,我把那一把丢了。
Where are *the other* students? 其他学生去哪儿了?
One of the murderers was caught, but *the other* is still at large. 一个凶手被抓住了,另一个却依然逍遥法外。

④ others 是 other 的复数形式,指"其他的、另外的人或物"

We should not think only of our children, there are *others* to be cared for also. 我们不应该只想到自己的孩子,还有别的孩子也需要照顾。
Others may object to this plan. 别人可能会反对这个计划。

⑤ the others 表示同类中余下的全部

The search party was divided into two groups. Some went to the right, *the others* went to the left. 搜寻小组一分为二,一部分人向右,另一部分向左。
Jenny is cleverer than any of *the others* in her class. 珍妮比班上的其他(任何)人都聪明。

(7) 复合不定代词

复合不定代词有 someone, somebody, something, anyone, anybody, anything, no one, nobody, nothing, everyone, everybody, everything 等。

① someone, somebody 某人; something 某物

Someone is asking to see you. 有人要见你。
Someone suggests putting off the meeting. 有人建议推迟会议。

There's *something* wrong with the machine. 机器出了毛病。
Something strange happened last night. 昨晚发生了件奇怪的事。

② anyone, anybody 任何人; anything 任何事情

Anybody can do this work. It's very simple. 这事太简单了,人人都能做。
Did you meet *anyone* on your way home? 你回家的路上碰到什么人了吗?
He faltered: Is *anything* wrong? 他支支吾吾地说:"有什么错吗?"
He did not say *anything* after that. 那以后他再也没说什么。

③ no one, nobody 没有人; nothing 没有东西

I'm not *somebody*. I'm nobody. 我不是重要人物,我是个无名小卒。
No one wants to do that. 没人愿做那种事。
Nobody is absent. 没有人缺席。
That's *nothing*. 那没有什么。
He said he knew *nothing* about it. 他说他对那事一无所知。

④ everyone, everybody 每个人;everything 每样东西,一切事物

She said good-bye to *everyone*. 她向每个人告别。
Everybody's business is nobody's business. 事关大家无人管。
Everything is ready for the experiment. 实验的一切事情都准备好了。
This news means *everything* to us. 这个消息对我们至关重要。

第 11 章 数 词

11.1 数词的分类

根据其特征,数词可分为基数词、序数词、分数词、百分数、成数、小数等;根据数字是否为整数,又可将它们分为整数、分数和小数;根据数字所表示的数是否确定,又可分为确数和概数。数词在句中可作主语、表语、宾语、定语、同位语、状语等。

在使用基数词时,要特别注意 hundred, thousand, million, billion 等几个词的用法:若其前用了基数词,则不论其后面是否有 of,都必须用单数形式(此时若带 of 则通常表示特定范围中的一部分);若泛指数百、数千、数百万等,则用 hundreds of, thousands of, millions of 等结构。

11.2 基数词

基数词用来表示数目,其形式有的是没规律的,有的是有规律的。

(1) 从 1—10

这些数词是无规律的:one, two, three, four, five, six, seven, eight, nine, ten。

(2) 从 11—19

这些数词中,有的有规律的,有的没规律:eleven, twelve, thirteen, fourteen, fifteen, sixteen, seventeen, eighteen, nineteen。从上面那些数词中可见,除 eleven, twelve, thirteen, fifteen, eighteen 为特殊形式外,fourteen, sixteen, seventeen, nineteen 都是由其个位数形式后添加后缀-teen 构成。

(3) 从 21—99

整数几十中除 twenty, thirty, forty, fifty, eighty 为特殊形式外,sixty, seventy, ninety 都是其个位数形式后添加后缀-ty 构成。表示几十几时,在几十和个位基数词形式之间要添加连字符"-":twenty-one, seventy-six, eighty-eight, ninety-nine。

(4) 百位数

个数基数词形式加 hundred,表示几百,在几十几与百位间加上 and:a/one hundred and one, three hundred and twenty, six hundred and forty-eight。

(5) 千位数以上

从数字的右端向左端数起,每三位数加一个逗号","。从右开始,第一个","前的数字后添加 thousand,第二个","前面的数字后添加 million,第三个","前的数字后添加 billion。然后一节一节分别表示,两个逗号之间最大的数为百位数形式。

2,648 two thousand, six hundred and forty-eight

16,250,064 sixteen million, two hundred and fifty thousand, and sixty-four
5,237,166,234 five billion, two hundred and thirty-seven million, one hundred and sixty-six thousand, two hundred and thirty-four

(6) 不用复数形式的基数词

基数词在表示确切的数字时,不能使用百、千、百万、十亿的复数形式;但是,当基数词表示不确切数字,如成百、成千上万、三三两两时,基数词则以复数形式出现。

There are *hundreds of* people in the hall. 大厅里有数以百计的人。
Thousands and thousands of people come to visit the Museum of Qin Terra-Cotta Warriors and Horses every day. 每天有成千上万的人来参观秦兵马俑博物馆。
They went to the theatre in *twos and threes*. 他们三三两两地来到了剧院。

(7) 不确切岁数或不确定年代表示法

在表示人的不确切岁数或表达不确定的年代时,要用"几十"的复数形式表示。

He became a professor in his *thirties*. 他三十多岁时成为教授。
She died of lung cancer in *forties*. 她四十来岁时死于肺癌。
It was in the *1960s*. 那是在20世纪60年代。

(8) 基数词的句法功能

基数词在句中可作主语、宾语、定语、表语、同位语等。

The two happily opened the box. 两个人高兴地打开了盒子。(作主语)
I need *three* altogether. 我总共需要三个。(作宾语)
Four students are playing volleyball outside. 四个学生在外面打排球。(作定语)
We are *sixteen*. 我们是16个人。(作表语)
They *three* tried to finish the task before sunset. 他们三个人尽力想在日落前完成任务。(作同位语)

11.3 序数词

序数词用来表示顺序。序数词的形式含有特殊形式和规律形式两种情况。

(1) 从第1至第19

特殊形式:one—first, two—second, three—third, five—fifth, eight—eighth, nine—ninth, twelve—twelfth
规律形式:four—fourth, six—sixth, seven—seventh, ten—tenth, eleven—eleventh, thirteen—thirteenth, fourteen—fourteenth, sixteen—sixteenth, eighteen—eighteenth, nineteen—nineteenth

(2) 从第20至第99

整数第几十的形式由其对应的基数词改变结尾字母 y 为 i,再加"eth"构成。twenty—twentieth, thirty—thirtieth 表示第几十几时,用几十的基数词形式加上连字符和个位序数词形式。
thirty-first 第31, fifty-sixth 第56, seventy-third 第73, ninety-ninth 第99

(3) 第100以上的多位序数词

由基数词的形式变结尾部分为序数词形式来表示。
one hundred and twenty-first 第121, one thousand, three hundred and twentieth 第1320

(4) 序数词的缩写形式

有时,序数词可以用缩写形式来表示,主要缩写形式有:first—lst, second—2nd, third—3rd, fourth—4th, sixth—6th, twentieth—20th, twenty-third—23rd。其中 lst,2nd,3rd 为特殊形式,其他都是阿拉伯数字后加上"th"而成。

(5) 序数词的句法功能

序数词在句中可作主语、宾语、定语和表语。
The second is what I really need. 第二个是我真正需要的。(作主语)
He choose *the second*. 他挑选了第二个。(作宾语)
We are to carry out *the first* plan. 我们将执行第1个计划。(作定语)
She is *the second* in our class. 在我们班她是第2名。(作表语)

Notes:① 在使用序数词时,通常前面要加定冠词 the;如果序数词前出现不定冠词 a 或 an 时,则表示"再一"、"又一"。

We'll go over it *a second* time. 我们得再念第2遍。
We've tried it three times. Must we try it *a fourth* time? 我们已经试过三遍了,还必须试一次(第4次)吗?

② 另外,基数词也可以表示顺序。只需将基数词放在它所修饰的名词之后即可,不需要添加定冠词:the first lesson—Lesson One, the fifth page—Page 5 (Five), the twenty-first room—Room 21 (Twenty-One)。

(6) 序数词与冠词

序数词一般与定冠词连用,但有时也有与不定冠词连用的情况。

① 序数词前通常要用定冠词。
It's *the third* time I've been here. 这是我第3次来这儿。
The second is better than *the first*. 第2个比第1个好。

② 表示考试或比赛等的名次时,通常省略定冠词。
She was (*the*) third in the exam. 她考试得了第3名。

③ 序数词用作副词时其前也通常不用冠词。
He came *first*. 他先来。
I'll have to finish my homework *first*. 我得先把作业做完。

④ 有些习语中的序数词前没有冠词。
at first 开始, at first sight 乍看起来, first of all 首先

⑤ 若序数词前有物主代词或名词所有格时,不能再用定冠词。
his second wife 他的第二个妻子, Tom's third book 汤姆的第三本书

⑥ 序数词前有时可用不定冠词,表示在原有基础上增加的次数。
A second student stood up. 又一个(第2个)学生站了起来。
I want to read the book *a third* time. 这本书我想读第3次。

⑦ 序数词前用定冠词和不定冠词有区别。
它们的区别在于:定冠词表示特指,不定冠词表示泛指,有类似 another 的意思,但比 another 的意思更明确。

I like *the third* girl. 我喜欢第3个女孩。(至少有三个女孩供选择,特指)
I saw *a third* girl. 我又看见了第3个女孩。(暗示原来已看见两个,这已是第3个)

11.4 数词的具体用法

(1) 表示生日

要注意,在汉译英时汉语中的基数词译成英语时往往要用序数词。
今天是我爷爷的60大寿。
误:Today is my grandfather's sixty birthday.
正:Today is my grandfather's sixtieth birthday.
汉语说"30岁生日"、"60大寿"等,其实指的是过第30个生日、过第60个生日等,所以要用序数词而不用基数词。

(2) 表示年龄

用英语数词表示年龄,大概有以下七种方法:

① **直接用基数词表示。**

Her daughter is *eighteen*. 她的女儿18岁。

② 用"基数词 + years old"表示,有时可将 years old 换成 years of age。

Her daughter is *eighteen years old*./Her daughter is *eighteen years of age*. 她的女儿18岁。

③ 用"基数词-year-old"表示,此结构常作(前置)定语。

Her *18-year-old* daughter is now in the university. 他18岁的女儿现在上大学。

④ 用"at the age of + 基数词"表示"在……年龄"。

Her daughter got married *at the age of eighteen*. 她的女儿18岁就结了婚。

⑤ 用"of + 基数词"表示,此结构常作后置定语。

Her daughter is now a pretty girl *of 18*. 她女儿现在是一个18岁的美少女了。

⑥ 用"aged + 基数词"表示,此结构常作后置定语。

Lying on the floor was a boy *aged about seventeen*. 躺在地板上的是一个约莫17岁的男孩。

⑦ 用"in one's + 几十的复数形式"表示某人大概的年龄。

He went to the United States *in his fifties*. 他五十多岁时去了美国。

(3) 表示倍数

用英语数词表示倍数时通常借助 half, double, twice, three times 等之类的词。
Half (of) the apples are bad. 一半苹果是坏的。
His homework is not yet *half* done. 他的作业还没完成一半。
He eats *twice* what I eat. 他的食量是我的两倍。
下面三句,表达形式不同,但含义相同
This rope is three times as long as that one. 这根绳子是那根的三倍长。
This rope is three times longer than that one. 这根绳子是那根的三倍长。
This rope is three times the length of that one. 这根绳子是那根的三倍长。

第 1 句和第 3 句的意思比较清楚,但第 2 句常容易误解,有人认为它与其他两句意思不同,应理解为"这根绳子比那根绳子长三倍",但绝大多数语法学家并不这样认为,而是认为以上三句意思相同。

11.5 分数词

分数词的表达有两种形式:一为基本形式,或叫常用形式,另一种叫简易形式。

(1) 基本形式

基本形式是分数词由基数词和序数词构成——分子用基数词,分母用序数词;分子超过"1"时,序数词分母要用复数。

a [one] sixth = 1/6, two thirds = 2/3, three fifths = 3/5

Three quarters of the students have passed the exam. 3/4 的学生考试及格了。

The WTO cannot live up to its name if it does not include a country that is home to *one-fifth* of mankind. 如果世贸组织不能容纳占世界人口 1/5 的国家,那它就算不上世界贸易组织了。

Notes:① 1/2 通常读作 a/one half,一般不读作 a second。② 1/4 可读作 a/one fourth,也可读作 a/one quarter。

(2) 简易形式

在数学上,为了简洁起见,分子和分母均可用基数词来表达,中间用介词 over。例如,3/4 读作 three over four,67/95 sixty-seven over ninety-five;尤其对于比较复杂的分数,我们通常采用此形式。

(3) 带分数的表达

带分数的表达是在整数与分数之间用 and 连接,如 five and two thirds,那就是 5⅔。

(4) 分数词在句中的功能

分数词在句中常用作主语、定语、宾语等,有时也可用作状语。

One fourth is equal to 25%. 1/4 等于 25%。(主语)

Two thirds students in my class are from the south. 我们班 2/5 的学生来自南方。(定语)

Houses cost *one third* more this year than they did five years ago. 今年房价比五年前上涨了1/3。(宾语)

China is *one-sixth* larger than the United States. 中国比美国大 1/6。(状语)

The bottle had been about *three-quarters* full then. 那时瓶子里大约装满了 3/4。(状语)

11.6 小 数

当我们在计算 41/7 =5.857, 其商读作 five point eight five seven,这就涉及"小数"。如何读小数? 小数点前的数按基数词读,小数点读 point,小数点后面的数按单个基数词一个一个单独念,如 9.65 读作 nine point six five,218.39 读作 two hundred and eighteen point three nine。

11.7 百分数

百分数由"基数词 + percent"构成,其中的 percent 可分可合。

With production up by 60 *percent*, the company has had another excellent year. 因为产量提高了 60%,所以公司那年又取得了很好的效益。

About 60 *per cent* of the workers in this company are young people. 这个公司约60％的工人是年轻人。

11.8 成 数

关于"成数"有关内容的介绍,一般语法书上很少见到。其实我们时不时地用到"成数"的表达。虽然在表达所占比例时,用分数和百分数最常见,但有时人们却用"成数"来表示,这是因为有时用成数表达更切题,或更符合某种场合。

Seven in ten students in their school are from the north. 他们学校的学生中七成是北方人。

One out of ten computers is now using Window XP. 现在一成的计算机使用Window XP操作系统。

Notes：（1）成数表示法中,前面用基数词,后面 in ten 或 out of ten,它们后再加复数名词,如：one in ten（boys）或 one out of ten（boys）一成的男孩,two/five/nine in ten（girls）或 two/five/nine out of ten（girls）二/五/九成女孩。

（2）由成数组成的短语作主语时,其谓语动词单复数的使用有所不同：表示一成的,单、复数均可,这主要取决于话语者的着重点；二成以上的都用复数。

（3）成数表示中,涉及内容还有很多,如复数名词的位置、复数名词的省略、成数表达的变异及成数短语表达中还可添加 every, of 等,由于篇幅关系,我们在这里就不涉及那些内容。对于那些问题,杨元兴先生在《新编英语句型句法全解》（北京语言大学出版社,2012）里的有关数词的章节中有全面、详细的论述。

11.9 表示约数的五种方法

（1）笼统数目的表示方法

笼统数目就是不确切数目。这些不确切数目可用 tens of, dozens of, scores of, hundreds of, thousands of, millions of 等表示数目几十、几百、上千、成千上万等。

I've been there *dozens of* times. 我那儿去过几十次了。

Thousands of people were gathered at the airport. 数千人聚集在机场。

There were *hundreds of* people on the beach. 海滩上有成千上万的人。

Millions of dollars have gone into the building of this factory. 数以百万计的美金被投入修建这座工厂。

（2）表示"少于"、"接近"的方法

表示"少于"、"接近"等时可用 less than, under, below, almost, nearly, up to 等来表示少于或接近某个数目。

It cost me *less than* 10 pounds. 我买它没花上10英镑。

There's nothing *below* 5 dollars. 没有一样东西价钱在5美元以下。

Almost/Nearly all the students passed the exam. 差不多所有的学生都通过了考试。

（3）表示"多于"、"超过"的方法

表示"多于"、"超过"可用 more than, beyond, or more, over, above 等来表示超过或多于某个数目。

He was away for *more than* a month. 他离开了一个多月。

There are ten chairs *or more* in the room. 房间里有十多把椅子。

The temperature is two degrees *above* zero. 温度是零上2度。

You have to be *over* 18 to see this film. 超过18岁的人才能看这部电影。

(4) 表示"大约"、"左右"的方法

表示"大约"、"左右"可用 or, or so, about, around, some, more or less 等。

They arrived *around/round* 5 o'clock. 他们大约 5 点钟到的。

It's an hour's journey, *more or less*. 大约有一个钟头的路程。

Take this medicine. You'll feel better in an hour *or so*. 把药吃了，过一个多小时你会感觉好些的。

(5) 表示"一两个"的方法

英语中表示"一两个"有两种方法：一是"a + 名词 + or two"，二是"one or two + 名词"。要注意两者不可混用(尤其注意不能将 a 与 one 用混)。

After *a minute or two* we saw him. 一两分钟后我们看见了他。

May I borrow the book for *a day or two*? 这本书我可以借一两天吗？

I would like to use the computer for *an hour or two*. 我想用一两个小时的电脑。

I want to put you right on *one or two matters*. 我想给你纠正一两个错误。

There is *one or two things* I'd like to know about. 有一两件事我很想知道。

11.10　表示"年代"、"公元"的方法

(1) 表示年代

① 年代表示法

表示某个世纪的几十年代，用"in the + 逢十的基数词的复数"。基数词的复数若用阿拉伯数字表示，可直接加 s，也可加 's，如"在 20 世纪 80 年代"是 in the 1980s 或 in the 1980's，读作 in the nineteen eighties。表示整十的基数词用复数形式可以表示人的岁数或年代，注意不要漏掉 the，如：in the sixties/in the 60s（在 60 年代），in one's thirties（在某人 30 多岁时）。

② 表示年代的词语可作定语的类型

A. 类似 1960 的词语作定语

He was awarded the *1960* Nobel Prize for peace. 他荣获 1960 年诺贝尔和平奖。

This is a *1979* recording with Ellison on bass guitar. 这是一部 1979 年埃利森演奏低音吉他的录音。

The new film is just a souped-up version of the *1948* original. 这部新电影只不过是在 1948 年的原版片中做些更动而已。

The *1992* Summer Olympics were held in Barcelona and the Winter Olympics were held in Albertville. 1992 年夏季奥运会在巴塞罗那举行，冬季奥运会在阿尔贝维尔举行。

B. 用 1980s 或 1980's 这样的词语作定语

It's an update of an old *60's* movie. 那是 60 年代一部老影片的更新版。

At that time, there was a great rage for *1920's* clothes. 当时，20 年代的服饰非常流行。

They decided to revive a *1930's* musical. 他们决定重新上演 20 世纪 30 年代的一个歌舞剧。

(2) 关于含 B.C., A.D.公元年份的表示

B. C.（念[bi: si:]，是"公元前"的意思，= before Christ），常写在年份之后。A. D.（念[ei di:]，是拉丁词"Anno Domimi"（in the year）since the birth of Christ），是指耶稣诞生之年起，意为"公元"。

A. D. 置于年份之前或后均可。A. D. 一般用于公元 1 年到 999 年之间的年份，超过了 1000 年一般就

不用。

Pompey died in 48 B.C., while Tiberius died in A.D. 37. 庞培于公元前48年逝世,而提比里阿斯于公元37年逝世。

From 300 B.C. to A.D. 500 is seven hundred years. 从公元300年到公元后500年,共为800年。

在表达1000年以后的年数,就不必在年份前或后加A.D.,如用了倒显得有点累赘。

His daughter was born in Beijing in 1993. 他女儿于1993年出生于北京。

Her grandfather was born in 1900. 她的爷爷生于1900年。

11.11 用英语数词编号

(1) 编房号

第305号房间:Room 305　　　　　第126号房间:Room 126

第1105号房间:Room 1105　　　　第2805号房间:Room 2805

(2) 编页码

第126页:Page 126　　　　　　　第308页:Page 308

第889页:Page 889　　　　　　　第902页:Page 902

(3) 编路牌号

五一路2230号:2230 Wuyi Road　　八一路696号:696 Bayi Road

蔡锷路195号:195 Cai'e Road　　　中山路256号:256 Zhongshan Road

(4) 编公共汽车号

第111路公共汽车:Bus Number 111　　第103路公共汽车:Bus Number 103

第905路公共汽车:Bus Number 905　　第704路公共汽车:Bus Number 704

(5) 编厂名

第一拖拉机厂:The No. 1 Tractor Works　　第九玻璃厂:The No. 9 Glass Works

第三造纸厂:The No. 3 Paper Factory

(6) 编车厢号

第10号车厢:Carriage No. 10　　　第12号车厢:Carriage No. 12

第18号车厢:Carriage No. 18　　　三号和四号卧铺:Berths 3 and 4

11.12 数学计算和公式表示

$5+6=11$	Five plus six is eleven.
$10-2=8$	Ten minus two is eight.
$2\times5=10$	Two times five (Two multiplied by five) is ten.
$9\div3=3$	Nine divided by three is three.
$a>b$	a is more than b.
$a<b$	a is less than b.

a≈b	a approximately equals to b.
a≠b	a is not equal to b.

11.13 日期表示和读法

(1) 日期的表示和要避免的写法

① 日期的表示

日期的表示法在英国和美国稍有不同,英国通常表示为"日—月—年",美国通常表示为"月—日—年",如"1985 年 10 月 10 日"可表示为 October 10, 1985(美)或 10(th)(of) October, 1985(英)。

② 要避免的写法

最好避免把整个日期都写成数字,因为这在英美英语中表示的含义并不相同,容易造成误解,如"2.7.97"、"2-7-97"、"2/7/97"这类表达,在美国英语中表示"1997 年 2 月 7 日",而在英国英语中却表示"1997 年 7 月 2 日"。

(2) 年份的读法

英语中"年份"的读法是这样的:四位数以下的年份,按基数词的读法读,如"(公元)689 年"直接读成 six hundred and eighty-nine;满四位数年份,一般是两位两位地读,即读作"几十几,几十几",如"1986 年"通常读作 nineteen eighty-six;若是整数为百的年份,通常读作"几十几—hundred",如"1900 年"读作 nineteen hundred;若是整数千的年份,通常读作"几千",如"2000 年"读作 two thousand。类似地,"2005 年"可读作 two thousand and five。

11.14 钟点的表示

钟点表示除纯粹用数词外,有时半小时用 half,一刻钟用 a quarter。用数词表达中,半小时以内用钟点数加 past,再加分钟数;超过半小时要用 to,即几点差几(十)分钟,其中的 to 表示"不足"。

08:00	eight o'clock/eight
09:15	nine fifteen/a quarter past/after nine
14:15	fourteen fifteen/2:15 p. m.
23:05	five past twenty-three
24:00	twenty-four hundred hours/midnight
02:30	two thirty/half past/after two
05:45	five forty-five/a quarter to six/fifteen to six
08:55	eight fifty-five/five to nine
11:40	eleven forty/twenty to twelve

Note:用 past 和 to 表示钟点时的读法也叫普通说法,直接念出数词来的说法也叫"时刻表"读法。

11.15 "度"表示法

要表示长度、宽度、高度、深度等,可用"基数词+单位名词(复数)+形容词"结构。

We need a rope about *10 meters long*. 我们需要一根约 10 米长的绳子。
The well is about *30 meters deep*. 这口井约 30 米深。

有时也可用"基数词＋单位名词(单数)＋in＋长度或重量的名词"表示长度、宽度、高度、深度等。

He is *six feet in height*. 他身高6英尺。

The fish is *two feet in length*. 这条鱼有2英尺长。

Note：表示重量时，可用 in weight 结构，不说"… heavy"。如要表示"这个箱子重10千克"，可说 The box is 10 kilos 或 The box is 10 kilos in weight, 但习惯上不说 The box is 10 kilos heavy。

11.16　dozen, score, hundred, thousand, million 的用法

(1) 这些词与具体数字连用时

在这些词与具体的数词连用时，它们后通常不加复数词尾-s，后面也不接介词 of。

I want *three score* eggs. 我要60只鸡蛋。

He is a man of *three score* years. 他60岁。

Two hundred (*thousand*) students went there. 有两百(千)学生去了那儿。

About *three million* workers were on strike. 参加罢工的大约有300万工人。

Note：有人认为 score, dozen 之后有时也接 of, 但惯用法认为省略 of 则常见。另外，当 million 用作中心词(即其后不接名词或数词)时，有时也可带复数词尾-s。

The population of New Zealand is now *three million*(*s*). 新西兰现有人口300万。

(2) 这些词不与具体数字连用时

这样用是表示不确定的泛指数字，则不仅要加复数词尾-s, 而且后面要接介词 of, 然后才能接名词。

I've read it *dozens* (*scores*) *of* times. 我读过它几十次。

Thousands of students entered the contest. 数千名学生参加了这次比赛。

Millions of people died in the war. 有数百万人在这次战争中丧生。

Note：若不出现名词，则不用介词 of。

Millions (*of* people) are homeless. 千千万万的人无家可归。

(3) 这些词与不很具体的数词连用时

当这些词与 a few, several, many 等数目不很具体的词连用时，带不带复数词尾 -s 均可，但若不带复数词尾 -s, 其后的介词 of 可以省略；若带复数词尾-s, 则其后介词 of 不可省略。例如，"我在那儿见到了数百外宾。"的翻译为：

既可说：There I saw several *hundred*(*s*) *of* foreign guests.

也可说：There I saw several *hundred* foreign guests.

Note：但 some hundred persons 与 some hundreds of persons 含义不同：前者指"大约100人"，其中 some = about, 后者指"几百人"。

(4) 这些词后面的名词有了限定词时

当这些词后面的名词有了 the, these, those 等特指限定词修饰，或其后的接的是 us, them 这样的人称代词时，此时则必须有介词 of, two dozen of them (它们中的两打), three scores of these eggs (这些鸡蛋中的三打), five hundred of the workers (这些工人中的五百人)。

(5) 注意以下与介词 by 连用的例子

The eggs are sold *by the dozen*. 鸡蛋按打出售。

The ants arrived at the picnic *by the hundred(s)*. 成群的蚂蚁来到野餐的地方。

They were sold *by the thousand(s)*. 它们被大批大批地(论千地)出售。

比较:Pack them *in dozens*. 把它们成打地包起来(即每12个一包)。

(6) dozen 与 score 的用法

① 一般用法

dozen, score 的用法与 hundred, thousand 等的用法相似:前面有基数词时,只能用单数作定语;若表示"几十"、"许多"时,用复数加 of。

I bought *a dozen* eggs and every one of them was bad. 我买了一打鸡蛋,每个都是坏的。

I said it was a secret but she's told *dozens of* people. 我说那是一个秘密,可她告诉了好几十个人。

They received *scores of* letters about their TV programmes. 关于他们的电视节目,他们收到了大批来信。

② 表示具体数量

上面提到,表示泛指意义的"许多"时,它们不仅要用复数,而且要接介词 of,方可在后接名词。但表示具体数量时,原则是这样的:dozen 后不加 of,但 score 后可以加也可不加 of。

We need to borrow *two dozen* coffee cups for the party. 我们必须去借两打咖啡杯,以备宴会之用。

The Tuscan coastline has *a score (of)* popular resorts. 托斯卡纳海岸线上有20个旅游胜地。

但是,当这些词后面的名词有了 the, these, those 等特指限定词修饰时,或其后接的是 us, them 这样的人称代词时,此时则必须用介词 of。

I want three *dozens of* these. 这些我要三打。

11.17 数词用法上的几个易错点

数词用法中,有几个常用且易出错的点,还得加以注意。

(1) "一两天"之类的表达

"一两天"可说 a day or two 或 one or two days,但不能说成 one day or two 或 a or two days。

类似的有:a year or two/one or two years (一两年)/a month or two/one or two months (一两个月)等。

(2) "一个半"之类的表达

表示"一个半"可用 a ... and a half 或 one and a half ...

We waited for *an hour and a half.*/We waited for *one and a half hours*. 我们等了一个半小时。

(3) "每隔几……"的表达

"每隔一天"的说法有:every two days, every second day, every other day,"每隔3天"的说法有:every three days 或 every third day。

(4) "另外几………"的表达

"另加2个星期"可说 another/a further two weeks 或 two other/more weeks。

(5) "数词 + more"的表达

Three more of the missing climbers have been found. 失踪的登山者又找到了3个。

How many more stamps do you want? —*Four more* please. —你还要多少张邮票？—请再给4张。
If he had received *six more* votes, he would be our chairman now. 如果他多得六票，现在就是我们的主席了。

(6) "another + 数词"的用法

I shall stay *another five* months. 我将再待5个月。
They drove for *another three* hours. 他们又行驶了3个小时。
The strike may last *another six* weeks. 罢工可能还要持续6个礼拜。
China picked up *another ten* gold medals. 中国又获得了10枚金牌。
The last time we talked, he said he needed *another two* days. 上次我们谈话时他说他还需要两天。
Notes：①当其中的数词为 one 时，我们可以说 one more，但一般不用 another one。
He decided to have *one more* try. 他决定再试一次。
Surely you can put it off *one more* week. 肯定你可以把它再推迟一个礼拜。
I was wondering if I must ask you *one more* question. 我不知道我是不是还需要再向你提一个问题。
②在意义上该用 another one 的地方，英语通常只用 another。
She's going to have *another* baby. 她又快有孩子了。
It's cold I need *another* blanket. 太冷了，我再要一条毯子。
如果其中的 one 不是数词，而是代词，则可以用 another one。
This pen doesn't work. I must buy *another one*. 这支钢笔坏了，我该另买一支了。
Your car, which I noticed outside, has been hit by *another one*. 我在外面看见你的汽车了，它给另一辆车撞了。
If your children closed up a bit there'd be room for *another one* on this seat. 你们几个孩子要是挤一挤，这座位上还能加一个人。
即使其中的 one 不是数词而是代词，英语也通常省略 another one 中的 one。
I didn't like the red skirt, so I asked to see *another* (*one*). 我不喜欢那条红裙子，所以我要求看另外一条。
③当其中的数词为 few 时，英语可以说 another few。
I'm staying for *another few* weeks. 我还要再呆几个星期。
I need *another few* days before l can make up my mind. 我还需几天才能决定。
对于 more 而言，英语通常的搭配是 a few more。
I advise waiting *a few more* days. 我建议再等几天。
Wet weather may continue for *a few more* days. 多雨的天气可能还要持续好几天。

11.18 英语中表达汉语"量词"的方法

英语中并没有具体的"量词"，而汉语中常有"个"、"次"、"把"、"只"、"匹"、"条"、"片"、"张"等量词说明事物的数量，如：一个人、(受了)两次伤、三把伞、四只老鼠、五匹马、六条长凳、七片肉、八张嘴等。对于这些量词，英语则用相关的词或某些词组来表达。

(1) 指事物形状的单位词

① 条状，块状
bar 较规则形状的长方块、长方条：a bar of chocolate/soap/goad/iron/candy
block 大块的木头/金属/石头等，常指至少有一面是平面的块：a block of ice（海中漂的大块

冰）/marble

　　cake 规则的方块,形似切好的方块蛋糕：a cake of soap/ice（冰冻而成的规则冰块）

　　lump 无固定形状的块状：a lump of sugar（散装的糖结成的块）/earth/coal loaf 规则形状的大长方块,常指未切片的大块长面包或腌肉：

　　　a loaf of bread/bacon

　　grain 细小的颗粒：

　　　a grain of salt/sand

　　strip 狭长的一块,常指土地、布匹等材料的形状：a strip of land/cloth

② 片状,薄页状

　　piece 从大的物体上分离下来的薄片状或一小段、一小截,也用来说明抽象名词的数,如一条新闻、建议等：a piece of bread/paper

　　sheet 原意指床单,用作单位词指床单状相似的薄片状物体：a sheet of paper

　　slice 从某物上切下来的薄片：a slice of bread/bacon

　　blade 原意指刀锋,作单位词用时指刀片状的狭长且薄的物体：a blade of grass

　　cut 原作动词"切",作单位词指用刀切一下的量：a cut of meat

③ 其他形状（都与单位词原始意义相关）

　　ear 植物长出的一部分,如人体与人耳的关系：an ear of corn/barley/millet/wheat

　　drop 水滴状（指液体）：a drop of blood/water/oil/rain

　　flight 排列有序的一段／一溜／队：a flight of stairs/steps/arrows

　　speck 斑点状大小：a speck of ink/dirt

　　stick 细长如短棍状：a stick of chalk/candle

（2）按事物排列、置放方式的单位词

　　bunch 一串／伙,指同一性质的事物串在一起的量：a bunch of keys/grapes/bananas

　　bundle 一捆／扎,指事物被绑缚在一起的量：a bundle of clothes/straw/sticks

　　cluster 一簇／团,指丛生的植物或密密匝匝在一起的群：a cluster of flowers/bees/islands

　　packet 一小包的量：a packet of cigarettes

　　series 相关的事物组成的一个系列：a series of films/lectures

　　tuft 一绺／撮,常指从同一底部而生的物：a tuft of hair/grass/feathers

（3）表示"人群"单位词

　　group 泛指各种群体：a group of people

　　army 为了某一目的自愿组成的团体：an army of volunteers/soldiers

　　band 常指为同一目的组成的乐队：a band of musicians

　　bunch 一伙干坏事的人：a bunch of rascals

　　gang 一帮／伙犯罪团伙：a gang of thieves

　　batch 指一批加入的成员：a batch of recruits

　　bench 常指一条长椅坐满的人的数：a bench of examiners/judges

　　board 常指会议或委员会全班人马或全体委员：a board of directors

　　choir 常指合唱团或唱诗班：a choir of singers

　　congregation 常指定期的宗教性质的集会：a congregation of prayers

　　crew 常指在一条船上或同一飞机上的工作人员：a crew of sailors

crowd 常指拥挤的人群：a crowd of people
mob 常指混乱无秩序的暴动的人群：a mob of demonstrators
pack 一伙（贬义）：a pack of thieves
party 指出席晚会的所有来宾：a party of guests
staff 常指一个单位所有的员工：a staff of teachers
team 常指参赛的团队：a team of players
troop 常指行军中的队伍：a troop of soldiers
troupe 常指演出的班子、团队，尤指芭蕾舞团、马戏团：a troupe of actors/dancers

(4) 表示"动物群"的单位词

brood 一窝孵出的幼小动物：a brood of chickens
litter 一窝胎生的幼小动物：a litter of puppies/little pigs
swarm 大量的、移动中的鸟类或昆虫，尤指蜂王后跟随的蜂群：a swarm of bees
bevy 叽叽喳喳的聚集在一起的大的群体：a bevy of birds
cluster 密密匝匝聚集在一堆的群：a cluster of bees/ants
flock 同一种类的禽类或兽类：a flock of birds/sheep
herd 放牧的动物群或群聚生存的动物群：a herd of cattle/deer
pack 野兽的群体：a pack of wolves
shoal/school 尤指鱼群：a shoal/school of fish
field 遍地的分散的群：a field of cattle

(5) 表示盛、装事物容积的单位词

bottle 细长的、有颈的瓶子盛的量：a bottle of milk/wine
cup 矮的瓷杯，有耳的杯子，常用来盛咖啡或茶的杯子的量：a cup of tea/coffee
glass 常用来盛水或酒的玻璃杯的量：a glass of water/wine
can/tin 常指铝质的装食品或饮料的罐的量：a can of food/a tin of peas
bucket 常指有提手的小提桶的量：a bucket of water/sand
bowl 一碗所盛的量：a bowl of rice/soup
jar 常指陶制的坛子或罐子：a jar of strawberry jam
truckload/trainload 一卡车或一火车所装载的量：a trainload of goods/coal

(6) 其他指方式或状态的单位词

fit 常指轻微的疾病如咳嗽的突发，较短暂，也指抑制不住的强烈的感情、冲动：a fit of temper/coughing/laughter
peal 常指发出的大而洪亮的声音：a peal of thunder/laughter/lightning
burst 常指突发的短暂而巨大的潜力或做的努力：a burst of cry/speed/energy
flash 常指如闪电般迅速短暂的一瞬：a flash of lightning/light
ray 一道/线，常指好事或所希望的事出现的点滴：a ray of hope/sunshine/comfort
roll 常指滚滚的大的声音：a roll of thunder

第 12 章　限定词(一)

12.1　限定词的定义

限定词(Determiner)是指对名词起限定作用而不起描绘作用的那些词语;说得更贴切些,就是对名词中心词起特指或泛指的、定量或不定量等起限定作用的一类词语。

12.2　限定词的范围

定冠词(Definite Article):the
不定冠词(Indefinite Article):a(n)
零冠词(Zero Article):"We need *trucks/help* from them."
指示限定词(Demonstrative Determiner):this, that, these, those
物主限定词(Possessive Determiner):my, his, her, our, your, their, one's, its
疑问限定词(Interrogative Determiner):whose, which(ever), what(ever)
关系限定词(Relative Determiner):whose, which
名词的属格(Genitive Noun):Tom's, his brother's
不定限定词(Indefinite Determiner):no, some, any, each, every, enough, either, neither, all, both, several, many, much, (a) few, (a) little, other, another
基数词(Cardinal Numeral):one, ten, two hundred
序数词(Ordinal Numeral):first, tenth, twentieth
分数词(Fractional Numeral):one-second, two-thirds
倍数词(Multiplicative Numeral):three times bigger than … (大两倍),three times as adj. /adv. as … (大三倍)
量词(Quantifier):a lot of, lots of, plenty of, a great/good deal of, a large/small amount of, a great/large number of

冠词是用在名词前对其进行修饰限制的,这个大概念对一般人来说是比较清楚的,但其具体用法比较复杂,为此,我们准备另辟一章加以阐述。this, these, that, those 这四个词可以是限定词,但也可能是指示代词,这要看它们在句中的作用如何:如对名词中心词加以限定性的是限定词,当它们单独用来代替名词(词组)时是代词。

This bike is mine. 这辆自行车是我的。(限定词)
This is her schoolbag. 这是她的书包。(指示代词)
Those shoes are man-made. 那些鞋子是手工做的。(限定词)
Those are imports. 那些是进口货。(指示代词)

物主限定词是指物主代词中的形容词性物主代词。
Our teacher is a young lady about thirty years old. 我们的老师是位30岁左右的年轻女士。(限定词)
Their car is old. *Ours* is a new one. 他们的车旧了。我们的(车)是辆新车。(their 是限定词,ours 是名

词性物主代词)

12.3 限定词的搭配

关于限定词的搭配,分两种情况:一是限定词与名词的搭配,二是限定词与限定词之间的搭配。

(1) 限定词与名词的搭配

限定词与名词的搭配是指有的限定词与单数名词搭配,有的跟复数名词搭配,有的又跟不可数名词搭配,还有的限定词可跟单复数名词和不可数名词三种名词搭配。

① 只能与单数名词搭配的限定词

这些限定词有:a(n), one, another, each, every, either, neither, many a, such a 等。

It is *an* interesting book. 这是本有趣的书。

Every worker must attend the meeting. 每个工人必须参加那个会议。

It is *such a* lovely dog. 真是条惹人喜爱的狗。

② 只能与复数名词搭配的限定词

这些限定词有:(a) few, both, two, five, another two, these, those, several, a (great) number of, many 等。

A few students were late for school that day. 那天有一部分学生上学迟到了。

These books were written by their teachers. 这些书是他们老师写的。

I have read *a number of* essays that he had written. 我已经看过了一些他写的论文。

③ 只能与不可数名词搭配的限定词

这些限定词有:a little of, a bit of, a large amount of, a great deal of, much, less, (the) least 等。

We don't make *much* money, but we are able to keep our heads above water. 尽管我们赚的钱不多,但是我们做到不欠债。(第二小句意为 We have enough money for our needs.)

There is *little* water in my cup. 我杯里没什么水了。

She has *a large amount* of money after her husband's death. 她丈夫死后她拥有了一大笔钱。

④ 与单复数和不可数名词都可搭配的限定词

这些限定词有:the, any, some, no, other, whose, (形容词性)物主限定词 my, your, our, their, his, 名词属格,它们可与单数名词、复数名词和不可数名词搭配。

The book, on the top shelf is my sister's. 书架顶上的那本书是我姐姐的。

The books on the desk are my teacher's. 办公桌上的那些书是我老师的。

The money on the table is my father's. 桌子上的钱是我父亲的。

Whose hat is it? 这是谁的帽子?

Whose textbooks are there on the floor? 地板上的那些课本是谁的呀?

Whose money is it? 这是谁的钱?

(2) 限定词与限定词之间的搭配

限定词与限定词之间的搭配实际上是限定词与限定词间的排列。限定词在修饰名词时根据其位置可分三种:前位限定词(Predeterminer)、中位限定词(Central Determiner)和后位限定词(Postdeterminer)。

第12章 限定词(一)

前位限定词	中位限定词	后位限定词
1. all, both, half 2. double, twice, three times, etc. 3. one-third, two-fifths, etc.	1. 冠词：a(n), the 2. 指示代词：this, that, these, those 3. 形容词性物主代词和名词所有格：my, your, etc; Tom's, etc. 4. 量词：some, any, no, every, each, either, neither, enough, much 5. wh- 开首的限定词：what(ever), which(ever), whose	1. 基数词：one, two, etc 2. 序数词：first, second, etc 3. 类序数词：last, next, other, another 4. such 5. 数量词：many, little, few, several, more, less, a lot of, a great deal of, a great number of, etc.

上表只是按照一般情况所做的分类。有的限定词单独出现在句中，这时就不易看出，有时是按前、中、后排列，有的又有重复排列，有的又有跨类的现象。

Write your answer on *every other* line. 每隔一行写上你的答案。
Both my brothers have left Beijing. 我的两个兄弟都离开了北京。
All *these last few* days we have been busy fighting drought(干旱). 最后的几天我们一直忙于对抗干旱。
在上面三句子中 both 与 all 是前位限定词，every, my, these 是中位限定词，other, last, few 是后位限定词，用在中位限定词的后面。

All your three books are wet. 你所有的三本书全湿了。(前、中、后排列)
The poor woman spent *all these last few* days alone. 那个可怜的老太独自一人度过了她最后的那几天。(前、中、后、后排列)

个别限定词有跨类现象，像 such 在 such a(n)搭配中是前位限定词，但在与 all, another, any, few, some, no, other, many, one, two 这些限定词搭配时又是后位限定词，如 any such, few such, no such, some such, one such。

① 前位限定词

A. all, both, half, 可以用于定冠词 the、指示词或形容词性物主代词之前。

You can find the girl among *all* the students. 你可以在所有的学生中找到那个女孩。
How much time will you take for *all* this work? 所有的工作你将花多少时间？
You should see *all* these (those) pictures. 你应该看见所有的画。
All his (my, her) brothers are teachers. 他所有的兄弟都是老师。
Both our teachers are from Shanghai. 我们两个老师都是上海人。
Women hold up *half* the sky. 女性撑起半边天。
I bought the book at *half* that (the) price. 我半价买了这本书。

Notes：a. all 后面的 the 常可以省略，在 all 所修饰的名词后面有定语时也是如此。
Check *all* (the) measurements, please. 请核对所有的尺寸。
The reading-room is open to *all* (the) students of the English Department. 阅览室对英语系的所有学生开放。

b. all 可以与基数词或 such 连用。
All four students are from Beijing. 所有的四个学生都来自北京。
All such factors should be considered. 所有这些因素应该被考虑。

c. all, both, half 不能与 every, either, neither, each, some, any, no, enough 等指量的中位限定词搭配。但 half 可以与中位限定词 a(n)搭配，如：half an hour（半小时），a half mask（一半的面具）。

d. all, both, half 都可以有 of 结构，后面是名词时, of 结构可有可无，后面是人称代词时则必须用，如：all (of) the water, all of it; both (of) the workers, both of them; half (of) the work, half of it。

- 说"一个半某物"时的两种表达

A month and a half/One and a half months has elapsed. 一个半月的时间过去了(消逝了)。

- half 与名词

half 与名词已结成一个概念,此时可以用连字符,冠词放在前面,如:a half-hour, a half-moon, a half-holiday。

B. double, twice, three times, one-third, two-fifths, etc.

这些词是倍数和分数词,它们也属前位限定词。

The cost of food is *double* what it was ten years ago. 食品的价格比10年前上涨了一倍。

I work *twice* as hard as you. 我工作比你勤奋一倍。

以上两例中的 double 和 twice 是副词性质的前位限定词。

② 中位限定词

中位限定词较多,它们有:a(n), the, zero, this, these, that, those, my, his, Rose's, his daughter's, some, any, no, every, each, either, neither, enough, what(ever), whose 等。

This is *an* English dictionary. 这是一部英语词典。

Those are *my brother's* books. 那些是我弟弟的书。

There are *some* girls in the classroom. 教室里有些女生。

冠词、指示代词、形容词性物主代词、名词所有格等互相排斥,在同一个名词词组中只能用其中的一个。

The
This, That, These, Those
My, Your …   } book(s) is/are on the table.
Tom's, The teacher's …

③ 后位限定词

A. 基数词

a. 基数词可以与前位限定词 all 以及后位限定词 last, next, other 序数词等搭配,位于这些词之后,但也可位于 last, next, other 和序数词之前。

All (the) *four* teachers were formerly foreign trade workers. 所有四个老师以前是从事外贸职业的。

His last (next) *two* books were novels. 他的下面两本书是小说。

There were *three* other girls at the meeting. 有三个其他的女孩在会议上。

b. 基数词还可以与 another 搭配,位于其后;与 such 和 more 搭配,位于其前。

We may take *another twenty* tons at this price. 我们以这个价格可以再拿20吨。

One *such dictionary* is enough for me. 这样一本字典对我来说已经够了。

May I have *two more* sheets of paper? 我可以再拿两张纸吗?

B. 序数词

序数词可以与前位限定词 all 以及后位限定词 another, few 等搭配,位于这些词之后,但与 few 搭配时,也可以位于其前。

The newsman is taking a picture of *all first* prize winners. 这个新闻工作者在拍获奖者的照片。

The first few evenings he did enjoy himself very much. 一开始的几晚他确实玩得很高兴。

C. 类序数词 last, next, other

类序数词 last, next, other 可以与后位限定词 few 搭配,位置在 few 之前或之后。

He often tells us about that (those) *last few* months of his college life. 他经常告诉我们关于他大学最后几个月的生活。

The few last comers could be put up at a hostel for the night. 最后到来的人可以在旅馆过夜。

Tom broke his leg on New Year's Day. It took him *the next few* weeks to get over it. 汤姆在元旦摔断了腿。这花了他接下来几个礼拜来恢复。

I saw most of the children waiting in the next room. But where are *the other few* children who are to take part in the dance? 我看见大多数孩子在隔壁房间等待，但是其他要参加跳舞的孩子在哪里？

D．such

such 可以与前位限定词 all 以及后位限定词 other，another，many，few，several 等搭配，位于其后。

All such offenders will be duly punished. 所有的罪犯应该实时地被处罚。

There have been *other (many) such* occurrences in the past. 在过去曾经有过许多这样的事件。

I hope never to meet with *another such* accident. 我希望永远不再遇到这样的事故。

Few (Several) such cases have been reported. 一些这样的案例已经被报道了。

E．more

more 可以与后位限定词 many，several 等搭配，位于其后。

How *many more* copies of the lecture notes do you want? 你想要多少更多演讲的册子？

There are *several more* books on that desk. 在那个桌子上有一些更多的书。

Note：more 还可与 a few, plenty, a lot 搭配，位于其后。

May I have *a few more* samples? 我可以拿一些更多的样品吗？

There are *plenty (a lot) more* eggs in the basket. 在篮子里有更多的鸡蛋。

F．several

several 的前面很少与其他限定词搭配，它的后面可以与后位限定词 other，hundred，thousand 等词搭配。

I saw the foreign expert and his wife and *several other* members of his family at a department store the other day. 前几天，我看见外国专家和他的夫人还有其他的家庭成员在百货公司。

Several hundred (thousand) foreign guests visited the exhibition last year. 去年好几百（几千）的外国客人参观了展览。

G．less

less 可以与 a little 搭配，位于其后。

This boiler consumes *a little less* fuel. 这样的锅炉消耗很少的燃料。

There is *a little less* alcohol in this bottle than in that one. 在这个瓶子里的酒精比那个瓶子里酒精少些。

④ 其他一些限定词之间的搭配

A．冠词与其他一些限定词的搭配

a. 不定冠词 a(n)

不定冠词 a(n) 可以与基数词、序数词及 few，little，such，many 等后位限定词搭配。

It's only *a two hours'* journey by bus. 乘公共汽车只有两个小时的旅程。

This raises *a second* question. 这引出了第二个问题。

Tom has *a few* tickets. 汤姆有一些票。

May I have *a little* ink? 我可以用一些墨水吗？

It was *such a* misfortune. 真是不幸啊。

Such an expression is never heard on British lips. 这种表达从来没有在英语口语中听到过。

Note：a 与基数词搭配时，这个基数词后面一般跟随一个名词，一同作定语修饰另一个名词。"many + a"的结构一般常为"many + 复数名词"的结构所代替。

He has been to Beijing many times. 他曾经去过北京许多次。

b. 定冠词 the

定冠词 the 可以与基数词、序数词、类序数词 next, last, other 以及 many, more, few, little 等后位限定词搭配。

The two visitors had a long talk with her. 这两个游客和她谈了很长时间的话。

This is *the second* time for you to try. 这是你第二次去试了。

The 53rd WTTC was held in Suzhou, China from April 26 to May 3, 2015. 第53届世界乒乓球比赛于2015年4月26日至5月3日在中国苏州举行。

You can find some useful material in *the next/last/other* book. 你可以在下一本/上一本/其他书上找到一些有用的材料。

The more drills you do today, *the less* mistakes you'll make tomorrow. 你今天做越多练习你明天就会犯更少的错误。

The little money that is left is not enough for the book. 留下的少许的钱不够买这本书。

B. 指示代词 this, that, these, those

a. 指示代词 this, that

指示代词 this 和 that 可以与基数词、序数词、类序数词 next, last, other 以及 few, several 等后位限定词搭配。

We are on duty *that* (*this*) six days. 我们值班六天。

That (*this*) *third* brother of his is such a spitfire. 他第三个兄弟是急躁的人。

b. 指示代词 these, those

指示代词 these, those 可以与基数词以及 few 等后位限定词搭配。

Please send *these five* samples to London by air. 请乘飞机把这五个样品送去伦敦。

Those three boxes have not been checked off yet. 那三个盒子还没有被核查。

C. 形容词性物主代词和名词所有格

形容词性物主代词(my, your, his, her, its, our, their)和名词所有格可以与基数词、序数词、类序数词 next, last, other 以及 many, few, little 等后位限定词搭配，也可与中位限定词搭配。

Their (Old Li's) *two* sons are both in the army. 他们的(老李的)两个儿子都在军队里。

The visitor found everything so new to him during *his first* weeks in China. 参观者发现他在中国的前几个礼拜中一切是如此的新奇。

His (John's, The writer's) *next* (*other*) book will come out pretty soon. 他的下一本书将很快出版。

His (John's) *many* (*few*) friends often speak highly of him. 他的许多朋友经常称赞他。

Her (John's) *little* knowledge of French has helped him greatly. 她对法语的少许的知识帮助了他很多。

Their/The enemy's every movement is being watched. 敌人的每个动作都在被监视着。

最后一句中 Their/The enemy's every 在这句中可用"all + 复数可数名词"的结构代替，成为：All their/the enemy's movements are being watched. (敌人的每个动作都正在被监视)。

My brother's dog is very lovely. 我兄弟的狗非常可爱。

Notes: a. 有的语法学者认为"名词所有格或代词 + every + 名词"的搭配不常见。

b. 可以说 his few friends，但不能说 his a few friends，因为 his 和 a 都是中位限定词，互相排斥。在这里 few 的意义与 a few 的含义差不多，不同于在通常情况下的 few (基本上有否定的含义)。

D. some, any, no

some, any, no 可以与基数词、序数词以及 other, more, such 等后位限定词搭配。

a. 与基数词搭配

Will you send a couple of students in your class to help pack the goods? *Any two* students will do. 你可以让你班上两个学生来帮忙包装货物吗？任何两个都行。

No two persons have exactly the same fingerprints. 没有两个人有完全相同的指纹。

Note：some three weeks, some few miles 等结构中的 some 用作副词,不算限定词。Some 在基数词和 few 之前用作副词,表示"大概"或"约"的意思,也要重读。

They learned the uses and dosage of *some fifty* kinds of medicine. 他们大约知道50种药的使用和下药剂量。

It took *some few* days to dismantle the machine. 花了几天拆除那台机器。

b. 与序数词搭配

Give me *any first* name/*some first* names of the English people you know. 给我一些你认识的英国人的名。

I never know he's a flutist. And he's *no second*-rate flutist, either. 我从来不知道他是个吹笛人。而且他也不是第二等的吹笛人。

c. 与 other 搭配

The monitor didn't ask Xiaoli but *some other* students to attend the meeting. 班长没有叫小李而是叫了其他一些学生去参加了会议。

There is *no other* use for it. 此外没有别的用处。

Ask *some other* people. 问别人吧。

Come *some other* day. 改天再来吧。

I have *no other* friend than you. 除了你我没有别的朋友。

d. 与 such 搭配

There is *no such* thing. 没有这么一回事。

e. any 与 no 还可以与后位限定词 less 搭配

I don't mean you could do it in *any less* time. 我的意思并不是你可以花更少时间做这个。

He has *no less* than seven daughters. 他有七个女儿之多。

f. every, each

every 和 each 都可以与后位限定词 such 搭配。此外,every 还可以与基数词、序数词以及 last, other, few, little 等后位限定词搭配。

Every such possibility must be considered. 每一个可能性都必须被考虑。

We must decide *each such* case on its merits. 我们必须以它的价值来决定每样事情。

There'll be only one copy for *every two* students. 每两个学生将只有一本。

I see the doctor *every second* day. 我每隔一天去看医生。

The heroic defenders will fight the enemy to *every last* (=single) drop of their blood. 英雄保卫者将流干他们每一滴血来对抗敌人。

I see Xiao Li *every other* day in school (=every two days 或 every second day). 我每隔一天在学校见到小李。

She visits her aunt *every few* days (weeks). 她每隔几天(礼拜)看她的姨妈。

Every little help you gave Xiaoli is appreciated by us all. 你给小李的每一点帮助都让我们所有人很感激。

"every other+单数可数名词" 的搭配可能有两种意义,此由读音来决定。

He come quite often—*every other* day, to be exact. 他时常来这里,准确地说,他每隔一天来一次。

He only comes on Mondays; he works *every other* day. 他只是星期一来,其他日子他都要工作。

g. much

much 可以与后位限定词 more 和 less 搭配。

She knows *much more* English than you suppose she does. 她比你以为的要认识更多的英国人。

They used *much less* coal for heating last winter. 去年冬天他们使用了少得多的煤来取暖。

h. what 与其他限定词的搭配

what 可以与后位限定词 other, few, little 等搭配;在感叹句中,what 可以与中位限定词 a(n) 搭配,位于其前。

What *other* novel has been annotated? 其他什么小说已经被作注解了?

What *few* suggestions he made have been extremely to us. 他做出的一些建议对我们来说比较极端。

What *a* fine example Lei Feng has set us! 雷锋给我们做了一个多好的榜样啊!

i. 一些分数词与其他限定词的搭配

分数词可以用在 a (n), the, this, that 等中位限定词之前。

The work took him *one-third* (*of*) *the* time it took me. 他做这个工作花了我1/3 的时间。

One-third (*of*) *that* (*this*) meat is tainted. 1/3 的肉腐烂了。

Note：分数词有时用在不定冠词之后。

The resolution requires *a two-thirds* majority to carry. 这个决定需要2/3 的成年人去做。

j. 倍数词与其他限定词的搭配

倍数词 double, twice, three times 等与其他限定词的搭配情况如下：

- 倍数词可以与定冠词、指示词、形容词性物主代词连用,位于这些词之前。

Beijing is now almost *three times* its original size. 北京现在几乎是原来的三倍大。

You can't do it even if you have *twice* your strength. 你即使有你两倍的力气也无法做到的。

- once, twice, three times 等能与 a, every, each, per(正式文体中)搭配,构成频率状语。

They come here	once twice three times four times	a every each per	day week month year

这种用法,在其他场合有时以 the 代替 a, every 等词,至少在美国英语中是如此,如：five dollars the head(每人五元)。

一个名词(词组)前只能用一个前位限定词,因为前位限定词之间是互相排斥的。还有,分数词和 half 有时也作名词用,此时前位限定词 all 放在它们前面。

—*That two-thirds* (*half*) of the canned(罐装的) beef is for you. 那2/3 的罐装牛肉是给你的。

—*All two-thirds* (*half*) of it? I don't need that much. 所有这些的2/3(一半)? 我不需要那么多。

第13章 限定词(二)——冠词

13.1 冠词的分类

冠词(Article)是虚词,本身不能单独使用,也没有词义,它用在名词的前面,帮助指明名词的含义。

传统语法通常将冠词分为不定冠词和定冠词两类,但现代英语已将冠词分为三类:不定冠词(Indefinite Article)、定冠词(Definite Article)和零冠词(Zero Article)。不定冠词用来表示这个冠词后面的名词是指某一类特定事物中的一个,但具体是哪一个并不重要;定冠词是用来限定这个冠词后面的名词是讲话者明确指出的某个特定的事物;零冠词是用来指既不用定冠词也不用不定冠词的情况。

13.2 冠词的用法

(1) 不定冠词的用法

不定冠词有 a 和 an 两种形式,其中 a 用于辅音音素前,an 用于元音音素前。

① 泛指某一类人或物中的任何一个。

I want to buy *a* hat. 我想买一顶帽子。

② 笼统指某类中的某一个,但又不具体说明是哪一个。

I met *a* lady at the gate. 我在门口遇到一位女士。

③ 表示数量"一",类似 one 的含义,但不与 two, three 等相对比。

I spent *an* hour doing my homework. 我花了一个小时在做作业。

④ 表示价钱、时间、速度等的"每一"(=per)。

She goes to cinema once *a* month. 她每月看一次电影。

⑤ 用于序数词之前,表示数量或序数的增加,即"又一"、"再一"。

Shall I ask her *a* second time? 我还要问她一次吗?

⑥ 用于某些物质名词前,使之转换为具体名词,表示"一杯"、"一种"等。

Please give me *a* coffee/tea. 请给我一杯咖啡/茶。

⑦ 用于具体化了的抽象名词前,表示与之相关的具体的人或事。

The party was *a* great success. 晚会开得很成功。

⑧ 在专有名词前表示"某一个"、"类似的一个"。

A Mr. Brown is waiting for you. 一位名叫布朗先生的人在等你。

⑨ 用于 of 短语中表示"同一"(=the same)。

They are of *an* age. 他们同年。

(2) 定冠词的用法

① 表示特指双方(讲话者和听话者)都明白的人或事。

Please give me *the* dictionary. 请把字典给我。

② 用于指上文提到过的人或事,即用于第二次出现的名词之前。

—Xiaoming is reading *a* book named *The Story of Mankind* by Hendrik Willem Van Loon. 小明正在读一本房龙写的《人类的故事》。

—I read *the* book last month. 我上个月看过那本书了。

③ 表示独一无二的人或事物。

the sun/*the* moon/*the* earth 太阳/月亮/地球

④ 用于可数名词前表示一类人或物。

The dog is *a* useful animal. 狗是一种有用的动物。

⑤ 用于序数词前表示顺序。

You are in *the* third group. 你在第三组。

⑥ 用于形容词和副词的最高级前面。

This is *the* most interesting novel I have ever read. 这是我所读过的最有趣一本小说。

⑦ 用于乐器名词前。

play *the* piano 弹钢琴　　play *the* guitar 弹吉他

⑧ 与姓氏的复数形式连用。

The Smiths came to Shanghai in 2001. 史密斯一家是2001年来上海的。

⑨ 与复数名词连用,指整个群体。

the students of Grade 3 三班的全体学生, students of Grade 3 三班的部分学生

⑩ 用于表示江、河、海、洋、山、沙漠、海湾、国家的名词前。

the Changjiang River 长江, *the* Taiwan Straits 台湾海峡, *the* Alps 阿尔卑斯山, *the* Sahara Desert 撒哈拉沙漠, *the* People's Republic of China 中国

⑪ 用于公共建筑、机关、团体名前。

the National Museum 国家博物馆, *the* State Council 国务院

(3) 零冠词的用法

① 表示独一无二的职务、身份前一般不用冠词。

Elizabeth II, *Queen* of England 英国女王伊丽莎白二世

Obama became *President* of the USA. 奥巴马当了美国总统。

② 在一日三餐名词前不用冠词。

have breakfast/lunch/supper　吃早饭/午饭/晚饭

③ 在非特指的季节、月份、星期、学科、语言前不用冠词。

We go to school from Monday to Friday. 我们从周一到周五都上课。

School usually begins in September. 学校通常在9月开学。

④ 在某些用介词 by 构成的表方式的短语中不用冠词。

by bus 乘公共汽车　　　　by plane/by air 乘飞机

by post 用邮寄　　　　　　　　by hand 用手工

⑤ 在某些表示学习、生活、娱乐等的单数名词前不用冠词。

go to school/bed/church/college/work 去上学/睡觉/教堂/上大学/工作

Note：不是指活动，而是指具体的实物，则要用冠词。

He went to *the* college to see his friend. 他去大学看他朋友。

Her grandmother is in hospital and she has been in *the* hospital to take care of her. 她奶奶生病住院了，她一直在医院里面照顾她。

⑥ 在球类、棋类、游戏以及含 day 的节日前不用冠词。

play football/chess 踢足球/下象棋

Christmas Day is an important holiday for Americans. 圣诞节对于美国人很重要。

⑦ 物质名词、抽象名词在表示泛指或一般意义的、复数名词之前不用冠词。

Gold is a precious metal. 金子是一种贵金属。

Those shoes are made of leather. 那些鞋子是皮革做的。

Knowledge is power. 知识就是力量。

Failure is the mother of success. 失败乃成功之母。

Man can't live without air. 人离开空气就无法生存。

⑧ 在 a kind/sort/type/form/variety of 后的名词前不用冠词。

a kind of animals 　一种动物

a variety of sports 　各种运动

⑨ 当不可数名词表示泛指时，其前通常用零冠词。

Bread is made from flour. 面包是用面粉做的。

⑩ 复数可数名词表示类别时，不用冠词。

They are teachers, not workers. 他们是教师，不是工人。

Books are essential to a student. 书对一个学生来说是不可缺少的。

13.3　冠词的位置

通常情况下，冠词出现在被修饰名词前，如：a computer, a book；若名词前带有形容词等修饰语时，冠词则放在相应的修饰语前，如：a new computer, an interesting book。

但是，当名词前的修饰语涉及以下几种情况时，冠词的位置有所变化。

(1) 不定冠词的位置变化情况

① 当单数可数名词前有 how, however, so, too, as 等修饰时

不定冠词通常放在形容词与名词之间。

It is *so interesting a book* that I like it. 这本书很有趣，我很喜欢。

She didn't know *how difficult a task* Tom had accomplished. 她不知道汤姆完成了一个困难的任务。

② 当单数可数名词前有 such, what, many 修饰时

这时的不定冠词就置于它们之间，也就成了"such a + 形容词 + 名词"，"what a + 形容词 + 名词"，"many a + 名词"。

I have never seen *such a big orange*. 我从未看到那样大的橘子。

What an interesting movie it is! 这本电影真有趣!
Many a student thinks highly of that lecturer. 很多学生对那堂课评价甚高。

③ **当单数可数名词前有 rather, quite 修饰时**

这时不定冠词通常放在它们之后。
It's *rather a* pity. 这真是遗憾。
Mr. Smith has been waiting for *quite a* while. 史密斯先生等了好一会。
Note：当名词除 rather, quite 外,还有形容词修饰,则不定冠词可放在 rather, quite 之前或之后。
It's *rather a* cold day. /It's *a rather* cold day. 天气真冷。
It's *quite an* interesting book. /It's *a quite* interesting book. 这是一本非常有趣的书。

④ **不定冠词与 half 的位置**

I'll come in *half an* hour. 我半小时后到。
不过在美国英语中也可将不定冠词放于 half 前,如 a half hour。同时,在以下情况下,必须说 a half。

A. 当构成复合词时
It's a half-hour interview. 这是一个半小时的采访。

B. 当 half 不表示"一半"时
a half sister 同父异母或者同母异父的姐妹。

C. 当表示"几个半"时
It will take about *an hour and a half* to Shanghai. 到上海大概需要一个半小时。

(2) 定冠词的位置

定冠词通常位于名词或者名词修饰语前,但是放于 all, both, half, twice 等词之后、名词之前。
All the students should go to visit the museum. 所有学生都要参观博物馆。
Both the students were late for school today. 两个学生今天上学都迟到了。
Half the staff are under 35. 半数的员工在 35 岁以下。
Your bedroom is *twice the* size of mine. 你的卧室是我的两倍大。

13.4 不定冠词 a/an 与 one 的异同

(1) 同

不定冠词 a/an 与 one 都可表示"一"的意思,有时可以互换,如:in a/one word（一句话,总而言之）。

(2) 异

① **词性不同,表义不同。**

从词性上看,不定冠词 a/an 主要表示类别,侧重于"类别"的概念,而 one 则主要强调"数量"概念。
Give me *a* dictionary. 给我一本字典。（表示我要的是一本字典,不是其他物品）
Give me *one* dictionary. 给我一本字典。（强调我要的是一本词典,不是两本或更多）

② **强调数量或回答 how many 的提问时,用 one。**

因为 one 着重"数量"的概念,所以当强调数量或回答 how many 的提问时,用 one,而不能用 a/an。
He has *one* dictionary, but I have two. 他有一本字典,我有两本。
—How many tickets do you have? —Only *one*. —你有几张票? —只有一张。

③ 当表示"类别"的概念时,只能使用不定冠词 a/an。

A *mobile phone* is useful. 手机是有用的。

She is *an outstanding student*. 她是一位杰出的学生。

④ 在某些短语中,两者都可使用,但表达的意思不一样。

at a time 每次,同时

at one time 一度,曾经

Note:在绝大多数习语中,两者不能互换。

as a result 结果是　　　one day 一天

a bit of 一点儿　　　　one another 互相,相互

⑤ 当修饰表示时间或度量衡的名词,表示"每"时,只用不定冠词。

twice a day 每天 2 次　　　a dozen 每打

13.5　冠词的省略、重复等

虽然冠词的用法有规律可循,但例外还是不少。一般来说,名词的词义比较具体时,需用冠词,而语义比较抽象时就不用冠词,有时用与不用冠词都可以,有时用与不用冠词意思又不同。

(1) 在报刊标题、文章、日记、商业信函及口语和正式书信里里,往往省去冠词。

(A) Plane crashes on (a) house. 飞机撞上民房。

(A) Full furnished flat to let. 配全套家具公寓出租。

Three thousand dollars followed details in (the) letter. 汇上三千美元详情见信。

(2) 并列名词前的冠词可以省略。

Then, together, (the) woman and (the) dog passed quietly into the sunset. 而后,一起,那女人和狗悄悄过去了,融入了夕阳里。

We don't know how (the) doctor, (the) nurse, (the) patient have become the best friends. 我们弄不清那个医生、护士和病人怎么会成了好朋友。

(3) 两个名词表示同一个人或物时,第二个名词前的冠词就省去。

I saw a man and painter. 我看见了一个画家的人。(一个人)

I saw a man and a painter. 我看见了一个人和一个画家。(两个人)

(4) 有时,指同一个人却用了两个冠词。

She is the doctor and the nurse here. 她是这里的医生,也是护士。(重复定冠词,并非指两人,而是一人身兼两职)

(5) 有时表示"每一"时,可用不定冠词或定冠词。

These apples cost/are five yuan a/the kilo. 这些苹果五元一公斤。

但在 by 后表示单位的名词前只能用定冠词。

His mother is paid by the day. 他母亲按日计薪。

(6) 有时名词带不带冠词意思相同。

from (the) beginning to (the) end 从头至尾

at (the) least/most 至少/多
from (the) left to (the) right 从左到右
from (the) south to (the) north 从南到北

(7) 在 what kind/sort of 后的名词前带不带冠词,有时意思相同,有时意思又不同。

What kind of (a) woman is she? 她是(个)什么样的女人?(指品质、行为、待人接物之类方面)
What sort/kind of a car is it? 这是一种什么样的车?(指性状)
What kind/sort of car is it? 这是一辆什么种类的车?(指车型类别,是上海大众,还是美国福特)

第14章 连词和感叹词

14.1 连词

连词是一种虚词,用于连接单词、短语、从句或句子。连词和感叹词一样在句子中不单独担当句子成分。
I went to bed early *because* I didn't feel well. 我很早就睡觉了,因为我觉得不太舒服。
连词不但具有连接从句的作用,同时能体现从句之间的逻辑关系。
I didn't go there *and* she didn't go there either. 我没有去那里,她也没有去那里。(这句中的 and 起着并列作用。)
She was young *but* she was brave. 她很年轻,但是她很勇敢。(此句中的 but 起了转折的作用。)
She doesn't go out now *for* she is very old. 她现在不出门了,因为她很老了。(句中的连词 for 起着原因的作用。)
连词按其性质可分为并列连词(Coordinating Conjunction)和从属连词(Subordinating Conjunction)。并列连词用于连接两个或两个以上并列的单词、短语、从句或句子,如:and, but, or, for 等;从属连词主要连接两个或两个以上的分句,如:that, whether, when, because, if 等。

(1) 并列连词的用法

① 表示并列关系的连词

这些连词主要有:and, or, either ... or, neither ... nor, not only ... but (also), both ... and, as well as 等。
He plays the piano *and* the guitar. 他弹钢琴,也弹吉他。
He plays *not only* the piano, *but (also)* the guitar. 他不但弹钢琴,也弹吉他。
It is *neither* cold *nor* hot today. 今天天气不冷也不热。

② 表示转折关系的并列连词

这些连词主要有:but, yet, while 等。
I wrote a letter to her, *but* she didn't reply. 我写了信给她,但是她没有回复。
Mary said she would come, *yet* she didn't. 玛丽说她会来的,但她没有。
The son was watching TV *while* his mother was busy working in the kitchen. 儿子在看电视,但他的母亲在厨房忙碌。

③ 表示因果关系的并列连词

这些连词主要有:for, so 等。
I won't go shopping today, *for* it's raining heavily outside. 今天我不去购物了,因为外面雨很大。
He didn't study hard, *so* he failed in final examination. 他学习不努力,所以期末考试考砸了。
Note:for 表示结果通常不能放句首,也不能单独使用。

(2) 从属连词的用法

从属连词是主要用来引导状语从句的词。这些状语从句有时间、条件、目的、结果、原因、让步、方式、地点、比较从句,从属连词还可用来引导名词性从句。

① **引导时间状语从句的从属连词**

A. 表示"当……时候"、"每当"的时间状语从句连词,如:when, while, as, whenever。

He was in the kitchen *when* the phone rang. 电话铃响时他在厨房。

Don't move *while* I take the photo. 我拍照时不要动。

She fell asleep *as* she was reading. 她看书的时候睡着了。

Please come to my office *whenever* you have time. 有空的时候到我办公室来。

B. 表示"在……之前(或之后)"的时间连词,如:before, after。after 也可作介词用,别混淆。

Please switch off the air-conditioner *before* you leave. 离开前请关闭空调。

Chen Jianming went to Sydney *after* he had graduated from Nanjing University. 陈建明从南京大学毕业后去了悉尼。

C. 表示"一……就"的时间连词,如:as soon as, the moment, the minute, the instant, the second, immediately, directly, instantly, once, no sooner … than, hardly … when。

I will give you a call *as soon as* I get to Beijing. 我一到北京就打电话给你。

I would like to see Mr. Bentley *the minute* he arrives. 班特利先生一到我就要见他。

Once you identify your goals, you will better understand what you need to do. 一旦你确立了自己的目标,你就会知道应该做什么了。

He had *no sooner* arrived *than* the meeting finished. 他刚到,会议就结束了。

D. 表示"自从"或"直到"的时间连词,如:since, until, till。

She has lived here *since* she came to Shanghai. 她从来上海后就一直住在这儿。

Linda didn't go to bed *until* her mother came back. 琳达直到她母亲回来才睡觉。

The matter will be discussed *till* next meeting. 这个问题到下次会议讨论。

E. 表示"上次"、"下次"、"每次"等的时间连词,如:every time, each time, any time, the first time, (the) last time, (the) next time。

Every time I go to his office, he is on the phone. 每次我去他办公室,他都在接电话。

He looks better than *the last time* I saw him. 他比我上次看到要好多了。

Please come and visit us *the next time* you're in Shanghai. 下次你到上海来看望我们。

Note:every time, each time, any time 前不使用冠词,(the) next time, (the) last time 中的冠词可以省略,而 the first time 中的冠词通常不能省略。

② **引导条件状语从句的从属连词**

引导条件状语从句的从属连词主要有:if, unless, as (so) long as, in case 等。

Would you mind *if* I turn off the air-conditioner? 你介意我关空调吗?

We'll miss the train *unless* we hurry up. 我们若不快点就会错过火车。

You will achieve your goal *as* (*so*) *long as* you work harder. 只要你多努力,一定会达到目标。

Take an umbrella with you *in case* it rains. 带把伞以免下雨。

Note:在条件状语从句中,通常要用一般现在时表示将来意义,而不能直接使用将来时间。不过,有时表示条件的 if 之后可能用 will,但那不是表示将来时间,而是表示意愿或委婉的请求(will 为情态动词)。

If you will wait a moment, I'll get you a coffee. 请稍等,我去帮你拿杯咖啡。

(3) **引导目的状语从句的从属连词**

常见引导目的状语从句的从属连词有 in order that, so that, in case, for fear 等。

I took a taxi this morning *in order that* I arrived at the meeting on time. 为了能准时参加会议,今天上午我

乘了出租车。

Please speak slowly *so that* I won't miss any information. 请说慢点,这样我就不会错过任何信息了。
Please speak in a low voice *in case* you should interrupt other students. 请小声说话,免得打扰其他学生。
Please give me your phone number *for fear* that I should miss my way. 请把你的电话给我,万一我迷路。

(4) 引导结果状语从句的从属连词

引导结果状语从句的从属连词主要有:so that, so … that, such … that 等。
It was very cold, *so that* the river froze. 天气很冷,河水都结冰了。
It is *so* hot today *that* I would like to go swimming. 今天太热了,我想去游泳。
She is *such* a smart girl *that* everybody likes her. 她很聪明,大家都喜欢她。
Notes:①so that 既可以引导目的状语从句,又可以引导结果状语从句。so that 引导目的状语从句时,表示"以便,为了",从句中常使用 can, could, may, might, will, would, should 等情态动词或助动词。so that 引导结果状语从句时,表示"因此,所以",陈述客观事实,因此从句中一般不用 can,may 等情态动词;在结果状语从句中,so that 前可以用逗号。同时,在口语中,so that 中的 that 通常省略。
We should take an early bus *so that* we'll get there in time. 为了能够及时到达,我们应该搭乘早一班车。(目的状语从句)
We took an early bus *so* (*that*) we got there in time. 我们搭乘了一辆早班车,所以我们及时到达了。(结果状语从句)
② so … that 和 such … that 都可以表示"如此……以至",用来引导结果状语从句,但两者用法不同。在 so … that 这一结构中,so 是副词,只能修饰形容词和副词,具体的搭配形式为:so + adj. /adv. + that; so + adj. (+ a/an) + n. + that。
Professor Ling is *so good that* every student respects him. 林教授非常好,以至每一个学生都尊敬他。
Mr. Ling is *so good a professor that* every student respects him. 林先生是一个这么好的教授,以至每一个学生都尊敬他。
在 such … that 这一结构中,such 是形容词,修饰名词,具体的搭配形式为:such + a/an + adj. + 单数可数名词 + that; such + adj. + 复数可数名词 + that; such + adj. + 不可数名词 + that。
Mr. Ling is *such a good professor that* every student respects him. 林先生是一个这么好的教授,以至每一个学生都尊敬他。
③ 如果 such 后面的名词前有 many, much, few, little 等词修饰的话,则不用 such 而用 so。
There are *so many* people in the meeting room *that* I can't find my friend. 会议室里有如此多的人,以至于我找不出我的朋友了。
We have *so little* money that we can't afford *that* car. 我们只有如此少的钱,以至于我们买不起那辆车。

(5) 引导原因状语从句的从属连词

引导原因状语从句的从属连词主要有:because, as, since, seeing (that), now (that), considering (that)等。
I didn't buy that car *because* it was too expensive for me. 我没有买那辆车,因为它太贵了。
As you were in the meeting, I left a message. 由于你在开会,我留了言。
Since we were at the same school, I have known her. 我们以前在一个学校,所以我认识她。
Now that you were wrong, you'd better apologize. 既然你错了,你应该道歉。

(6) 引导让步状语从句的从属连词

引导让步状语从句的从属连词主要有:although, though, even though, even if, while, however, whatever, whenever, whoever, wherever 等。

Although it was a very competitive championship, he won the first prize at last. 尽管这是一场激烈的比赛,最后他获得了第一名。

I'm sure he will come on time *even though* it rains. 我确信他会准时到的,即使在下雨。

She always disagrees with me *whatever* I say. 无论我说什么她都会反对。

(7) 引导方式状语从句的从属连词

引导方式状语从句的从属连词主要有:as, as if, as though, the way 等。

It seems *as if* it will snow. 天气似乎要下雪。

Don't treat others *the way* you don't want to be treated. 己所不欲,勿施于人。

(8) 引导地点状语从句的从属连词

引导地点状语从句的从属连词主要有:where, wherever, everywhere 等。

There was a big shopping mall *where* I lived. 我住的地方有个大型购物大厦。

He always takes his notebook *wherever* he goes. 无论到哪里,他都带着笔记本。

I've looked *everywhere* for my USB drive, but I didn't see it. 我找了所有地方,但依然没有找到我的U盘。

(9) 引导比较状语从句的从属连词

引导比较状语从句的从属连词主要有:than, as … as 等。

He works harder *than* other students. 他比其他学生都努力。

Tom can run *as* fast *as* Jim. 汤姆和吉姆跑得一样快。

(10) 引导名词性从句的从属连词

引导名词性从句的从属连词 that, whether, if, as if, because 等用于引导主语从句、表语从句、宾语从句和同位语从句。其中 that 在句子中只起连接作用,没有词义;whether, if 表示"是否";as if 和 because 只能引导表语从句。

It is true *that* we should finish the task before this Friday. 没错,我们必须在周五前完成任务。

It doesn't matter *whether* you can answer the question or not. 你是否能够回答问题没有关系。

14.2 感叹词

感叹词也是一种虚词,也不能在句中构成任何句子成分,主要是用来表达说话时产生的喜、怒、哀、乐等感情或情绪的词。

Oh! So you are here! 啊!你也在这里!

Ah! I told you before! 哎!我早告诉你了!

(1) 感叹词的位置

感叹词通常位于句子前面,用逗号或者感叹号隔开。感叹词也可以放在句子中间。

(2) 一些常用的感叹词

① oh 表示惊讶、恐惧、懊恼、高兴等。

Oh, who was that? 哦,是谁啊?

Oh! It's so beautiful! 啊！太漂亮了！

② ah 表示惊奇、高兴、痛苦、遗憾等。

Ah! How wonderful! 啊！多么神奇啊！

Ah! That's right! 嗯,那样就对了！

③ dear (me), (my) goodness 表示惊异、赞叹、难过、吃惊等。

Dear (me), what terrible weather! 哎呀！多糟糕的天气啊！

(My) Goodness! How could you finish it in one hour! 天哪！你怎么能在一个小时内完成！

④ well 表示犹豫、解释、让步等。

Well, finally we come here! 好了,我们终于到了！

Well, maybe you are right. 好吧,也许你是对的。

⑤ now 表示请求、说明、命令等。

Now, let's go shopping. 好了,我们去购物吧。

Now, it's all right! Don't cry. 好了,没事了,别哭了。

⑥ there 表示鼓励、同情、不耐烦等。

There! Don't worry, you'll be fine. 好啦,别担心,你会好的。

There, *there*, we spent too much time on it. 好啦,我们在上面花太多时间了。

⑦ come 表示鼓励、安慰、引起注意等。

Come, we must hurry up! 喂,我们要抓紧啦！

Come! What are you doing there? 喂,你在那干嘛呢?

⑧ man 表示兴奋、不耐烦、引起注意等。

Come on, *man*! 嗨,快点！

What're you saying, *man*? 嗨,你在说什么呢?

⑨ boy 表示兴奋、高兴、惊奇等。

Boy, it's exciting! 嘿,太刺激了！

Boy! We won the game! 嘿,我们赢了！

⑩ 其他常用的感叹词有:

ha 表示惊奇、疑惑 *Ha*, that's it!

hey/hello 表示打招呼 *Hey/Hello*, how are you?

why 表示吃惊、抗议 *Why*, what's the point?

Nonsense 意为"胡说" *Nonsense*, it's impossible!

good heavens 表示惊讶、不高兴 *Good heavens*! What are you saying!

(3) 感叹词 what, how

what 和 how 也可以是感叹词,它们组成的感叹句是整个感叹句中的主力军。

What an interesting book it is! 这是一本多么有趣的书啊！

How time flies! 时间过得真快啊！

这两词组成了众多的感叹句。感叹句表示说话时的惊异、喜悦、气愤等情绪,句末用感叹号。

(4) 由 how 构成的感叹句

how 用作感叹副词,在句中作状语以强调形容词、副词或者动词。

① How + adj!

How beautiful! 真漂亮!

② How + adj./adv. + 主语 + 谓语!

How delicious it is! 真好吃!

How beautifully you sing! 你唱的真好听!

③ How + adj. + a/an + 单数可数名词 + (主语 + 谓语)!

How wonderful a movie you recommended! 你介绍了一部多么精彩的电影!

④ How + 主语 + 谓语!

How he's changed! 他的变化真大!

(5) 由 what 构成的感叹句

① What + a/an + adj. + 可数名词单数(+ 主语 + 谓语)!

What a nice day it is today! 今天天气真好!

② What + adj + 复数可数名词 (+ 主语 + 谓语)!

What excellent solution you made! 你的解决方案真完美!

③ What + adj. + 不可数名词 (+ 主语 + 谓语)!

What good news it is! 这是多好的消息啊!

(6) 由 so 和 such 构成的感叹句句式

① so + adj.

You're *so warmhearted*! 你太热心了!

It's *so dangerous*! 太危险了!

② such + a/an (+ adj.) + 单数可数名词

He's *such a kind boy*! 他是个那么好的男孩子!

It's *such a delicious cake*! 这块蛋糕太好吃了!

③ such (+ adj.) + 不可数名词/复数名词

It's *such great* news! 这真是个好消息!

Those are *such beautiful* flowers! 那些花真漂亮!

(7) 否定疑问句构成的感叹句

① 在英语表达中,常可以用否定疑问句表示感叹句。

Isn't the movie exciting! 影片多精彩啊!

Isn't it hot today! 天气好热啊!

② 美国人和一些英国人也会使用一些普通的疑问句(非否定形式的)来表示感叹。

Did he look angry! 他真的生气了!

Who would have done such a thing! 谁会那么做!

第 15 章 介 词

15.1 介词概述

介词(Preposition),又称之为"前置词"。介词是表示它与其他词或短语之间关系的词。它必须与名词、代词等组成词组。因介词是一种虚词,所以它在句中也不能单独作任何成分,也不重读。介词的用法、搭配也比较复杂:多数介词的意义是肯定的,但也有表示否定意义的;多数介词后跟名词、代词,还有数词,that 和 wh-引导的宾语从句也可作介词的宾语;有些介词可与动词搭配组成短语动词。

15.2 介词的分类

(1) 按结构划分的 7 种介词

① **简单介词(Simple Preposition)**

即单一介词,此类介词几乎都可以与一些词或短语自由组合,如:at,in,of,since 等。

He used to get up *at* six every morning. 他以前每天早晨 6 点起床。

Her father has worked *in* the factory for twenty years. 她父亲在那个工厂工作了 20 年。

② **复合介词(Compound Preposition)**

复合介词可分成两类:一为双词介词,二为双重介词。

A. 双词介词（Two-word Preposition）

双词介词由两个介词组成,如 as from,but for(若非), such as, out of 等。

You've been hired *as from* last Sunday. 从上星期日起你已被告雇用了。

But for your help, I should have failed. 要不是你的帮助,我早已失败了。

There are languages coming from Latin in the world *such as* French, Italian and Spanish. 世界上有些语言源于拉丁文语言,诸如法语、意大利语和西班牙语。

Out of debt, *out of* danger. 无债一身轻。

像 as from, but for, such as, out of 等双词介词,粗略计算一下不下三十多个,如:ahead of; apart from; as of; because of; away from; except for; as for; as to; save for; upwards of; depending on; according to; close to; contrary to; due to; next to; on to; opposite to; owing to (=because of); prior to (=before); relative to; subsequent to (随后,接着); thanks to (=owning to, because of); up to; along with; together with 等。

B. 双重介词（Double Preposition）

双重介词是指两个用在一起,但属同一范畴的介词,它们在意义上所表达的角度不同,或者准确程度不一致,如同时表示空间位置的 in 与 among/between,表示地点位置的 from 与 round,表示上下位置的 on 与 to。

He put more than twenty bookmarks *in among* fifty pages. 他在 50 页中竟夹了 20 多个书签。

The poor woman fainted and fell *on to* the ground suddenly, and two schoolboys nearby went to help her at once. 那可怜的老太突然跌倒在地,就近两个小学生很快跑去搀扶她。

The three groups continued working in the workshop *from before* sunrise *till after* midnight. 那三个小组(的人)在车间里从日出以前一直工作到午夜之后。

以上三句中都用了双重介词,使意思表达得更精确、明了。第 1 句中的 in,among 虽同属空间位置的介词,但所表示的位置角度不同;第 2 句中的 on 意为"在……表面上",to 表示"向……",这更凸显出那老太跌倒的全过程;第 3 句中的两组表时间的 from before 和 till after 的合用,更显示出了时间的精确度。

③ 合成介词(Composed Preposition)

合成介词是由两个介词合并在一起成了一个独立介词,它们的意思几乎是原两个介词的合一,如:into(进入),outside(在……外边),within(在……内),alongside(在……旁边;沿着……),upon(在……上)等。

Two policemen rushed *into* the dark room. 两个警员冲进了那黑屋。

He lives *within* his income. 他量入为出。

Once *upon* a time, there lived a very old man named London. 从前,那里住着一个名叫伦敦的古稀老人。

④ 分词介词(Participle Preposition)

分词介词由现在分词转化而来的介词,如:concerning,including,pending(在等待……之际;在……期间;直到……为止;在……过程中)等。

Considering her age, she's very bright. 就她的年龄而言,她是极聪明的。

Pending her return, we must get everything ready. 在她回来之前,我们必须把一切都准备好。

They will arrive at noon *barring* accidents. 若无意外发生,他们将于中午到达。

We know nothing about him, *saving* that he was in the army during the war. 我们除了知道他战时在陆军服务外,其他一无所知。

常见的分词介语还有:concerning, excepting, following, including, regarding, touching 等。

⑤ 三词介词 (Three-word Preposition)

三词介词的结构常是"介词+名词+介词"。

She could not speak, but made her wishes *by means of* signs. 她不会说话,靠手势示意。

I wish I could do something *in return for* the kindness I have received from him. 我希望我能干点什么来报答他对我的一番好意。

三词介词 by means of 意为"用;凭借;通过", in return for 意思是"作为……的报酬;作为交换"。像 by means of, in return for 这样的三词介词还有很多,如:as opposed to, by way of, by/in virtue of (= because of), in accordance with, in exchange for, in need of, in place of, in search of, in spite of, in terms of, in view of, on account of, on behalf of, on ground of, on top of, in addition to, in/with reference to, in/with regard to, in relation to, in comparison with, in contact with, in line with 等。

⑥ 多词介词(More Than Three-Word Preposition)

多词介词通常有四个词组成,即"介词+冠词+名词+of",如:as a result of(因此,结果;由于……,作为……的结果),for the sake of (= for sb's/sth's sake)意为"为了某人或某事起见;出于对某人某事的考虑"。

He was late *as a result of* the snow. 因为下雪,他来晚了。

For the sake of peace and quiet, she let him have his way. 为了和睦和安静,她让他为所欲为。

像以上的 as a result of, for the sake of 的 多词介词还有:at the cost of, in (the) light of, at the expense of, in the case of, in the company of, in the face of, in the event of, on the face of, on the part of, on the point of, on the grounds of, with the exception of 等。

⑦ 特殊介词(Special Preposition)

之所以称它们是特殊介词是因为那些介词要与某些特定的动词、形容词、名词或过去分词相搭配起来。

A. 与动词搭配,如：insist on（坚持）, laugh at（嘲笑）, persist in（坚持）。

She *insisted on* our going by train. 她坚持我们乘火车去。

B. 与形容词搭配,如：be fond of（爱好）, be good at（善于）, be interested in（感兴趣）, be capable of（有做某事的能力和力量）, be eager for/about/after（对……有强烈的愿望）。

Show me what you *are capable of* and how well you can work. 让我看看你有什么本事。

C. 与名词搭配,如：conformity to（符合）, contrbution to（对……的贡献）, struggle against（与……战斗）。

Conformity to fashion is essential to the happiness of some women. 对某些妇人之快乐,合乎时髦是必要的。

D. 与过去分词搭配,如：be dotted with（星罗棋布,散布）, be/get caught in（遇上）, be covered with（覆盖）。

The sky *was dotted with* stars. 繁星满天。

We *had been caught in* a traffic jam. 我们碰到了一次交通阻塞。

(2) 按词义划分的 13 种介词

① 表示地点

表示地点的介词有：at, in, on, off, across, about, around, between, among, throughout, over, above, below, under, beneath, underneath, inside, outside 等。

The lid is *on* the pan. 盖在锅上。

The post office is *across* the street. 邮局在街对面。

② 表示位置

表示位置的介词主要有：above, over, on (the) top of, inside, outside, at the bottom of, under, underneath, beneath, below 等。

The electric light hanging from the ceiling is just *over* your head. 从天花板上悬挂下来的电灯正好在你头顶上。

The sky *above* our heads is a deep blue. 我们头顶上的天是深蓝色的。

The football was *under/underneath/beneath* the table. 足球在桌子下面。

The temperature is *below* freezing today. 今天温度在零度以下。

介词 above 与 over 都表示"高出……；在……正上方",在句中可互换。在表示"低于……；在……的下方"时,under, underneath, beneath 三词均可用。

③ 表示时间

在表达时间时最常用的介词为 at, in, about, 等。

The meeting will begin *at* 2 p.m. 会议将于下午两点开始。

Can you drive to Nanjing *in* half a day? 你能用半天时间开车到南京吗?

表时间的介词还有：after, around, as, before, by, during, for, from … to, since, on, over, past, through, throughout, till (until), within 等。

④ 表示除去

表示此义的介词有：besides, but, except 等。

There will be five of us for dinner, *besides* Tom. 除汤姆外,还有我们五个人一起吃饭。(besides 是"除……外还有"的意思)

Everyone was there *but/except* him. 除了他之外,大家都在。(but 除……之外, = except)

⑤ 表示比较

表示比较的介词主要有：as，like[像（某人，某事物）；类似，相似]，above，over 等。

They entered the building disguised *as* cleaners. 他们化装成清洁工人模样进了大楼。

This dress is twice as expensive *as* that. 这件连衣裙比那件贵一倍。（as ... as 同等比较，第一个 as 是副词，第二个 as 是介词）

I've always wanted a garden *like* theirs. 我总想有一座像他们那样的花园。

Should a soldier value honor *above* life? 军人应视荣誉重于生命吗？

⑥ 表示反对、赞成

表示反对、赞成的介词主要有：against，for，with。

Are most people *against* the proposal? 是大多数人反对这项提议吗？

Are you *for* or *against* the new road scheme? 你赞成还是反对这项新道路修建计划？

I'm *with* you in all you say. 我同意你所说的一切。

He had an argument *with* Tom. 他跟汤姆吵了一架。

⑦ 表示原因、目的

表示原因、目的的介词主要有：for，with，from 等。

You can't see the wood *for* the trees. 你只见树木不见森林。（for 表示原因）

As the storm burst the shoppers made *for* shelter. 暴风雨突然来临时，购物者纷纷跑向避雨的地方。（for 表示目的或某种活动、某种心情所向往的目标）

The small child trembled *with* fear. 小孩吓得打哆嗦。（with 表示原因）

He did it *from* kindness/spit/sheer stupidity. 他做这件事出于好意/恶意/十足的愚蠢。（此句中的 from 指一个事件或情况发生的原因、理由或动机）

⑧ 表示手段、方式

表示手段、方式的介词有：by，in，with 等。

Jim and Jack came to the west coast *by* car. 吉姆和杰克是乘汽车到西海岸的。（by 表示方式）

They always addressed each other *by* their Christian names. 他们彼此总用教名相称。（by 表示方式）

We stood *in* queue. 我们排队等候。（in 表示方式）

She lay back in the chair *with* her eyes closed. 她闭着眼睛背靠在椅子上坐着。（with 短语作方式状语）

⑨ 表示所属、拥有

表示所属和拥有的介词有：of，with 等。介词 of 表示所属，即表示所有关系，也常称"属格"。

The surface *of* the road is slipper. 那路的路面湿滑。

The name *of* the owner is Smith. 物主的名字叫史密斯。

介词 with 所表示的"拥有"是指"拥有某种财物或具有某种特征"的意思。

Robert is a man *with* a large fortune. 罗伯特是个拥有大批财产的人。

The house *with* a bay window is a church. 有凸窗的房子是个教堂。

⑩ 表示条件

表示条件的介词有：on，without，considering 等。

I can only do it *on* the understanding that I am not held responsible for the outcome. 只有在我对后果可以不负责任的条件下，我才能做这件事。（on 表示条件）

I cannot do it *without* your help. 你要不帮助我，我可干不了。[without 表示条件，此句中的 without 用作 unless（除非），= I cannot do it without you help me. 不过这种表达比较粗俗。]

That child read quite well, *considering* his age. 按那个孩子的年龄来说，他读得相当好。

第 3 句中的介词 considering 是来自动词 consider 的现在分词,它后面也可跟一个从句,如:Considering she is only six years old. 其实,在口语中,介词 considering 后不用带名词,而常把它单独置于句末,意为 considering the circumstances(就情况而论),如:You've not done badly, considering（照目前情况来看,你们干得不坏）。

⑪ 表示让步

表示让步的介词有:despite, in spite of, in despite of, notwithstanding 等。

She insisted on going her own way, *despite* my warning. 她不顾我的警告,仍然执意自行其是。

They went out *in spite of* the rain. 尽管下雨,他们仍然外出。

Bob still went to the concert *in despite* of his father's warning. 鲍勃不顾他父亲的警告,还是去听了音乐会。

They came *notwithstanding* the snow. 尽管下雪,他们还是来了。

需要说明的是第 1 句和第 2 句中的介词 despite 与 in spite of 同义,可以互换,只是 in spite of 语气比 despite 强些;第 3 句中的 in despite of 作"尽管"讲时是个相当正式的表达,显得文质彬彬,不过现在已较少用它了;第 4 句中的 notwithstanding 也与第 1 句和第 2 句中的"尽管"同义。

⑫ 表示方向和运动

表示方向和运动的介词主要有:in, into, to, out of, from, toward, by, by way of, via 等。

He arrived *in* Beijing on the morning of May 1. 他 5 月 1 日早晨到北京的。

We returned *to* Shanghai *from* Nanjing. 我们从南京返回上海。

Jim dived *into* the swimming pool. 吉姆一个猛子扎进游泳池。

They came *out of* the hall. 他们从大厅里走出来。

He jumped away *from* the falling wall. 他从正在倒塌的墙上跳开。（向相反方向）

The bus conductor said, "Please leave *by* the rear door." 公共汽气汽车售票员说:"请从后门下车"。（by 表示"途径,通过"）

The Whites went to Beijing *by way of* Nanjing. 怀特一家路经南京到北京。（句中 by way of 可用 via 替代）

⑬ 表示动作发出者或工具

这类介词有:by, with, in, like 等。

A. 介词 by 与其后面的名词或代词表示施动者,也就是发出行动、动作的人或物,通常用于被动语态。

This play was written *by* Shakespeare. 这个剧本是莎士比亚写的。

The window must have been broken *by* a baseball. 这扇窗户一定是被垒球打破的。

These shoes were made *by* hand. 这些鞋是手工做的。

B. 表示工具的介词常是 in, with。用 in, with 表示工具时,in 和 with 后的名词前不用冠词。

That picture seems to have been painted *in* oil, not *in* watercolour. 那张画看起来似乎是用油彩画的,不是用水彩画的。

She looked at her bank balance *with* satisfaction. 她怀着满意的心情看着她的银行存款余额。

C. 介词 like 的意思是"像"。

She speaks English like an American. 她说起英语来像个美国人。

15.3 表示否定意义的介词

多数介词的意义是肯定的,但也有少数是否定的。这些否定介词主要有 without, before, against, above, behind, from 等,其中 without 是最明显的表示否定,其余的否定意义常在实际语言表达中体现出来。

Liu Hulan would die *before* yielding. 刘胡兰宁死不屈。（before 意为"与其……宁愿"）

I didn't say anything *against* you at the meeting. 我在会上没说不利于你的话。（against 是"不利于"的意

思,它还可意为"提防")

The manager of the department is *above* taking bribery. 那个部门的经理不会受贿。(above 表示"不屑做某事")

His son is *behind* the others in his class in school. 他的儿子在学校里不如同班的学生。(behind 是"不及;落后于"的意思)

Her father persuaded her *from* going there alone. 她父亲说服她别独自去那里。

要注意,第5句中的介词 from 要与某些动词搭配,如"persuade/entice + 宾语 + from doing sth"才表示否定。

15.4　介词词组的句法功能

介词是虚词,在句中不能单独出现,它们必须与名词或代词组成词组才行,所以它们在句中的功能也只能说是"介词短语"在句中的功能。

(1) 作状语

Towards midday the fog began to disperse. 将近中午时分,大雾开始消散。
His eyes were red *with excessive reading*. 由于看书过度,他的眼睛都红了。
In spite of old age he is still working hard for the people. 尽管年事已高,他仍在为人民努力工作。
In all probability, the mail will arrive this afternoon. 很有可能,邮件将在今天下午到达。

(2) 作表语

He was *out of breath* when he reached the station. 当他到达车站时已是上气不接下气了。
His father is *in good health*. 他爸身体很好。

(3) 作名词的定语(或"名词修饰语")

He is a man *of wealth*. 他是个富有的人。
Let me have a look *at the car*. 让我瞧瞧这辆车子。
A day *in the open air* will do you a lot of good. 在露天度过一日会对你身体有许多好处。
She lived in a village *near the seaside*. 她住在靠近海边的一个村庄里。

(4) 作复合宾语

He always considers *himself in the right*. 他总是认为自己正确。
We found *the map out of date*. 我们发现地图已经过时了。
He thought *it beneath him* to do such a thing. 他认为自己不屑于做这种事。
When I came back home, I found everything *in good condition*. 我回到家时发现每件东西都完好无损。

15.5　介词的双词性或多词性

介词有时可能还是副词或连词,甚至还有其他词性,这是英语词性的多见现象。这种情况一般不说是介词或其他词的兼职功能,因那些词性是各自独立,并不存在依附关系。对于那些不同的词性只有在具体的句子中才能看出。

(1) 有些介词有副词及其他词性

有些介词(如 before, in, over, on, down, up 等)还有副词词性或其他词性,使用或阅读时均须注意。

I met him *before* the war. 战前我见过他。(介词)
We've met *before*. 我们以前见过。(副词)
My mother is *in* the house. 我母亲在屋里。(介词)
Is there anybody *in*? 里面有人吗？(副词)
The program was broadcast *over* the radio. 这个节目是通过电台广播的。(介词)
The program is *over*. 这个节目播完了。(副词)
I'm *on* your side. 我支持你。(介词)
The old man was standing in the blazing sun with no straw hat *on*. 那个老人没戴草帽,一直站在烈日下。(副词)
The boat moved slowly *down* the river. 那船沿河缓缓而下。(介词)
The sun went *down* below the horizon. 太阳落山,消失在地平线下。(副词)
We *downed* our beer and left. 我们一口气把啤酒喝光就走了。(动词)
She's got a *down* on me; I don't know why. 她很讨厌我；我不知道为什么。(down,名词,意为"讨厌或敌视某人某物")
He climbed *up* the tree. 他爬上了树。(介词)
Lift your head *up*. 把你的头抬起来。(副词)

(2) 有些介词有连词词性

有些介词(如 after, before, since, until 等)既可是介词也可是连词,在实际使用中和翻译时须好好区别。

The ball goes up very high *after* it hits the ground. 这球着地后蹦得很高。
It will not be long *before* they come back. 他们不久就回来。
I can't make you out. You've changed so much *since* last we met. 我认不得你了。自上次见面后,你可变多了。
Will you be all right *until* I get back? 在我回来之前你会一切都好吗？

15.6 介词后的宾语

(1) 名词和代词

She lived in *Beijing*. 她以前住在北京。(名词)
—What can I do for *you*? 您要什么东西？(代词)
—Two pencils. 两支铅笔。

(2) 数词

The little girl can count from *one* to *one hundred*. 那小女孩能从一数到一百。
His grandfather was born in *1941*. 他祖父生于 1941 年。

(3) v-ing 分词(动名词)

Thank you for *giving* me so much help. 谢谢你给了我这么多帮助。
He entered Mary's bedroom without *knocking* at the door. 他没敲门就径直进入了玛丽的房间。

(4) 动词不定式及其短语

动词不定式及其短语指两种：一是带 to 和不带 to 的动词不定式（短语）；二是 wh- + 动词不定式。
She seldom comes but/except *to see her father*. 她除了看她父亲外，很少过来。
She did nothing but/except *watch TV* at night. 她晚上没事做，就是看电视。（介词前面有 do，后面的动词不定式就省 to）
Then I really didn't *know what to do*. 那时我真的不知道怎么办。

(5) 形容词和副词

少数介词可带形容词和副词作其宾语。

① 形容词作介词宾语

可作介词的宾语的形容词主要有 well（指身体好），beautiful, blue, crazy（疯狂的；发狂的），happy, useless 等。
The young woman looks nothing *but well*. 那少妇看上去身体绝不健康。
The thief ran *like crazy* as soon as he saw the policeman. 小偷一看见警察就拼命地跑。
I'm sure that she was *far from happy*. 我敢肯定她非常不幸福。

② 有些介词后可接副词作其宾语

这些介词主要是表示地点和时间的。
What can you do *in here*? 你在这儿能干什么？
One of the windows suddenly opened *from within*. 其中一扇窗突然从里面打开了。

(6) 复合宾语

有少数介词（如 for, instead of, on, upon, with, without 等）能带复合宾语作其宾语。
I'm waiting *for Professor Liang to come*. 我在等梁教授的到来。（句中的动词不定式作宾语补足语）
The old town looks more beautiful *with all the lights on*. 华灯齐明，那古镇看上去更加美丽。（句中的副词 on 作宾语补足语）

(7) 从句

以从句作介词的宾语主要有以 wh-和 that 引导的从句。

① 以 wh-引导的从句作介词宾语。

I'll pay attention *to whatever* you may say. 你不管说什么，我都会注意的。
We are puzzled *about what* we should do next. 我们不知道下一步该怎么办。

② 可以以 that 引导的从句作宾语的介词并不多，它们是 but, except, for, in, rather than 和 save/saving。有时 that 可省去。

He would have helped us but (*that*) he was short of money. 要不是他那时没有钱，他会帮助我们的。
I shouldn't care *for that* doctor to be my doctor. 我不要那个医生给我看病。
I knew nothing about her *save/saving that* she graduated from Beijing Language and Culture University in 1990. 我除了知道她 1990 年从北京语言大学毕业外，其他便一无所知。

15.7　与动词搭配组成短语动词的介词

一些介词与某些动词搭配起来可组成短语动词。这些短语动词数目巨大，如在杨元兴先生所著的《英语短语用法比对大词典》里就涉及 800 余个,如:abide at/in, accept as, assist with, advance (up) on, hand in, insist on, mail from, reach for, persist in, safeguard against, write to。

15.8 介词的省略

(1) as 的省略

as 作介词用,常与某些动词搭配组成一些特定词组,如:accept/reguard/consider/acknowledge/characterize + 宾语 + as。当 as 的宾语是名词时,as 也有省去的情况。

The king accepted the girl his daughter. 国王把这女孩收做女儿。

I consider him an expert. 我认为他是一位专家。

上例中的 daughter 和 him 前可有介词 as ,那就是介词短语作宾语补足语,省去 as 之后成了名词作宾语补足语。

(2) at 的省略

介词 at 常与时间名词连用,作表示时间的状语。有时,介词 at 省略后成了时间名词作时间状语。

What time did you arrive home? 你什么时候到家?(what 前省去 at)

It is hard work keeping the grass green this time of year. 一年中这个时节保持绿草不枯,要费很大气力。(this time 前省去 at)

(3) from 的省略与否

介词 from 在"prevent/stop sb/sth from doing sth"结构中,往往省略。

Illness prevented him (*from*) going. 疾病使他未能成行。

Can't you stop the child (*from*) getting into mischief? 你就能使孩子不淘气?

(4) in 的省略

介词 in 在:spend some time in doing sth, have difficulty/trouble in doing sth, There be no hurry/use/sense(道理)/point in doing sth, in + 限定词 + way, be interested in doing sth 中,in 也常用省略。

Mr. Young spent nearly twenty years writing the book *A Guide to the Use and Contract for English Phrases*. 杨先生花了将近二十年时间才写成了《英语短语用法比对指津》那本书。(writing 前省了 in)

I have been some time answering this question. 我想了一些时候才回答这个问题。(answering 前省去 in)

When work on the television series began in 1982, director Young had trouble casting the man character. 1982 年开始制作这部电视连续剧时,杨导演在选这个男演员时曾遇到了麻烦。(casting 前省去 in)

She was busy preparing lessons. 她忙于备课。(preparing 前省去 in)

I think there's no use complaining now. 我认为现在抱怨没用。(complaining 前省了 in)

Do it your own way if you don't like my way. 如果你不喜欢用我的方法做事,那你就用自己的方法做吧。(own way 前省了 in)

Who is interested doing the work in this strange way? 谁有兴趣用这种怪方法做这事?(doing 前省了 in)

"keep/deter/hinder + 宾语 + from doing sth"中,介词 from 不可省。

They are doing something to keep the child from going to sleep. 他们在做着一些事不让那小孩睡着。

They were hindered from going there earlier. 他们受阻不能早些到那里。

(5) of 的省略

of 常在"of + 限定词 + 名词 age/design/size/weight"的结构中可省略。

He is tall for a child his age. 从他的年龄来说,他是长得高的。(his age 前省去 of)

The small box is a very smart design. 这小盒子设计精美。(a very smart 前省去 of)

The Pacific Ocean is so big that it could hold twenty countries the size of the United States. 太平洋很大,它可以装得下 20 个美国那样大的国家。(the size 前省去 of)

(6) on 的省略

on 的省略主要出现在表示特定的日子前。

The police arrested him on an assault charge (on) the evening of November 18. 警察于 11 月 18 日以殴打罪逮捕了他。

Who was born (on) September 9, 1999? 谁出生在 1999 年 9 月 9 日?

15.9 介词的后置及介词与其宾语的分离

有时,介词与其宾语分开,置于句尾,有时与其宾语分离。在下列情况下,介词置于句尾或与其宾语分离。

(1) 介词宾语为疑问句时

What are you talking *about*? 他们在谈什么?

Where are you *from*? 你是哪里人?

What *for*? 为什么? (= What do you work *for*? 你为什么而工作?)

I don't know what you are talking *about*. 我不知道你们在谈什么。

(2) 介词宾语为关系代词或连接代词时

Do you remember the book which the teacher refereed us *to*? 你记得老师叫我们看的那本书吗?

That's what he is talking *about*. 那就是他所谈的事。

(3) 在其他情况下

"There's nothing to be afraid *of*," Mother said. "没有什么可怕的,"妈妈说道。

It is a fact that here I could not find one garbage can to throw trash *in*. 确实,我在这里连一个倒垃圾的垃圾桶都找不到。

We helped the troupe avoid the kind of trouble it had met *with* elsewhere. 我们帮助这个剧团避免了它在别处曾遇到过的那种麻烦。

I will try to get it over with as quickly *as* possible. 我一定尽快地把它结束。(to get it over with 是一固定说法)

第16章　句子移位

16.1　移位概述

对英语句子移位(Dislocation)现象的研究起始于20世纪70年代。移位是一种句法结构,其中一个带有名词核心成分的句子成分被移至句首或句尾,此时原来的位置往往通过一个替代成分标出。移位属于有标记的句法结构。凡含这种结构的句子我们管它们叫移位句。移位是世界上绝大多数语言中都存在着的句法现象。对英语中的移位,也许是Rose(1967)首先注意到的,而后是Quirk, et al.(1985),文旭(2005),仇伟、张法科(2006),杨元兴(2007,2012)等。我国汉语界的知名学者王力(1985)、吕叔湘(1986)也曾提出了汉语中的移位现象。

16.2　移位的分类

移位,从其结构和形式上讲,一般可分为右移位(Right Dislocation)和左移位(Left Dislocation)两种;其实,最近研究证实,还有一种形式叫虚拟移位(Subjunctive Dislocation),也叫零移位(Zero Dislocation)。

（1）虚拟移位

人类语言客观性与主观性的对立直接决定了语言表达中真实和虚拟的对立。我们对真实条件句和虚拟条件句比较熟悉,而移位理论上也有虚拟移位和真实移位之分。对虚拟移位,李秋杨、陈晨曾在《山东外语教学》上著文,做过较详细的论述。

① 虚拟移位的定义

虚拟移位是一个物体或一种抽象概念在空中发生的隐喻化运动(Ramscar, et al., 2009; Matlock, 2004; Talmy, 2000),这种运动形式已成了心理语言学和认知语言学的研究内容之一。

② 虚拟移位的表现形式

虚拟移位是以运动形式来描写静止状态的。尽管其中存在运动动词,但不产生真实运动(李秋杨、陈晨,2012)。

The fence *goes from the plateau to the valley.* 栅栏从高地一直延伸到山谷。

上面那句子足以说明"虚拟移位"这个概念。句中的fence是移位的主体,plateau和valley是相应的参照物,介词from ... to是移位的方式。句子的主语fence其实没真正发出goes这个动作,所谓的goes from the plateau to the valley只是一种想象而已,像这样的句子就叫虚拟移位句。

③ 虚拟移位的功能

根据李秋杨、陈晨(2012)的观点,虚拟移位是语言使用者用来表达或者推断有关场景的物理状态。虚拟移位能反映出人的身体感知和空间感知延伸到人的心智、向外延伸到外部环境的体验性认知规律。

有一些虚拟移位是现实世界中真实位移的经验在说话人认知意象上的投射,是现实移位的隐喻,也就是现实物理世界中实体的移动经验在抽象范畴里的映射结果。

The tree threw its shadow into the valley. 那树把它的影子投射到山谷。

Soon the fresh air entered the room through the open window. 很快,新鲜空气通过打开的窗子进入房间内。
The light is shining into the cave. 光照亮着洞穴。

上面三例的位移主体是影子、空气和光线,它们的位移过程是"源域—路径—目标物体",这就反映了虚拟动态本身是存在的,只不过它们在人类视觉感知的限度之外了。尽管光线、影子的运动、路径已有科学验证,但因其速度太快而无法让人们感知,所以语言所表达的不是人们的实际所感到的运动,而只是一种想象的运动,这当然还叫虚拟移位。

更多的虚拟移位是通过视觉器官来体验的。
The wide road runs along the coast. 那宽阔的路一直延伸到海岸。
The field spreads out in all directions from the granary. 田地从谷仓那里向四面八方蔓延出去。

从上面例句可见,有一些虚拟移位表达客观物体并未发生真实运动,所谓运动是通过人体本身或人的视觉来实现的。人的视觉对客观物体进行一次顺序式的扫描,使得那些道路、山脉、田地等具有空间延伸或展开这一类物体,由此而发生虚拟移位现象。

(2) 右移位

右移位指小句中的一个组成成分移至句尾位置,而其原位置[学术语叫"典范"(Anonical)]则由一"同指的"(Co-Referential)代词或一个完整的词汇名词短语补充(仇伟、张法科,2006)。上面所说的典范位置就是指原位置。右移位不同于虚拟移位,它是一种真实移位。

① 右移位的功能

A. 澄清功能

日常的口语交际多数情况是应时即景的。在话语人用代名词指称某些实体,且把它作为已知信息置前之后,可能会意识到言而无尽,这时话语者就借助名词短语附加语来补充和澄清(Clarifying)前面代词的指称对象以满足听话者希望得到清晰的要求,这样就会使会话进展得顺畅。

At length *it* was over, *the big meal*. 它最后结束了,那顿大餐。
I know *her* better *your favorite student—Chang Zhuhuao*. 我比较了解她,你最喜欢的那个学生——张志华。
At last *he* turned out just before the first bus began to start, *the laz-bones*. 他总算在头班车发动前到了,这个懒虫。
"*It*'s beautiful—" Martin murmured, watching her, "*your yellow hair*". "它漂亮——"马丁看着她,自言自语道:"你的黄头发。"

例句 1 中的主语 the big meal 右移至句尾,原处用 it 指代。而 the big meal 是对 it 加以补充和澄清。例句 2 中的宾语 her 是指代 your favorite student—Chang Zhuhuao 的,它也是对 her 加以补充和澄清的。例句 3 的主语 he 是指代后面的 the lazy-bones;例句 4 中的主语 it 是指代右移主语 your yellow hair 的,当然 your yellow hair 也是对直接引语中的主语 it 加以补充说明的。例句 4 稍复杂些,就是把直接引语分开成两部分,主句插在中间,后还带一个作状语的 v-ing 分词短语。

B. 强调功能

有时,右移位结构的名词短语附加语占据突出的位置,易于引起听话人的注意,此乃话语人以后移的名词短语附加语对前面相关的实体进行"加强"处理,让听话人再次引起注意,这就是右移句的强调功能。

It is useful *that dictionary* anyway. 无论怎样,它是有用的,那本词典(不是这本词典)。
It was a good watch *this*. 它是一块好表,这块(不是那块)。

② 右移位句的特点

右移位句的特点有两个,即"松"和"紧"。当右移成分表示澄清和补充功能时,那与前面句子间有逗号分开,也就是说与前面句子结构上比较疏松;当右移成分表示强调时,与原句子结构上比较紧密,其前就没有逗号。

(3) 左移位

相比之下,左移位情况更复杂,表达更丰富,使用更广泛。然而,迄今为止,国内外语言专家、学者对英语中的左移位句的注意不多,对其进行深入研究的更是寥寥无几。国外提出英语左移位句的现象的也只有 Ross, Prince, Quirk, Radfordy 等人。在 1985 年和 1986 年,我国汉语界的王力、吕叔湘先生也先后提到过汉语中的左移位现象。欣慰的是,20 世纪 80 年代,我国英语界也有几个学者提到左移位句(如:文旭,2005;仇伟、张法科,2006;杨元兴,2007,2012)。1987 年,Langacker 在他的 *Information Structure and Sentence Form* 一书中,对左移位句进行过分析研究,但研究的深度和广度似乎还不够有好些方面还未涉及。杨元兴在 *A Complete Collection of English Sentence Patterns* 里的 *Left Dislocation Sentence* 中,对英语左移位句进行了全面、系统地论述,还提出了一些以前中外学者未涉及的新观点,得出了一些令人信服的新结论。

① 左移位句的定义

左移位句式(Left Dislocation Construction)是指一种句法结构,在该结构中一个名词短语向左移到句首,而其原位置则由一指称相同的代名词或名词短语填充(文旭,2005)。其实,上面的代名词或名词短语后应加或相应的副词(填充)(杨元兴,2007)。

② 左移位句的结构

左移位句也是通过位移来表达句子焦点的一种方法。左移位句的具体的结构是"左移位成分 + 原句子 + 指代成分",即指代代词/指代名词词组/指代副词(其位置由左移成分而定)(杨元兴,2007)。

Obama, he gave Martin's son a beautiful fountain-pen. 奥巴马,他给马丁的儿子一支漂亮的自来水笔。

The handsome man, we met *him* at the foot of the hill yesterday. 那个英俊男人,我们昨天在那小山脚下遇到他的。

In Beijing, Percy worked and lived *there* for ten years. 在北京,勃西在那里工作和居住了十年。

In 2010, Ms Jing Lili began to work in Nanjing University *then*. 在 2010 年,金丽丽女士那时开始在南京大学工作。

显而易见,例句 1 的左移位成分是句子的主语,原主语处用代词 he 指代 Obama。例句 2 的左移位成分是句子的宾语,原宾语处用 him 指代。例句 3 是地点状语左移至句首,原处用地点副词 there 指代。例句 4 中原句末的时间状语左移至句首,原处用时间副词 then 指代。

从上述四例中可以看出,左移位部分与原位置部分虽在语音上完全不同,但在语义上却具有相同的指称对象。

④ 左移位句的特征

从语音、句法、语义、认知等方面来讲,左移位句都有它自身的特征,在使用时必须加以注意。

A. 左移成分必须置于句首

左移成分必须置于句首,这是左移位句的首要特征。而且,在原处必须要有一个相关的代词、副词或一个完整的名词词组指代。

These beautiful mobiles, they made *them* in their factory. 这些漂亮手机,他们在他们的工厂把它们制造出来的。

These beautiful mobiles they made in their factory. 这些漂亮手机,他们在他们的工厂制造出来的。

上面,例句 1 中,These beautiful mobiles 原是 made 的宾语左移,made 后用了代词 them 指代它,them 与 these beautiful mobiles 两者有共指关系,因此这是左移位句。而例句 2 中,These beautiful mobiles 虽也是 made 的宾语左移至句首,但 made 后没有相应的指代词语,只有一个语迹,所以此句不是左移位句,而叫主位性前移。

B. 左移的成分与原句子间须用逗号隔开

左移位成分与原句子间必须用逗号隔开,这是第二个特征。

Neil's younger brother, he is playing with his friends. 尼尔的弟弟,他在跟他的朋友玩着呢。

Zhang Lian's daughter, we met *her* in the People's Park this morning. 张莲的女儿,我们今天上午在人民公园碰到了她。

C. 左移的成分与原句子结构间的关系疏松

由于左移成与原句子间要用逗号隔开,所以它们之间在结构上比较疏松。而且因为在原位置有与左移成分共指的名词、代词、名词短语或副词,所以如把左移的成分省去,句子的意思还是完整的。有时候,在左移成分与原句子间可插入别的词语,要分清它们之间的语法关系。

The book, *it* is written by my father and published by Shanghai Foreign Language Education Press in 2007. 那本书,它是我父亲所写,于2007年由上海外语教育出版社出版。

The pretty girl behind Rose, I know *her*. 在罗丝后的那个漂亮女孩,我认识她。

Tom—the strong boy, you know, *he* has a love for football. 汤姆,那强壮男孩,你知道,他喜爱踢足球。

上面例句1中,如省去左移位成分 the book 后,句子结构不错,意思也清楚,因为原句子里还有一个指代前面左移成分的共指代词 it。例句2中左移成分是 the pretty girl,如省去它,I know her 意思还是明白,句子结构也不错。例句3中,Tom—the strong boy 是带有同位语的原主语左移,后插入了插入语 you know,后面的 he 与前面的左移成分有共指关系,如省去 Tom—the strong boy 后,后面的句子结构仍然完整,意思也还清楚。

D. 左移人称代词时必须用宾格

如左移位句的左移成分是人称代词时,必须用宾格,这是因为在早期英语中,左移位句常是介词短语或介词宾语。

Me, I love Rose. (至于)我,我爱罗丝。

Her, she's gone mad. 她(怎么了),她已发疯了。

Her, she's good at cooking. 她(怎么样),她精于烹调。

E. 左移成分与其后的指代词必须是同一语法成分

左移位成分的原位置上的相应指代词——代词、副词、名词词组在语法上必须是同一成分,不然就不是左移位句。

Angus, *he* has made so much progress in his studies this term. 安格斯,他这学期学习上取得了如此大的进步。

Its pleasant environment and special animals, *like the Kangaroo and the koala bear*, Australia is a country famous for *them*. 她的优美环境和像袋鼠及无尾熊那样的特殊的动物,澳大利亚就是一个由于它们而闻名的国家。

Professor Chen Zaina, *some English novels* on the shelf were written *by* in 2010. 陈在娜教授,书架上有些英语小说是她在2010年写的。

上面例句1中的 Angus 与后面的 he 同是主语,它们有共指关系,因此是左移位句。例句2中的 Its pleasant environment and special animals, like the Kangaroo and the koala bear 与后面的 them 同是介词宾语,它们有共指关系。例句3中,Professor Chen Zaina 与 some English novels 不属同一语法成分,前者是 by 的宾语(施动者),by 后有它的语迹,而后者是句子的主语,它们不属同一语法成分,因此不是左移位句。

F. 表示的是确定的已知信息

左移位句中的左移位成分必须是确定的、已知的信息,或者是类属的内容。它们多数是显性的,偶尔在表面上是隐性的。

West, did you see *him* before? 威斯特,你以前看见过他吗?

Chen Yi, she post Mary a letter last week. 陈屹,她上星期寄给了玛丽一封信。

The yellow mobile, my father bought me *that* as a present for my birthday. 那只黄色手机,我父亲买它给我作生日礼物的。

Money, they don't want *any*; *help*, they do need *some*. 钱,他们不想要;帮助,他们真的需要(一点)。

上面例句 1 中的 West 与例句 2 中的 Chen Yi 虽表面上隐性,前面没表示确定的词限定,但他们都是说话者心目中所确定的人,它们分别与后面的 him 和 she 有共指关系,因此是左移位句。例句 3 中的 the yellow mobile 前面有限定词,当然是指确定的事物。例句 4 中的 money,help 都是不确定的名词,它们与 any,some 都没有共指关系,所以它们都不能被认定为左移位句。

④ **左移位句的功能**

我们可以从语用和语篇的角度来分析左移位句的功能,就如 Quirk 等在 *A Comprehensive Grammar of the English Language*(p.1417)上所说,左移位成分作为特示主位,显然为整句标出了出发点。在随便的谈话中,这样处理非信息中心的长名词短语并非少见,对听者(他可以提早听到一个复杂的词项)和说话者(他不必把这个复杂的词项放在句子的语法结构中)都比较方便。

A. 起强调作用

句首在信息传递中起着重要的作用,是传递信息的出发点。而左移位句把句子某个成分移到句首也就起了强调的作用。从语用角度上讲,左移位起到了加强语气、突出左移位成分的作用。

Edith, I saw *her* clean the windows this morning. 伊迪丝,我看见她今天上午擦了窗子。

Mary, we do like *her* to go there with us. 玛丽,我们的确喜欢她与我们一起上那儿.

上面例句 1 中强调的是(我看见的是)伊迪丝,(不是别的什么人),她今天上午擦了窗子。显然,这比用无标记 I saw *Edith* clean the windows this morning 语气更强,强调作用更明显。同样,例句 2 中强调的是"玛丽",(不是别人),我们的确喜欢她跟我们一起去那儿。

B. 表示对比

要进行对比,一定得有两个以上的对象才能进行。

His father is an engineer, and his mother is a doctor. 他的父亲是个工程师,他的母亲是个医生。

His father, *he* is an engineer, and *his mother*, *she* is a doctor.

上面例句 1 为无标记的并列句,语气极其平淡。例句 2 是从例句 1 转变来的左移位句,把两个分句的主语都左移到了句首,原来的主语位置分别用了 he 和 she 指代,形成共指关系,表现出了鲜明的对比关系,突出了句首信息焦点。

C. 平衡结构

有时,左移位也是为了起到平衡句子的作用。如果不用复指的词语(指称词语),让左移成分自己充当句子成分,就会使所要表达的主语或宾语不能这样集中、明显,不但会显得零散,而且还会给人一种脉络不清的感觉[仇伟、张法科,西安外国语学院学报,2006(1):2]。

The strong man who is often late for work, *you know*, *the poor man with blue tire*, *he* will be dismissed next week. 那个上班常迟到的壮汉,你知道,就是那个戴蓝领带的可怜人,他下星期要被解雇了。

上面例句的左移主语中,既有定语从句,又有插入语 you know,后面还有 the strong man 的同位语 the poor man with blue tire 这样一连串的东西,如不以左移位句形式表达,把左移的主语恢复到指代词 he 的位置,变成"The strong man who is often late for work, you know, the poor man with blue tire, will be dismissed next week."验证了"显得零散,给人一种脉络不清的感觉"。

使用左移位结构后,句子显得既平衡流畅,又凸显了句首的信息焦点。

D. 语篇衔接功能

我们认为,衔接概念是用来解释话语的语义关系的。衔接的范围不只局限于所指、省略、替代、连接和词汇衔接五个方面。所以说,任何表达句子之间语义关系的特征都应该被看作衔接特征。

杨元兴先生在 A Complete Collection of English Sentence Patters 中的 English Left Location Sentence（2007）有一段有关左移位衔接功能的短文及其说明，颇能说明问题。

People in our neighborhood like dogs more than anything else, especially ladies. They raise many kinds of dogs. And our landlady also breeds three foreign dogs. *The three dogs*, *they* are taken good care of. *They* have bread and milk in the morning, *they* eat rice and meat at noon, *they* dine on noodles and sausages for supper. What's more, our fashionable landlady never forgets to play with *them* in the neighborhood after breakfast and supper. 我们街区一些人，特别是女士们，爱狗如命。他们养了很多种狗，我们女房东也养了三只外国种狗。这三只狗，它们受到细心的照料，早餐牛奶、面包，中餐猪肉、米饭，晚上香肠、面条。而且，每天早、晚饭后，我们那时髦女郎绝不忘记与它们一起在小区里跑跑跳跳。

很清楚，文中的 the three dogs 是左移位成分，后面的四个 they 和一个 them 是指代前面出现的 the three dogs，它们形成了共指关系，组成了五句左移位句。这四个 they 把这篇短文紧密地连接起来，最后一个 them 又反馈到了上面的左移位成分 the three dogs。这短短 70 个词的小文充分反映出了我们这个街区的一些 ladies 爱狗如命、与狗为伍，人狗合一的"逍遥自在，无所事事"的西洋式富婆生活。

E. 标记出一个独立的信息单位

因为左移位成分有一个独立的语调曲拱，所以它的左移位成分可以标记出一个独立的信息单位。

The teacher my father worked with him in Soochow University, he has written a book about *English Syntax*. 那个以前与我父亲在苏州大学一起工作的老师，他已经写了一本关于《英语句法》的书。

上例中的 The teacher my father worked with him in Soochow University 是一个独立的新信息与后面的句子主语 he 有共指关系。

⑤ 可被左移的句子成分

从句法角度讲，可左移位的句子成分可以是主语、宾语、复合宾语中的宾语、宾语补语、介词宾语、状语、定语，还有名词同位语。

A. 左移主语

Mr. Green likes skiing in winter and swimming in summer. 格林先生喜欢在冬天滑雪，夏天游泳。
Mr. Green, he likes skiing in winter and swimming in summer. 格林先生，他喜欢在冬天滑雪，夏天游泳。
Chu Fu is our maths teacher. 朱复是我们的数学老师。
Chu Fu, he likes skiing in winter and swimming in summer. 朱复，他喜欢在冬天滑雪，夏天游泳。

以上四句例句中，例句 1、3 分别为无标记句，2、4 例句是左移位句。例句 2 把原句的主语 Mr. Green 左移至句首，原主语的位置由人称代词 he 替代，指称 Mr. Green。同样，例句 4 中主语 Chu Fu 被左移至句首，原句中的主语位置由人称代词 he 指代。

B. 左移宾语

可被左移的宾语有一般宾语、介词宾语、复合宾语中的宾语。

a. 左移一般宾语

The red apple, I gave *it* to the crying boy. 那只红苹果，我把它给了那个哭着的男孩。
English, we all like *it* very much. 英语，我们都很喜欢它。
This dictionary, I bought *it* for Betty as her 15th birthday present. 这本词典，我买了它给贝蒂作她 15 岁的生日礼物。

b. 左移介词宾语

Its pleasant environment and special animals, like the Kangaroo and the koala bear, Australia is a country famous for *them*. 它的优美环境和像袋鼠及无尾熊那样的特殊的动物，澳大利亚就是一个由于它们而闻名的国家。
Alan, *a handsome man*, I borrowed the car from *him* last week. 艾伦，一个英俊男人，我上星期向他借的

车。(带有同位语的介词宾语左移)

c. 左移复合宾语中的宾语

We noticed Li Hua enter the house. 我们看见李华走进那房子。

Li Hua, we noticed *her* enter the house. 李华,我们看见她走进那房子。

Paul turned all the lamps on in the room. 保罗把屋里的灯都全开了。

All the lamps in the room, Paul turned *them* on. 屋里所有的灯,保罗把它们全开了。

在把复合宾语中的宾语左移时,应把宾语补足语保留在原处,而原宾语位置要用相应的代词填入,如例句 2 中用 her 指代 Li Hua;例句 4 中的左移位宾语中的 in the room 与 all 一样,是 lamps 的定语,所以一起左移,原宾语位置由 them 指代 all the lamps in the room 这个整体。

C. 左移状语

左移状语中可分左移时间状语和地点状语。

In 1978, Professor White published his first article *then*. 在 1978 年,怀特教授那时发表了他的第一篇论文。(左移时间状语)

In the ten bookcases, Bob keeps most of his books *there*. 在这十只书橱里,巴勃把他的大部分书放在那里。(左移地点状语)

D. 左移定语

左移定语时要特别注意,千万不能把"'s"一起移至句首。这样的左移乍看起来有点不顺眼,这需要仔细体会。

Dick's wife went to New York to see her mother. 狄克的妻子去纽约看她的母亲了。

Dick, *his wife* went to New York to see her mother. 狄克,他的妻子去纽约看她的母亲了。

Xiaoling's father was my father's teacher. 小林的父亲是我父亲的老师。

Xiaoling, *his father* was my father's teacher. 小林,他的父亲是我父亲的老师。

如把例句 1 中的定语 Dick's wife 一起左移,就成了 *Dick's wife*, she went to New York to see her mother,那是左移主语的左移位句。例句 3 中主语的定语左移,也是同样道理。

E. 左移宾语补足语

根据左移位句的定义,这种可左移的宾语补足语应是名词(短语)形式。

We call Hunt lazy-bones. 我们称呼韩特懒骨头。

Lazy-bones, we call Hunt *that*. 懒骨头,我们那样称呼韩特。

They named the little girl Kitty. 他们把这小女孩取名吉蒂。

Kitty, they named the little girl *it*. 吉蒂,他们给这个小女孩取了这个名字。

We all think Mr. Liang a man of talent. 我们都认为梁先生是个有才干人。

A man of talent, we all think Mr. Liang *that*. 一个有才干的人,我们都认为梁先生是那样的人。

上面例句 2、4、6 是由例句 1、3、5 变来的左移位句。这些左移位句都是把原句中的名词(短语)宾语补足语左移至句首,它们的原位置均由相应的指代词语填入,而后成了左移位句。

F. 左移同位语

杨元兴先生指出,"名词性同位语左移及宾语的同位语左移都可看作左移位句,因为它们左移时,与后面的部分也可用逗号分开,它们的原位置上也有同一语法成分的名词指称词组或代词指称词。"这些都与左移位句的定义相吻合。左移位的同位语中,非但有名词词组的,也有代词的名词性同位语。

A very interesting novel The Three Musketeers by Alexandre Dumas, was published in 1844. 一部非常有趣的小说,大仲马所写的《三个火枪手》是在 1844 年闻世的。(可把 A very interesting novel 视为主语左移,原主语位置 The Three Musketeers by Alexandre Dumas 为左移主语的指称名词词组)

Intellect, imagination, power of expression, humor, taste, truth to life, and truth to human nature—these are the qualities which make a writer popular. 才智、想象力、表达能力、幽默感、审美力、忠于生活、忠于人

性——所有这些都是使一个作家受人欢迎的品质。(可把 Intellect, imagination, power of expression, humor, taste, truth to life, and truth to human nature 视为左移的主语,而原句子主语处有 these 指称。)

⑥ 左移位句与某些句子的比较

我们把左移位句与其他一些句子进行的比较是以认知语言学为框架的,以结构、语义、"突显"(Prominence)为理论基础,以语言事实为本,对它们在句法特征、话语意义、句子内涵、所起作用等范围进行讨论。这样,读者会加深对左移移位句的理解,逐步消化,以致最后能掌握、运用它们。

A. 与含呼语句子的比较

由于含有置于句首的呼语的句子,呼语与句子之间也用逗号分开,这是其一,其二是含句首呼语的句子后面也有貌似左移位句那样指代前移位成分的代词或名词词组,所以含呼语的句子与左移位句极容易混淆,使人难于区分。

a. 分清呼语的作用

首先,我们应该分清的是,呼语在句中是独立成分。呼语的作用是引起被呼唤人的注意,尤其要把被呼唤的人从那些听得见的人中间找出来,如 Eda, you are wanted on the phone.(埃达,有你的电话。)句中的 Eda 是呼语,作独立成分。You 并非 Eda 的指代词,而是我(I)呼唤的对象,也就是我对着 Eda 说:"Eda, you are wanted on the phone"。

b. 区分呼语中酷似左移位句的指代词

其次,句首含呼语的句子中酷似左移位句中的指代词总是 you,句首含呼唤语句子的呼唤人常是 I。被呼唤人是"you"。在使用这种句型时,我们常用表示"人"的名字,如 Rose, Tom, John, Eda, Dr. Smith 等这样的呼语。呼语的功能是表示说话人对被呼唤人的态度的,所以在朗读这种句子时的语音、语调明显有别于一般句子。对呼语的朗读声音一定提高、拉长,且常用升调,这是焦点手段表达中的语音手段。请再看下面这些句子:

Rose, have *you* got a minute? 罗丝,你有空吗?

Mr. White, have *you* finished your composition? 怀特先生,你的作文写完了吗?

What time, *Dr. Smith*, will you come this afternoon? 斯密斯先生,今天下午你什么时候来?

从上面的那些例子可见,例句1、2 句首含呼唤语句子中的酷似左移位句中的指代左移成分的填入语是 you,而不能是其他词。因此,我们如把 Rose, have you got a minute? 改成 Rose, I don't know if she has got a minute 这样的句子后,Rose 就不是呼语,而是宾语从句中主语左移,原主语的地方用 she 指代 Rose,这是名副其实的左移位句。例句3是含呼语的特殊疑问句,呼语 Dr. Smith 插在中间了,不要误认为是左移位句。要注意的是,呼语有时也可置于句末。

Hurry up, *boys and girls*. 孩子们,快点。

c. 识别连贯对话中的呼语

如何识别连贯对话中的呼语与左移位,关键看句首的词语与后面极像左移位句的指代词语是否有共指关系。试看下面对话:

——Wilson, will you go to meet Mr. White at the airport? 威尔逊,你要去机场接怀特先生吗?

——Monitor, I won't. I have to finish the article this morning. 班长,我去不了。我今天上午必须完成这篇论文。(下午一定要交的)

很清楚,上面例句1中的 you 虽然与 Wilson 是指同一人,但 Wilson 是"我"呼唤的对象 monitor,并不是左移位句中的指代词,也没有共指关系。例句2是对例句1那句问话做出的反应,Monitor 是呼语,与后面的 I 没有共指关系,当然也不是左移位句。

B. 与语题化句的比较

Michaelis 和 Gregory 两位学者指出,左移位句与语题化句是不同的。对左移位句与语题化句的比较可归纳为12个字:"作用相同,结构有异"和"一不两可"。对于这些,我们可以从对它们的详细比较中就能看出。

a. 作用相同

也就是说把它们句子的某部分前移,都是为了强调。

b. 结构有异

左移位句与话题化句在结构上有差异:把左移位句中的某个成分左移至句首,其原来位置上由一个替代名词/副词或名词短语填入,也就是说左移位句是由基础生成的。而语题化句只是把句子的某成分移位到句首,其原处只留下了一个语迹,在语迹这地方绝不能用任何词或词组填入,这是因为它仅是一个句子成分的向前移位。请比较下面句子:

The handsome man, he married a handsome girl last week. 那英俊男子上星期与一身材秀丽的姑娘结了婚。

The handsome girl, Tom married last year. 汤姆去年跟那身材秀丽的女孩结了婚。

从上面两个例句中可见:例句 1 中的 The handsome man 是原句子中的主语被提前到句首,原来的主语地方由 he 填入,这显然是左移位句。而例句 2 中的 The handsome girl 是句中谓语动词 married 的宾语,移位到句首,它原来的宾语位置上只留下了宾语的语迹。这当然是语题化句。

c. 在某些语境下不能用语题化句

"一不两可"有两层意思:"一不"指在某些语境下,不能用语题化句子,而只能用左移位表示;"两可"是指表达某些句子的意思时,话题化句式可使用,左移位句式也可使用。

- 现在先谈"一不"的内容。大家可能知道,由于左移位句与话语化句均为人们对语言情景进行识解的不同产物,因此就会出现在某些情况下可使用左移位句式,却不可使用话语化句式情况。

Alison, Dr. White thinks that she is the suitable woman for the job. 艾丽森,怀特博士认为她是干这工作的合适人选。

*Alison, Dr. White thinks that is the suitable woman for the job.

This purse, to whom should we give it? 这个钱包,我们该把它交给谁呢?

*This purse, to whom should we give ?

上面例句 1、3 均为左移位句。例句 1 中的 Alison 是原宾语从句中的主语,原处由 she 指代,使用合理。例句 3 中 This purse 是左移成分,它是原句中的 give 的宾语,现由代词 it 指代它,使用也合理。例句 2 表面上看似乎是例句 1 的语题化句,但结构不对,that is the suitable woman 难于理解,因此不可接受;例句 4 表面上看似乎是例句 3 的语题化句,但句子结构也不对,因此也不可接受。

- 有时两种句型均可使用

所说的"两可"是指在言语表达时,有时可使用话题化句式的句子,左移位句式也可使用。请观察下面四例:

This new sample you should send to Belinda immediately. 这个新样品,你应该马上给碧林达送去。

This new sample, you should send it to Belinda immediately. 这个新样品,你应该马上把它送给碧林达。

The English novel—The Return of the Native by Thomas Hardy, Ned has read. 托马斯·哈代的英语小说——《还乡》,内德已经看过了。

The English novel—The Return of the Native by Thomas Hardy, Ned has read it. 托马斯·哈代的英语小说——《还乡》,内德已经看过它了。

很清楚,上面例句 1、3 是话题化句,语迹分别在 send 和 read 后;例句 2、4 是左移位句,it 分别是 The new sample 和 The English novel—The Return of the Native by Thomas Hardy 的指代词。

C. 与主位性前移句子的比较

在对这两种句子进行比较之前,我们要先解释一下什么叫主位和主位性前移。所谓主位是指句子的句首部分(一般不包括原句首状语)。而主位性前移是指把正常语序中位于句子后面的成分提到句首作为主位。拿主位性前移(Thematic fronting)句子与左移位句相比,它们有"同",也有"异"。

- 相同点
  * 位置都在句首

Excellent food our hotel serves here. 我们酒店供应美味食物。（主位性前移，serve 的宾语前移，serve 后留下宾语的语迹，且前移部分后没有逗号）

The charming young lady, they found her in the lonely village yesterday. 那个娇媚少女，他们昨天在那僻静的村子里发现的。（左移位句，强调宾语，her 是前移宾语 The charming young lady 的指称代词，前移部分后面有逗号分开）

  * 都可以强调多种成分

左移位句子和主位性前移句子所强调的句子成分可以是宾语、状语和宾语补语。

Tom, I hate *him* asking me for money. 汤姆，我讨厌他向我借钱。（左移位句，强调复合宾语中的宾语。him 是前移宾语 Tom 的指代词）

An interesting novel Wang Shouzhi lent me this morning. 王守志今天上午借给了我一部有趣的小说。（主位性前移，me 后有前移宾语的语迹）

Through the crowd, the young man rushed. 那年轻人匆忙通过人群。（主位性前移，强调状语，rushed 后有前移状语的语迹，因 through the crowd 与 rushed 的关系密切，它不算句首状语）

In 1964, Wang Shouli graduated from Jiangsu Teachers' College *then*. 1964 年，王守礼那时从江苏师范学院毕业。（左移位句，强调状语，then 是左移状语 in 1964 的指代副词）

Old Jiao, we call Jiao Gueifu that. 老乔，我们那样叫乔桂覆的。（左移位句，宾语补语中的名词短语 old Jiao 左移，原处用代词 that 指代）

Old Jiao we call Jiao Guifu. 老乔，我们那样叫乔桂覆。（主位性前移，强调宾语补语。原宾语补语 Jiao Guefu 后留下了语迹。）

- 不同点
  * 左移位句和主位性前移与其后面句子的关系

左移位句的左移成分与句子的关系疏松，因此左移成分与句子间必须用逗号隔开。主位性前移成分与句子关系十分密切，因此前移部分与后面不用逗号隔开。

Erica, Tony has fallen in love with her. 艾丽嘉，托尼已经爱上了她。（左移位句，强调宾语，her 是 Erica 的指称代词）

A beautiful bike his father brought him. 他父亲买给他一辆漂亮自行车。（主位性前移，强调直接宾语）

  * 左移位句可以左移主语进行强调，原处用指代词替代；主位性不可前移主语

Victor, *he* is the only person who was against the plan. 维克多，他是唯一反对这计划的人。

  * 左移位句不可强调谓语，但主位性前移可左移谓语。

Lift the box, I can't, but I can remove *it*. 我举不起那箱子，但可以把它移开。

  * 主位性前移可将表语置句首，但左移位句还未见过

Poor Wang Xiaowei is, but beggar *he* is not. 王小薇是穷，但他不是乞丐。

D. 与分裂句的比较

左移位句与分裂句很有可比性。它们有三个"同"，即目的相同——都为了强调，语义基本相同，功能相同——都可强调主语、状语、宾语等；一个"不同"，那就是强调的手段不同。众所周知，句首是传递信息的出发点，左移位句是通过移位手段达到强调的目的，而分裂句则是通过语法结构手段达到强调目的的。分裂句的结构是"It be + 被强调的成分 + that（/who/when）+ 句子的其他成分"。

下面，我们列出数组以无标记句开头的句子，然后把它们分别用左移位句和断裂句进行转换表达：

- 强调主语

Wang Ming often plays chess with Huang Zunren. 王明常与黄遵仁下象棋。（无标记句）

Wang Ming, *he* often plays chess with Huang Zunren. 王明，他常用与黄遵仁下象棋。（左移位句，主语

Wang Ming 左移,原处用 he 指代)

It is Wang Ming who often plays chess with Huang Zunren. 是王明,他常与黄遵仁下象棋。(分裂句,强调句子主语)

- 强调宾语

We can see Gu Hao watering flowers in the garden every morning. 我们每天早晨能见到顾豪在花园里浇花。(无标记句)

Gu Hao, we can see *him* watering flowers in the garden every morning. 顾豪,我们每天早晨能见到他在花园里浇花。(左移位句,Gu Hao 是左移了的宾语,原处用了 him 指代他)

It is Gu Hao that we can see watering flowers in the garden every morning. 是顾豪,我们每天早晨能见到在花园里浇花。(分裂句,强调宾语)

- 强调介词宾语

Dr. Godwin often talked with Zhou Xingkang last year. 哥德文医生去年常与周新康闲谈。(无标记句)

Zhou Xingkang, Dr. Godwin often talked with *him* last year. 周新康,哥德文医生去年常与他闲谈之人。(左移位句,介词宾语左移句首,原处用代词 him 指代)

It was Zhou Xingkong that Dr. Godwin often talked with last year. 哥德文医生去年常与之闲谈的人是周新康。(分裂句,强调介词 with 的宾语)

- 强调状语

∗ 强调时间状语

Zhuang Kunshi graduated from Nanjing Normal University in 1965. 庄坤石 1965 年毕业于南京师范大学。(无标记句)

In 1965, Zhuang Kunshi graduated from Nanjing Normal University *then*. 1965 年,那时庄坤石毕业于南京师范大学。(左移位句,强调时间状语,原处用副词 then 指代)

It was *in 1965* when Zhuang Kunshi graduated from Nanjing Normal University. 庄坤石是 1965 年毕业于南京师范大学。(分裂句,强调时间状语 in 1965)

∗ 强调地点状语

Cheng Yuzhen keeps almost all her books in her study. 程玉箴几乎把她所有的书都保存在书房里。(无标记句)

In her study, Cheng Yuzhen keeps almost all her books *there*. 在她书房里,程玉箴几乎把她所有书都保存在那儿。(左移位句,强调地点状语,原处用副词 there 指代)

It is in her study where Cheng Yuzhen keeps almost all her books. 是在书房里,程玉箴几乎把她所有的书都保存在那儿。(分裂句,强调地点状语)

从上面三组例句可见,无标记句的语气最平淡,左移位句的语气强于无标记句,而分裂句比左移位句还要强些。所以说,有些左移位句能与断裂句进行转换,意思基本不变。不过,由于用分裂句表达在语气上更强,信息更突出,因而达到的话语效果更显著。

E. 左移位句与同位语倒装句的比较

我们说,任何一个事物都是多方面的,而且有时多方面的事物会存在于一个统一体中。当我们将注意力投放在某个方面时,常会出现置其他方面于不顾,这也就是认知凸显概念上所讲的强光化(highlighting)。

- 同位语的倒装与左移位句

一般语法书上都说,同位语跟在中心词后面进行说明的。但有时为了强调,同位语可以位于中心词前,成了同位语与中心词的倒装(Inversion of the Apposition and the Head Word)。我们先看下面两例:

The electronic computer, the marvel of our age, has been widely used now in the world.

→The marvel of our age, the electronic computer has been widely used now in the world.

电子计算机,我们时代的奇迹已在世界上得到广泛的应用。→我们时代的奇迹——电子计算机已在世界上得到广泛的应用。

上面那组句子第一句的主语是 The electronic computer，而 the marvel of our age 是前面主语的同位语。第二句是倒装句，原句中的主语同位语已提前至句首，成了倒装语序。我们认为，按左移位句的定义完全可以把第二句理解成 The marvel of our age 是句子的主语，左移至句首，而把 the electronic computer 是指代前面左移部分的完整名词短语替代它，因此这也是左移位句。

- 倒装后的同位语句与左移位句

在强调同位语时，要把它置于中心词前。特别当中心词是代词时，用这种语序更常见。在这里，我们特别要提醒，人们在理解一个事物时往往聚焦于某个方面而忽视或根本注意不到其他事物的存在，或是由于人的视觉角度的不同，而得出不同的结论。请看下面例句：

Financial expert, Mrs. Green will begin writing a weekly column on the national economy. 财政专家格林太太将开始就国民经济问题每周写一篇专栏文章。

A child labor in the old society, she was now studying in Nanjing University. 昔日旧社会的童工，她那时在南京大学学习。

Your friend Vic, I saw *him* here last night. 你的朋友维克，我昨天晚上在这里见到过他。

从以上三例可见，例句 1 的 Financial expert 是句子主语 Mrs Green 的同位语；例句 2 中的 a child in old society 是句子主语 she 的同位语；例句 3 中的 your friend Vic 是 him 的同位语，把它们提高前至句首都是为了强调。然而，我们为什么不可以把上述三句看成是左移位句呢？我们可把 Financial expert 和 A child labor in the old society 看作是原句子的主语，your friend Vic 看作是原句子的宾语，现在左移至句首，原主语的地方分别由 Mrs Green 和 she 指代，your friend Vic 由 him 指代。由此，杨元兴先生指出，像这样句子既可看作是同位语倒装句，也可看作左移位句。

第 17 章　语气、虚拟语气

17.1　语　气

语气(Mood)是一种动词形式,具体地说是谓语动词用来表示说话人对动词表示的动作或状态的看法或者态度的形式。同一件事,或许因说话人的看法或态度不同,所用的谓语动词的语气也就不同。英语中的语气分为三种:陈述语气(Indicative Mood)、祈使语气(Imperative Mood)和虚拟语气(Subjunctive Mood)。

(1) 陈述语气

陈述语气是表示说话人认为谓语动词所表示的动作或状态是事实或可能是事实而对其加以陈述、询问或表示感叹。陈述语气用于陈述句、疑问句和感叹句。陈述语气中,动词具有二时六体,而且还有人称和数的变化等。详见第 20 章。

He is never late for work. 他上班从不迟到。
We didn't see Mr. Green. 我们没见到格林先生。
Where is she living now? 她现在住在哪儿?
How pretty the girl is! 那女孩多么漂亮啊!

(2) 祈使语气

祈使语气是表示说话人的请求、指示、劝告、建议、命令等,使听话者把话语者动词表示的动作或状态成为事实。祈使句只有一种时态,动词用原型,没有人称和数的变化。详见第 22 章。

Give the boy an apple, please.　请给那个男孩一只苹果。
Be quiet, please. 请安静!
You *go* out! 你给我出去!
Everybody *shut* their eyes. 大家都闭上了眼睛。

17.2　虚拟语气

虚拟语气所表示的是说话人认为动词表示的动作或状态不是事实或可能不是事实,或者说,虚拟语气重在表现在动词表示的动作"非真实"(Unreality)或"不确定"(Uncertainty)。

I wish I *were* young. 但愿我还年轻。
Jim insisted that Tom *stay* there for another week. 吉姆坚持汤姆在那里面再待一个星期。
If I had wings, I *could fly* to the sky. 如果我有翅膀,我就能飞向天空。
虚拟语气的动词没有时态范畴,也是没人称和数的范畴。

She looks/looked/has always looked as if $\begin{cases} \text{he } needed \text{ sleep.} \\ \text{he } hadn't\ slept \text{ for a week.} \end{cases}$

(1) 虚拟语气的动词形式

虚拟语气的动词有三种形式：原形形式、一般式和完成式。

① 原形形式

原形形式(Base Form)是指所有的动词都用原形，包括 be 动词。

It is/was necessary that we/you/she *start* at once. 我们、你们、她有必要马上出发。

He urges/urged/has urged that we/you/he *accept* the post. 他敦促/敦促过/已经敦促过我们/你们/他接受那工作。

A．原形形式的被动式

其形式是"助动词 be 的原形形式 + 主动词的过去分词"。

Professor Ma insists/insisted that Xiaoli *be punished*. 马教授坚持小李应该受到惩罚。

B．原形动词的否定式

虚拟语气原形动词的否定式比较特别，不须用助动词 do 或 does，而是直接在动词前加 not。

He insisted that we *not eat* meat. 他坚持我们不要吃肉。

C．not 对 be 动词的两种位置情况

如果动词是连系动词 be，那 not 的位置在 be 后；如谓语含有助动词 be 了，那 not 在 be 前后均可。

If that *be not* the case, I shall leave. 如果不是那种情况，那我要离开。

Professor Dong recommended that Qiu Shasha {not be punished. / be not punished.} 董教授建议邱莎莎不该受到处罚。

② 一般式

虚拟语气一般式(Indefinite Form)也叫一般体(Indefinite Aspect)，表示主观设想在说话或主句表示的时间的同时或之后发生的动作或存在的状态，其时所有的动词都用动词的(-ed)过去式，be 动词用 were，在口语和非正式文体中，第一、第三人称单数可用 was。

I wish I *were/was* in Beijing. 但愿我在北京。

If I *were/was* you, I would refuse his invitation. 如果我是你的话，我会拒绝他的邀请。

If a serious crisis *were/was* to raise, the government would have to act swiftly. 如果暴发一场严重的经济危机，政府必须会迅速做出反应。

Notes：对第一、三人称后用 were/was 需要作一说明。

A. 在"It is time that I … "后只能 I was，不能用 I were。

B. 在 as it were 中，were 不可改成 was，因为这是个固定搭配。

C. 在"If Mary were/was here, we would learn the truth."（如果玛丽在这里，我们就知道真相了）中，省略"if 从句"中的"if"成倒装句时，就只能是"Were Mary here … "，绝不可说"Was Mary here … "。

D. 当谓语动词含有情态动词时，其虚拟语气的一般式是"情态动词的过去式形式 + 主动词的一般不定式"构成。

If I were to do so, what would you say? 如果是我要这样做，你会说什么？

③ 完成式

虚拟语气有完成体(Perfective Form) 和进行体(Perfective Aspect)，此表示主观设想在说话或主句所表示的时间之间发生的动作或存在的状态。这种虚拟式与过去完成式相同，即"had + 主动词的过去分词"，有时是"could/would + have + 过去分词"。

I wish/wished I *had been* to Guilin. 我去过桂林就好了。

If I *had known* him, I *would have told* him the news. 如果那时我认识他，我就把那消息告诉他了。

We talked as if we *had been* good friends for years. 我们就像多年的老朋友那样地交谈着。

I wish I *could have finished* my essay yesterday. 我能在昨天完成了我的论文就好了。

（2）虚拟语气在句中的运用

有好多语法书把虚拟语气以谓语动词变化形式的不同来讲解，如有的就分作 be 动词形式和 were 动词形式来讲解，be 形式就是动词原形虚拟语气，或叫虚拟现在时，不管主语是何人称，是何数，谓语动词一律用原形，而 were 形式虚拟句就是我们常说的虚拟语气在三种条件句中的运用，当然还涉及其他一些从句。

今天，我们把虚拟语气的运用分为简单句和复合句两个大类讲。

① 虚拟语气在简单句中的运用

虚拟语气在简单句中常用动词的原形形式。这些简单句常表示祝愿、诅咒，还用于一些公式化的结构中。这些简单句中也可以用"情态动词 may＋不定式"代替；"部分情态动词的过去式＋动词原形"也可表示虚拟语气。

A．用于表示祝愿、诅咒的简单句

God *bless* you. 上帝保佑你。

Long *live* world peace! 世界和平万岁！

Heaven *help* you! 老天帮助你！

Long *live* the People's Republic of China! 中华人民共和国万岁！

B．用于一些公式化的结构中

Devil *take* the hind most. 落后者遭殃。

So *be* it. 就这样吧。（＝I accept/let it be）

C．用"情态动词 may＋不定式"代替动词原形

May you *be* happy! 祝您快乐！

May god *bless* you! 但愿上帝保佑你！

May there never *be* another world war! 但愿再不会有一场世界战争！

部分情态动词的过去形式（could, might, should, would）用在一些句中，表示想象或猜测。

There *could be* something wrong with the tape recorder. 这台录音机可能出毛病了。

He *might have said* so. 他可能这样说过。

D．表示委婉或客气

虚拟语气"could, would, might＋动词原形"可使说话者的口气变得委婉客气，有时表示惋惜或责备。

a．口气变得委婉客气

You *could answer* this email for me. 你可以替我回这个电子邮件。

Would you *mind* opening the window? 劳驾把窗子打开，好吗？

Could you *leave* me your telephone number and address? 你能将电话号码和地址留给我吗？

You *might* as well *put off* the discussion till next week. 你们不妨把讨论推迟到下个星期。

b．表示惋惜或责备

Given more time, we *could have done* better. 如果给我们更多时间，我们能够干得更好些。（我们并没有得到更多的时间）

You could have got up a little earlier! 你完全可以早点儿起来！（实际上没有早起）

It was cold yesterday. I *should have worn* a heavy coat. 昨天很冷，我该穿件厚外套的。（但我没穿）

This wall *shouldn't have been painted* blue. 这墙不应该漆成蓝色。（但已漆了）

② 虚拟语气在复合句中的运用

虚拟语气用于复合句，情况比较复杂，除了用于条件状语从句中外，还有其他一些状语从句，以及主语从句、宾语从句、表语从句、同位语从句、定语从句等。

A. 虚拟语气用于 if 引导的条件状语从句.

	从句（条件句）	主句（结果句）
与现在事实相反的假设	• 动词过去式 • be 一般用 were	should ought to would　　 ＋动词原形 could might
与过去事实相反的假设	had＋动词过去分词	should ought to would　　 ＋have＋动词过去分词 could might
与将来事实相反的假设或实现的可能性很小	• should＋动词原形 • were to＋动词原形	should ought to would　　 ＋动词原形 could might

a. 表示与现在事实相反的情况

其基本句型为：If＋主语＋动词过去式，主语＋(would, could, might, should, ought to)＋动词原形。

If I *were* rich, I *would help* you. 如果我有钱,我就会帮助你。

＝As I am not rich, I cannot help you. 因为我不富有,所以无法帮助你。

If she *knew* it, she *would tell* me. 如果她知道,她会告诉我。

＝But I know she does not know it. 事实是她不知道,因此她不会告诉我。

If I *had* the novel at hand, I *would read* the story to you. 如果我手边有这本小说,我会读这个故事给你听。

＝I do not have the novel at hand, so I cannot read the story to you. 事实是我手边没本小说,所以不能读这篇故事给你听。

Notes： • 不论主语是第几人称,if 从句中如出现 be 动词一般用 were。但在口语和非正式文体中,第一、三人称后可用 were/was。

If you *were* in my shoes, what *would* you *do*? 如果你站在我的立场,你会怎么做?

If everything *were* ready, we *should start*. 如果一切就绪,我们开始吧。

If I *were/was* you, I *would not do* it. 如果我是你,我不会做这事。(用 were 比较正规)

• 主句中的助动词一般不用 must，must 表示现在或将来的真实状况。

If you *had* money, you must help the poor.（误）

If you *had* money, you *should help* the poor.（正）如果你有钱,就应该帮助穷人。

• 在同一句子里要保持事实情况的一致性,不能一部分表示真实情况,一部分表示非真实情况。

If it *rains* tomorrow, I should stay home.（误）

If it *rains* tomorrow, I *will stay* home.（正）如果明天下雨,我会待在家里。(主句和从句表示真实条件)

If it *rained* tomorrow, I *should stay* home.（正）如果明天下雨,我会待在家里。(主句和从句表示非真实条件)

b. 表示与过去事实相反的情况

其基本句型为：If + 主语 + had + 动词过去分词，主语 + (would, could, might, should, ought to) + have + 过去分词。

If *I had* arrived earlier, *I could have met* him. 要是我当时早点到，就可以见到他。

= As I did not arrive earlier, I did not meet him. 因为当时我没有早点到，所以我没见到他。

If he *had known* it, he *would have told* me. 如果他当时知道，他会告诉我。

= But I know he did not know it. 事实是他当时不知道。

If you *hadn't been studying* so hard, you *might have failed* the exam. 如果你当时没有努力学习，你有可能考试不及格。

= You were studying so hard, so you didn't fail the exam. 事实是你当时学习努力，因此你通过了考试。

Note：注意以下例句中 had 的用法。

If he had money, he would have bought a house. (误)

If he *had* money, he *would buy* a house. (正)如果他现在有钱，他就会买房。(与现在事实相反)

If he *had had* money, he *would have bought* a house. (正)如果他当时有钱，他就会买房了。(与过去事实相反)

c. 表示与将来事实相反的情况

此情况表示成为事实可能性小和大两种情况，表示与将来可能相反的情况时，可以与祈使句连用。

● 表示可能性小的基本句型是：If + 主语 + should + 动词原形，主语 + (would, could, might, should, ought to) + 动词原形。

If you *should fall* ill, the meeting *would be put off*. 如果你生病，会议将延期。(生病的可能性低，故会议延期的可能性也低)

● 表示可能性大的基本句型是：If + 主语 + should + 动词原形，主语 + (will, can, may, should, ought to) + 动词原形。

If it *should rain*, I *will stay* home. 如果下雨，我就会待在家里。(下雨的可能性较大，故待在家里的可能性较大)

● 表示与将来事实相反的情况时，可与祈使句连用。

If I *should be late*, *be sure* to wait for me. 如果我迟到，务必等我。(我有可能会迟到，你务必等我)

If you *should see* him, *give* him my regards. 如果你见到他，请代为致意。(你有可能见到他，请你代我向他致意)

If she *should fail* this time, *tell* her to try again. 如果她这次失败了，告诉她再试一下。(她这次可能失败，请告诉她再尝试一下)

● 表示将来情况，还可用"were + 不定式"形式。

If he *were to come*, I *should be* away from home. 如果他回家，我就离开。

= But I know he will not come. 他回家的可能性极小。

If he *were to study* math, he *would have* a hard time. 如果他学数学，他将很痛苦。

= he will not study math. 他学习数学的可能性极小。

d. 表示错综时间的情况

有时，条件状语从句中所表示的动作和主句所表示的动作在时间上不一致，在表示错综时间时，要根据实际情况把两个不同的句型用在同一个句子里。

If you *had taken* the medicine, you *would be* well now. 要是你当时吃了药(表示过去)，你现在已经好了(表示现在)。

= You did not take the medicine, so you are not well now. 事实是你当时没吃药，所以你现在没好。

If he *were* honest, he *would have told* the truth. 要是他老实的话(表示现在)，他早已说出事实真相了(表

示过去)。

= He is not honest, so he did not tell the truth. 事实是他不老实,所以他之前没说出事实。

If I *had started* saving money then, I *would have been* able to buy a house now. (误)

If I *had started* saving money then, I *would be* able to buy a house now. (正)如果当时我存钱,我现在就能买房了。

Notes: • If it were not for/that ... (如果没有……)表示同现在事实相反的假设;If it had not been for/that ... (如果当时没有……)表示同过去事实相反的假设。

If *it were not for your help*, I *should be* in a very awkward position. 如果没有你的帮助,我现在处境会很尴尬。

= You help me, so I am not in an awkward position now. 你帮了我,所以我现在才没有很尴尬。

If *it were not that he works hard*, I *wouldn't like* him. 如果不是他努力工作,我才不会喜欢他。

= He works hard, so I like him. 他努力工作,所以我喜欢他。

If *it had not been for Dr. Li*, my father *would have died* of heart disease. 如果不是当时李医生的医治,我父亲会死于心脏病。

= Dr Li treated my father in time, so he did not die of the heart disease. 李医生及时医治了我父亲,所以我父亲没有死于心脏病。

If *it had not been that he lent me the money*, I *could not have bought* that book. 如果不是当时他借钱给我,我是无法买到那本书的。

= He lent me the money in time, so I bought that book. 他当时及时借给我钱,所以我才买到了那本书。

• 如果条件状语从句中包含 were, had, should, could, 连词 if 有时可以省略。这时,条件从句要用倒装语序,即把谓语动词或其中一部分移到主语前面,这种情况主要用于书面语。

Were Joan here now (= If Joan were here now), I would explain the whole matter. 如果乔安现在在这里,我会向她解释整件事。

Had she done it (= If she had done it), she would have felt sorry. 如果她当时做了这件事,她会后悔的。

Should Tom tell lies (= If he should tell lies), I would punish him. 如果汤姆说谎,我会处罚他。

B. 虚拟语气用于其他条件状语从句

a. 虚拟语气用于其他一些条件句

虚拟语气除了用于 if 从句外,还可以用于一些其他连词或短语引导的条件状语从句,如 unless, provided/providing (that), supposing/suppose (that), in case, so/as long as, on condition that, imagine that, given that, in the event that 等。此类连词通常引导真实的条件句,部分情况下引导非真实的条件句。

I cannot write to John unless (= if not) you give me his address. 我无法写信给约翰,除非你给我他的地址。(真实条件)

You will pass the examination unless (= except that) you don't work hard for it. 你能通过考试,除非你不认真进行复习。(真实条件)

Unless (= If not) you had lent me a hand, I should not have completed my task. 除非你当时帮助我,不然我无法完成我的任务。(表示与过去事实相反)

I could not fly unless I were a bird.

= I could fly if I were a bird. 我不会飞,除非我是只鸟。(表示与现在事实相反)

I will leave provided/providing (that) (= if) my expenses are paid. 倘若我的费用已被付清,我就会走。(真实条件)

Suppose/Supposing (that) it rains, what shall we do? (真实条件)

Suppose/Supposing (that) it rained, what should we do? (对未来的假想)假如下雨的话,我们该做些什么?

In case he comes, let me know. 如果他来了,让我知道一下。(真实条件)

You may borrow this book as/so long as you keep it clean and tidy. 只要你保持书本整洁,你就可以借这本书。(真实条件)

I will take the trip with you on condition that you pay the expenses. 如果你出旅费的话,我就和你同行。(真实条件)

Imagine that we were at the top of the mountain now. 想象我们现在在山顶。(对现在的假设)

Given that the city government approves the project, we shall have a new hospital here. 只要市政府同意这个项目,我们将会在这儿有个新医院。(真实条件)

In the event that Mr Smith refuses to meet us, what shall we do? 如果史密斯先生拒绝会见我们,我们将怎么办。(对事情发生可能性的假设)

Notes:• unless 既可以引导真实条件句,也可以引导非真实条件句。引导真实条件句时,可用 if not 替代,但需要注意的是,当 unless 后面接带有否定谓语动词的从句时,不能用 if not 所替代,而是表示 except that 的含义。引导非真实条件句时,通常可以和 if not 互换使用,但有时根据上下文 unless 的含义是 but if 或 except on condition that。

• provided 原是"规定"的意思,它引导的从句表示一种规定。所以一般来说,规定者总希望自己的规定能够实现,而 if 是表示假设的情况,provided/providing (that) 不能在所有情况下替换 if,而 if 能在所有场合替换 provided/providing (that)。

You will be dismissed provided (that) you make the same mistake again. (误)

You will be dismissed if you make the same mistake again. (正)如果你再次犯错,你将被解雇。(规定者不希望再次犯错的情况出现)

I will take part in the work provided/providing (that) (=if) I am fine. 只要我身体状况好,我将参加工作。

b. 与并列连词 and 或 or, or else, otherwise 一起连用的条件句

Try again, and you will succeed. 再尝试一下,你将会成功。(真实条件)

Try again, and you would have succeeded. 如果你再尝试一下,你会成功。(事实是过去没有再尝试)(非真实条件)

= If you had tried again, you would have succeeded.

I did not know the situation, or/or else/otherwise I would have helped him. 我不知道情况,否则我会帮他。

= If I had known the situation, I would have helped him.

c. 虚拟语气用于含蓄条件句

虚拟条件句中的条件从句有时没有直接表达出来,只暗含在上下文中,这种句子叫作含蓄条件句。含蓄条件句大体有三种情况。

• 条件暗含在短语中。

But for your help we couldn't have succeeded in the experiment. 如果没有你的帮助,我们的实验是不会成功的。(暗含在分词短语 but for your help)

What would I have done without you? 如没有你,我会怎么办呢?(条件暗含在介词短语 without you 中)

It would be easier to do it this way. 这样做会比较容易。(条件暗含在不定式短语 to do it this way 中)

• 条件暗含在上下文中。

You might stay here forever. 你可以永远待在这儿。(可能暗含 if you wanted to)

We would have succeeded. 我们本来是会成功的。(可能暗含 if we had kept trying)

Your reputation would be ruined. 你的名誉会损坏的。(可能暗含 if you should accept it)

• 在不少情况下,虚拟式已变成习惯说法,很难找出其暗含的条件。

You wouldn't know. 你不会知道。

I would like to come. 我愿意来。

d. if only 引导的虚拟条件句

非真实的条件句如省去结果主句,则表示一种不可能实现的愿望。这种条件句常用 if only 来引导。If only 位于句首引起的感叹句用虚拟语气,动词用一般过去时表示目前的愿望,用过去完成体表示过去的愿望,用 would 或 could 表示将来。

If only he knew the answer. 他要是知道答案就好了。(用过去时表示现在)

If only I could speak several foreign languages! 我要是能讲几种外语就好了!(用 would/could 表示将来)

If only you had told me the truth before. 要是你以前告诉我真相就好了。(用过去完成体表示过去)

Note:if only 和 wish 的用法相同,表示的意愿也基本相同。

If only it would rain. 但愿天能下点儿雨!

= How I wish it would rain.

If only I had known her earlier! 要是我早点儿认识她就好了!

= I wish I had known her earlier.

C. 虚拟语气用于目的状语从句

a. 用于以 in order that, so that 引导的目的状语从句

此时从句中的谓语多用"could/might + 动词原形"。

He goes closer to the speaker so that he could hear him clearer. 他走近说话的人以便能听得更清楚。

He read the letter carefully in order that he should not miss a word. 他把信读得很仔细以便不漏掉一个字。

b. 用于以 lest, for fear that 和 in case 引导的目的状语从句

此时的谓语动词多用"should + 动词原形",should 往往省略。

She examined the door again for fear that a thief (should) come in. 她又把门检查了一遍,以防盗贼的进入。

He started out earlier lest he (should) be late. 他早早地就出发了,以防迟到。

D. 虚拟语气用于方式状语从句

as if (as though) 引导的方式状语从句可用陈述语气,也可用虚拟语气。

a. as if 引导的从句用陈述语气的情况

当说话者所述的是真实的或极有可能发生或存在的事实时。

It sounds as if it is raining. 听起来像是在下雨。

b. as if 引导的从句用虚拟语气的情况

当说话人认为句子所论述的是不真实的或极少有可能发生或存在的情况时,as if 引导的从句用虚拟语气。从句虚拟语气动词时态的形式有三种:

• 从句表示与现在事实相反,谓语动词用一般过去时。

He talks as if he knew where she was. 他说话的样子,好像他知道她在哪里似的。

• 从句表示与过去事实相反,谓语动词用"had + 过去分词"。

He talks about Rome as if he had been there before. 他说起罗马来好像他以前去过似的。

• 从句表示将来发生的可能性不大,谓语动词用"would (could, might) + 动词原形"。

It looks as if it might snow. 看起来好像要下雪了。

E. 虚拟语气用于让步状语从句

让步状语从句指事实时,从句谓语动词用陈述语气。若从句内容表示现在和将来的假设情况,从句谓语动词用虚拟语气。

a. even if/even though/即使

even if/though 有假设之义,主从谓语可用直接陈述语气,也可用虚拟语气。用虚拟语气时,主从时态呼应与 if 条件句相同。

The boy couldn't have been saved even if he had been tended without delay. 即使当时那个男孩得到及时照

顾,他的生命也未能被挽救。

I wouldn't be angry with her even if I tried. 我即使想生她的气,也做不到。

I should say the same thing even if he were here. 即使他在这里,我还是要这么说。

b. though, whether ... or, however, no matter ... 等引导的让步状语从句

Though he (should) fail, there would still be hope. 即使他失败了,仍有一线希望。

Whether he (should) succeed or fail, we shall have to do our part. 不管他成功还是失败,我们还是要做好自己的事。

However hard it might rain/rains, we shall go there together. 不管雨下得多么大,今晚我们还是要去那里。

No matter what his social position (might) be, a man is equal in the eye of the law. 一个人不论其社会地位如何,在法律面前都是平等的。

F. 虚拟语气用于表语从句

当主句主语为 wish, suggestion, proposal, decision, aim, plan, idea, condition, request, arrangement, necessity, demand, recommendation, advice, motion, advocation, agreement, belief, desire, determination, instruction, direction, order, proposition, regulation, requirement, resolution, rule, stipulation 等名词时,从句的谓语动词可用"should + 动词原形"型虚拟语气,should 可以省略。

My suggestion is that we should tell him. 我的建议是我们应该告诉他。

Our only request is that this should be settled as soon as possible. 我们唯一的请求就是尽快解决这个问题。

His only condition was that we should keep the place clean. 他唯一的条件是要我们保持那个地方的清洁。

Our demand is that a simpler wedding ceremony should be held. 我们的要求是举办更简单的婚礼。

The regulation is that no candidate should take a book into the examination room. 规定是任何考生都不能带书进入考场。

My idea is that we (should) get more people to attend the conference. 我的主意是我们应该让更多的人与会。

G. 虚拟语气用于同位语从句

在同位语从句中,当先行词表示命令、建议、愿望、同意、决定或意图,如 suggestion, order, request, requirement, recommendation, understanding, decision, agreement, wish, desire, ambition 等名词时,从句可以使用"should + 动词原形"的虚拟语气结构,should 往往可以省略。

We are all for your proposal that the discussion (should) be put off. 我们都赞成你提出的将讨论延期的建议。

The suggestion that the mayor (should) present the prizes was accepted by everyone. 由市长颁发奖金的建议被每个人接受。

He spoke about his country's desire that friendly relations (should) be established. 他说出了他的祖国希望建立友好关系的愿望。

Many congressmen seconded Jefferson's motion that a special committee should be set up to look into the problem. 许多国会议员附议了 Jefferson 关于设立特殊委员会来调查问题的动议。

H. 虚拟语气用于主语从句

虚拟语气用于主语从句中时,通常以"it is ... that ..."结构出现,it 为形式主语,句子真正的主语是后面 that 引导的从句。在这种结构中,主句中 it is 后常跟一些标志性形容词或名词,提示句子可能用到虚拟语气,后面所接的 that 从句中的谓语动词一般用"should + 动词原形"结构,而 should 常可以省略。

It is necessary that a doctor (should) be sent for at once. 立刻叫医生来很有必要。

It was important that the money (should) be collected for the cause. 为了事业筹钱很重要。

It is quite natural that unexpected difficulties (should) arise. 不可预见的困难会出现是很自然的。

a. 常见标志性形容词

It is (was) necessary (有必要的) that ...

It is（was）imperative(有绝对必要的) that …
It is（was）essential（不可或缺的)that …
It is（was）important(很重要的) that …
It is（was）urgent（紧急的）that …

除了上面形容词之外，还有 strange, natural, adamant, anxious, appropriate, proper, careful, compulsory, crucial, vital, eager, expedient, keen, monstrous, odd, obligatory, rational, sorry, sufficient, right, wrong 等。

还有一些动作形容词(一般以动词的-ed 或-ing 形式或以动词派生出的形容词形式出现）：amazing, amazed, ashamed, arranged, decided, demanded, disappointing, disappointed, advised, advisable, agreeable, desired, desirable, desirous, determined, incredible, insistent, ordered, preferable, proposed, requested, required, recommended, rejoiced, resolved, shocking, shocked, stipulated, surprising, surprised, suggested, unthinkable, recommended, recommendable 等。

b. 常见标志性名词

It is（was）a pity that …
It is（was）a shame that …
It is（was）no wonder that …

It is a pity that Lewis should be so careless. 露易斯竟然如此粗心真可惜。
It is a shame that Judith should be so cheap. 朱迪斯竟然如此小气真遗憾。
It is my proposal that he be sent to study further abroad. 我建议派他去国外进一步学习。

I. 虚拟语气用于宾语从句

a. 用在 wish 引导的宾语从句中

当动词 wish 表示不太可能实现的假想或愿望时，它引导的宾语从句用虚拟语气。表示现在不能实现的愿望，从句的谓语动词用过去式，表示将来不可能实现的愿望用"would/could + 动词原形"，表示过去不可能实现的愿望时用"had + 过去分词"。

I wish I were better-looking. 要是我长得再漂亮些就好了。
I wish I had brought a pen with me. 我希望我带了笔。
I wish you would not listen to his words. 我希望你没有听他的话。

Notes： • wish 与 hope 接宾语从句的区别在于：hope 表示一般可以实现的希望，宾语从句用陈述语气。wish 表示很难或不大可能实现的希望，宾语从句用虚拟语气。试比较：

We hope they will come. (We don't know if they can come.)
We wish they could come. (We know they are not coming.)

• wish 后面宾语从句中的虚拟语气要按"后退一步法"处理从句中谓语动词的时态。表示何时的愿望，与那个事实相反，不能以主句的时态为判断依据，而应根据从句的意义判断。

b. 用在表示要求、命令、建议等动词所引导的宾语从句中

在表示建议、要求、愿望、命令、坚持、想法（advise, command, demand, decide, desire, insist, order, prefer, propose, request, require, suggest）等动词后面的宾语从句，从句谓语用"should + 动词原形"，其中在美国英语中，should 常省略。

The young man insisted that I (should) go with his fellows. 这个年轻人坚持要我同他的同伴们一起去。
The doctor advised that he change his job. 医生建议他换工作。

Notes： • insist 表示"坚称，主张"时，宾语从句要用陈述语气。

She insisted that she had seen a thief climb into the house through the window. 她坚持说她曾看见一个小偷从窗口爬进了房间。
He insisted that he was honest. 他坚持认为自己是诚实的。

- 当 suggest 表示"表明,暗示"时,宾语从句也要用陈述语气。

The smile on his face suggested that he had passed the exam. 他脸上的微笑表明他已通过了考试。

The look on his face suggested that he was quite satisfied with what I had done for him. 他的表情暗示出他对我为他所做的事非常满意。

c. 用于 would rather, would sooner, would prefer 后的宾语从句

在 would rather, would sooner, would prefer 后的宾语从句中,谓语常常用过去时来表示现在或将来的情况,用过去完成体表示过去的情况。

I would rather you came tomorrow. 我宁愿你明天来。

I'd sooner she left the heavy end of the work to someone else. 我宁愿她把重活留给别人。

I would prefer he didn't stay here too long. 我倒希望他不要在这儿待得太久。

Wouldn't you rather your child went to bed early? 为什么你不愿让你的孩子早点上床睡觉呢?

I would just as soon you had returned the book yesterday. 我真希望你昨天把这本书还了。

J. 虚拟语气用于定语从句

在"It is (high) time (that)…"结构中,that 定语从句的谓语动词用过去式或"should + 动词原形",但 should 不能省略,表示"到某人该做某事的时间了"。

It is time that the children went to bed. 到孩子们睡觉的时间了。

It's time that we began our meeting. 是该开会的时候了。

It is high time that we should tell him the truth. 是我们该告诉他真相的时候了。

第18章　句子的倒装

18.1　句子倒装概述

所谓倒装,就是句子的结构不是按照主语、谓语的正常语序排列,而是把谓语的部分或全部提到主语的前面。所以倒装主要是为了结构或修辞的需要。对于句子倒装,我们应掌握以下内容:一是写作上的技巧问题;二是语法上的规则问题;更重要的是通过那些生动形象的倒装表达手段可达到作者和读者之间的感情上的沟通,使读者能理解作者所要表达的内在含义及感情色彩。

18.2　倒装的需要

(1) 句子结构的需要

句子结构的需要是指在不同的语言环境中为了准确无误地表达出话语者的意思,其时句子本身就是一些倒装句。这种倒装大致有疑问句、there be 句型、省略 if 的非真实条件句、省略 whether 的让步状语从句、以 be 开始的由动词命令引导的让步状语从句、由 as,that,no matter what/whatever 等引导的让步状语、由分词引导的原因状语从句、表示祝愿的句子和 how/what 引导的感叹句、the … the … 句型等。

① 疑问句中除了问主语或主语的定语的特殊问句外,都是倒装句。

这些疑问句是特殊疑问句、一般疑问句、选择疑问句和附加疑问句。

What did he say at the meeting last night? 他昨天晚上在会上说了些什么?

Has Rose left her phone number with you? 罗丝给你留了电话号码吗?

Are you eighteen or nineteen this year? 你今年 18 岁还是 19 岁?

You are interested in English, aren't you? 你喜欢英语,是不是?

② 表示客观存在的 there be 句子是倒装句。

there is (+单数名词),there are (+复数名词),其开头的 there 是引导词,也可说是形式主语,没有实际词汇意义;后面的 be 动词是谓语,再跟着的名词、代词或其短语才是真正的主语,所以说它们是倒装句。

There *is a map of the world* on the wall. 墙上有幅世界地图。

There *are a lot of Englsh books* in our school library. 我们学校图书馆有很多英语书。

There *is a box*, *two pencils and three bottles* on the desk. 办公桌上有一只盒子、两支铅笔和三只瓶子。

There *is plenty* to eat, isn't there? 有好多吃的东西,不是吗?

There *has been much talk* about the matter. 关于这件事议论很多。

There *appeared to be* no better way. 看来没有更好的办法。

Will there *be a meeting* tomorrow morning? 明天上午开会吗?

上面例句 3 中,因首先出现的是 a box,所以前面用的 is,这种句子更多出现在口语中;例句 6 证实 there be 中的 be 还有其相似的动词形式;例句 7 还是按一般疑问句的变法对待,因为 there 是形式主语。

③ 非真实条件句可以省略 if。

if 可引出非真实条件句,在省去 if 时,原 if 后的 were, had, should 就提前至句首。

Were I you, I would go there with them. 要是我是你的话,我就与他们一起去那里了。(原句是 If I was/were you, I …)

Had she not been working so hard, she wouldn't have achieved so much. 如果她不那样努力地工作,就不可能取得如此多的成就。

Should something go wrong with the machine, they would have nothing to do today. 如果机器出了毛病,他们今天就没事可做了。

④ 部分状语从句需要倒装。

不带连词的让步状语从句、as 引导的方式状语从句、as 和 than 引出的比较状语从句、一些时间状语从句等,都用倒装语序。

A. 不带连词的让步状语从句

凡不带连词的让步状语从句都用倒装语序。

Be a man ever so learned, he ought not to proud. 一个人不管多么有学问,(他)也不应该骄傲。(→Even if a man be ever so learned, he ought not to be proud.)

Be a man ever so rich, he should not sit idle and do nothing. 无论一个人多么富有,也不应该坐着无所事事。

Be he king or peasant, he shall be punished. 无论他是国王还是农民,他都必须受到处罚。

Even *had he had* money, he would not have bought the expensive car. 即使他有钱,他也不会买那昂贵的小汽车。

B. as 引导的方式状语从句

as 引出的方式状语从句用倒装语序是因为句子的主语较长。

He is unusually thin, *as are both his parents*. 他特别瘦,他的双亲也是的。

Air is attracted by earth, *so is every other substance*. 像其他物质一样,空气也受到地球的吸引。

C. as 和 than 引出的比较状语从句

当要强调 as, than 比较状语从句中的主语时,就用倒装语序。

No substance so completely permeates our lives *as do water*, *air and the like*. 没有物质像水、空气那样为我的生活所必不可少。

Silver allows a larger current than *does iron*. 银比铁允许更多的电流通过。

D. 以 whatever, however 等引出的让步状语从句

Whatever advice she may offer, it will be of value to me. 不管她提出什么样的建议,对我都是有价值的。

Brave as he is, he trembles at the sight of a snake. 他虽然勇敢,可看到蛇仍然会发抖。

E. 一些时间状语从句

对于时间状语从句中的倒装,看起来好像是错句,实际上并不错,要多加注意。

My grandfather will be seventy *comes August*. 我祖父到 8 月份将满 70 岁了。(句中的 comes August = when August comes)

⑤ 结构性前移需要倒装。

把定语从句中含有关系代词的介词短语移至句首,叫结构性前移。这些关系代词是介词的宾语。这些介词与代词组成的短语常用的有:about which, by which, from which, of which, with which 等。

The cells *of which* each organ is made are different. 构成每一器官的细胞是不同的。

That was a mysterious phenomenon *about which* men understood nothing for more than 1,000 years. 那是1000多年来人们一无所知的神秘现象。

⑥ 直接引语的陈述部分主谓倒装。

除非主语是代词或陈述部分带有宾语，直接引语的陈述部分主谓倒装。

"Your son has passed the exam in English, I think," *said Mr. Green.* "我想，你儿子通过了英语考试了。"格林先生说。

"Did you hand in your term paper?" *asked Mary.* "你学期论文交了吗？"玛丽问道。

"Get out of here!" he shouted to Tom. 他大声对汤姆说"滚出去！"（陈述部分的主语是代词，不倒装）

"Our English teacher has written fourteen books." Robert told me in low voice. "我们的英语老师已写了14本书。"罗伯特小声对我说。（陈述部分带有宾语，不倒装）

⑦ 分词可引导原因状从句。

Standing *as it does* on the top of the hill, the temple has a full view of the city. 那寺庙位于山顶上，可以俯视整个城市的全景。

Situated *as he is*, he has difficulties to deal with. 他处在这种境地，有很多困难需要应付。

⑧ 表示祝愿的句子倒装。

May you succeed! 祝你成功！

May God bless you! 愿上帝保佑你！

Long live the friendship between our two countries! 我们两国的友谊万岁！

⑨ 由方位副词和地点副词引出的感叹句倒装。

方位副词和地点副词引出的感叹句主谓语常倒装，但主语如是代词就不倒装。常用的方位副词有：away, back, down, in, off, up 等；常用的地点副词有：here, there 等。

Away went Li Na to Shanghai! 李娜去海了！

Away she went to Shanghai! 她去机场了！

There comes the bus! 公共汽车来了！

Here she comes! 她来了！

⑩ "the … the … "句型需要倒装。

在"the more … the more … "句型中，主句有时可用倒装语序。

The more we practise, the better is our skill. 我们越练，技术越好。

The better I know him, *the more do I* learn from him. 我越了解他，我从他那里学到的东西越多。

The harder she works, the happier she feels. 她工作越努力，就越觉得快乐。

The more I study, the more I know. 我学得越多，知道得越多。

（2）行文的需要

行文的需要所指的内容包括为了强调、渲染气氛或为了语流需要以达到某种写作效果时把某些特殊的词、短语置于句首形成倒装，或因主语较长非得把其移后形成倒装。

① 强调同位语时的倒装

此时，要把同位语置于中心词前，特别当中心词是代词时，用这种语序更常见。

Chen Caihong—Mr. Li's wife, *she* was then studying in Beijing University. 李先生的妻子陈彩虹那时在北京大学学习。

Financial expert, Professor White will begin writing a weekly column on the national economy. 财政专家怀特教授将开始就国民经济问题每周写一篇专栏文章。

从上两例可见，例句 1 中的 Chen Caihong—Mr. Li's wife 是句子主语 she 的同位语，把它们提前至句首都是为了强调。例句 2 的同位语 financial expert 是句子主语 Professor White 的同位语。

② **同位语与中心词的倒装**

通常情况下,同位语跟在说明的中心词后面。但有时为了强调,同位语可以位于中心词前,成为同位语与中心词的倒装(Inversion of the Apposition and the Head Word)。

The electronic computer, the marvel of our age, has been in use only in 1946. 电子计算机,我们时代的奇迹,是在1946年才得到应用的

→The marvel of our age, the electronic computer has been in use only in 1946. 我们时代的奇迹——电子计算机是在1946年后才得到应用的。

③ **当as, however 等引导让步状语从句时,其宾语补足语必须置于从句首的倒装**

Charming as I found her, she had struck me as rather presumptuous. 尽管在我看来她是可爱的,我仍然觉得她相当高傲。

Mrs Wu, you have nobody to love you; and however *miserable* you made us, we shall still have the revenge of thinking that your cruelty arises from your greater misery. 吴太太,你可是没有一个人爱你呀,你无论把我们搞得多么惨,一想到你心肠狠毒是因为你受的罪加倍地深,我们也就出了这口气。

④ **复杂的同位语倒装**

当某个同位语比较复杂,为了使句子结构平衡,同时起到强调的作用,可以把同位语置于句首,用逗号分开。

Intellet, imagination, power of expression, humor, taste, truth to life, and truth to human nature—these are the qualities which make a writer popular. 才智、想象力、表达能力、幽默感、审美力、忠于生活、忠于人性——所有这些都是使一个作家受人欢迎的品质。

⑤ **宾语的同位语的倒装**

为了强调,也可以把宾语的同位语提前至句首。

Your first teacher—Wu Ming, I saw *him* here last night. 你的启蒙老师——吴明,我昨天晚上在这里见到他了。

Our gold and silver and valuables and clothes—you can have *them* all, only let us live. 我们的金银财宝、衣服全都给你们,只要饶我们几条命。

上面例句1中的 Your first teacher—Wu Ming 是 him 的同位语,例句2中的 our gold and silver and valuables and clothes 是 them 的同位语。

⑥ **以 only 开头作为状语的短语或句子的倒装**

Only then did he realize the seriousness of his mistake. 只有到了那时,他才认识到他的错误的严重性。

Only in this way can we advice him to give up smoking. 只有用这种方法,我们才能劝说他戒烟。

Only when the war was over was he able to go back to his own country. 只有到了战争结束时他才能回到他自己的祖国。

Only after he was gratulated from college could he go to the large firm to work. 只有在他大学毕业后他才能进那家大公司工作。

像 only then 的短语还有 only by chance, only by luck, only on rate occasion, only today/yesterday, only with difficulty 等。

⑦ **在以 often, little, never, scarcely, no sooner … (than), hardly … (when), well, rarely, scarcely, seldom 等开头的句子倒装**

Often did he go to the computer house to play last year. 他去年常去电脑房玩。

Little did she sleep last night. 昨晚她睡得很少。

Never have I in my life *attended* an international conference on such a big scale. 我一生中从未参加过如此

255

大规模的国际会议。

Well do I remember the first day when I go to school. 我非常清楚地记得我第一天上学的情境。

Rarely have I seen such a beautiful sunset. 这样漂亮的落日,我很少见到。(正常语序为 I have rarely seen such a beautiful sunset, 但意气较倒装的要弱得多)

Scarcely did he speak about the difficulties in his work. 他很少谈到自己工作中的困难。

No sooner had they got to the plant than they started to work. 他们一到工厂就开始工作了。

Hardly had I finished my homework *when* someone kocked at the door. 我一做完作业就有人敲门。

⑧ 以 not only ... but (also) 开头的句子倒装

这里所说的以 not only ... (but also) 置于句首是指它们连接的两个分句要用倒装语序。

Not only is this problem very important, but it is a difficult problem to be solved at once. 这个问题不仅非常重要,而且还是一个难于马上解决的问题。

Not only does the sun give us light, but it gives us heat. 太阳不仅给我们光,而且还给我们热。

Not only is he a scientist, but he also a fighter. 他不仅是个科学家,而且还是个战士。

但 not only 置于句首时,可连接主语,此时句子就不倒装,如:Not only Rose but also Mary went to the concert last night. (不仅罗丝,而且玛丽昨晚也去听音乐会了。)。not only ... but also 还可连接其他同等句子成分, 如: Water is not only the most common liquid in the world, but it is also the most important liquid. (水不仅是世界上最普通的液体,而且也是最重要的液体)。

⑨ 在诸如 many a time, to such an extent/a degree 等开头的句子倒装

Many a time have I come across this expression. 我有好多次见到这种表达法。

To such an extent is he mad that he beat his father. 他竟疯到打起父亲来了。

To such a degree was I excited that I could not fall into asleep that night. 我激动得如此程度以致那夜睡不着觉。

⑩ 在含有以 not 开头的短语状语置于句首的句子倒装

这些短语数量较多, 如: not a (word), not often, not a soul, not a single, not for the life of, not even then, not even if 等。

Not a single word has he written. 他一个字也没写。

Not a finger did I lay on the boy. 我碰都没碰一下那个男孩。

Not on my life would I risk putting money into that type of business. 我一生中不会冒险把钱投资到那种生意上去。

⑪ 含有"so + adj.,""so + adv."的句子倒装

在"so + adj."和"so + adv."的两种倒装句中,前者是主语补足语的前移,后者是状语的前移。它们都是为达到另一种强调效果,后面的 that 从句均为结果状语从句。

So small was the mark that I could hardly see it. 符号如此之小,我几乎看不见它。(so + adj. + that 从句)

So fast does light travel that it is difficult to imagine its speed. 光传播的速度如此之快,以至于难以想象出其速度。(so + adv. + that 从句)。

⑫ 把定语置句首实施强调性的倒装

把定语置于句首实施强调,这是一种常见的修辞手法。

Scattered in museums around the world there are other early manuscripts which give us a glimpse into the mathematics of Egypt. 世界各地的博物馆还收藏着其他一些早期的手稿,从中我们可以窥见古埃及数学的一斑。

Of everything that she saw she made extremely careful drawings, which she explained with copious notes. 她把

看到的每一样东西都仔细地画下来,并做了大量的注释。

从上面两句中可见,例句 1 是过去分词短语形式的定语前移至句首,与其中心词 manuscripts 分离,另一 which 引导的定语从句保留原处。例句 2 中句首的 of everything that she saw 是 drawings 的定语,第二个定语——非限制性定语从句,保留在原处。

⑬ 为加强主语语势的倒装

一些表示地点的介词短语位于句首时使用倒装句。

Near the church was an old ruined house. 靠近教堂是一座古老的废屋。

Below the house ran a little stream. 那房子的下面是小河流水。

Through the open window came the sounds of the explosion. 爆炸声从敞开的窗户传来。

(3) 上下文衔接的需要

我们常用倒装手法使句子、篇章间的衔接更加紧密。

① 用特殊形式的倒装句

我们常使用一些特殊形式的倒装句以实现这个目的,同时也达到某种特殊的修辞作用。

She was born poor and *poor she remained* all her life. 她生来贫穷,而且一生贫穷。

He is already very nervous and *still more nervous would he become* if he knew you were here. 他已经很紧张了,如知道你在这里的话会变得更紧张。

② 用排比形式的倒装句

排比形式的倒装句可说是起衔接作用的又一奇妙手法。下面有篇选自杨元兴先生的 *New Horizon English Syntax* 短文,很能说明问题。

"*Not until* I became a mother *did I* understand how much my mother had sacrificed for me; *not until* I became a mother *did I* feel how hurt my mother was when I disobeyed; *not until* I became a mother *did I* know how proud my mother was when I achieved; *not until* I became a mother *did I* realize how much my mother loves me."

此文用了四句"not until … did … "排比形式的倒装句,使我们俗话所说的"不养儿女不知父母恩,不当家不知柴米贵"的深奥而朴实的哲理跃然纸上。这连续的四个"not until … did …"把这篇短文非常自然地融为一体,非但不显得累赘,反而使作者所要表达的感情更亲切、贴人、明了、易懂。就这样简单的四句通俗话,充分反映了对母爱的深刻理解,把对母亲发自内心的爱自然、生动地表现了出来,由此使读者也骤然产生了一种感情的共鸣,同时也对作者产生了几分敬意。这是倒装句语言表达所显示出来的一种衔接上的奇特功能、表达上的特殊效果,最终凸显出了修辞学上所说的话语和篇章中的语言使用技巧。

③ 前移部分句子成分

为使句子衔接紧密,我们可以把宾语、表语或状语置句首,引起句子倒装。

The committee have asked him to resign. *That he will not do.* 委员会已要求他辞职。那他是不答应的。(宾语移前)

There is a sketch chart of foot reflecting zones on the front wall. *Above the sketch chart of foot reflecting zones is a big clock.* 前面墙上有一幅足部反射区示意图。足部反射区示意图上面是只大钟。(表语移前)

Of education he had only three years. 他只有受过三年教育。(定语提前)

Talent, Maria has; *capital* Maria has not. 说到天才,玛丽亚是有的;谈到资本,她没有。(宾语提前)

④ 名词中心词的定语提前

把第二分句中的定语前移,这种倒装是指为了使上下文更紧密地连接起来。

A few facts are at our disposal, and *of these* I shall try to give you a trustworthy account. 一些事实可供我们利用,我将如实向你汇报。

And they need strength; *of that* he has enough. 他们需要力气,那个,他有的是。(enough *of strength* = of that)

(4) 特定词置于句首时的需要

在英语中,一些特定的词置于句首时常须用倒装语序。这些词有 so, nor, neither, 还有一些表示地点和时间的副词。

① 以 so 或 neither/nor 开头的倒装句型

这种句型有其特点,那就是它们都以上文为前提,接着用 so 或 neither/nor 开头;它们均为省略句型,其中 so 和 neither/nor 分别替代前句中的谓语或谓语的一部分,意思分别是"也"、"也不"。neither 与 nor 相比,前者在正式文体中较多,后者比较通俗。

Jim was hungry and *so was I*. 吉姆饿了,我也饿了。
Julia hasn't left for New York. *Nor/Neither has* Mary. 朱丽娅没有去纽约,玛丽也没去。
Tom can speak Chinese, French and English, and *so can* his father. 汤姆能讲汉语、法语和英语,他父亲也能。
They didn't know the good news, *neither/nor did* we. 他们不知道那个好消息,我们也不知道。

还有以 such 开头的句子也用倒装语序。
Such was the force of the explosion. 这就是爆炸的威力。

A. 在使用 so am I 和 so do we 时,有四点要注意:

a. 为表达方便,我们把 so 开头的省略倒装句型具体化为两种形式:so am I 和 so do we。那句型就是"so + 助动词 + 主语",里面的助动词要与前面句中的助动词一致。如果前面句中没有助动词,那 so 后用 do(does, did),以此指代前面的谓语动词。再比较两句句子:

—I'll have whisky.　　　　　　—So will I.
—我要威士忌。　　　　　　　—我也要。
—I like whisky.　　　　　　　—So do I.
—我喜欢威士忌　　　　　　　—我也喜欢(威士忌)。

b. 在 be 和 have 不是助动词时,有时也可用"so + be/have + 主语"。
He is tired and *so am I*. 他累了,我也累了。
He has a headache. *So have I*. 他头痛,我也头痛。

c. 其他普通动词不能用这个结构,如不能说:He likes bananas and so like I. 要把 like 改成 do 才对。

d. 也有"so + 主语 + 助动词"结构,这种结构表示听话人赞同说话人的话语,有时可能带有惊异的意味。

—It's snowing. 天下雪了。　　　　　—So it is. 果然下雪了。
—Wang Li is a good teacher. 王丽是个好教师。　　—So she is. 可不是。
—Bober has already finished his homework. 巴勃已经完成了家庭作业。
—So he has. 他完成了。

B. neither/nor 结构可用 not … either 结构替代,意思相同,但此时的句子用正常语序。

—Jack didn't like the play.　　　　　杰克不喜欢这出戏。
—Nor did we.　　　　　　　　　　　我们也不喜欢。
—I can't skate.　　　　　　　　　　我不会溜冰。
—His brother can't either.　　　　　他弟弟也不会。

② 以副词 out, away, up 等及其短语开头的句子

以 out, away, up, in, down, back, off 等副词及其短语作状语置于句首时,还有 here, there, now, then 等词,都要用倒装语序。还得说明一下的是,这种用法在口语中见得更多;而且这种句子常用于一般现在时和一般过去时;再者,如主语是人称代词时,只把副词提前至句首,其余不变。

Out jumped a lion from the woods. 从树林里窜出了一只狮子。

Up went the model plane. 模型飞机飞上去了。

Away hurried the soldiers. 战士们匆匆地离开了。

In the southern suburbs of the city is a little hill and an ancient temple is on the half way up the hill. 这城的南郊是一座小山,一座古寺就在上山的半路上。

On one side of square stands the Great Wall of the People. 广场的一边是人民大会堂。

Out he rushed as soon as he heard the terrible voice. 他一听见那可怕声音就冲了出去。

③ 以拟声词开头的句子

英语有一种拟声词,它们常置于句首,后面就是倒装语序。这种倒装能使语言更加生动、情景更加逼真、表达效果更为惟妙惟肖。

Crack goes the whip. 啪的一声抽了一鞭!

Bang came another shot! 砰!又是一声枪响!

Boom went the cannon! 轰隆一声加农大炮开了火!

④ 为使句子平衡的倒装

特别在主语较长时,或当一个名词中心词有两个或两个以上的后置定语时,为使句子平衡,有时就得使用倒装这一手法。

A. 当主语较长时

当主语较长时,不用倒装,就会显得头重脚轻。这时,就要对主谓语进行调整,把主语置后,引起倒装,这样就使整个句子显得平衡。

Gone were three hundred acres of crops. 300亩地的庄稼没有了。

Many are the moving instances of selfless contributions made by the Learning-From-Lei Feng Group in our school. 我们学校的学雷锋小组所做的无私贡献的动人事迹有很多。

Ahead sat an old lady with black glasses. 前面坐着一个戴着黑眼镜的老妇。

On the ground were *shoes*, *socks*, *bags and several basketballs*. 地上有鞋子、袜子、袋子及几只篮球。

B. 当一个名词中心词有两个或两个以上的后置定语时

在一个名词中心词有两个或两个以上的后置定语时,它们都放在后面会显得脚重头轻,这时可把一个后置定语移至中心词前,引起中心词与后置定语的倒装。

And there, glowing with a faint light in the glass test-tubes on the table, was the mysterious something which they had worked so hard to find-radium. 在桌上的玻璃试管里闪耀着微弱蓝光的就是他们付出了极其艰辛的劳动要寻找的那种神秘的东西——镭。

句中的现在分词短语 glowing with a faint light in the glass test-tubes on the table 是 something 的定语,现移至 be 动词 was 之前,使句子在结构上平衡、语义表达上更生动逼真。

第 19 章　句子的强调

英语中表达强调的手法多种多样,具体可归纳为四大类:语音强调、词汇强调、语法强调、修辞强调。

19.1　语音强调

语音强调当然是指口头语言而言。如果话语者要强调句中某一部分内容,可以采用增加音高(Pitch)、增加音长(Length)、提高音调(Strength)等语音手段来达到强调的目的。

所谓语调,就是语音的高低变化。每一个句子都有一个或多个语调组(Tone Unit),这种语调组就是指包含信息片断的词、词组、分句或句子,每一语调组中发音最高的部分叫作调核(Nucleus),代表一个信息焦点,说话者可以移动调核的位置,即增加音高,来实施对同一语调组中不同词语强调。英语中词的重读或轻读就是音调的变化,语句中重读的词便是说话人强调的内容所在。此外,话语者通过增加音长（即放慢语速）来表示强调。

(1) 句子重音——最基本的语音强调手段

我们口头表达思想感情时,表示强调的最基本的语音手段就是句子重音。在英语中,普通的单词都有其自己的重音,但在每个句子中,不可能保持每个单词的重音,而是话语者对其认为或需要突出某些意思时,那些词就会被重读,那些被重读的词语就是句子重音(Sentence Stress),其他的就失去了重音。就像在 On that occasion there was nothing to be done 一句中的 that, occasion, nothing, done 四个词都有句子重音。

能在句中独立担任句子成分的实词(Notional Words),如名词、形容词、数词、代词、动词、副词等,能有句子重音;不能在句子中独立担任成分的虚词(Form Words),如冠词、介词、连接词等,没有句子重音;当然也有一些例外。

(2) 代词的重读与否

代词中,物主代词、指示代词、反身代词、不定代词、相互代词、疑问代词等一般有句子重音;人称代词、物主限定代词、关系代词和连接代词就没有句子重音。但在关系代词之前有非重读的介词,之后又有两个或更多的非重读词,那么关系代词就要重读。

He 'sent for the 'boy who 'lost his 'textbook. 他派人把那个丢了练习本的男孩找来。

She has 'given up his incor'rect 'viewpoints on 'which he has insisted so 'far. 他已放弃了他坚持至今的错误观点。

(3) 动词 be, have 以及助动词和情态动词的句子重音

这些词在句尾(包括分局句尾)有句子重音,在句首可有可无,但在句中则没有;它们的否定简缩形式由于副词 not 弱化成 n't 而取得句子重音。

——He is a 'pupil. ——Is he a 'pupil? Yes, he 'is.

——他是个学生。——他是个学生吗?是的,他是。

A 'week has 'seven days. I shouldn't have 'thought so.

一星期有七天。我不这么认为。

(4) 其他一些词的重读与否

① 副词失去重音的情况

A. 副词词义弱化后失去重音

副词一般要重读,但在某些副词在本身词义弱化以后只起引导句子的作用时,则就失去重音。试比较下列句子:

I must 'start' now. 我必须现在开始。
Now 'listen to me. 现在听我说。
Then 'why did you 'go? 那么你为什么去?
Since 'then we 'haven't heard of her. 从那时起我们就没听到过她的音讯。

B. 句末的副词在其前有一个重读词时失去重音

句末的副词通常是程度副词,如果前面有一个重读音,有时它也会失去重音,如 much, enough, 地点副词也是这样,如 there, here 等。

The 'classroom isn't 'large enough. 那教室不够大。
He can't see that it 'matters much. 他看不出那有多大关系。
It was the 'last thing he ex'pected to 'find there. 这就是他期待在那里发现的最后一样东西。

② 关系副词及连接副词不重读

'Is it the 'place where her 'father 'works? 这就是她们父亲工作的地方吗?
'Tell him when you 'get there. 告诉他你什么时候到达那里的。

③ 单音节介词一般不重读,但在句首可以重读

'On the way 'home I 'met 'one of my 'old ac'quaintance 在我回家的路上遇到了我的一个熟人。

双音节介词通常要重读。

'What's it 'all a'bout! 全关于什么方面的?
The 'dog is 'running after him. 那条狗在他后面奔跑着。

④ 连接副词一般不重读,但在复合句句首的连接词后跟着不重读的主语时可以重读

When 'mother 'comes, … 在母亲来的时候……
When she 'comes, … 在她来的时候……

(5) 加强重音

加强重音(Intensified Stress)是指在句子重音的基础上,某些词的重音可以加强,表示这个词所含的意义受到进一步强调。加强重音用" "表示。这种强调有时可分为程度上的强调和语气上的强调两种。

There was an "enormous 'queue 'waiting at the 'theater. 剧院前排着特长的购票队伍。(从程度上予以强调,表示"特别长"的 queue)

"Do "stop "talking. (从语气上予以强调,表示"绝对不能再讲话")

这里,加强重音的语句部分通常放慢语速,即增加音长以达到特别强调的目的。但是,原来没有句子重音的词,如 I, the, at, and 等,是不可使用加强重音的。

加强重音可以用于一个词,也可以用于几个词,有时整句都可以加强。

"Plenty. 多得很。
It's "perfectly ab"surd! 真是荒唐到极点!
"How "very in"genious! 真是太机灵

(6) 用逻辑重音进行强调

逻辑重音(Logical Stress)就是话语者从词的意义上着眼,认为句中某一个词隐含着对比(Contrast)而使句子有某种含蓄或言外之意,就把它读得特别重;而句子重音是由词在语句中的重要性,即词在句中的语法作用来决定的,而这种重要性取决于词性,因此并不一定能反映出词在意义上的重要性。

"He is a handsome fellow. 他是个漂亮的男子。

逻辑重音 He 隐含一个对比 somebody else, 全句的言外之意是:It is he, not somebody else, who is a handsome fellow。根据末端焦点(End Focus)的原则,调核通常位于语调单位的最后一个重读音节,但是此句中话语者为了突出信息的最重要部分,把调核前移,起到对比的作用,形成对比焦点(Contrastive Focus)。

逻辑重音不但与句子重音不同,而且与加强重音也无关。没有句子重音的词也可以获得逻辑重音。有时甚至还可以对那些一般不该重读的人称代词、冠词、助动词等重读。对比焦点可以落在话语者所要强调的任何一种词类上。

Give "him the pen. 给他(而不是别人)这支笔。
Give him "the pen. 给他这支笔(而不是其他笔)。
I "can do it. 我(真的)能做这事。(强调情态动词 can)
We travel "to and "from the airport. 我们往返于机场。(强调了介词 to 和 from)

比较下列各句,不同的词具有逻辑重音,句子的含义也就各不相同。

"We don't know what he wants. 我们不知道他要的是什么。(其他人可能知道)
We don't "know what he wants. 我们真不知道他想什么。(含有我们想知道而没法知道之意)
We don't know "what he wants. 我们不知道他究竟要什么。(这样也不要,那样也不要,他到底要什么呢?)
We don't know what he "wants. 我们不知道他究竟想要什么。(含有我们不耐烦之意)

19.2 词汇强调

用词汇手段实施强调就是指用某些词、短语或者习惯用语来对句子的某个词语进行强调。我们可以用助动词 do 对句子的谓语进行强调,除此之外,还可用强化形容词和强化副词、形容词和副词的比较级和最高级来进行强调等来进行强调。

(1) 用助动词 do 强调

用助动词 do 进行强调是最常用的词汇手段强调方法。用 do 进行强调有其特点。

① 用助动词 do 强调的条件

助动词 do 表示强调时,其条件是只用于不含有助动词、情态动词或系动词 be 的肯定陈述句中。而且 do 跟它作其他用法时一样也有人称和数的变化,还有时态的变化。

I don't like biology, but I *do* enjoy chemistry. 我不喜欢生物,不过我确实喜欢化学。
Brenda *does have* her own room now. 布伦达现在确实有她自己的房间了。
She *did* say she would be here at nine. 她确实说过她在9点钟到这儿。

② 助动词 do 可用于强调祈使句

Do let's go to the pictures! 走吧,还是去看电影吧!
Do come if you have time! 有空一定来啊!

(2) 用强化形容词强调

强化形容词(Intensifying Adjective)可分为两类:强调语和增强语。

① 强调语

起强调语(Emphasizer)作用的形容词主要由 certain, clear, definite, mere, plain, pure, real, sheer, simple, such, sure, true 等担任。

She is a *mere* child. 她不过是个孩子。

Jim won by *sheer* luck. 吉姆全靠运气获胜。

It's *such* a good chance (that) we mustn't miss it. 机会这么好,我们一定不要错过。

② 增强语

增强语(Amplifier)是起加强程度的作用。这类形容词有 absolute, entire, complete, extreme, great, last, perfect, single, strong, total, utter, very 等。

What he said was *utter* nonsense. 他所说的一切全是胡诌。

You are the *last* man (who ought) to make a remark like that. (= You oughtn't to make a remark like that.) 你最不应该那样说话。

You've said the *very* thing I had been trying to say. 你正好说出了我一直想说的话。

(3) 用强化副词强调

强化副词(Intensifying Adverb)与强化形容词一样可以分为两类:加强语意的强调语、增强程度的强调语。

① 加强语意的强调语

用于加强语意的强化副词,常见的有 actually, definitely, ever, indeed, just, fairly, honestly, literally, really 等。

Have you *ever* been to Xining? 你真的到过西宁?

I *just* want to read the novel that he is reading. 我真的想读他在读的那部小说。

Do you *definitely* want him to be elected? 你们真的想让他入选?

Make an effort this time. But *really* make an effort. 这次要努力了,确实要加把劲了。

大多数强调语的位置在被它们强调的动词之前(像上面4例)。除 fairly 以外,多数强调语都可以置于被否定的动词短语前面;除了 certainly 和 surely,有的强调语都能用于疑问句(如例句3)。通常,强调语不用于祈使句,但是有时候 actually, definitely, really 这些词也可以用在祈使句中(如例句4)。

此外,fairly 要求它所修饰的谓语动词含有某种程度的夸张。

In his anger, he *fairly* screamed at her. (BrE) 他很生气,简直是对她大喊大叫。(而在 In her anger, she *fairly* spoke to him. 一句中用 fairly 则不合适。这也许女人的脾气不会这么坏的道理。)

honestly 倾向于与表示态度或认识的动词连用。

They *honestly* admire her courage. 他们真诚地称赞她的勇气。

② 增强程度的强调语

用于增强程度的副词加强语常用见的有 badly, never, deeply, quite, much, far, highly, bitterly, severely, terribly, violently, well 等。

She *quite* forgot about my birthday. 她把我的生日忘得一干二净。

They paid for the damage *fully*. 他们全部赔偿损失。

We enjoyed the play *extremely*. 我们非常喜欢这个剧本。

大多数作增强语的副词置于句中或句末均可(如例句1、2),但副词 extremely 只限于放在句末(如例句3)。

Notes: A. 在肯定的陈述句分句中,如果增强语在句中,一般就表示语意加重的程度;如果增强语在句末,那就表示其本意,因而不起强调作用。

She *completely* denied it. 她全盘否定这一点。(= He strongly/really denied it. 加强语意)

She denied it *completely*. 她否认一切。(= She denied all of it. 表示本意)

B. 还有,utterly 和含有贬义的动词连用,greatly 常和含有褒义的动词连用,deeply 往往和表示感情的动词连用。

The second failure discouraged him *utterly*. 他的第二次失败使他信心全失。

I know I gained *greatly* from my experiment in novel writing. 我知道我从写小说中获益匪浅。

They wounded her *deeply*. 他们深深地伤害了她。(感情上的创伤)

They wounded her *badly*. 他们深深地伤害了她。(肉体上的创伤)

C. much 的前面常有 so, too, very 等加以修饰,如果它单独修饰动词,只能用于非断定句,或把它放置于句中。

Do you like him *much*? I don't like him *much*. 你很喜欢他吗?我并不太喜欢他。

I *much* appreciate your invitation. 我十分感激你的邀请。

(4) 用形容词、副词的比较级和最高级形式强调

用形容词、副词的比较级和最高级形式强调,这只能说是用某些形容词和副词的比较级、最高级形式表示强烈的肯定或否定概念,如"can't + be + 比较级"结构、"more than any-"结构、"be/v. (not) + the least/the slightest/the faintest"构结等。

Rose can't be more careless. (= Rose is very careless.) 罗丝太粗心了。

Mary did more work than any others. (= Tom did the most.) 玛丽做的工作比其他任何人都多。

King Midas loved gold better than anything else in the world. (= King Midas loved gold the best.) 迈德斯国王爱金子胜过世上的一切。

The old man is the meanest of the mean. 那老头是吝啬人中最吝啬的。

I did not take the slightest notice of her. 我丝毫也没注意到她。

很清楚,在上述的前三句例句中,每一句都比括号内的句子语意强烈、感情色彩浓厚。其他的则通过那些特定结构表达出强烈的语意感情。

(5) 用反身代词强调

反身代词有非强调性用法和强调性用法两种,常见的强调用法有三种。

① 当反身代词用作同位语时这时反身代词要重读,在句中作主语的同位语时位置也比较灵活。

The president *himself* will attend the opening ceremony. 总统将亲自参加开幕式。

The president will attend the opening ceremony *himself*. (译文同上,只是主语同位语置于句尾)

② 反身代词作动词和介词宾语时也可以表示强调。

He thinks of *himself* but not of you. 他只考虑自己,并不为你着想。

I don't know anything about it, why don't you ask *himself*? 对这件事我一无所知,你为什么不问问他自己?

虽然反身代词一般不能单独作主语的,而在非正式文体中可以以"名词 + and/or + 反身代词"组成主语后也表示强调。

His son and *himself* went sailing yesterday. 他儿子和他本人昨天去航行。

His colleague or himself will attend to the work. 他的同事或者他本人将用心做这项工作。

③ 反身代词与某些介词搭配时也可以表示强调,产生特殊的意义。

Jim painted the house all *by himself*(=completely alone). 吉姆完全靠自己漆那房子。

This type of machine works *by itself*(=automatically). 这种型号的机器自动运行。

Remember, this matter is *between ourselves*(=without anyone else knowing). 记住,这件事只有你我两人知道。

(6) 用微量名词强调

表示微小数量概念的名词叫微量名词(Micromeaning Noun)。表示微量意义方面的词语约有六种之多,它们有:表示微量固体的词 atom, bit, grain, jot, morsel, particle, pin, pinch, scrap, shred, speck, straw, thing 等;表示微量液体的词 drop;表示微量时间的词 minute, while, moment;表示微量语言单位的词 word, syllable;表示微量货币的词 penny, cent;表示微小动量的词 wink。利用微量名词可以表达强调的肯定性概念(every+微量名词)和否定性概念(not+微量名词)。这些词的运用可以获得较好的具体、生动、形象的效果。

We are glad that we can understand *every word* she says. 我们很高兴能听懂她说的每一句话。

I didn't sleep *a wink* last night. 昨晚我一宿都未曾合眼。

There isn't *a spice* of humor in his talk. 他的言谈没有丝毫幽默味。

The boys ate up *every bit* of food that had been served. 男孩子们把送上来的东西吃得精光。

(7) 用习惯短语强调

一般用于加强语意的习惯短语有 the hell, the deuce, the devil, on earth, in the world, in existence, in heaven's name 等,用它们可以表达出强烈的惊讶、愤怒、厌烦等情感,它们的位置常在助动词或主要动词前。例如:

What *the hell* are you doing? 你究竟在干什么呀?

Where *the devil* did you go yesterday? 你昨天到底上哪儿去了?

When *in the world* does the bus start? 公共汽车到底什么时候启程?

Who *on earth* told you the news? 究竟是谁告诉了你那个消息的?

(8) 用介词短语强调

我们常用 at all events, at all costs, by all means, in any case, at any rate, under any circumstances, on every and any occasion, (not) at all, (not) on any account, (not) by any means 等介词短语来表达在数量、程度、频度等方面强调肯定性或否定性(前面加 not)的概念。

We had to complete the task *by all means/at all costs*. 我们得不遗余力地完成这项任务。

She had a terrible accident, but *at all events/in any case* she survived. 她出了一次可怕的事故,不过她总算活了下来。

Don't *on any account* leave the baby alone in the room. 切不可将婴儿单独留在房间里。

They have run out of bread. They do not have any *at all*. 他们的面包已经吃完了,一点也不剩了。

(9) 用"all+名词"强调

"all+名词"结构表示强调常用在口语交际中。

We were *all tears*. 我们都热泪盈眶。

She is *all talk* and no deed. 她只说不做。

Mary is *all astonishment*. How can such a child be a favorite of all? 玛丽大为惊讶,这样的孩子怎能成为大

家的宠儿?

In the hall the young teacher was nearly knocked over by a boy illegally running. She should have told him off, instead, she apologized. She was, inwardly, *all white flag*. 在大厅里,年轻女教师差点被一位违反纪律到处乱跑的男生撞倒。她本应该训斥他一顿,然而她道歉了。她在内心里已完全(向学生)投降了。

(10) at all 用在否定句、疑问句和条件句中加强语气

① 用于否定句,意为"一点也不,完全不"。

They weren't *at all* the kind of books Lei care to read. 它们根本不是蕾所喜欢读的那种书。
Tom doesn't think that would do *at all*. 汤姆认为那是根本行不通的。
Henry doesn't seem *at all* sorry for the things that he has done. 亨利对于他干的事似乎一点也不感到难过。

② 用于肯定句和疑问句,意为"真地/的,究竟,到底,竟然"。

It's a miracle that you returned *at all*. 你竟然回来了,这真是个奇迹。
Are you going to do it *at all*? 你到底打算干不干这件事?
Does he come to school *at all*! 他究竟来不来上学?
Whatever is worth doing *at all* is worth doing well. 凡是值得做的事情都值得好好地做。

③ 用于条件句,意义为"真的,确实"。

If you know anything *at all* about it, you should tell me. 如果你真的知道此事,你应该告诉我。
If you do it *at all*, do it well. 如果你真要干此事,就干好。

(11) 用带-ever 的强式词强调

这种用带有-ever 的强式词 whatever, whenever, whichever, whoever, whenever, however 等可以加强语势,也起强调作用。

Goats eat *whatever* (food) they can find. 山羊找到什么(食物)吃什么。
Whichever of us comes late for work will be criticized. 无论我们谁上班迟到都要受批评。
Whatever were you thinking of to suggest such a plan? 你究竟在想些什么,提出这样的计划?
Whenever we see him, we speak to him. 每次我们看见他,都要同他说话。
However did you do that? 你到底是怎么做的?

(12) 用作副词用的 way(远远地)加强语气

Mary is *way* behind you in her studies. 在学习方面玛丽远远落后于你。
The result *was* way beyond my expectation. 其结果远远超出我的预料。
Jane got the news *way* in advance. 简事先早早就得到了消息。

(13) 用意义为"更不用说"的词语表示强调

英语中常用 let alone, even less, much less, much more, not to mention, not to speak of, still less, still more, to say nothing of 等意义为"更不用说"的词语表示强调。

We had no hospital, *let alone* an isolation ward. 我们没有医院,更不用说有隔离病房了。
He could barely pay for his own meal, *much less* for mine. 他连自己的饭钱几乎都要付不起,更不用说为我付钱了。
She cannot afford the ordinary comforts of life, *to say nothing of* luxuries. 她连普通的舒适生活都维持不了,更谈不上奢侈豪华了。

（14）用分词表示强调

英语中有少数分词，如 biting（刺骨的），blazing（烤人的，酷热的，熊熊燃烧的），burning（强烈的，激烈的），dazzling（炫目的），freezing（冰冻似的），piercing（刺骨的，透骨的），raging（发狂的），raving（疯狂的/地，胡言乱语的），scorching（像火烧似的），steaming（冒热气的）等，可用作形容词或副词来加强语气。

She had a *burning* desire to be an actress. 她强烈地渴望成为一名演员。

It is *biting/piercing* cold today. 今天冷得刺骨。

I wiped my *steaming* forehead. 我擦了擦冒着热气的前额。

19.3 句法强调

句法强调的形式较多，有多种句子成分的移动，有利用某些句型来达到强调。句子成分的移动有右移位、左移位和主位性前移和倒装；句型方面有如分裂句、感叹句、祈使句、尾重句等也可达到强调的效果。

（1）通过"右移"进行强调

右移（Right Location），或叫后移（Postponement），是指把某一句子成分从正常位置移至句子后部。为了避免句子头重脚轻，使句子结构变得匀称，我们通常将文字较多或结构较复杂的主语从句、宾语从句、同位语从句、比较状语从句、不定式短语、现在分词短语等后移。这样，使后移部分得到强调。

① "先行代词 it 结构"的右移句

用这种结构就是把用作主语、宾语的不定式短语、现在分词短语或从句移至句末，在原来的位置以先行代词 it 指代，成为形式主语或形式宾语。这样，后移部分也得到强调，句子也显得平衡。

It's a pity *to make a fool of himself.* 他愚弄自己，真是遗憾。

It doesn't matter *what he is doing.* 他在做什么没关系。

You must find *it* enjoyable *working with us.* 你在这儿与我们一起工作准会感到愉快。

我们常说当句子是"主语 + 动词 + 宾语 + 宾语补足语"，而宾语是动词不定式短语、现在分词（动名词）短语、从句时，我们常把动词不定式短语、现在分词（动名词）短语或从句放在宾语补足语后，而原来宾语的位置用形式宾语 it 指代。上面 2、3、4 例句属于"S + V + it（formal object）+ Oc + Real O"结构。这样处理后，句子就显得比较均衡。

② 名词性修饰语的右移

作名词的定语或同位语的不定式短语、现在分词、介词短语、从句等可以与它所修饰的名词分隔开，移至句末，同样也能起到强调的作用。如不这样做，句子就显得别扭，而且头重脚轻。

The problem arose *of what to do with the money.* 问题出现了：这笔钱究竟该怎么用。（of what to … 是 problem 的定语）

The time has come *to decorate the house for Christmas.* 该是装点屋子过圣诞节的时候了。（动词不定式短语 to dedicate … 是 timer 的定语）

About 85 *papers* were published *reporting the results of the experiment.* 大约有85篇论文发表，报告该实验的结果。（现在分词短语 reporting the results of the experiment were published 是 papers 的定语）

All of them were captured *except the leader of the gang.* 除了帮主之外，所有的人都被抓住了。（比较：All of them except the leader of the gang were captured 头重）

An order came from Berlin *that no language but German be taught in the school.* 柏林来令：除德语外，学校里不许教任何其他语言。（此句把 an order 的同位语从句 that no languages but German be taught in the school 置后，起强调作用。比较：An order that no language but German be taught in the school came from

Berlin.）

③ 比较状语从句的右移

根据末端重心原则，比较状语短语或比较状语从句通常右移至句末，与它所修饰的比较项分隔开，达到强调的效果。

Smith has spent *less time* on his work *than he ought to have done*. 史密斯在工作上花的时间比他应该花的时间要少。

More people own houses these days *than used to years ago*. 如今拥有房子的人比几年前多。

④ 其他成分的右移

通常情况下，在含有双宾语的句子中，直接宾语常位于间接宾语之后，含复合宾语的句子中，宾语补足语常在宾语之后，状语也在宾语之后。若是话语者要强调间接宾语，或带有补足语或状语的宾语时，都可以将所强调的这些成分右移，这也完全符合末端焦点和末端重心原则。

Her mother showed her old stamps *to her friends*. 她母亲拿她的邮票给她的朋友们看。

Please explain to him *what this means*. 请向他解释，这到底是什么意思。

She has proved wrong *the forecasts made by the leading economic experts abroad*. 她已经证明，国外的那些知名经济学家所做的预测是错误的。

有时，这样做也是为了使句子匀称。如上面例句 3 不把宾语后移的话成了 She has proved the forecasts made by the country's leading economic experts wrong 那样中间大两头小的一句别扭句。

还有，当表示强调的反身代词用作主语的同位语时常常后移成为末端焦点。

Did you paint the portrait *yourself*? 这幅肖像是你自己画的吗？

（2）通过"左移"进行强调

① 主位性左移

我们把句子的句首成分叫作主位。主位性前移（Thematic Fronting）就是把在正常词序中位于后面的成分提前至句首作为主位而不作主语。虽然末端焦点原则表明后移句子成分能达到强调的作用，但是因为句首是传递信息的出发点，它在信息传递中也起重要的作用，所以主位性前移也可以用来强调。通常前置作主位的句子成分有宾语、谓语、状语、补足语等。

Poor Joe may be, but *thief* he is not. 乔可能穷一些，但他不是贼。（主语补语，也叫表语）

Leave him I couldn't, but at least I could make his life a misery. 我无法摆脱他，但我至少可以使他日子不好过。（谓语）

Chairman of the committee they have elected Eleanor. 他们已经选举埃琳娜任委员会主席。（宾语补语）

Her face I'm not fond of. 她那副面孔我不喜欢。（介词宾语）

Excellent food they serve us here. 他们这里供应给我们美味食品。（宾语）

Into the thick of the smoke we plunged. 我们陷入了浓烟之中。（状语）

我们从这一类句子可以看出，话语者首先说出主位成分，突出最重要的事，而后标出句子的其余部分。因此，这类句子往往有两个信息焦点：一个是左移的主位成分，有调核，表示主要信息；另外一个是句尾成分，也具有调核，表示的是次要信息。

② 左移位

左移位，就是把句中要被强调的成分提到句首，原处用相应的替代词语加以指代，用这种句法手段来进行强调还是现代英语中新提出来的语言现象。当然，起强调作用是左移位句众多功能中的一种。

A. 可左移位的句子成分

可被左移位的强调成分可以是主语、宾语、复合宾语中的宾语、状语、定语等。

A group of girls, they have already collected outside the school gates. 校外已经聚集了一群女孩子。(左移主语)

A fat man, she saw *him* wandering in the park. 一个胖男人,她看见他在公园里漫步。(左移宾语)

In her study, she keeps her laptop *there*. 在她书房里,她把笔记本电脑放在那里。(左移状语)

Mary, they noticed *her* enter the house. 玛丽,他们看见她进那房子。(左移复合宾语中的宾语)

Evelyn, *her husband* went to New York on business. 伊夫琳,她的丈夫去纽约出差了。(= Evelyn's husband went to New York on business. 伊夫琳的丈夫去纽约出差了。)(左移定语)

要注意上面最后一例,左移的是主语的定语,原主语处用 her husband 指代;我们绝不能把 's 一起移动,说成 Evelyn's husband, he went to New York on business。

B. 使用左移位进行强调的注意点

a. 左移成分必须置于句首

b. 左移位成分与原句子间要用逗号

c. 左移的成分与原句子结构疏松,因为在原位置有与左移成分共指的名词、代词、名词短语或副词,所以如把左移的成分省去,句子的意思还是完整的。

d. 左移位成分的原位置上的相应指代词代词、副词、名词词组在语法上必须与左移的部分是同一句子成分,不然就不是左移位强调句。

C. 行文需要的倒装

主位性左移可以不引起倒装,但在下面几种情况下也可以引起倒装。倒装的目的同样是为了强调。

a. 强调表语

当主语较长时,我们可以把表语置于句首,形成倒装,同时也强调了表语。

Next to it is another restaurant where we can have Chinese food. 隔壁也是一家餐馆,那里可以吃上中餐。

Especially popular are the musical and theatrical groups. 特别受欢迎的是那些音乐和戏剧团体。

b. 强调状语

当状语是副词或介词短语时,我们也可把它们置于句首,形成倒装,也起到强调的作用。

Well do I remember the first day when I came to this city. 我清楚地记得我来这城市的第一天。

There was a sudden gust of wind and *away* went her beautiful hat. 突然刮起一阵风,吹掉了她漂亮的帽子。

c. 用"强调否定意义"的词

我们常用把像 few, little, hardly, scarcely, seldom, rarely, never, neither, nowhere, not until, in vain, at no time, under no circumstances 等否定词或含有否定意义的词放到句首进行强调时,句子也引起倒装。

Under no circumstances must we drive too fast. 在任何情况下我们都不得开快车。

Hardly could he recognize me. 他差点认不出我了。

In vain did we try to persuade her to give up her plan. 我们努力劝说她放弃计划,然而一切都是徒劳。

D. 局部倒装的几种情况

表示强调的局部倒装有两种情况:

a. 以 only + 副词/介词短语/状语从句开头或者以"not only + 分句",so/such ... (that) 结构开头的句子,通常都引起局部倒装, 这种局部倒装也起着强调的作用。

Only on Sundays do we meet him. 只有星期天我们才见到他。

Only when the war was over could he go back to his research work. 只有战争结束,他才能回到他的研究工作上去。

Not only did he see her in the park, he also spoke to her. 他不仅在公园里看见了她,还跟她说了话。

So absurd did Jim look that everyone stared at him. 吉姆显得如此愚蠢可笑,以致大家都盯着看他。

b. Not until ... 句式是从强调句 It is (waw) not until ... that ... 演变而来,其目的是为了强调 until 后

的内容,其结构也是局部倒装。

Not until 1983 did he graduate from Beijing University. 直到1983年他才从北京大学毕业。(来自 It was not until 1983 that he graduated from Beijing University.)

Not until our teacher came did we begin the experiment. 直到我们老师来了以后我们才开始这个实验。(来自 It was not until our teacher came that we began the experiment.)

要注意的是,一般情况下 till 与 until 可交替使用,但 Not until ... 句型中只能用 until,不能用 till。

E. 为了强调的分裂句

分裂句(Cleft Sentence)结构通常是:It + be 的一定形式 + 被强调部分 + that 从句。它也是一种主位性前移的结构,当然也是一种强调句型。所以称作分裂句,是因为它把一个句子分裂成两个独立部分,每一个部分都有自己的动词。

分裂句可以强调主语、间接宾语、直接宾语、介词宾语、表语、宾补、状语等,但谓语除外。使用这种句型既可突出信息焦点,又能保证末端重心。

a. 把普通句变为分裂句的情况

我们可以把下面那句普通句子结构改变为下面断裂句强调形式的四种句子,各强调句子的一个成分:

Smith saw your uncle in the park this morning. 史密斯今天在公园里碰上了你叔叔。

- →It was *Smith* that/who met your uncle in the park this morning. 是史密斯今天早晨在公园遇到你叔叔的。(强调主语)

- →It was *your uncle* that/whom Smith met in the park this morning. 史密斯今天早晨在公园碰到的是你叔叔。(强调直接宾语)

- →It was *in the park* that(不用 where) Smith met your uncle this molning. 史密斯今天早晨是在公园里碰上你叔叔的。(强调地点状语)

- →It might be *this morning* that(可用 when) Smith met your uncle in the park. 史密斯可能是在今天早晨在公园里碰见你叔叔的。(强调时间状语)

b. 对间接宾语、介词宾语和宾语补足语的强调

间接宾语、介词宾语和宾语补足语也可以作为分裂句的焦点而被强调。

It's *him* that she gave the book (to). 她把书给的是他(不是别人)。(强调间接宾语)

It's *the book* that she gave him. 她给他的是那本书(不是别的什么东西)。

It's *dark green* that they've painted the kitchen. 他们把厨房涂成的是深绿色。(强调宾语补足语)

It was *you* that I thought of all the time. 我一直在想念的是你。(强调介词宾语)

c. 分裂句强调状语时的注意点

分裂句强调状语时,要注意可以强调 because 引导的原因状语从句,但不可以强调由 as 或 since 引导的原因状语从句。

It was *in 1941* that/when he was born in a poor family. 1941年他出身在一个贫穷的家庭。(强调时间状语)

It was *in this house* that she was born. 她出生地是在这个屋里。(强调地点状语)

It is *only through a great deal of practice* that we shall be able to operate the machine well. 只有经过大量实践我们才能熟练操作机器。(强调方式状语)

误:It was *as/since* she worked hard that she passed the mid-term examination.

正:It was *because* she worked hard that she passed the mid-term examination. 是因为学习努力,她才通过了期中考试。

Note:让步状语从句、比较状语从句和表语不能作为分裂句的中心成分被强调,因此下面三句均不成立:

* It was *although it was raining* that they went out.

* It was *whereas David was a Londoner* that Peter was a Parisian.

* It is *a teacher* that he is.

d. 分裂句的疑问式

分裂句的疑问形式有两种:一种是一般疑问句句式,另一种是特殊疑问句式。

● 一般疑问句的强调形式

Was it Henry that broke the window last night? 是亨利昨晚打破了窗子吗?

Was it last night that Henry broke the window? 亨利是昨晚打破了窗子吗?

Was it the window that Henry broke last night? 昨晚亨利打破的是窗子吗?

● 特殊疑问句的强调形式

Who was it that Jane met with last night? 昨晚简遇到的是谁?

Why is it that copper is not widely used? 为什么铜不被广泛使用?

How is it that Lei wants to leave? 蕾怎么会想离开的?

What is it that Mary wants you to do? 玛丽要你做的是什么事?

(3) 由 what 从句引导的强调结构

A. What 从句 + be + 表语

What caused the accident was Tom's driving a car carelessly. 造成事故的原因是汤姆驾车太鲁莽。

What dissatisfied the listeners so much was Mary's poor oral English. 使听众非常不满意的是玛丽的英语口语太差。

B. 主语 + is/was + what 从句

Quality is what counts most. 最为重要的就是质量。

Power is what they are out for. 他们一心追求的就是权力。

(4) 带有 if 条件句的强调句型

在陈述句后加一个"if + a/an/one + 表示时间、次数、高度、深度、距离等名词"结构,可用来强调度量或数量的准确性,意义为"一定,无论如何应该是,至少有"。

Tom has said one hundred times, *if he has said once*, that he doesn't believe Mary. 汤姆已说过不下百次,他不相信玛丽。

This mountain is 1,800 meters high, *if an inch*(= if it is an inch high). 这座山足有1800米高。

She is eighty-one, *if a day*. 她确确实实是81岁了。

He has come five miles, *if a yard*(= if he has come a yard). 她走了足足有5英里路。

(5) 感叹句式强调句和尾重句

① 感叹句也是一种强调句

感叹句虽然表示的是情感,但也是一种强调句。

What a handsome man he is! 多帅的男子啊!

What a difficult situation we are in! 我们现在的处境多难啊!

How strange a feeling it was! 这是一种多么奇怪的感情啊!

How we miss you! 我们多么想念你!

How time flies! 时间过得真快啊!

其实,陈述句、疑问句、祈使句,甚至一个从句、一个短语、一个单词,都可以通过加强音高、音长、音强,再伴以相应的表情和动作,使之变成感叹句(后面加上感叹号),表示强调的感情。

I wish I had his brain! 要是我有他那样聪明的脑袋就好了!

Mind your head！可要小心你的头啊！

(He says it's cheap.) Nonsense!（他说这很便宜。）胡说八道！

② 尾重句

这里所说的尾重句（Periodic Sentence）是指那种直至句末才出现主要信息或实质性部分的句子。这种句子也完全符合末端信息焦点和末端重心的原则。尾重句的语言效果是使读者一开始便产生悬念，因为主要信息迟迟不出现，这样会使读者一口气地读下去，而当最终出现主要信息时，其脑子里便会留下更深刻的印象。这样，末端焦点就能得到了充分的强调。下面，我们来看一组松散句（即普通表达句）和尾重句的对比例子：

松散句：*Tom and Robert reached the village* after a day's walking.

尾重句：After a day's walking,, *Tom and Robert reached the village.*

19.4 修辞强调

在英语中，除了用上面所说的语音、词汇、句法等手段表示强调外，可用修辞手段进行强调。英语中表示强调的修辞手段很多，它们可以是重复、层进、反问、夸张等。

(1) 重复

① 词、短语、句子的重复

It was on a *very, very* cold night that we were walking in the street, bare-headed and barefooted. 一个很冷、很冷的冬夜，我们光着头、赤着脚走在大街上。

Anyway, kindness isn't enough, I want *a real man, a real man*. 而且，光体贴是没有用的，我要嫁的是一个男人，一个男人。（重复名词短语）

② 词义的叠用

They arrived *safe* and *sound*. 他们平安到达。

Robert's dealt *fair* and *square* with me. 罗伯特对我很公平。

There are *no* notebooks in her schoolbag. There are *none*. 她书包里没有练习本。一本也没有。

③ 句子的重复

I say to you, my friends ... in the *American dream.*

I have a dream ...

I have a dream ... I have a dream

That one day even the state of ... *I have a dream ...*

That my four little children ... *I have a dream* today.

I have a dream ... I have a dream today.

I have a dream ...

and all flesh shall see it together.

以上是美国黑人运动的著名领袖马丁·路德·金在"自由进军"的黑人集会上的演讲。演讲稿从 American Dream 起，引出了八个"I have a dream ..."句子，以逐渐加强的情感把听众引向光明美好的未来，从而使其演说富有更强烈的感染力，具有更强大的号召力。

(2) 层进

层进（Climax）是一种有效的强调方法。它讲的是一种以语意的轻重、范围的大小、程度的深浅、数量的多少或时间的先后为顺序,将词组、分句或句子排列在一起,层层递进,步步深入,使语意逐渐加强。

The young man was handsome, well-mannered and kind-hearted. 那青年男子长相帅气,举止优雅,而且心地善良。

如果把上句任意颠倒词序,不按照层进的原则,那就无法取得加强语意的效果,而且还变成语义序次上的病句。

The young man was handsome, kind-hearted and well-mannered.

严格地说,这种句子程序上是不合逻辑的。描写一个人应该是先外表后内在,在 handsome(帅气)后应是 well-mannered(举止行为),最后才涉及 kind-hearted,这也叫"由表及里"、"步步深入"。

(3) 反问

反问(Rhetorical Question)就是反问疑问句。反问包含了答案,暗示了结论,作者的态度已明确地在问句中表示出来。虽然句子采用了疑问句的方式,但句子表达的还是陈述句的内容。用反问句比起直接用陈述句的语气更加强烈。

If autumn comes, *can winter be far behind*? (= Winter will not be far behind.) 秋天到了,冬天还会远吗?

Mr. Li, *when are you going to stop being so bad-tempered*? (= You should stop being so bad-tempered.) 李先生,你什么时候才能不再有这么火爆的脾气。

一般来说,肯定意思的反问句表达强烈的否定含义,如上面的例句1;否定意思的反问句则表达强烈的肯定含义,如上面的例句2。

(4) 夸张

在英语中,为了更加突出、鲜明地强调某一事物,我们也常用夸张(Hyperbole)的手法来扩大事物的某些特征,增强语言的感染力,达到强调这一目的。夸张通常用于文学作品或日常口语中,不适用于准确性要求较高的文体。

A thousand thanks. 千多万谢。

The waves were *mountain high*. 海浪如山一般高。

We *almost died* laughing. 我们差点笑死了。

Her eloquence would *split rock*. 她的雄辩会劈开坚石。

Rose again made *a thousand and one* excuses. 罗丝又找到了种种借口。

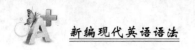

第20章　陈述句

20.1　陈述句的概述

陈述句(Declarative Sentence)用来说明一个事实或陈述说话人的看法,句尾用句号。陈述句包括肯定和否定句二类,语调通常用降调。

说到陈述句,就要涉及动词。一般来说,句子通常由主语和谓语两个部分构成。由于谓语动词的不同,谓语动词短语的构成也就不同,因此句子的结构也不同。据杨元兴 A Complete Collection of English Sentence Patterns 中讲,英语里有五种主动词,它们是:不及物动词(Intransitive Verb)、单宾语及物动词(Monotransitive Verb)、双宾语及物动词(Ditransitive Verb)、复合宾语及物动词(Complex-object-transitive Verb)、连系动词(Link Verb)。

20.2　陈述句的七个句型

以五个主动词为主构成了英语里七种基本的句子结构,也就是陈述句的七种基本句型。这些基本句型可以转换成否定句、疑问句或祈使句,有的可以转换成被动句,通过增加修饰语、使用从属和并列等手段组成多种多样的句子,表示各种各样的意思。因此,陈述句也是其他句子的渊源。

(1) SV(主语＋不及物动词)句型

此种句型是英语里最简单的句型,其谓语由不及物动词(Intransitive Verb)及其短语构成。
Who cares? 管它呢?
The sun rose. 太阳升起了。
Nobody laughed. 没有人笑。
It's raining. 在下雨了。
Tom has come. 汤姆已经来了。
Everyone breathes, eats and drinks. 每个人都要呼吸、吃饭、喝水。
It doesn't matter whether they start now or later. 他们现在或过一会儿出发都无所谓。

(2) SVA (主语＋不及物动词＋状语)句型

上面的句型常常带有状语,因而由两个成分扩展到三个成分,成了 SVA 句型。这种句型中状语前的介词 for 常常省略。
They walked (for) five miles. 他们走了五英里。
It snowed all day. 雪下了一整天。
Won't you stay for the night? 你不留下过夜吗?
The stone weighs five kilos. 这个石头重五公斤。
She waited (for) two hours. 她等了两个小时。
The bus leaves at 10. 公交车十点钟开出。

少数不及物动词,如 sit, live, sell 等,不能单独用作谓语,必须带状语或用于否定式,否则意思不完整。

⎧ She sat down. 她坐下来。
⎩ * She sat. （不能成立）

⎧ She lives in Shanghai. 她住在上海。
⎩ She lived to be ninety. 她活了九十岁。

* She lives/lived. （不能成立）

⎧ This dictionary sells well. 这本词典好卖。
⎩ This dictionary doesn't sell. 这本词典卖不出去。

* This dictionary sells. （不能成立）

根据末端重心的原则,英语里一般不用两个词构成的句子,除非是特殊情况,而要改用较长的形式表示。

⎧ They took a walk. 他们散步。
⎩ They walked along the street. 他们沿街散步。

They walked. （不合习惯）

⎧ I had a rest. 我休息了一阵。
⎩ I rested for a while. 我休息了一会儿。

* I rested. （不合习惯）

(3) SVO(主语+单宾语及物动词+宾语)句型

① 单宾语及物动词

这种句型的动词后只带一个宾语,因此称为单宾语及物动词(Monotransitive Verb),其中包括简单动词和短语动词。

He hurt himself. 他把自己弄伤了。
You didn't tell me. 你没有告诉我。
They often listen to BBC. 他们经常听 BBC 广播。
My aunt brought up four children. 我的婶婶抚养了四个孩子。
She should pay attention to her health. 她应该注意她的健康。

② 单宾语及物动词宾语的位置

A. 视其关系的亲疏

宾语和动词关系密切时两者之间通常不能插入其他成分。但宾语较长、状语较短时,宾语常常置于状语之后。

Mary found for the first time the necessity of learning foreign languages. 玛丽第一次发现了学习外语的必要性。
Tom's aunt has translated into French *War and Peace*, the great novel by Lev Tolstoy. 汤姆的婶婶把列夫·托尔斯泰的著名小说《战争与和平》译成了法文。
I remember so well my impression that never had the *Internationale* carried such a message of hope and triumph. 我清楚地记得,在我的印象中,《国际歌》还从来没有这样让人充满希望和胜利的感觉。

B. 宾语置动词前的情况

宾语通常位于动词之后,但在下列情况下必须移至动词前:

a. 强调宾语时,可以把它放在句首。

Not a single word did Tom speak. 汤姆一句话也没有说。
So many things we can do with bamboo! 我们可以用竹子做多少东西啊!
These two picture books I'll give to you, and these two to your sister. 这两本画册我给你,这两本给你妹妹。

b. 在感叹句中,宾语或表语含有感叹限定词或感叹副词时,宾语或表语移至动词前。
What a simple life they lived! 他们过着多么俭朴的生活啊!
How terrible Mr. Lu's hamdwriting! 陆先生的书法多么糟啊!
What a dreadful act she has committed! 她做了一件多么可怕的事啊!
c. 在定语从句中,宾语是关系代词或含有关系限定词时,宾语移至动词前。
The woman whom they are going to visit is the chairman of the department. 他们要见的那个女士是该系的主任。
The dictionary that I borrowed from Rose is a great help to me. 我从罗丝那里借的那本字典对我的帮助很大。
The building whose roof we can see from here is a school. 我们从这儿看得见屋顶的那座大楼是一所学校。
d. 在名词从句中,宾语是wh-词或含有wh-词时,宾语移至动词前。
I don't care what you said. 我不在乎你说什么。
They don't know which plan I am going to take. 他们不知道我打算采用哪个方案。
Do you know how many grammar books he has written? 你知道他已经写了多少本语法书吗?
e. 在状语从句中,宾语是wh-词或含有wh-词时,宾语移至动词前。
Whatever you do, do it well. 无论你做什么,都要把它做好。
No matter what you say, I won't change my mind. 无论你说什么,我都不会改变主意。
You will be there by five, whichever train you (may) take. 无论你乘哪班火车,五点以前你都可以到那里。
f. 在特殊疑问句中,宾语是疑问代词或含有疑问限定词或疑问副词时,宾语移至动词前。
Who(m) did you see? 你看见了谁?
What is she doing? 她在做什么?
Which book do you like best? 你最喜欢哪本书?
How many books has he read on English grammar? 他读过多少有关英语语法方面的书?
g. 宾语在上文已提到时,常常可以把它放在句首,使上下文联系得更加紧密,而且还含有强调的意味。
That film he doesn't see at all. 那部影片他根本没看过。
All these books they have read. 所有这些书他们都看过了。
His passions and prejudices had led him into great error. That error he determined to recant. 他的激情和偏见使他出了大错。这一点他决心公开承认。

(4) SVOA(主语+单宾语及物动词+宾语+状语)句型

① 少数单宾语动词用于这种句型必须带状语,否则意思不完整。

{ She treats us very well. 她待我们很好。
{ * She treats me. (不能成立)

{ She put the food in the refrigerator. 她把食物放在冰箱里。
{ * She put the food. (不能成立)

{ He showed me into the manager's office. 他把我领进经理办公室。
{ * He showed me. (不能成立)

{ This bicycle has carried me 500 miles. 这辆自行车已经载我走了500英里。
{ * This bicycle has carried me. (不能成立)

② 有一些单宾语及物动词后面只跟动词不定式作其宾语。
这些动词常见的有 ask, wish, hope, expect, agree, learn, refuse, decide, care, mean(意为),

promise(承诺),pretend,manage(设法得以……)等。

  Jane asked to join our club. 简要求参加我们的俱乐部。
  He wishes to visit the island. 他渴望去参观那个岛屿。
  Henry is hoping to spend a few days in the mountains. 亨利希望到山里过几天。
  I didn't expect to see you today. 我没料到今天能见到你。
  When do you expect to be in? 你估计什么时候能回来?
  How can you expect to make headway if you don't work hard? 你不下苦功怎么能有进步呢?
  I agreed to accept the offer. 我同意对方的出价。
  The name of the book is *Learning to Speak English*. 这本书的名字是《学习讲英语》。
  We worked round the clock, refusing to go home. 我们日夜不停地干,家都不肯回了。
  She wishes very much you could manage to come over. 她非常希望你能设法来一趟。

③ 有一些单宾语及物动词后面只跟动名词作其宾语。

这些动词主要有 mind, risk, practice, delay, miss(错过,没赶上), suggest, enjoy, escape, finish, advise, excuse(使……成为理由), avoid, consider, admit(承认,供认)等。

  I wouldn't mind having a try myself. 我也愿意自己来试试。
  You can't risk getting caught in a storm. 你不能冒受暴风雨袭击的危险。
  Practice remembering what you read. 要养成把你读过的都记得的习惯。
  I decided to delay (going on) our holiday until next month. 我决定推迟到下个月再出去休假。
  John missed going to the meeting on Saturday. 星期六约翰没能去开会。
  Who suggested doing it this way? 谁提出这样做的?
  You were lucky to escape being killed. 你很幸运,没有丢性命。
  I advise reading the letter carefully before answering it. 我建议在回信前先把来信仔细读一遍。
  Nothing can excuse lying to your parents. 没有任何理由对父母撒谎。
  We just avoided running over the cat. 我们差一点儿轧着猫。
  They first considered writing to her, but then decided to go and see her. 起先他们考虑写信给她,后来决定去看看她。
  The thief admitted having stolen the gold watch. 那小偷承认偷了那块金表。

下面这些短语动词后也接动名词作它们的宾语或组成一些特殊表达。它们是:give up(停止,中断), keep on, succeed in, insist on, look forward to, be used to, be busy, be worth, can't help(禁不住)等。

  I have given up smoking on medical advice. 我遵医嘱戒了酒。
  Mary keeps on changing her mind. 玛丽老是改变主意。
  At last he succeeded in passing the exam. 最后他终于通过了考试。
  I was perfectly well five minutes after my fall, but my hostess insisted on sending for a doctor. 我摔倒五分钟后就完全好了,但我的女房东坚持要我看医生。
  We did not look forward to living in the splendor of Government House. 我们并不盼望住在显赫的政府大楼里。
  I am/get used to looking after myself. 我已习惯于照顾自己了。
  They are busy getting ready for their journey. 他们那时正忙于准备旅行。
  Is such a person worth knowing? 这种人值得结识吗?
  She could not help laughing. 她禁不住笑了。

(5) SVOO(主语+双宾语及物动词+双宾语)句型

用于这种句型的动词带有两个宾语,因此称为双宾语及物动词(Ditransitive Verb)。英语里的双宾语及物动词不多,常见的有:accord, allow, answer, ask, assign, award, build, bring, buy, call, catch, cause, charge, choose, cook, cost, cut, deal, deny, do, envy, fetch, find, fine, fix, forgive, get, give, grant, grudge, hand, kiss, leave, lend, make, offer, order, owe, pass, pay, post, prepare, promise, reach, read, recommend, refuse, render, reserve, return, save, sell, send, show, spare, strike, take, teach, telephone, tell, throw, wish, write 等。

We wished you a long life. 我们祝你长寿。

I'll give her something to eat. 我将给她点吃的东西。

They refused me permission to leave earlier. 他们不允许我们早点走。

They promised me that everything would be ready by five o'clock. 她们答应我五点钟以前一切都会准备好。

上述动词中的 answer, ask, envy, forgive, grudge, owe, pay, teach, telephone, tell, write 等后面的两个宾语都可以看作直接宾语,因为省去其中任何一个宾语,意思依然完整,句子可以成立。

She writes me a letter every day. 她每天给我写一封信。

She writes a letter every day. 她每天写一封信。

She writes me every day. 她每天给我写信。

间接宾语(Indirect Object)通常指人,它几乎总是位于直接宾语之前。

We don't grudge him his success. 我不忌妒他的成功。

His elder sister made herself a new dress. 他的姐姐给自己做了一件新衣。

I bought my children some pencils and exercise books. 我给孩子们买了一些铅笔和练习本。

When will you return me the bike I lent you last month? 你什么时候把我上月借给你的自行车还我?

当强调间接宾语时,也可以把它置于句首。

Mary gave many gifts, but me nothing. 玛丽,他给了许多礼物,我,他什么也没有给。

此句如写成 Mary, he gave her many gifts, but me nothing. 就成了左移位句。因原宾语的位置有指代代词。

① 间接宾语有时可以转换成介词宾语

这就是"主语 + 双宾语及物动词 + 双宾语"句型向"主语 + 单宾语及物动词 + 宾语 + 状语"句型转换。

A. 在 accord, allow, assign, award, bring, cause, deal, deny, do, fetch, give, grant, hand, kiss, leave, lend, offer, owe, pass, pay, post, promise, reach, read, recommend, render, return, sell, send, show, take, telephone, teach, tell, throw, wish, write 等动词后的间接宾语可以转换介词 to 的宾语。

{ He gave me these books. 他给了我这些书。
{ He gave these books to me. 他把这些书给我了。

{ We wrote her a letter. 我们给她写了一封信。
{ We wrote a letter to her. 我们写了一封信给她。

{ Jane told him the whole story. 简告诉了他整个事情。
{ Jane told the whole story to him. 简把整个事情告诉了他。

B. 动词 build, buy, call, catch, choose, cook, cut, find, fix, get, keep, make, order, prepare, reserve, save 等后的间接宾语可以转换介词 for 的宾语,这介词短语成了谓语动词的目的状语。

His mother bought him a car.
His mother bought a car for him. } 他母亲给他买了一辆轿车。

We chose him a good one.
We chose a good one for him. } 我们给他挑了一个好的。

They have got me a ticket.
They have got a ticket for me. } 他们给我弄到了一张票。

C. 有些动词的间接宾语应根据动词和介词的习惯搭配关系转换成其他介词的宾语。

She asked me a question.
She asked a question of me. } 她问了我一个问题。

Mary bears him no grudge.
Mary bears no grudge against him. } 玛丽对他不怀恨。

John struck the table a heavy blow.
John struck a heavy blow on the table. } 约翰重重地击了一下桌子。

D. 少数动词的间接宾语可以转换成不同介词的宾语，但意思仍相同。

She sang us a folk song.
She sang a folk song for us. } 她给我们唱了一支民歌。

She played me a trick.
She played a trick on me. } 她捉弄我。

Henry played me a game of chess.
Henry played a game of chess with me. } 亨利和我下了一盘棋。

E. 有些动词的间接宾语只能转换成某一介词的宾语；如换用其他介词，句子虽然成立，但意思不同。

{He read me the letter.
He read the letter to me. } 他把信念给我听。

He read the letter for me. 他替我念信(给别人听)。

{Jane sold him her bicycle.
Jane sold her bicycle to him. } 简把自行车卖给他了。

Jane sold her bicycle for him. 简为了他卖掉了自行车。

② **少数动词后的间宾不能转变成介宾**

但有少数动词(如 cost, refuse, reach, spare, take, wish 等)后的间接宾语就不能转换成介词宾语。

The meal cost me ＄30. 这顿饭花了我 30 美元。

She refused me admittance. 她拒绝让我进去。

Lei wished me a pleasant journey. 蕾祝我旅途愉快。

③ **在下列情况下，间接宾语必须转换成介词宾语**

A．强调间接宾语时

Who(m) did you give the book to? 他把书给谁了?

It is Jim that I bought this for. 我买这东西是给吉姆的。

To him Mary told the story, not to his younger brother. 我把事情告诉了他，而不是他的弟弟。

B．直接宾语是代词时

We sent it to the police station. 我们把它送到警察局去了。

I gave it to Mr White, the manager. 我把它给经理怀特先生了。

C．间接宾语比直接宾语长时

He showed the picture to all those who visited him. 他把那张照片拿给所有去看望他的人看。

John bought the English grammar book for his son who was a college student. 约翰给在读大学的儿子买了一本英语语法书。

④ **有些不是双宾语及物动词，要用 to 表示动作的对象**

有些动词，如 announce, dedicate, demonstrate, describe, disclose, explain, express, introduce, mention, mutter（嘟囔）, point out, relate, repeat, report, submit, say, shout, suggest, whisper 等，不是双宾语及物动词，不能带间接宾语，要用介词 to 表示动作的对象。

She explained to me why she was late. 她向我解释了她迟到的原因。
John mentioned to me that he had seen Jane. 约翰向我提到他见过简。
I can't express to you how grateful I am for your help. 我难以向你表达我是多么感激你的帮助。

(6) SVOC(主语＋复合宾语及物动词＋复合宾语)句型

用于这种句型的动词带有复合宾语，即宾语和宾语补足语，因此称为复合宾语及物动词（Complex-object-transitive Verb）。

① 复合宾语及物动词

A. 表示"感觉"、"视听"等生理活动方面的动词，如 catch (＝find), discover, feel, find, hear, listen to, look at, notice, observe, overhear, see, smell, watch 等。当然，如这些动词后的宾语补足语为动词不定式时，要省去不定式符号 to。

Many people caught them trying to corner the rice market. 人们发现他们企图垄断大米市场。
I discovered him stealing public property. 我发现他盗窃公共财产。
Lei felt somebody touch her on the shoulder. 蕾感到有人碰她的肩膀。
We saw someone move about. 我们看见有人走动。
We smell something burning. 我们闻到什么东西烧起来了。
She found a stranger entering the office. 她发现一个陌生人正走进办公室。

B. 表示"爱憎"等心理活动的动词，如 can't bear, dislike, hate, like, love 等。

I could not bear my comrades to be attacked like that. 我不能看着我的同伴受到这样的攻击。
I hate you to be selfish. 我讨厌你自私。
I would like you to meet a friend of mine. 我想让你和我的一个朋友见见面。
I couldn't bear Lei to be away. 蕾不在我受不了。
Mary loves me reading to her in bed. 玛丽喜欢躺在床上听我念书给她听。
She likes her room (to be) tidy. 她喜欢她的房间整整齐齐。

C. 表示"相信"、"认为"等思维活动方面的动词，这些动词有：acknowledge, assume, believe, consider, count (＝consider), deem (＝consider), feel (＝think), find (＝consider), hold (＝consider), imagine, judge, know, presume, remember, suppose, suspect, think, trust, understand 等。

They believe John to be honest. 他们相信约翰是诚实的。
Do you consider her trust-worthy? 你认为她靠得住吗？
I know her to be a good woman. 我知道她是个好女人。
We thought the grammar book worth publication. 我们认为这本语法书值得出版。

D. 表示"指望"、"依靠"等意向方面的动词，如 count on, depend on, desire, expect, intend, long for, mean (＝intend), prefer, rely on, want, wish, would/should like 等。

We should/would like him to stay a bit longer. 我们想要他再待一会儿。
What does she desire me to do? 她要我做什么？
I want the work to be finished this week. 我要求在本周内完成这项工作。
We should prefer Lei not to stay there too long. 我们希望蕾不要在那里待得太久。

E. 表示"宣布"、"任命"、"称谓"、"选举"等意义方面的动词，如 appoint, assert, call, choose, declare, elect, name, nominate, proclaim, pronounce, report 等。

We call him Old John. 我们叫他老约翰。
I declare what she said to be false. 我宣布她说的是假话。
The doctor reported the patient fit and well. 医生报告说，病人健康状况很好。

The Prime Minister nominated Tom Ambassador to China. 首相任命汤姆为驻中国的大使。

F. 表示"要求"、"允许"、"教导"、"强迫"、"命令"、"警告"、"禁止"、"使"、"让"等意义的动词,如 advise, allow, ask (for), beg, request, require, teach, tell, get, lead, leave (=let), let, make, oblige, bid, call on, cause, command, compel, direct, drive (=compel), empower, enable, encourage, entice, entreat, forbid, force, have, imply, implore, incite, induce, instruct, invite, order, permit, persuade, pray, press (=urge), prevail upon, recommend, remind, tempt, urge, warn 等。

We often advised people to use their brains. 我们常常劝人多用脑子。

Allow me to introduce you to the head of our department. 请允许我介绍你见见我们的系主任。

The old man told me to go away. 那位老人叫我走开。

I must get John to come over here. 我必须设法让约翰到这里来。

Leave her to do it hesself. 让她自己去做。

Hunger drove them to sell their children. 饥饿迫使他们卖儿卖女。

Praise makes good men better and bad men worse. 表扬使好人更好,使坏人更坏。

My father warned me not to be late again. 我的父亲警告我不要再迟到。

G. 表示通过某种动作使宾语处于某种状态或产生某种结果方面的动词,如 beat, boil, cut, drive, dye, get, knock, paint, polish, push, put, render, set, shout, turn 等。

I have already put it right. 我已经把它弄好了。

Who set her free the next day? 谁第二天就把她放了?

I'm going to paint the wardrobe white. 我打算把衣柜漆成白色。

The hot weather has turned the milk sour. 天气热,使牛奶变酸了。

H. 表示使宾语保持、开始或终止某一动作或状态方面的动词,如 hold, keep, leave, start, stop 等。

Good food keeps you healthy. 吃得好,身体好。

The young actress held the audience spellbound. 那个青年女演员使观众着了迷。

We stopped her going there alone. 我们阻止她一个人到那里去。

The news started us thinking seriously. 这消息引起我们认真思考。

I. 表示其他意义的动词,如 dare (=challenge), deny, determine, entitle, help, prove, trouble, wait for 等。

Lei denied it to be the case. 蕾否认那是事实。

I dare you to do it again. 我谅你不敢再干。

This determined me to act immediately. 这使我下决心马上采取行动。

What entitled you to criticize her? 什么使你有权批评她?。

Henry helped me (to) repair my bicycle. 亨利帮我修理自行车。

He proved himself (to be) an outstanding fighter. 他证明自己是一个出色的战士。

Can I trouble you to pass me the sugar? 劳驾把糖递给我。

J. 另外,有些动词可以用 as 或 for 组成的短语引导宾语补足语。关于这种情况,我们可以把 as/for 看作结构词;也可以把 as/for 看作介词,那就是介词短语作状语,补充说明宾语,属句型"主语+单宾语及物动词+宾语+状语"。常见的这类动词有下面四类:

a. 表示"认为"、"看成"、"说成"等的动词,它们有:accept, acknowledge, characterize, class, consider, count, define, describe, depict, express, imagine, interpret, look upon, quote, read, recognize, refer to, regard, remember, see, speak of, take, think of, treat, view 等。

We regard this as of great importance. 我们认为这一点很重要。

Lei treated me as a distinguished guest. 蕾把我待若贵宾。

Everyone recognized me as the lawful heir. 大家都不得承认我是合法继承人。

We would interpret her silence as a refusal. 我们认为她的沉默是拒绝的表示。
b. 表示宣告、声称的词，这些词有：declare, denounce, represent 等的动词。
They declared the election as legal. 他们宣布选举是合法的。
He denounced his own brother to the police as a criminal. 他向警方告发他的亲兄弟为罪犯。
Jane represented herself as an expert. 简称自己是个专家。
c. 表示"任命"、"选举"等的动词，它们有：appoint, choose, name, nominate 等。
They appointed him as chairman. 他们指派他当主席。
They choose Mr Dick as their leader. 他们选狄克先生做他们的领导。
The board nominated me as the new director. 董事会提名我为新董事。
d. 动词 take 和 mistake 后用 for 引导。
She took him for her brother. 她把他当成她弟弟了。
We mistook him for the mayor. 我们把他错当成市长了。
有时，动词 nominate 后也可以用 for 引导。
The President nominated her for Secretary of State. 总统任命她为国务卿。

② 形式宾语

复合宾语（Complex Object）的位置通常宾语在前、宾语补足语在后。但在下列三种情况下需用先行代词 it 作形式宾语（Formal Object），而把真实宾语置于宾语补足语之后。

A. 宾语是不定式及其短语时，需用先行代词比作形式宾语，而把真实宾语置于宾语补足语之后。
Mary does not think it wrong to tell lies. 玛丽不认为撒谎是错误的。
I count it an honor to serve you. 我认为为你们服务很光荣。
We found it impossible to keep silent any longer. 我们觉得不能再保持沉默了。

B. 宾语是动名词短语时，需用先行代词比作形式宾语，而把真实宾语置于宾语补足语之后。
We think it worthwhile discussing the question again. 我们认为再讨论一下这个问题是值得的。
You must find it rather dull living here all by yourself. 你一定会感到一个人生活在这里很无聊吧。
I think it most dangerous your climbing the mountain alone. 我认为你一个人去爬山非常危险。
动名词短语比较简短时，也可以把它放在宾语补足之前，而不用先行代词 it 作形式宾语。
You must find working here exciting. 你一定会觉得在这里工作很令人兴奋。

C. 宾语是从句，特别是 that 引导的从句时，需用先行代词比作形式宾语，而把真实宾语置于宾语补足语之后。
采用这样的结构表达，能使句子达到平衡的效果。
He has not made it clear whether I am to go or not. 他还没有说清楚我是否应该去。
They consider it a great compliment that the President should visit them. 他们认为总统去看望他们是莫大的荣幸。
We think it impossible that the meeting will be put off. 我们认为会议延期是不可能的。
但是，以 what 引导的从句可以直接放在宾语补足语之前，而不必用先行代词 it 作形式宾语。
She believe what he said to be true. 她相信他说的话是真的。
We found what we had learned to be useless. 我们发现我们以前学的东西没有用。

③ 宾语补足语的位置

通常，宾语补足语（Object Complement）位于宾语之后，即使宾语带有较长的定语时也是这样，尤其在较严谨的科技英语中。
We regard anything which takes up space and has weight as matter. 我们把任何占有空间和具有重量的东西都看作物质。

为了使宾语和宾语补足语更接近，可以把宾语的定语移到宾语补足语之后，或把宾语补足语提到宾语之前。如上一句就可以改为：

We regard anything as matter *which takes up space and has weight*.

We regard as matter anything *which takes up space and has weight*.

例句1中 anything 的定语从句被宾语补足语 as matter 所分隔；例句2把宾语补足语提前后，虽句子结构不算错，但念起来似乎不怎么通顺。因此，在实际使用中还是少用为妙。

A．宾语是 wh-词引导的从句时，宾语置后。

We should not consider impossible *what is really possible*. 我们不应该把真正可能的事情看作不可能。

You should make clear *which is correct, which is not correct*. 你应该说清楚哪一个对、哪一个不对。

B．宾语较长而宾语补语较短时，宾语置后。

We pronounced guilty *every one of the accused*. 我们宣布所有被告都有罪。

I have put in order all the books he has left. 我把他留下来的书都整理好了。

C．宾语补足语是疑问代词、连接代词、或被疑问限定词、连接限定词修饰时，宾语置后。

What did you name your daughter? 你给你女儿取了什么名字？

I don't care *what* she call me. 我不在乎她叫我什么。

What colour will you paint the window? 你把窗户漆成什么颜色？

I'd like to know *what colour* he is going to paint the window. 我想知道他打算把窗户漆成什么颜色。

D．在分裂句和感叹句中，宾语补足语受到强调时，宾语置后。

What a fool you would think me if I agreed to go. 如果我同意去，你会认为我多么傻啊。

It is *yellow* that they have painted the walls. 他们把墙漆成了黄色。

E．在其他情况下强调宾语补足语时，宾语置后。

"Old Fox" I call him. 我叫他"老狐狸"。

In a blur, *rushing at her*, she saw a white face, a club upraised, and heard heavy footfalls behind him. 在朦胧中，她看见一个白人朝他冲过来，手里拿着一根木棒，还听见他身后沉重的脚步声。

F．有些动词加复合宾语结构，由于省去宾语或颠倒词序，已经转化成了短语动词。

He didn't *see* (it) *fit* to adopt my suggestion. 他认为采纳我的建议不合适。

Rose *made* (herself) *bold* to ask her father for a gold watch. 罗丝冒昧地叫他父亲给他买只金手表。

We have *heard* (someone) *say* you've got married and moved to New York. 我们听说你已经结婚并搬迁到了纽约。

Celia will never *let slip* such a golden opportunity. 西莉亚绝不会放过这种好机会。（= Celia will never let such a golden opportunity slip.）

④ **复合宾语与其他结构的区别**

有些结构外部形式即表层结构相同，但内部关系即深层结构不同。比较下列结构，注意它们之间的区别：

A．动词＋宾语＋名词(短语)

She made him a good husband. 她使他成了好丈夫。（复合宾语 = She caused him to become a good husband.）

She made him a good wife. 她成了他的好妻子。（间接宾语 + 直接宾语 = She became a good wife for him.）

Note：有时，同一个句子具有不同的内部关系，表示不同的意思，如

They call John a porter. 这句子可有三个层面的意思：

a. 作"复合宾语"型，= They consider John a porter. 他们认为约翰是搬运工。

b. 作"间接宾语+直接宾语"型，= They call porter for John. 他们为约翰喊来一个搬运工。
c. 作"宾语+同位语"型，= They call John, (who was) a porter. 他们叫约翰，一个搬运工。（书写时通常用逗号隔开，说话时稍有停顿）

B. 动词+宾语+形容词(短语)

We found him one-handed. 我们发现他只有一只手。（动词+复合宾语 = We found that he was one-handed.）

They caught him red-handed. 他们当场抓住了他。（动词+宾语+状语 = They caught him when he was doing something wrong.）

She ran the shop single-handed. 她一个人经营那个商店。（双重谓语 = She ran the shop and he was single-handed；动词+宾语+状语 = Single-handed, she ran the shop.）

C. 动词+宾语+不定式(短语)

I asked him to help her. 我叫他帮助她。（动词+复合宾语，to help her 是宾语 him 发出的动作）

He promised me to help us. 他答应我要帮助我们。（动词+间接宾语+直接宾语，to help us 是主语 he 发出的动作）

I sent her to help him. 我派她去帮助他。（动词+宾语+状语，to help him 修饰 I sent him，表示目的）

D. 动词+宾语+v-ing 分词(短语)

I saw the girl crossing the street. 可分拆成下面两种结构：

复合宾语 = I saw that the girl was crossing the street. 我见那个女孩正在横穿街道。

宾语+定语 = I saw the girl who was crossing the street. 我看见那个正在横穿街道的女孩。

E. 动词+宾语+-ed 分词(短语)

句子 He got the picture mounted on a stout paper. 也可分拆成下面两种结构：

复合宾语 = He got someone to mount the picture on a stout paper. 他找人把那幅画裱糊在厚纸上了。

宾语+定语 = He got the picture which was mounted on a stout paper. 他买到了那幅裱糊在厚纸上的画。

F. 动词+宾语+介词短语

I found some people in the garden. 可分拆成下面两种结构：

复合宾语 = I found that some people were in the garden. 我发现有些人在园子里。

宾语+状语 = In the garden I found some people. 我在园子里发现一些人。

I found the girl in blue. 可分拆成：

复合宾语 = I found that the girl was in blue. 我发现那姑娘穿着蓝衣服。

宾语+定语 = I found the girl who was in blue. 我找到了那个穿着蓝衣服的姑娘。

⑤ **动词+宾语+副词**

I found her there. 可分拆成：

复合宾语 = I found that she was there. 我发现她在那里。

宾语+状语 = There I found her. 我在那里找到了她。

从以上例子可以看出，复合宾语和其他结构的区别在于宾语和后面的词语是否是一个整体、它们之间是否存在逻辑上的主谓关系。如果是，就是复合宾语；如果不是，就不是复合宾语。

⑥ **动词+宾语+从句(宾语补足语)**

这是以从句作为宾语补足语，它具有宾语补足语的特征。特别要注意，宾语补足语从句不可用 that，而应以 what 引出。

You may call me what you like. 你愿意叫我什么就叫什么吧。

Her parents have made her what she is. 她双亲使她成为现在这个样子。

(7) SVC (主语 + 连系动词 + 表语)句型

这种句型含有"连系动词 + 表语"构成的复合谓语,主要说明主语的身份和性状特征,即说明主语是什么或怎么样。

① "主语 + 系动词 + 表语(补语)"句型的意义

A. 某人、某物是/成为……

Life without friend is death. 没有朋友的生活等于死亡。

Naturally he became chairman of the commission. 自然他就成了委员会的主席。

B. 某人/物在……/发生在

在表示存在意义时,"主 + 系 + 表"句型一般只用在主语为特指的句子中,如果主语是泛指,则用 there be 句型来表示存在。

It must be 10 years ago. 这事一定发生在 10 年前。

There are more ways to the wood than one. 车到山前必有路。

C. 用于完成体,意义为"去过,到过,来过"

She has only been there two or three times. 她只去过那里两三次。

Who has been here? 谁来过这里?

② "主语 + be + 表语"中的表语

系动词 be 后可跟名词、形容词、现在分词、过去分词、动名词(短语)、动词不定式(短语)、介词短语、代词、数词、副词和从句作表语。

A. 名词(短语)作表语

Beijing is China's greatest political, scientific and cultural center. 北京是中国最大的政治、科学和文化中心。

The railway station is no distance at all. 火车站一点也不远。

B. 形容词作表语

He's sorry that you can't come. 你不能来他很遗憾。

It would be better for me to write to her. 我最好给她写封信。

C. 介词短语作表语

My memory is at fault. 我记错了。

Everything between us was at end. 我们之间的一切关系都结束了。

D. 代词作表语

You took that old man to be him/he. 你把那位老人当作他了。

You thought it was her/she. 你想那就是她。

E. 数词作表语

You are always the first to arrive and the last to leave. 你总是第一个到达、最后一个离开。

You were about six when you came here. 你来这里时大约 6 岁。

F. 副词作表语

Tom hasn't been up yet. 汤姆还没有起床。

The key you are looking for is here. 你找的钥匙在这儿。

G. 动词不定式、分词、动名词(短语)作表语

Tom's desire is to be a doctor. 汤姆的愿望是当个医生。

The situation is encouraging. 形势喜人。

Linda's work in the hospital is raising rabbits. 琳达在医院长里面的工作是养兔子。

H. 从句作表语

That is where you differ. 这正是你们的不同之处。

That's why they decided to put the meeting off. 那就是他们推迟会议的理由。

③ 主语 + 状态/行为系动词 + 表语

这类状态或行为概念的动词主要有 act, blow, break, burn, continue, die, hold, keep, lay, lie, live, marry, remain, rest, return, shame, sit, stand, stay, test 等,其后可跟形容词、过去分词、名词作表语。

The window blew open. 窗吹开了。

Your motives lay hidden. 你的动机不明。

He married young. 他结婚时很年轻。

Henry lived a hero and died a martyr. 亨利生为英雄,死为烈士。

④ 主语 + 表状态变化的系动词 + 表语

这类系动词主要有 become, break, burn, come, drop, fall, feel, grow, make, prove, run, turn, wear 等,其后常跟形容词、过去分词或名词作表语。

Mary became accustomed to her new work. 玛丽已习惯了新工作。

She went red with anger. 她气得满脸通红。

You have grown a good fighter. 你成长为一名优秀战士。

The stone steps have worn smooth. 石阶走得久变得光滑了。

⑤ 主语 + 表示感觉概念的系动词 + 表语

这类系动词表示人对外界事物特征或状态的感受,主要有 feel(表示感觉),ring/sound(表示听觉),smell(表示嗅觉),taste/eat(表示味觉)等,其后主要跟形容词或过去分词作表语。

Cotton feels soft but iron feels hard. 棉花摸起来很软,而铁很硬。

The flower smelt fresh and sweet. 这花发出清新的香气。

⑥ 主语 + appear/seem/look 系动词 + 表语

与视觉有关的系动词 appear, seem, look 后可跟形容词、过去分词、现在分词、名词、动词 不定式(短语)等作表语。

This appears to be the only exception to the grammar rule. 这一条似乎是语法规则的唯一例外。

She appeared unable to get out of her habit. 她似乎改不掉她的习惯。

You appeared quite touched at the words. 你似乎对那话十分感动。

He seems a nice boy. 他看来是个好男孩。

第 21 章　疑问句

21.1　疑问句概述

英语句子就其表达的意思上来讲有陈述句、疑问句、祈使句和感叹句。在使用频率上讲，陈述句居首，疑问句其次；但就其多变性和复杂性来说，疑问句又要居首了。疑问句除了表示疑问外，也可以表示"请求"、"看法"、"建议"、"赞叹"、"惊奇"、"责备"等意思。就其句法结构和交际功能来说，疑问句可分为一般疑问句(General Question)、特殊疑问句(Special Question)、选择择疑问句(Alternative Question)、附加疑问句(Tag Question)、陈述疑问句(Declarative Question)、回响疑问句(Echo Question)、修辞疑问句(Rhetorial question)等。

对于前四种疑问句，英语学习者也许并不陌生，因一般语法书上都有所阐述，然而那些阐述多数都过于简单；对于后三种疑问句，一般语法书上述及不多，还有像感叹疑问句(Exclamatory Question)、重叠疑问句(Reduplicative Question)推理疑问句(Ratioinative Question)等类疑问句在一般语语法书上很难见到。

21.2　一般疑问句

按照语言实际来讲，一般疑问句是用来询问一件事情或一个情况是否属实，其回答可用 yes/no 或者相当于 yes/no 的词语或以直接意思作答的疑问句。一般疑问句句尾用问号，朗读时多数情况下念升调(杨元兴，2007)。

（1）一般疑问句的语序

一般疑问句的语序是"功能词 + 主语 + 谓语（含表语）"，即"助动词/情态动词、动词 be 或 have（has）等开头 + 主语 + 主动词 + 其他成分"。

　　—Is Rose a teacher? 罗丝是个教师吗？
　　—Yes, she is. 是的，她是。
　　—No, she's not. 不，她不是。

　　—*Must* she be back before ten? 她十点前必须回来吗？
　　—No, she needn't. 不需要

　　—Is that Li Hua? 那是李华吗？
　　—He is Chen Ming. 他是陈明。

　　—*May* I leave now! 我可以走吗？
　　—No, you mustn't. 你不能走。

　　—Are they upstares? 他们在楼上吗？
　　—They are having a meeting in the dining hall. 他们在饭堂开会。

　　—Is she going to Nanjing tomorrow? 她打算明天去南京吗？
　　—Her elder sister is going there. 她姐姐要去那里。

{ —*Has* the boy been out of danger? 孩子脱离了危险吗?
 —Not yet. 还没呢。

{ —*Are* they doing their homework now? 他们现在在做作业吗?
 —They've finished. 他们已经做完了。

{ —*Won't* you go and see the film? 你不去看电影吗?
 —I think I will. 是呀,我想要去的。

(2) 含情态动词的一般疑问句

① 含情态动词一般疑问句的结构

这种句子一般也是将有关的情态动词提前至句首,但有的可以借用助词 do/does/did,有时也有否定形式的一般疑问句。

Can you drive a car? 你会开车吗?(这句话的意思是"你有没有能力开车",即 Do you know how to drive a car? 或 Have you learned how to drive a car?)

Can/Could I borrow your umbrella (please)? (请问)我能借用你的雨伞吗?(这句不表示"能力",而是征求对方的"许可")

May I go out? 我可以出去吗?

Dare you do it? 你敢做这事吗?

Do you *dare* (to) do it? (译文同上)

Used her father live in Beijing? 她父亲以前住在北京吗?

Did her father use to live in Beijing? (译文同上)

② 不同的情态动词表达不同的意义

这些不同的意义是指这些情态动词本身的不同意义。

A. 一般情况下,用情态动词放置句首,表达其本身意义。

Can you run 1,500 metres in five minutes? (= Are you able to run … ? 或 Are you capable of running 1,500 metres in 5 minutes?) 你能在五分钟内跑1500米吗?(此句表示天生的能力)

Can the boy find his way home? 那男孩找得到回家的路吗?(此句表示某一具体的能力)

B. 如果在表示迫切想要得到肯定答复的请求时的那种特殊情况下,可用 can't 或 couldn't 代替 can 或 could。

Can't/Couldn't you look after my children till this afternoon? (请问)你可不可以把我的小孩照看到今天下午吗?

Do you think I *might* use your mobile phone? 你看我可以用一下你的移动电话吗?(表示很客气的请求)

{ —*Must* I be quiet? 我必须安静吗?
 —Yes, you must. /No, you needn't. 是的。/不必要。

{ —Does she *dare* (to) tell you? 她敢告诉你吗?
 —She doesn't dare (to) tell you. 她不敢告诉你。

③ 注意某些含特殊情态动词的一般疑问句的结构

像含 had better, have (got) to, ought to, used to 等情态动词短语的一般疑问句的构成形式与一般的一般疑问句的形式有所不同。

I often get up at 5:30. *Do* you ever *have to* get up at at 5:30! 我经常在5:30起床。你有不得不在5:30起床的时候吗?

Have they *to* finish the work this week? 他们必须在本周完成那工作吗?

Used they *to* live in London? 他们以前住在伦敦吗? *Did* they *use* to live in London? (译文同上)

Had I *better* start at once? 我是不是该马上开始?
Hadn't you *better* do the work with them, Tom? 你跟他们一起做那工作不是更好吗,汤姆?
Ought you *not* to see a doctor? 难道你不该去看医生吗?

(3) 一般疑问句中的否定词和肯定词的使用

一般疑问句中否定词和肯定词的使用情况有两种:当问话人吃不准答话人会作肯定或否定的回答时,句中就用否定词;当问话人认为答话人会用肯定意思作答,那就用肯定词。

① 当问话人吃不准答话人会作何种回答时

在问话人吃不准答话人会作何种回答时,问句中常用非肯定词(Non-assertive Word),如 any, anything, anybody, anyone, ever, yet, at all 等词。

Do you see *any* soldiers? 你看到士兵了吗?
Is there *anything* else to do? 有什么事情要做吗?
Do you have *any* questions to ask? 你有什么问题要问吗?
Can you see *anybody* on the top of the hill? 你能看到山顶上有什么人吗?
Have you finished your homework *yet*? 你回家作业做完了吗?
Does this kind of medicine work *at all*? 这种药管用吗?

② 问话人认为答话人会用肯定意思作答时

当问话人认为答话人会用肯定意思作答时,问句中常含 some, always, someone, already 等肯定词(Assertive Word)。

Do you have *some* information about our monitor? 你有关于我们班长的消息吗?(被问人是消息灵通人士)
Do they *always* do their work like that? 他们总是那样做事吗?
Have you *already* finished your homework? 你作业已经做完了吗?
Is there *something* important to tell me? 有重要事情告诉我吗?

(4) 一般疑问句的省略

在非正式英语中,特别是在口语中,一般疑问句常出现省略现象,句中的功能词(如 do, have, be, will)的省略很常见,在不影响句意的前提下,还有省略句中的其他词的情况。

① 省略功能词

在口语中,把一般疑问句的功能词省去的例子比比皆是。
Rose is lying in bed. (*Is*) She ill! 罗丝躺在床上。她病了吗?
(*Is*) Anything wrong? 出错了吗?
(*Have*) You finished your paper? 你的论文完成了吗?
(*Will*) He leave at once? 他马上要走吗?

上面例句 1、2 为现代英语句法研究称为无动词简单句(杨元兴,2007);例句 3 中,如 you 大写,那就是陈述句式疑问句;例句 4 只能是省略了功能词的一般疑问句,因 leave 后没"s"之故。

② 省去主语与功能词

为了简洁、省时,在口语中也有省去主语和功能词的。
(*Have you*) Ever been to London? 你去过伦敦吗?
(*Are you*) Looking for your glasses? 你在找眼镜吗?
(*Is there*) Anything I can do for you! 我能为你做点什么吗?
(*Are you*) Tired? 你累了吗?

例句 4 中的 tired 是省略了主语和功能词的独词句(杨元兴,2007)。

③ 仅保留主语和功能词

一般疑问句的省略也有只保留主语和功能词的情况。

I don't like swimming in winter. *Do you*? 我不喜欢在冬天游泳,你呢?
I want to have a cup of tea. *Don't you*? 我想喝杯茶。你也来一杯吗?
I have missed the lecture given by Professor Green. What a pity! 我没听到格林教授所做的那讲座,太可惜了!
—*Is it*? 是吗?

Note：这类一般疑问句的省略很容易与附加疑问句相混,如上面例句 1 和例句 2,初看起来像附加疑问句,前半部分肯定,简略问句用肯定形式;前半部分肯定,简略问句用否定形式。但要注意的是,在书写上,附加疑问句的后半部分前用的是逗号,也就是说附加疑问句前后两部分是一个整体,而例句 1、2 中的一般疑问句的省略部分与前面句子是两个独立句子,句子的开头都是大写,这就是省略的一般疑问句与附加疑问句最明显的区别。

④ 其他的省略形式

一般疑问句还有其他一些省略形式,如有的只保留下了状语、表语、主语、宾语等。

—What's your dog's name! 你的狗叫什么名字?
—Robert. 罗伯特。
—*Really*? My dog's name is Robert, too. 真的? 我的狗的名字也叫罗伯特。(此句仅保留了状语)

—Do you know my neighbour—Huang Fu robbed somebody again last night? 你知道我的邻居黄福昨晚又抢劫了吗?
—(Is it) *the man* (who is) *often in red*? 是那个常穿红衣服的那个人?
(此句保留的是分裂句中的被强调的主语及其省略了的定语从句中的表语)

—Do you often visit your maths' teacher? 你常用去看望你的数学老师吗?
—(Do you refer to) *Mr. White*? 你指的是怀特先生?
(此句中保留的是介词 to 的宾语,言外之意是我的数学老师有几个,问话者可能对 Mr. White 比较熟悉,所以答话者就问"(Do you refer to) *Mr. White*?"。

(5) 一般疑问句的答语

一般疑问句答语有很多形式,用 yes/no 开头作答的约有 5 种,不用 yes/no 开头回答的大致有 8 种。

① 5 种以 yes/no 开头的答语

用 yes/no 开头作答的形式大致有 5 种。就是以 yes/no 开头作答,yes/no 后也有多种表达形式。

A. 后跟简略的主谓结构

—Did you spend last weekend with Mr Millton? 你上个周末与密尔顿先生一起度过的吗?
—Yes, I did. 是的,我与他一起度过的。

B. 后跟完整的主谓结构

—Have you read the book—*The Story of Mankind*? 你看过《人类的故事》这本书吗?
—Yes, I have read the book—*The Story of Mankind*. 是的,我看过《人类的故事》。

C. 后跟反问

—Have you been to Harbin? 你去过哈尔滨吗?
—Yes, why? 去过,怎么啦?

D. 后跟补充说明

—Did you see Ms White in the park this morning? 你今天上午在公园里见到怀特女士了吗?

—No. She's gone to her daughter's. 没有。她去她女儿家了。

E．有时用 Yes,please. 或 No,not at all. 作答

{—Can I take a message? 我可以带个口信吗?
—Yes, please. 好的。

{—Would you mind if I open the window? 我开窗你介意吗?
—No, not at all. 不，一点也不(你开吧)。

② **不用 yes/no 作答的情况**

在日常口语中,不用 yes/no 开头作答一般疑问句的情况好像比用 yes/no 开头作答的情况要多一些。我们粗略归纳一下有如下 8 种:

A．为了加强语气或表达某种感情

有时为了加强答话者肯定或否定的语气,或表示某种感情,就不用 yes/no 作答。

—May I have a look at your new mobile? 我可以看看你的新手机吗?
—Sure! Here you are. 当然啦! 给你(看)!
—Do you love me, dear? 亲爱的,你爱我吗?
—Why, of course, Mary. 哎,当然啦,玛丽。

B．用 All right, Certainly, Of course, OK 等作答

如表示听话者乐意接受对方的请求、建议、劝告等时,常用 All right, Certainly, Of course, OK 等作答。

{—Will you take a walk with me after supper? 晚饭后与我一起去走走,好吗?
—OK. 行。

{—Will you go swimming with us tomorrow? 明天愿意与我们一起去游泳吗?
—Certainly. I'd be glad to. 当然,我很想去。

C．回答侧重于事实的陈述时

当答话人的回答侧重于事实的陈述时,就做直接回答。

{—Will you please turn off the radio? 请你关上收音机好吗?
—All right. 行。

{—Do you know why she didn't come to the party yesterday? 你知道她为什么昨天没来参加聚会?
—She went to Beijing on business. 他出差去北京了。

D．用 I'm sorry, I'm afraid not 作答

当听话者要婉言谢绝对方要求、建议时,可用 I'm sorry, I'm afraid not 作答。

{—Do you know whose hat it is? 你知道这是谁的帽子?
—Sorry, I don't know. 对不起,我不知道。

{—Can you type this article within twenty minutes? 你能在 20 分钟内把这篇文章打出来吗?
—I'm afraid not. 恐怕不行。

E．以"言外之意"的句子作答

这种答语表面上看是答非所问,但实际上却是"言外之意"的婉转答法。

—Do you know who broke my glass on the desk? 你是否知道谁打破了我桌子上的玻璃杯?
—I noticed little Tom and Rose playing in your study this morning. 我注意到今天上午小汤姆和罗丝在你书房玩的。(可能是那两个小家伙闯的祸)

F．含"责备"意思的一般疑问句不用 no 开头的言语作答

对含有"责备"意思的一般疑问句,常用带有说明或申述意思的言语,而不用以 no 开头的言语做否定回答。

{—Is it the article you wrote? Terrible! 那就是你写的文章？太差了！
—Oh well, I have tried my best, but … 哎，我已尽力了，但是……
(还没写好，怕的是我就这么点水平，实在对不起……)

{—Did you take two hours to get there by bus? 你坐公交车去那儿花了两个小时？
—Well, it wasn't that, but … 噢，不是那儿事，但是……

G. 用反问、重复作答
在听话者听到对方所提出问题感到惊奇、出乎意料时，用反问、重复作答。

{—May I listen to the music now, Mum? 妈妈，我现在可以听音乐吗？
—What? have you finished your composition? 什么(听音乐)？你的作文完成了吗？

{—Can you give me a key to the car? 能给我一把汽车钥匙吗？
—Key? 钥匙？(你要把汽车钥匙？我可不放心给你，让你去乱开，出了事怎么办？)

H. 以特殊疑问句作答
此种答话表示答话者想听听原问话人的意见、想法、建议等。

{—Are you playing computer games again? 你又在玩电脑游戏了？
—What else can I do next? I have finished my homework. 那接下来我能做什么呢？
(你说说看。)我已做完作业了。

{—Is this the picture you drew yesterday? 这是你昨天画的画？
—How is it? (这画)怎么样？
—Oh, beautiful. 喔，很漂亮。

(6) 一般疑问句的否定形式

① 一般疑问句的否定形式

一般疑问句的否定形式有三种：由"句首的动词、助动词或情态动词 + not 的缩略形式"构成，这主要用于主语较长的非正式文体中；不用缩略形式，这主要用于主语较长的正式语境中；动词、助动词或情态动词 + 一般疑问句的主语 + not，这也常用于正式文体中。

Isn't Robert watching TV in the living room? 罗伯特不是在起居室看电视吗？
Don't you know the fat man standing there? 你难道不认识站在那里的那个胖子吗？(你应该认识)
Are there not more than enough weapons of destruction on earth? 难道地球上毁灭性武器还不够多吗？
Was the fifteenth century not an age of great discoveries? 难道15世纪不是一个有重大发现的时代吗？
Did not a single student come to the lecture? 连一个学生都没有来听讲座吗？
Is not English a social science? 英语不是一门社会科学吗？

② 否定一般疑问句的作答

对于否定一般疑问句的作答要求大致有四种，这四种要求所表达的意思又各不相同。

A. 期望得到肯定的回答
期望得到肯定的回答的否定一般疑问句常表示提出疑问、试探性的建议、有礼貌的邀请、请求等意思。
Don't you have a cup of tea? 你不喝杯茶吗？(提出疑问)
Won't you help us? (= Please help us.) 帮我们一下好吗？(要求)
Don't you think we should bring umbrellas with us? 我们带上雨伞吧？(建议)

B. 不需要正面回答
表示"失望"、"艰难"、"恼怒"或"批评"意思的否定疑问句一般不需要正面回答。
Aren't you ashamed of yourself? (You ought to be ashamed of yourself.) 难道你不害羞吗？(表示失望)
Can't you stop talking? 你们不能不说话吗？(我听不见，表示批评)

Didn't I tell you not to do that again? 我不是告诉过你不要再做那事了吗？（表示恼怒或批评）

C. 不需要回答

表示强烈的感叹意义的否定一般疑问句相当于感叹句,而且在句尾用感叹号。只是此种句子是以"动词、助动词或情态动词 + n't + 主语"的结构出现,但不需要回答。

Isn't it a lovely night! 多美的夜晚啊！

Isn't it the marvel of our age, the computer! 电子计算机,我们时代的奇迹啊！

Wasn't it a marvelous concert! 那场音乐会多么美妙啊！

D. 对陈述句作答

否定一般疑问句有时可以表示同意刚才别人说的话（陈述句）,也就是对陈述句作答,此表示回话人与说话人有同感。

{ —Mr. Li has been very successful. 李先生非常成功。
  —Yes, *hasn't he*? 是的,非常成功。

{ —Their performance in Capital Theatre was outstanding. 他们在首都新剧院的演出十分出众。
  —Yes, wasn't it? 可不是吗？

Note：要是答语用 Yes, wasn't it?（可不是吗？）,这表示说话人也去看演出的,他同意上文说话人的意见。要是听话者说 Was it? 那表示说话人没有去观看演出,因此就不必表示出意见。

21.3 特殊疑问句

对句中特殊成分提出疑问的句子叫特殊疑问句。特殊疑问句一般都是以一个疑问代词或疑问副词开头,再加上一般疑问句的语序；除了疑问词直接作主语或主语的定语的句子外,一般都用倒装语序；句末用问号,朗读时通常用降调。特殊疑问句中的疑问词不仅起着引导特殊疑问句的作用,而且在句中还充当一定的句子成分。

What happened last night? 昨晚发生了什么事？（主语）

Whose glasses are broken? 谁的眼镜破了？（主语的定语）

Whose watch is this? 这是谁的表？（表语的定语）

What would you like for supper, Mr. Zhang? 张先生,晚饭你想吃点什么？（宾语）

Who do you write the letter to? 你写信给谁？（介词的宾语）

What's your name? 你的名字叫什么？（表语）

Which university do you study in? 你在哪一所大学读书？（介宾的定语）

What kind of books do you want to read? 你想看什么样的书？（宾语的定语）

How much money do you spend a month? 你每月花多少钱？（主语的定语）

Which way did you go last night? 昨晚你走的哪条路？（状语的定语）

（1）特殊疑问句的疑问词

特殊疑问句的疑问词有：疑问代词,如 who, whom, what, which；疑问形容词,如 which, what, whose；疑问副词,如 where, when, why, how。因为特殊疑问句的那些疑问词,除 how 外,都是以 wh-开头的疑问词中,所以特殊疑问句又叫"wh-"疑问句。

（2）含有两个以上疑问词的特殊疑问句

在实际的语言表达中,特殊疑问句往往会同时出现两个以上的疑问词问及不同的内容。

① 询问句子中两个或两个以上的成分时

如要询问句子中两个或两个以上的成分时,一个疑问句中就可能会有两个或多个疑问词,此时作主语用的疑问词要放在句首,其他的可置后,甚至置于句末。

Who said *what* to the old woman? 谁对那个老太说了什么?

Where and *when* did you put your mobile phone? 你在什么地方、什么时候把你的手机搁下了?

Who sent *what* to *whom*? 谁寄给谁什么东西?

Who said *what* to *whom*? 谁对谁说了什么?

Where have you hidden *what*? 你在什么地方藏了什么?

② 两个疑问词放置句首的排列问题

一般情况下只用一个疑问词放在句首,但如对状语提问,那两个疑问词可并列置于句首,其顺序按习惯排列,有时也可采用把一个疑问词置于句后。

Where and when/When and where shall we meet you this afternoon? 今天下午我们在什么地方、什么时候(什么时候什么地方)与你碰头?

Where did you meet the first time, and when? 你们第一次在什么地方见的面,什么时候?

(3) 疑问词 what,why,how 的用法

① 以 what 开头的特殊疑问句中,what 问的是内容。

A. what 作主语时所问的意思是"什么事情"。

—*What* caused the damage? 什么造成了损坏?

—Typhoon. 是台风(造成的)

B. 用 what 问句子的谓语时,问的是"做什么"的意思。

—What is he doing now? 他现在在做什么?

—He is typing an article for me. 他在给我打篇文章。

C. 用 what 提问句子的宾语时,what 表示"什么事物"。

—What is he holding? 他拿着什么?

—He is holding a bag. 他拿着一只包。

D. 用 what 作表语时,问"人名"、"物名"。

{ —What's your name? 你叫什么名字?
  —My name is Chen Zaina. 我的名字叫陈在娜。

{ —What's that (called) in English? 那个用英语怎么说?
  —It is (called) peach (in English). 用英语说叫桃子。

E. 用 what 询问职业、国籍、数字计算、号码等有关的情况。

{ —What's your mother? (= What does your mother do?) 你母亲干什么工作?
  —She is an engineer. 她是个工程师。

{ —What nationality is Peter? 皮特是哪国人?
  —He's English. 他是英国人。

{ —What is twelve and twelve? 12 加 12 是多少?
  —Twenty-four.

{ —What's her telephone number? 她的电话号码是多少?
  —One three one one five one zero zero nine eight nine. (她的电话号码是)13115100989。

F. 询问描述人或事物的价格、尺度等时,其句型常是 What colour/size/age/length/width/depth/height/price/weight … ?

{ —What color is her coat? 她的外套是什么颜色?
  —It's yellow. 是黄色。

{—What price is the hat? 那帽子多少钱？
 —It's ￥68. 人民币 68 元。

G. 用 what 提问人或事物的特征、天气、原因等。

a. What ... like 是用来询问人或事物的外貌或特征，也可以用来问天气、气候等。

{—What does her son look like? 她儿子长得怎么样？（问人的外表、长相）
 —He is tall and handsome. 他个子高，而且也很帅。

{—What is Ms White like? 怀特女士这人怎么样？（问人的性格特征）
 —She is modern and beautiful. 她时髦、漂亮。

b. （进一步）问及人或事物的性质、特征方面的确切情况，就用 What kind/sort of ...。

{—What sort of (a) woman is his elder sisiter? 他姐姐是种什么样的人？
 —She is a quiet, serious, young woman. 她是个文静、严肃的年轻女人。

{—What kind of (an) English book do you want to buy? 你想买一本什么样的英语书？
 —I want to buy an English book on English sentence patterns. 我想买本关于英语句型方面的书。

c. What if ... ? What though ...? 特殊疑问句在现代英语研究中被称之为无动词主句。

What if she is ill? 如果她病了，那会怎么样？

What though it's raining? 下雨又有什么关系？

上面例句 1 中的 What 是 What will happen/What would be the result 的省略，而 if ... 是条件句；例句 2 是一句含有让步状语从句的特殊疑问句，句中的 What 无动词主句是 What does it matter 的缩略，后面的 though ... 要变成 if it is raining，这是形式上的条件句、实际上的让步句。

② 以 Why ...? 开头的特殊疑问句

以 Why ...? 开头的特殊疑问句多数用作询问原因，也可询问其他一些内容。

A. 问原因时，答语常用 because。

{—Why does she speak so low? 她干吗说话这么轻？
 —Because her throat is sore. 因为她的喉咙疼。

{—Why does Peter often come late for school? 皮特干吗上学总是迟到？
 —Because he has a sick grandfather to look after. 因为他有一个生病的祖父要照料。

B. 有时 Why ...? 可问目的，也可问原因。

询问目的时，答语可直接用带 to 的动词不定式作答，此时动词不定式就是表示目的；询问原因时，仍用 because ... 回答。

—Why did he buy so cheap clothes? 他干吗买如此便宜的衣服？

—To save money./Because he wanted to save money. 为了省钱。／因为他想省钱。

C. 用"Why not ＋不带 to 的动词不定式"表达两种意思。

a. 表示提出建议、劝告或赞同

Why not let me go out to play? 为什么不让我出去玩呢？

{—Let's go out to eat at noon. 我们中午出去吃饭吧。
 —Yes, why not? (why not = why not go out to eat) 好的，为什么不呢？

{—Are you really going to lend him so much money? 你真的打算借那么多钱给他吗？
 —Yes, why not. He is short of money to run his firm. (why not = why not cend him monoy?)
  是的，为什么不呢？他缺资金经营他的公司。

b. 表示"不值得费力去……"或"我认为不应该……"

Why stand up if we have benches to sit on? 如果我们有凳子坐，干吗要站着呢？

Why pay more (money) at other shops? We have the cheapest good clothes in town. 为什么到别的商店去多

花钱呢？全城数本店的衣服价廉物美。

D. Why don't / doesn't … ? 以现在时表示将来或过去不久的事情。

Why don't you see your mother tomorrow? 你明天去看看你母亲好不好啊？

Why doesn't her brother go with her father? 她弟弟怎么没跟她父亲们一起去呢？

E. Why don't you …? 表示的意思在听话者没有遵照建议去做时，常用这种句型来表示"邀请"、"建议"、"指导"，"含有批评或不耐烦的劝告"或"含有命令意味的询问"。

Why don't you paint the windows yourself? 你为什么不自己漆窗呢？（劝告）

Why don't you go and see the doctor? 你为什么不去看医生？（劝告）

Why don't you buy a new dictionary for her? 你为什么不给她买本新词典？（建议）

Why don't you telephone me? 你为什么不打电话给我呢？（批评,你该打电话告诉我）

F. 表示我或我们主动提供帮助的方法时，可用 Why don't I …? 或 Why don't we …? 句型。

Why don't I go there to help them? I know how to operate the new machine. 我去帮助他们如何？我知道如何操作这部新机器。

Why don't we go out to eat for a change? 我们为什么不出去吃一次饭换换口味呢？

Why don't we open the window to let in some fresh air? 我们为什么不打开窗子让新鲜空气进来呢？

③ 以 how 开头的特殊疑问句

以 how 引出的特殊疑问句表达的意思很多，它们可用来询问目前（健康）状况、方式、过程等；how 也可与其他一些词合起表达另外的一些意思。

A. how 与某些情态动词组成疑问句。

How 可跟一些情态动词组成疑问句,表示"责备"、"气愤"、"感叹"等。

How can you say such an unkind thing? 你怎么能说这么不客气的话呢？（气愤）

How could you copy my composition? 你怎么能抄我的作文？（感叹）

How dare he say such a thing to his father? 他怎么敢对他父亲说这样的事？（责备）

B. 用 how 询问目前情况。

以 how 开头,对形容词或副词进行提问,用于询问目前情况。

{ —How is your mother? 你母亲可好？
—She's very well, thank you. 她很好,谢谢。

{ —How are you? 你好吗？
—Fine, thank you, and you? 我很好,谢谢,你呢？

(Mr. Lu Ming's handwriting is *terrible*. 陆明先生的书法糟糕透顶。)

{ —How is Mr. Lu Ming's handwriting? 陆明的书法怎么样？
—Terrible. (And his moral quality is more …). 很糟。(他的人品更……)

{ —How are they traveling? 他们怎么去旅游的？
—By train. 乘火车。

{ —How did you finish the job so soon? 你怎么能这么快就干完了？
—With the help of my elder sister. 我姐姐帮忙一起干的。

C. 用 "how+某些形容词或副词" 句型表示年龄、程度等。

用 how + adj. /adv. …? 句型可表示年龄、程度、时间、距离等。

{ —How old is your daughter? 你女儿多大？
—Eighteen. (她)18 岁。

{ —How wide is the street? 这街多宽？
—It's 50 metres. 50 米宽。

{—How well do you know her? 你对她了解如何？
{—Not very well. 不怎么深。

{—How long will it take us to get there by train? 我们乘火车要多长时间才能到那里？
{—One and a half hours. 一个半小时。

{—How far away does he live? 他住的地方离这儿多远？
{—About five miles. 大约五英里。

D. 如何问体积、价格、程度等。

用 How much …? 句型问不可数物质名词的数量或液体的体积、价格、程度等；how much 也可问数学运算结果。

{—How much salt did you put in the soup? 你在汤里放了多少盐？
{—Half a spoon. 半汤匙。

{—How much time did Yang Yuanxin spend on the book *21st Century's Four-Purpose Guide to English Phrasal Verbs*? 杨元兴写那本《21世纪英语短语动词四用指南》花了多长时间？
{—Five years! It was published by Nanjing University Press in 2008.
  5年！它于2008年由南京大学出版社出版。

Note：how many times 与 how much time 不能相混，前者是"多少次"的意思。

{—How much does he love her? 他爱她爱得如何？
{—He loves her deeply. 他深深地爱着她。

{—How much rent did you pay for the house every month? 你以前每个月付多少房租？
{—Two thousand five hundred and fifty yuan. 我们每月付2550元人民币。

{—How much is twenty times five? 20 乘 5 是多少？
{—Twenty times five is one hundred. 20 乘 5 是 100。

E. how many 与复数名词连用，询问人或物的数目

{—How many students are there in your class? 你班有多少人？
{—There are forty-one in my class. 有四十一个。

F. How long/often/soon …？用来询问什么

a. How long …？问"持续多长时间"。

{—How long will your father stay in Shanghai next month? 下个月你父亲将在上海待多长时间？
{—About three weeks. 大约三个星期吧。

{—How long ago did your grandfather live? 你祖父生活在多久以前？
{—He lived sixty years ago. 他生活在六十年前。

b. How often …？问频度时间状语。

这些频度状语是 once a week/a month/year, evry day/week/month/year 和 sometimes 等。

{—How often do you go to see your grandparents? 你每隔多久去看望你祖父母？
{—Twice a month. 每月两次。

{—How often do you have a bath in winter? 你冬天多长时间洗一次澡？
{—Three times a week in winter. 冬天一周三次。

c. 用 How soon …？来对"in/within + 一段时间以后或以内"，或对 in a moment, in a short time, right away 进行提问；这些所说的时间是预期某事发生的速度快慢，也就是要多长时间……。

(Peter will leave for New York *in a moment*. 皮特一会儿就动身去纽约。)

How soon will Peter leave for New York? 皮特多久动身去纽约？

(Mr. Green will be back *in a month*. 格林先生一个月后回来。)

How soon will Mr. Green be back? 格林先生多久后回来？

G. How …? 用于日常交际语中
a. 表示问候
{—How is your father? 你父亲身体好吗?
 —He's fine, thank you. 他很好,谢谢。

b. 用于初次见面时的介绍
{—How do you do? 你好!
 —How do you do? 你好!

c. 用于表示建议、邀请
{—How about a cup of tea? 喝杯茶怎么样?(建议)
 —OK, that's fine. /That's a good idea. 好的。/真是个好主意。

{—How would you like to come and have supper tomorrow? 明天来吃晚饭行吗?(邀请)
 —Thank you. I'd like very much. 谢谢,我很愿意。(肯定)
 —I'm afraid I can't. /I'm sorry, I can't. 我恐怕来不了。/对不起,我不能来。(否定)

H. How come …? 用于口语中
How come …? 意思为"怎么会,……是怎么回事,为什么"。
How come he isn't here? 他为什么不在这里?
How come you don't come to our party? 你为什么不来参加我们的聚会?
How come you didn't call me last night? 昨晚你为什么没有给我打电话?

(4) 几组疑问词的用法

英语中有几组疑问词在实际使中不易区别,如表示选择含义时,什么情况下用 what,什么时候情况下用 which,如在表示数目时,如何确定用 which 还是 what 等。

① 表示选择时,who 与 which 的选择

这两个词的区别在于:which 具有选择的含义,而 who 有一定的广泛性。试比较:
Who would like to go shopping with me this afternoon? 谁愿意今天下午与我一起去购物?
Which (of you) would like to go shopping with me this afternoon? 你们中谁愿今天下午与我一起去购物?
上面例句 1 说明没有数量限制,愿意去的人都可去;例句 2 的意思是有一定的数量限制,你们中有哪几个愿意跟我一起去购物,但不要太多。

② 表示数目时,what 与 which 的选择
A. 在没有限制的数目中,用 what;在有限制的数目中选择时用 which (of)。
{—Which of the subjects do you like best? 哪一门课你最喜欢?
 —English, of course. 当然是英语。

{—What would you like to study in next year's English course? 明年的英语课你选学什么?
 —American literature. 美国文学。

B. 当 what 指人时,问何内容,此时只限于询问职业、职务、社会地位等方面的内容。
{—What's his wife? 他妻子干什么工作?
 —She's a nurse. 她是个护士。

{—Which is her husband among them?
 —The third one from left. 左边第三个。

{—Who's his son? 他儿子是谁?
 —He's Paul Jone, one of the most famous professors in Hong Kong University.
   他是保罗·琼斯,香港大学最有名的教授之一。

③ why 与 what ... for 的等同与否

当 why = what ... for 时的意思是"为什么",但 what ... for 有时意为"作什么用;有什么用途"。

—*Why* did he buy a book on English syntax? (= *What* did he buy a book *On English Syntax for*?)
　他为什么买了本《论英语句法》的书?
—Because he wanted to write an essay "*on the Change of English Syntax*".
　因为他想写一篇《论英语句法变化》的论文。

—What did you buy it for? 他买它干啥用?
—I bought it for building up my body. 我买它用来锻炼身体。

④ 主格 who 与宾格 whom 的使用

很明显,who 是主格,whom 是宾格,但有时 who = whom。

Who is going to meet our teacher at the station? 谁到车站接我们的老师?(理所当然用 who,因其在主语的位置,不用 whom)

Who(m) do you think we saw? 你以为我们见到了谁?(句中用 whom 是正规的用法,用 who 是口语用法)

Who(m) did you give your cellphone to? 你把手机给了谁?(理由同上句)

但 To whom did you give your cellphone 中的 whom 不可改为 who,因为它与介词 to 在一起,作 to 的宾语。

Who do you think he is? 你以为他是谁?(句中 who 是表语)

Note：明明听见有好些人在外边说话,发问时却用 Who is there?,而不用 Who are there。who 作宾语用是非正式英语。直接作介词宾语用时一定用 whom,但如介词留在句末,那句首用 who 或 whom 均可,如上例句 3,如作动词的宾语时也是这个道理,见例句 2。

⑤ what ... like 与 how ... 句的用法区别

what ... like 用于询问人天生的特征、容貌或长相,How ... 用于询问身体健康状况、对事物的评价等,但有时两者可交替使用,有时又有其他表达法。

A. what ... like 结构示例

—What is Alice like? 艾丽斯(她)人怎么样?
—She is very clever and pretty. 她很机灵、漂亮。

—How is your brother-in-law? 你姐夫身体怎么样?
—He is well. Thank you. 他身体很好。谢谢。

—How is the new book *English Sentence Patterns and Syntax* by Yang Yuanxin?
　杨元兴的那本新书《新编英语句型句法全解》怎么样?
—Excellent. It was published in 2012, and was reprinted in 2013.
　好极了。它于 2012 年出版,2013 年就重印了。

B. 何时 How ...? = What ... like?

用来询问个人反应时,How ...? 和 What ... like? 可以交换使用。

—How was the play? (= What was the play like?) 那本剧怎么样?(此句还可说成 Did you enjoy it or not?)

C. How ... 与 What ... like? 用来问天气

How is the weather today? (= What is the weather like today?) 今天天气怎么样?

Note：在表达"提议"、"征询"、"询问"时,可用 How about ...? 或 What about ...?。

How/What about hearing a concert this afternoon? 今天下午去听一场音乐会怎么样?

How/What about a drink? 喝点饮料如何?

(5) 复杂特殊疑问句

在日常会话中,常用一种以疑问词开头,其后有一个 do you think/believe/imagine/propose/reckon/

say/suppose 的插入句的疑问句,这就是复杂特殊疑问句。在这种句子中,疑问词同在简单特殊疑问句中一样,可以充当不同的句子成分。该句型可以用来征询对方对某事的看法、判断、意见或要求复述等。

Who do you think is the best salesperson this year? 你认为今年谁是最佳销售员?(主语)

What do you think she should do? 你认为她应该做点什么事?(宾语)

What did you say Tom's name was? 你说汤姆的名字是什么?(表语)

How fast would you say he ran? 你说他跑得有多么快?(状语)

Which way do you imagine Jane went? 你能想象出简走的哪一条路吗?(定语)

在询问第三者对某事的看法时,也可以用此结构。

When *does the letter say* Mary will start? 信中说玛丽什么时间动身了吗?

How long *did she say* she waited? 她说她等了多久吗?

(6) 省略型的特殊疑问句

与一般疑问句一样,特殊疑问句也有省略的情况。省略型的特殊疑问句(Elliptical Patterns of Special Questions)在日常交际会话中出现得很多。

① 省略型的特殊疑问句的类型和表义

这类省略型特殊疑问句有时仅是单个疑问词,有时是"疑问词 + 修饰成分",有时是"介词 + 疑问词",有时是"疑问词 + 介词",有时是"疑问词 + 不定式",有时又是"陈述句 + 疑问词"。这些省略的使用主要要求对方重复或简要说明、澄清、进一步解释等。这些特殊疑问句省略句多数是无动词句。

{—He's off to Nanjing. 他要到南京去?
—When? 什么时候?(单个疑问词)

{—Borrow a bike to go there. 借辆自行车去那儿。
—Whose? 借谁的?(单个疑问词)

{—There are several bottles of milk on the desk. 办公桌上有几瓶牛奶。
—How many bottles? 多少瓶?(疑问词 + 修饰词)

{—Frankly, I am a bit doubtful. 坦白地说,我有点怀疑。
—About what? 关于什么?(介词 + 疑问词)

{—I'm reading an interesting novel. 我在看一本有趣的小说。
—Who by? 谁写的?(疑问词 + 介词)

{—What to do next? 下一步该怎么办?(疑问词 + 带 to 的动词不定式)
—Why not swim with him? 为什么不跟他一起去游泳?(疑问词 why 后跟不带 to 的动词不定式)

{—My old friend, Professor Leech, came up to me and said …
我的老朋友,李奇教授,走过来跟我说……
—He said what? 他说了什么?(陈述句 + 疑问词)

② 以 what about, how about, what if 等引出的疑问句

它们表示询问、命令、建议等。

What about a glass of grape? 喝杯葡萄酒怎么样?

How about going for a walk after supper? 晚饭后去散步怎么样?

How about your family? Are they well? 你全家人怎么样?他们都好吗?

What if you have lunch with us? 你与我们一起吃饭怎么样?

What if it snows? (= What will happen if it snows?) 下雪的话怎么办?

What though the way is long? (= What does it matter if the way is long?) 路长又怎么样?

③ What about it?, What of it? 和 So what? 作答语用

此时是表示说话人对前面说话人所讲的内容有疑问。美语中用 How about that? 作答语表示听话者怀有"惊奇",并含有赞同或不以为然的意思。

{—It is said that Henry was arrested yesterday. 据说亨利昨天逮捕了。
—What about it? 你说的什么呀?(意思是"他怎么会被逮捕呢?")

{—He took a drink now and then. 他有时喝杯酒。
—So what? He is a man. 那又怎么样? 他是个男人。

{—Fred and Pam have just got married. 弗雷德和帕姆刚结婚。
—Well, how about that? 噢,那又怎么样呢?(不以为然?)

④ 省略型的特殊疑问句还常出现在一些习语和套语中

What else? 还有什么呢?
What next? 接下来怎么办?
Who else? 还有谁呢?
What matter? 有什么关系呢?

(7) 特殊疑问句的强调

特殊疑问句的强调就是加强特殊疑问句的语气。这种疑问句常用来表示"钦佩"、"惊奇"、"责备"、"愤慨"等意思。

① 疑问词 + 加强语气的副词 exactly, just, actually 等

这属于比较正规的用法。

{—Just who is "she" in your story? 你故事中的"她"是谁呀?
—My beloved girl-friend. 我亲爱的女友。

{—What exactly is she up to? 她究竟想干什呢?
—Who knows? 谁知道?

② 疑问词 + ever 型

不要误认为这种句型是 whatever, whichever 等的分离形式。这种结构可以作主语、宾语,也可以作状语,有时作答语用。

A. 作主语、宾语或状语

{—Who ever told you that Mr. Wu and his wife passed away last month?
  究竟是谁告诉你吴先生和他太太上个月去世了?(作主语)
—Their neighbours. 他们的邻居。

{—What (contents) ever did he write in the book?
  他在那本书里到底写了些什么(内容的章节)?(作宾语)
—Nothing. 什么也没写。

Where ever did you see him? 你到底在什么地方看见他的?(作状语)
How ever did Mr. White manage to get the book? 怀特先生到底怎么搞到那本书的?(作状语)

B. 用作答语

有时,"疑问词+ever"用于答语中。

{—I sent them a donation. 我给他们寄去了一笔捐款。
—What ever for! 究竟为什么要这样做呢?

③ 有时,重复 why, where, 其后常带 oh,可加强语气

Why, (oh) why did he do that? 为什么,(呵)他究竟什么干那事?

Where,(oh) where has she been? 哪里,(呵)她到底去过哪里?

④ 用"疑问词+介词+世界上独一无二的事物"表示强调

Where in the world did you find your purse? 你到底在哪里找到你的钱包的?

Who in heaven's name does he think he's doing? 他究竟想干什么?

像上例中的 in the world, in heaven's name 的"介词+世界上独一无二的事物"的词组还有:in hell, in nature, on earth, in (under, beneath) the sun, in (under) heaven, in heck 等。

⑤ 在正式场合,可用 It is ... that 结构组成特殊疑问句

这些疑问词可以充当主语、宾语或状语。

What is it that makes you headache often? 是什么使你经常头痛?（作主语）

Who was it that interviewed her? 到底是谁会见了她?（作主语）

Whom is it that the strong cold wind makes headache often? 究竟强冷风使谁经常头痛?（作宾语）

When was it that the Long March started? 长征是什么时候开始的?（作状语）

21.4 选择疑问句

当说话人提出两个或两个以上的方案,供听话者选择时,我们就要用选择疑问句(Alternative Question)。选择疑问句的最后两部分由 or 连接。朗读时,or 前用升调,or 后用降调。连词 or 连接的可以是状语、宾语、表语、谓语、分句等。选择问句的答语也比较灵活。

(1) 选择疑问句的形式

选择疑问句有两种形式:一种是一般疑问句形式,另一种是 wh-疑问句形式。

① 一般疑问句形式

一般疑问句类型的选择疑问句(Alternative Question with the Structure of General Question)实际上是由两个或两个以上的一般疑问句组成,只不过第二个起的一般疑问句用简略式。

A. 一般疑问句类型的选择疑问句的表达形式

a. 把选项全列出,其中只有一项是真实的。

—Is the pencil red, black or blue? 这支铅笔是红的、黑的还是蓝的?
—It's blue. 是蓝的

—Did Li Ming, Chen Ming or Chang Hua call me this morning?
 今晨是李明、陈明还是张华打电话给我的?
—Chen Ming, I suppose. 我想是陈明吧。

b. 肯定和否定形式的选择疑问句。

有时在一般疑问句后加 or ... 或 or not (...),也可组成选择疑问句。

Is she ready or isn't she ready? 她准备好了还是没有准备好?（两者必居其一）

Is she ready or is she not? (译文同上)

Is he ready or not? 他准备好了没有?

Is he coming or isn't he coming? 他来还是不来?

Is she or isn't she coming? (译文同上)

—Is she or not coming? (= Is she coming or isn't she coming?) 她打算不打算来呀?
—Yes, she is./No, she isn't. 她打算来。/她不打算来。

以上这种选择疑问句常表示带有不耐烦、急躁、催促等语气,它们可以用 Yes-No 开头的形式作答。但其他形式的选择疑问句是不可以用 Yes-No 开头的词语来回答的。

c. 无动词一般疑问句型

一般疑问句型的选择疑问句，有时还有以无动词句型的形式出现，它们是一种省略形式。

- 一项选择

Tea？/Coffee？/Milk？/Right？/Ready？/Now？ 茶？/咖啡？/牛奶？/对？/准备好了吗？/现在？/
上述的 Tea？… ＝Would you like tea？… 喝茶吧？……

- 二项选择

Milk or coffee？/True or false？/Yes or no？/牛奶还是咖啡？/正确还是错误？/是还是不是？

- 三项或多项选择

Today，tomorrow or the day after tomorrow？ 今天，明天，还是后天？
Pen，pencil，ball pen or crayon？ 自来水笔、铅笔、圆珠笔还是彩色铅笔？

- 下面是不重复主谓语等的并列无动词省略式。

Do you want a black and white film or colour？你要黑白胶卷还是彩色胶卷？

此句中 colour 的完整式是 Do you want a colour film，所以可以说 colour 是一句省略了主谓语、不定冠词 a 和宾语 film 的并列无动词句。

B．一般疑问句与一般疑问句型选择问句的区别

在语调上可以对一般疑问句和一般疑问句型选择择问句进行区别。如果句末用升调时就是一般疑问句，用降调时就是选择问句。

Will you go there this morning or this afternoon↗? 你今天上午去那儿还是下午去？（一般疑问句，因句末用的是升调）

Will you go there this morning or this afternoon↘? （译文同上。这是选择疑问句，因为句末用的是降调。）

② 特殊疑问句型的选择疑问句

除了疑问词作主语的特殊选择疑问句子外，特殊疑问句型的选择疑问句（Alternative Question with the Structure of Special Question）从结构上说是"特殊疑问句＋省略型的一般疑问句"句型，从意义上讲，or 连接的并列选项是疑问词的同位语。

{ —Who wants to go swimming this weekend, you or your younger brother？本周末谁想去游泳，你还是你弟弟？（疑问词作主语，you 和 your younger brother 是 who 的同位语）
—Both of us. 我们俩都去。

{ —Where are you supposed to spend your summer vacation, in Qingdao or in Dalian？你打算在哪儿度暑假，青岛还是大连？（疑问词加一般疑问句，in Qingdao 和 in Dalian 是 where 的同位语）
—In Qingdao. 青岛。

（2）选择疑问句中的 or 可以连接的成分

选择疑问句中 or 连接的句子成分可以是主语、谓语、状语、宾语、表语、分句等。

{ —Which is bigger, the sun or the earth？哪一个大些，太阳还是地球？（连接主语）
—The sun, of course. 当然是太阳。

{ —Shall we go home or stay here for the night？我们回家还是待在这里过夜？（连接谓语）
—We'd better go home. 我们最好回家。

{ —Is your father a teacher or an engineer？你父亲是老师还是工程师？（连接表语）
—An engineer. 是工程师。

{ —Is the delegation leaving today or tomorrow？代表团今天走还是明天走？（连接状语）
—Probably tomorrow. 可能明天。

{ —Do you want tea or coffee？你要茶还是咖啡？（连接宾语）
—Tea, please. 要茶。

Are you ready or aren't you ready? 你准备好了还是没有准备好？（连接分句）

21.5 附加疑问句

附加疑问句（Tag Question），传统语法书上称之为反意疑问句（Disjunctive Question）。

附加疑问句由两部分组成：第一部分是陈述句，第二部分是根据第一部分而来的简略短疑问句；如前面的陈述句是肯定形式，那简略问句是否定式，如陈述部分是否定式，那简略短问句是肯定式。一般来说附加疑问句是说话者提出情况和看法，问对方同意不同意，也就是表示"反意"的意思。要注意的是，附加疑问句并非完全遵循其结构原则和表达"反意"的意思，有时有些句子只是提出来一个事实，让听话人承认。从结构上来说，有的附加疑问句是以"同向"的方式出现的，这就是杨元兴先生在《英语句型大全》（上海外语教育出版社，2007）里称之为"同向附加疑问句"（The Same-way Tag Question），与此同时杨先生还提出了把原传统附加疑问句为"逆向附加疑问句"的观点。所谓的同向附加疑问句就是"陈述句部分肯定＋肯定形式的简略问句"和"陈述句部分否定＋否定形式的简略问句"两种；这种附加疑问句用来表达得出结论或者关注或有挑衅的意思。

（1）使用附加疑问句时的相关问题

在使用附加疑问句时，涉及很多问题，这些问题有些语法书提到过，有些压根儿没提，这使读者在实际使用时深感迷惑。

① 前后时态上的一致

附加疑问句前面陈述句部分的时态与后面简略问句部分的时态要保持一致，前部分是一般现在时，后部分也用一般现在时，前部分是过去时，后部分也用过去时，如此等等。

Robert is a good student, isn't he? 罗伯特是个好学生，是吗？

Everyone present made a wild rush for the door, didn't they? 在场的人都拼命向门口拥去，对吗？

That old woman wouldn't believe your words, would she? 那个老太不相信你的话，是吗？

Clare has finished her work, hasn't she? 克莱尔已完成了她的作业，是不是啊？

They are watching TV, aren't they? 他们在看电视，是不是？

She was watching TV at eight last night, wasn't she? 她昨晚八点在看电视，是吗？

② 汉英语答语意思的不同

回答附加疑问句时，肯定答语要用 yes 开头，否定则用 no 开头；但要注意，在"前半部分否定，简略问句肯定"的情况下，其答语的汉译与英语是不同的。

—His sister goes to school on foot, doesn't she? 他妹妹步行上学，是不是？
—Yes, she does. /No, she doesn't. 是的，她步行上学。/不，她不是步行上学。

—She didn't do her homework yesterday, did she? 她昨天没做家庭作业，是吗？
—Yes, she did. /—No, she didn't. 不，她做了。/是的，她没做。

③ 期待得到证实的简略问句

有时，附加疑问句可用 am I right/don't you think/is that so/OK 等之类的词语，表示期待得到证实。这时附加疑问句就不表示反意的意思。

She forgot to bring money with her again, am I right? 她又忘记带钱了，对不对？

We'll meet at the gate of Dahua Cinema at seven tonight, OK? 那么我们今晚七点在大华电影院门口见，好吗？

④ 附加疑问句的主语及其后面的简略问句中代词的指代

附加疑问句的主语及其后面的简略问句中代词指代情况复杂，初步统计了一下，可达 17 种。

A．普通的一致表达

如陈述句部分的主语是 I, you, he, she, it, we, they 时，那简略问句的主语与前面的主语保持一致。

Celia just managed to get there on time, didn't *she*? 西莉亚就是设法准时赶到了那里，是吗？

They are not interested in music, are *they*? 他们对音乐不感兴趣，是吗？

B．用 it 指代的情况

附加疑问句的主语一定要用与第一部分的主语相应的代词。但是，指示代词 this, that 作主语时，附加问句的主语要用 it 指代。

Rose and Tom went to visit Mr. Green, didn't *they*! 罗丝和汤姆去探望格林先生了，(他们)是不是？

Mr. White never works on Saturdays, does *she*? 怀特先生星期六从不上班，是吗？

These are not English dictionaries, are they? 这些不是英语词典，是不是？

This is your Maths teacher, isn't it? 这是你们的数学老师，对吗？

That's not correct, is it? 那不对，是吗？

C．当陈述部分的主语是 one 时的指代词

此时后面简略句的主语可用 you 或 he，也可以仍用 one，前者在美语中用得较多。

One can't be always young, can one/can you/can he? 人不可能一直年轻，对吗？

D．当陈述部分是 there be 形式的情况

此时后面简略问句根据 there be 变化。

There is a pencil on the desk, isn't there? 书桌上有支铅笔，不是吗？

There will not be anything to do this afternoon, will there? 今天下午没什么事要做，是吗？

There had been a tall building in front of the church, hadn't there? 以前教堂前有座高大楼，不是吗？

E．以 each of 作陈述句的主语的情况

此有两种情况：如强调个别时，简略问句的主语可用单数代词，如强调全体时，则用复数代词。但在 each 作陈述句的主语定语时，谓语动词一定要用单数，简略问句的主语也用单数。

Each of the girls has a red flag in her right hand, doesn't she/do they? 每个女学生右手拿着一面红旗，是不是？

Each of the children had an apple, didn't he/didn't they? 儿童们每人都有一个苹果，是吗？

Each students is in his/her school uniform, isn't he/she? 每个学生都穿着校服，不是吗？

F．用 every-, some-, any-, no- 等构成的复合不定人称代词作陈述部分的主语

此时，简略问句的主语用 they。但要注意，用 nobody 或 no one 作主语时可用 he 或 they。

Eveyone knows the news, don't they? 每个人(大家)都知道这件事，是吗？

Somebody used my computer yesterday, didn't they? 昨天有人用了我的电脑，是不是？

Nobody likes to stand in cold, do they/does he? 没人乐意站在寒风中，对吗？

No one answered the question, did he/did they? 没人答出这问题，对吗？

G．凡是用 some-, any-, every-, no- 等与 -thing 构成的复合不定代词作陈述部分的主语

此时，简略问句的主语要用 it。

Everything is all right, isn't it? 一切顺利，对吗？

Something had gone wrong with the machine, hadn't it? 机器出过毛病，是不是？

H．以 neither, either, none 等作陈述部分主语的情况

此时，简略问句部分的主语可用作 he 或 they。

Neither of my friends came to see me, did he/they? 我的两个朋友谁也没来看我，是不是？

Either will be satisfactory, won't he/won't they? 两个都会满意/合适，是吗？

None have/has arrived, have/has they/she (or he)? 一个都没有到，是不是？

I．以"none/some of＋名词或代词"的单数（或不可数）名词或复数名词作陈述部分的主语

此时，简略问句的主语分别用 it, they, you 或 we。

None of it is yours, is it? 这全不是你的，是吗？

None of the food is delicious, was it? 没有一个菜是可口的，是吗？

Some of the students are playing on the playground, aren't they? 一些学生在操场玩耍，是吗？

J. 陈述句部分的主语是动名词短语（或其词组）、不定式（短语）、从句时

它们的简略问句的主语都用 it；当然，以 it 为形式主语代替以上三种结构的，简略问句中的主语也用 it。

Swimming is the best sport in summer, isn't it? 游泳是夏天最好的运动，是吗？

To hear the matter with her own ears made her change her mind, didn't it? 亲耳听到那事后使她改变了主意，是不是？

That Dora couldn't answer the simple question surprised us all, did it? 多拉(她)竟回答不出这么简单的问题使我们大家吃惊，是不是？

It surprised us that their party won the selection, didn't it? 他们的党赢得了大选，这使我们大吃一惊，是不是？

K. 当陈述部分的主语是一个"名词＋介词短语"时

此种情况下后面不管带一个介词短语，还是几个，附加问句的主语用单数。

Bob, with Mary and Tom, often goes to the river near the People's Park, fishing, doesn't he? 鲍勃经常跟玛丽、汤姆一起到人民公园附近的河里去钓鱼，是吗？

She as well as the other students has learned how to intall this electric equipment, hasn't she? 她和其他学生一样，也学会了如何安装这种电气设备，是不是？

L. 陈述部分主语是"两个或两个以上的 each, no 或 many a＋单数名词"的词组时

此时，简略问句的主语用复数，其谓语也做相应变化。

Each boy and each girl was given a pen and some paper to have a dictation, didn't they? 男女学生均发了一支笔和一些纸进行听写，是不是？

No man and no woman is admitted to enter the hall, aren't they? 男女都不能进入大厅，是吗？

Many a ship has been wrecked on those rocks, haven't they? 很多船撞上那些岩石而毁坏，是不是？

M. 以"the＋形容词"表示一类人的短语作陈述句部分的主语时

此时，简略问句的主语用复数。

Only the rich had the right to speak at that time, didn't they? 那时只有有钱人才有权利说话，是吗？

N. 当陈述部分的主语后由连词 but, as well as, no less than 等连接两个或两个以上的主语时

此时，后面附加问句的主语应取用第一主语。

His father, but you and I knows the secret, doesn't he? 除了你和我，他的父亲知道这个秘密，是不是？

You, no less than Zhang Ming, Li Liang and Chen Na, are good students, aren't you? 你和张明、李良、陈娜一样，也是好学生，对吗？

O. 连词 not ... but, not ony ... but also, either ... or, neither ... nor, or, both ... and 连接陈述部分的主语时

此时，其主语的谓语动词采用靠近法；简略问句部分主语要应根据陈述部分的主语及句子的意思而定；一般常采用"意思上靠近'我'为中心"的方法定法，即，并列主语中有 I 的，简略问句主语用 we, 有 you 的，那就用 you, 只有 he, Tom, Mr. White, etc.（他、汤姆、怀特先生等）的，那简略问句的主语当然要用 they 了。

Not she but her younger brother is going to be sent for the doctor, aren't they? 不是她而是她弟弟要被派去请医生，是吗？

Not only you but also I am interested in music, aren't we? 不仅是你，而且是我也对音乐感兴趣，对吗？

Neither you nor he is right, are you? 你和他都没有对，是吗？

P. 当陈述句部分主语有 (a) few, (a) little 修饰时

此时简略问句的主语分别用复数和 it。

A few teachers will go to visit London, won't they? 有些老师要去游览伦敦,是吗?

Little has been done to stop polluting the city, has it? 几乎没有采取什么措施阻止污染这城市,是吗?

Q. 陈述部分是祈使句时

简略问句的主语可用 you 以外的其他不定代词。

Close the door, won't somebody? 谁去关门,好吗?

Turn down the TV set, will someone or other? 不管哪一个请把电视机关低一点,行吗?

Go and get me a piece of chalk, can one of you? 你们中谁给我拿支粉笔,好吗?

(2) 不变附加疑问句

附加疑问句中还有一种不变附加疑问句。这种附加疑问句的结构是:不管前面是肯定的陈述句还是否定的陈述句,后面简略问句却完全不变,而且一般都念升调。具体情况是这样的:

He {forgot to attend / didn't forget to attend} the lecture {isn't that true? / am I right? / don't you think/agree? / wouldn't you say?}

(3) 附加疑问句中简略问句里的动词

一般来说,除了时态一致外,简略问句的动词也要根据陈述部分的动词而定,但有时简略问句可以用不同的动词。

① **当 have 作"有"用时,后面简略问句的动词形式**

此时用 have 或 do 均可。但是,陈述部分的 have 作"有"的否定式时,那简略问句的动词与陈述部分保持一致。

Mrs. White has two children, hasn't she/doesn't she? 怀特太太有两个小孩,是吗?

Abe hasn't a lot of time to read many books about the subject, has he? 阿贝没有很多时间看这一课题方面的书,是吗?

Mrs. Obama doesn't have any money in her pocket, does she? 奥巴马太太口袋里没有钱,是吗?

② **在 have 不作"有"时,后面简略问句的动词形式**

此时一般用 do 的形式。

The boy had too much, didn't he? 这孩子吃得太多了,是吗?

Jim had a good time in the party last night, didn't he? 昨天晚会上吉姆玩很痛快,是吗?

③ **在陈述句部分有 had better 时,后面简略问句的动词形式**

此时用 had 或 should 的有关形式。

You had better copy down these sentences on the blackboard, hadn't/shouldn't you? 你最好把黑板上的句子抄下来,对吗?

We had better start at once, shouldn't/hadn't we? 我们最好马上动身,对吗?

④ **在陈述部分的情态动词表示推测时,后面简略问句的动词形式**

对现在情况推测时,简略问句动词要用第二动词的限定形式;在表示对过去情况的推测时,附加问句动词可以用第二动词的限定式,也可以用 do 的限定式。

There may be several children playing in the room, isn't there? 教室里也许有几个小孩在玩耍,是吗?

He must be joking, isn't he? 他一定在开玩笑,对吗?

His mother can't be a teacher, is she? 他的母亲不可能是教师,对吗?

Her head might have left for Shanghai, hasn't he/didn't he? 她的上司到上海去了,是吗?
You must have seen the film, haven't/didn't you? 你以前一定看过那部电影了,是吗?
显然,上面例句4、5所表达的意思是对过去情况的推测,因此简略问句用第二动词的限定式。

⑤ 情态动词 must 表示"必须"、"有必要"时,后面简略问句中的动词形式

此时可用 mustn't 或 needn't ;但当 must + be 表示对现在情况的推测时,简略问句不用 must,而要用 be 的相应形式。

We must study English well, mustn't/needn't we? 我们必须学好英语,对吗?
Charles must finish the work tonight, mustn't/needn't he? 查尔斯必须今晚把这工作完成,是吗?
It must be Mary, isn't it? 一定是玛丽,对吗?
Rose and Mary must be in the office, aren't they? 罗丝和玛丽一定在办公室,是吗?

⑥ 表示否定的推测,后面简略词句的动词形式

此时一般不用 mustn't 而要用 can't be,简略问句的动词仍用 can。

Tom can't be a teacher, can he? 汤姆不可能是个教师,对吗?

⑦ 在陈述句部分用表示禁止的 mustn't 时,后面简略词句的动词形式

简略问句动词要用 may,不能用 must。

You mustn't do such thing again, may you? 你不得再做这种事,不是吗?

⑧ 在"must + 现在完成体"表示对过去发生的情况的推测时,后面简略词句的动词形式

简略问句中的动词可根据情况分别用 did 或 has/have,难得也有用 mustn't 的, 其中包括"must + 现在完成进行体"。

You *must have lived* in Suzhou for a long time, *haven't* you? 你肯定在苏州住了很长时间了,不是吗?
Dora *must have attended* the meeting yesterday, *didn't* she? 多拉昨天一定参加了那个会议,是不是?
They *must have visited* the Great Wall, *mustn't* they? 他们一定游览过长城了,对不对?
Mary *must have been working* very hard, *mustn't* she? 玛丽肯定一直学习很努力,是吗?

⑨ 当陈述部分 must 表示向对方发出邀请或表示应该时,后面简略词句的动词形式

表示发出邀请时,简略问句的动词要用 will;当陈述部分的 must 表达"应该"时,简略问句该用 mustn't。

You *must* go to see me next week, *will* you? 你下周一定要来看我,好吗?
They *must* study hard, mustn't they? 你应该努力学习,是吗?

⑩ 在陈述部分有 need, dare 时,后面简略问句的动词形式

要是它们作实义动词用,那简略问句用 do 形式;要是它们是作情态动词用,那简略问句要用 need, dare;但在陈述部分是 needn't 时,简略问句用 need 或 must。

She *needs* money, *doesn't* she! 她需要钱,是吗?
He *dares* to insult her, *doesn't* he? 他竟敢侮辱她,是吗?
She *dare not* do it again, *dare* she? 她不敢这样做,对吗?
They *neednot* do it again, *need* they? 他们不必再做一次了,是吗?
We *needn't* do that, *must/need* we? 我们不必做那事,是吗?

⑪ 如陈述部分谓语是 would like to do … 或"would rather + 动词原形"时,后面简略问句的动词形式

此时简略问句用 wouldn't;陈述部分是"I'd/We'd like to do sth"时,简略问句也可用 shouldn't,这是因为"I'd/We'd like …"中的"'d"也可以是 should 的缩略形式。

You'd like to have apples, wouldn't you? 你想吃苹果,是吗?

Ada, she would rather read the text ten times than copy it five times, wouldn't she? 埃达，她宁愿把这课文念十遍也不愿抄五遍，是吗？

We'd like to start our work at once, shouldn't/wouldn't we? 我们马上开始工作，好吗？

上面例句 2 是一左移位句，原句子的主语 Ada 提前置句首，用逗号与新主语分开，新主语 she 指代前面的原主语，这样的目的是强调原主语，也表明了 Ada 是个女性。此种结构是近年来现代英语语言研究的新内容。

⑫ **在陈述部分是 ought to do sth 时，后面简略问句的动词形式**

此时简略问句可用 oughtn't（英国），也可用 shouldn't（美国）。

The naughty boy ought to be punished, oughtn't he? 那调皮鬼应当受到惩罚，不是吗？

We ought to go there, shouldn't we? 我们应当去那里，对吗？

⑬ **当陈述部分是 used to do sth 时，后面简略问句的动词形式**

此时简略问句用"didn't 或 usedn't 或 used + 主语 + not"。

His father used to work till 12:00 at night, use(d)n't/didn't he? 他父亲过去常在晚上工作到 12 点，是吗？

They used to play basketball together, used they not? 他们以前常在一起打篮球，是吗？

⑭ **当陈述部分的谓语 wish 是用来表示询问或征求对方意见时，后面简略问句的动词形式**

此时简略问句要用 may。

I wish to watch TV, may I? 我想看电视，可以吗？

（4）附加问句中的肯定与否定

一般来说，陈述句部分肯定，简略问句否定，陈述部分否定，简略问句部分肯定，但也有些特殊情况。

① **如陈述句部分有了否定词或半否定词，后面简略问句用肯定还是否定**

如陈述句部分有了像 hardly, seldom, never, no, not, rarely, few, little 等否定或半否定词时，简略问句就用肯定式。如否定词置于陈述部分的句末，简略问句还可以用否定式。

He *seldom* goes to the cinema, does he? 他难得看电影，是吗？

This kind of bird *rarely* builds nets in our garden, do they? 这种鸟很少在我们花园里筑巢，是吗？

Amy had *little* money in his pocket that day, did/had she? 埃米那天口袋里没什么钱，是吗？

He sees his grandparents *rarely*, doesn't he? 他很少看望他祖父母，是吗？

② **在陈述句部分的句首有否定意义的状语（短语）时，后面简略问句用肯定还是否定**

如状语不是否定句子，而且句子也没倒装，那简略问句还用否定式。

Not long ago, the Whites moved to Montreal, didn't they? 不久前怀特一家搬到了蒙特利尔，是不是？

Not surprisingly, Anna is on diet, isn't she? 不奇怪，安娜在减肥，不是吗？

③ **当陈述部分有 dis-, im-, in- il-, un-, ir-等否定前缀或否定后缀-less 等构成的派生词时，后面的简略问句用肯定还是否定**

因为它们虽在意义上讲是否定，但其结构还是肯定的，所以简略问句还要用否定式。

It's unfair, isn't it? 这不公平，是不是？

They dislike it, don't they? 他们不喜欢它，是吗？

He is helpless, isn't he? 他真无可救药，是不是？

④ **在 no one, none, nothing, nobody, neither 作陈述句主语时，后面的简略问句用肯定还是否定**

在陈述部分的主语是 no one, none, nothing, nobody, neither 等时，简略问句要用肯定式；但在上述词作宾语时，简略问句也可用否定式。

Nobody came to my study while I was out, did they? 我外出时没人来过我书房，是吗？

Neither of my classmates could answer the question, could they? 他们两位同班同学谁也不能回答这个问题,是吗?

She has nothing to do, does(n't) she? 她无事可做,是吗?

(5) 一些特别句型的附加疑问句

有时,一些特殊句型的附加疑问句会使我们犯糊涂,对它们要认真对待。

① I am …型陈述句后的简略问句

当陈述部分是 I am …时,简略问句有三种形式,即 aren't I(英国英语)、ain't I?(美国英语),有时也有用 am I not?。但陈述部分是 I'm not 时,简略问句当然用 am I?。

I'm late, aren't/ain't I? 我迟到了,是不是?

I'm your close friend, ain't/aren't I? 我是你要好的朋友,是吗?

I'm a prince, am I not? 我是一位王子呀,是吗?

I'm not an engineer, am I? 我不是个工程师,对不对?

② 祈使句型的附加疑问句

这类疑问句很多,用法也比较灵活,其后的附加疑问句也有其自身的特点。随着说话人所要表达的意思不同而要采用不同的形式。在祈使句后的简略问句可有:will you?, won't you?, can you?, can't you?, could you?, would you?, wouldn't you? 等。

A. 表示说话人"厌恶"或"不耐烦"时的简略问句

用 will/won't/can't you?,而且要念升调。

Stop talking, will/won't/can't you ↗? 别说话,行不行?

Shup up, can't you ↗? 别说了,行吗?

Be seated, will you ↗? 请坐,好不好?

B. 表示一般请求和礼貌请求时的简略问句

在表示一般的请求时,简略问句用 will/can you?;在表示比较客气的请求或表示礼貌一些时,简略问句就用 won't/could you? 例如:

Close the window, will/can you? 关窗,好不好?

Come here, would you? 来这儿,好吗?

Open the front door, won't/could you? 打开前门,好不好?

C. 表示建议或礼貌上的鼓励时的简略问句

此时用 will/won't you? 。

Be sure to get there on time, will you? 一定准时到达那里,好吗?

Sit in the armchair, won't you? 您请坐在扶手椅里,好吗?

D. Don't …, will you? 句型

否定祈使句 Don't …, will you? 句型用来表示要求或争取对方合作。表示此意时一般不用 won't you? 之类的其他形式。

Don't look out of the window, Miss Green, will you? 格林小姐,别看窗外,行吗?

Don't stand there, will/can you? 不要站在那里,行吗?

E. Somebody 作祈使句的主语时,后面简略问句的指代词

祈使句一般省略 you,但有时其主语可以是 somebody,此时的简略问句的主语可以用第二人称,也可用第三人称复数。

Somebody answesrs the call, will you/they? 谁去接一下电话,好吗?

F. 关于 Let ... 句型的简略问句的形式

这种句型常有" Let's ...；Let us ...；Let me ...；Let's not do sth"等形式。它们的简略问句形式也有多种。

a. Let's ... 句型

要注意的是，Let's ≠ Let us。Let's 句型包含听话者在内，意为"让我们……"，因此简略问句中的主语应是 we。它的简略问句是 shall we？或 shan't we？。

Let's go shopping after supper, shall/shan't we? 晚饭后我们去买东西，好吗？

Let's not play table tennis, shall/shan't we? 我们不要打乒乓了，好不好？

b. Let us ... 句型

请注意，Let us 不能缩写成 Let's。此句型是说话人要征得听话人允诺，或表达说话人的建议。它的简略问句一般是 will/won't you？。

Let us know your name, will/won't you? 告诉我们你的名字，好吗？

Let us go to the playground to play, will/won't you? 让我们到操场上去玩，好吗？

c. Let me ... 句型

像此种句型的简略问句可用 will you？也可用 may I？。

Let me help you (to) solve the matter, may I? 让我帮你解决这问题，好吗？

Let me help your son with his homework, will you? 让我来帮助你儿子做家庭作业，好吗？

Let me do the work, will you? 让我来干这工作，行吗？

d. Let him/her ... 句型

这种句型用于说话人征求对方(听话人)的意见，让第三者做什么事，因此简略问句一般用 will you，也可用 won't you？。

Let her enter the room, will/won't you? 让她进教室，好吗？

e. 否定形式的 Let's 祈使句后的简略问句

否定形式的 Let's 祈使句可以是 Let's not do sth ...或 Don't let's do sth ...（英国英语）及 Let's don't do sth(美国英语)。其简略问句可用 Ok？或 all right？。

Let's not go to the library, ok/all right! 咱们别去图书馆，好不好？

Let's don't listen to the music, all right! 咱们别听音乐了，行吗？

G. 当陈述部分的主语是"第一人称单复数＋心理活动的动词"时

这些心理活动的动词是 believe, expect, fancy, guess, imagine, suppose, think, etc. , 后再加 that 从句时，其简略问句的主谓语要与从句保持一致；当陈述部分的主语也是第一人称单复数，但心理活动的动词是否定式时，那就是俗称的否定转移，其后的简略问句的主谓语也要与从句一致，但要按照否定转移的意思那样用肯定式。

I think she will be back in half an hour, won't she? 我想她半小时后会回来，对吗？

We believe that all of the students in his class had passed the exam, hadn't they? 我们相信他班上所有的学生都通过了考试，对吗？

I don't believe Robert will pass the exam, will he? 我相信罗伯特不能通过考试，是吗？

We don't think Professor Jiang is a qualified teacher, is he? 我们认为蒋教授不是个合格教师，是不是？

H. 陈述句部分是复合句时，后面简略问句的一致问题

陈述句部分是复合句时，那后面的简略问句一般要与主句保持一致。但如果说话者的重点放在从句上，那简略问句也可与从句保持一致。

They wouldn't go there if it rained, would they? 如果下雨他们就不去那里了，对吗？

The guard will let me go in if I show him my pass, won't he? 如果向卫兵出示证件，他就会让我进去，对吗？

Robert told me that you were going to take a trip to London, weren't you? 罗伯特告诉我你要到伦敦去旅游，是吗？

I. 陈述部分是并列分句时，后面简略问句的一致问题

通常与邻近的保持一致；但在说话者把言语的重点放在前面一句上时，那简略问句的主谓语就与那句保持一致。

They kept singing songs, but *nobody* liked them, did *they*? 他们不停地唱着歌，但是没人喜欢(那些歌)，不是吗？

Rose is a good student, but she has some shortcoming, isn't *she*? 罗丝是个好学生，但她有些缺点，是吗？

J 陈述部分是省略句时，简略问句部分要补全省略的内容

Terrible weather we are having, isn't it? 我们碰上了坏天气，不是吗？

Speaking French, are they? 他们在讲法语，是吗？

(6) 感叹句后的附加问句

这种附加问句常用 be 现在时否定式，中文仍译成感叹句。

What a stupid fellow, isn't he? 多蠢的家伙啊！

How beautiful the painting is, isn't it? 这幅画多漂亮啊！

(7) 同向附加疑问句

所谓的附加疑问句的同向是与指传统的附加疑问句相对而言。我们把传统的附加疑问称为逆向附加疑问句(Conversing Tag-question)。同向附加疑问句就是"陈述部分肯定＋简略问句部分肯定"、"陈述部分否定＋简略问句否定"型的附加疑问句。这些附加疑问句不仅在结构上与传统的附加疑问句不同，而且它们所表达的意思也是不同的。

① "陈述部分肯定＋简略部分肯定"型

这种同向附加疑问句的陈述部分前面有时有 oh 或 so，表示说话人经过推断或者回忆对已经说过的情况做出结论，或用来表达训斥、讥讽、轻蔑、愤怒、惊奇等情绪，有时也可表达证实、认可之意。

You have made another serious mistake, have you? 你又犯了个严重错误，对吗？（表示训斥）

He's Ming Ming, is he? 想不到他就是明明。（表示惊奇）

So they're getting married, are they? 那么说，他们就要结婚了，是吗？（表示推断或要求证实）

② "陈述部分否定＋简略问句否定"型

这类附加疑问句虽然不多，但在语言实际中还是存在的。此类附加疑问句在表示挑衅时，含咄咄逼人那种感情色彩，有时表示不服气，有时也可表示猜测。

So she won't pay her bill, won't she? We'll see about that. 这么说她不会付账了，是不是？我们倒要看看。（表示挑衅）

This isn't the last bus, isn't it? 这不是最后一班车，是不是？（表示猜测）

I can't do that work well, can't I? 什么？我干不好那工作？（表示不服气）

③ "祈使句＋简略问句"型的同向附加疑问句

此类附加疑问句能表达多种意思，如"请求"、"建议"、"询问"、"厌恶"等。

Lend me a hand, will you? 帮我个忙，好吗？（表示"请求"）

Have a little more drink, will you? 再喝点(酒)吧，好吗？（表示"询问"）

Somebody answer the door, will you/they! 谁去开门，好吗？（表示"请求"）

Be quiet, will you? 别作声，行吗？（表示"厌恶"）

Let us know where you are going to spend your summer holiday, will you? 告诉我们你打算到哪儿去度暑

假,好吗?(表示"请求")
Let me help you with your Chinese, may I? 我来帮你补习中文,好吗?(表示"商量")
Let's go for a walk after supper, shall we? 晚饭后我们去散步,好吗?(表示说话人的"建议",包括听话人在内一起动作。后面简略问句不可用 will you? 或 may I?)
We have worked for three hours. Let's stop to have a rest, shall we? 我们已经工作了三个小时了;休息一下,好不好?(表示"商量")
Note:上面例句7、8中的简略问句也可用 shan't we?,但此已不属同向附加问句了。

(8) 陈述句+答语附加疑问句

在英语口语中,有一种很特别的附加疑问句表达形式:第一句是陈述句形式的问句,接下来是用附加疑问句作答语。

{—He's won $1,000. 他赢了1000美元。
—Has he? 真的?

{—They aren't moving to Nanjing. 他们不打算搬到南京去。
—Aren't they? 不打算搬吧?

21.6　陈述疑问句

陈述疑问句(Declarative Questions)表示说话人事先已倾向于他所需要的那种期望的回答,希望得到听话人的证实。它在结构上与陈述句一样,词序不用倒装,不同之处只是它的句末用问号,语调用升调。

He is the chief-editor of the English grammar book? 他是这本英语语法书的主编?(表示"惊讶";言外之意可能是此人英语水平平平、专业造诣浮浅、写作水平差劲,怎能担当起主编呢? 可能是个冒牌货,或顶替者! 也还有一种可能是……)
You are going to get married next month? 看来下个月你打算结婚了?(推断)
Henry has spoken to the teacher, of course. 亨利肯定对老师讲过了吗?(证实)
Then you think Mary would make a good teacher? 那么你认为玛丽会成为一个好老师?(询问)

21.7　回响疑问句

英语中的回响疑问句(Echo Question)主要用于口语中。人们在连续不断地交谈中,一方紧接着对方的话语提出反问,以此表示另一方对对方所讲的内容的怀疑、反驳,有时也表示没听清对方所说的话而要求重复等情态和意味之类的疑问句。由此,回响疑问句也叫重复或反问疑问句。

回响疑问句可分四类:重复对方的整个句子;衔接反问;重复对方句子中某部分;对对方句子中的某个词语提问。

(1) 重复对方的整个句子

说重复对方的整个句子,实际上有点不完全切合实际,因为听者重复对方的话语时要改变人称,另外,为了不显俗套,还可在所重复的句子前或后加上 Did you say, (Do) You say, 或 Do you mean, you mean 等话语,有时也有在重复的句中加上相关的词语,表示对对方话语意思的深化。

{—You have used my computer. 你用了我的电脑。
—I have used your computer? 我用了你的电脑?

{—Leave the light on. 让灯开着。
—You say leave the light on? 你说要把灯开着?

{ —It is a book—*A Complete Collection of English Sentence Patterns*. 这是一部《英语句型大全》的书。
　　　—It is a real complete collection of English sentence patterns? (It contains more than forty sentence patterns.) 这是一部真正的句型大全？（它包含了四十多种句型。）

(2) 衔接反问

　　衔接反问就是根据对方的话语，在意思上衔接起来进行反问。衔接反问常用倒装语序，读时用升调，如是特殊问句，那疑问词要重读。

　　{ —Mary is ill. 玛丽病了。
　　　—Is she (ill)? 是吗？

　　{ —Mr White was put into prison. 怀特先生坐牢了。
　　　—Really? Did he steal something again? 真的吗？他又偷东西了？

　　{ —She said she has seen his lost son yesterday. 她说她昨天看见了他丢失的儿子。
　　　—Whom did she see, his lost son? 她看见谁了，他丢失的儿子？

(3) 重复对方句子中的某部分

　　这个"部分"可以是一个词，也可以是一个词组。

　　{ —I bought a new bike. 我买了辆新自行车。
　　　—A new bike? 一辆自行车？

　　{ —I am going to skate this afternoon. 我今天下午要去溜冰。
　　　—To skate? 去溜冰？

　　{ —I don't know he has got the job. 我不知道他已有了工作？
　　　—You don't know? 你不知道？

(4) 对对方句子中的某个词语提问

　　这种提问相当于小学生平时所做的对画线部分提问。这种提问有时可能是特殊疑问句，有时仍是陈述句，只是被问部分用疑问词代替。

　　{ —It took him *four years* to write the book. 写那部书花了他四年时间。
　　　—*How long* did it take him to write the book? 他写那部书花了多长时间？

　　{ —His mother is *a doctor*. 他母亲是个医生。
　　　—*What* is his mother? 他母亲干什么工作？

　　{ —He told me *the good news*. 他告诉了我那个好消息。
　　　—He told you *what*? 他告诉了你什么？

21.8　修辞疑问句

　　修辞疑问句(Rhetorial Question)也是一种不表示疑问意思的疑问句；也就是说，其形式上是疑问句，但是用来表示特殊感情，起强调作用，或起暗示、祈使、感叹等的修辞作用。修辞疑问句可分为一般疑问句式和特殊疑问句式两种。

(1) 一般疑问句式修辞疑问句

　　一般疑问句式修辞疑问句表意特别，如以肯定形式表示，那就相当于强调的否定陈述句；如以否定形式出现的，那就是强调的肯定陈述句。这种疑问句语调常用升调，偶尔用降调。

　　Is that the reason for stopping doing your work? 难道这就是停下那工作的理由？(＝Surely that is not the reason for stopping doing your work. 那绝不是停下工作的原因。)

Do you have any right to put your own name to the article? 难道你有权利在这篇文章上署上你自己的名字吗？(= You have not any right to have put your name to the article. 你没有权利在这篇文章上署上你自己的名字。)

Isn't it silly to do such a thing? 做这样的事情不是太蠢了吗？(= It's really silly to do such a thing. 做这样的事情真是太蠢了。)

Haven't you got any information about the test in geography from Professor Green? 难道你没有从格林教授那里得到地理考试的消息？(= Surely you have got some information about the test in geography from Professor Green. 你一定从林教授那里得到了一些关于地理考试的消息。)

(2) 特殊疑问句式修辞疑问句

特殊疑问句式修辞疑问句的结构同特殊疑问句，其语调多数用降调，偶尔用升调，其句子形式也有肯定和否定两种，肯定形式的特殊疑问句修辞句表示否定意思，否定形式的特殊疑问句修辞句表示肯定意思。

Who can do it within half an hour? 谁能在半小时内做好这事？(= Nobody can do it within half an hour. 没人能在半小时内做好这事。)

{—What is Jane doing now in the study? 琼妮在书房间做什么？
—Why should I know? (= There's no reason why I should know) 我哪知道？

Who can't anwer this kind of question? (= Everyone can answer this kind of question.) 谁不能回答这样的问题？(谁都能回答这样的问题，意思是问题太简单了。)

How couldn't remember the day when we first met? (You certainly should remember the day …) 你怎能会不记得我们第一次见面的日子呢？(你一定记得我们第一次见面的日子的。)

第 22 章 祈使句

22.1 祈使句概述

祈使句(Imperative Sentence),即以动词的原形起首,用来表示命令、请求、恳求、要求、劝告、忠告、叮嘱、强调、警告、建议、号召、指示、邀请、准许、禁止、祝愿、诅咒等。祈使句的特征有三个:一是第一、第二人称主语是任选的,通常不表示出来,如果需要把主语表示出来,那要有一定条件的限制;二是谓语动词不带屈折词尾,也就是无时态标记;三是谓语动词(含动词 be 和 have)的否定式和强调式都不需要用助动词 do 或 does。

22.2 祈使句的主语

一般语法书上只讲祈使句的主语常是 you,其实祈使句的主语除了 you 外,还有第三人称不定代词、数量词、指示代词、带有定冠词的名词词组、不带定冠词的复数名词及专有名词等。

(1) 祈使句的主语 you 常被省略

多数情况下,祈使句的主语是听话人 you,但一般不表示出来。
Open the windows. 请(你)打开那些窗子。
Give the boy an orange. 请(你)给那男孩一个橘子。
Be sure to get to the station before ten o'clock. 请(你)务必十点钟到达车站。

(2) 祈使句主语要表示出来的条件

祈使句的主语在下列情况下可以或需要表达出来,这样做能使意思更清楚。

① 有几个人在场的情况下不省略

在有几个人在场的情况下,为了指明向谁提出请求或发命令,需要把主语表达出来。
You put the book away right now. 你马上把那本书放到一边去。
You and William do the cooking and I'll provide the wine. 你和威廉烧菜,我去备酒。
You make the dinner and John do the washing up. No? All right, then, John cook and you wash up. 你来做饭,约翰洗餐具。不行吗?那好吧,约翰来做饭,你洗餐具吧。

② 为避免歧义时不省略

当祈使句的主语为 you 以外的其他词时,主语需要表达出来,否则会引起歧义,试比较:
Someone lend me his coat. 谁把大衣借给我。
Lend me her coat. 请(你)把她的大衣借给我。

从上面两句的中译文可看出它们的意思不同。第一句中的 his 与主语 someone 同指一个人,起到互相照应的作用。第二句中的 her 是另外一个人,不回指主语 you。

祈使句的主语除 you 以外,还可以是:

A．第三人称不定代词、数量词或指示代词

Someone help me. 来个人帮帮忙。

Nobody move. 大家不要动。

Two of you fetch some water. 你们中去两个人打些水来。

A few of you stay behind to help me clear up. 你们中留下几个人帮我收拾一下。

Those near the front please wait until the others have left. 靠近前面的那些人待其他人走后再离开。

B．带有定冠词的名词词组、不带定冠词的复数名词或专有名词

The man with the list come up here. 拿着名单的那个人请到这里来。

The tallest of you stand at the back. 你们中个子最高的那个站到后面去。

Visitors please use the other entrance. 来访者请从另一个入口进来。

People with questions stay behind afterwards. 有问题的人随后留下来。

Joyce hold one end of the rope and Rance hold the other. 乔埃斯握住绳子的这端，兰斯握住另一端。

③ 为了加强语气时不省略

为加强语气，表示说话人不高兴、厌烦、轻蔑、鄙视等情绪，常要把主语表达出来。

You mind your own business! 你别管闲事！

You get out of here! 你给我滚出去！

{—I'll tell him if you don't stop it. 你再干，我就要告诉他了。
—OK, you tell him then—I don't care. 好啊，那你去告诉他，我无所谓。

{—I'm going to report you to the boss. 我要向老板汇报你的情况。
—You do that then—it doesn't bother me. 你汇报去吧，这对我无妨。

（3）祈使句主语与呼语的区别

祈使句的主语和呼语都表示向谁提出请求或发出指示。它们之间的区别在于：

① 主语与呼语在结构、语调、标点符号使用上均不同

祈使句的主语在句中是不可分割的部分，朗读时无须停顿，书写时不用逗号与其他成分隔开；呼语是一个独立的语法单位，它与句子的其他成分之间有语气停顿，书写时通常用逗号隔开。试比较：

You take that bench. 你坐那条长凳。（主语）

You, stand there. 你，站那边去。（呼语）

Girls go into the classroom, boys don't move yet. 女孩们进教室去，男孩们暂不要动。（主语）

Girls, go into the classroom; boys, don't move yet. 女孩们，进教室去；男孩们，暂不要动。（呼语）

当第三人称不定代词作主语时，其照应词应该与主语相呼应；不定代词（包括名词）作呼语时，它照应词不必与呼语相呼应。试比较：

Someone lend me his English dictionary. 谁把英语词典给我用一下。（主语）

Don't anyone forget his room number. 任何人不要忘记自己住的房间号。（主语）

John, don't forget her room number. 约翰，不要忘记她的房间号码。（呼语）

Darling, remember her umbrella. 亲爱的，别忘记她的雨伞。（呼语）

上面前两句中的 his 分别和 someone, anybody 照应，即指代主语的所有格。后两句的 her 不是 John 和 darling 的所有格照应词，指代它们的所有格应是 your。另外，呼语通常也可以置于句末，一般应用逗号隔开，有时也可以不用逗号隔开。

Answer the phone, someone. 去个人接电话。

Don't get yourself into trouble anybody. 大家不要自找麻烦。

Lend me your jacket one of you. 你们中谁把夹克衫借我穿穿。

很清楚,上面第一句中的 someone 为呼语。第二句中的 anybody 和第三句中的 one of you 虽然没有逗号和其他成分隔开,但还应看作呼语,因为指代它们的自身代词和所有格代词分别是 yourself 和 your。换句话说,这两句话的隐含主语是 you,相应的照应词当然是 yourself 和 your。

从上面的分析可见,祈使句的主语是句子不可分割的部分,句中的照应代词必须与它一致,而呼语是一个独立的语法单位,也叫独立成分(Independent Element)。句中的代词 his,him,himself 等不与它照应,不表示它们之间格的关系。例如,下面句子是错误的:Don't say a word about himself anybody. 应该改为:

Don't anybody say a word about himself. 关于自己的事,大家要只字不提。(主语)

Don't say a word about yourself(,)anybody. 诸位,关于自己的事,大家要只字不提。(呼语)

② someone 作主语及呼语时,在句中的位置不同

主语和呼语在一定情况下受到不同分布条件的限制:someone 可以位于句首,作祈使句的主语,但作呼语时却只能位于句末。

Someone answer the phone. 谁接一下电话。(主语)

Answer the phone, someone. 诸位,接一下电话。(呼语)

* Someone, answer the phone. (错误)

专有名词作呼语比作主语较为常见,特别是带有附加问句时,只能作呼语。试比较:

Li Na, bring the glasses in, will you? 李娜,请你把玻璃杯带进来,好吗?(呼语)

* Li Na bring the glasses in, will you? (错误)

相反,有些代词或名词词组又只能作主语,不能作呼语。试比较:

Nobody make a noise. (= Don't make a noise.) 大家不要吵闹了。(主语)

* Make a noise, nobody. (错误)

You and Fred go and fetch help. 你和弗雷德去找些帮手来。(主语)

* Go and fetch help, you and Fred. (错误)

Those children of yours keep out of my garden, or I'll send the dog on them. 你的那些小孩不要到我的花园里来,否则我要放狗咬他们。(主语)

* Keep out of my garden, those children of yours, or I'll send the dog on them. (错误)

有时呼语和主语可以同时出现在一个句子里。

Mary, you come to my office at ten. 玛丽,你10点钟到我的办公室来。

Tom, you turn the radio off. 汤姆,你去把收音机关掉。

(4) 带主语的祈使句需要倒装

在带有主语的简单祈使句中,如果谓语动词带有 away, back, in, off, out 等副词时,它们常可倒装,置于主语之前。

Off you go! 你滚吧!

Up you come! 你到这里来。

Back you go! 你回去吧!

Out you come! 你出来

Away you go! 你走开吧!

22.3 祈使句谓语动词的特点

(1) 祈使句谓语的动词用原形

祈使句的谓语动词只用原形,不受主语人称、数的限制,没有屈折变化,也不与助动词连用。在与陈述

句比较时,只有在主语为第三人称单数、谓语动词为 be 的情况下才明显地体现出来。试比较下列例句:

You go and John stay with me. 你,去吧;约翰,和我待在一起。(祈使句)
You go and John stays with me. 你去吧,约翰和我待在一起。(陈述句)
You be quiet. 你,安静下来。(祈使句)
You are quiet. 你很安静。(陈述句)
Don't be late. 不要迟到。(祈使句)
You aren't late. 你没有迟到。(陈述句)

在某些情况下,祈使句的谓语动词与陈述句、疑问句、虚拟句的谓语动词形式相同。这要从句子结构与所表达的意义去判断。

You come with me. 你,跟我来。(祈使句)
You look pale. 你脸色苍白。(陈述句)
Don't you tell him about that. 你,可别把那件事告诉他。(祈使句)
Why don't you tell him about that? 你干吗不告诉他那件事?(疑问句)
If you be quiet, you can stay here. 如果你安静的话,你可以呆在这儿。(虚拟句)
If you don't be quiet, I'll send you away. 如果你不安静,我就把你打发走。(陈述句否定强调式)

上面第1、2句所属的句子类型不言而喻。第3句为否定祈使句。第4句语言学家们的看法不一致:Huddlestone(1976)把它看作疑问祈使句(Interrogative Imperative),Quirk (1972)把它看作准祈使句(Quasi-imperative)。我们认为,从句子的使用目的来看,把它看作疑问句更为妥帖。第5句中的 be 用于推测条件句,是一种比较古老的虚拟式,在现代英语中可用陈述式代替。第6句的 be 与 don't 连用构成否定强调式。

(2)祈使句的谓语动词可用于进行体、完成体和被动语态

① 用于进行体

此时表示请求、指令马上行动或赋予感情色彩。
Be waiting on the corner at six. 请6点钟在拐角处等候。
Be working when she comes in—then she will be impressed. 她进来时你务必正在工作,这样会给她留下好印象。
Don't be messing about when the bell rings. 铃响时,可别还在荡来荡去。
Up! Be doing everywhere, the hour of crisis has really come. 起来,到处都要动起来,危机的时刻真的到来了。

② 用于完成体

此时表示要求听者在某一时间前完成某事。
Have done with it. 把它做完了吧。
Start the book and have finished it before you go to bed. 现在就开始读这本书,要求在睡觉前读完。
For heaven's sake, do have completed at least the first part by them, so you'll have something to show them. 务请到那时至少完成第一部分,这样你就有东西拿给他们看了。
Don't have tidied up before he comes, or you'll have nothing left to do when he leaves. 在他到来之前,可别把什么都整理好;否则,他走后你们就没有什么事可干了。

③ 用于被动语态

A. 用于行为被动语态和状态被动语态

祈使句用于行为被动语态多为否定式,表示被动;用于状态被动语态,含有主动意义。
Don't be deceived by his look. 可别为他的外表所欺骗。

Don't be made to look foolish. 不要被弄傻了。

Don't be bullied into signing. 不要受威胁而签字。

Don't be fooled by his mild manner. 不要因他态度温和而上当。

Be guided by what I say. 请按我的话去做。

Be seated. 请坐。

Be reassured. 请放心。

Be checked over by a doctor, then you'll be sure there's nothing wrong. 请让医师检查,你就会确信没有什么毛病。

Be elected chairman—that's the way to make sure your reforms are carried out. 愿你当选主席——这是确保你的改革得以进行的条件。

B. 用"get＋过去分词"构成祈使句的被动语态

在现代英语口语中,常用这种被动语态。

Got washed. 洗一洗吧。

Don't get worked up over such a trifle. 别因这点小事就如此激动。

Don't get caught in the storm. 不要让暴风雨淋着了。

Get prepared for your paper. 准备好写论文吧。

C. "Let…型"祈使句被动语态

Let me be heard. 听我说。

Let the prisoners be brought in. 把犯人带进来。

Let the study of Latin be dropped from our school, and the English of next generation will reach a level unknown heretofore. 如果让学校不再开设拉丁语,下一代英国人的拉丁语水平将从此不得而知了。

(3) 祈使句的谓语动词不能与情态动词连用

祈使句的谓语动词前不能加情态动词构成合成谓语,如不可以说 Can open the door。但是,祈使句的谓语动词可以置于一些含有情态意义的词组的后面,常用于以 and 连接的并列句的第一个分句。这个分句相当于一个条件状语从句。

Be able to speak Welsh and you get offered all kinds of jobs. 如果你会讲威尔士语,你就会有各种样的供职机会。

Have to leave early and you miss all the fun. 如果你必须早离开的话,你就会失去很多乐趣。

Be willing to discuss things frankly and you may find a solution. 如果你愿意坦率地讨论问题,你也许会找到解决的办法。

以上斜体部分均不可改为相应的情态动词 can, must, will 等。dare, need 只有作为实义动词时才能用于祈使句。

Dare to speak to her and you might be pleasantly surprised. 要是你敢对她说话,就会有惊喜的。

Need to leave early and you have to get special permission. 如果你需要早些儿离开,你就必须得到特别的允许。

22.4 祈使句与词汇意义的关系

(1) 静态动词和静态形容词不用于祈使句

英语中的一些动词、形容词,就其词汇意义来说,可以分为动态和静态两类。Quirk 等人(1972)认为,静态动词和静态形容词不用于进行时和祈使句。像下面的句子都是错误的:

* I'm knowing the language.
* I'm being tall.
* Know the language.
* Be tall.

（2）转化为动态动词的静态动词和转化为动态形容词的静态形容词可用于祈使句

Quirk 等人认为，许多不用于进行体的静态动词和静态形容词又可以解释为动态词而用于祈使句，如下面句子都是可以接受的（Quirk et. al. 1985）：

Forgive us. 请原谅我们。
Love your enemies. 爱你的敌人吧。
Owe nobody anything. 不要欠谁任何东西。
Be early. 请早一点。
Be glad that you are escaped without injury. 你安然逃脱，应该高兴。
Don't be a stranger. 别像陌生人似的。

从以上例句可以看出，一个动词或形容词（与 be 连用）能否用于祈使句，不在于它们是表示动作还是状态，而在于所表示的动作或状态是否可以被听话人理解为受到主观意识的支配。在下面这些例句中，前 4 句是不可以接受的，后 4 句又显得十分自然。

* Understand the answer.
* Want more money.
* Hope it rains.
* Be big.

Know the poem by Friday. 请在星期五前背熟这首诗。
Stop moaning and hope for the best. 不要唉声叹气，要持乐观态度。
Just understand this——I never meant to hurt you. 只要了解这一点就行——我从来都无意伤害你。
Be intelligent. 请明智一点。

前 3 句的动词不用于祈使句，是因为这些动词所表示的动作不受听话人主观意识的控制。我们不能请求、批示或说服别人做无法支配的事情。听话的人连题意也不理解，你就不能要求他知道这一问题的答案；他也许希望有更多的钱，但他并不能真的就能拥有；你可以希望下雨，可是你不能指望今天下雨。但是在一定的语境里，原来一些动词所表示的动作不受主观意识的支配，可以转变为受到主观意识的支配，后 3 例的谓语动词就属于这种情况。要求听话人"请在星期五以前背熟这首诗"、劝说别人"持乐观态度"、请求他"了解自己的意图"等都是听者的主观意识能支配的，因而这几个句子都是正确的。至于 big 和 intelligent，前者是一个具有相对稳定、持续状态比较长久的形容词，后者是一个表示心理状态的暂时性形容词。我们可以请求、指示或说服别人保持暂时的心理状态，但却不能用同样的方式要求他改变客观静止状态，因而 be intelligent 是正确的，而 be big 却是错误的。

（3）某些动态动词和动态形容词有时不用于祈使句

有些动词和形容词原来是具有动态意义的，由于受到语境的制约，也不能用于祈使句。例如，不说：

* Fall ill.
* Go mad.
* Be dull.

很显然，说话人不能请求或批示别人"生病"、"发疯"、"呆头呆脑"，这是违背别人的意愿的。值得注意的是，有些谓语动词在肯定的祈使句中是不可接受的，在否定祈使句中又可以接受。反过来，亦是如此。

* Feel disappointed.

Don't feel disappointed.
* Don't know what's going on around you.
Know what's going on around you.

要求别人"感到失望"是违背他人意愿的,忠告别人"不要感到失望"是理在其中。劝告别人"了解周围的情况"是一番好意,听者愉悦;而要他"不要了解周围的情况"就是要求作用于大脑的客观事实被涂抹掉,这是不可能的。

22.5 祈使句的强调式

祈使句的强调式(Emphatic Form of Imperative Sentence)主要用来加强语气,表示说话人的强烈请求、劝说、愿望等,一般不表示命令。祈使句的强调式由"助动词 do + 动词原形"构成。do 没有人称、数、时态的变化。

(1) 不带主语的强调式

这种情况"用"于主语为不必表示出来的 you,其强调形式是在动词前加上 do。
Do drive slowly. 车子千万要开慢些。
Do stay two hours, then you'll be able to catch a direct train home. 务必待两个小时,然后你就能够搭直达快车回家。
Do be careful all the time. 务必要时时小心。
Do be happier that she is here. 她在这里务必要高兴些。

要注意,作强调用的助动词 do 不用于两个并列的表示动作先后发生的祈使句。例如,下面两个句子是不可接受的:
* Do show him the way and come back.
* Do read a while and then go to bed.

但是,如果将 do 置于第二个分句之前,表示第一个动作完成后,强调第二个动作,又是可以接受的。我们可以将上面两句改写为:
Show him the way, and do come back. 给他指指路,随后一定要回来。
Read a while, and then do go to bed. 先读一会儿书,然后可要去睡觉。

两个并列的分句同时受到强调也很常见。
Do give my regards to Fred, and do try to see Angela. 千万代我向弗雷德致意,千万设法去看安吉拉。
Do write that letter, and do stay for dinner tonight. 一定要把那封信写好,也一定要留下来吃晚饭。

(2) 带主语的强调式

① 将 do 置于主语之前

这种情况多见于主语为第三人称单数不定式代词。
Do someone help him quickly. 务必快去找个人帮他的忙。
Do every body sit down. 大家务必请坐下。

一般说来,在单独的句子里,当主语为 you 时,由于某种原因它本身已有强调作用,即说话人已经指明向谁提出请求或发出指示,因此 do 不宜用在它的前面表示再次强调。例如,不说:
* Do you go out tonight.
* Do you sit down.
* Do you blow your horn when you see the enemy.

但是,"不定代词 + of you"作主语时,do 置于它的前面表示强调却又很常见。

Do all of you let me know your decisions. 你们中所有的人务必要让我知道你们的决定。

Do at least some of you have a try. 你们中至少一定要一些人去试一试。

在含有对比意义的上下文中,do 也可以置于 you 的前面,表示说话人对听话人(you)明确提出请求,以区别于其他人。这时句中常有 at least, at any rate 等状语。

Do at least you have a go, even if the others won't. 即使别人不愿意去,至少你一定要去。

I know there may not be time for everyone to examine the report, but do at any rate you have a look at it. 我知道可能没有时间让每个人都来审查这个报告了,但是无论如何你还得过过目。

在上下文已经清楚地表明 you 与其他人含有对比意义时,也可不用 at least, at any rate 等状语。这时 do 和 you 要重读。

I know I can't expect the rest of them to understand this, and wouldn't ask them to try. But do you be sympathetic, please—it's the support of people like you I really need. 我知道我不能指望其他人理解这一点,我也不要求他们设法理解。但是,请你千万予以同情——我的确需要像你这样人的支持。(E. Davies, 1986)

② 将 do 置于主语之后

这种情况不仅适用于主语为第三人称单数不定代词,也适用于主语为其他形式的名词短语。

Everybody do sit down. 请大家务必坐下。

Somebody do answer the telephone. 务必让一个人去接电话。

The boy in the corner do stop writing on the desk. 坐在角落的那个男孩千万不要再在书桌上写字。

Those with cars do bring them along. 有汽车的那些人务必把汽车开来。

前面两句的 do 置于这个位置上比置于主语前更为常见。后面两句由于句中的主语只是一个名词词组,强调的对象不必和其他人区别开来,因此 do 只宜放在主语和动词之间,而不能放在主语的前面。

Whoever's talking do shut up. 谁在谈话都要住嘴。

Passengers on international flights do ensure that all their documents are in order. 乘国际航班的旅客务必保证所有证件都要符合要求。

但是,如果上下文提及别人,说话人要表明向谁发出指令,则不宜用上述形式,而改用将 do 置于主语的前面。

I don't want you all to come, but do those with cars turn up. 我并不要你们都来,但是那些有汽车的人务必要到场。

I don't care what you do to those old desks in the front, but for heaven's aske, do the boy in the corner stop writing on the desk—that's a new one. 你们这些人把前面那些旧桌子弄成怎样我也不在乎。但是,坐在角落那个男孩务必不要再在书桌上写字——那是一张新的书桌啊。

22.6　祈使句的否定式

祈使句的否定式有三种:一是省略了主语否定式,二是带主语的否定式,三是其他形式的否定式。

(1) 省略了主语的祈使句的否定式

① 省略主语

在谓语动词的前面加上 don't(有时也用 do not)。

Don't tell him. 不要告诉他。

Don't stay too late, John. 约翰,可别待得太晚了。

Do not do that. 别再做那事了。

Don't be reckless. 不要粗心大意。

Don't be too dishonest, but don't be too truthful either. 不要太不诚实,也不要太诚实。

在古英语中,有时可用 do no 构成或只是在动词之后加 not。这否定式现在几乎不用,只是偶尔见于文学作品中。

Do no go. 不要去。(Onions, 1971)

Be not anxious for the morrow. 勿忧明日。

② 有时可用 never 代替 don't

这种形式具有更强烈的否定意义。

Never complain and never explain. 不要抱怨,也不要解释。

Never mind what I said yesterday. 千万不要介意我昨天说的话。

Never fear. 别怕。

③ 有时不加任何否定词

直接由含有否定意义的动词构成。

Stop being so silly. (=Don't be so silly.) 不要那样傻里傻气的。

Distrust him. (=Don't trust him.) 不要相信他。

Do have done with nonsense. 别胡闹了。

④ 以 have done 起首

这种结构相当于 stop (doing),有时表示"结束,停止"。

Have done scolding her! 不要再责备她了!

Have done running! 不要跑了!

(2) 带主语祈使句的否定式

① 这种句式通常将 don't 置于主语的前面

要注意,句号中的 don't 不能用 do not 代替。

Don't you tell him. 你可别告诉他。

Don't you ever do that again! 你可别再干那种事了!

Don't you go and tell him the secret. 你可不要告诉他这一秘密。

Don't anybody touch this wet paint. 谁也不要碰这未干的油漆。

但是下面两句祈使句否定句是错误的:

* Don't those with luggage leave it unattached.

* Don't anyone who has a radio use it for the next half hour.

Huddlestone (1971) 认为,这两句祈使句的否定式之所以错误在于它们的主语太长,且都有定语修饰,这样置于前面会头重脚轻。诚然,在多数情况下,祈使句的这种否定式主语都较短,但是 E. Davies (1986) 认为,主语的长短并不是判断 don't 能否置于主语前面的决定因素。

Most of you will be very welcome, but don't that boy over there with the long hair and dirty jeans dare to show his face there. 你们中大多数是非常受欢迎的,但是站在那边那个长头发穿着牛仔裤的男孩看他敢露面。

Don't the boy who whistled come; it's the one who sang I want to see. 那个吹口哨的男孩可别来;我要见的只是唱歌的那个。

从以上例句的对比中可以看出,E. Davies 的例句可以接受是因为上下文中存在着对比,发话人所指令的对象只是特定的人：that boy over there, the boy who ...，而不是在场的其他人：most of you, the one who ...。don't 位于主语之前，该分句就成了否定的中心，不只是否定动词所表示的行为，而且还强调了这一行为的特定执行者。Huddlestone 的例句不能接受，是因为句中的主语没有对比，说话人向谁发出指令不明确。虽然主语 those 带有定语 with luggage, anyone 带有定语 who has a radio，但仍然是泛指，"带有行李的那些人"和"有收音机的人"可以是在场的，也可以是不在场的。说话人到底向谁发出指令还是不明确。因此，主语如系泛指，即使在有对比的情况下，也不宜将 don't 置于主语的前面。下面两个句子均不正确：

* Don't non-members forget their tickets.
* Girls go into the hall, don't boys move.

但是下面两个句子又是可以接受的：

The girls can ran about as much as they like, but don't the boys move yet. 女孩们可以随意走动，可男孩们先别动。

It doesn't matter about the members, because we'll recognize them, but don't the non-members forget their tickets. 至于会员那是没有问题的，因为我们认识他们，但是非会员可别忘了带入场券。

② 带主语的祈使句的否定式有时也可将 don't 置于主语之后

这时，谓语动词之前，而且在主语为泛指的情况下也可以采用这种形式。例如前面举的那两个例子可以改写为：

Girls go into the hall, boys don't move. 女孩们请进大厅，男孩们不要动。

Non-members don't forget their tickets. 非会员们不要忘记带入场券。

但是有时 don't 置于主语和谓语动词之间与置于主语之前意思略有不同。试比较下面两对例句：

Don't one of you forget the money.

One of you don't forget the money.

Don't some of you talk to him.

Some of you don't talk to him.

上面各对句中的两个例句否定的范围不同。前一对例句中的第一句表示说话人要求在场的每个人都带钱来，任何人都不得忘记；第二句表示只要求在场中的一个人不要忘记把钱带来，其他的人不作要求。第二对中的前一句表示说话人怀疑在场的人中"可能已经与他谈论过"，因此他希望"不要有任何人与他交谈"；后一句则表明说话人只向其中一些人而不是全部提出"不要与他交谈"的要求。

(3) 除否定祈使句谓语动词外的其他否定形式

祈使句的否定式除了否定谓语动词外，也可以否定其他成分。

Tell him not to forget his duties. 告诉他不要忘记自己的职责。（否定不定式）

Ask no questions and you'll be told no lies. 如果你不提问，别人就不会向你撒谎。（否定宾语）

Try not to put on weight and so will I. 你要设法不要增加体重，我也设法这样。（否定动词不定式宾语）

Be there not at ten o'clock. 不要在 10 点钟到那里。（否定状语）

22.7 祈使句与状语

祈使句与状语连用的问题比较复杂。它的一条铁律是不可与表示过去的时间状语连用，也就是说状语的使用与祈使句的句子结构及所表达的语义内涵有关：一方面，它排斥某些状语，而另一方面又与一定的状语连用；另一方面，同一类状语也需视语境而定，在一些情况下可以使用，在另一些情况下又不能使用。

(1) 为何祈使句不与表示过去的时间状语连用

这是因为祈使句是表示说话人请求或指令别人马上或以后做某事,因此不与表示过去的时间状语连用。例如,不说:

* Come to see me yesterday.
* Open the door just now.

(2) 祈使句与其他状语连用情况

Quirk 等人(1985)认为,祈使句不与表示习惯的时间状语或频度的时间状语连用。例如,不说:

* Usually drive your car.

M. Frank (1972)认为,祈使句可以与频度时间状语连用。下面是他举的两个例子:

Always open that door slowly. 总要慢慢地开那门。

Don't ever open that window. 任何时候不要把那窗子打开。

我们认为,在没有上下文的情况下,祈使句一般不与频度时间状语连用,Quirk 所举的例子就属于这种情况。Frank 所举的两例中,前一句用了 always,同时又用 slowly,可以推知,听话人平时可能是砰的一声把门打开,因此说话人用 always 和 slowly 两个状语以便提醒他"开门时每次都要慢慢地打开"。第二句中的 ever 虽然是频度副词,但是只起加强语气的作用,因而是可以接受的。

(3) 祈使句与程度状语连用的情况

Lees (1964)认为,祈使句的谓语动词不能与程度状语连用。例如,下面几个句子都是错误的:

* $\begin{Bmatrix} \text{Hardly} \\ \text{Scarcely} \end{Bmatrix}$ touch your food.

* Almost be there at five.

但依 E. Davies (1986)的观点,在特定的上下文中,祈使句可以带程度状语。

Be very careful when you dust machinery—*scarcely* touch it. 掸机器上的灰尘时要非常小心——几乎不要碰着它。

I want you to whisper very softly. That's right, *hardly* make a sound. 我要求你们低声耳语。对了,几乎不要发出声音。

Bend over as far as you can, and *almost* touch the ground with the palms of your hands. 要尽量地把腰弯下,差不多要让手掌着地。

后面 3 句之所以可以带程度状语,是因为带有那些状语的部分所表达的意义跟前面部分趋于一致,即前部分是前提,后部分对前部分做补充说明,更加确切地表明说话人的行为。

(4) 评注性状语在祈使句中的使用与否

表示命令的祈使句一般不与评注性状语连用。例如,不说:

* Unfortunately, pay your rent now. (Quirk et. al., 1985)
* Frankly, come down from there this instance. (E. Davies, 1986)

但在表示劝告的祈使句里,评注性状语可以使用。在这里可以把它看作一个独立的语言单位,表示说话人的态度和看法。

Frankly, be glad that we are coming. 坦率地说,你应该为我们到来而感到高兴。

Seriously, do give the matter some thought. 严肃地说,你务必考虑这件事。(Davies, 1986)

(5) 祈使句可以与某些方式状语连用的情况

祈使句可以与某些方式状语连用,此时的方式状语也在句首,但与后面不用逗号分开。

Quickly run and fetch some help. 快去请人来帮忙。
Kindly tell me your address. 请把你的地址告诉我吧。
Carefully remove the lid. 小心地把盖子打开。
Simply shut up and get on with your work. 别讲啦,继续工作吧。

22.8 祈使句的表达形式

(1) 一般表达形式

祈使句的一般表达形式除了用动词的原形外,其意思上主要用来表示请求、邀请、命令、警告、叮嘱、批示、规劝、强调、轻蔑、鄙视等。

Do please leave him alone. 请让他独处吧。(请求)
Spare a penny, sir, for a starving man. 先生,请省一便士给饥饿的人吧。(恳求)
Come inside and meet my father. 请进屋里见见我的父亲吧。(邀请)
Go and fetch me some chalk. 去给我拿些粉笔来。(命令)
Take plenty of exercise if you want to stay slim. 你要保持苗条,就得多做些运动。(忠告)
To obtain attention ring twice. 要引起注意,就得按两次铃。(忠告)
Watch out for the dog! 当心那只狗。(警告)
{—Where can I find Mr. Smith? 我在哪儿可以找到史密斯先生呢?
 —I'm not sure. Try his office or ring up his house.
  我说不准,你试试给他的办公室挂个电话,或者把电话打到他家里吧。(建议)
{—I'm going to report you. 我要告发你。
 —OK, report me then. 好呀,去告吧。(鄙视)
{—I'll tell Father if you don't stop that. 你再不停止,我就去告诉父亲了。
 —Go and tell her then. I don't care. 去告诉她吧,我不在乎。(轻蔑)
Catch me gambling. (= I never gamble.) 我绝不赌博了。(强调)
Come if you want, but I'm not telling you what I want you to do. 你想来就来吧,但我不会告诉我要你来干什么事。(允许)

(2) 特殊表达形式

祈使句的特殊表达形式是指不像上面所说的那种形式,而且在意思上表示祝愿、目的、让步、条件等意思,而这种意义体现在具体的句子中。

① 祝愿形式祈使句

英语中有表示祝愿形式的句子表示祈使意思。
Have a lovely day. 祝今天愉快!
Sleep well. 祝睡个好觉!
Get well soon. 祝早日康复!
Enjoy yourself and come back quite well again. 祝你玩得愉快,回来时身体健康。

② 目的性祈使句

通常用 and 连接两个并列的谓语动词,后一个动作动词表示前一个动词的目的,相当于一个动词不定式。

Go and ask him when he'll be back. (= Go to ask him when he'll be back.) 去问他什么时候回来。
Come and help him to lift these boxes. (= Come to help him to lift these boxes.) 过来帮他抬起这些箱子。
Write and ask him when he is coming. (Write to ask him when he is coming.) 写信问问他打算什么时候来。
像上述 ask, help 之类的动作动词还有很多,如 come, fetch, go, have, send, thank, write 等。

③ **让步性祈使句**

所谓的表示让步意义的祈使句是说那些祈使句可以解释成让步状语从句。这样的句型有下面几种。

A. 祈使句＋不用连接词连接的分句

这时的祈使句可以解释为一个由 even if 引导的让步状语从句,而分句就是主句。
Offer us five thousand for it (= Even if you offer us five thousand for it), we still won't sell. 即使你出价 5000 元,我们也不卖。
Tell me a hundred times (= Even if you tell me a hundred times), I won't believe it. 即使你告诉我 100 次,我也不会相信。

Note:像上面的那种句子也有含有让步意义否定形式。
Don't invite him, he'll still turn up. (= Even if you don't invite him, he'll still turn up.) 即使你不请他,他也会到场。

B. 含有 wh- 从句的祈使句＋不用连接词连接的分句

此时的祈使句可以解释为"no matter + wh-"或"wh- + ever"引导的让步从句,而后面的分句就是主句。
Come whenever you will (= No matter when you come), you are welcome. 不管你什么时候来,都受欢迎。
Everyone say what they like (= No matter what everyone likes to say), we won't change our minds. 不管大家说什么,我们都不会改变主意。
One of you offer to take me there by taxi (= No matter which one of you takes me by taxi), I won't go. 不管你们中谁用出租车送我,我也不愿去那儿。

Note:从上述那些例句中可以看出,含有让步意义的祈使句的主语应为第二人称(常省略)或第三人称单数不定代词,谓语动词为原形,否则不应看作祈使句。下面这些句子虽然也以原形动词开头,也表示让步意义,但都不宜看作祈使句,而是将动词置于连接词前面的倒装让步状语从句。
Come what may, we shall not give up. 不管发生什么事,我们也绝不让步。
Detest him as we may, we must acknowledge his greatness. 虽然我们憎恨他,我们也不得不承认他是伟大的。
Be that as it may, the problem still remains. 尽管这样,问题仍然存在。

事实上,这些句子动词并不是动词原形,而是主动词置前的倒装让步状语从句。因此,句中的谓语动词并不是原形,主语也不是可以省略的 you。再比较下面几个含有让步意义的祈使句和让步状语从句:
(You) Offer me a thousand dollars for it, I still … 即使你出价 1 000 美元,我也不(卖)……
(You) Say what you will, I'll get to finish the work. 不管你说什么,我都要把这工作做完。
﹡(You) Try though you may, you won't …
﹡(You) Detest him as we may, we must …

很显然,可以补加 you 的是含有让步意义的祈使句,见上面例句 1、2。不可以补加进 you 的只是让步状语从句,而不是祈使句,如上面例句 3、4。

④ **条件性祈使句**

条件性祈使句是以祈使句的形式表示条件句的内容。条件性祈使句的结构有下面三种:

A. 用 and 连接两个并列分句

这时,第一句为祈使句,第二句为陈述句。and 的前面通常有逗号,有时可以没有。第一个分句在意义上相当于一个条件状语从句。

第22章 祈使句

Work hard, and you'll pass the final examinations. (= If you work hard, you'll …) 努力学习,你就能通过期终考试。

Give in to her, and you'll never have your way again. (= If you give in to her, you'll never have …) 如果你对她让步,你就再也不能按照自己的意志行事。

Don't buy now and you'll miss the bargain of the year. (= If you do not buy now, you'll…) 如果你现在不买,你就错过一年一度的减价机会。

One more step, and you'll be a dead man. (= If you go one more step, you'll…) 再往前走一步,你就没命了。

B. 用 or 连接两个并列分句

这时,前一句为祈使句,后一句为陈述句。从表达的意思上来说,如果祈使句是肯定的,那条件意思是否定的;如果祈使句是否定的,那条件意思是肯定的。

Do it quickly or you'll be punished. (= If you don't do it, you'll …) 快做吧,不然你要受到处罚的。

Stop doing that or I'll call the police. (= If you do not stop doing that, I …) 如果你不住手,我就叫警察了。

Don't take too long in dressing or you'll be late for the party. (= If you take too long in dressing, you'll be late …) 如果你花太多时间化妆打扮,你参加晚会就会迟到了。

Notes: a. 有时,在省去第二个并列分句的主语后,句子含义与不省去主语相同。

Give me liberty or give me death. 不自由,毋宁死。

Say something sensible or be quiet. 要么讲些有理智的话,要么保持沉默。

b. E. Davies (1986)指出,有时省去主语与不省主语含义就不同。试比较:

Stay away from there or you'll get blown to pieces. 快离开那儿,否则你就会被炸得粉身碎骨。

Stay away from there or get blown to pieces. 你再不走,就把你炸得粉身碎骨。

从上面的两句中译文可见,第一句表示说话人对正在无意识向雷区走去的听者提出有礼貌的、善意的忠告;而第二句中说话人对听者的恐吓,带有敌意的、威胁性的口吻。

c. 大多数情况下,or 后面的陈述句不能改作省略主语的祈使句,如下面第二个句子是错误的:

Hurry up or you'll have to walk. 赶快,不然你就得走路了。

*Hurry up or have to walk.

C. 用 or else, otherwise 等连接

Hurry up *or else* you'll be late. 赶快,不然你就要迟到了。

Do what I say—*or else*! 按照我说的去做,否则!

Get up right now, *otherwise* you'll be late for the bus. 现在就起床,要不你就赶不上末班公共汽车了。

22.9 Let 祈使句

由 let 引起的祈使句是以第一人称代词单复数、第三人称代词或名词为祈使的对象,表示建议、请求等。在 let 引起的祈使句中,后面所接的人称(包括人称形式)不同,含义和用法也都不同,它们所构成的否定式也不尽相同,诸如此类的情况还较复杂。

(1) Let 祈使句的形式

① let's 和 let us

let's 是 let us 的缩略式,通常用在口语中。

Let's/Let us try again. 让我们再试吧。

Let's/Let us work hard. 我们努力工作吧。

Let's/Let us not say anything about it. 对于这件事我们什么也不要说。

但是 Let's 和 let us 在一定的上下文中是有区别的。它们的区别在于：

A．Let's 通常包括听话人在内

表示说话人建议听话人一道做某事。祈使句的隐含主语为 we。

Let's spend a day or two in the country. 咱们在乡下待一两天吧。

Let's have dinner. 咱们开饭吧。

Let's do the invitation right away. 我们马上发邀请吧。

Let's call him ourselves instead of sending B over. 咱们自己打电话叫他过来吧，用不着派 B 过去请。

Let's 的这一特点尤其突出地表现在附加问句的使用上。例如：

Let's go again, shall we? 我们再去吧，好不好？

Let's give him some help, shall we? 我们给他些帮助，好吗？

虽然偶尔 let's 也可指第一人称单数，但还是少用为妙。

Let's give you a hand. 让我来给你帮忙吧。

Let's have a look. 让我看一看。

B．let us 通常不包括听话人在内

这种表达多用于表示请求，let 在意义上相当于 allow, permit，隐含的主语为 you。

Let us go through the list and then we'll let you know. 让我们先把单子查对一下，然后再告诉你吧。

Let us now turn to the second question. 让我们讨论第二个问题吧。

因此，let us 祈使句的附加问句为 will you 或 won't you。

Let us know the time of your arrival, will you? 请告诉我们你(们)到达的时间，好吗？

Let us try again if you don't want to, will you? 如果你不愿干，就让我们试吧，好吗？

let us 有时也可能包括对方，这时可缩略为 Let's。但是它们的附加问句仍然是 will/won't you 或 shall we。

Let us have a look, will/won't you? 让我们看一看，可以吗？

Let's have a look, shall we? 让我们看看，好吗？

② Let me/him/them … 结构

A．在 Let me … 结构中

let 在意义上相当于 allow 或 permit，表示请求。隐含的主语为 you，附加问句用 will you，有时也可用 may I。

Let me try again. 让我再试一试。

Let me think what to do next. 让我想想下一步怎么办吧。

Let me have a try, will you? 让我试一试，行吗？

Let me help you, may I? 让我来帮你的忙，好吗？

B．在 Let him/them … 结构中

除了用第三人称单复数代词外，还可用名词或别的代词。这一结构可以表示多种意思。

a．表示建议

Let him come in. 让他进来吧。

Let everyone sign his name. 让每个人都签名吧。

b．表示间接命令或吩咐

Let her read it through and then let her form an opinion. 让她先读完，然后提建议。

Let the porter carry these wooden boxes. 让搬运工人来搬这些木箱子吧。

Let someone try explaining that to you. 让个人设法把这点向你们解释清楚。

Let all his things have their places. 把他所有的东西放在适当的位置上。

c. 表示轻蔑、警告、无可奈何

Let him do his worst. 让他尽管瞎干好啦。

You say they will launch an attack against us? Let them! 你说他们要向我们发动进攻？让他们来吧！

Let those who think I have an easy time try living on my salary for a month! 让那些认为我的日子过得安逸的人拿着我的工资过一个月的生活看看吧。

d. 表示假设

Let X be the unknown quantity. 设 X 为未知量。

Let ABC be a triangle. 设 ABC 为三角形。

e. 表示条件

这多是"let + 第三人称祈使句 + and + 陈述句"句型。

Let her make them an offer and they won't refuse. 如果让她向他们提建议，他们是不会拒绝的。

Let him help you and you'll succeed. 如果让他帮助你，你会成功的。

Let an honest man enter politics of this kind, and all the established groups will be at his throat. 如果让一个诚实的人进入这样的政界，所有既有的集团都会攻击他。

f. let us 表示条件

Davies (1986) 认为，let us 可表示条件，而 let's 不表示条件。

Let us make the tiniest mistake and he used to get mad at us. 我们如果犯了最小的错误，他也总是大为恼火。

Let us be in trouble and he wouldn't lift a finger to help us. 要是我们遇到困难，他也不愿尽举手之劳帮助我们。

g. 表示让步

这多见于"let + 第三人称代词或名词结构 + 不用连接词连接的陈述句"句型。

Let Joe do his worst, he won't upset us. 尽管乔治使出最卑劣手段，他也不会使我们难堪。

Let him say what he likes, I still believe we were right to act as we did. 不管他想怎么说就怎么说，我还是认为我们这样做是对的。

Let her say what she will, he doesn't mind her. 不管她怎么说，他总是不听她的。

（2）Let + there be 结构

这一结构主要用来表示希望或不希望存在或出现某事。

Let there be no more complaints of this type. 但愿不再有这样的抱怨。

Let there be something to do. 有些事情做就好了。

（3）Let 祈使句的宾语补足语

Let 祈使句的宾语补足语有不带 to 的动词不定式，有副词、介词短语等充当。

Let me see. 让我想想。

Let the cat out. 把猫放出去。

Let him off this time. 这次就放过他吧。

Open the door and let the dog in. 把门打开，让狗进来。

Let him out of the prison. 让他出狱吧。

Let a piece of lace into a dress. 在衣服上镶一条花边吧。

Don't let the cat into my kitchen. 别让猫进我的厨房。

（4）Let 祈使句的强调形式

此种强调式也用 do 来实施。这时 do 可以放在 let 之前，也可放在动词不定式前。

Do let's be friends. 让我们务必做朋友吧。

Do let him come to see us. 务必让他来看我们。

Do let promises be kept. 一定要遵守诺言。

Let's do come to see him. 让我们务必去看他吧。

Let him do come to dinner today. 叫他今天一定来吃饭。

(5) Let 祈使句的否定

① 否定不定式，即把否定词 not 置于不定式之前。

Let's not get angry. 咱们别发火。

Let us not be disappointed. 咱们不要灰心。

Let me not believe such accusation. 别叫我相信这样的控告吧。

Let him not disturb us. 叫他别打扰我们。

② 把 not 置于 let 的后面是古体用法。

Let not anyone fool himself that he can get away with it. 别让任何人糊弄自己以为做了坏事而不被发觉。

Let not those in authority abuse their power. 不要让那些当权的人滥用职权。

③ 在非正式语体(特别是英国英语)中，可将 don't 置于 let 的前面。

Don't let's quarrel. 咱们别争吵了。

Don't let us be down hearted. 咱们不要闷闷不乐。

Don't let me do it again. 别让我再做这件事了。

Don't let them disturb me. 别让他们打扰我。

Don't let anyone fool himself that he can get away with it. 别让任何人糊弄自己,认为做了坏事而不被发觉。

Notes：A. 如果第三人称祈使句在表示说话人对对方的反应持冷淡、鄙视、轻蔑态度时不宜用"don't let him/her/them + 不定式"结构,而要用"let him/her/them not + 不定式"结构。

—Henry says he doesn't speak to you any more unless you apologize to him.
亨利说除非你向他道歉,否则他不会和你讲话。
—Well, let him not speak to me. It doesn't matter to me at all.
好啦,那就不说吧。这我一点也不在乎。

—Some of the staff are refusing to work on Saturday morning. 有些职员不愿在周六上午上班。
—Let them not work then. Why should I care whether they work or not?
就让他们不上吧,这与我有什么关系呢？

B. 含有条件意义的第三人称祈使句的否定式也只用"let … not"结构,而不用"don't let …"结构。

Let John not feel better by Friday, and he'll have to stay at home. 如果到星期五约翰没感到好转,他将不得不待在家里。

Let it not be fine tomorrow, and we shall all have to carry umbrellas. 如果明天天气不好,我们都得带雨伞。

④ 在 let's 的后面加上 don't,这种形式多见于美国英语中的非正式语体。

Let's don't say anything about it. 关于这件事咱们什么也不要讲。

Let's don't be serious. 咱们别当真啦。

Let's don't make a mistake. 咱们一个错误也不能犯。

(6) 相当于陈述句的 Let 祈使句

Let this be a warning to her. 这件事就当作对她的警告。

Let young people bear this in mind. 年轻人应铭记此事。
Let others say what they will, I will go my own way. 走自己的路，让别人去说吧。

22.10　无动词祈使句

前面讨论的祈使句的谓语均为原形动词，但是英语中还有一种没有动词的祈使句，其中有些省略了谓语动词，有些用法约定俗成，在一定的场合使用。它们常用作表达请求、建议、命令、忠告等意思。对于无动词祈使句，我们根据杨元兴先生的观点做一简单的介绍。

(1) "名词 + 副词/介词短语"型

Hats off！脱帽！
Faces to me！面对我！

(2) "名词/形容词/副词/"型

Peace！静一些！。
Splendid！太好了！
Exactly！正是（这样）！
（Sit）Down！坐下！

(3) "副词 + with + 名词/代词"型

Off with your glasses！取下眼镜！
Out with it（= bring it out）！把它拿出来！

(4) "介词短语"型

At ease（= Stand at ease）！稍息！
Off the road！离开马路！

(5) "名词短语"型

Double time！跑步前进！（命令）
Another coffee, if you don't mind. 如果你不介意的话，请再给我杯咖啡。（请求）
Another round？再打一轮好吗？（提议）
The police！警察来了！（警告）

(6) "否定的名词短语"型

No bear feet！禁止赤脚！
No smoking！禁止吸烟！
No bicycle against the wall！靠墙禁止放自行车！

(7) "none of + 名词或代词"型

None of your little tricks！不要再玩弄鬼把戏！
None of your nonsense！不要胡说八道！
None of that again！不要再那样！

第23章 感叹句

23.1 感叹句的分类

感叹句(Exclamatory Sentence)是用来表示说话人的惊奇、厌恶、焦急、喜悦、热情等情绪的句子。感叹句书写时句末用感叹号,语调用降调。

根据句子的结构,我们把感叹句分为一般型(What 型和 How 型)、回响型、动词不定式型、转化型等几种。转化感叹句就是指那些由陈述句、疑问句和祈使句转化而来的感叹句。

(1) 一般型感叹句

① What 型感叹句

这是我们最为熟悉的感叹句,其结构是"What + 被强调或被感叹的成分 + 主语 + 谓语 + 状语"等。
What an interesting novel it is! 这是一部多么有趣的小说啊!
What terrible handwriting Mr. Lu writes! 陆先生写的字多么可怕呀!

A. what 的句法作用

在 What 型感叹句中,感叹词 what 可以是感叹代词,在句中作宾语、表语,也可以是感叹限定词,作定语等。
What a nice voice she has! 她的嗓子真好!(what 作宾语)
What a fool you are! 你真是个蠢蛋!(what 作表语)
What a pity it is! 这是多可惜的事啊!(what 作定语)

B. What 型感叹句的省略

a. 省掉 SV

What 型感叹句省略掉 SV(主谓语)是常事,这样的句子也叫无动词感叹句。
What heavy traffic! 交通真拥挤呀!
What a lovely day! 多好的天气啊!

b. 省掉 what 和 SV

有时,What 型感叹句还可省去 SV(主谓语)和 what,这也是无动词感叹句。
A good idea! 好主意!
Nonsense! 废话!

C. "What + 句子"型感叹句

这种句子是在一般的句子前加上感叹词 what 而成,用来表示值得注意的事。
What Gorky suffered in his childhood! 高尔基在童年时代真够受苦的!
What these ancient walls could tell us! 这些古城墙能告诉我们多少往事啊!

D. What 型感叹句中介词的位置

当在 What 型感叹句中的名词是介词的宾语时,介词一般在句末,但在非正式英语中也有出现在句首。
What disorder the office is *in*! 这办公室里真是乱七八糟!
With what amazing skill the young artist handles the brush! 这位青年画家的运笔技巧真是非凡!

② How 型感叹句

A．How 型感叹句中，how 的句法作用和句子语序

这种句子中的 how 是感叹副词，用来强调形容词、副词、动词、句子等。句子的主谓语用正常语序。

How beautiful the dress is！这女装多漂亮啊（How 修饰形容词 nice）

How well George writes！乔治写得多好啊！（how 修饰副词 well）

How fast the boy runs！那男孩子跑得多快啊！（how 修饰副词 fast）

How I love her！我多么爱她啊！（how 修饰后面整个句子 I love her）

B．How 型感叹句的省略

a．省略 SV 与 What 型感叹句一样，How 型感叹句也可省去 SV

How encouraging！多么令人鼓舞呀！

How hot today！今天多热啊！

b．省去 SV(主谓语)和 how

How 型感叹句不但可省去主谓语，还可连感叹副词 how 一起省，这就成为简洁的独词句。不过它们与省去主谓语和感叹词 what 的 What 型感叹句不同，它们留下的是形容词或副词，其意思可视上下文而决定。

Wonderful！妙！

Good！好！

(How) Fast (he is running)！（他跑得）多快啊！

C．"How ＋句子"型感叹句

感叹副词 how 后可跟一个句子，不过这种情况下的 how 是修饰后面句子中的谓语动词的。

How I miss you！我多么想念你啊！

How the old woman snored！那老太打鼾打得多响啊！

Notes：使用 What 型和 How 型感叹句的 9 个注意点：

a．感叹词通常置于句首，但有时也可把带有感叹词的整个介词短语置于句首。

In what poverty these people live！这些人生活多贫困！

For how many years I have waited！我等了多少年了！

b．没有否定式。我们不能说"What a lovely day, it *isn't*！"之类的句子。

c．对表示确定的人或事物的名词，普通感叹句不能进行强调，如不能说 What *the fine day* it is！

d．当被强调的是单数可数名词时，其前要用不定冠词；当被强调的是复数可数名词时，那其前不用冠词。

What *an* interesting book！多么有趣的书啊！

What strange *clothes* she is wearing！她穿着多奇怪的衣服啊！

e．感叹副词 how 不能修饰不可数名词或复数名词前的形容词，但可修饰单数可数名词前的形容词。

What beautiful weather！（正确）

＊How beautiful weather！（错误）

What funny stories he tells！（正确）

＊How funny stories he tells！（错误）

What an astonishing sight！（正确）

＊How astonishing sight (it is)！（错误）

f．被感叹词强调的成分的位置常在主语前，但在感叹副词 how 强调句子的谓语动词及其短语时，被强调的成分不能置于主语前。

How they shout！（正确）

＊How shout they！（错误）

How I used to hate history！（正确）

How used I to hate history! （错误）

g. 当强调谓语动词或状语时,谓语动词用一般体表示动作正在进行;当强调宾语时,谓语动词用进行体表示动作正在进行。

How she runs! 她跑得多快啊!
What noise the children are making! 孩子们多吵啊!

h. 谓语动词用现在时较多,也可用过去时;体态方面,用一般体较多,也可用进行体、完成体或完成进行体。

How hard she *works*! 她工作多卖力啊!
How he *missed* you! 他多么想念你!
What a time we've *had* today! 今天我们多倒霉啊!
What a long time I've *been waiting*! 我已等了多长时间了!

i. 一般感叹句用正常语序,但在强调主语或主语比较长时,可用倒装语序。

What a poor fool is he! 他是个多可怜的傻瓜!
How strange is her appearance! 她的外貌多奇特!

（2）回响感叹句

回响感叹句是指那些重复对方话语中的全部或部分,以表示怀疑、惊奇等意思。

{ —What a lovely day! 多好的天气!
　—*What a lovely day*! You must be joking. 多好的天气啊! 你一定在开玩笑。

{ —Have you been to Shanghai? 你到过上海吗?
　—*Been to Shanghai*! I'll say I was born in Shanghai. 到过上海! 我要说我生在上海。

（3）动词不定式感叹句

动词不定式感叹句就是省去了 I'm astonished 或 It surprises me 的感叹句。这种感叹句可分为:"to think + that 从句"、"to think of + 动名词短语"、"(to) fancy + 动名词短语"等。

① to think + that 从句

(I'm astonished) To think that you are so foolish! 没想到你这么蠢!
You people! (I'm astonished) To think (that) we have to support your kind with taxes! 你们这些人! 想想看,我们竟然得纳税养活你们这种人!

② to think of 动名词短语

(It surprised me) To think of her leaving us without a word! 没想到她一句话没说就走了!
(It surprised me) To think of all the money that he has! 没想到他有那么多钱!

③ (to) fancy + 动名分词短语

(It surprised me to) Fancy your having seen her somewhere! 没想到你在某个地方见过她!
(I'm astonished to) Fancy that! (= Indeed! What a curious happening!) 那真是怪事!

（4）其他形式的感叹句

① 其他感叹词引出的感叹句

Well, here we are at last! 咳,我们总算到这里了!
Ah, there you are! 啊! 你在那儿!
Hum, you're lying! 哼! 你在撒谎!

② 方位副词引出的感叹句

方位副词 away, back, down, in, off, up 和地点副词 here, there 等可引出感叹句。

Away she went to the airport! 她去机场了!
Away went Linda to the airport! 林去机场了!
Off you go! 你走开!
There goes the bus! 公共汽车去那儿了!
Here he comes! 他来这儿了!

③ 单词和短语型感叹句

一些单词和短语可作感叹句,其中一些句子可以说是一些完整感叹句的省略形式。

Nonsense! 胡扯!
Excellent! 好极了!
Just fancy! 多奇怪啊!/真想不到!
Hush, not a word! 嘘!别说话!
Bravo! Well done! 好啊!好极了!

(5) 双重感叹句

双重感叹句是指那些感叹句还带了感叹词,而这些感叹词不是句子成分,但在意思上与句子融为一体,感叹词宣泄情绪,它们前或后的感叹句说明所泄情绪的性质或原因。

Oh, how lovely the little girl is! 啊,多可爱的小女孩!
My goodness! How could you work so fast? 啊呀!你怎么干得这么快!
Her mother, *alas*, isn't out of danger yet! 唉,她母亲还没有脱离危险期!

(6) 转化感叹句

这里讲的转化感叹句是指那些原是陈述句、祈使句、疑问句,甚至一个从句、一个词组或一个单词,通过增强语气,加上相应的表情、动作,都可表示说话人的喜、怒、哀、乐等各种情绪,具有感叹的作用,在它们后面加上感叹号就是感叹句。

① 陈述句型感叹句

He is so kind! 他如此仁慈!
The old woman is so good-natured! 那老太多么善良啊!
Our country is a great socialist country! 我们的国家是个伟大的社会主义国家!

② 祈使句型感叹句

Mind that step! 小心那个台阶!
Do tell us the truth! 说实话!
Take care you don't catch cold! 你要当心别受凉!

(7) 祝愿句型感叹句

好多表示祝愿的句子是感叹句,它们的语序是倒装的。

Long live world peace! 世界和平万岁!
May you succeed! 祝你成功!
O were he only here! 啊,要是他在这里就好了!

(8) 疑问句型感叹句

疑问句型感叹句在书写时还是疑问句词序,只是句末一定要用感叹号。

Isn't her handwriting beautiful! 她的书法真漂亮!

How can you be so lazy! 你怎么这样懒呢!
Have you ever seen any one like her! 你见到过谁像她这样的人!

(9) 从句型感叹句

O that I could swim like you! 啊,但愿我能像你一样会游泳!
If I could see her once! 我只要见到她一次就好了!
To think that she should succeed! 想不到她竟会成功!
由 if (…) only 引导。实际上省去了主句 How nice it would be 之类的句子。
Oh, (how nice it would be) if he could only come! 啊,要是他能够来该多好啊!
(How nice it would be) If only it would stop raining! 要是雨停了该多好啊!
(How nice it would be) If only he had seen me! 要是他看见我该多好啊!
(How nice it would be) If only he had arrived in time! 要是他按时到了该多好啊!

(10) 单词型和词组型感叹句

Exactly! 正是这样!
Not likely! 不见得!

23.2 感叹句型的转换

我们把感叹句的转换分两种情况:一是感叹句型之间的转换,二是感叹句型向其他句型的转换。

(1) 感叹句型之间的转换

这里指"What …!"与"How …!"之间的转换。有时候,有些"What …!"和"How …!"句型可互相转换,它们的意思基本相同。
What a pretty girl she is! 多漂亮的女孩!
→How pretty the girl is! 那女孩多漂亮啊!
What an interesting story it is! 多有趣的一部小说啊!
→How interesting the story is! 这部小说多么有趣啊!

(2) 感叹句型与其他句型的转换

感叹句型与其他句型的转换就是指"What …!"和"How …!"两种句型向间接引语句型转换。特别要注意的是,在转换时必须增添主谓语,有时甚至还要加进适当的状语,而原来的感叹句却常作为宾语从句出现在句中。尽管感叹句向间接引语的转换并不多见,但还是能碰到。当然,转变后的间接引语句所表达的意思没有原来那样真切,也不能再现原感叹句的那种喜、怒、哀、乐的激动情感。下面两组句子可证实上面所述:
How beauteous mankind is! 人类多么美丽啊!
→ Donald/Linda/Mary/Jim exclaimed with delight that mankind was so beauteous. 唐纳德/琳达/玛丽/吉姆高兴地喊道:人类多么美丽。
What a lovely garden! 多可爱的花园啊!
→She/Tom/Mary/Jim remarked with admiration that it was such a lovely garden. 她/汤姆/玛丽/吉姆赞叹这花园多么可爱。

第24章　形容词、形容词(定语)从句

24.1　形容词的定义

形容词(Adjective),简称 adj. 或 a.,是英语中很重要的词类,用于修饰名词或代词,表示人或事物的性质、特征、状态、程度等,在句中可作定语、表语、补语等多种成分。

24.2　形容词的分类

形容词的分类可从两个方面进行:一是从其构成形式分类,二是从其词义上分类。

(1) 就其构成形式分类

① **单词形容词**

单词形容词就是仅有一个自由词素构成的形容词,如 big, short, beautiful 等。

② **复合形容词**

复合形容词是由两个或两个以上的单词组成。组成复合形容词的每个形容词之间要用连字符。复合形容词在句子中只作定语,不作表语或补语。复合形容词的构成方式主要有以下 14 种:

A. 数词＋名词

one-child (独生子女的)　　two-hour (两小时的)

B. 数词＋名词(单数)＋形容词

three-year-old (三岁的)　　seven-foot-wide (七英尺的)
8,000-meter-long (8000米长的)　　six-meter-tall (六米高的)

C. 数词＋名词＋-ed

one-eyed (独眼的)　　four-storeyed (四层的)
two-faced (两面的)　　four-footed (四只脚的)
three-legged (三条腿的)

D. 形容词＋(普通)名词

full-time (全日制的)　　high-class (高级的)
second-hand (二手的)　　part-time (业余的)
mid-term (期中的)　　final-term (期末的)
first-class/rate (一流的)

E. 形容词＋名词＋-ed

kind-hearted (好心肠的)　　cold-blooded (冷血的)
warm-hearted (热心肠的)　　blue-eyed (蓝眼睛的)
middle-aged (中年的)　　red-lipped (红嘴唇的)

F. 形容词/副词动名词

good-looking（长相好看的）　　ugly-looking（长相丑陋的）
easy-looking（长相随和的）　　tired-looking（面容疲劳的）
hard-working（勤奋的）　　　　ever-lasting（永恒的）

G. 形容词/副词＋过去分词

new-born（新生的）　　　　　so-called（所谓的）
hard-won（来之不易的）　　　well-dressed（衣着好的）
ready-made（现存的）　　　　newly-built（新建的）
recently-built（刚建的）

H. 形容词/副词＋形容词

dark-blue（深蓝的）　　　　　light-green（浅绿的）
all-round（全面的）　　　　　red-hot（灼热的）

I. 名词动名词

English-speaking（说英语的）　peace-loving（爱好和平的）
world-shaking（震惊世界的）　grass-eating（食草的）
mouth-watering（流口水的）　meat-eating（食肉的）

J. 名词＋-ed 分词

hand-made（手工制作的）　　heart-broken（极其伤心的）
man-made（人造的）

K. 名词＋形容词

life-long（毕生的,终生的）　　world-famous（世界著名的）
world-wide（世界范围的）　　ice-cold（冰冷的）

L. 名词＋名词

X-ray（X 光的）　　　　　　　English-language（英国语言的）

M. 形容词＋名词＋-ed

long-winged（长翅膀的）

N. 名词＋介词

child-like（像小孩似的）

（2）就其意义分类

形容词,就其词汇意义来分,有动态形容词和静态形容词两种。

① 动态形容词

带有动作含义的形容词叫动态形容词。它们为数不多：abusive, ambitious, awkward, adorable, careful, conceited, disagreeable, enthusiasitc, friendly, helpful, impudent, irritable, mischievous, obstinate, playful, rude, sensible, shy, spiteful, stubborn, tactful, talkative, timid, thoughtful, unfaithful, vain, vicious, witty 等。

② 静态形容词

静态形容词是描写人或物的静态特征,指描述人或事物所固有或持久性质,如 tall, short, big, small, ugly, beautiful, shallow, deep, blue, white 等。英语中的形容词绝大部分是静态的,只有少数是动态的。动态形容词和静态形容词在用法上有所不同。

③ 动态形容词和静态形容词的区分

A．静态形容词不能用于进行体，而动态形容词可以。

误：He is being *beautiful*.（beautiful 是静态形容词）

正：He is being *nervous*. 他显得很紧张。（nervous 是动态形容词）

B．静态形容词不能用于以主要动词为 be 的祈使句，而动态形容词可以。

误：＊Be *tall*.

＊Don't be *short*.

（因 tall 和 short 是静态形容词）

正：Be *polite*. 有礼貌点。

Don't be *rude*. 不得无礼。

（因 polite 和 rude 是动态形容词）

C．静态形容词不能用于 What he did was to be 这类句型后面作表语，而动态形容词可以。

误：What he did was to be *tall*.（tall 为静态形容词）

正：What he did was to be *careful*. 他所做的是就是要认真。

D．静态形容词大多用于 "It's + adj. + for …" 结构，而动态形容词则大多可用于 "It's + adj. + of sb …" 结构。

It was *difficult* for him to finish it in time. 要他按时完成它有困难。

It was *clever* of him to finish it in time. 他很聪明，按时完成了它。

E．一些主动性较强的语境中可用动态形容词，但不用静态形容词。

误：You must be *beautiful*.（must 若表示肯定推测，此句则正确）

正：You must be *careful*. 你必须仔细。

F．动态形容词可用于使役结构，而静态形容词不可以。

误：I persuaded her to be *pretty*.

正：I persuaded her to be *generous*. 我让她大方点。

(3) 中心形容词和外围形容词

形容词，就其句法功能来说，分为中心形容词和外围形容词。大多数形容词都是既能作名词修饰语，又能作主语补足语和宾语补足语，这种形容词构成本词类的主体，故称"中心形容词"。只能作修饰语或只能作补足语的形容词叫外围形容词。

① 中心形容词

下面，我们就以中心形容词 green 为例，说明中心形容词的三种句法功能：

Green apples are sour. 绿色的苹果是酸的。（作名词修饰语）

Pillar-boxes are *green*. 邮筒是绿色的。（作主语补足语或叫表语）

They have painted the windows *green*. 他们把窗户漆成了绿色。（作宾语补足语）

② 外围形容词

外围形容词中，有的只能作修饰语，不能作补足语；有的又只能作补足语，不能作修饰语。

A．只能作修饰语的外围形容词

{ 正：This is *utter* nonsense. 这完全是一派胡言。
  误：The nonsense is *utter*. }

{ 正：His *elder* brother is fifteen. 他的哥哥 15 岁。
  误：His brother is *elder*. }

$\begin{cases} 正：His\ left\ hand\ is\ \textit{wounded}.\ 他的左手受伤了。\\ 误：His\ \textit{wounded}\ hand\ is\ left. \end{cases}$

$\begin{cases} 正：He\ has\ a\ wooden\ house.\ 他有个木头房子。\\ 误：His\ house\ is\ \textit{wooden}. \end{cases}$

像 utter, elder, left, wooden 这样的形容词还有：right, inner, outer, upper, hinder, utter, former, major, latter, lesser, earthen, woolen, brazen, golden, leaden 等。

B．只能作补足语的外围形容词

有些形容词只能作补足语，不能作前置修饰语。这里所说的补足语包括表语（或叫主语补足语）和宾语补足语。这些形容词有 well（表示健康，只作表语）及多数以 a-开头的形容词 asleep, afraid, aware, awake, alike, alone, ashamed, alive, away, alert, averse（反对的，不乐意的）agape, astir（惊惶的），afloat（飘浮的），afire（着火；燃烧的）等。

She is not *well* today. 她今天身体不舒服。

He is *alone*. 他单独一人。

I saw him *alone*. 我看他单独一人。

The old man, alone on the island, looked like a beast. 那个老人单独一人生活在这个岛上，看上去像个野兽。（alone on the island 是 man 的后置定语）

$\begin{cases} 正：This\ child\ is\ \textit{asleep}.\ 这个小孩睡着了。\\ 误：This\ is\ an\ \textit{asleep}\ child. \end{cases}$

Note：上述带 a-的形容词不能"单独"作前置修饰语，但是如果它们不是单独使用，而是带有其他修饰语时，那就可以作前置修饰语。

a *somewhat afraid* soldier 一个稍微有点害怕的士兵

the *fast asleep* child 那个熟睡的小孩

a *really alive* student 一个相当活跃的学生

the *wide awake* patient 那个清醒的病人

③ 还有少数形容词作补足语和定语时的意义不一样

Her aunt was *ill*. 她姨妈病了。

She has an *ill* aunt. 她有一个凶狠的姨妈。

The boss was *hard*. 这个老板很厉害。

He was a *hard* worker. 他是一个勤奋的工人。

24.3 描绘性形容词和限定性形容词

从实用角度考虑，形容词可分为描绘性形容词和限定性形容词。

（1）描绘性形容词

描绘性形容词又称非限定性形容词，它主要起描绘性作用，它们可能表示有关人的品质，也表示某些东西的特点，可以是指性质或表达情绪，也可以与某些地名或材料有关。这些词如果省去不用，通常不会影响所修饰名词的本意。

The French horn has a *beautiful* sound. 那法国喇叭有着美妙的声音。

The house has got a *wonderful* atmosphere. 屋子里有着美妙的氛围。

A *good* dictionary is necessary. 一本好的字典是必要的。

They are having a *working* lunch in Mr. Smith's office. 他们在史密斯先生的办公室享用午餐。

描绘性形容词可以有多种位置,可置于名词前后,这样并不影响名词的单复数表意。

(2) 限定性形容词

限定性形容词用于表示事务的本质,其位置紧挨着它所修饰的名词。这类型的形容词不多。它们可以表示数量,或"哪个"。与描绘性形容词的可有可无不同,限制性形容词通常是必不可少的,如果去掉则会影响所修饰名词的意义。如果和描绘性形容词同时用来修饰一个名词,它们都放在描绘性形容词前面。

Some dictionaries are very useful. 有些字典非常有用。

You may ask me *any* questions. 你可以问我任何问题。

His faults are very *few*, and mine are *many*. 他的错误几乎没有,但我的很多。

He has *many* good friends. 他有许多好朋友。

He knows *some* such honest northern people. 他认识一些这样诚实的北方人。

24.4 形容词的前缀与后缀

英语单词由三部分组成,即前缀(prefix)、词根(stem)及后缀(suffix)。有的形容词是由名词、动词、形容词等加上词缀后派生而来。一个单词中位于词根前面的部分就是前缀,位于词根后面的部分就叫后缀。

(1) 常见的形容词前缀

常见的形容词的前缀有:a-、un-、im-、in-、il-、ir-、dis-、mis-、non-、anti-、counter-、super-、over-、hyper-、under-、sub-等。具体用法见下表:

前缀	规律	举例
a-	①主要用在较文的词或科技词之前,表示"缺乏"或"无" ②与动词结合构成形容词,表示"处于……状态或过程中"	amorphous 无定形的 anarchic 无政府状态的 awake 醒着的 asleep 睡着的
un-	加在形容词前,表示与原词相反的意义,使用较为广泛,无特定规律可循	uncertain 不确定的 unhappy 不开心的
im-	一般加在以 p 开头的形容词前,表示与原词相反的意义	impossible 不可能的 improbable 不可能的
in-	加在形容词前,表示与原词相反的意义,无特定规律可循	infinite 无限的 inactive 不活跃的
il-	一般加在以 l 开头的形容词前,表示与原词相反的意义	illogical 不合逻辑的 illegal 不合法的
ir-	一般加在以 r 开头的形容词前,表示与原词相反的意义	irregular 不规则的 irresponsible 不负责的
dis-	加在形容词前,表示与原词相反的意义,无特定规律可循	dishonest 不诚实的 disobdient 不顺从的;抗命的
mis-	加在形容词前,表示"坏,错,不,无,没"	misleading 误导的
non-	加在形容词前,表示"无"	non-existent 不存在的 non-alcoholic 无酒精的

续表

前缀	规律	举例
anti-	加在形容词前,表示"反对"	antibiotic 抗生的
counter-	加在形容词前,表示"方向或作用相反"	counterproductive 事与愿违的,产生相反结果的
注意:anti-和counter-都有反对之意,anti-指的是反对的态度,而counter-指为防止某事物或针对某事物而采取的行动。		
super-	加在形容词前,表示"极端的,非常的,超级的"	super-intelligent 超级聪明的
over-	加在形容词前,表示"在上,超过,过度,过多"	overdue 到期的 overbearing 蛮横的 overblown 盛开过的
hyper-	加在形容词前,表示"过度,在……之上,高于"	hypercritical 吹毛求疵的 hypersensitive 过度敏感的
under-	加在形容词前,表示"不足"	underripe 不够成熟的 underdeveloped 发育不全的,不发达的
sub-	加在形容词前,表示"在……之下,次于,不完全的,近似的"	submarine 海面下的 subnormal 正常以下的 subtropical 亚热带的

(2) 常见的形容词后缀

常见的形容词后缀各带其自身的含义。它们分别有:

① 带有"属性,倾向,相关"的含义

-able -ible movable, comfortable, applicable, visible, responsible

-al natural, additional, educational

-an urban, suburban, republican

-ant, -ent distant, important, excellent

-ar similar, popular, regular

-ary military, voluntary

-ic -ical politic, systematic, historic, physical

-ine masculine, feminine, marine

-ing moving, touching, daring

-ish foolish, bookish, selfish

-ive active, impressive, decisive

-ory satisfactory, compulsory

-ile -eel fragile, genteel(文雅的)

② 表示"相像,类似"的含义

-ish boyish, childish

-esque picturesque

-like manlike, childlike

-ly manly, fatherly, scholarly, motherly

-some　troublesome, handsome

-y　milky, pasty

③ 表示"充分的"含义

-ful　beautiful, wonderful, helpful, truthful

-ous　dangerous, generous, courageous, various

-ent　violent

④ 表示由某种物质形成、制成或生产的含义

-en　wooden, golden, woolen

-ous　gaseous

-fic　scientific

⑤ 表示方向的含义

-ern　eastern, western

-ward　downward, forward

⑥ 表示"倍数"的含义

-ble　double, treble

-ple　triple

-fold　twofold, tenfold

⑦ 表示"数量关系"的含义

-teen　thirteen

-ty　fifty

-th　fourth, fiftieth

⑧ 表示国籍、语种、宗教的含义

-an　Roman, European

-ese　Chinese

-ish　English, Spanish

⑨ 表示"比较程度"的含义

-er　greater

-ish　reddish, yellowish

-est　highest

-most　foremost, topmost

⑩ 表示否定

-less　countless, stainless, wireless

⑪ 表示以某方式方法, 或沿着某方向

-wise　clockwise, lengthwise

Note：有些形容词虽然词根一样，但是前后缀不同，意思就完全不同。例如，valuable 表示"有价值的"，而 valueless 表示"毫无价值的"；economic 表示"经济学的，与经济有关的"，而 economical 表示"节俭的"。

24.5 -ing 形容词与-ed 形容词的区别

(1) 常见的-ing 形容词

常见的由-ing 分词转化而来的形容词有：absorbing, alarming, amusing, annoying, astonishing, boring, challenging, changing, charming, comforting, confusing, convincing, daring, disturbing, exciting 等。

(2) 常见的-ed 形容词

常见的由-ed 分词转化而来的形容词有：alarmed, amazed, balanced, bored, civilized, disappointed, embarrassed, excited, pleased, satisfied, shocked, interested, fascinated, uncovered, unknown 等。

(3) -ing 结尾和-ed 结尾的形容词主要区别

① -ing 结尾的形容词表示正在进行、-ed 形容词表示动作已经完成

boiling water 正在沸腾的水　　boiled water 已经烧开的水
sleeping baby 正在熟睡的小孩　　finished job 已经完成的工作

② -ing 结尾的形容词表示主动意义，-ed 结尾的形容词表示被动意义

a charming girl 一个迷人的姑娘　　a charmed girl 一个着了魔法的姑娘

③ -ing 形容词表示激起情绪，-ed 形容词表示感到情绪

-ing 结尾的形容词表示感到情绪，意为"让人觉得……"，-ed 结尾的形容词意为"感到……"。

amusing 引人发笑的　　amused 觉得好笑的
interesting 好玩的　　interested 感兴趣的
shocking 令人震惊的　　shocked 感到震惊的
astonishing 令人震惊的　　astonished 感到震惊的
disgusting 让人厌恶的　　disgusted 觉得恶心的
annoying 让人觉得讨厌的　　annoyed 恼怒的
gratifying 令人满足的　　gratified 觉得满意的
fascinating 令人着迷的　　fascinated 着迷的

24.6 形容词的排序

当出现几个形容词同时修饰一个名词时，这几个形容词需要按如下的顺序排列：限定词(determiner) + 一般描绘性形容词(observation) + 表示大小、形状的形容词(size and shape) + 表示年龄、新旧的形容词(age) + 表示色彩的形容词(color) + 表示国籍、地区、出处的形容词(origin) + 表示物质、材料的形容词(material) + 表示用途、目的、类别的形容词(purpose) + 名词。具体如下表：

THE ROYAL ORDER OF ADJECTIVES							
Determiner	Observation	Physical Description			Origin	Material	Qualifier	Noun
	Size	Shape	Age	Color				
a	beautiful		old		Italian		touring	car
an	expensive			antique		silver		mirror
four	gorgeous		long-stemmed	red		silk		roses
her			short	black				hair
our		big	old		English			sheepdog
those		square				wooden	hat	boxes
that	dilapidated	little					hunting	cabin
several	enormous		young		American		basketball	players
some	delicious				Thai			food

Note: 一般来说在句中连续出现三四个形容词修饰某词已经差不多了,如用多了形容词会显得累赘。当两个形容词属于同一类别时,一般在两个形容词之间加个逗号。比如 the inexpensive, comfortable shoes,或者加个 but,说成 inexpensive but comfortable shoes。当三个形容词属于同一类别时,就加两个逗号,如 a popular, respected, and good looking student。

24.7 形容词的大小写问题

当某个形容词是由一个地名、人名、地名等引申而来时,首字母要大写,一般形容词只要小写,如 Christian music, French fries, the English Parliament, the Ming Dynasty, a Faulknerian style, Jeffersonian democracy, the Nixon era, a Renaissance/Romantic/Victorian poet。

24.8 "the + 形容词"表示某类人

(1) "the + 形容词"表示某一类型的人

He set up a school for the deaf and the dumb. 他为聋哑人建立了一个学校。
He stole from the rich to give to the poor. 他劫富济贫。
Those who are sighted don't understand the problems of the blind. 那些看得见人不能明白盲人的困难。
这类结构常见的有:the rich(富人), the poor(穷人), the blind(盲人),the sick(病人), the old(老人), the young(年轻人),the dumb(哑巴), the deaf(聋子), the dead(死者),the weak(弱者), the strong(强者), the wealthy(富人)。

(2) "the + 分词形容词"表示某一类型的人

Times are hard for the unemployed. 对于失业者来说,日子很艰苦。
Many of the wounded died on their way to hospital. 大多数受伤的人在去医院的路上去世。
这类结构常见的有:the wounded(伤员), the injured(伤员), the killed(被杀者), the employed(被雇佣者), the unemployed(失业者), the jobless(失业者),the accused(被告), the learned(有学问的人), the aged(老年人),the missing(失踪的人), the living(活着的人)。

(3) "the + 国籍形容词"表示全体国民

The Chinese are a friendly people. 中国人民是友好的人民。
The French are famous for their cooking. 法国人以他们的餐饮而著名。
The British are very proud of their sense of humor. 英国人对他们的幽默感很自豪。

(4) "the + 形容词"表示抽象概念

One must learn to take the bad with the good. 一个人必须接受事情的好坏两个方面。
He wants to make the impossilbe possible. 他想让不可能变成可能。
这类结构常见的有：the true（真），the good（善），the beautiful（美），the right（是），the wrong（非），the false（伪），the impossible（不可能做到的事），the unknown（未知的事情）。

24.9　形容词的比较等级

形容词的比较等级与副词一样，有三级：原级、比较级和最高级。

(1) 比较级和最高级的构成

① 单音节形容词以及少数以-er, -ow 结尾的形容词的比较级和最高级

这些形容词的比较级和最高级是在词尾加-er, -est。

原　形	比较级	最高级
great	greater	greatest
tall	taller	tallest
fast	faster	fastest
narrow	narrower	narrowest
clever	cleverer	cleverest

② 以-e 结尾的单音节形容词以及少数以-able, -ple 结尾的双音节形容词的比较级和最高级

这些形容词的比较级和最高级是在词尾加-r, -st。

原　形	比较级	最高级
wise	wiser	wisest
large	larger	largest
able	abler	ablest
simple	simpler	simplest

③ 结构为"辅音 + 元音 + 辅音"的单音节形容词的比较级和最高级

这些形容词中间的元音字母发短元音时，双写最后一个辅音，然后加-er, -est，构成比较级和最高级。

原　形	比较级	最高级
hot	hotter	hottest
thin	thinner	thinnest
flat	flatter	flattest
big	bigger	biggest

④ 以"辅音+加 y"结尾的形容词的比较级和最高级

这类形容词在变化成比较级和最高级时要将 y 改成 i，再加上-er, -est。

原　形	比较级	最高级
easy	easier	easiest
happy	happier	happiest
angry	angrier	angriest

⑤ 一般多音节形容词的比较级和最高级

这类形容词都在前面加 more 和 most 变成比较级和最高级：

原　形	比较级	最高级
beautiful	more beautiful	most beautiful
careful	more careful	most careful

⑥ 由现在分词和过去分词演化而来的形容词的比较级和最高级

这类形容词,不管单音节还是多音节,都在前面加 more 和 most 变成比较级和最高级。

原　形	比较级	最高级
tired	more tired	most tired
pleased	more pleased	most pleased
interesting	more interesting	most interesting
interested	more interested	most interested
astonishing	more astonishing	most astonishing

⑦ 有双重变化的形容词的比较级和最高级

有些形容词,它们既可以在后面加-er,-est 变成比较级和最高级,也可以在前面加 more, most 构成比较级和最高级。

原　形	比较级	最高级
cruel	crueler/more cruel	cruelest/most cruel
friendly	friendlier/more friendly	friendliest/most friendly

⑧ 不规则变化的形容词比较级和最高级

原形	比较级	最高级
good/well	better	best
bad/ill/evil	worse	worst
many/much	more	most
little	less	least
old	older/elder	oldest/eldest
far	farther/further	farthest/furthest

⑨ 有些以-or 结尾的形容词没有比较级和最高级

这些形容词有：interior, exterior, ulterior, minor, major, inferior, superior。

⑩ 有些形容词没有比较级和最高级

有些形容词本身已经包含最高级的含义,也没有比较级和最高级的变化,如:complete, perfect, unique, excellent, absolute, impossible, principal, adequate, nevitable, stationary, chief, irrevocable, sufficient, main, unanimous, devoid, manifest, entire, unbroken, fatal, paramount, final, perpetual, universal, ideal, preferable。

(2) 形容词比较级的用法和表达形式

① 同等程度比较

同等程度相比用"as+形容词原形+as"结构,否定时在第一个 as 前加进 not,有时也用"not so … as"结构。

She is as tall as her sister. 她与她姐姐一样高。

This pencil is as long as that one. 这支铅笔与那支一样长。

This building looks not as high as that one. 这幢楼看上去没有那幢高。

My bike is not so clean as yours. 我的自行车没有你的干净。

② 两者比较

两者比较有两种情况:一为甲方超过乙方,二为甲方不如乙方。

A. 甲方超过乙方

表示一方超过另一方时,用"比较级+than …"。

The pen is better than that one. 这支笔比那支好。

She is more beautiful than she was. 她现在比过去漂亮了。

"more … than …"结构除了在两样东西之间进行比较外,还可在同一个人或物的本身做不同方面的比较。

John is more daring than quick-witted. 与其说约翰脑子灵活,不如说他胆大。

George is more intelligent than aggressive. 与其说乔治言行放肆,不如说他聪颖过人。

The present crisis is much more a political than an economic crisis. 当前的危机与其说是经济危机,不如说是政治危机。

当要表示超过的程度时,可以在比较级前面加表示程度的副词,如 even, much, many, far, by far, still, a lot, a little, a great deal 等。

She is much taller than her sister. 她比她姐姐高很多。

Air in the country is much cleaner than that in the city. 乡下的空气比城市要好很多。

B. 甲方不如乙方

双方比较,表示一方不如另一方时,用"less+形容词原形+than …"结构。

Mr Wu is less old than Mrs Wu. 吴先生比吴太太显得年轻。

This room is less big than that one. 这个房间没有那个大。

其实,"more … than …"与"less … than …"是"正反"两种表达。

John is less daring than quick-witted. 与其说约翰胆大,不如说他脑子灵活。

George is less intelligent than aggressive. 与其说乔治聪颖过人,不如说他言行放肆。

The present crisis is much less a political crisis than an economic crisis. 当前的危机与其说是政治危机,不如说是经济危机。

C. 表示一方随另一方的变化而变化

在要表示一方随另一方的变化而变化时,可用"the+比较级, the+比较级"。

The warmer the weather, the better the plants grow. 天气越暖和,植物生长越好。

The harder she works, the more progress she gets. 她工作越努力，取得的成绩越多。

D. 表示本身程度的改变

不与其他事物相比而只表示本身程度的改变时，用"比较级＋and＋比较级"。

The weather is getting warmer and warmer. 天气变得越来越暖和了。

The girl becomes more and more beautiful. 这个女孩变得越来越漂亮了。

E. 某些以-or结尾的形容词进行比较

某些以-or结尾的形容词进行比较时，用to代替than。

He is superior to Mr. Wang in mathematics. 他在数学方面要比王先生强。

F. 表示倍数的比较级

表示倍数的比较级，可有以下几种情况：

a. A is three times (four times, etc.) the size (height, length, width, etc.) of B.

The new building is four times the size of the old one. 新大楼是旧大楼的四倍。

b. A is three times (four times, etc.) as ＋形容词原形＋as B.

Asia is four times as large as Europe. 亚洲是欧洲的四倍。

c. A is three times (four times, etc.) ＋形容词比较级＋than B.

Your school is three times bigger than ours. 你的学校比我们的大三倍。

（3）the ＋比较级＋of ＋比较范围（通常用于两者）

He is the cleverer of the two boys. 他是这两个男孩中比较聪明的那个。

（4）"not ＋比较级＋than"和"no ＋比较级＋than"的区别

John is not better than Tom. 约翰没有汤姆好。

John is no better than Tom. 约翰和汤姆一样不好。

前者是"约翰不比汤姆好"，是一般的比较结构；后者用了no better than，相当于as bad as，含义是两人一样坏。这里"no ＋比较级＋than"所表示的是该形容词的反义。

（5）形容词最高级的用法和表达形式

① **三者或三者以上相比较。**

表示最高程度时，用"the ＋最高级＋of (in, among, etc.) ＋比较范围"。

Among the three girls, Louise is the most capable. 在三个女孩中，路易斯是最能干的。

② **最高级可以被序数词以及much, by far, nearly, almost 等表示程度的词所修饰。**

This hat is by far the biggest. 目前这个帽子是最大的。

How much did the second most expensive hat cost? 第二贵的帽子要多少钱？

③ **most 有时不指最高级，而是表示"非常"。**

The telephone is a most useful tool. 电话是非常有用的工具。

（6）使用比较级时的一致性和排他性

① **一致性**

错：Her English is as fluent as her teacher.

对：Her English is as fluent as her teacher's. 她的英语和她老师的一样流利。

错：The weather is colder in Beijing than Shanghai.

对:The weather is colder in Beijing than in Shanghai. 北京的天气比上海的冷。
第一组里,因为比较的是两个人的英语,所以后面要用 her teacher's (English);第二组里,因为比较的是两个地点状语,所以 Shanghai 前的 in 不能漏掉。

② 排他性

错:Tom is more diligent than any student in his class.
对:Tom is more diligent than any other student in his class. 汤姆比他班上的其他学生要更用功。
Tom 也属于 any student in his class,所以比较时要注意排除 Tom,所以加一个 other,表示其他。

(7) 关于比较级中的替代问题

为了避免重复,在比较从句中也常用一些另外的词替代前面出现过的词。

① 用助动词代替主句中的有关动词

I earn more than I did in the past. 我现在比以前赚的钱更多。
John spends as much time watching TV as he does writing. 约翰花在看电视上的时间和花在写作上的时间是一样的。

② 用代词代替主句中的有关名词

that 代替指物的单数可数名词或不可数名词,一般是特指的;those 代替指人或物的复数名词,一般是特指的;one 代替指人或指物的单数可数名词,一般是泛指的;ones 代替指人或指物的复数名词,一般是泛指的。

The output of coal this year is twice as much as that of last year. 今年的煤产量是去年的两倍。
The books on this shelf are more interesting than those on that shelf. 这个架子上的书比那个架子上的书好看。
A bridge built of iron is much stronger than one built of stone. 钢铁造的桥要比石头造的结实。
Small bananas are often better than bigger ones. 小的香蕉要比大的好。

24.10　形容词的句法功能

形容词在句中可作定语、表语、补语、状语、感叹语等多种成分,而且其间涉及很多问题。

(1) 作定语

形容词主要的句法功能之一就是作名词修饰语,在语法上叫作定语。作定语时通常放在限定词之后和它所修饰的名词前面,被修饰的名词称为中心词。

He is an intelligent boy. 他是个聪明的男孩。
It is a rainy day. 这是个雨天。

但有时,形容词也能作后置定(修饰)语。形容词在下面几种情况下后置:

① 遇到由 some-, any-, no-, every- 构成的合成词,形容词要放在这些合成词的后面。

Have you read anything interesting? 你有没有读什么好玩的东西?
I'd like something cheaper. 我喜欢便宜一点的东西。
He has nothing pleasant to say to you. 他没有什么好事跟你讲。
He wants everything good. 他想要一切好的东西。
This isn't anything important. 这不是什么重要的东西。
Anyone intelligent can do it. 任何聪明的人都可以做这事。

② 在法律文件中，由于受到法语的影响，形容词也可以后置。

He is the Consul General. He showed his letters patent in the court martial as proof positive. 他是总领事。他在军事法庭上亮出专利证作为铁证。

③ 某些由专有名词，特别是人名后，形容词后置。

He was Alexander the Great. 他是"伟人"亚历山大。

④ 成对的形容词作定语时，考虑到句子的节奏和平衡，可以把它们置后。

There was a huge cupboard, simple and beautiful. 那里有个大的碗橱，简洁漂亮(的碗橱)。

She has many pencils, blue and red. 她有许多铅笔，蓝的，红的(铅笔)。

⑤ 有时形容词作定语时，置前、置后均可。

有些形容词，如 past, last, next, nearby, following 等，它们可放在被修饰名词之前，也可放在被修饰词之后，如：in past years/in years past (过去的年月)，the following days/the days following (以后的日子)。

形容词 enough, opposite 等修饰名词时也可前置或后置。

If we had enough time (time enough), things would be easy. 如果时间足够，事情就好办了。

The people in the house opposite (the opposite house) never draw their curtains. 对面房子里的人从来不把窗帘拉上。

Note：有的形容词虽然前置和后置均可，但含义不同。

What's your present feeling? 你现在感觉如何？(present = 现在的)

He was the only Englishman present. 他是唯一在场的英国人。(present = 在场的)

overseas students 外国留学生 (= students from overseas, 指外国到本国来求学的学生)

students overseas 出国留学生 (= students who are overseas, 指本国到外国去求学的学生)

(2) 作表语(补语)

形容词放在系动词后面作表语(也可称主语补语)，修饰主语或说明主语的情况。补足语形容词主要有三类：

① 表示健康状况的词

He is very well. 他很健康。

You look ill. 你看上去病了。

② 以前缀 a-开头的词

The two brothers are very much alike. 那两个兄弟非常像。

I was alone in the house. 我单独一人在房子里。

He was asleep. 他睡了。

Although old, he is very much alive. 尽管年纪大了，他还是很活跃。

The sky was aglow with the setting sun. 天空由于晚霞而放出光芒。

Note：当这些带 a-的补足语形容词不能"单独"作前置修饰语，但它们可以与其他修饰用在一起时可作前置于定语。

③ 补语，对前面的名词、代词等加以修饰或说明的词

A．作宾补

They make me angry. 他们让我生气。

I thought it easy. 我觉得它很简单。

He likes his coffee hot. 他喜欢热咖啡。

They left their son ignorant. 他们让他们的儿子(对此事)一无所知。
They called his work great. 他们称赞他的工作很好。
Mother keeps the floor clean. 妈妈保持地上清洁。
They find John honest. 他们发现约翰很诚实。

B. 当修饰语本身带有不定式、介词词组、that 分句等补足成分时

I know of a man ready to help us. 我知道一个可以帮助我们的人。
Marriage is a matter hard to handle. 婚姻是件很难处理的事情。
He is a man deserving of sympathy. 他是个值得同情的人。
It was a conference fruitful of results. 这是个富有成效的会议。
I think he is a man suitable for the job. 我认为他是适合这个工作的人。
We need a place twice larger than this one. 我们需要一个两倍于这个地方的地方。
I'm sure that we'll succeed. 我确信我们会成功。
I'm glad that you like it. 我很高兴你喜欢它。
She was amazed that he should arrive so soon. 她很惊喜他能这么快到达。

C. 在"数词 + 名词 + old（long, high, deep, tall 等）"结构中

Her husband is 55 years old. 她丈夫 55 岁。
The well is 25 meters deep. 井深 25 米。

(3) 作状语

① 说明性状语

形容词的主要功能是用作定语和表语,但有时也可用作状语(有人也称之为主语补足语,因为它们是补充说明主语的)。

He lay in bed, awake. 他躺在床上,没有睡着。(表示伴随)
He arrived home, hungry and tired. 他回到家里,又饿又累。(表示结果)
Unable to afford the time, I had to give up the plan. 由于抽不出时间,我不得不放弃这个计划。(表示原因)

形容词用作状语的特点是该形容词的逻辑主语就是句子主语,并且通常可以用并列句或主从复合句来改写。如以上各句可分别改写为:

He lay in bed and he was awake. 他躺在床上,很清醒。
He arrived home and he was hungry and tired. 他到家了,既饿又累。
Because I was unable to afford the time, I had to give up the plan. 因为我没有时间,我不得不放弃了计划。

② 程度性状语

有少数形容词,如 red, boiling, freezing, icy, bitter 等,它们在某些搭配中可以起副词作用,用作状语,表示程度,意为"很"、"非常"等。

The stove was red hot. 火炉是炽热的。
It's boiling hot. 它是滚烫的。
His face was bright red. 他的脸是鲜红的。
The weather is freezing /icy/ bitter cold. 天气冷极了。

但这样的用法非常有限,并往往只用于某些特定搭配中,如可说 bitter cold（冰冷）, bitter wind（寒风）等,但习惯上却不说 bitter hot（炽热）, bitter busy（极忙）等。

③ 承上启下性状语,以独立成分出现

有些形容词在某些固定结构中可用作独立成分,起承上启下的作用,也可视为一种状语。如:
Sure enough, she was there. 果然她在那里。

Strange to say, he did pass his exam after all. 说也奇怪,考试他竟然通过了。
He may be late. Worse still, he may not come at all. 他可能会迟到。更糟的是,他可能根本不来。
More important, he's got a steady job. 更重要的是他得到了一个稳定的工作。
Most remarkable of all, he never suffers from nerves on the stage. 最了不起的是他从不怯场。

④ 作感叹语

形容词有时用作感叹语,表示一时的情绪。
Stupid! He must be crazy. 愚蠢! 他一定是疯了。
Very good! Say it again. 很好! 再说一遍。
Right! So what is wrong? 正确! 所以什么出了问题?
Wonderful! It's so wonderful. 太好了! 这太好了。
Shocking! I have never seen such a thing. 震惊! 我从没见过这样的东西。
How dangerous! 多危险啊!

24.11 形容词(定语)从句

形容词从句也叫定语从句。因形容词作定语是其最突出功能之一,所以形容词(定语)从句也可说是形容词作定语的扩大。定语从句跟起定语作用的词语一样,也是用来修饰和限制名词、代词、名词短语的成分。杨元兴先生把含有定语词语的简单句称作简单句式定语句,把含有从句的定语句称为复合句式定语句(2012),这里,我们也沿用此说。定语从句有两大类:限制性定语从句和非限制性定语从句。定语从句还有存在的两个条件:必须有先行项,也就是被修饰的对象;必须要用关系词(关系代词和关系副词)引出。

24.12 简单句式定语句

说含有定语的简单句为简单句式定语句,就是因为这些句子中作定语用的都是一些词、词组。这些词、词组与各式各样的简单句组成了数量众多的简单定语句。这些用作定语的词语有限定词、名词及其短语、数词及其短语、不定式及其短语、现在分词和动名词及其短语、-ed 分词及其短语、副词及其短语、介词短语等。

Mary has *a* pen, and *the* pen is red. 玛丽有一支铅笔,那支铅笔是红的。(限定词冠词作定语)
Jim's father is a professor. 吉姆的父亲是个教授。[名词所有格(限定词)作定语]
There's *a flower* garden in front of the house. 那房子前有个花园。(名词作定语)
He has a *grammar* book written by Professor Li. 他有部李教授写的语法书。(名词作定语)
The war lasted *five* years. 那场战争持续五年。(数词作定语)
The *swimming* pool is at the foot of the hill. 那个游泳池位于一座小山的脚下。(动名词作定语)
There's a *broken* glass on the table. 桌子上有一只破玻璃杯。(-ed 分词作定语)
Have you anything else *to say*? 你有什么话要说吗? (动词不定式作定语)
It was an *out-and-out* liar. 这是个彻头彻尾的谎言。(副词作定语)
His mother is a teacher *of English*. 他的母亲是个英语教师。(介词短语作定语)
Did you see a man *standing* at the gate? 你见过站在门口的一个男人没有? (现在分词短语作定语)

24.13 复合句式定语句

上面说到复合句式定语句必须有先行项,也就是被修饰的对象,还必须有引出从句的关系词。这种先行项可以是一个词(名词或代词),也可以是一个词组,甚至可以是一个句子。引出复合定语从句中的关系词有两种:一种是关系代词,另一种是关系副词。另外,复合句式定语句还有限制性定语从句和非限制性定语从句之分。

(1) 定语从句的关系词

引出复合句式定语句中的定语从句的关系词有关系代词和关系副词两种。这两种关系词在定语从句中又担当一定的句子成分。

① 关系代词及其在从句中担当的成分

关系代词有 who, whom, whose, that, which, but 等,它们在从句中可作主语、宾语、定语等。

A. 一般关系代词引出定语从句

He laughs best *who* laughs last. 谁笑到最后,谁笑得最好。(who 作从句中的主语)

The head *whom* you are looking for went to Harbin on business. 你要找的那个头儿去哈尔滨出差了。(whom 作从句中的宾语)

I do like the book *that/which* was written by him. 我真的喜欢他写的书。(that/which 在从句中作主语)

Do you know the boy *whose* father is a professor *who* has written a book named *Modern English Syntax newly edited*? 你是否认识那个学生,他的父亲是个教授,写了一部名为《新编现代英语句法》的书?(此句中的第一个 whose 在第一个定语从句中作定语,第二个 who 在第二个从句中作主语)

B. 由 but 引出定语从句

一般语法书上对用关系代词 but 作引出定语从句很少讲到。要记住,把 but 作关系代词用时,有四个注意点:a. but 引出的是限制性定语从句,其意思是"无不"(=who not, which not),也就是含否定意义;b. but 在从句中只作主语;c. but 的先行词可以是人,也可是物;d. but 的主句(也可称先行项)中常带有否定词或否定意义的词(如 few, little, not, no),因 but 本身具有否定意思,所以这种复合句往往表示肯定意思。

There are few of us *but* admire your determination. 我们中间很少有人不钦佩你的决心。

There is not one of us *but* wishes to visit London. 我们没有一个不想去游览伦敦。

There is no rule *but* has exception. 没有无例外的规则。

Nobody knew him *but* respected him. 认识他的人都尊敬他。

C. 由关系词 as 引出定语从句

as 既可作关系代词,也可作关系副词,引出限制性定语从句。它在从句中作主语、宾语或状语。

Such women *as* knew Tom thought he was handsome. 认识汤姆的女人都认为他帅。(关系代词 as 的先行词是 women, 它在定语从句中作主语。其实,句中的 such women as knew Tom = Those women who knew Tom)

She likes the same hat *as* he does. 她喜欢像他的那顶帽子。(先行词是 hat, 关系代词 as 在从句中作宾语,一般不省略)

You should do it in the same way *as* I did. 你应该像我那样做此事。(关系副词 as 的先行词是作状语用的介词短语中的 way, 因此 as 引出的定语从句是前面状语中的一部分,那 as 在从句中当然叫作状语。)

从上述例句可见,用 as 引出定语从句时,前面常有 same, such 等词与其搭配。

② 关系副词及其在从句中担当的成分

引出定语从句的关系副词有 when, where, as, that, why 等。关系副词在从句中作状语,分别表示时间、地点、原因等。

The October 1, 1949 was the day *when* the People's Republic of China was founded. 1949年10月1日是中华

人民共和国成立的日子。(when 在从句中作时间状语)
This is the house *where* his father was born. 这房子是他父亲出生的地方。(where 在从句中作地点状语)
The reason *why* she didn't attend the meeting was that her mother was ill. 她为什么没有参加那个会议的原因是她们的母亲病了。(why 在从句中作原因状语)

③ 关系代词和关系副词的使用选择

如何选用关系代词和关系副词取决于定语从句中的谓语动词的及物与否。如在先行词是表示地点的名词 house, town, place, village 等,而且从句中的谓语动词是不及物的,那就用 where 引出定语从句;如先行词是表示时间的名词 day, occasion, season 等,而且从句里的谓语动词是不及物的,那就用关系副词 when 引出定语从句。要是从句里的谓语动词是及物的,那要用 which 或 that 引出定语从句。同样,如先行词表示原因方面的名词的,如 reason,那引导词用 why;但从句中的谓语动词如是及物的,那也要用 that 引出定语从句。请看下面两组句子:

{ This is the *house where* Jim *lived* last term. 这是吉姆上学期住过的房子。
  This is the *house which/that* Jim *visited* last term. 这是他上学期参观过的房子。

We will never forget the happy *days when* we *lived* and *worked* together. 我们永远也不会忘记我们一起生活、工作的那些快活日子。

We will never forget the happy *days that/which* we spent together. 我们永远也不会忘记那些一起度过的那些快活日子。

从第 1 组可见,两句的先行词都是 house,但句 1 用关系副词 where 是因为从句中的谓语动词是不及物动词 lived, where 在从句中作地点状语;而句 2 用了关系代词 which/that 引出定语从句,因为从句中的谓语动词 spent 是及物动词,which/that 在从句中作宾语。第 2 组中的先行词都是 days,因句 1 中的谓语动词是不及物动词 lived 和 worked,所以用关系副词 when 引出定语从句,它在从句中作状语;而句 2 用 that/which 引出定语从句,因从句的谓语动词 spent 是及物动词,在从句中作宾语。

(2) "介词 + 关系代词 which, whom, whose/which" 结构

在定语从句中,常常涉及一些介词与 which, whom, whose, which 等词的搭配问题。这些关系代词与哪些介词进行搭配取决于定语从句中本身名词、动词或形容词的搭配要求,或根据句意而确定搭配的介词。其实,这些介词的选用也有一定规律可循。

① 根据定语从句名词先行词的搭配确定介词

当先行词是名词时,引出后面的定语从句的介词(+ 关系代词)要根据前面的先行词而定。
Her uncle bought her a grammar book *with which* she can look up sentence patterns and sentence structure easily. 她叔叔给她买了本语法书,用它她可方便地查阅英语句型和句子结构。(= Her uncle bought her a grammar book *which/that* she can look up sentence patters and sentence structure with)
The person *to whom* we should *write* first is Mr. White. 我们应该先给其写信的人是怀特先生。(= The person who(m)/that *we should write to* first is Mr. White.)

② 根据定语从句中的形容词的搭配要求确定介词

定语从句中的形容词要与一定的介词进行搭配的,如 fond 要与 of、interested 与 in 搭配等。
The ice-cream *of which* you are fond is on the desk. 你喜欢的冰淇淋在书桌上。(= The ice-cream *which/that* you are fond *of* is on the desk.)

③ 如表示所有关系或整体中的一部分时,关系代词前的介词要用 of

He lived in that house, the door *of which* faces north. 他住在那房子里,它的门朝北。(= He lived in that house *whose door* faces north.)

There are twenty-eight students in her class, twenty *of whom* are boys. 她班有二十八个学生,其中二十个是男生。(= There are twenty-eight students in her class *among whom* are twenty boys.)

④ 根据定语从句中谓语动词的要求确定介词

这种句式的情况是指引出从句中的"介词+关系代词"中的介词要以从句中的谓语动词合理搭配而锁定,如 talk with (to), speak to, lend … to, borrow … from, turn to (sb for help)等。

There was nobody there *with* whom she could *talk*. 那里没人她可与之交谈。(= There was nobody there whom/who/that she could talk with.)

In the dark street, there was not a single person *to* whom Mary could *turn* for help. 在这样一个漆黑的街上,没有一个人玛丽能求得帮助。(= In the dark street, there was not a single person whom/who/that Mary could turn *to* for help.)

Note:要是介词与关系代词不分开时,先行词如是人,那关系代词要用 whom(因是介宾),不能用 who 或 that;分开时,先行词如是人,那关系代词可用 who/whom/that。先行词是物时,不分开的话,关系代词要用 which;分开时,关系代词可用 which/that,而且可以省略。

The old woman *to whom* he *spoke* is Rose's grandmother. 他刚才与之说话的那老太是罗丝的祖母。[= The old woman (who/whom/that) he spoke to is Rose's grandmother.]

⑤ 根据从句句义灵活选用介词

这就是说根据从句句义比较灵活地来确定介词的选用,这种搭配是自然组合,并不是固定习语。

Li Na, *with whom* I went to visit the Great Wall last week, enjoyed herself very much. 李娜,上星期我与她一起去游览长城的,她玩得很开心。

The ancient city, Suzhou, *in which* we arrived last night is famous for its gardens and towers. 我们昨晚到达的那个古城苏州,以它的楼台园林而闻名。

This is the house *in which* I used to live when I was a child. 这就是我孩童时曾住过的房子。

上面例句 1 中的 went with sb 是"与人一起去"的意思,例句 2 中的 arrive in 是"到达一个较大的地方"的意思,它们都是自然组合。

(3) 限制性定语从句和非限制性定语从句

① 限制性定语从句

The woman who told me this refused to give me her name. 告诉我这件事的那个女人拒不说出她的名字。
The noise he made woke everybody. 他弄出的响声把所有的人都要闹醒了。

Note:限制性定语从句与被修饰的名词间没有逗号;限制性定语从句不可省略,如被省去意思就不完整。

② 非限制性定语从句

非限制性定语从句置于性质已经明确的名词后面。因此,它对这类名词不做限定性描述,仅对该项作进一步的说明予以补充而已。像这样的从句就是省去也不会引起语意混乱。还有一点是这种句子与被说明的名词之间有逗号隔开。

My master, who has written many books, often says hard work leads to success. 我的导师,他已写了很著作,常说勤奋出成果。

The experiment, which Professor Young has been making for many years, will come to an end successfully. 那个试验,杨教授已将其进行了好多个年头,将成功结束。

③ 限制性定语从句与非限制性定语从句的区别

A. 意义方面

限制性定语从句是句子的一部分,不能省去,省去后意思不完整。而非限制性定语从句被省去后意思仍完整,因为它是补充说明先行词的。

He has a daughter who is at school. 他有一个上学的女儿。(可能还有一个女儿或儿子)

He has a daughter, who is at school. 他有个女儿,还在上学。(只此一女,没有其他儿女了。)

B. 所涉及的先行项方面

限制性定语从句的先行词或词组是名词性的,而非限制性定语从句限制的可以是名词性的词或词组,也可以是主句中的部分或全句的抽象内容。

He wears a red shirt which makes him like a girl. 他穿着一件红衬衫,看上去像一个女孩。(其先行词是 shirt)

He wears a red shirt, which makes him like a girl. 他穿着一件红衬衫,看上去像一个女孩。(其先行项是前面的整个句子。)

C. 所选用的关系词方面

在限制性定语从句中,指物时可用 which 或 that;关系代词作定语从句的宾语时,可以省去,在口语里 that 可替换 whom, who, which;而在非限制性定语从句里,不能用 that 引导从句,也不能省去关系代词,可用 which, as 指代主句的部分或全句。

This/that is the book which/that I bought yesterday. 这/那是我昨天买的书。

Do you know Tom (whom/who/that) we talked about? 你认识我们谈论的汤姆吗?

I like the book, which I bought yesterday. 我喜欢这本书,我昨天买的。

Do you know Tom, whom we talked about? 你认识汤姆吗? 我谈论的汤姆?

She has to work on Sundays, which she doesn't like. 她必须周日工作,她不喜欢。

D. 汉译意义方面

限制性定语从句常译作"……的",而非限制性定语从句常另译成一句,与主句并列。

He has a daughter who is at school. 他有一个在上学的女儿。

He has a daughter, who is at school. 他有一个女儿,她还在上学。

④ **限制性定语从句中关系代词只能用 that 的四种情况**

A. 先行词前有"形容词最高级"、"序数词"等修饰时

在先行词前有形容词最高级、序数词或 all, no, only, every, little, much, the very 等修饰时,只能用 that。

This is the best film (that) I've seen. 这是我看过的最好电影。

That's the second bicycle (that) I have lost. 那是我丢失的第二辆自行车。

This was the only problem that was settled at the meeting. 这是会上落实的唯一问题。

B. 先行词本身就是 all, few, little, much, any, everything

I'm interested in all (that) you've told us. 我对你告诉我的一切感兴趣。

She saw much that was bad. 她看到很多坏的方面。

There's little (that) we can do besides wait. 除了等候,我们能做的事很少。

Don't throw away anything that may be of any use. 只要有用的东西就别扔掉。

但先行词是 something 时,关系代词可以用 that,也可用 which。

I saw something that/which was of great importance. 我看见非常重要的方面。

C. 全句开头已用疑问词 who, which 等后

Who is the man (that) we met just now? 我们刚刚遇到的那个人是谁?

Which of the books that were borrowed from him is the best? 我从他那儿借来的哪本书最好?

Where is the place (that) she used to hide? 我过去常常隐藏的地方在哪儿? (that = where)

D. 先行词同时是指人和物的两个或更多的单词时

They are talking about the school and the students that they visited. 他们正在谈论他们参观过的那所学校和学生。

第 25 章 副词、副词(状语)从句

25.1 副词

副词的英文单词 adverb 就是 ad-verb,即补充动词的意思。它用来修饰动词,告诉我们某事是如何、何时、何地发生或进行的,这反映出动词在句中的情况。除此之外,副词还可用来修饰副词、形容词、甚至句子,表示程度、看法、态度等;有时甚至还可用来修饰名词、代词、限定词、连词等,表示强调查。副词虽然不是句中必不可少的成分,但有了它们,句子表达的意思会更清楚。

(1) 副词分类

副词可分为简单副词、复合副词和派生副词三种。

① 简单副词

简单副词是指由单个词表达副词词义的词,如:fast(快;迅速地)(与形容词同形),there(那里)(地点副词),then(然后)(时间副词),often(经常)(频度副词),perhaps(也许)(观点副词)等。

② 复合副词

复合副词是指由两个词组成的副词,如:somewhere, therefore, however, hereby, herewith, whereto 等。

③ 派生副词

派生副词就是在某些词后加上副词后缀而派生出来的副词。它们主要是由在形容词后加-ly 和一些名词加一些副词组成。

A. 以-ly 结尾的副词

a. 在形容词词尾直接加-ly,如:clear→clearly, great→greatly, mad→madly, near(几乎)→nearly(几乎地), patient(耐心的)→patiently(耐心地), slow→slowly, usual(通常的)→usually(通常地)等。

b. 辅音字母加 y 结尾的形容词变成副词时,把 y 变成 i,再加 ly,如:easy→easily, heavy→heavily, happy→happily, hungry→hungrily, ordinary→ordinarily 等。

c. 以辅音字母加 y 结尾的形容词变成副词时,直接加 ly,如:spry(活泼/跃的)→spryly, wry(扭曲的)→wryly 等。

d. 以-le 结尾的形容词变成副词时,去 e,再加-y,如:gentle→gently, simple→simply, possible→possibly 等。

e. 结尾是-ue 的形容词变成副词时,去-e,再加-ly,如:due(应给予的)→duly, true-truly 等。

f. 以-ll 结尾的形容词变成副词时,在后面直接-y,如:full→fully, dull(不清楚的)→dully 等。

g. 以 ic 结尾的形容词变成副词时,通常加 ally,如:economic→economically, scientific→scientifically, politic→politically(例外:public→publicly)等。

h. 以-ed 结尾的形容词变成副词时,直接加-ly,不过原词的-ed 要念成/id/,最后念成/idli/,如:learned→learnedly(/-idli/), marked→markedly, assured→assuredly 等。

B．名词＋副词后缀

a．-wards（向）：back→backward(s)（向后），north→northwards（向北）

b．-ways（沿某方向）：side→sideways（斜向一边），cross→crossways（成十字形地）

（2）副词的句法功能

① 作状语

副词作状语,可说是其主要功能。副词作状语有多种表达内容。

A．表示时间、地点、频度、方式、程度等

We are having a meeting *now*. 我们现在在开会。（表示时间）

Do you know *where* Miss Li lives? 你知道李小姐住哪里？（表示地点）

How often does he go to see his grandfather? 他间隔多久去看望他爷爷？（表示频度）

His uncle used to smoke *heavily*. 他叔叔以前抽烟很厉害。（表示程度）

She has told me *how* to operate the machine. 她已经告诉过我如何操作那部机器了。（表示方式）

They *entirely* agree with me. 他们完全同意我的看法。（表示程度）

B．修饰形容词、副词或动词，表示程度。

Robert is a *very* careful writer. 罗伯特是个很细心的作家。（但请注意：This room is large *enough*.）

Rose was *greatly*（*all*）excited. 罗丝非常激动。

Her father smoke *heavily*. 她的父亲以前抽烟相当厉害。

He played *surprisingly* well. 他演奏得出奇地好。

C．修饰整个句子，表示说话人的看法或态度

They are *probably* at office. 他们大概在办公室。

Perhaps her suggestion will be accepted. 或许她的建议会被接受。

Obviously they are against the plan. 显然,他们反对这个计划。

Clearly, he's a very stupid person.（＝It is clear to me that he is a very stupid person.）很明显,他是个傻瓜。

D．修饰名词、代词、限定词、连词、介词短语等,表示强调

Only Chen Ming finished his homework that day. 那天只有陈明完成了他的作业。

Nearly everybody went to see the film. 几乎大家都去看了那部电影。

There is *hardly any* water left in the thermos. 保温瓶里几乎没水了。

She received *about double the amount* of reward she expected. 她收到了她所预料的大约两倍数字的报酬。

Just when I left the store, it began to rain heavily. 就在我离开商店时,天下起了大雨。

The tank went *right through the shop*, and three men in it was killed. 那辆坦克正好穿过那家商店,里面三人丧生。（副词right修饰介词短语 through the shop）

The lecture is *almost at an end*. 讲座差不多要结束了。（副词almost修饰介词短语 at an end）

② 作表语

Autumn is *in*. 秋天到了。

What's *up*? 发生了什么事啦?

③ 作定语

The girls *there* are sweeping the floor. 那里的女孩子在扫地。

We met Rose on our way *home*. 我们在回家的路上碰到了罗丝。(home 作副词用)

④ 作介语宾语和宾语补足语

I didn't know her until quite *recently*. 我直到最近才认识她。（副词recently作介词until的宾语）

Mark, ask them *in*, please. 马克,请他们进来。(副词 in 作宾语 them 的补语)

⑤ 起强调作用

有的副词可起强调作用,这种副词也叫强调副词。它们用来修饰名词短语。此种强调副词有 quite 和 rather.

They had *quite* a party. 他们办了一个相当不错的晚会。

It was *rather* a mess. 这真糟糕。

(3) 副词的比较等级

① 副词的比较等级与形容词一样,多数可分为原级、比较级和最高级三种。

A．单音节和少数双音节词比较等级

单音节和少数双音节副词级的比较级和最高级是在原级后加-er,或把 y 变 i,再加-er;最高级是在原级后加-est,或把 y 变成 i,再加-est;最高级前可加定冠词 the,或省去。

hard—harder—hardest　　　soon—sooner—soonest
fast—faster—fastest　　　　slow—slower—slowest

B．大多数副词是在它们前面加 more, most 构成比较级和最高级。

quickly—more quickly—most quickly　　carefully—more carefully—most carefully
fluently—more fluently—most fluently　　obviously—more obviously—most obviously

② 几个不规则变化的副词比较等级

well—better—best　　　　badly—worse—worst
little—less—least　　　　　much—more—most
far $\begin{cases} \text{farther—farthest} \\ \text{further—furthest} \end{cases}$

(4) 副词和形容词同形

这样的同形词有:better, best, bright, cheap, clear, close, deep, direct, early, fair, far, fast, full, high, ill, just, late, long, loud, low, near, sharp, slow, soft, straight, well, wide, wrong 等。

She was quite *right*（adj.）to refuse his invitation. 她拒绝他的邀请是完全正确的。

You must put it *right*（adv.）in the middle of the desk. 你必须把它放在办公桌的中间。

(5) 用"副词比较级+than …"表示两者之间的比较

Bob swims *faster than* I do. 伯勃比我游得快。

Mary paints better thar Rose does. 玛丽画得比罗丝好。

(6) 表示同等比较和同等比较的否定形式

在表示同等比较时,用"as + 原级 + as",表示否定时用"not as … as"或"not so … as"结构。

I can run *as fast as* he. 我能和他跑得一样快。

The foreigner speaks Chinese *as fluently as* we. 那个外国人讲汉语和我们讲得一样流利。

Usually adults don't learn a foreign language *as quickly as* children. 通常成年人学习外语没有小孩子快。

(7) 副词最高级的范围

副词最高级的范围与形容词一样,必须三者以上,它们在句中的表达跟形容词一样为"the + 最高级 … in（表示范围的状语）…"。

She works (*the*) *hardest* in her class. 她是班上学习最用功的。
Of all his books, I like this one *best*. 他所有的书中,我最喜欢这本。

25.2 状语从句

(1) 时间状语从句

时间状语从句用来表示主句动作发生的时间。表示句子动作发生的时间也可用单词、词组、短语来表示,如:*When* did he go to see his English teacher? (时间疑问副词 when 作状语), I think you can reach Suzhou *by noon*. (介词短语 by noon 作时间状语), Lei doesn't know *when* to start her work. (句中的 when 作时间状语,修饰 to start our work,整个 when to start our work 是 know 的宾语)。

① 同时性从句

同时性从句是指与主句动作同时发生的从句。

A. "同时性从句"的连词

引导"同时性从句"的连词有:as, as long as, so long as, while, whilst, when, whenever, now (that) 等。有时 as, when, while, whilst 等连词可以互换。

Tom read a book *as/when/while/whilst* we watched television. 我们在看电视时,汤姆在煮饭。

I saw Mary *as/when/while/whilst* I was walking to the station. 当我上火车站时,看见过玛丽。

Notes: a. 在上面两句中,例句 1 的从句与主句的动作是平行同时发生的。例句 2 主句的动作是在从句动作的过程中发生的。

b. as 有时可译为"随着……"。

We will grow wiser *as* we grow older. 我们将随着年龄的增长而越来越聪明。

As the sun rose, the fog disappeared. 随着太阳的升起,雾渐渐地消失了。

c. 有时,连词 while 引导的从句与主句都用进行时以表示持续性的动作或状态。

While I was watching television, he was reading an interesting story. 我在看电视时,他在看一部很有趣的小说。

B. as 与 while 表示"段同时"

在"同时性从句"中,虽然 as 与 while 都可指一段时间内主句和从句动作同时进行,但 as 从句强调的是平行动作,而 while 从句强调动作持续的全过程。它们均可译成"一边……一边……"。

She sang *as* she read. 她一边看书一边唱歌。(强调平行动作)

She sang *while* she read. (译文同上)(强调动作持续全过程)

C. as 与 when 表示"点同时"

在"同时性从句"中,连词 as 和 when 用来表示"点同时",即表示从句与主句中两个短暂的动作同时发生。从句和主句中都用瞬时动词(或叫点动词),但 as 连词引导的从句表示更短暂的时间,所以常在 as 前加上 just 来加强其更短暂的动作。

She arrived *as/when* we stepped out of the car. 我们下车时,她就到了。

Henry went out just *as* Mary entered. 玛丽进来时,亨利正好出去。

when 引导的从句也可以表示"段同时",这时从句谓语动词用持续性动词或状态动词。

有时,when 从句的动作与主句的动作同时发生,有时主句的动作出现在 when 从句的一段时间内。

When it is wet, the buses are crowded. 下雨时,公共汽车总是很拥挤。(when 从句与主句动作同时发生,从句用状态动词)

When she lived in Shanghai, she often went to see her aunt. 她住在上海时,常去看她婶婶。(主句动作重复出现在从句表示的一段时间内)

D. as,when 和 while 的用法比较

as,when 和 while 用来引导时间状语从句时,都有"在……时候"之义,但是其内含语义不完全相同。三词中,引导的从句主要表示从句动作与主句动作相互发生,强调从句的动作发生后,主句的动作随之发生,两者一先一后,十分紧凑,从句与主句的动作同时发生,从句先于主句动作,且常表示动作的过程,而不表示状态,所以常译作"一边……一边"。when 有时可用来代替 while,但 while 不能用来代替 when。while 引导的时间状语从句只可指一段时间,不可指一点时间,while 从句与主句的动作总是同时发生,但强调的多为动作的过程,所指的时间比 as 要大一些。

As the temperature increases, the volume of a gas becomes greater. 随着温度的增加,气体的体积变大。(动作一先一后,十分紧凑)

I'll let you know *when* it is arranged. 此事安排好后,我会告诉你。(从句动作在主句之前)

While she sang, she danced. 她边唱边跳。(主从句动作同时发生,指一段时间)

While the child was playing with his toys, his parents were reading books. 孩子在玩玩具,他的父母在读书。(主从句动作同时发生,指一段时间)

当表示一段时间时,三个连词常常可以互换使用。

When/While/As I was walking down the street, I noticed a police car in front of No. 37. 沿街而行时,我注意到一辆警车停在 37 号门前。

I entered *while/when/as* the meeting was going on. 会议正在进行时,我进了会议室。

在指一点时间时,as 常常与 when 互换使用。

As/When he stood up, he dropped the glass. 起立时,他放下了玻璃杯。

② 先时性从句

先时性从句是指从句的动作发生在主句之前。

A."先时性从句"的连词

引导"先时性从句"的连词有:after, as soon as, as often as(每当), each/every time, now (that), when, whenever, directly, immediately, instantly, the instant/moment/minute/second, once, since。

B. 先时性从句动作的先与后

先时性从句的动作不仅表示从句的动作发生在主句前,有时也表示从句的动作发生后瞬间,主句的动作就紧接着发生了。请看下面例句:

She found her pen was *gone after Jane had left the room*. 简离开房间后,她发现钢笔不见了。

I will tell her the good news *as soon as I see her*. 我一看见她就会告诉她这个好消息。

He came *directly he got my message*. 他一得到我的口信就来了。

She recognized me *immediately she saw me*. 她一看见我就认出我来了。

Lei made me feel at home *the moment/instant/minute/second I arrived*. 我一到,蕾就使我感到像在自己家里一样。

Once you arrive, we can start. 你一到,我们就可以开始了。

I will come *as son as I've finished supper*. 我一吃过晚饭就来。

They told me the news *immediately they got the message*. 他们一得到口信,就把消息告诉我了。

C. 有时,when 相当于 after,也表示从句动作先于主句的动作

When/After she had had her breakfast, she began to work. 她吃过早饭后开始工作。

D. as often as 相当于 whenever

whenever 是"每逢"、"每当"的意思,有时 as often as 相当于 whenever。

Whenever that man says "To tell the truth", I suspect that he's about to tell a lie. 每当那人说"说实在话"的时候,我猜想他就要说谎了。

We shall finish it *as often as we can*. 能够完成它时我们就会完成它。

As often as John came, he stayed with us. 约翰每次来总住在我们家。

E．each/every time

在 each/every time 所表示的从句的动作发生后，主句的动作紧接着就发生。

Each time I go to Beijing, I would visit the Great Wall. 每次到北京，我都要去游览长城。

Every time the little boy listens to you, he gets into trouble. 那个小男孩每次听你的，总招来麻烦。

③ 后时性从句

后时性从句是指从句的动作发生在主句之后。

A．"后时性从句"的连词

引导"后时性从句"的连词常用：before, till, until, when, hardly/scarcely … when/before, no sooner … than。

B．连词 before 引导的后时性从句从其本身的词汇意义上就可看出从句的动作发生在主句之后

I had finished my work *before you got here*. 你到这里前我已完成了我的工作。（从句用过去时，主句用过去完成体）

She knocked several times *before a little girl answered the door*. 她敲了几次门，一个小女孩才来开门。

C．hardly/scarcely … when/before, no sooner … than 是"一……就……"的意思

这几个连词词组都是表示主句和从句动作随即相继发生，主句动词用过去完成体。如果 no sooner, hardly 或 scarcely 位于句首，主句要倒装，即把 had 放在主语前。

I had *hardly/scarcely* finished my homework *before/when* the light went out. 我刚做完作业，灯就熄了。

We had *no sooner* reached home *than* it began to rain. 我们刚到家天就下雨了。

No sooner had he got off the train *than* his daughter ran towards him. 他一下火车，他女儿就朝他跑去。

Note：hardly … when 和 scarcely … when 有时可同 not … before 换用。

They had hardly talked for half an hour when she entered. (= They had not talked for half an hour befoe she entered.) 他们才谈了不到半小时她就进来了。

④ 时间从句的时与体

在时间从句中，动词的时态与主句的时态有紧密的联系，而不同连词引导出的从句中时态用法也不相同。

A．时间从句中的将来意思

时间从句中用将来意思有两种情况：一是用一般现在时或现在完成体代替将来意思；二是可用或必须用 shall 或 will 表示将来意思。

a．用一般现在时或现在完成体代替将来意思

一般现在时表示说明将来的事实或动作，其时现在完成体所表示将来是强调动作的结果或完成。

The Chen's will move to a new flat *when their baby is/has been born*. 陈先生一家在孩子出生后将搬进一套新公寓去住。

When we have finished our letters, we usually take them to the post ourselves. 写完信后，我们通常都是亲自去邮寄。

He will go *directly he has finished his homework*. 他一做完功课就直接去。

They often play chess *after they have had supper*. 他们晚饭后经常下棋。

b．可用或必须使用 shall/will 的情况。

• 用在 before 时间从句里表示说话人的意愿，这时 before 相当于 rather than,常译成"宁愿"。

I will die of hunger *before I will steal*. 我宁愿饿死也不愿偷东西。

Tom will do anything *before his family shall want*. 汤姆宁愿做任何事情也不愿家里受穷。

- 用在 before 时间从句中是"过一段时间才……"的意思。

It will be long *before she will come back.* 她要过很久才会回来。

Will it be a long time *before you will/shall see me again?* 你要过很久才能见到我吗？

- 有时，用于 until 时间从句中表示时间的延续。

Mr. Green is to be held until an investigating officer will come. 格林先生将被拘留到调查官到来为止。

- 当 when 时间从句置于主句后，且前面有逗号与主句隔开，此时的 when 就相当于 and then，主句中常陪伴如 till 之类的表示时间界限的词。

We must wait till noon, *when*(= and then) *Professor Zhang will be here.* 我们必须等到中午，那时张教授就会到了。

You'd better stay here till eleven, *when*(= and then) *Lei will come back.* 你最好等到十一点，那时蕾就回来了。

Note：当 when 前没有逗号时，其后可用现在时或将来时间表示法。

We shall be on holiday till the end of August *when we return/shall return to Beijing.* 我们休假到八月底，之后我们将返回北京。

⑤ 一些常用连词从句中的时与体

A. before 时间从句中的时与体

a. 主从句都用过去时和主句用过去完成体，从句用一般过去时。

Mary finished her article *before John arrived.* 在约翰到达之前，玛丽已写完了那篇文章。

Mary had finished her article *before John arrived.*（译文同上）

上面例句 1 虽用了一般过去时，但 before 这词本身词义就明确表示出动作的先后关系；而例句 2 中的主句用了过去完成体，从句用一般过去时就更明确了主从句动作的先后关系。

b. "It was(n't) long/a long time + before 从句"中，主句必须用一般过去时替代过去完成体，以此表示主句的动作先于从句的动作，而从句用一般过去时。

It was a long time *before I got her another letter.* 过了很长时间，我才收到她的第二封信。

It wasn't long *before you were able to stand up.* 不久，你就能站起来了。

c. 主句用一般过去时，before 从句用过去完成体，这是过去完成体的一种特殊用法。其实这时的 before 从句中用的过去完成体是表示一个过去没有完成或没有及时去做时间顺序在后的动作。在这种情况下，before 从句还是可以用一般过去时的。

The old man died *before his daughter had had/had a chance to speak to him.* 他女儿还没来得及跟他说话，老人就死了。

We went out *before the bell had rung/rang.* 铃还没有响，我们就出去了。

Note：before 从句只能用于肯定式，但译成汉语时却要译成"还没来得及……"这样的否定式。

d. before 从句用一般过去时，有时可用"could + 不带 to 的动词"构成谓语，主句用过去完成体或一般过去时。

It began to rain *before I got to the top of the hill.* 我还没爬到山顶，天就下起雨来了。

Before Henry could have his breakfast, the bell had rung/rang for class. 亨利还没来得及吃早饭，上课铃就响了。

B. after 从句与主句的时与体

a. 如 after 从句的时态在主句动作之前，此时从句用过去完成体，主句用一般过去时；由于 after 连词的词汇意义已明确表示出动作的先后关系，所以主从句均可用一般过去时。

They reached the airport *after the plane had left/left.* 飞机起飞后他们才到机场。

I told her the news *after you had left/left.* 你走了之后我才告诉她那个消息。

b. 当 after 从句用来表示自然规律时，主从句用一般现在时，从句也可用现在完成体。

第 25 章　副词、副词(状语)从句

After it leaves the blades, the steam passes out to the atmosphere. 蒸气离开叶片后,释放到大气中。

Water becomes steam *after it is heated to over* 100℃. 水被加热到摄氏 100 度以上就会变成蒸气。

C. when 从句与主句的时与体

a. 当 when 从句和主句的动作同时发生时,主从句都用一般时或进行体,或者可以一个用一般时态,一个用进行体。

Mike came back to his home town *when he was seventy*. 迈克七十岁时回到了家乡。

They have been working *when I've been sitting here talking*. 我坐在这里谈话,他们一直在干活。

When Grace returned from work at four, her daugter was watching TV in the hall. 格蕾丝四点下班回家,她女儿在客厅看电视。

b. 当 when 从句和主句动作先后发生时,主句和从句都可用一般过去时。如果强调两个过去的动作的先后顺序时,那发生在先的用过去完成体,另一个用一般过去时。

When I opened the window, a beautiful butterfly flew in. 我打开窗户,一只漂亮的蝴蝶飞了进来。

When she came home, her son had gone to bed. 她回家时,她儿子已上床睡觉了。

c. when 从句中所用动词类型不同,所选用的时与体也不同

when 从句中用终止性动词时,可用一般过去时替代过去完成体;when 从句中用的是持续性动词,那就不能用过去时代替过去完成体,以免使人产生主句和从句的动作同时发生的歧义。

When he had got/got home, everybody went to bed. 他回家后,我们就上床睡觉。

When she had sung, she sat down. 她唱完了歌,然后坐下。

D. while 从句与主句的时与体

a. 主从句都用过去进行体,表示主从句的两个动作持续时间大致相等。

Mary was doing her homework *while you were playing pingpong*. 你在打乒乓时,玛丽在做作业。

b. 主句用一般过去时,从句用一般过去时或过去进行体。

Mike read a newspaper *while he waited/was waiting for the bus*. 迈克在等汽车时就看报纸。

c. 当主从句动作持续的时间有长短时,那时间长的动作用过去进行体,持续短的动作用一般过去时。

I broke a glass *while I was cooking the supper*. 我煮饭时打破了一只杯子。

E. till/until 从句与主句的时与体

a. 在表示两个过去动作或状态时,till/until 从句用一般过去时或过去完成体,主句用一般过去时。

I waited *till/until the rain stopped/had stopped*. 我一直等到雨停。

We didn't go *till/until the rain stopped/had stopped*. 我们等到雨停才去。

b. 但有时为了强调 till/until 从句的动作完成在先,那也可以在 till/until 后加 after 这词加以突出。

She didn't find her seats *till/until after the play had begun*. 戏开始后她才找到自己的位子。

F. since 从句与主句的时与体

主句用现在完成体(非正式语体中也有用一般过去时的),since 从句用一般过去时或现在完成体。要特别注意的是,在 since 从句中,终止性动词表示肯定意义;持续性动词的一般过去时表示否定意义,那就是与词汇的字面意义相反,但持续性动词的现在完成体则表示肯定的意思,也就是与该动词字面词义相一致。

a. 主句用现在完成体,从句也用现在完成体。

She met me often *since I have moved to her block*. 自从我搬到她的街区之后,她常见到我。

b. 主句用现在完成体,从句用一般过去时。

I haven't seen her *since she left*. 自从她走了以后,我一直没有看见过她。

c. 主从句都用一般过去时。

I lost (= have lost) fifteen pounds *since I started running and swimming*. 我开始跑步和游泳以来,体重减轻了十五磅。

d. 有时,主句用现在完成进行体,从句仍用一般过去时。

I have been feeling much better *since I saw the doctor*. 自从求医以来,她感觉身体好多了。

e. 如主从句都表示过去动作,主句可用过去完成体,since 从句用一般过去时或过去完成体。

Robert had written two books about love *since he was a friend of hers*. 自从罗伯特与她断交后,他写了二本关于爱情方面的书。

Since John (had) improved his methods of study, he had made rapid progress in his studies. 约翰自改进他的学习方法后,他在学习上取得了飞快的进步。

f. 在 ever since 引导的从句中,ever 是用来加强语气的。在这种情况下,ever since 从句用一般过去时,表达肯定的含义,主句用现在完成体或现在完成进行体。

She has worked as one of the managers in our shop *ever since she graduated from Beijing University*. 她从北京大学毕业以来,一直在我们店里任一经理。

Mary hasn't written anything *ever since she was ill*. 自从玛丽病好后,她就再也没有动过笔。

Ever since I saw the film, I've been having night mares. 从看那部电影以来,我一直做噩梦。

g. since 所引导的从句一般要用非延续性动词,主句用完成体。

Since he graduated from the college, he has worked in this city. 他大学毕业后一直在这个城市里工作。

Jack came to see me last month. *Since we left school (till then)*, we had not seen each other. 杰克上个月来看我。自从我们离开学校(直到那时),我们一直没有见面。

Notes:● since 所引导的从句如果用延续性动词或状态动词的过去式,所表示的就是动作或状态的完成或结果。

Since he lived in Nanjing, I have not heard from him. (= Since he left Nanjing …) 自从他离开南京以来,我没有收到过他的信。

Since she was in Yangzhou, she has kept correspondence with her former friends. (= Since she left Yangzhou, …) 她离开扬州以来,一直同过去的朋友保持着通信联系。

● 作介词时,since 后要接时间点,不接时间段,since 还用作副词。

＊He has been writing the book since five years. (错误)

He has been writing the book since five years ago. 五年前他就已经写书了。(正确)

He has been writing the book for five years (since he retired). 他写书已经五年了。(正确)

h. It + be + 一段时间 + since 从句

● 在这个句型中,主句常用一般现在时,偶尔用一般过去时、完成体和将来时,从句用一般过去时。

It is thirty years *since they saw each other*. 他们已有 30 年没见面了。

Next Monday it will be/will have been forty years *since I became a teacher*. 到下星期一我成为一名教师已有四十年了。

● 当 since 从句中有 last 之类明显的表示时间点的标记时,也可用现在完成体,不过从句中的持续性动作是肯定形式、否定含义,但绝不能用否定式表达。

It has been two years *since we last saw you*. 我们已有两年没见到你了。

It is thirty years *since you have seen each other*. 你们已有 30 年没见面了。

● 当主句中的谓语是 be, seem 之类的状态动词时可用非完成体或完成体形式,since 从句用一般过去时。

Things are/have been much better *since he left*. 自从他走了后,事情更加好了。

She feels/is much better *since he took the medicine*. 她服药以来,感到身体好多了。

● 当 since 从句中用了 can remember 和 could remember,那是表示人的记忆所及的时间跨度。在这样的表达中常把 ever since 合起来用。

Grace has had such impression *ever since she can remember*. 格蕾丝从能记事时起就有了这种印象。

Ever since she could remember, the summer in her home town has been very hot. 从她能记事以来,她家乡的夏天是非常炎热的。

G．as, when 和 while 状语从句中动词的时与体

a. 持续性动词和终止性动词在 as 从句中使用时,如 as 从句指一段时间时,要用持续性动词,如指一点时间时,那要用终止性动词。

He sang *as he worked*. 他一边干活,一边唱歌。

As you left the house, you remembered the key. 你离家时,记起了钥匙。

b. 持续性动词和终止性动词在 when 从句中使用时,如 when 从句指一段时间时,要用持续性动词,如指一点时间时,那要用终止性动词。

When Jane was walking down the street, she met one of her old schoolmates. 简在街上走的时候,碰见了她的一位老同学。

When I arrived, he was writing. 我到的时候,他在写东西。

c. 持续性动词和终止性动词在 while 从句中使用时。

- 通常,连词 while 引导出的从句中的动词是持续性动词。

They sang happily *while they walked home.* 他们走回家时高兴地唱着歌。

- 现代英语中,while 从句也有用终止性动词的。

Mike put the newspaper on the toilet tank beside him *while he finished washing.* 迈克洗好脸后把那张报纸放在身边的洗槽上。

⑥ 时间句的强调形式

时间句的强调一般用三种形式实施:把副词 only 置于句首;把否定词置于句首;用"It is/was … that"结构。这种强调形式也包含时间状语的简单句。

A．把副词 only 置于句首

在强调 after/when/then 短语和从句时,经常把 only 置于句首实施强调。此时,主句的主谓语要部分倒装。

Only after the war was over, she able to go back to her work. 只有在战争结束后,她才能回去继续工作。

Only then can I do the work myself. 只有到那时我才能自己做那个工作。

Only after we had performed hundreds of experiments did we succeed in solving the problem. 只有在做了几百次实验后,我们才把这一问题解决了。

Only when we gets there will we telephone you. 只有我们到达了那里,我们才会打电话给你。

B．把否定词置于句首

以 not until 开头的从句(因为从句可以置于主句前,从句不倒装)及像 hardly/scarcely … when/before, no sooner … than 开头的句子,它们的否定词放在句首时,主句的主谓语须部分倒装。

Not until the sun had set did I go home from work. 到太阳下山,我才下班回家。

Not until she comes back will the children leave the house. 直到她回家,孩子们才会离开那屋子。

Hardly/Scarcely had their father entered the room *when/before* the children rushed out. 他们的父亲进屋,孩子们就冲了出去。

No sooner had I said hello to Lei *than* tears came from her eyes. 我一对蕾说再见,她就热泪盈眶。

C．用"It is/was … that"结构

以 after, when, before 和 not until 开头的那些句子中都可以用"It is/was … that"句型实施强调。

It was after the sun had set that the workers went home from work. 太阳落山后,工人们才下班回家。

It was when the moon had risen that the farmers left their fields. 月亮升起来时,农民才离开他们的土地。

It was not until the clock had struck seven that she got the children up and dressed for school. 直到时钟打了

七下,她才让孩子们起床,穿好衣服去上学。

⑦ 时间句的省略和替代

A. 时间句的省略

当时间从句的主语与主句的主语一致而且谓语动词又是 be 时,从句的主语和动词 be 通常省略,有时它们就是无动词句。

When angry (= When you are angry), count a hundred. 生气时,数一百。

While still at college (= While she was still at college), Miss Mary had her first novel published. 还在上大学时,玛丽小姐就出版了她的第一部小说。

B. 时间句的替代

有时,为了使句子简洁明了,节省时间和笔墨,用介词短语、分词短语、独立结构等形式替代时间句是很常见的现象。

a. 用"连词 when, while, once + 介词短语"替代。

She always sings when doing her homework (= when he is doing his homework). 她做作业时经常唱歌。

While waiting to see the doctor (= While she was waiting to see the doctor), Mary finished reading a short story. 在候诊时玛丽看完了一篇短篇小说。

Once published (= Once it was published), the English grammar book caused a remarkable stir. 这本英语语法书一出版就引起了异常轰动。

b. 用介词短语替代。

Before taking meals (= Before we are going to take meals), we are asked to wash their hands. 吃饭前,要我们洗手。

Since arriving in this foreign city (= After I have arrived in this foreign city), I have tried my best to "do as the Romans do". 来到那个外国城市后,我已尽力做到"入乡随俗"。

c. 用分词短语替代。

Walking along the river (= While she was walking along the river), she met a friend of hers. 在河边走时,她碰到了她的一个朋友。

Having done our homework (When/After we have done their homework), we went to see a film. 我们做完功课后,去看了部电影。

d. 在从句的主语与主句的主语不相同时,从句部分可以用独立结构来代替。

The job finished (= After the job was finished), Mr. Green left the room and went home. 工作干完后,格林先生离开那房间回家去了。

The lamp having been lit (= When the lamp had been lit), Mr. White produced his daughter's letter. 电灯亮后,怀特先生拿出他女儿的信。

(2) 原因状语从句

原因状语从句(Adverbial Clause of Cause)表示主句中动作或状态发生的原因或理由。原因状语从句的位置可以在主句之前也可以在主句之后,还可插在主句中间。这种句子常用"why …?"进行提问。当然,表示原因除了用从句之外,也可以用词语、短语来实施。用从句表达原因,除了直接的原因状语从句外,还可用并列句中的分句、虚拟结构、"It is … that"强调结构等表示原因。

① 用单词表示原因

这种单词要算数量巨大的介词(短语)了。这些介词有简单介词和复合介词两种。确切地说,这些介词必须与相关的词语组成介词短语方可履行其表示原因的职能。

A．简单介词短语表示原因

这些简单介词有：after, as, by, at, from, in, for, of, on, over, through, to, under, with, without 等。

After standing for hours on the bus, Henry felt very tired.（由于）在汽车上站了几个小时，亨利感到很累。

Mike ought to succeed *after his painstaking efforts*. 迈克付出了艰苦的努力，所以应该成功。

Note：上例中的介词 after 虽然字面意义是"在……之后"，但其深层含义上表示时间上先出现的情况是后一种情况的原因。

As a professor of English language, he is naturally very much interested in English sentence patterns and syntax, and has written some books about them. 由于他是英语语言教授，所以他对英语句型和句法很感兴趣，并且写了几部那方面的专著。

She is the dean of the department, and *as such has to sign this paper*. 因为她是系主任，因此她必须在这个文件上签字。

上两例中 as 意为"由于（某种身份）"，与 in the capacity of 相当。

She felt glad *at what I said*. 听了我的话，她感到高兴。

You were ashamed *at being unable to give an answer*. 你因回答不出而感到羞愧。

Li Li wept with joy *at the sight of her long-lost child*. 见到丢失了很久的孩子，丽丽高兴得哭了起来。

Lei wondered *at his rudeness*. 蕾对他的粗鲁感到惊讶。

从上述例句可见，介词 at 常与表示情感的形容词和分词搭配使用，说明产生某种感情的原因。除上述的这些常见的形容词和分词外，还有 aghast, surprised, alarmed, frightened 等。at 也常与表达情感的动词 blush, cry, grieve, hesitate, marvel, rejoice, shudder, weep, wonder 等连用，表示产生某种感情的原因。

Jim and his brother succeeded *by hard work*. 吉姆和他弟弟因勤奋工作而获得了成功。

By good fortune, you succeeded the first time. 由于运气好，你第一次就成功了。

Many birds know how to build nests *by instinct*. 很多鸟完全是因为本能而会筑巢的。

Note：by 介词短语表示由某种行为或由于某种手段或方法的作用所形成的原因，或由某种因素造成的原因。

Suzhou is famous *for its beautiful gardens*. 苏州以其美丽的园林而闻名于世。

Einstein is best known *for his theory of relativity*. 爱因斯坦主要因为他的相对论而闻名。

Professor Li was respected *for his achievements* in the fields of science. 李教授因为他在科学领域取得的诸多成就而受到尊敬。

Xiaowang shed tears *for anxiety about his mother's sickness*. 小王因母亲的病焦急得落泪。

Notes：a. 从上面的例句1、2中，介词 for 与其后面的词语组成的短语说明出现某种情况的原因；而例句3、4 的 for 短语是说明产生某种情感或与情感有关动作的原因。

b. 介词 for 前用动词 die 表示死亡原因，这种原因常表示为某一事业、理想、追求、信仰等而献身。

Liu hulan would rather *die for* my ideas than give in. 刘胡兰宁愿为她的理想而死也不屈服。

To *die for* one's motherland is an honour, not a misfortune. 为国捐躯是一种荣誉，而不是一种不幸。

c. 还要指出的是，一些与 for 组成固定搭配的短语表示原因，如：all the more for（因……而更），for a change（为了改变），for fear of/that（怕……），for the good of（为……的利益），for lack（因缺少），for the sake of（为了……缘故），not the less for（不……而减少）等。

He devoted his whole life to working *for the good of the poor*. 他一生都在为穷人谋福利。

She cited the example *for the sake of comparison*. 她为了对比而举这个例子。

He does not work the less hard for his repeated failures. 他不是因屡屡失败而减少对工作的努力。

B．复合介词短语表示原因

as a result of（由于，作为……的结果），because of（因为，由于），due to（由于，应归于），by reason/

occasion of（由于，因为，凭……的理由）, by right of（由于，凭借，以……理由）, in consideration of（考虑到……，由于，鉴于）, in consequence of（考虑到……，由于，鉴于）, in/by the light of（由于，按，因为，考虑到）, in view of［因为，由于，鉴于（看到某种情况）］, on account of（为了……的缘故，因为，由于）, on the score of（因为，由于）, owing to（亏得，归功于）, thanks to（由于，全靠，幸亏）等都是用来表示原因的复合介词。在这众多表示"原因"的表达中，有的意思相差较大，有的几乎相同，但其中还有差异。要确如其分地使这些表达，得视不同的语境、场合及话语者说话的动机等选择使用。

As a result of his hard work, he has made great progress. 由于学习努力，他进步很快。

The flight was delayed as a result of fog. 因有雾该航班误点。

His son didn't go to school today because of illness. 因为生病，他儿子今天没去上学。

Because of his wife being there, I said nothing about it. 因为他妻子在场，我对此事一字未提。

I should say his success is due to chance. 我认为他的成功是由于机会好。（言外之意，并不是能力强，技术好，水平高……）

The team's success was largely due to her efforts. 该队的成功在很大程度上是由于她的努力。

By reason of her health, she was excused from the meeting. 由于健康原因，她获准免于参加会议。

Mr York's lawyer also pleaded him not guilty by reason of insanity. 约克先生的律师也以精神错乱为他作无罪辩护。

By occasion of his lameness the boy could not play games. 由于跛足，那男孩不能参加游戏。

She is British by right of marridge. 她由于结婚而成了英国人。

The Normans ruled England by right of conquest. 诺曼人籍征服的力量统治英国。

He was pardoned in consideration of his youth. 考虑到年幼，他被宽恕了。

In consideration of her long service, the company granted her a pension of 8,000 dollars a year. 由于她服务时间长，公司每年付给她8,000美元养老金。

She didn't join in boating that day in consequence of her sudden illness. 由于突然患病，她那天没参加划船。

In consideration of the long drought, we are extremely short of water. 由于长期干旱，我们非常缺水。

In the light of these changes, we must revise our plan. 由于出现了那些情况，我们必须修改我们的计划。

He reviewed his decision in the light of recent developments. 他根据最近的事态发展重新考虑自己的决定。

I had told Alexander privately that in view of my promise to the soldiers, I refused to attack before October. 我私下告诉亚历山大，鉴于我对战士们的许诺，我不愿在10月前发动进攻。

In view of the recent developments, we do not think this step advisable. 由于最近事态的发展，我们认为这一步不可取。

These errors are owing to sheer carelessness. 这些差错完全是由于粗心大意造成的。（作表语）

The service is poor owing to a shortage of staff. 服务之所以差是因为缺少工作人员。

Thanks to the traffic jam on the way to the airport, I missed my plane. 由于去机场的交通阻塞，我误了飞机。（表示消极因素）

Thanks to a good teacher, she passed the examination. 幸亏有位好老师，她通过了考试。

C. 用动词表示原因

用动词表示原因有两种情况：一种是动词先表示"因"，而后带出果；另一种是动词先表示"果"，而后显示出"因"。

a. 用简单动词直接表示原因，如 cause, spark, stand 等，而后得出结果。

Don't you think what you did will cause much confusion? 难道你不认为你所做的事会引起很大的混乱吗？

All her unhappiness was caused by her beauty and wealth. 她所有的不幸都是由于她的美丽和财富引起的。

Who could tell the reason standing behind the successful young man's suicide? 谁能说出为何这位有成就的

年轻人要自杀呢?

We all know what *stands* behind the principal's resignation. 我们大家都知道校长为何要辞职。

Note：不及物词 stand 常与介词 behind 连用,表示因果关系,其意思可译为"导致"、"造成"。

The essay published in *China Daily* has *sparked* a major discussion on how to improve the system of education. 发表在《中国日报》的那篇论文引起了对教育制度改革的广泛讨论。

The move *sparked* violent anti-Japan demonstrations in China. 这一行动在中国引发了强烈的反日示威游行。

上例的 spark 作及物动词用；spark 与副词 off 搭配成短语动词,意思也是"引发"、"引起"的意思。

Border clashes have *sparked off* an all-round war between the two countries. 边界冲突已导致了两国的全面战争。

b. 英语中有很多短语动词也用来表示原因,它们是 account for, arise/rise from, ascribe to(把……归于), attribute to, come from/of/out of, ensue from, impute to, issue from, lead to, lie in, refer to, result from/in, set up, spring from, stem from 等。这些短语动词中有的是先表示原因,后得出结果；有的是先给出结果,后说明原因。

• 先原因,后结果

这样的短语动词也是很多,常用的有：account for 意为"是……的原因"、"说明……的原因",它的用法是 C accounts for R,也就是"前因后果"。

This might *account for* his optimistic view. 这大概是他持乐观观点的原因。

Tom's convincing analysis *accounted for* Grace seeing the point and acknowledging the corn. 汤姆那令人信服的分析使得格蕾丝对问题有了认识并承认了错误。

短语动词 lead to 的意思是"导致"、"使得"、"造成"等。它可有以下几种表示法：

* lead sb/sth into 意思是使某人/物处于某种状态。

His careless spending *led him into debt*. 他的乱花钱使他负上了债。

* 某人/某物 lead sb do sth, lead 后是复合宾语,意思是"使某人/物做某事"。

Hard work *leads him to make progress* every day. 勤奋学习使他学习天天向上。

Curiosity *led her to observe and study* the lives of the wild animals. 好奇心使她对野生动物的生活加以观察和研究。

• 先结果,后原因

下面这些短语动词是表示先结果后原因。

* arise/rise from 的意思是表示先结果后原因。"起因于",现多用 rise from, 因 arise from 用法陈旧。

Her being late for school *rose* partly *from* her oversleeping. 她上学迟到有几分是因睡过头所致。

Quarrels between them often *rise from* trifles. 他们之间的争吵常由小事引起。

The country's present difficulties *rise from* the reduced value of its money. 该国目前的困难是货币贬值引起的。

* ascribe to 的意思是"认为……是由 …… 造成的"、"把……归因于",语气比较肯定。

We *ascribed* the forest fire *to* carelessness. 我们认为这次森林大火是由粗心造成的。

She *ascribed* her failure *to* bad luck. 她把失败归咎于运气不好。

* originate 是不及物动词,常与介词 from 或 in 连用,意思是"起源于"、"由……引起"。

The quarrel between you *originated in* a misunderstanding. 你们之间的争吵由误会引起。

Do you know coal of all kinds has *originated from* the decay of plant? 你是否知道各种煤是由腐烂的植物形成的?

* attribute to 的意思是"把…… 归因于"、"认为……是……的结果"、"认为……的原因是",这意思含有个人的判断和看法。

We *attribute* Edison's success *to* intelligence and hard work. 我们把爱迪生的成功归因于他的智力和艰苦

工作。

He *attributed* his success *to* hard work and a bit of good luck. 他认为他的成功是由于勤奋加上一点儿好运气而得来的。

* come from/of/out of 的意思是"由……引起"、"是……的结果"、"由……造成"。

What results do you expect to *come from* all this activities? 你预计这一切活动将会引起什么结果？

Poverty often *comes of* idleness. 贫困往往产生于懒惰。

This is what *comes of* being overconfident. 这就是过于自信的结果。

* ensue from 的意思是"随……而起"、"由……而产生"、"因……而发生"。它是"前果后因"句，即 R ensues from C。

The floods *ensued from* heavy rain. 出现洪涝是因为下了大雨。

Bitter arguments *ensued from* this misunderstanding. 这一误会引发了激烈的争论。

* lie in 的意思是"……的原因在于"。

Her sadness *lies in* her failure in the exam in maths. 她的悲伤原因在于数学考试不及格。

The root of all these events *lay in* history. 所有这些事件都源于历史。

* refer to 意思是"把……归(功)于"、"将……归(咎)于"，它的用法就是 refers R to C。

Many successful businessmen *refer* their success *to* hard work and good judgment. 许多有成就的企业家认为他们的成功与勤奋工作和正确判断有关。

He *referred* the team's defeat *to* poor training. 他把球队的失败归因于训练不力。

* result from/in 中不及物动词 result 可与 from 和 in 两个介词搭配，表达不同的意思。

result from 的意思是"……是由……造成的"，result in 意思是"产生于/起因于"，也就是"前果后因句"。

The accident *resulted from/in* her carelessness. 事故是由于她的粗心大意造成的。

Many illnesses *result from/in* lack of exercise. 很多疾病是由于缺少锻炼所致。

D. 用非谓语动词表示原因

非谓语动词不定式、现在分词和过去分词在句中都可作状语，表示原因。

a. 动词不定式表示原因

● 在感情动词和感情形容词后面的动词不定式常表示原因。这些感情动词常见的有：weep, shudder, rejoice, blush, wonder 等；这类形容词常有：happy, sorry, glad, proud, indignant, furious, content 等；还有一些由-ed 过去分词转化来的形容词，如：amazed, bored, depressed, embarrassed, frightened, grieved, hurt, overjoyed, puzzled, relieved, shocked, thrilled, worried 等。

We all *wept* to see many many Chinese people were killed and shot by the Japanese soldiers in the film "Nanjing! Nanjing!" 当看到"南京！南京！"电影里如此之多的中国人被日本鬼子屠杀我们都哭了。

They feel much *honoured to* have you come to visit their school. 您能到他们学校访问，他们深感荣幸。

Henry is *glad to* be well again. 恢复了健康后，亨利很高兴。

I was *depressed* to learn of her illness. 我得知她生病后感受到沮丧。

注意：不要混淆 too … to (do sth)与 only too … to (do sth)，前面结构的不定式表示否定意思，后面的 only too = very，其后动词不定式表示原因。比较下面两句句子：

I am *too weak to* carry the heavy box. 我身体太弱，搬不动那只重箱子。

Tom is *only too glad to* be of service. （因为）能帮上忙，汤姆十分高兴。

● 动词不定式复合结构表示原因

如果动词不定式的逻辑主语不是句子的主语，而是由介词 for 或 with 引出的名词或代词作其逻辑主语，这个动词不定式和这个名词或代词组成了动词不定式复合结构。

She is sorry *for me to have been so careless*. 我这么粗心，令她遗憾。

第 25 章 副词、副词(状语)从句

He was ashamed *for you to have made such a serious mistake*. 他因为你犯了这么一个严重的错误而羞愧。
With nobody to help her, she had to work into the night. 由于没人帮她忙,她只好工作到深夜。

b. 现在分词表示原因

现在分词句中可作状语说明原因或理由。表示现在分词是由状态动词或静态动词转化而来,如 be, believe, feel, find, hope, live, lose, think, want, wish 等。现在分词作原因状语可分三种情况:一是它的主动式;二是它的被动式;三是它的复合结构。

- 现在分词主动式作原因状语

* 表示动作或状态现在分词一般式与谓语动词的动作同时发生,或在谓语动词的动作之前发生。

Being a member of the club, I must attend the meeting once a week. 因为是俱乐部成员,我必须每周参加一次会议。
Living in the countryside, John knows almost every kind of plants growing there. 由于生活在农村,约翰几乎知道生长在那里的每一样植物。
Not knowing what to do next, she telephoned her father for help. 由于不知道接下来做什么,她打电话给她父亲求助。

* 现在分词的完成体表示原因时,其动作发生在谓语动作之前。

Having seen the film, Mary stayed at home reading an interesting story. 因为看过了那部电影,玛丽待在家看一部有趣的小说。
Not having received an answer, they had to put off the meeting they proposed. 由于没有收到答复,他们只好把提议的见面推迟了。
Having never used a computer, Grace met with many difficulties at first. 由于从没使用过计算机,格蕾丝在刚开始时遇到很多困难。

- 现在分词被动式作原因状语

* 现在分词一般体被动式表示原因。

Being done in a hurry, the exercises were full of mistakes. 那些练习做得匆忙,所以错误百出。
Being written in good English, the book is recommendable to all. 这本书是用很漂亮的英文写的,因此值得向大家推荐。

* 现在分词的完成体被动式表示原因。

Having been asked to give a lecture, the professor is busy preparing it. 这位教授被邀做讲座,所以忙着做准备。
Having been robbed and raped, the young lady hanged herself. 那名年轻妇女既被抢劫,又被施暴,因而上吊自尽了。

- 现在分词的复合结构表示原因

假如现在分词的逻辑主语不是句子的主语,那就要在分词前加上逻辑主语(常是名词或代词),组成现在分词的复合结构,或叫现在分词独立结构。用这种结构表示原因,也有一般体、完成体、主动式、被动式。

Some students either talking or laughing, the room was noisy. 一些学生又说又笑,教室里一片喧闹声。(一般体主动式)
The question being settled, they went home from work. 问题(被)解决了,他们下班回家。(一般体被动式)
The teacher having left, the students resumed their discussion. 老师走了以后,同学们又继续讨论。(完成体主动式)
John's health having been impaired by years of over work, he retired ahead of the time. 多年的劳累把约翰的身体搞坏了,所以他提前退休了。(完成体被动式)

英语中有一些现在分词复合结构可由介词 with 引出,成为 with 复合结构。

With the price of oil going up constantly, Mary can not afford a car. 由于油价的不断上涨,玛丽用不起小汽车了。

With so many people showing their care and contributing their share, the "Hope Project" is full of hope. 有这么多人关心出力，"希望工程"充满希望。

there being 结构和 it being 结构作原因状语。实际上，这两个结构是现在分词的特殊结构，它们也可用来表示原因。

There being no further business, the chairman closed the meeting. 由于没有其他事情，主席宣布散会。

It being known that he was an expert in English teaching, many English teachers wrote to him asking some questions. 由于大家都知道他是英语教学专家，所以许多英语教师写信向他讨教。

c. 过去分词短语表示原因

在用过去分词表示原因的句子中，有一般结构和复合结构两种。

● 过去分词的一般结构表示原因。作原因状语的过去分词的动作与句子主语具有意义上的动宾关系。

Discouraged by one failure after another, Xiaoli finally gave up the plan. 接二连三的失败使小李灰心丧气，她最终放弃了这个计划。

Encouraged by his parents, the little boy contributed all his savings to the "Hope Project". 在父母亲的支持下，那小男孩把全部存下的钱捐赠给了"希望工程"。

● 过去分词的复合结构表示原因

＊过去分词复合结构与过去分词结构不同。作原因状语用的-ed 分词复合结构与主语之间没有意义上的动宾关系，也就是说过去分词前要有自己的逻辑宾语（名词或代词）组成过去分词复合结构。有时，逻辑宾语可用宾格。

The bridge destroyed, they had to swim across the river. 由于桥梁被毁，他们只好游泳过河。

His partners arrested, he could do nothing but give herself up to the police. 由于同伙被捕了，他只好投案。

Jane insulted by her boyfriend, her elder brother decided to give him a lesson. 由于简受到男友的侮辱，她的哥哥决定教训他一番。

＊用介词 with 引出过去分词复合结构。

With a gas main in this district cracked, they had to dine out for a week. 由于该小区一条煤气主干道破裂，他们只好一周外出就餐。

② 用从句表示原因

这里所说的用从句表示原因，不但指我们比较熟悉的状语从句，还有不是状语从句而起原因状语作用的句子，它们是并列句中的分句，有些是虚拟结构，还有"It is ... that"强调结构等。

A. 原因状语从句表示原因

原因状语从句是说明产生某种情况的原因。原因状语从句的功能有两种：一是用于说明缘由或事理进行推理或判断；二是回答问题。

She failed to pass the final examination in English *because she had not worked hard*. 她英语期终考试没通过因为她不努力。（说明原因）

It must have rained at night, *because the road is wet*. 晚上一定下雨了，路这么湿。（推理判断）

—Why are they laughing? 他们为什么笑？

—Because the story I'm telling is very funny. 因为我讲的故事很可笑。（产生原因）

—Why do you want to learn a foreign language? 你为什么要学外语？

—Because a foreign language is a useful tool. 因为外语是有用的工具。（说明事理）

—Why is he absent today?

—He's ill.（回答问题）

B. 原因状语从句的类型

a. 关于 because 从句

- because 从句有以下特点:because 是引导原因状语从句最常用的词语;最直接地对 why 提出的问题进行回答;它在口语和书面语中均可使用;它的语气比 since,as 强;它的位置一般在句子后面,强调时置于句首;because 从句不在句首时,用与不用逗号均可,如在句首时,常用逗号与主句分开;because 从句的话语重点在 because 从句上。

- because 从句不在句首时,其前用与不用逗号均可;但在句首时常用逗号与主句分开。

He distrusted me(,) because I was young. 他因为我年轻而不相信我。

Because I was young, he distrusted me. 因为我年轻,所以他不相信我。

- because 从句前的修饰语需要时,可在其前加修饰语 merely, just, only, simply, solely, the more 等对原因状语从句加以修饰,以加深程度。

He went there with her *merely because he had to*. 他与她一起上那里纯属无奈。

She has been married to the old man *only because he has much money*. 她嫁给那老头只是因为他有很多钱。

Just because his father is mayor of the city, he thinks he is so superior. 只是因他父亲是这个市的市长,他就以为高人一等。

- 含有 because 的主从句的原因与结果间要合理,因为 because 从句表示的是原因,所以主句当然是由于原因而产生的结果,那原因和结果应该合理,不然尽管语法结构没问题,而在意思上却是讲不通的。

* It will rain because the barometer is falling. 因为气压计的降低不是下雨的原因。(错误)

* It is morning, because the birds are singing. 因为鸟叫不是天亮的原因。(错误)

上面例句 1、例句 2 中的 because 从句可分别改成:

It will rain, because it is getting dark. 天将下雨,因为天变黑了。(乌云密布是大雨来临的预兆)

It is morning, because the cocks are crowing. 天亮了,因为公鸡在啼叫。(公鸡叫,天亮了)

- because 从句的否定及有关的问题

* 以否定转移形式进行否定。这种否定就是把否定词 not 对主句的谓语进行否定,或用其他形式对主句进行否定,但实际上否定的是 because 从句。这时主从句连接紧密,没有停顿,因此 because 前不加逗号。

The country *is not* strong because it is large. (= The country is strong not because it is large.) 国家不是因为大而强大。

The motor *did not* stop running because the fuel was used up. (= The motor stopped running not because the fuel was used up.) 马达停并不是因为燃料用尽了而是其他原因。

I *don't* teach because teaching is easy for me. (= I teach not because teaching is easy for me.) 我之所以教书并不是因为教书轻松。

The flowers *are not* fragrant because they are numerous. (= The flowers are fragrant not because they are numerous.) 花香不在花多。

* 有时候,主句里的否定并不一定转移到 because 从句,这时就要根据语境和上下文的情况进行理解。当否定不包含从句时,because 从句前加上逗号更好。

I didn't go swimming with them, because I was very busy those days. 我没有与他们一起去游泳,因为那些天我非常忙。

We can't see the stars in the daytime, because the sun is much brighter than the light of the stars. 白天我们看不见星星,因为太阳光比星星的光要亮得多。

- "because … not because"和"not because … but because"结构,这是含有两个原因句的表达形式:前一个是肯定第一个原因,否定第二个原因;后一个是否定第一个原因,而肯定第二个原因,但要注意的是,其结构上不是 not because … because,而是 not because … but because。

I study Russian *because* I thinks it is useful, *not because* I want to show off. 我学俄语是因为觉得它有用,不是因为想炫耀自己。

He studies French *not because* he wants to show off, *but because* he thinks it useful. 他学习法语不是想炫耀自己,而是觉得它有用。

• 用逗号界分"not ... because"歧义句。

I didn't leave home because I am afraid of my father.

* 我并不因为怕父亲才离开家的。

* 因为我怕父亲,所以没有离开家。

很清楚,第一个汉语的意思是按否定转移的形式理解而得出句意;第二个汉语的意思是按不否定转移的形式而得出句意。我们认为,如句子中 because 前没有逗号,这时否定点就在后面的 because 从句上,如有了逗号,那理解成第二种意思,"因为我怕父亲,所以没有离开家。"这样的处理可说简单易行。

• 一般情况下不要把 because 与 so 连用在一句中,因为 because 是从属连词,而 so 是并列连词。

• because 从句与 for 从句的区别

* because 是从属连词。而 for 如后跟的句子表示"附加说明理由,追忆"时,把它当作从属连词更为恰当。

* because 与 for 的意义在 A Dictionary of English and American Usage (1991) 上讲得比较贴切: because 与 for 都可引出表示原因的句子,但 because 引出的原因表示"直接而又明显的原因",for 在近代用法中比 because 直接感少些,它往往"表示追忆,用于附加说明理由";因此,也可以说 because 说的是因果关系的必然推断,for 用于普通理由的说明。

I hid myself, *because* I am afraid. 因为我害怕,所以我躲起来。(直接理由)

I hid myself, *for* I was afraid. 我躲起来,是由于我害怕。(附加理由)

The light went out, *because* the oil was out. 由于油尽了,所以灯灭了。(原因)

The oil must be out, *for* the light went out. 一定是油尽了,因为灯灭了。(表示推断的理由)

* because 与 for 从句的位置 because 从句可以在句首,也可不放在句首,不放在句首时,用与不用逗号均可,如在句首时,常用逗号与主句分开;for 引出的从句不置于句首,它与前面的主句常用逗号分开。

b. as 引导的原因状语句

• as 引导的原因句有五个特点:

as 意为"因为"、"由于",意义接近 since,但比 since 轻;

as 提及的原因比较明显,或者对方已经了解;

as 提出原因时,只是附带提及,话语重点在主句;

as 引导的从句不可回答"why 问句";

as 从句多用于非正式文体;

as 可以用来提出非直接原因。

• as 从句可以放在句首、句后均可,但置于句前较多,这时表达的语气也强些。

As Jim wasn't feeling well, I went there alone. 由于吉姆身体不适,我就一人去那里了。

As they object, we'll reconsider the plan. 他们既然反对,我们将重新考虑这个计划。

She is going to bed, *as she is dead tired*. 她要去睡了,因为她累死了。

• 引出原因状语从句时,有四种情况要注意:

* as 在口语中可以省略。

Mr White can't go with us, (*as*) he is busy preparing his speech for the meeting tomorrow. 怀特先生不能与我们一起去,他忙着准备明天的发言。

* 有时 as 可引出省略性状语。

His teacher criticized him *as showing* (*as he showed*) *no interest in his study*. 他的老师批评他,因为他对学习没兴趣。

* 在加强语气时,as 引出的原因状语从句可用倒装语序。

Clever as he was, he found little difficulty in solving the problem which was none to easy. 因为他很聪明，所以不费什么劲就把这个绝非容易的问题解决了。

* 关于"as … so"结构问题。

对这种结构，有些语法学家认为不正统，就像 because 引出的从句后不可以用 so（但可接 therefore）一样。其实这种用法非但在谚语中存在，在口语中也存在。

As you sow, so shall you reap. 种豆得豆，种瓜得瓜。（谚语）

As you make your bed, so you must lie on it. 既然床是你铺的，好坏都得往上躺。（谚语）

As a man lives, so he dies. 有生必有死。（口语）

As our speech, so we are. 言如其人。（口语）

"as … so"结构可用来表示"正如 A……，B 也……"这样的比较意思。A 和 B 意思的区别主要在意义上进行仔细区分。如果你对上面四个例句的意思推敲一下，就不难得知都是"正如……，也……"的意思了。

As rust eats iron, so care eats the heart. 正如锈可蚀铁，忧亦能伤身。

As I would not be a slave, so I would not be a master. 正如我不想当奴隶一样，我也不想当主子。

如果把上面例句 1 译成"因为锈可蚀铁，所以忧亦能伤身。"意思上就讲不通了；把例句 2 译成"因为我不想当奴隶，所以我也不想当主子"，那是对"as … so"结构的误解。"as … so"要译成"正如……，也……"，绝不能把这结构中的 as 误认为"因为"。

* 英语中各种结构的表达也存在着错综复杂的交织现象。关系代词 which, who, whose 和关系副词 where 引导的非限制性定语从句有时含有原因意义，而且可与 because/as 互换。

She should thank you, *who* (= because you) *did so much for her.* 她应该感谢你，因为你为她做了那么多。

There was no difficulty in finding the city, *whose* (= because its) *smoke was discernible* 50 *miles away.* 找到那座城市毫不困难，因为该城市里的烟在 50 英里之外就可辨别出来。

I often go to the countryside, *where* (= as) *I can learn a lot.* 我经常去农村，因为在那里我可以学到许多东西。

c. 关于 since 从句

在这从句中，从属连词 since 意为"因为"、"既然"，其引出的原因一般是已知的、明显的，也可能是靠分析推断出来的。从主句的意义关系上讲，since 从句只起附带说明的意思，像 as 主从句一样，话语的重点在主句上。从语气上来说，since 比 as 强，但比 because 轻。在多数情况下，since 从句置于主句前，此时用逗号与主句分开，如置于主句后，逗号可用可不用。

Since she doesn't want to go with us, Let her stay at home. 既然她不想与我们一起去，那就让她留在家里。

You'd better go to bed earlier(,) *since you don't feel well.* 你觉得身体不好，最好早点睡吧。

• since 从句的用法注意点

* since 从句一般不省，但 since 从句的表语是表语形容词或主从句有相同的词语时，可以省略。

He doesn't need the old laptop, *since he has got a new one.* 他已有了一部新的笔记本电脑，那旧的就不需要了。

这句不可省略成"… since having got a new one"，但下面两句可以省略。

This is useless, *since impossible* (= since it is impossible), proposal. 这个建议既然行不通，也就毫无用处。

Since Henry can't (*teach French*), Harden will teach French. 既然亨利教不了法语，哈登将教法语。

* since 从句不可用在"It is … that"结构中，原因是其语气比较轻，如下面的句子是不对的：

It is since you don't understand that I will explain again.（句中的 since 该换成 because 就行，意为"既然你不懂，我就再解释一次"）

* since 不可与 so 或 then 同时使用，但可用 therefore。例如，Since you don't feel well, so you'd better go to bed earlier. 是不对的，应去掉 so，或换成 therefore。

d. lest 从句

lest 的意思是"因怕"、"唯恐",相当于 be afraid that 或 for fear that,此属书面语,现在用得较少。

lest 从句中的谓语动词常是"should/might + 动词原形",但在美语中常省略,只用其动词原形。lest 从句一般置于主句的后面,与主句可用逗号分开,也可相连,如 lest 从句置于主句前是为了突出原因。

We all took our umbrellas(,) *lest it should rain*. 因为担心下雨,我们都带了伞。

I did not go to bed, *lest I might be needed*. 恐怕有需要用上我的时候,我没上床睡觉。

He formed wild resolution, and, *lest he should wave from it*, he set about at once to realize it. 他做出了一个大胆的决定,并立即着手去实现它,因他怕自己会动摇。

Note: lest 还可以引导目的状语从句和名词从句。

I hid the book *lest he should see it*. 我把书藏起来以免他看见。(目的状语从句)

句中的 lest 可用 for fear that, so that ... not, in order that ... not 取代。

We were afraid lest (= that) he should get here too late. 我们恐怕他会来得太迟。(名词从句)

e. whereas 从句

whereas 的意思是"由于"、"鉴于"、"因为"等,相当于 seeing that。在现代英语中,它只用于法律条文、决议、告示、合同等公文写作中。

Whereas it is dangerous to cross the railway, crossing it except by the bridge is prohibited. 因为跨越铁轨是危险的,所以禁止不走天桥而横跨铁轨的行为。

Whereas they said tenant damaged the property, she is required to pay 100 dollars. 由于租用人损坏了财物,她应赔偿 100 美元。

f. that 从句

that 引导原因状语从句时是从属连词。还要注意的是 that 从句前常是一些表示情绪、感情的形容词或-ed 形容词,这些词常见的有:afraid, angry, amazed, content, disappointed, hurt, glad, irritated, proud, thankful, overjoyed, annoyed, surprised, ashamed, delighted, pleased, worried, satisfied 等。that 从句说明产生某种情绪或感情的原因。这种从句中的 that 相当于 because,在口语中往往省略。

I'm so thankful *that nobody was hurt*. 我感到欣慰没人受伤。(感到欣慰的原因是没人受伤)

He is proud *that his son has won the first prize in the contest*. 他为他儿子比赛得了第一名而感到自豪。(感到自豪的原因是他儿子比赛得了第一名)

Tom was ashamed *that he could not answer the question*. 汤姆因回答不出那问题而感到羞愧。

g. in as much as 从句

in as much as 也可写成 inasmuch as,它是个复合从属连词,意为"因为"、"由于"。

• inasmuch as 从句的特点 inasmuch as 是语气最强、最正式的说明原因的词语。它所引出的句子是为了说明主句所讲的情况是必要的或正确的。它的位置可置主句前,也可置于主句后。

Inasmuch as you have grown up, you shouldn't do nothing all the day. 因为你已经长大成人,不能整天无所事事。

I'm ready to accept your proposal, *in as much as it is practical*. 鉴于你的建议是切合实际的,我准备接受它。

• in as much as 是正式用语,所以常用于书面语。由于其结构累赘,又与 as 连用,所以现在常被 since 替代,这样就简单明了。

Inasmuch as (Since) you have seen the film, you should stay at home to do some other things. 你既然已经看过那部电影了,就待在家做些其他事吧。

Chang Hua and Li Ming had to be given extra coaching, *since* (*in as mush as*) they had too poor a start. 李明和张华需要给予额外辅导,他们因为起点太低。

h. considering that 从句

considering that 的意思是"鉴于"、"由于"、"考虑到"、"就……而论"等。它是个复合连词,其中的

considering 是动词 consider 的现在分词转化而来。

● 这种原因从句是对主句给出的情况或做出的判断提供依据或说出原因。它在书面语和口语中均可使用。它的位置可在主句前或后。considering 已失去了分词的功能，所以不存在与主句主语上的逻辑主谓关系。有时，considering that 中，可省去 that。

Rose has done the work well, *considering that she is only eighteen.* 考虑到她只有十八岁，罗丝做到这一步已经不错了。

Considering (that) she was young, they did not allow her to go there alone. 考虑到她年轻，他们不允许她独自去那里。

● considering that 一般可以与 in that、seeing that 替换。因此，上面两句中的 considering that 可以换成 in that 或 seeing that，意思不变。

i. seeing that 从句

seeing that 在意思、特点方面与 onsidering that 一样，其中的 seeing 是动词 see 的现在分词转化而来，与 that 一起组成复合连词，不过 seeing that 还包含"目睹"的含义。

j. in that 从句

in that 意思是"因为"，偏重于说明某方面的理由或原因，有比较浓的书面语意味。它的位置在主句前、后均可。其实，此结构是个固定搭配，因此两个词中一个也不能省。in that 相当于 for the reason that，可与 considering that 和 seeing that 交替使用。

The new book written by him is unsatisfactory *in that it lacks a good index.* 他写的那本新书不太令人满意，因为缺少一个好的索引。

In that her mother is ill, she cannot continue doing the work. 她因母亲病了无法继续干那工作。

k. now that 从句

now that 也是复合从属连词。因为 now that 中的 now 是从时间副词 now 演变而来，所以与"现在"这一时间概念有联系，由此 now that 的意思是"既然（现在）"、"鉴于（眼下）"、"由于（至今）"、"因为（目前）"等。这种从句通常以某种事实作为理由或原因对主句所陈述的情况或结论作衬垫。now that 从句的位置在主句前、后均可，在实际使用中 that 可以省去。

Now (that) everybody is here, let's begin the meeting. 既然大家都到了，我们开会吧。

You should allow us some discount *now that we have ordered such a large quantity.* 我们既然订了这么多货，你们应当给一些折扣。

l. 并列句中的分句表示原因

表示原因的并列分句有 and 和 so 前的分句、but 和 for 引导的分句、only 引导的分句。

● 并列连词 and 连接的两个分句常有因果关系，and 前的句子为因，后面的句子为果，这些在上下文中意思显得更清楚。and 前有无逗号均可。

We drank in excess that day and three of us were sent to the hospital nearby. (= Three of us were sent to the hospital nearby because we drank in excess that day.) 那天我们饮酒过量，其中三人被送到了附近的医院。

It was very cold, *and* we had some difficulty in starting the engine. (= We had some difficulty in starting the engine because it was very cold.) 天气很冷，因此我们在发动引擎时有些困难。

* 如果 and 前后两分句的主语相同，那第二个主语往往省略。

The peasants in the fields were wearing raincoats, *and (they)* didn't get wet. 田地里的农民穿着雨衣，因而没有淋湿。

* 并列连词 and 常与 so, therefore, consequently, hence, thus, accordingly, thereby 等副词连用，这样能使两分句的因果关系显得更明显。

I'm behind with my study, *and so* I must catch up with the other students. 我在学习上落后了，因此必须赶上其他同学。

The documents were not ready, *and consequently* we could not sign them. 文件尚未准备好,所以我们无法签署。

Note:一般来讲,两个分句间用逗号,但如副词前没用 and,那就可用分号或仍用逗号。

I was told to speak briefly; *accordingly* I cut short my remarks. 人家叫我说话简短些,于是我把话删减了。

They were walking in the teeth of the wind, *so* they made slow progress. 他们迎风而走,所以速度很慢。

● 因为并列连词 so 所引导的分句表示结果,所以另一分句是表示原因或理由的。从逻辑上讲,so 分句常置于第一分句后。

He had broken his glasses, *so he could not see what was happening.* 他的眼镜打破了,所以他没看到当时发生的情况。

It was rather cold outside, *so they closed all the windows.* 因为外面很冷,所以他们把窗子全关上了。

● 通常,but 引出的分句表示转折关系,但有时也有说明原因、含蓄表达结果的意思。这一类句子的特征是前一分句常由表示计划、愿望的及物动词+(表示要做某事的)动词不定式,说明主语想做而没有做成的事;第二分句是陈述第一分句没做成某事的原因。这样的情况有两种:一种是"表示现在无法实现的愿望和原因",另一种是"表示过去未能实现的愿望和原因"。

* 表示现在无法实现的愿望和原因:这种句子的特点是第一分句用现在时,其宾语的不定式用一般式;第二分句也用现在时范畴。

He wants to have a laptop, *but he has not enogh money to buy one.* 他很想买台笔记本电脑,但手头没有足够的钱。

I'd like to go for a walk with you, *but I have to finish my paper tonight.* 我很想与你一起去散步,但是我今晚必须完成这篇论文。

* 表示过去未能实现的愿望和原因:这种句子的特点是第一分句中谓语动词用过去时,其宾语的不定式用完成体,第二分句也用过去时。

He meant to have returned you the money this morning, *but he forgot to bring it here.* 他本想今天早晨把钱还给你,但忘记带来了。

We expected to have reached Shanghai on April 23, *but the ship stranded somewhere near it for* 20 *hours.* 我们本来预计 4 月 23 日抵达上海,但轮船在上海附近某处搁浅了 20 个小时。

● 在并列连词 for 连接的两个并列句中,for 前的分句表结果,for 后的分句表原因,对前面分句所说的情况做推断或说明、解释。for 分句主要用于书面语中,for 前可用逗号或分号。

* 表示推断

She must be ill, *for she's looking pale today.* 她一定病了,因为她今天脸色苍白。

Autumn has come, *for the leaves of the trees are falling.* 秋天到了,因为树叶在飘落。

The laboratory was broken in last night, *for a valuable instrument was found missing this morning.* 实验室昨晚被盗窃了,因为今天早晨发现丢失了一台贵重仪器。

* 表示说明或解释

She felt no fear, *for she was a brave woman.* 她毫不惧怕,因为她是个勇敢的女人。

His father looked older than his age, *for he had had a hard life.* 他爸看上去比实际年龄要老一些,因为他曾经历过艰苦的生活。

I must hurry, *for it is going to rain.* 我得抓紧,天要下雨了。

● 表示转折意思的副词 only,意为"只是"、"只不过",其引出的分句也有说明原因、暗示结果的作用。

He would help you to finish the work in time, *only he was not feeling well those days.* 他很想帮你按时完成工作,只不过那些天他身体不舒服。

I would do it with pleasure, *only I was too busy.* 我很乐意做那件事,只是我现在太忙了。

m. 虚拟结构表示原因

有些虚拟句从表面上看表示的是"要不是……就会",但从深层意思看,所表示的意思是"正是因为……"、"……才"。这些虚拟句主要是某些假设条件句和结果句,表达与之相应的真实原因和结果。

If it hadn't been for the heavy rain, we should have arrived earlier. 正是因为遇上了大雨,我们才来迟了。(这句的原意是"要是没遇上大雨,我们早就到了。")

If the expert had not helped me, my experiment would have failed. 由于有了那专家的帮助,我的实验成功了。(这句的原意是"要是那专家不帮助我,我的实验就不会成功。")

But for an unexpected emergency, I should have visited their factory. 由于发生了意外情况,我没去参观他们工厂。(句中的 But for = If there had not been an unexpected emergency …)

I could not have done the work well without your help. 由于有了你的帮助,我才能把工作做好。(句中的 without your help 是一句无动词句,= if there had not been your help)

But that she was prevented, she would have accomplished her design 由于受到阻碍,她没有完成她的设计。(根据句意,句中的 But that … = If she had not been prevented, …)

从上述例句可见,表示原因的虚拟句常有以下几种句型:If it were not for (=Were it not for) +名词;If it had not been for (Had it not been for) +名词;But for (or without) +名词;But that +名词。

n. "It is … that"强调结构表示原因

这种结构表示原因,被强调的是原因短语或从句,或是"-ing 分词 + as sth/sb does"结构。

- 被强调的是表示原因的短语或从句

It was owing to her kindness that I obtained a good post. 由于她好心相助,我获得了一个好职位。

It was by slip of pen that her letter was addressed to a wrong place. 由于笔误,她的信投错了地方。

It was because he wanted to buy a dictionary that he went to town yesterday. 因为想买词典,他昨天上了城。

- 现在分词 + as sth/sb does 结构

这是一种表示原因的强调结构,其中 sb/sth 是句子后面的主语。

Living, as he does, so remotely from the town, He rarely has visitors. 因为他住在离城很远的地方,所以很少有人拜访。

Wearing, as he did, the seat belt, he was not hurt in the accident. 由于他系上了安全带,所以在事故中没有受伤。

o. 过去分词 + as it is(was)结构

This essay, published as it was in a small magazine, remained unknown for a long time. 这篇论文由于发表在一个小杂志上,所以很长时间没有人知道。

③ 一句中多种原因的表达法

英语中,有时在同一个句子中需要表达两种以上的原因,这样的表达法最常见的有以下几种句型:

A. 表示"部分(或一半)因为(或由于)……部分(或一半)因为(或由于)"可分两部分:

a. partly because … and partly because …的意思是"部分由于……部分由于……"。

She wants to buy a computer *partly because* it is useful and *partly because* it is in fashion. 她想买部电脑,一方面因为它有用,一方面也因为这东西眼下很时髦。

The patient is isolated *partly because* she must be kept quiet and *partly because* the desease she has caught is infectious. 该病人被隔离,部分原因是要让她保持安静,部分原因是她得的病是传染病。

b. "partly + 原因介词短语… and partly + 原因介词短语"表示"一半由于(或因为)……,一半(或因为)……"。句型中原因介词可以是 because of, through, owing to, by 等。

Robert fell ill *partly because of* the heat, and *partly because of* the long journey. 罗伯特病倒了,一半是天气炎热,一半是长途跋涉。

She became rich *partly because* by industry and *partly because* by good luck. 她发财致富了,勤劳是一个原

因，运气好也是一个原因。

B. either because/for ..., or because/for

这句型的意思是"或是因为……或是因为……"或"不是因为……就是因为……"。

The little boy was beaten by his father *either because* he forgot to do his homework, *or because* his homework was full of mistakes. 那小男孩被他父亲揍了，或是因为他忘了做作业，或是因为他作业中满是错误。

Rose disliked him *either for* his appearance *or for* his laziness. 罗丝不喜欢他，或是因为他的外貌，或是因为他的懒惰。

C. not only because（of）... but also because（of）

这短语的意思是"不仅因为……而且因为……"。

Why the ladies have chosen these hats is *not only because of* the colours *but also because of* the style. 女士们为什么选择那些帽子不仅因为它们的颜色，而且因为它们的式样。

He can't writer anything *not only because* he is ignorant *but also because* he is full of conceit. 他写不出什么东西，不仅因为他无知而且因为他太自负。

D. not that ... but that

这个句型的意思是"不是因为……而是因为……"，那就是否定前一个，肯定后一个。

I felt a bit worried, *not that* my fellow workers were not working hard, *but that* they did not pay enough attention to safety. 我有点担心，不是因为我的同事们工作不卖力，而是因为他们对安全不够重视。

④ 名词 + that + 句子

Fool that he was, he believed what she said. 他是个蠢人，所以相信了她的话。

John did not quarrel with her, *gentle man that he was*. 约翰没同她争吵，因为他是个性情温和的人。

（3）结果句与原因句的关系

在英语中，表示结果意思的句子中往往含有原因，而表示原因的句子中又往往含有结果的意思，所以原因与结果有着相当密切的关系。表示结果的形式众多，有词、短语，也有句子，句子中有简单句、并列句、从句，有时还有定语从句或其他句子表示结果。在句子表未结果中，结果状语从句最为复杂。结果状语从句（Adverbial Clause of Result）表示主句中某一动作或状态所产生的结果。结果状语从句有时与原因句同时存在于一句中，表达原因的句子里往往含有结果。但在位置上，结果状语从句却只能位于主句之后，原因状语从句可位于主句之前或之后。

① 结果状语从句的特点

结果状语从句有其自身的特点，它有专门的连词或引导词引出；有的结果句也并不依附原因句子或原因短语；有些集因与果于一身的结果句是简单句，它们借助非谓语动词、介词短语或句中的复合结构来表达结果；表示结果的有直接的结果状语从句，也有结果句是定语从句，而不是状语从句；有些结果句所表达的结果是以一定的条件为前提的。

② 结果状语的表达方式

A. 以短语、复合结构或动词形式表达结果

a. 介词短语表示结果可分简单介词短语和固定介词短语两种。

• 介词 for 用于一些成语中表示某一情况的"结果"、"后果"。

Tom has been working on this book for six years, and all *for nothing*. 他在那部书上花了六年时间，却毫无收获。

We have had our trouble *for nothing*. 我们吃了苦头，却一无所获。

• 介词 into 常用于某些动词后表示某种情况或动作行为所引起的结果或产物。

It is said that the book will be *translated into* several languages. 据说那部书将被译成好几种文字。

Cotton is first *spun into* thread and then *woven into* cloth. 棉花先被纺成纱,然后被织成布。
- 介词 to 表示结果可有以下几种情况:
* 介词 to 表示某一动作行为或情况的结果。

She was so angry to tear the letter *to pieces*. 她气愤得把信撕成碎片。

The map of the world is not hung *to advantage*. 这幅画挂得不是地方。

* 介词 to 表示感情上的结果。

The audience were all moved *to tears*. 观众都感动得热泪盈眶。

To my surprise, she picked the one I thought that he was a handsome good for nothing to marry. 使我吃惊的是,她挑了我认为是仪表堂堂的二流子结了婚。

b. 一些固定介词短语表示结果,这些表示结果的固定介词短语常有:as a result, as a/the result of, in the result, with the result that, as a consequence (of), in consequence, in the end, in the sequel, in the issue, in the long run, in that case。

- as a result 作结果状语,意思是"结果"。在使用时,as a result 后常用逗号,然后接一个具体表示结果内容的句子。有时,as a result 前面有一个陈述原因的句子,这句子与 as a result 之间可用标点隔开或用 and 连接起来。

As a result, the whole class rushed out of the classroom. 结果,全班冲出了教室。

She refused to have medical attention in the early stages of her complaint, *and as a result* she became seriously ill. 她生病初期拒绝接受治疗,结果病情严重恶化。

We follow up the suggestions, and have had satisfying experiences *as a result*. 我们按照建议办事,故而一直得到满意的结果。

- as a/the result of 作"作为……的结果"用。它们用作状语时可以置于说明结果句子的前或后,如在句首,那就用逗号与后面分开。

As a result of what we saw we decided to change the rules. 鉴于我们所看到的情况,我们决定更改规则。

He was late *as a result of* snow. 因为下雪,他来迟了。

- 作状语用的 in the result 引出具体说明结果的句子,其意思是"结果"、"最后"。例如:

His father had too much work and too little rest, *in the result* he fell ill. 他的父亲工作太繁重而休息又少,结果病倒了。

You took a great risk, though *in the result* it did not turn out so badly. 你冒的风险太大了,纵然后来事情并没弄到糟透的地步。

- with the result that 后面接句子,它的意思是"其结果是",其中的 that 可以省略。

He was watching TV, *with the result that* he didn't hear the telephone. 他那时在看电视,结果没有听见电话铃响。

I was in the bath, *with the result that* I didn't hear the doorbell. 那时我正在洗澡,结果就没有听见门铃声。

- as a consequence (of) 或 in consequence 这两个短语用法相同,引出的句子都陈述具体的结果。

As a consequence, they were hung up at the crossroads for half an hour. 结果他们在十字路口受阻半小时。

In consequence, we could spend only two days in Guilin and all we could do was to hit the high spots. 结果我们只能在桂林待两天,只能拣一些主要景点游览一下。

You studied hard, and *in consequence* you passed the test. 你学习努力,所以通过了考试。

- in the end/in the sequel/in the issue/in the long run 这四个短语都可作状语,表示"最终"、"结果"。但要注意,被这些句子所修饰的句子与其前面的句子并非都存在因果关系。

He worked very hard and *in the end/sequel/issue* he reaped his reward. 他努力工作,最终获报偿。(因努力工作而后得到报偿是因果关系)

Learning a foreign language may be difficult in the beginning, but you will benefit *in the long run*. 刚开始学

外语可能有困难，但最后你会受益的。（学习困难与受益没有因果关系）

● in that case 作状语，意思是"如果这样"、"这样"。它引出结果句时，前面往往有一个说明原因的句子。

You don't like your job? *In that case* why don't you leave? 你不喜欢这份工作？那你怎么不辞掉呢？

The lecture given by Professor Li Yuehua is above my head, *in that case* I had to leave earlier. 李月华教授做的讲座我听不懂，于是我只好先走了。

c. 用非谓语动词表示结果。对于非谓语动词的定义及其有关的一些问题，我们已经在第 5、6、7 章中做过详细的介绍，现在只说非谓语动作结果状语的情况。

● 动词不定式表示结果

＊动词不定式表示的常是一种事先没料到的情况或令人失望的结果。

The scientist entered the office *to find a window was broken and some important design drawings were missing.* 那位科学家进办公室发现一扇窗户被打破，一些重要的设计图纸不翼而飞。

After two years of marriage they parted company, *never to see each other again.* 结婚两年后，他们就离异了，从此再也没有见过面。

Note：动词不定式表示结果时的位置总在被修饰动词的后面，这是因为动词不定式作结果状语用时，总以前面被修饰动词为前因而产生动词不定式这个结果的。

The old woman hoped that she could live *to see her grandson return from abroad.* 那老妇人希望能活着看到她孙子从国外回来。

＊动词不定式与 so/such ... as 连用时，表示某个行为或状态达到某种程度之下所产生的结果，其结构是 so/such ... as to do sth，意思是"如此……以致"。

The population was increasing *so rapidly as to cause a food shortage.* 人口增长太快，引起了食品短缺。

The hall of the building was *so built as to admit plenty of light as well as fresh air.* 那座大楼的礼堂建成这个样子，空气流通，光线充足。

Jane was *such a fool as to believe what Tom said.* 简真是个笨蛋，竟然相信汤姆的话。

Books are now so expensive *as not to be within the reach of everyone.* 现在的书很贵，不是人人都买得起。

在 so/such ... as 结构中，such 后接名词，so 后接形容词或副词，有时也可接动词，如上面例句 2。例句 4 是动词不定式前加了否定词 not，as not to be within the reach of everyone 之意也就是结果成了否定："有些人就买不起（那些书了）"。

＊动词不定式可以与副词 enough, sufficiently 等副词连用，表示在前述情况下足以产生的结果。

She was *sufficiently* awake *to hear what the boys said.* 我十分清醒，听到了孩子们的全部说话。

His shout was loud *enough to wake up the dead.* 喧闹声之大连死人都能吵醒。

＊too 与动词不定式连用，构成 too ... to (infinitive) 结构，此时的不定式含否定意义，表示否定的结果，它的整个意思是"太……以至于不……"。

John speaks English *too fast to be understood.* 那外国人英语说得太快，让人听不懂。

The news was *too good to be true.* 那消息好得令人难以相信。

但是在 too ... to (infinitive) 结构中的不定式前加了 not 后，动词不定式就失去了否定意义，那时的意思是"太……以至于会"或"太……不能不"，也就是我们在数学上所说的"负负得正"。

He should say some expressions of yours are far too good *not to be quoted in his essay.* 他的一些话说得太好了，我不得不在我的文章中引用一下。

We have read too many novels and seen too many films *not to know a good deal about love.* 现在的学生小说看得多，电影看得多，所以对恋爱的事懂得相当之多。

● 现在分词表示结果时，有很多特点，如位置常在后部，分词前可以用 thus, thereby 等副词，分词的逻辑主语并不都是句子的主语。

* 现在分词表示结果时,其位置常在句子的后部,并且与前面常用逗号分开。

It rained for ten days, *causing floods in the low-lying parts of the town*. 一连下了十天雨,使这个城市的低洼地方一片汪洋。

We hope the new machine will work faster, *reducing our costs*. 我们希望新机器将工作得更快,从而降低成本。

以上两句的 -ing 分词短语都在句末,它们的逻辑主语是前面整个句子。按传统语法讲,它们是现在分词短语作结果状语。

* 用副词 thus, thereby 等加强后面的语气,thus, thereby 意思是"因此(而)"、"从而",属正式用语。现在分词(短语)前用了 thus, thereby 等后,可以加强后面与前面部分的因果关系。

A number of new machines were installed in the factory, *thus resulting in an increase in production*. 这工厂安装了一些新机器,因而增加了生产。

She became an American citizen, *thereby gaining the right to vote*. 她成了美国公民,因此有了投票权。

* 表示结果的现在分词可转变成非限制性定语从句,因为现在分词的逻辑主语一般是前面整个句子,而后面的分词短语是由于前面句子所述情况而产生的,所以后面的分词短语相当于一个非限制性定语从句,因此这种结构可以转变成非限制性定语从句。

It rained heavily for a week, *completely ruining* (which completely ruined) *my holidays*. 大雨下了一周的时间,把我的假期给破坏了。

B. 一些连系动词表示结果

常见用来表示结果的连系动词有:become, come, fall, get, grow, prove, run, turn 等,它们都表示结果的意思。

His father *has become* an expert at troubleshooting. 他的父亲已成为解决棘手问题的专家。

We all *fell asleep* one after another. 我们先后都睡着了。

She *has grown* big enough to wear her mother's dresses. 她已经长大,可穿她母亲的衣服了。

We have run *short of money*. 我们缺钱花。

The milk turned *sour* after three hours. 三个小时后,牛乳变酸。

C. 一些短语动词表示结果

常见表示结果的短语动词有:bring about, end in, end up, come to … end, come out, fall out, give rise to, lead to, result in, turn out 等。

a. 短语动词 bring about 的意思是由主语的"因"而引出了"带来"、"引起"、"造成"的"果"。

Hitler's invasion of Poland *brought about* the Second World War. 希特勒对波兰的侵略导致了第二次世界大战。

The Liberals wish to *bring about* changes in the electoral system. 自由党人想要改变选举制度。

b. 短语动词 end in 的意思是"以……为结局"、"以……告终"。

The battle *ended in* a victory so glorious for our army. 这场战争以我军的光荣胜利而告终。

He went on from theft to theft, till he *ended in* prison. 他不断地扒窃作案,结果被关进监牢。

c. end up 是"结束"、"告终"的意思。在表达这些意思时,它后面可跟介词 as, with, in 及 v-ing 分词,形容词等。

● end up 与介词 in 组成短语时,多数表示以某种状态告终。

Wasteful people usually *end up in debt*. 挥霍浪费者最后往往负债。

He didn't listen to anyone and *ended up in prison*. 他谁的话也不听,结果被关进了监牢。

● end up 与介词 with 组成短语时,作"以……结束(告终)"讲。

The meeting *ended up with the song* "The Internationale". 会议以高唱《国际歌》结束。

And one named Robert *ended up with a badly cut head*. 一个名叫"罗伯特"的人被砍头而死。

● end up 与 as 组成短语时,表示"最后成为"、"结果当上"之意。

She tried several different jobs and *ended up as a lawyer*. 她做过几种不同的工作,最后当了律师。

He *ended up as head of the firm*. 他最后成了商行的主管者。

- end up+现在分词这种短语表示"以做某事而结束"或者"最后有某种结果"的意思。

I never dreamed that I could *end up owing such a lot of property*! 我做梦也没想到我会拥有这么一大笔财产。

Somewhat to his own surprise he *ended up designing the whole car and putting it into production*. 连他自己也有点惊讶,他最终竟设计了整辆汽车并把它投入生产。

d. come to (a) ... end 这短语的意思是"有……结果"、"有……结局(下场)",它不能写成 come to an end (to stop 停止; to finish 结束)。

Bob's son didn't review English and the final examination *came to a bad end*. 鲍勃的儿子没有复习英语,结果期末考试没有通过。

In history, past and present, those who start an aggressive war all *come to no good end*. 历史上,无论是过去还是现在,发动侵略战争者都没有好下场。

e. come out

- 表示一般意义的"结果"、"结局"。

The answer to the problem *came out* wrong/right. 问题的答案错/对了。

Everything will *come out* all right. 到头来一切都会好的。

- 表示考试的"结果"时,后面接名次的词语。

Mary, Mr. Green's daughter, *came out* second in the final examination. 格林先生的女儿——玛丽,期末考试名列第二。

He *came out* in the top three in the mid-term examination. 他在期中考试中进入了前三名。

- 表示"透露出"、"揭晓"、"(最终)传出"的意思。

It *came out* that the girl had been stealing money from her classmates. 原来那女孩一直在偷她同班同学的钱。

The news has just *come out* that Frank will be punished because of his gosiping. 有消息说弗兰克因搬弄是非将受到惩罚。

要注意,come out of 作"由……产生出的结果"讲,它表达"先果后因"。

Something good *came out of* the sinking of the "Titanic". 泰坦尼克号的沉没也促成了一些好事的产生。

f. fall out 表示的结果是具体的,它常用在"As it fell out"和"It fell out that"句型中,意为"结果是"。

As it fell out, their firm was run in the red. 结果,他们的公司经营出现了赤字。

Things fell out just as he had expected. 事情的结局正如他所预料的那样。

It fell out that they were late for the train. 他们终于没有赶上火车。

g. give rise to 引出前因后果句,意思是"导致"、"造成"、"引起"。

The world depression *gave rise to* widespread unemployment. 世界经济萧条造成了广泛的失业。

Poverty *gives rise to* the desire for change. 穷则思变。

h. result in 表示的是在前述情况下引起的结果,它的意思是"结果是"、"导致"(见原因状语从句)。

i. turn out 意思是"结果是,发展为,原来是"。此短语有较强的出乎意料的意味。

Who would know the examination *turned out* so easy? 谁会知道考试会这么容易?

It *turned out* that this method does not work well. 结果证明这个方法效果不好。

As we entered the office, I found that the newcomer had *turned out* to be one of my old acquaintances. 当我们走进办公室时,我发现新来者竟是我的一个熟人。

D. 一些名词表示结果

这里所说的名词表示结果是指,在判断句中,主语或表语是表示结果的名词,如 consequence, issue

(结果,后果),result,outcome(结果,成果,结局),product。

The *result* of the driver's carelessness was the traffic accident and five deaths. 驾驶员的粗心大意造成了那次交通事故和5人死亡的后果。

The book is the *outcome* of a tremendous amount of scientific work. 这本书是大量科学工作的成果。

The paper was the *product* of my half a month's hard working. 那篇论文是我半个月辛勤工作的结果。

E．一些副词、固定副词短语表示结果

英语中也有一些副词表示结果或结局,如 finally, ultimately, eventually 和 at last,用在句中,表示结果。

Finally we got to the top of the high mountain. 最后他们终于到达了那座高山的顶上。

She did not doubt that you would *ultimately* (= finally) succeed. 她没有怀疑我终将成功。

All the contradictions *eventually* were greatly sharpened. 所有这些矛盾被激化了。

F．补足语表示结果

a．一些表示"致使"意义的动词(如 make, have, leave, get, keep, set, render 等)所带的宾语补足语可以说明结果。这些表示宾语补足语的词语常是名词、形容词、动词不定式(短语)、分词、介词短语、从句等。

They made him their team *leader*. 他们选他当队长。

Can you make yourself *understood in English*? 你能用英语表达自己吗？

John managed to have Jane *believe what he said at the meeting*. 约翰设法让简相信他在会上说的话。

I have got the film *developed*. 我已把胶卷洗出来了。

She always keeps her room *in a good order*. 她总是把房间收拾得井井有条。

Modesty helps one *to go forward*, whereas conceit makes one *lag behind*. 虚心使人进步,骄傲使人落后。

b．用被动句中的主语补足语表示结果。被动句中的主语补足语实际上是由原主动句中宾语补足语转化而来。它表示主语在某动作的作用下所产生的结果。

Henry was made *to leave his own country*. 亨利被迫离开自己的祖国。

My teacher said my article must be cut *short*. 我的老师说我的文章得缩短。

Grace was left *an orphan* after the death of her parents. 父母双亡后,格蕾丝成了孤儿。

G．以分句表示结果

用分句表示的结果句常是由并列连词 and, and 与某些表示结果的副词或介词连用引出,或用 so 引出。

a．用并列连词 and 引出表示结果的分句不同于一般的分句。试比较下面两个句子：

The heavy rain had been on the rampage for four days *and a lot of crops were destroyed*. 大雨肆虐了四天,许多庄稼都被毁坏了。

Some supermarkets have opened, *and many little stores are soon on the ropes*. 一些超市已开始营业,许多小商店生意一落千丈。

b．并列连词 and 可以与某些表示结果的副词或介词连用,引导出表示结果的分句。

They have never been to Vienna *and they don't know much about this city*. 他们从没去过维也纳(奥地利首都),所以对这个城市了解不多。

You were always diligent in your study and as a consequence you received high marks. 你一向用功学习,因此而得高分。

c．并列连词 so 引出的并列句表示结果。以 so 引导的分句表示结果时分句与前面的分句常用逗号或分号隔开,有时也有不用标点与第一分句隔开。

She has a tendence to retire into herself, so *I know little about her*. 她不大和别人来往,所以我不怎么了解她。

Jane didn't study hard;*so she didn't pass her examination*. 简学习不努力,所以她考试不及格。

I forgot to close the gate of the coop *so all the chickens were on the loose.* 我忘了关鸡窝门,结果鸡全都跑出来了。

有时,so 可以引出独立句子,但在意义上还与前面句子相连。

I don't use the computer by day. So you can use it if you want. 我白天不用电脑。所以,你如果想用就可以用。

H. 以从句表示结果

以从句表示结果的从句常见的有状语从句、定语从句及连接性因果副词引出的句子表示。引出状语从句的主要从属连词有:so that, so … that,such that, such … that, so, that 等。

a. so that 引导结果状语从句

● 从属连词 so that 引导的状语从句表达的意思是"以致"、"因而"、"结果"。这种句子只位于主句后,中间有逗号分开。在口语中,可用 so 或 that 替代 so that。

My son had done well in the company, *so that he was given a promotion and an increase in salary.* 我儿子在公司干得很出色,所以获得了提升和加薪。

We have spared no effort in planting trees, *so that the streets have now improved beyond recognition.* 我们不遗余力地植树,结果街道大为改观,使人认不出来了。

What has he done (*so*) *that the boss should fire him?* 他做了什么(不好)事老板竟然解雇他?

● so that 引导结果状语从句与目的状语从句的区别

* 结果句是表示已经发生的事实或以前一种情况为前提而发生后一种情况,而目的句是表示某一件事的出发点、愿望或尚未形成的事实。

It was very cold, *so that all of us wore cotton-padded clothes.* 天气很冷,我们都穿上了棉衣。(结果句)

I stepped aside *so that you might go in.* 我站到一旁好让你进去。(目的句)

* 因为结果句表达的是已经或者将会产生的结果,所以极少用情态动词,而目的句所表达的是可能性、愿望,所以常用情态动词以表达委婉的语气。

We started very early, *so that we arrived there before noon.* 我们很早就出发了,所以中午前就到了。(结果句)

I asked them to keep quiet *so that they might not disturb others.* 我要他们保持安静,以免打扰别人。(目的句)

* 在位置上,结果句不可以放在句首,而目的句却可以。

She missed the train *so that she was late for the work.* 她误了火车,结果上班就迟到了。(结果句)

此句不可说成: So that we were late for work, we missed the train.

但可说: So that we might get there before noon, we got up early in the morning. 为了在中午前赶到那里,我们早晨一大早就起身了。(目的句)

* 结果句与主句之间一般用逗号分开,朗读时在主句后稍有停顿;而目的句与主句之间一般不分开,读时也不停顿。

The boy stood on a bench, *so that he saw clearly.* 那个男孩站在一条长凳上,所以他看得很清楚。(结果句)

The boy stood on a bench *so that he could see clearly.* 那男孩为了看得清楚些就站在了一条长凳上。(目的句)

* 目的句可以放在"It is … that"句型中进行强调,但结果句不可以。

It is *so that he will pass the college entrance examination* that he is working hard. 正是为了通过大学入学考试,他正在刻苦学习。(此句原为:He is working hard so that he will pass the college entrance examination.)

像 The day is cloudy so that we can not take good pictures. (天气阴,我们拍不出好照片。)这样的结果句就不能改成:It is so that we can not take good pictures that the day is cloudy.

b. so … that 引导结果状语从句

其中 so ... that 是关联从属连词,意思是"如此……以致"。要注意,句中的 so 属主句部分,其后常接形容词或副词,有时也可不接,说明主语的状态或者动作方式;that 引导出结果状语从句说明主句中的动作或状态到达某种程度而导致的结果。

You were all *so* tired (*that*) *you could do nothing but yawn*. 你很累,以致做不了什么事,只是打哈欠。
Mike speaks Chinese *so* fluently *that everybody believes that he was brought up in China*. 迈克汉语说得很流利,大家都以为他是在中国长大的。

- so ... that 引导的结果状语从句的特点

∗ that 从句表示实际结果,常用陈述语气。

The little dog ran so fast *that Mary could not overtake him*. 那只小狗跑得太快,玛丽逮不住它。
I was so surprised *that I couldn't say a word*. 我激动得连一句话也说不出来。

∗ 常与表示推测的情态动词(如 may, might 等)连用,that 从句表示可能的结果。对现在情况的推测用"may/might + 原形动词"对过去情况的推测用"may/might + have + 过去分词"。用 might 比用 may 的语气弱些,而且所指的结果出现的可能性也小些。

It is raining so heavily *that Xiaozhang may not come*. 雨下得这么大,小张可能不会来。
Mr Li left so early this morning *that he might have arrived in the city*. 李先生今天早晨走得那么早,可能已经到达那个城市了。

∗ 在 that 从句表示不可避免的结果或者根据逻辑推断时,表示现在情况肯定用"must + 动词原形",否定式要用"can't + 动词原形";表示过去情况时,肯定式用"must + have + 过去分词",否定式用"can't/couldn't + have + 过去分词"。

The girl was so injured *that she must die*. 那个女孩伤得这么重,肯定会死的。
You are so weak *that you can't swim across the river*. 你身体这么弱,不可能游过这条河。
Her daughter is so sensible *that she can't (couldn't) have done such a foolish thing like that yesterday*. 她的女儿是很明智的,她昨天不会做出像这样的蠢事。

∗ 在 so ... that 句型中,有时 so 后可接动词。

The strange bridge is so *built* that it can open in the middle when necessary. 那座怪桥是这样建的,需要时可以在中间开启。
Things were so *arranged* that everybody was pleased. 事情处理得皆大欢喜。

∗ 常见在书面语中,把 so 提前至句首,这是为了强调达到的程度。要注意,这时主句要用倒装语序。

So highly praised was Lei's paper that the university council proposed to offer her an award. 蕾的那篇论文得到很高的评价,大学理事会建议奖赏她。

∗ 与 so that 引导的结果状语从句不同,so ... that 句型中,that 引导的结果从句可以置于句首,但 that 常略去,而后面的 so 从句起补充说明的作用。

She doesn't know what to say, she felt so happy. 她高兴得不知说什么才好。
The old man could scarcely stand, so faint was he from illness. 那老人因病而虚弱得几乎不能站立。

- so ... that 引导程度状语从句与引导结果状语从句有区别

这句型中的 that 引出的程度状语从句往往有具体的有时甚至是夸张的描述。要区别它们,只有注意分析 that 从句的内在含义和它在具体语言环境中的作用,熟记上面结果状语从句的几个特点。

c. such that 从句

这里的 such that 是个复合从属连词,一般用在系动词之后引出结果状语从句。such that 中,such 表示到达某种程度的某种情况,that 引出前述情况所带来的结果。因为 such 本身意思含糊,不明确,这需取决于上下文,所以在朗读时 such 后要稍作停顿。

Mike's progress was *such* (= so great) *that it* surprised the teacher. 迈克的进步如此大,使他的老师感到吃惊。
The situation is *such* (= so unfavourable) *that* agreement is unlikely. 形势如此,达成一致意见不大可能。

My courage is *such* (= so great) *that* I do not know the meaning of fear. 我的勇气很大,不知道什么叫害怕。
The weather was *such* (= so hot 或 so cold) *that* we all kept indoors. 天气如此坏,我们都待在家。
在强调时,也可把 such 提前,后面倒装。
Such was the the force of the explosion *that* all the windowns were broken. 爆炸力如此之大,竟使所有的窗子都震破了。
Such was her anxiety *that* she couldn't stop trembling. 她十分焦虑不安,以至于禁不住全身发抖。
d. such ... that 引出结果状语从句
● such ... that 是个关联从属连词,意思是"如此……以致"。such 在表示原因的主句里,that 在从句里,引导出结果状语从句。
I gave *such* important reasons *that* I was excused. 我说出了很多重要理由,得到了谅解。
Mr. Wu was *such* a selfish man *that* nobody would help him. 吴先生是个自私人,所以没人愿意帮助他。
● 在口语中,such ... that 结构中 that 可以省略。
Miss Lei had such confidence in herself she did not consult anybody about the matter. 蕾小姐是那样地自信,以致没跟任何人商量过这件事。
● such ... that 与 so ... that 都用来引导结果状语从句,但它们的搭配并不一样。such ... that 中,such 修饰的是名词,这名词可以是单数,可以是复数,也可以是不可数名词,名词前面可以有形容词修饰;so ... that 中,so 修饰的是形容词或副词。
Your proposal was *such* a good one *that* they all agreed to it. 你的建议很好,他们都表示同意。
You shut the window with *such* force *that* the glass broke. 你用力关窗,把窗玻璃都打碎了。
My proposal was *so good* that you all agreed. 我的建议这样好,你们都表示同意。
The border area is *so dangerous* that it may be blocked. 边境地区十分危险,可能会被封锁。
The girl got up *so early* that she caught the first bus to the Town Hall to listen to the concert. 那女孩早晨起得特早,赶上了头班公共车到市政厅听音乐会。
e. so much so that 引导结果状语从句
这句型的意思是"太……以至于"。so much so that 可以连在一起用,也可以分成 so much ... so that 用。so much so that 引出的结果状语从句与前面主句子可以连接在一起,也可以用逗号、分号或破折号相隔开。
Mrs Wu is very ignorant *so much so that* she does not know how to take after a child. 那个吴太太无知,连怎么照料小孩都不知道。
Tom longed to go abroad, *so much so that* he often dreamed about it. 汤姆极想出国,以至于常做这方面的梦。
You are weak—*so much so that* you can hardly walk. 她太弱了,几乎无法走路。
f. that 引导结果状语从句
that 引出的结果状语从句可说是 so that 的省略形式,因此也是"而"、"以致"、"结果"之类的意思。
Her son does very well in school *that* he is often praised by teachers. 他的儿子在学校学得很好,所以常得到老师的表扬。
My second English grammar book is written in easy English *that* beginners can understand it. 我的第二部书是用浅显的英语写的,因此初学者可以读懂。
g. but, but that 和 but what
如果主句含有 never, never so, not so, not such 等否定词,可用 but, but that 或 but what 引导表示结果的状语从句,构成双重否定,相当于 that ... not 或 unless,可译成"没有……不"。
Henry never comes *but he borrows*. (= Henry never comes unless he borrows.) 亨利不借东西不来。
Mary is not so old *but that she can read*. (= Mary is not so old that she can not read.) 玛丽并未老到不能读书。
Mike is not such a fool *but that he knows it*. (= Mike is not so foolish that he does not know it.) 迈克并非笨

得不知道这个。

There is no man so learned *but what he can learn something from this book.* (= There is no man so learned that he can not learn something from this book.) 再博学的人都会从本书中学到一些东西。

I. 原因和结果融于简单句

这种句子更常见于以动词或短语动词所表达的原因句中。

The worker on duty imputed the accident *to his own oversight.* 值班工人把事故归因于他的疏忽。(结果是 accident,介词 to 后是造成这结果的原因。)

Too much work and too little rest often *lead to illness.* 多劳少逸往往导致生病。(句中的 too much work and too little rest 是原因,lead to 后的 illness 是结果)

J. 原因和结果融于主从复合句

这类句子也常见于以动词或短语动词所表达的原因句中。

Tom's arthritis began to act up again, *which accounted for his absence from school.* 汤姆的关节炎又开始发作了,这是他不能到校的原因。(此句中的主句是原因,从句是结果)

It rises from the fact that the two sides cut each other's throats in their business competition. 这是双方在商业竞争中相互拆台所致。(句中的 the fact that … 是原因,it 是结果)

K. 隐含因果句

隐含因果句就是指那些既没有表示因果的词汇,也没有通过因果结构的手段来表达因果关系的句子,也就是这种句子的因果意思完全通过句子中的前后意思表达出来的。这种句子可分前因后果句和前果后因句两种。

It was so noisy, how could you sleep well? 如此吵闹,你怎能睡得好?(前因后果句)

John's arguments rested upon sound facts, no one challenged him. 约翰的论点基于可靠的事实,所以无人表示异议。(前因后果句)

Henry was asked to go away, Grace didn't like someone looking on while she was writing. 亨利被要求走开,因为格蕾丝不喜欢写东西时有人旁观。(前果后因句)

She doesn't believe what you said, you often tell lies. 她不相信你说的话,因为你经常说谎。(前果后因句)

L. 定语从句表示结果

这种定语从句多数是非限制性的,其修饰的多数是前面整个句子或句子中的某个部分。

Mr John turned a deaf ear to your demands, *which enraged you.* 约翰先生对你的要求置之不理,这使你很气愤。

Their products now sells much more widely, *which enables them to make more money.* 他们的产品现在销路广多了,这使他们能赚更多钱。

The clerk explained in an impatient manner, *which offended the customer deeply.* 那店员以一种不耐烦的态度做解答,令顾客十分气愤。

M. 连接性因果副词引出的句子表示结果

有些连接性副词可以用来说明事情所发生的因果关系。这类副词既可连接简单句或并列句中的因果并列成分,也可以连接在结构上相互独立而意义上却有因果关系的前后两个句子。有时,为了进一步突出主从句的因果关系,这些连接性副词还可与表示因果关系的从属连词 since, as 等配合使用。这种连接性因果副词所引出的结果句与前面的句子间一般用逗号连接,也可用句号把它们分开。

- accordingly 的意思是"于是"、"所以"、"因此",是书面用语。它以两种方式出现:一是引出结果分句,二是连接两个结构上独立即意思上有因果关系的句子。

He was tired out; *accordingly*, we sent him to bed. 他累坏了,于是,我们就送他上床休息。(此属第一种)

She was too sick. *Accordingly* we sent her to the hospital nearby. 她病得很厉害,于是我们就把她送到了附近的医院。(此属第二种)

Accordingly, many teachers devote a part of each class to audio-lingual activities. 于是, 许多老师每节课都将一部分时间用于开展听说活动。(此属第二种, 不过前面表示原因的那句隐去了)

The bill has entered into force. *Some people's interests will suffer accordingly.* 该法案已开始生效, 有些人的利益将受到损失。(此属第二种, 不过 accordingly 已置于结果句的末尾)

- consequently 的意思是"所以"、"因此"、"结果", 属书面语。它也有两种用法:一是与 and 连用, 引出结果分句, 或者单独使用引出结果分句;二是与 and 连用, 连接两个有因果关系的并列成分。

She was a bright and eager student and, *consequently, did well in school.* 她是个聪明好学的学生, 因此学习成绩很好。

Corn was in long supply. *Consequently there was no famine after the severe drought.* 谷物供应充足, 所以大旱之后未出现饥荒。

He missed the first bus, *and consequently was late for work.* 他没乘上早班公共汽车, 因此上班迟到了。

- 副词 hence 的意思是"于是"、"因此"、"所以"、"由此(而有了)……"。它常用于书面语或论说文中。hence 的用法有两种, 一是连接有因果关系的两个独立句子;二是连接两个有因果关系的分句。hence 后还可用省略形式。

The aircraft's speed is limited. *Hence it will soon become obsolete.* 这种飞机的速度有限, 因此很快将淘汰。(第一种用法)

Newton discovered them; *hence they are called Newton's Laws.* 这些定律是牛顿发现的, 所以叫作牛顿定律。(第二种用法)

It's handmade *and hence expensive.* 这是手工制作的, 因此价钱很贵。(省略形式, hence 后只接了个形容词。)

- 连接副词 then 表示结果时的意思是"于是"、"那么"。then 有时用于独立句或者是并列句中, 此时表示在前述的前提之下产生的结果;有时, then 可与从属连词 if 结合使用, 表示在 if 从句的条件下产生相应的结果。

I, *then*, made this decision. 于是, 我做出了这个决定。(用于独立句)

The sun rose, *and the frost then melted.* 太阳出来了, 于是霜化了。(用于并列中)

If she is honest, *then her word is true.* 如果她是诚实的, 那么她的话也是真实的。(以 if 从句条件下产生的相应结果)

- 连接副词 therefore 的意思是"因而"、"因此", 是书面语。它在句中的位置较灵活, 句首、句中、句末均可。它的作用可连接两个有因果关系的并列句, 也可用于独立的句子中, 使其在意思上与前面的句子连接, 并表达出因果关系, 还可连接同一句子中含因果关系的两个成分。

He is in the right, *therefore we should support him.* 他是对的, 所以我们应当支持他。(连接两个因果关系的并列句)

It rained heavily, *the football match therefore was put off.* 下大雨了, 因此足球赛推迟了。(用于两句表示因果关系的并列句)

The new car is smaller *and therefore cheaper.* 这辆新车比较小, 因此就比较便宜。(省略形式, therefore 后只接了个形容词。)

- 连接副词 thus 的意思是"因而"、"因此"、"从而", 书面语和口语中都常见。它可连接有因果关系的两个分句, 也可连接一个独立的与上文有因果关系的句子, 还可连接同一句子中两个因果关系的成分。

Her father had left all his property to the church, *and thus she had to shift for herself.* 她父亲把全部财产捐给了教堂, 因此她只好自行谋生了。(连接有因果关系的两个分句)

Their plane was two hours late; *thus, they did not arrive in time for the conference.* 他们的飞机晚点2小时, 所以他们没能按时到会。(连接有因果关系的两个分句)

There has been too much rain this spring. *Thus the crops are likely to suffer.* 今春雨水太多, 所以庄稼可能

要受损。(连接一个独立的与上文有因果关系的句子)
We hope the new machine will work faster, *thus reducing our costs*. 我们希望新机器将工作得更快,从而降低成本。(连接同一句中含因果关系的成分)
● 连接性副词 whence 的意思是"由此"、"因此",现在用得较少。
It feeds on small birds, *whence it is called the butcher bird*. 它吃小鸟,因此叫作屠夫鸟。
That's the source *whence these evils spring*. 那就是滋生这些罪恶的渊源。
● 连接性副词 wherefore 的意思是"因此"、"为此",可以引出表示结果的句子。
She often gives a false colour to her statements, *wherefore nobody believes in her* even when she speaks the truth. 她常说假话,因此当她说真话时也没人相信她。
That's the reason *wherefore we have met*. 那就是我们之所以会见面认识的原因。

N. 条件性结果句
有些结果句的出现取决于或依附于一定的条件或假设。
If you keep on shouting, your throat will ache. 如果你继续高叫,你的喉咙会痛的。
As long as Mark studies hard, he will surely pass the final examinations. 只要马克努力学习,他会通过期末考试的。
We will let you use the room *on condition that you keep it clean and tidy*. 我们可以给你用这房间,只要你能保持这房间整洁。

(4) 条件状语从句
表示前提或条件的从句称为条件状语从句(Adverbial Clause of Condition)。条件句有四类:事实条件句、直接条件句、间接条件句和修饰条件句。

① 事实条件句的特点和功能
事实条件句(Factual Condition)用来表示习惯性的动作、科学真理、客观事实等。它的特点是都用 if 引出,此时的 if 相当于 when 或 whenever。从其动作的时间上看,主从句里的动作可以均用一般现在时,或均用一般过去时。事实条件句有两个功能:一是表示习惯动作,二是表示客观现实及不受时间限制的科学真理和自然法则。

A. 表示习惯动作
表示习惯动作指的是有了分句的动作或状态,就必定有主句的动作或状态出现。
If it rains, Henry goes to work by car. 如果天下雨,亨利总是乘车去上班。
If Tonny was hungry, he usually had a full meat. 如果饿了,我通常饱餐一顿。
If Rose makes a promise, she keeps it. 只要罗丝做出承诺,她就会遵守。
If it snowed, the road got very slippery. 如果下雪,路总是很滑。

B. 表示客观现实、不受时间限制的科学真理和自然法则
If you pour oil on water, it floats. 油注入水中,油浮在上面。
If we mix red with yellow, we get orange. 红色与黄色调成橘黄色。

C. 暗指事实条件句 (Factual Conditionals of Implicit Inference)
表达与具体时间有关的推测,主从句中的谓语动词的时态和所用的情态动词要一致。
If it's Monday, it's Mike's birthday. 如果那天是星期一,那就是迈克的生日。
If it froze outside last night, our roses were dying. 如果昨晚外边冷得结冰,我们的玫瑰花就要冻死。

D. 明指事实条件句 (Factual Conditionals of Explicit Inference)
表达与具体时间有关的推测,所不同的是,在时态或情态动词上无须与主句保持一致。
If Mary borrows money, she must get into debt. 如果她借钱,她一定会负债。

If John was there, he must have seen the painting. 如果约翰当时在那里,他一定已看到了那幅画。

② 直接条件句

直接条件句(Direct Conditional Sentence)即直接引起某种结果的条件句。这类句子内容众多且较复杂。

If I work hard, I will succeed. 如果我努力工作,我会成功。

If you catch the 8 o'clock train, you can get there by lunch-time. 如果你们赶上8点钟的火车,午饭前你们能到达那里。

A．真实条件句

If she comes here, she can see it. 如果她到这里来,她就看得见它了。

If Lei needs money, I'll give her some. 如果蕾需要钱,我就给她一些。

If the stamp is not torn, it's good for my collection. 如果邮票没破,我收集起来是有用的。

Note：真实条件可以实现,但是否实现的问题没有解决,如 If she comes here, she can see it. 意味着它的反面 If she doesn't come here, she cannot see it.（如果她不到这里来,她就看不见它。）所以真实条件又叫作开放条件（Open Condition）。

B．非真实条件句

非真实条件又叫假设条件(Hypothetical Condition),即假设不能实现或没有实现的条件,动词用虚拟语气形式。

If Tom were here, I would give it to him. (= Tom is not here and I will not give it to him.) 要是汤姆在这里,我就把它给他。(意味着:汤姆不在这里,我不把它给他。)

If it rained tomorrow, I would stay at home. (= It will not rain tomorrow and, therefore, I will not stay at home.) 要是明天下雨,我就待在家里。(意味着:明天不会下雨,因此我不会待在家里。)

If Mike had worked harder, he would have succeeded. (= He didn't work hard enough, so he didn't succeed.) 要是迈克工作更努力一些,他就成功了。(意味着:他努力不够,所以他没有成功。)

这种句式传统语法也叫与现在事实相反的条件句,如上面例句1；与将来事实(可能)相反的条件句,如例句2；与过去事相反的条件句,如例句3。

C．真实条件句的表示法

真实条件句的表示法有两种：一种用从句表示,另一种用并列句的分句表示。

用从句表示真实条件时,谓语动词用陈述语气。引导这种真实条件句的连词常有以下几种：

a. 用 if 引导的从句表示真实条件句

if 是最常用的引导条件状语从句的连词。它常表示下列这些意义：

● 表示"如果"

If I am tired, I will sit down and have a rest. 如果我累了,我就坐下来歇一歇。

If you demand Jane's presence, warn her in advance. 如果你们要简来,就事先通知她。

Notes：情态动词 will/shall 通常不用于状语从句表示单纯的将来,但在下列情况下要用 will：

* 当表示从句主语的意愿时

Ask, *if you will*, who the manager is. 如果你愿意,去问一问经理是谁。

If you will do the beds, Tonny will wash the dishes. 如果你愿意理床,托尼就洗碗。

* 当从句表示说话人对将来情况的预测时

If they definitely won't win, why should they bother to play? 如果他们肯定赢不了,我们又何必打呢?

If the crops will be ruined by next week's drought, you'll have to buy in extra food. 要是庄稼会被下周的旱灾毁掉,你们得多买点食物存起来。

* 当从句表示主句动作的结果时

Lei can lend me 20 pounds *if that will help.* 蕾可以借二十镑给我,如果那样会有用的话。

If it will make Mary happier, Mark'll stop smoking. 如果马克戒烟能使玛丽高兴一些,那他就戒吧。

* 为了使语气委婉时

I would not like to buy this book *if it will cost too much.* 我不想买这本书,如果太贵的话。

If Rose won't be here before midnight, there's no need to rush. 如果罗丝半夜前到不了这里,就不必急了。

● 表示"如果(说)",主句表示推论,通常不含情态动词。

If she's here, she is in the garden. 如果说她在这里,那她就在花园里。

If Robert is mistaken, Grace is mistaken, too. 如果说罗伯特错了,那格蕾丝也错了。

If that was what she told you, she was telling lies. 如果那是她告诉你的,那她就是在撒谎。

If you saw Mr. Huang yourself, surely you can tell us what he looks like. 如果你亲自见到了黄先生,那你一定能告诉我们他像什么样子。

● 在表示"每当"时,等于 when (ever),从句和主句都表示习惯的或必然的情况,不含情态动词。

If you do not understand, you ask questions. 你不懂就问。

If you are tired, you have a short rest. 你累了就稍微休息一下。

If metal gets hot, it expands. 金属变热就会膨胀。

She glares at me *if I go near her desk.* 每当我走近她的书桌,她就向我瞪眼。

Oil floats *if you pour it on water.* 把油倒在水里,油会浮在上面。

● if 有时候相当于 since 或 seeing that,可译为"既然"。

If you like the English grammar book, why don't you buy it? 你既然喜欢这本英语语法书,为什么不买呢?

If Tom doesn't want to stay with me, he may leave at any time. 汤姆既然不想同我在一起,他可以随时离开。

● if 可在简单句中表示与事实相反的愿望,谓语动词用虚拟语气,相当于 I wish, if only …,多以感叹句的形式出现,意义为"要是……多好"。

If she were here with me! 她要是在这里同我在一起该多好!

If she had been warned! 要是有人提醒她该多好!

b. 用 if only 和 only if 引导的从句表示真实条件

if only 和 only if 均是 if 的强调形式,表示"要是"、"只要"的意思,前者常常含有希望的意味,if 和 only 可以分开。

If only it clears up, I'll go shopping. 只要天放晴,我就去购物。

You shall do better *if only you have another chance.* 要是你再有一次机会,你会干得更好。

You shall do better *only if you have another chance.* 只要你再有一次机会,你就会干得更好。

I will succeed *if I only do my best.* 要是我尽最大努力,我会成功。

I will *only* succeed *if I do my best.* 只要我尽最大努力,我会成功。

She'll *only* stay *if I offer her more money.* 只要我给她更多的钱,她就留下来。

If only I can get to the next petrol-station, I'll be all right. 要是我能到达下一个加油站,我就没有问题了。

Note: if only 引导的从句可以单独用,这时谓语动词用陈述语气,表示可能实现的愿望。但 if only 引导的从句也常常用虚拟语气,意义为"但愿……要是……就好了"。

If only she will listen to me. 要是她能听我的话就好了。

If only he will come. 要是他能来就好了。

If only that photograph weren't missing! 要是那幅照片没丢失该多好!

If only I had known it, I wouldn't have troubled him. 要是我早知道那件事,我就不会麻烦他了。

c. 用 unless 引导的从句表示真实条件

对于 unless 的用法及 unless 与 if … not 的用法区别等,杨元兴先生曾经在《山东外语教学》上作过详细的论述。现在我们沿用其观点并结合现代语言的发展简述如下：

- unless 是否定连词，表示"除非"、"如果不"的意思。

Don't come *unless we call*. 我们不喊你就不要来。
Unless you try, you will never succeed. 除非你们试一试，否则你们就绝不会成功。
Lei won't write *unless you writes first*. 蕾不会给她写信，除非你先给她写信。
There is no real courage *unless there is real perception of danger*. 对危险没有真正的认识，就不会有真正的勇气。

- unless 和 if ... not 常常可以交替使用，但 unless 比较正式。

Come tomorrow { *unless I phone*. 除非我打电话，否则你明天来吧
              { *if I don't phone*. 如果我没有打电话，你明天就来。

Note：unless 和 if ... not 用法上的区别：

* unless 引导的从句中通常用肯定词而不用非肯定词，if ... not 引导的从句中通常用非肯定词而不用肯定词。例如：

I will be angry *unless you have already finished your work*. 我会生气的，除非你已经把活干完。
I will be angry *if you haven't finished your work yet*. 如果你还没有把活干完，我就要生气了。

* unless 引导的从句中可以再用其他否定词，if ... not 引导的从句中不可再用其他否定词。由此下列句中的从句不能交换：

We won't explain to you *unless you really don't understand*. 我们不给你解释，除非你真的不懂。
We will explain to you *if you really don't understand*. 如果你真的不懂，我们会给你解释。

* 表示后来想起的补充说明只能用 unless，不能用 if ... not。

Lili hasn't got any hobbies—*unless you call watching TV a hobby*. 丽丽没有任何嗜好——除非你把看电视也叫作嗜好。
Have a cup of coffee—*unless you'd prefer a cold drink*. 喝杯咖啡吧——除非你想喝冷饮的话。

* unless 只用于结果没有受到条件的阻碍而发生时；结果因条件实现而发生时只能用 if ... not，不能用 unless。

I'll be quite glad *if Robert does not come this evening*. 今晚上他不来我才高兴呢。
I'll be surprised *if Robert doesn't have an accident*. 他要是不出事故，我倒会感到奇怪。

* if 引导的从句可以表示非真实条件（用虚拟语气），而 unless 引导的从句一般不可表示非真实条件。下面一句只能用 if ... not：

I would lend him the money *if he didn't break his promise*. 如果他不违背诺言的话，我就会把钱借给他。

d. 用 so long as 或 as long as 引导的从句表示真实条件

so long as 和 as long as 的意思均为"只要"，两者可以互换，但后者多见于口语。

So long as we are innocent, we need not fear. 只要我们是清白的，我们就不必害怕。
I don't care, *so long as Mary lets me be with her daughter*. 我不在乎，只要玛丽让我和她的女儿在一起。
As long as I persevere, I will succeed in the end. 只要我坚持下去，我终究会成功。
She can go out, *as long as she promises to be back before 11 o'clock*. 她可以出去，只要她答应在十一点钟以前回来。

e. 用 on condition that 和 in the event that 引导的从句表示真实条件

- on condition that 多用于正式场合，意思为"如果"、"条件是"。

We'll come *on condition that Rose is invited*, too. 如果你们也邀请罗丝，我们就来。
Mike may borrow the book *on condition that he doesn't lend it to anyone else*. 迈克可以借这本书，条件是他不借给其他任何人。
I will lend her the money *on condition that she pays it back in one month*. 如果她在一月内归还，我就把钱借

给她。

Little Tom was allowed to go swimming *on condition that he kept near to the other boys*. 小汤姆允许去游泳，条件是他得一直靠近其他男孩。

• 在正式场合，in the event that 也可以用来表示条件，但不多见。

In the event that our team wins, there will be an celebration. 如果我们队赢了，将要举行庆祝会。

f. 用 in case 引导的从句表示真实条件

in case 表示的是不确定的条件，含有"假如"、"万一"的意思。

In case she comes, let me know. 假如她来了，给我说一声。

In case I forget, please remind me of it. 万一我忘了这件事，请你提醒我。

In case you fail, you must try again. 万一你失败了，你必须再试一试。

In case the house burns down, you'll get the insurance money. 万一这房子烧掉了，你们会得到保险金。

但 in case 还可以表示目的。

He doesn't dare to leave the house *in case he can be recognized*. 他不敢出门，怕被人认出来。（in case 引出的目的句可用陈述语气）

g. 用 once(if once) 引导的从句表示真实条件

once 是 if once 的省略，表示"（如果）一旦"，并兼有时间含义。

Once Xiaowang hears the story, he will never forget it. 小王一旦听了这个故事，他永远也不会忘记。

Once I understand this rule, I'll have no difficulty. 我一旦理解了这条规则，我就不会有困难了。

Once you reach the village, you are safe. 你们一旦到了那个村子，你们就安全了。

Once Mr. Zhang has learned Spanish, he will find Italian easy. 张先生一旦学会了西班牙语，他就会发现意大利语好学。

h. 用 provided/providing(that) 引导的从句表示真实条件

provided/providing (that) 是"如果"或"只要"的意思，多用于正式场合。

Provided/providing (that) there is no opposition, we shall hold the meeting here. 如果没有反对意见，我们就在这里开会。

I will pardon him *providing/provided that he acknowledges his fault*. 只要他承认错误我就原谅他。

We'll visit Europe next year, *provided/providing we have the money*. 只要有钱，我们明年就去欧洲。

i. 用 suppose/supposing(that) 引导的从句表示真实条件

* suppose/supposing (that) 表示假设的条件，常译为"假如"、"假设"，主句多为疑问句。

Suppose/Supposing (that) it snows, what shall you do? 假如下雪，你们怎么办？

Suppose/Supposing (that) all the doors are locked, how will I get into the house? 假如所有的门都锁上了，我怎么进到房子里去？

Suppose/Supposing that you fail, don't lose heart, but try again. 假如失败了，不要丧失信心，而要再试验。

* suppose/supposing 引导的从句可以单独使用，表示建议。

assuming that 和 presuming that 也可以表示假设的条件，但不像 suppose/supposing (that) 常用。

Assuming that I am right, we'll make a great deal of money from the project. 假如我是对的，我们会从这个项目上赚很多钱。

Presuming that you are innocent, you must be set free. 假如你是无辜的，你就应该被释放。

j. 用 given that/granted/granting that 引导的从句表示真实条件

given that 和 granted/granting that 表示假设的条件，有时含有让步意义。

Given/Granted that we have the means enough, we'll make the attempt. 假如我们有足够的资金，我们会试一试。

Given that Rose is interested in children, I am sure teaching is the right career for her. 假如罗丝对孩子感兴

趣,我相信教书是她适合的职业。

Granting/Granted that what he said is right, what follows? 假如他说的是对的话,下一步将如何呢?

k. as far as 和 so far as 表示"只要"的意思,还兼有程度意义

I will help *as far as I can*. 只要我办得到,我会帮忙的。

So far as you can believe these facts you will use them. 只要你们相信这些事实,你们就会加以利用。

(5) 程度状语、程度状语从句

所谓程度就是指事物发展到某一程度,即"a point on an imaginary line, which is used for measuring ability, progress, etc."。我们把英语中含有程度状语的句子称为程度句。程度句中的程度,有的是以词汇手段表达的,有的是以语法手段表达的;以词汇手段表达的句子是一种简单句,以语法手段表达的句子是复合句,其表示程度的句子叫程度状语从句(Adverbial Clause of Degree)。像结果状语从句表示主句动作或状态到某种程度时所引出的结果,所以结果状语从句中 so ... that, such that, such ... that 等与程度状语从句是相互交叉的。

① 用词汇手段表达程度

用词汇手段表达程度状语时,可用副词、形容词、名词词组、介词短语表达。

A. 用副词表达程度

英语中,表示程度的状语大多数由副词充当。但在程度副词的分类上,我们根据著名语法学家 M. Frank(1972)的观点把程度副词分为两类:一类是表示程度有多大的程度副词(Adverbs of Degree Denoting How Much),另一类是表示完成情况如何的程度副词(Adverbs of Degree Denoting How Complete)。

a. 表示程度有多大的程度副词

表示程度有多大的程度副词常见的有:very, too, quite, extremely, somewhat, rather, exceedingly, dreadfully, fairly, more, awfully, so, pretty, terribly, horribly, really 等。这类副词主要用来修饰形容词或副词,而且可以相互代替。

Lei felt *terribly* tired that night. 那晚蕾感到非常疲倦。

Mary became *very/quite/awfully/really* angry with the insolent boy. 玛丽对那傲慢的小孩非常/十分/很/真的生气。

My mother always walks *rather* quickly. 我的母亲总是走得相当快。

That grammar book was *pretty* bad. 那本语法书相当糟。

Grace is *breathtakingly* beautiful. 格蕾丝漂亮得惊人。

Tom works *devilishly* hard. 汤姆工作非常努力。

We've been working *awfully* hard lately. 我们近来一直非常努力工作。

Note: much 在意义上也属于这类副词,但它不用于修饰形容词和副词原级,而是修饰它们的比较级。不过它可用来修饰纯粹分词、表语形容词或某些表示感情的动词。

Jane's room is *much* bigger than yours. 简的房间比你的房间大得多。

She works *much* harder. 她工作努力多了。

I was *much* tired by the work. 干这工作使我很劳累。

The window was *much* damaged. 这窗户损坏得很厉害。

She is *much/very/very much* afraid of me. 她很怕我。

She doesn't like him *much/very much*. 她不是很喜欢他。

I *much* prefer the old method. 我很喜欢那种老方法。

b. 表示完成情况如何的状语

●常见表示完成情况如何的程度副词有：almost, enough, entirely, half, fully, nearly, partially, practically, utterly, wholly, hardly, scarcely, slightly, absolutely, perfectly, greatly, thoroughly 等。这类副词的构成形式大多数与方式副词一样，在形容词后加-ly。这些副词主要用来修饰动词、形容词。

They have *almost* finished the work. 他们差不多做完了这工作。

He *completely* misunderstood his wife's remarks. 他完全误解了他妻子的话。

Henry has *partially* recovered from his illness. 亨利的病已经好些了。

We paid for the damage *fully*. 我们赔偿了全部损失。

Lili is *practically* ready to begin the show. 丽丽差不多准备好要开始表演。

The builders were *utterly* exhausted. 那些建筑工人完全筋疲力尽了。

Entirely obvious of all protests, the manager went ahead with his plan. 尽管市长完全知道所有的抗议，但他仍然继续执行他的计划。

The mural was *one-third* completed before the painter received part of his fee. 画家需要完成壁画的1/3后才能领到部分酬金。

●有个别表示完成情况如何的程度副词如 almost, nearly 等的位置比较灵活，当位置不同时，意思也不同。

Nearly everybody loves a bargain. 几乎每个人都喜欢讨价还价。

The farmer *nearly* lost two hundred cattle in the flood. 农场主在洪涝中差点儿损失了200头牛。

The farmer lost *nearly* two hundred cattle in the flood. 农场主在洪涝中损失了差不多200头牛。

She does't *completely* agree. 她不完全同意。

She does't agree *completely*. 她完全不同意。

●程度副词中，有些有交叉现象，同一个词在不同的语境里可属于不同的类型。

The grammar book is *quite* interesting. 这本语法书相当有趣。（属第一类）

She *quite* forgets about his birthday. 她完全忘记了他的生日。（属第二类）

You were *utterly* hopeless. 你非常绝望。（属第一类）

I stopped loving her *utterly*. 我一点也不爱她了。（属第二类）

B．用形容词表达程度

a. 英语中，有些形容词与副词同形，其中有些也可以充当程度状语。这些状语常置于被修饰词（组）之前。

She knows the job is *terrible* hard. 她知道这工作十分艰苦。

Mr Zhu was *dead* drunk. 朱先生喝得酩酊大醉。

Xiaocheng took *precious* good care to stay away. 小成非常小心地离开了这里。

Xiaoli is *plain* silly. 小李糊涂透顶。

The door was *wide* open. 这门开得很大。

Little Tom climbed *clear* to the top of the tree. 小汤姆一直爬到树顶。

b. 有些副词、形容词可与另一些形容词、分词构成合成形容词，其中有些副词、形容词可作程度状语而修饰另一形容词或分词。

The window is *wide-open*. 这窗户开得很大。

The old man was *dead-alive*. 那老人半死不活。

She wore a *light-blue* suit. 她穿着一套浅蓝色衣服。

I am a *hard-working* man. 我是个工作努力的人。

You have won a *clear-cut* victory. 你们已经取得了彻底的胜利。

She is already a *full-grown* person. 她已经是个成年人。

c. 有几个含有赞赏意味的形容词与另一形容词连，在意义上相当于一个程度副词，对后一形容词起修饰作用,其意思常可译成"非常,很,十分"等,有时也可根据句子情况灵活翻译。

The building stands *nice and* high. 这建筑坐落的位置很高。

I am *rare and* hungry. 我很饿。

The house is *nice and* warm. 这房屋很暖和。

It was *lovely and* cool. 天气舒适凉爽。

Xiao Ma drove *good and fast*. 小马把车子开得挺快。

Lei prepared a cup of tea for me, *good and strong*. 蕾给我沏了杯茶,味道挺浓的。

d. 一些形容词、副词与某些词语搭配表示程度

● too … to 结构

在这一结构中,too 修饰形容词或副词,不定式表示否定的意思。

The boss was *too* angry *to* speak. (= The boss was so angry that he cannot speak.) 那老板气得说不出话来。

The desk is *too* heavy *to* move away. 这张桌太重搬不开。

The tea is *too* hot *to* drink. 这茶烫得不能喝。

Note:不定式如有逻辑主语,那要用介词 for 引出。

It's raining *too* hard *for* Mr. Yu *to* go out. 雨下得太大,于先生出不去。

He walked *too* fast *for* his friends *to* keep pace with him. 他走得太快,他的朋友跟不上。

＊在 not too … to, only toop … to, but too … to, all too … to 等结构中,不定式不表示否定,而是表示肯定的意思。

Lili is *not too* old *to* do it. 丽丽年纪不太老,可以做这事。

Xiaoliu is *only too* glad *to* accept it. 小刘非常高兴接受它。

Mike is *all too* satisfied *to* take the opinions of others. 迈克很高兴接受别人的意见。

I know *but too* well *to* hold my tongue. 我深知少说为好。

当然, too 不一定与不定式搭配,too 的前面可有像 all, none, quite, much 等别的词。

The holidays were *all too* short. 假期实在太短了。

He is *only/but too* satisfied. 他太满意了。

They got to the station *none too* soon because there were a lot of other people waiting to buy tickets. 他们到车站一点也不太早,因为那儿已有许多人在等着买票。

It was quite *too* bad. 太糟了。

Paul has become so naughty recently—he really was *too much*. 保罗近来变得如此调皮——昨天到了不能容忍的地步。

● enough to 结构

＊在这种结构中,不定式表示肯定的意思,enough 的位置总在它所修饰的形容词或副词的后面。

The auditorium is large *enough to* hold one thousand people. (= The auditorium is so large that it can hold one thousand people.) 这个礼堂很大,能够容纳 1000 人。

Paul ran fast *enough to* catch the bus. 保罗跑得很快,赶上了公共汽车。

＊要是 enough 的前面有否定词,那它后面的不定式则表示否定的意思。

He was *not* old *enough to* understand all that. (= He was too young to understand all that.) 他的年龄还不够大,不了解这一切。

We found the room *not* big *enough to* hold so many people. 我们发觉这房间不够大,容纳不下这么多人。

I *didn't* know him well *enough to* marry him. 我对他了解不够,不能嫁给他。

＊在 enough 修饰不可数名词和复数名词时,置于名词的前面或后面均可。

He has *enough money* (*money enough*) for his son to buy a house. 他有足够的钱让他儿子买房子。

Have you got *time enough* (*enough time*) to go to the bank? 你有足够的时间上银行去吗?
They have *enough seats* (*seats enough*) for everyone to sit on. 他们有足够的位子让每个人入座。

　＊ enough 与单数可数名词搭配时通常后置,此时总省去冠词。这里的名词实际上起了形容词的作用。

He was *fool enough to* believe what the cheat said then. 那时他竟然蠢到相信了那个骗子的话。
Mr chen is not *scholar enough to* name this plant. 陈先生学识不够,说不出这植物的名称。
Xiaodiao was *gentleman enough to* help her. 小刁绅士派头十足地帮助她。

● "such＋名词＋as to"结构中,such 表示程度,as to 表示结果。

Peter is *such a fool as to* believe what the man said. 皮特真是个笨蛋,竟然相信别人的话。
Bob can't have done *such a dreadful thing as to* put off going for my sake. 鲍勃不能做出这样糟糕的事,为了我竟然拖延着不去。

　有时 such 可作代词与 as to 搭配使用,也表示程度。

Her stupidity is *such as to* fill me with despair. 你的愚蠢竟然达到使我失望的地步。

● "so＋形容词/副词＋as to"结构表示行为或状态达到某种程度而产生的结果,意思是"到……以致"。

John wouldn't be *so careless as to* forget his key. 约翰不会粗心到连自己的钥匙也忘记。
Outside, the storm drove *so fast as to* create a snow-mist in the hall. 外面,暴风雪吹得很急,以致大厅里起了雪雾。

● "sufficiently＋形容词＋to"结构的意思是"够……以至"。

I was *sufficiently* awake *to* hear what the boys said. 我完全醒着,听到了那些男孩们所说的话。

C. 用名词词组表达程度

某些名词有时也可作程度状语修饰形容词、副词或动词。

The wire was only *house* high as it crossed the road. 横过马路的电线只有房子高。
The mountain is *snow* white. 这山像雪一样白。
The river is *fifteen meters* deep. 这河有 15 米深。
The temperature dropped *five* degrees. 温度下降了 5 度。
Bob is *three inches* taller than his mother. 鲍勃比他母亲高 3 英寸。
He met Lili *three times* last moth. 他上个月碰见了丽丽 3 次。
A *paper* thin sheet of copper separates the two layers. 两层之间隔着一张薄如纸的铜片。
I walked *a long way* to the station. 我们走了一大段路来到车站。
Does he know the box weighs 10 *pounds*? 他可知道这盒子有 10 磅重?

D. 用介词短语或固定词组表达程度

这些常见的介词短语有:according to, as good as, at least, at all, all of, by far, in part, to some extent/degree, kind/sort of, more and more, more or less, in some respects, in the least, a bit, all for, anything but, beyond one's ability, none the least, the best part of, or so, like anything, by no means 等。

You don't support them *at all*. 你一点也不支持他们。
Our town is *a great deal* poorer than yours. 我们镇比你们镇穷得多。
From each *according to* his ability, to each *according to* his needs. 各尽所能,按需分配。
I don't mind *in the slightest*. 我一点也不介意。
You *as good as* ruined the farm. 你们几乎把农场毁了。
Peter didn't enjoy it *in the least*. 皮特一点也不喜欢它。
In another year *or so*, Jane will have forgotten all about me. 大约再过一年,简将会把我全忘了。
I'll do it *to the best of my ability*. 我将尽我所能做好此事。

The little girl is *anything but* polite. 那小女孩一点也不礼貌。

The naughty boy ran *like anything* when he saw his father. 那调皮鬼见到他父亲就拼命地跑。

Little by little, Grace revealed her ambitions. 格蕾丝逐步地暴露了自己的野心。

We are *all for* selling the old car and buying a bicycle. 我们完全赞成把旧汽车卖掉,买一辆自行车。

The little girl was *all of a tremble*. 那小女孩冷得全身发抖。

Lili is blushed *to the roots* of her ears. 丽丽羞得红到耳根。

The orange is rotten *to the core*. 这橘子烂透了。

I was *at my happiest* among my students. 和学生们在一起我最高兴。

The tasks you faced seemed *far beyond your ability*. 你面临的任务似乎远远超出你的能力。

② 用语法手段表达程度

用语法手段表达程度就是用程度状语从句表达程度。这种从句是以从属连词或关联词的形式引出程度和结果相结合的状语从句。

A. 由从属连词引导的程度状语句

这些常见的从属连词有:as, as … so, in proportion as, … (so), to the extent that, according as, as/so far as, insofar as, to the degree that, as … as can be 等。

a. 以 as 引导的程度状语从句:在 as 引导的程度状语从句中,从句和主句常有形容词或副词的比较级,相当于 the more … the more 结构。

As Mark acquires more power, he becomes more unscrupulous. (= The more power Mark acquires, the more unscrupulous he becomes.) 马克的权力越大,他就越是无所不为。

They get wiser *as they get older*. 随着年龄的增大,他们就越聪明。

b. 以 as … (so) 引导的程度状语从句:在 as … so 中,as 在意义上相当于 in the same proportion, in the same way, 说明主句所表示的内容在程度上与从句是一样的。

As Bob treats Mary, *so* Mary will treat him. 鲍勃怎样对待玛丽,玛丽也怎样对待他。

As you like music, *so* I like poetry. 正像你喜欢音乐一样,我喜欢诗歌。

c. 以 in proportion as …(so) 引导的程度状语从句:in proportion as … (so) 的意思是"按……比例"、"依……的程度而变"。如后面用 so 时,该从句常用倒装语序。

Man is free *in proportion as* his surroundings have a determinate nature. 人类的自由与环境的约束成比例。

In proportion as the land value increased, *so* too did taxes become higher. 税率也是按照土地价值增长的比例而提高的。

d. 以 to the extend that 引导的程度状语从句:to the extend that 与 to the degree that 同义,都表示"到……程度",that 引起的是同位语从句。

The project will succeed only *to the extent that each of us puts his best efforts into it*. 这项工程成功的程度如何,仅在于我们每个人所下功夫的大小。

Xiaoji will succeed *to the degree that he applies himself diligently*. 小季的成功与否在于他努力的程度。

有时也用 to such a degree/an extent that。

You were tired *to such a degree that you fainted*. 你疲倦得昏了过去(程度)。

These villages are small *to such an extent that they cannot be shown in the map*. 这些村庄小得无法在地图上显示。(程度)

从上述两例句可以看出,程度状语从句往往也可以表示达到某种程度时所引出的结果,因此两者之间可以交替使用,上述两句可交替为:

You were so tired *that you fainted*. (结果)These villages are so small *that they cannot be shown in the map*. (结果)

e. 以 as/so far as 引导的程度状语从句

as/so far as 可以表示距离"远至"、"直到",也可以表示程度、范围"就……而论"、"尽"、"至于"。

As far as Mike can see Xiaoyang appears satisfied with the arrangement. 就迈克所知,小杨对这样安排显得很满意。

As far as illness was concerned, Tate was even worst off than most others. 就其疾病而言,泰特比其他多数人甚至更为严重。

In one year, dust from these farm lands was carried *as far as the Atlantic Ocean*. 一年里风就把尘土从这些耕地吹到远至大西洋。

She followed me with her eyes *as far as she could*. 她目送我直到看不见为止。

f. according as 引导的程度状语从句:according as 的意思是"根据"、"要看在眼里……来决定"。

He may go or stay, *according as he decides*. 他或去或留由他决定。

You will be praised or criticized *according as your work is good or bad*. 根据你工作的好坏你将受到表扬或批评。

g. 以 insofar as（in so far as）引导的程度句:insofar as 也可以写成 in so far as,表示"就……而论"、"尽"、"至……程度"。

You will learn your lessons *only insofar as you are willing to keep studying them*. 这些功课你学得如何,决定于你诚心坚持的程度。

I will help you in so far as I can. 我一定尽力帮助你。

h. 以 as ... as can/may be 引导的程度句:as ... as can/may be 的意思是"到不能再……的程度"。两个 as 后用同样的形容词,第二个形容词是对第一个起强调作用的。

Tone is as happy *as happy can be*. 托恩快乐极了。

You are as wrong *as wrong can be*. 你大错特错。

Yale is as thirsty *as thirsty can be*. 耶鲁渴得不得了。

i. 形容词和副词的某些比较结构:as ... as, more ... than, -er ... than, "the + 最高级形容词/副词 + 比较范围"等表示程度。

B. 以"the + 比较级,the + 比较级"引导的程度状语从句

a: "the + 比较级,the + 比较级结构"表示程度。在这种结构中,the ... the ... 为关联词,第一个 the 为关系副词,引导状语从句,第二个 the 为指示副词,含有"到那个程度"的意思,通常可译成"越……越……"。

b. 在使用这一结构时,应该注意以下几点:

• 在这一结构中可用屈折词尾构成的比较级,也可以用分析形式构成的比较级。

The {more old / older} we are {the more wise / wiser} we become. 我们年龄越大,越有智慧。

• 在正式语体中,that 可以插在第一个比较级的后面。

The sooner (that) a man begins to enjoy his wealth, *the better*. 人越早享有自己的财富,就越好。

The more (that) life disappointed Scott, *the more* he sought refuge in books. 生活越使斯格特灰心失意,他就越是从书本里寻找安慰。

The more money (that) Sulla makes, *the more* he wants. 苏拉挣的钱越多,奢望就越大。

• 有时主句(第二个结构)可以在前,从句(第一个结构)在后。这时主句需用正常语序,the 往往可以省去。但翻译时,仍要先译从句,后译主句。

Xiaoli wrote *the better*, *the more* she practiced. 小丽越练习,就写得越好。

I liked the book *better*, *the more* it made me cry. 这本书越是催人泪下,我就越喜欢它。

Sulla became (*the*) *more cynical*, *the older* he grew. 苏拉年纪越大,就越是玩世不恭。

They became (*the*) *hungrier*, *the harder* they worked. 他们越是努力干,就越饥饿。
有时主句还可用比较级的重叠结构表示相同的意思。
Soddy gets *more and more restless*, *the longer* she stays in the same place. 苏迪待在同一地方的时间越长,越感到焦虑不安。

• 比较部分可以是补足语、状语、宾语和主语。
The less Suzan worried, *the better* she worked. 苏珊担忧得越少,工作得就越好。(the less 和 the better 充当状语)
The more grain they produce, *the greater* will be their achievement. 他们生产的粮食越多,他们的成就就越大。(the more grain 充当宾语, the greater 充当补语)
The more hydrogen is compressed into the balloon, *the larger* it will become. 打进气球里的氢气越多,气球就越大。(the more hydrogen 充当主语, the larger 充当补语)

c. 主句在后,谓语动词为 be 时, be 常可倒装,置于主语的前面。
The noisier the children were, *the better* was their mother pleased. 孩子们越吵闹,他们的母亲就越高兴。
The more people that sign up for the trip, *the cheaper* will be the price. 报名参加旅游的人越多,票价就越便宜。
要注意,如果主句的主语为代词,则不可倒装。
The sooner I decide, *the better* it will be. 我决定得越快就越好。

d. 从句和主句可省略某些成分,其中最常见的是省略动词 be,有时也省略其他成分。
The prettier the girl (is), *the more foolishly* he acts. 在越是漂亮的女孩子面前,他表现得越笨拙。
The nearer the bone (is), *the sweeter* the meat (is). 越靠近骨头的肉,其味越美。
The smaller the village (is), *the friendlier* the people (are). 村子越小,人们越友好。
The more (*money*) he makes, *the more* (*money*) he spends. 他挣钱越多,花钱越多。
The more guests that come, *the better* (it will be). 来的客人越多越好。
有时只剩下两个比较级,其他成分都省略。
The more, *the better*. 越多越好(多多益善)。
The sooner, *the better*. 越快越好。
The earlier, *the better*. 越早越好。
The more haste, *the less speed*. 欲速则不达。

C. "关联词 so 等 ... that +结果句"结构
含有关联词 so ... that, such (a) ... that, so much so that, not so ... but that/what 的句子结构是一种程度与结果相结合的结构。so, such 后面的词语表示程度,that 引出的则是结果从句。

a. so ... that 结构:在 so ... that 结构中, so 的后面可接一个"形容词、副词、分词或限定词+名词"结构,表示主语的动作或状态达到某种程度, that 引出的从句则是由于这种程度导致的结果。
There were *so many people* in the hall *that* Lili could not find me. 大厅里人这样多,丽丽找不到我。
Grace is *so emotional that* every little thing upsets her. 格蕾丝多愁善感,以致一点小事也使她焦虑不安。
Henry behaved *so emotionally that* we knew something terrible had upset him. 亨利的行为如此激动以至于我们看出肯定是一些可怕的事扰烦了他。
In clouds, condensation may be *so rapid that* millions of droplets of water are formed. 云里,凝聚作用之快,可以构成数以百万计的微滴。
Rose's book is *so written that* it gives a quite wrong idea of the facts. 罗斯的书的写法使人对事实产生误解。
It was *so warm a day that* we decided to go to the sea. 天气这样暖和,我们决定去海边游玩。
The car costs *so much money that* Scott won't buy it. 这汽车要价太高,斯格特就不买了。

b. such ... that 结构:在 such ... that 结构中, such 后可接"a +可数名词单数"、"复数名词或不可数名词"。

This is *such an ugly table that I am going to give it away*. 这张桌子这样难看,我要把它处理掉。
These are *such ugly chairs that I am going to give them away*. 这些椅子这样难看,我要把它们处理掉。
This is *such ugly furniture that I am going to give it away*. 这家具这样难看,我要把它处理掉。

c. so much so that 结构:so much so that 是复合强调连接词,so much so 表示主句或前面分句动作或状态达到某种程度,that 引出结果从句也作"达到……程度,以致……"解。
He felt happy, *so much so that he didn't know what to say*. 他感到高兴,高兴得不知道说什么好。
Taylor hates his work, *so much so that he is thinking of resigning*. (= Taylor hates his work so much so that he is thinking of resigning.) 泰勒很讨厌他的工作,以致考虑把它辞去。

D. not so … but that/what 结构

not so … but that/what 中的 but that/what 相当于 that … not。有时候可把 that 和 what 省去,只剩下 but。not so 引出的词语表示主语的动作或状态达到了某种程度,but that/what 从句则是由这种程度引起的结果。
On the whole that task is *not so difficult but that I may try it*. (= On the whole that task is not so difficult that I may not try it.) 一般说来,那个任务并没有难到我不能试的地步。
They all know things are not *so bad but what they might be worse*. 他们都知道事情不能糟到再糟的地步了。
I shall never be *so busy but that/what I shall find time to answer your letters*. (= I shall never be so busy that I shall find no time to answer your letters.) 我不会忙到抽不出时间给你回信的地步。
在这一结构中,so 有时可以换成 such (a),such 后接的成分与 such (a) … that 相同。
There is *not such a fool but that/what he can see*. (= There is not such a fool that he can not see.) 没有人傻到连那点也看不出来。

(6) 让步句的定义及类型

凡含让步意义的句子称为让步句。让步状语从句(The Adverbial Clause of Concession)表示主句中的情境与从句中所说情况产生的预期情境相反,但不影响事情的进行或实现。从句子结构上说,含让步意义的句子可以是简单句,也可能是复合句;是复合句时,那就是通过从句表达让步意义。让步的表达类型有:通过词汇手段表示;用短语表示;通过上下文表示;用让步状语从句表示。

① 通过词汇手段表示让步

这里所说的用词汇手段是指用有让步意义的单词、短语等,而使整个句子成为让步句。

A. 用副词表示让步意义
用于让步的副词主要有:anyhow, however, though, nevertheless, still, yet, notwithstanding 等。

a. 表示让步副词的位置
● 一般副词位置:表示让步意义的连接副词常放在第二个句子的开头,也有放在第二个句子中间或末尾的。它们通常被用逗号与句子的其他部分隔开。
I may not like her visit, but she shall come and see me, *anyway*. 我可能不喜欢她来探访我,尽管如此,她还是要来看我。
This essay is all right; *however*, there is still much room to improve. 这文章不错;尽管如此,还大有改进的余地。
What she said may be unexpected; *nevertheless*, it is true. 她说的也许突然,尽管如此,却是真的。
I did wrong. *Still*, she's ready to forgive me. 我犯错了。尽管如此,她还是宽恕我。
You have made great progress; *yet*, you should be modest and prudent. 你已经取得了巨大的进步;然而,你应当谦虚谨慎。

I tried to prevent the marriage, but it didn't take place *notwithstanding*. 我尽力阻止这桩婚事,但它终究没有成功得了。

Lili said she would come, she didn't, *though*. 丽丽说她会来;然而她没有来。

You denied yourself everything. *Notwithstanding*, the old skinflint complained without ceasing. 你放弃了一切。尽管如此,那个老守财奴还是不停地抱怨。

● 副词 though 的特殊位置:副词 though 的位置比较特殊,它通常放在第二句的句末,但有时也可放在第二句的中间,但它不可以像副词那样放在第二句的开头。

It's hard work. She enjoys it, *though*. 这是苦活。然而,她喜欢它。

Mike is a dangerous element. There is no reason to shoot him, *though*. 迈克是一个危险分子。虽然如此,没有理由枪毙他。

Mike is a dangerous element. There is no reason, *though*, to shoot him. 迈克是一个危险分子。虽然如此,没有理由枪毙他。

但不能说:

* He is a dangerous element. Though, there is no reason to shoot him.

b. 含 notwithstanding 的让步句:notwithstanding 虽与 in spite of 同义,但它是较为正式的用语,有较重的法律语体味。它的特殊之处是有时候可置于它的受词后。

John Smith, *notwithstanding his tedious rhetoric*, is a master of the sublime in prose style. 约翰.史密斯,尽管他喜欢用冗长的修辞,在散文风格上是出类拔萃的大师。

The law will go into force, any other agreements *notwithstanding*. 尽管有其他的协议,该法律仍将生效。(此句相当于 The law will go into force, notwithstanding any other agreements.)

The cool weather *notwithstanding*, Rose was perspiring freely. 尽管天气凉快,罗丝仍大汗淋漓。(此句相当于 Notwithstanding the cool weather, Rose was perspiring freely.)

B. 用短语表示让步

表示让步意义的短语常有:介词短语、分词短语、独立结构、无动词短语四种。

a. 介词短语表示让步:用作表示让步意义的介词短语通常有:in spite of, despite, for all, with all 等。

● 一般来说,介词短语表示让步意义时可以前置,也可以后置。

Despite the bad weather, they had a wonderful holiday. 尽管天气不好,他们的假日还是过得极为愉快。

Ruth went with us *in spite of* her cold. 尽管感冒得很厉害,露丝仍和我们一起去了。

● 一些介词短语表示让步意义的情况

* 含 in spite of 短语的让步句

in spite of 常置于句后,有时也可置于句子前。

We admire him, *in spite of his faults*. 尽管他有缺点,我们还钦佩他。

In spite of what you say, I still believe he is honest. 不管你说什么,我还是相信他是诚实的。

Xiaochen decided to go to the East Lake *in spite of the great distance*. 尽管路途遥远,小陈还决定去东湖。

● despite 引导的介词短语让步句

despite 与 in spite of 同义,但前者较为正式。despite 所引导的介词短语通常置于句前,但也有置于句后的情况。

Despite strong pressure from her parents, Xiaolei has refused to break with her boyfriend. 尽管有父母方面来的压力,小蕾还是拒绝与男友断绝关系。

Xiaohai attended the important meeting *despite* his illness. 小海尽管生病了,但还是参加了那个重要会议。

● 含 for all, with all 的让步句

for all 与 with all 两短语的意思一样,两者后接名词时可以互换。它们多见于口语。要注意的是,for all 或 with all 表示让步意义时,其后一定要附加限定词。

For all that Rose seems to dislike him, he still like her. 尽管罗丝似乎不喜欢他，他仍然喜欢她。
With (for) all his wealth, Mark is not happy. 尽管马克富有,他并不幸福。
For (with) all his boasting, Tonny was knocked out in the first round by a man lighter than him. 尽管他牛皮十足,托尼在第一回合就被体重比他轻的人击倒。

b. 表示让步意义的分词短语、独立结构或无动词短语

● 分词短语表示让步意义

分词短语指现在分词短语和过去分词短语。用分词短语可以表示让步意义,此种情况有两种:

* 无连词分词结构表示让步

Weighing almost fifty pounds, the little Tom moved the stone alone. 尽管石头差不多五十磅,那小汤姆还是一人把它搬动了。
Born of the same parents, Mary bears no resemblance to her sisters. 尽管是同父母所生,玛丽与她的几个姐妹一点不像。

* "连词+分词短语"表示让步

有时,可用"连词+分词短语"结构表示让步。这种结构实际上是省略了与主句相同的主语和助动词 be 的缩略的让步状语从句,用这种结构表示让步意义更明确、语气更强烈。

Although invited, I didn't go to the party. 虽然我们被邀请了,但我们没有去参加派对。
Even though given much money the little boy was not satisfied. 虽然给了许多钱,那个小男孩还不满意。
Although impressing the examiners, she nevertheless failed. 虽然她十分打动考官的心,但还是失败了。

● 独立结构表示让步:表示让步意义的独立结构也常置于主句之前,它们可以是分词独立结构和介词独立结构。

* 分词独立结构表示让步

Granting/Granted that Bob has enough money to buy the car, it doesn't mean he is going to do so. 即使买得起这辆汽车,鲍勃也并不意味着他会这样做。
Granting all those facts, I still have not convinced her. 就算那些全是事实,我仍然没有说服她。

* 介词独立结构表示让步

Even with conditions quite favorable, you would not succeed. 即使条件十分有利,你们也不会成功。
For all the barometer falling, it hasn't rained. 尽管晴雨表下降了,可是没有下雨。

● 无动词短语表示让步:含让步状语的无动词短语是根据杨元兴先生的无动词句的观点而来,此指短语中的实义词是名词或形容词,而不是动词。无动词短语实际上是连词引导的让步状语从句的省略形式,其省略的情况是让步状语从句的主语与主句的主语一致,谓语是动词 be 时,该从句的主语的动词 be 同时省略,有时甚至连接词也同时省略。

* 省略主语和动词 be

Although a doctor by training, John became a great statesman. 虽然约翰学的是医,却成了伟大的政治家。
Xiaoli was happy, *though broke*. 小丽虽然身无分文,却很快乐。
It is one of the most spacious, *if not the most spacious of salons*. 它即使不是最宽敞的客厅,也是最宽敞的客厅之一。

* 省略主语、be 动词及连词

A timid young man, Neil nevertheless jumped into the water and rescued the girl from drowning. 尽管是一个害羞的年轻人,然而尼尔跳入水中救起了那溺水的女孩。
No swimmer, Lili splashed about happily in the sea. 虽然不会游泳,丽丽在海里拍水拍得很畅快。
The rumor, *however incredible*, was believed by Neil. 谣言,尽管它无论怎样不可信,尼尔还是相信了。

② 用词序手段表示让步

这里所说的词序手段就是倒装语序。下面这些句子中的从句都用了倒装语序,所表达的意思是让步。

Late as it was, they continued the work. 时间尽管不早,他们仍然继续工作。

Complicated as the problem is, we can solve it in only two seconds with an electronic computer. 虽然这个问题复杂,但我们用电子计算机只需两秒钟就能解决。

However hard she tries, she cannot understand this question. 尽管她费了好大的劲,这个问题她还是不理解。

Close though the union of small particles is, you have found ways of breaking it. 虽然微粒子结合得很紧密,你们还是找到了分裂的方法。

Standing as it does at the top of the hill, the house is well preserved. 这个房子虽然坐落在小山的顶上,但却保存完好。

Try as she might, she could not solve the problem. 虽然努力过,她却无法解决问题

Be it ever so late, they must do another experiment. 时间虽晚,但他们必须再做一个实验。

Much as he likes physics, he likes mathematics better. 虽然他喜欢物理,但更喜欢数学。

Child as Grace is, she knows something of physics. 虽然格蕾丝还是个孩子,但她懂得一些物理的知识。

Come what may, we must go there. 不管发生什么情况,我们都必须去那里。

Go where Henry will, he will find many good things. 无论到什么地方,亨利都会发现许多好事物。

③ 通过上下文表示让步概念

让步句中的让步概念除了用词汇手段、词序手段外,还可用其他的方法,那就是在特定的上下文中也可表示让步意义。某些表面结构是定语从句和时间、地点、程度状语从句,还有某些并列分句等,在特定的上下文中也能表示让步的意思。

A. 定语从句起让步作用的让步句

Many people *who had few advantages in their youth* have done great things for their country. 许多在年轻时没啥有利条件的人,倒已经为他们的国家做出了伟大的业绩。

B. 时间、地点、程度状语从句起让步作用

You stopped trying, *when you might have succeeded next time*. 当你下一次可能成功时,你反倒不试了。

Unfortunately, *where I should expect gratitude*, I often find the opposite. 不幸的是,在我应该期待感激的地方,反倒经常碰到怨恨。

As bad as Tonny is, he is not without merits. 坏到像托尼那样子,他不是没有优点。

C. 并列分句起让步从句作用

We cannot keep these trees alive *and we have watered them well, too*. 我们不能保住这些树不死,我可是浇好了水的。

It was difficult, but I accomplished it. 这是困难任务,然而我完成了。

④ 用让步状语从句表达让步

让步状语从句表达让步意思用得最多,也较复杂。对于让步状语从句,还得述及让步状语从句的种类、使用的从属连词以及让步状语从句在句中的位置等。

A. 让步状语从句的种类

让步状语从句可分一般让步状语从句、特殊让步状语从句、选择让步状语从句和普遍让步状语从句四种。

B. 引导让步状语从句的从属连词

这些连词有:although, though, if, even if, even though, while, as, that; whether ... or ..., no matter whether ... or ..., ... or ..., be ... or ...; whoever, whatever, whomever, whichever, whenever, wherever, however, no matter who (whom, what, which, when, where, how)等。而这些不同的从属连词所引导的让步状语从句由于位置的不同而含义也有所差异。

C. 让步状语从句在句中的位置

让步状语从句的位置有前置、后置，有时也可置于中位做附加说明，里面的省略部分显而易见。

Though it was late, we went on working. 虽然很晚了，我们还在继续工作。（前置）

They'll try to finish the work in time *although they are short of manpower*. 虽然他们十分缺乏劳力，他们要设法按时完成这项工作。（后置）

Our tent, *though light as a feather*, remained firm. 他们的帐篷虽然轻得像羽毛，却很坚挺。（置中）

D. 让步状语从句的语气

让步状语从句的语气也分直陈和虚拟两种。如所指的是事实时，从句的谓语动词就用陈述式；但如果让步状语从句的内容是现在或将来的假设情况，那从句的动词就要用"should + 动词原形"，或者省掉 should，用动词原形；有时也可以用 were，或者 were 加带 to 的不定式。

Though I stand (should stand) alone, I will never yield. 就算我孤立，我也不会屈服。

I shouldn't have time to see her *even if she were here*. 就算她在这里，我也没有时间见她。

Even if you were to object, that would not change matters. 就算你反对，那也无济于事。

E. 让步状语从句的使用特点

让步状语从句的使用特点表现在所使用的从属连词上，使用的连词不同，意义也就不同。

a. 引导一般让步状语从句的从属连词

它们是：although, though, if, even though, even if, while, notwithstanding 等。

● although, though 引导的让步状语从句及其差别

由 although, though 引导的让步状语从句是纯粹表示让步意义。although 与 though 都作"虽然"解，在一般情况下可以互换。

We didn't close the doors at night *although (though) it was cold*. 虽然天气很冷，我们晚上没有关门。

Though she is poor, she will be happy. 尽管她穷，她会幸福的。

● though 用得较普通，显得口语体；although 的强调语气较重，显得正式些。

Though we know the war is lost, we continue to fight. 虽然我们知道这场战争输了，但仍继续战斗。

I insisted on doing it *although my husband warned me not to*. 尽管我丈夫警告我不要那么做，我仍坚持说要那么做。

● though 能与 even 连用，而 although 不能，因此有 even though，而没有 even although。

Xiaowang sometimes takes a shower *although/even though he perfers a bath*. 尽管小王更喜欢洗盆浴，他有时洗淋浴。

Even though/although the traffic held us up, we got to the station on time. 尽管我们遇到交通堵塞，我们还是准时到达车站。

● though 可以用来表示对现在或将来的假设，although 却不能。

Though she may fail, she will try. 尽管她也许失败，但她仍愿意试一试。

Though all the world were against Lei, she should still hold to her opinion. 就算全世界的人反对蕾，蕾仍坚持她的意见。

Though everybody (should) desert me, Lei will not. 即使大家都抛弃我，蕾不会。

Let's start as arranged *though it (could) rain tomorrow*. 即使明天下雨，我们仍按原计划安排开始行动。

上面的例句 3 中的 desert 不可用 deserts，例句 4 中 rain 不可用 rains，因为它们是表示将来的虚拟句与主句陈述句混用。

● 以 though 引出的让步从句除了置于句首外，其位置还可以移动以表示对让步的强调，但 although 不能移动。

Foolish though you may be, you are kind of heart. 虽然你也许傻，但心肠相当好。

Difficult though the task was (= Although the task was difficult，不说 Difficult although the task was)，I managed to accomplish it in time. 虽然任务困难,我还是设法按时完成了。

- though 可以作副词,放在句末作连接性状语,表示让步;但 although 却不可以。

Your food is rather a problem. They look fit, *though*. 你们的食物相当有问题。不过,它们看起来很健康。

Jane would like to see the inside of my house *though*. 尽管如此,简要看看我房子的里面。

- though 和 although 都能用在置于主句后的从句句首,引出补充说明的从句,其意思是"可是"、"然而"、"不过"。

It was not entirely his decision—*though I think that generally he agrees with it*. 这不完全是他的决定,不过,我想大体上他同意这一决定的。

上面这一英语句子可以理解成"It wasn't entirely his decision. I think that generally he agrees with it, though."(这不完全是我的决定。尽管如此,我想我基本上是同意这一决定的。)

We are poor—*although we are satisfied with our condition*. 我们很穷,可是我们满足于我们的现状。

上面这一句子可以理解为"Although we are poor, we are satisfied with our condition."(虽然我们很穷,但我们满足于我们的现状。)也可理解为"We are poor. We are satisfied with our condition, though."(我们很穷。不过,我们满足于我们的现状。)但要注意,上面的句子里的 though 不能被改成 although,这是因为 although 不能当作副词作连接性状语用。

当 though 和 although 引导的让步从句置于句首时,后面主句前不能用 but;这是因为 but 是并列连词,不可用来连接从句和主句,但可用表示让步转折意义的连接副词 till, yet 或者 nevertheless 是可以用的。

Although it was already seven o'clock in the evening, the lights were not yet on. 虽然已经是晚上7点钟了,但灯还没开。

Though the pain was bad, still the little boy did not groan. 虽然疼得厉害,那个小男孩仍然没有呻吟。

Although I believes it, yet I must consider. 虽然我相信,但我还得考虑考虑。

b. if, if any 等引导的让步状语从句:由 if, if any, if ever, if anything, if at all 引导的让步状语从句除了表示让步的意义外,其本身仍含有条件意义。

- if 主要用来引导条件状语从句,有时也可用来引导让步状语从句。假如句子里两个分句的意义是顺势的,那么其引导的是条件状语从句;假如是逆势的话,那其引导的就是让步状语从句。试比较下列句子:

If you are inexperienced, you won't be able to accomplish it. 如果你没有经验,你将不能完成它。(顺势,是条件句)

If you are inexperienced, you are at any rate eager to learn. 如果说你没有经验,至少你迫切要求学。(逆势,是让步句)

If Tonny is poor, how can he buy the house? 如果托尼穷,他怎么能买房子?(顺势,是条件句)

If Tonny is poor, at least he is honest. 如果说托尼穷,至少他是诚实的。(逆势,是让步句)

- if any, if ever, if anything, if at all 引导让步状语从句,都是省略了某些词的从句。它们多用来表示让步,有时也表示条件,杨元兴先生称之为"无动词让步状语从句"和"无动词条件状语从句"。

须注意的是,假如主句里有 few, little, seldom, rarely 等准否定词时,上述从句为让步状语从句,从句省略掉的词恰恰就是主语及除去 few, little, seldom, rarely 以外的其他词。这类省略型从句的使用是为了节省笔墨,表达简洁,避免重复。假如主句里没有 few, little, rarely, seldom 等准否定词,上述从句则为条件状语从句,其中 if any, if anything 更为常用。此时的 if any 相当于"if there is any ..."的省略式,意思是"如果有……的话", if anything 相当于 if there is anything 或 if there is anything different,意思是"如果有什么的话"、"如果有什么不同的话"。

There is very little ink in the bottle, *if any*. 瓶里即使有墨水,也不多。(让步)

It happens seldom, *if ever*. 即使有其事,也很少见。(让步)

There is little, *if any*, difference between you. 你们之间即使有差别也是很小的。(让步)

Seldom, *if at all*, do we go to the film. 我们即使去看电影,也只是偶尔去。(让步)
True greatness has little, *if anything*, to do with rank or power. 真正的伟大与地位和权力无关,即使有关,那也是极少的。(让步)
Correct mistakes, *if any*. 如果有错,改过来。(条件)
If anything, her new job is harder than her old one. 要说有什么不同的话,她的新工作比原来的要难做一些。(条件)
You are, *if anything*, a shade better today. 如果说有不同的话,你今天稍微好了点。(条件)
I am a hero, *if ever* there was one. 倘如有过英雄,我便是一个。(条件)(注意此句里的 if ever 不是省略型从句)

c. even though, even if 引导让步状语从句

一般来说,even though 与 even if 所引导的让步从句意义相同,且它们都是强调让步意义。
She borrowed his laptop, *even though Tom told her not to*. 尽管汤姆叫她不要那么做,她还是硬借走他的手提电脑。
I believe he's on duty—*even though he's in plain-clothes*. 尽管他着便衣,我相信他在值勤。
We'll come *even if it rains*. 即使下雨,我们也会来。
Even if Mr. Ma dislike ancient interesting places, Warrick Castle is worth a visit. 纵然马先生不喜欢古迹,但瓦里城堡还是值得一游的。

d. even though/if, although, though 表示让步的比较

这三个词语都表示让步,但它们所表达的让步程度略有区别。even though/if 具有强调的特点,让步语气最强,although 次之,though 为最弱。even though/if 引导的从句中,谓语动词可用陈述语气,也可用虚拟语气,although 和 though 引出的从句通常用陈述语气。
Even though/if I had been there yesterday, I would not have told them the news. 即使我昨天在那里,我也不会把这消息告诉他们。
Even if it's hard work, I enjoy it. 即使那是艰苦工作,我也喜欢。
It was cold, *though it was sunny that day*. 那天虽然天气晴朗,却很冷。
当让步状语从句表示一种臆想的情况时,通常用 though,而不用 although。这时从句的动词通常用虚拟语气。
Though all the world were against him, he should still hold his opinion. 即使全世界的人都反对他,他仍然会坚持他的意见。
though 可用作副词,意义为"然而",通常位于句中或句末,作表示让步的连接性状语,although 则不能。
It was a quiet party, Lili had a good time, *though*. 晚会并不很热闹,但丽丽玩得很痛快。

e. while 引导让步从句

while 引导让步状语从句时,意义相当于 although。但是这种让步状语从句只置于主句前,不能置于主句后。
While he may be right, Jane can't altogether agree. 虽然他也许对,但简不能完全同意。
While I admit that the problems are difficult, I think that they can be solved. 我虽然承认这些是难题,但我认为这些问题是可以解决的。
当 while 作从属连词用时,既可以引导让步状语从句和时间状语从句,也可以连接并列分句表示转折对比,意思相当于 but,但要注意不同用法。试比较:
While he doesn't really like modern art, he finds this work impressive. 虽然他不是真正喜爱现代艺术,但他发现这件作品挺动人。(让步)
While I was reading, she came in. 在我阅读的时候她进来了。(时间)

She was famous and rich in her life time, *while many artists die in poverty and obscurity*. 她活着的时候有名气又富有,而许多艺术家却默默无闻贫穷地死去。(转折对比)

f. "be 型"让步从句

这种从句不用连词引导,直接将动词位于句首,用倒装语序表示出来。从句可位于主句之前或之后,其句型有以下五种:

- "be + 主语 + ever so + 表语",意义为"尽管,无论"

Be a man ever so learned, he must not be conceited. 无论一个人有多大的学问,也不能骄傲自满。

- "be + 主语 + 表语",意义为"不管,无论"

Be it gaseous, liquid or solid, all substances are made of atoms. 不管是气体、液体或固体,所有的物质由原子构成的。

- "let + 名词 + be ever so + 表语",意义为"不管,不论"

Let a man be ever so learned, he must not be conceited. 无论一个人有多大的学问,也不能骄傲自满。

- "let + 名词 + 动词 + 宾语",意义为"不管,不论"

Let people say what they would, Jane would be what she ought to be. 不管人们怎么说,简还是该怎么样还怎么样。

- "主动词 + what/when/where/which/who/whom + 代词或名词 + may/will + 主句",意思是"尽管,不论"

Say what Mary will, in his heart he knows that she is wrong. 不管玛丽说什么,他内心里明白她错了。

g. 连接词 as, that, though 等常用来引导特殊让步状语从句

- as 所引导的让步状语从句语气庄重,语体正规

* 当 as 引导的从句是"主语 + 系动词 + 表语"结构时,表语要提至 as 前,成为"表语 + as + 主语 + 系动词"。假如表语是名词,前置时要省去名词前的冠词。

Rich as she is, she is not happy. 尽管她富有,但并不幸福。

Short as little Mike was, he managed to get the apple. 尽管小迈克身材矮小,他还是设法拿到了那苹果。

Clever as I may be, I cannot do that. 尽管我聪明,我也干不了那事。

Child as you are, you know a lot of things. 虽然是个孩子,你却知道很多事情。

Note:当 as 引导的让步状语从句的主语是名词时(不是代词),那从句的主谓要倒装或不倒装。

Difficult as was the work/the work was, it was finished in time. 工作虽然困难,还是按时完成了。

Difficult as the situation was, nobody had the thought of giving in. 虽然处境困难,但无人想到屈服。

- as 引导的让步状语从句的两种情况

如果是"主语 + 谓语"或"主语 + 谓语 + 副词状语"的话,要将副词状语提前成为"副词状语 + as + 主语 + 谓语";无副词状语时,原形动词提前,留下主语和助动词在后成为"原形动词 + as + 主语 + 助动词";谓语动词有宾语时,原形动词和宾语同时提前,留下主语和助动词在后成为"原形动词 + 宾语 + as + 主语 + 助动词"。

Little Tonny was unable to make more progress, *hard as he tried*. 小托尼不能取得更多的进步了,虽然他做出了很大的努力。

Hard as she tries, her paintings are no good. 虽然她做了努力,还是画得不行。

Much as Mark should like to see you, he is afraid you may find it inconvenient to come in this hot weather. 虽然马克想见见你,又恐怕你这么热的天来不方便。

Much as the dogs look alike, there is a difference between them, and Henry knows one from another. 虽然这些狗看起来很相像,它们之间有不同之处,亨利能辨别它们。

Try as she would, she could not lift the rock. 虽然她尽了努力,仍不能搬起那石头。

Search as you would, you could find nobody in the house. 你们虽然搜索,但在屋子里找不到人。

Detest him as we may, we must acknowledge his greatness. 虽然我们也许讨厌他,但我们必须承认他的伟大。

从上面的最后三个例子可见,原形动词或者"原形动词+宾语"提前时,后面的助动词通常是may, might, will, would 等表示假设的助动词。

as 引导的倒装句可以是让步状语从句,也可以是原因状语从句;如从句和主句之间在意义上有转折关系,那从句则为让步状语从句;如果从句和主句之间有因果关系,那从句为原因状语从句。

Tired as she was, she talked with us late into night. 她虽然累了,但还是和我们谈到深夜。(让步)
Tired as she was, she went to bed early. 因为累了,她早早睡觉去了。(原因)
Young as Lei is, she is equal to the task. 蕾虽然年轻,但能胜任这项任务。(让步)
Young as Jim is, She is not equal to the task. 由于年轻,吉姆不能胜任这项任务。(原因)

- though, that 也可以用于上述特殊的句型结构,表示强调意义的让步句。

Clever though he may be, he cannot do that. 他虽然聪明,却做不了那事。
Difficult though the task was, we managed to accomplish it in time. 任务虽然困难,我们却设法及时完成了。
Miraculous though your survival seemed, it was nothing to what lay ahead. 虽然你们活下来似乎是奇迹了,但比起往后的困难根本不算啥。
Naked that John was, he braved the storm. 尽管约翰赤身裸体,他仍与暴风雨搏斗。
Child that she was, she knew what was the right thing to do. 她虽是个孩子,但知道什么该做。
Fool that he was, he took her word for it. 尽管那时他是傻瓜一个,他却没有轻易放过她说的话。
Sneer unkindly though she may, Tom is very popular. 虽然她会不友好地嗤笑他,但汤姆很受人欢迎。

h. 选择条件让步状语从句

引导选择条件让步从句的连词有:whether … or …, no matter whether … or …,… or …,be … or … 它们引导的从句同时存在条件和让步的意义;从句同时提供两个或两个以上的让步条件供选择。

- 用"whether … or … 引导让步状语从句

whether … or …引导的让步状语从句提出正反两种甚至多种情况作假设,但不管哪种情况,都不影响后边的结果。这种句子表达出很强烈的让步语气,而且假设的情况可以是真实的,也可以是虚拟的。

Whether I can see the stars or not, they are always in the sky. 不管我是否能看见星星,它们总在天上。
Whether she believes it or not, it is truth. 不管她信不信,反正是事实。
She said it didn't matter *whether I stayed or went*. 她说不管我是去还是留,都没关系。
We'll resolutely wipe out the intruders *whether they come from the land, the sea or the air*. 我们将坚决消灭来犯之敌,不管他们从陆上来,从海上来,还是从空中来。
Whether you drive or whether you take the train, you shall be here on time. 不管你骑马还是乘火车来,你必须准时赶到。
Whether you go, or whether she go (goes), the result will be the same. 不管你去,还是她去,反正都一样。
All matter, *whether it be (is) gas, liquid or solid*, is made up of atoms. 所有物质,不管是气体、液体、还是固体,都由原子组成。

有时在从句里可以省略掉某些词。

Whether by accident or by design, you arrived too late to help me. 不管是碰巧还是故意,你来得太迟,你没有帮我的忙。

- 用 no matter whether … or … 引导让步状语从句,no matter whether … or …与 whether … or …意思一样,不过前者语气更庄重。

No matter whether Tonny studies natural or social science, the object of his study is for the service of the people. 不管托尼学自然科学还是社会科学,目的都是为人民服务。

此结构中 no matter whether 没有变通写法,不能写成 whetherever。

● 用... or ...引导出让步状语从句, 用... or ...引导的让步状语从句实际上就是"whether ... or ..."中省略了 whether, 有时甚至在从句里有些词也被省略, 但意思不变。

Believe Tom or not, something is in his pocket. 相信汤姆也好, 不相信也好, 反正有东西在他口袋里了。(省略了 whether you ...)

Waking or sleeping, this subject is always in my mind. 醒着也好, 睡着也好, 这个问题总是在我的脑海里。(省略了 whether I am ...)

Right or wrong, this is Jane's temper. 不管对不对, 这是简的性格。(省略了 whether it is ...)

Rain or no rain, we're going to swim. 不管下不下雨, 我们都要去游泳。(省略了 Whether there is ... there is ...)

● 用 be ... or ...引导让步状语从句

在省略了 whether 后, 如果从句里的谓语是系动词, 那系动词就用原形 be, 主语和谓语要倒装。

Be she friend or enemy, the law regards her as criminal. 不管她是朋友还是敌人, 法律认为她是罪犯。

All magnets behave the same, *be they large or small*. 所有磁体, 不论大小, 性质一样。

i. 普遍条件让步从句

普遍条件让步从句是指这些让步状语从句既表示让步, 同时又表示在任何条件中的自由选择。引导普遍条件让步从句的连词有: whoever, whomever, whatever, whichever, whenever, wherever, however 或者 no matter who (what, which, when, where, how 等)。

● 用 whoever, whichever 等引导普遍让步状语从句并在从句中作主语、宾语、表语、定语、状语。

Whatever happened, you must be calm and quiet. 不管发生什么情况, 你必须镇静。(主语)

Whatever you do, do it well. 不管你做什么, 都要做好。(宾语)

Whatever the cost may be, the building must be saved. 不管费用是多少, 这楼必须抢救。(表语)

Whatever difficulties she met, she was going to be a singer. 不管遇到什么困难, 她决心成为一名歌手。(定语)

Whenever it rains, the underpass is flooded. 无论什么时候下雨, 这地下过道都积水。(状语)

Wherever you go, I'm right here waiting for you. 无论你到哪里, 我都依然在这里等着你。(状语)

However imperfect the book (may be), it is the fruits of her five years' toil. 这本书无论怎样不完美, 却也是她五年辛劳的成果。(修饰形容词 imperfect)

However much it cost, he had to get the car fixed. 不管花多少钱, 他也得把车子修好。(修饰副词 much)

Note: however 可用作连接性副词表示让步。

Henry had promised to meet me at the airport. *However*, he was not there. 亨利答应来机场接我。然而, 他却没在那里。

上面各句的连词可以分别用 no matter who (what, which, when, where, how) 来替换。用 no matter ... 句型更口语化些。no matter ... 引导的普遍条件让步从句也可以位于主句之后或主句之中。

Keep calm, *no matter what he said*. 无论他说什么, 保持冷静。

Every substance, *no matter what it is*, is made up of atoms. 每一种物质, 不管它是什么, 都由原子组成。

No matter where and how the invaders come, they will be wiped out clean. 无论入侵者何地以何种方式来犯, 都将被彻底消灭。

no matter what, whatever 等引导的让步状语从句可以转换成动词命令式引导的让步状语从句。

No matter what you do, do it well. 不管你做什么, 都要做好。(宾语)

Whatever you do, do it well.

Do what you will, do it well.

No matter what happened, you must be calm and quiet. 不管发生什么情况, 你必须镇静。(主语)

Whatever happened, you must be calm and quiet.

Happen what may, you must be calm and quiet.

No matter what the cost may be, the building must be saved. 不管费用是多少,这楼必须抢救。(表语)
Whatever the cost may be, the building must be saved.
Be the cost what it may, the building must be saved.

● 普遍条件让步状语从句里的谓语动词是系动词 be 时,这个系动词可以省略。
Whatever her problems, they can't be worse than yours. 不管她有什么问题,都不会比你们的问题更糟。
However great the pitfalls, I must do my best to succeed. 无论意想不到有多大的困难,我必须尽最大努力争取成功。
No matter how high one's official position, one should act as an ordinary worker among the people. 不管一个人官职多高,在人民中间都应该以普通劳动者的姿态出现。

● 普遍条件让步从句的谓语动词有时表示假设,这时可有下列三类句型:
＊whatever（或 no matter what）等 + 主语 + may/might + 原形动词
No matter what she may say, I'll do it. 不管她会怎么说,我一定要干。
However annoying his behavior may be, I can't get rid of him. 无论他的行为多么令人厌烦,我不能摆脱他。
＊原形动词 + 疑问词 + 主语 + will/would/may/might/can/could 等
Do what he could, the king could neither soothe nor quell the nation as he wished. 无论怎么做,国王都不能如愿地安抚或镇压全国的老百姓。
Go where you will, you find a house full of peace and cordiality. 无论走到哪里,你都会看到充满和平与温情的家庭。
Come when I may, I will find you in the workshop. 无论我什么时候来,我会发现你总是在车间。
Come what may, she is prepared for it. 无论发生什么,她都准备好对付。
Here, *wake at what hour Lei may*, early or late, she lies amid gracious stillness. 在这里,无论蕾何时醒来,是早还是晚,都躺在舒适的静寂之中。
Doubt whom you will, but never yourself. 无论你怀疑谁,绝不要怀疑自己。
＊以原形动词 be 或 let 开头的让步从句
be + 主语 + 副词 so
Be it so, you must continue to do the test. 尽管如此,你们得继续进行试验。
be + 主语 +（ever）so + 形容词
Be it so humble, there's no place like home. 无论怎样简陋,还是家好。
Be the rain ever so heavy, Lei must come to see me. 无论雨下多大,蕾一定来看我。
Be a man ever so learned, he ought not to be proud. 一个人不管多么有学问,也不该骄傲。
let + 主语 + be ever so + 形容词
Let it be ever so humble, home is home. 无论怎样简陋,家总归是家。
Let it be ever so weak, there is nobody who does not love his country. 无论祖国多弱,没有人不爱祖国。
Let your occupation be what it may, you must devote yourself if you are to succeed. 无论你干哪一行,如果要成功,必须全身心地投入。

以原形动词开头引导的从句书卷气重,多用于书面表达中,口语都用"no matter + 疑问词"的形式。

(7) 地点状语从句、方式状语从句

① 地点状语从句

地点状语从句是表示空间关系的从句,确切地说是表示位置或方位的从句。其实,地点状语从句是从地点状语的基础上引申出来的,如 She lived there ten years ago.（她十年前住在那里。）句中的地点副词 there 起状语的作用;而 She lives where her father lived ten years ago.（她住在她爸十年前曾住过的地方。）

句中的 where her father lived ten years ago 可说是 there 引申出来的。

A. 作地点状语的词语

能作地点状语的词语主要有 here, there, upstairs, downstairs 等及介词 in/by/on/above/over 等加地点名词所组成的短语。特别要注意的是，地点副词绝不位于主语和动词之间，但可用于句首。

—My spectcals are *here* just now. Where are they? 我的眼镜刚才在这儿的，它们在哪儿呀？

—*In your school bag.* I saw you put them *in it*. 在你书包里。我看见你放进去的。

Indoors it was nice and warm. *Outside* it was snowing heavily. 室内非常温暖，室外大雪纷飞。（地点副词用于句首）

All the teachers and students are having a meeting *in the hall*. 全校师生在礼堂开会。（介词短语作状语）

The small village stands *by the river* named Heaven River. 那小村庄坐落在一条名叫"天河"的河边。（介词短语作状语）

John lives *about five miles from our school*. 约翰住在离学校五英里的地方。（名词短语作状语，其中 about 为副词，作"大约"讲）

B. 一些含地点状语的简单句

● 主语 + 不及物动词/be + 地点状语

The boy was forced to stand *there* for two hours. 那男孩被罚站在那里两个小时。（副词作状语）

A peach tree stood *in front of our house*. 以前我们房子前有一棵桃子树。（介词短语作状语）

They are all *upstairs* to watch TV. 他们都在楼上看电视。（方位副词作地点状语）

Our school is situated just *outside the town*. 我们的学校就在镇外。（介词短语作状语）

Poor Jim had to work *there* till morning. 可怜的吉姆不得不在那里干到天明。（地点副词作状语）

● there be + 主语 + 介词短语

这类句型是表示人或事物的处所的。要注意，这种句中的 there 是先行主语，而作其真实主语的是 be 后的名词或名词短语；这 be 动词有时可用像 stand, come, spring, live 等替代。这种句子后通常用介词短语作地点状语。

There will be a concert tonight *in the Grant Palace*. 今晚格兰特宫有一场音乐会。

There are two milk bottles *in the basket*. 篮子里有两只牛奶瓶。

There stood a boy named Zhang Hua *at the door*. 门口站着一个名叫张华的男孩。

Many many years ago, there lived a woman known by the name of Ah Liao Sha *in a small wooden house*. 很久很久以前，那小木屋里住着一位名叫阿辽莎的女人。

● 主语 + 动词(不及物) + from 短语 + up to/down to 短语

这句型中的前两项后面的 up to 与 down to 分别表示"上……"和"下……"，像汉语里所说的"北上"、"上城里"、"南下"、"下乡去"这类表达。

Grace is flying *up to Beijing from Suzhou*. 格蕾丝从苏州乘飞机北上北京。

We are flying *down to Shanghai from Beijing*. 他们从北京乘飞机南下上海。

They will drive *down to the countryside* to spend their holiday. 他们要驾车去农村度假。

● 主语 + 动词(不及物) + from 短语 + to 短语 + by the way of 短语

我们常用上述句型表达主语起止地点和路经某地到某地去。句中的 from 短语表示行程的起点，不过常被省略，to 短语表示目的地，by the way of 引出的是途经的地点；我们可以用拉丁文的 via 代替 by the way of，但 by the way of 显得正式、庄重。

She is going (*from Shanghai*) *to Harbin by the way of Tianjing*. 她准备(从上海出发)途经天津，到哈尔滨去。

Chang Ming drove *up to the police station via Modern Road*. 张明驾车穿过现代大道，来到警察局。

● 关于方位句

方位句属地点句中一支流，或是地点句的深入。它是用来表示人或物的存在或行为发生的地点范围内的方位。其中最关键的因素体现在方位词上。有时候方位副词与地点副词不加区分,如上面的例句 Indoors it was nice and warm. Outside it was snowing heavily.(室内非常温暖,室外大雪纷飞。)句中的 indoors 和 outside 当然是方位副词。由此,有的语法书不另列方位句这一内容。方位句基本上都是简单句。这些简单句大致有以下六种类型:

* 主语+谓语+方位副词:这一类句型属泛指。句型中的方位副词是由方位名词转化而来,或是由"方位词+ward(s)"构成方位副词,这些方位副词也作地点状语。

Tom went *east* in order to stay with his relatives. 为了与他的亲戚在一起,汤姆向东走去。

They walked *south* along the road. 他们沿着那条路向南走去。

Did they sail *southeastward*? 他们是不是向东南方向航行?

* 主语+谓语+介词+the+方位词:这种句型并不表示具体的地点,只表示泛指的东南西北。句型中的介词常是 in, from, to(wards) 等。

The sun rises *from the east* and sets *in the west*. 太阳从东方升起,在西方落下。

When the wind blows *from the west*, we call it westerly wind. 风从西方吹来时,我们称之为西风。

Henry would like to live, *at the sea-side.* 亨利想住在海边。

There was a lamp *over the table.* 桌子上方有盏灯。

* 主语+谓语+(表示上、下;边上、中间等位置的)介词+名词:这种句型所表示的方位较具体些。介词与后面的名词一起组成短语,作方位(地点)状语。此类介词常见的有:above, below, under, over, beside 等。

They were flying *over the clouds.* 我们飞行在云层之上。

The sky is *over (above) our heads.* 天在我们的头顶上。

When the sun sets, it goes *below the horizon.* 当太阳落下时,它就到地平线下面去了。

* 主语+谓语+at/on/to+the+right/left of+地点名词

这种句型用来表示"左右"方位。如表示泛指的"左"、"右",那后面就不接 of 短语;如指具体的某地的左右,那就要接 of 短语。其中的介词 at, on, in, to 的意思也有所不同。如把左右当作一个点来看,那就用 at;如把左右当成一个空间来看,那就用 in;如把左右看成是一个平面或一条线,那就用 on 和 to。在这四个介词中,on 用得最普通。

I will see the the cinema *on my left.* 在左边我会看到电影院。

The library is *on the right of the teaching building.* 图书馆在教学大楼的右边。

In China we drive *on the right* while in Britain *on the left.* 在中国,汽车靠右行驶,在英国靠左行驶。

In the United States traffic keeps *to the right.* 在美国,汽车靠右通行。

Note:其实,介词 on 表示紧接着,to 不表示紧接。如要同时表示"左"、"右",那我们要先说"右",再说"左",就像我们中文说东南,而英语却说 southeast(南东)一样的道理。

She sat *on my left* that night. 那天晚上她紧挨着坐在我的左边。

Mike was seated *on the right of Grace* that night. 迈克那天晚上坐在格蕾丝的右边。

Tom was seated *on my right*, Rose *on my left.* 汤姆坐在我右边,罗丝坐在我左边。

I can see two bookcases in her study, one is *at (on) the right*, and the other *on (at) the left.* 在她的书房里我能看到两个书柜,一个在右边,另一个在左边。

* 主语+be/lie+in/on/to the+方位词

这种句型用来表示"在某一地点的某一方位",里面的三种动词互换时,意思不变,但它们后面的介词不得互换,因为这些介词的意思各异,in 是表示在某一地点的境内,on 表示在边界上,to 则表示在地点的境外。

Suzhou is *in the east of Jiangsu.* 苏州在江苏的东部。

Korea is *on the northeast of China.* 朝鲜与中国东北接壤。

Japan lies *to the southeast of Korea*. 日本在朝鲜的东南方。

Our college is situated *to the west of the city*. 我们大学位于该市的西面。

＊ 主语＋face/front/look … ＋（宾语）＋ …

上面所列的句型表达"朝……方向"的意思。其中 face 意作"面向"、"朝着……方向"讲，front 作动词用，与 face 的意思相当，表示"面对"、"前面是……"，动词 look 作"朝着……"用。

China *faces* the Pacific *on the east*. 中国东临太平洋。

The park *fronts southwards*. 那个公园朝南。

Their old house *looks to the west*, so it is very hot in summer. 他们的老宅朝西，所以夏天很热。

C．地点状语从句

地点状语从句常用 where, wherever, whence［旧用法＝(from) where］及由 where 组成的复合词 anywhere, everywhere 等引导。其位置可以在主句前，也可以在主句后。现在，我们把地点状语从句分为一般地点状语从句、含条件意味的地点状语从句和含让步意味的地点状语从句三个方面来讲。

a．一般地点状语从句

一般地点状语从句是那些从句作主句中的地点状语而言，它们的汉译文也较直接地译成地点状语。

Where I live there are plenty of sheep. 我住的地方有着很多的绵羊。

You have the right to live *where you want*. 你有权利住在你想住的地方。

They went *wherever they could find work*. 哪里能找到工作，他们就去哪里。

Let's meet *where we first met you*. 我们在我们第一次相见的地方见。

You can go *anywhere you want*. 你想去什么地方就去什么地方。

We were warmly welcomed *everywhere we went*. 无论到哪里，我们都受到热烈欢迎。

Go back *whence you came*.（＝Go back where you came from.）你从哪里来就回到哪里去。

b．含有条件意味的地点状语从句

这种句子往往先以 where 引出地点从句，而后加上"there＋主句"。这种句子是一种加强语气的表达。由于 where 从句置句首，所以含有较强的条件意味。这种句子常被被译成"（如果）哪里……，哪里就……"。

Where there is a will, there is a way. 有志者，事竟成。

Where bees are, there is honey. 哪里有蜜蜂，哪里就有蜜。

Where we are needed by our motherland, there we should go. 哪里祖国最需要我们，我们就应该到那里去。

Note：where 除表示地点外，还可以表示条件、对比、让步、处境等。

Where men are greedy, there is never peace. 人类贪欲不止，世界和平无望。（条件）

We want to stay at home, *where children would rather spend the holiday in the country*. 我们想留在家里，而孩子们却宁愿去乡下度假。（对比）

Unfortunately, *where we should expect gratitude*, we often find the opposite. 遗憾的是，虽然我们本该得到感激，却常常得到的是怨恨。（让步）

Mary said that she was happy where she was. 玛丽说她对现在的处境很满意。（处境）

It's Tom's fault that Jane is where she is. 简今天落到这个地步都怪汤姆。（处境）

c．含有让步意味的地点状语从句

在口语中，人们常用 wherever 引出地点句，而后加上"there＋主句"来强调从句的语气。这种 wherever 句意思是"无论何处"、"不论到哪里……，哪里就……"，有让步的意味。句中的 there 可以省略。

Wherever there is a quarrel, there she is sure to be. 无论是何处，只要有口角，她肯定在场。

Wherever the sea is, you will find seamen. 无论何处，只要有海就有海员。

Note：where 和 wherever 引导的地点状语从句可以省略某些成分。

Wherever (it is) possible, all moving parts should be tested. 只要有可能，所有活动部件都应该检验。

Supply suitable determiners in the following blanks *where* (*it is*) *necessary*. 在下列空白处需要的地方填上适当的限定词。

② 方式状语从句

方式状语从句(Adverbial Clause of Manner)是用来描述主句中动作或状态发生的方式或方法的从句。表达方式状语可以用方式副词,也可用从句。

A. 用于表达方式状语的副词

这些副词常见的有:carefully, heavily, bravely, clearly, angrily, very, well, badly, foolishly, naturally, quietly 等。

Xiaoling, look at the cover of the book *carefully* and then read it. 小林,仔细看看这书的封面,然后阅读。

You must see *very clearly* what you can do, and what is above your ability. 你必须非常明白你能做什么,什么又是你力所不能及的。(即"人要有自知之明")

His son behaved *foolishly* at the party. 他的儿子晚会上举止可笑。

Quietly, she moved forwards to get a better view. 为了看得更清楚些,她悄悄地往前挪动。

从上述例句可知,方式副词作状语可以在句首、句中或句末。但下面两句中的 badly 因在句中的位置的不同而意义和功能就有别。

Tom, you typed this letter *very badly*. 汤姆,这封信打得很糟。(方式状语)

He *badly* needs knowledge, not money. 他非常需要知识,而不是金钱。(badly 起强调作用)

B. 方式状语从句的表达形式

方式状语从句主要有三种表达形式:以连词 as 引出;以(in) the way 之类的词语引出;以 as if 和 as though 引出。

a. 以连词 as 引出

• 位置在主句后

Mr. Green wrote the article *as I had told him*. 格林先生按我的吩咐写了那篇文章。

• 可用 how, the way 或 like 替代 as

The room is decorated just *how* I like it. 这房间正是按我喜欢的样子装饰的

The room is decorated just *the way I like it*. (译文同上)

They didn't do it *like/as we do it now*. 他们当时的做法和我们现在的做法不一样。

上面例句 1、2 中的 how, the way 与 like 仍可用 as 替代,句意不变。

• 用 as … so, what (= as) 引出方式状语从句

Air is to man *as water is to fish*. (= As water is to fish, so air is to man. = Air is to man what water is to fish. = What water is to fish, that is air to man = What water is to fish, that air is to man.) 空气之于人,犹如水之于鱼。

• 以 as 引出的方式状语从句的省略

as 引出的方式状语从句常可省去一些成分后变成名词短语、过去分词短语、介词短语、副词短语等。

You talked *as old friends* (*did*). 你们像老朋友样交谈过。(名词短语)

Henry is returning my book *as* (*he was*) *requested* (*to do*). 亨利按我的要求会把书还给我。(过去分词)

Spell the word *as* (*she did*) *in French*. 像她那样用法语把这词拼出来。(介词短语)

You had better manage the business *as* (*you did*) *before*. 你们最好像以前那样经商。(副词)

• 有时 as 从句也可用来在行为方式上与他人进行示比较

Only Grace understands him *as I do*. 只有格蕾丝像我一样了解他。

Mary is a hard-working student, *just as her elder brother used to be*. 玛丽是个勤奋的学生。就像她的哥哥以前那样。

● 关于用 like 替代 as 表示方式和行为的问题

虽然有人认为用 like 对方式、行为进行比较不恰当,但在美国口语中用得很多。

Nobody love you *like* (*as*) *he does.* 谁也没有像他那样疼你。

Do it *like* (*as*) *she does.* 像她那样做。

b. 用(in) the way 之类的词语引出

方式状语从句也常见用(in)the way, (in) the way that, the way in which, (in)the same way, (in) the same way as 等词语引出。

I may do it *my own way.* 我可用自己的方法做这事。

You fixed things (*in*) *the way* (*in which*) *he wanted.* 你以他所希望的方式安排(处理)好了事情。

I can't read the article *the way she did.* 我不能像她那样读出那篇文章。

You were looking at her *in a way* (*that*) *she did not recognize.* 你那样瞧着她,让她认不出来。

Our chemical teacher said, "Boys and girls, do the experiment (*in*) *the same way* (*as I did just now*)." 我们的化学老师说:"同学们,照我刚才做的那样做这实验。"

I don't like *the way she walks.* (= I don't like the manner of her walking.)我不喜欢她走路的方式。

Notes: ● 当方式从句由上述这些词语引出时,有时也表示比较。

He's behaving (*in*) *the same way his elder brother used to.* 他的举止与他哥哥过去一模一样。

● way 作"方法,手段,方式"用时,其后接不定式或从句作定语时,具有连接副词 how 的功能。

That's *the way* (*in which*)*she did it.* (= That's how she didit.) 她就是那样做的。

● 用 as if/though 引出,此时 as if/though 从句可以跟在任何表示举止、行为的动词后面,也可以跟在 be, seem 等动词后面。

* 表示举止、行为的动词 + as if/though:从句表示举止和行为的动词很多,如 talk, look, fall, pause, shake, strive, act 等后面都可跟 as if/though 引出方式句。

She talks *as if/though she knew all about it.* 她说话的口气好像她什么都已知道了。

Rose looks as *if/though she had seen a ghost.* 罗丝的脸色看起来好像她见到了鬼。

Jane opened her lips *as if/though she were to say something.* 简张开嘴巴好像要说什么。

* 在 be, seem 等词后 as if/though 从句:这些动词除 be, seem 外还有 appear(出现),behave(举动),feel(感觉), look(看),smell(闻),sound(听起来),taste(尝起来)等。

Tonny feels *as if/though he's floating on air.* 托尼感到好像飘浮在空中一样。

Now it was *as if he had known Mary for years.* 他似乎已认识玛丽多年了。

In fact, it seems *as if/though computer will become more popular than ever.* 事实上电脑将比以往更普遍。

Lei took her face in her hands *as if/though she was feeling its lovely shape.* 蕾用双手捧着自己的脸,好像抚摸着她那可爱的脸庞。

You work very hard *as if/though you never intended to sleep.* 你工作非常努力,仿佛你永远不打算睡觉似的。

It sounds *as if/though the situation will get better.* 听起来好像情况好起来似的。

Some flowers shut up at night *as if/though they were going to sleep.* 有的花晚上收缩了,就好像睡觉似的。

C. as if/though 从句的省略问题

由 as if/though 引出的方式句可以省去一些成分而变成"as if/though + 形容词短语、介词短语和非限定动词短语"等。

He remained motionless, *as if/though* (*he was*) *asleep.* 他一直一动也不动,好像睡着了。(as if/though + 形容词)

I shook her head *as if/though* (*I was*) *to say* "*No*". 我摇头好像要说"不"。(as if/though + 动词不定式短语)

We glanced about *as if/though* (*we were*) *in search of something.* 我们四处环视好像在找东西。(as if/

though + 介词短语)

Mark fell off the horse *as if/though* (*he was*) *shot*. 马克从马上跌下,好像被击中了。(as if/though + 过去分词)

Grace paused *as if/though* (*she was*) *expecting Mary to speak*. 格蕾丝(说着)停下来,好像期待玛丽说话。(as if/though + 现在分词短语)

Tonny made that remark *as though absently*. 托尼好像漫不经心地说了那样的话。(as if/though + 副词)

从上面这些例子可见,as if/though 后的省略是有条件的:一是后面谓语是 be 动词;二是主语与主句的主语要一致。

D. 在现代英语中可用 like 替代 as if

关于 like 替代 as if,我们可在 Michael Swan 的 *Practical English Usage*(Oxford University Press,1987)中看到有关的论述,他说在非正式的文体里,特别在美国英语里,可用 like 代替 as if。

He sat there smiling *like it was his birthday*. 他面带笑容坐在那里,好像过生日似的。

She started kissing me *like we were on our honeymoon*. 她不停地吻我,好像我们在度蜜月似的。

E. as if/though 的语气

as if/though 从句常用虚拟语气,即用过去时表示现在,以表示所说的动作"不真实";在非正式文体中表示一种实现可能性较大的情况或者说话者认为近乎事实时,也可用陈述语气。

Jane looks *as almost if she were drunk*. 简看上去就像喝醉了似的。

Mike looks *as if/though he'd seen a ghoast*. 迈克好像见了鬼似的。

You looked *at me as if I were/was mad*. 你那样看着我,好像我是个疯子。

He looks *as if he has been running*. 他好像刚跑完了一阵似的。

You look *as if you know each other*. 你们好像彼此认识。

It looks *as if/though it's going to rain*. 天好像要下雨了。

上面例句 1、2、3 中,as if/though 从句中用了过去时或过去完成体表示与事实不相符,句中的 were 可用 was 替代,特别是在口语中。例句 4、5、6 中是直陈语气,表示事情的可能性很大。

F. as if/though 引导的从句前可以与副词 as 连用

John continued working *as happily as if nothing had happened to him*. 约翰继续愉快地工作,好像什么事也未发生过。

Lei remembers it *as vividly as though it were today*. 此事蕾记忆犹新,就像发生在今天。

(8) 比较等级句

根据杨元兴先生在 *English Sentence Patterns and Syntaxh*(2012,北京语言大学出版社)中的观点,我们把比较等级句分为狭义比较和广义比较两种。狭义比较就是我们平时所说的比较等级。它们可分为原级比较(Absolute Degree)、比较等级比较(Comparative Degree)和最高等级比较(Superlative Degree)。广义比较就是不用形容词、副词的比较形式来表达比较等级意思的句子。

① 狭义比较句

A. 原级比较

a. 原级比较的概念与构成

原级比较是指用形容词或副词的原级,其前后均用 as 构成,即"as + 形容词/副词的原级 + as",这也叫同等比较(Same Degree of Comparison)。它表示"与/像……一样"之意。

His handwriting is *as good as mine*. 他的书法与我的一样好。

Mr. Li studies *as hard as his sister does*. 李先生与他妹妹一样学习努力。

John is *as good a hunter as his father*. 约翰和他的父亲一样是个好猎手。

He's *as bad-tempered as his father*. 他和他的父亲脾气一样坏。

b. 原级比较的否定"not as/so + 形容词/副词原级 + as "

Jane is *not as/so tall as her elder sister*. 简没有她姐姐高。

She *doesn't sing so/as beautifully as Mary does*. 她没有玛丽唱得漂亮。

Note：虽然，在现代英语中，not as … as … 与 not so … as … 两者都可使用，但事实上还有一些差别，那就是前者强调程度不同，后者强调程度不及。

c. 原级比较中的一些问题

原级比较并不像上述例句中表示的那样简单，它还涉及带修饰语、省略现象及要引起注意的情况等。

● 程度修饰语"as + 形容词/副词原级 + as"结构中，第一个 as 前常可用像 almost, exactly, half, just, quite, nearly, nowhere, still, by no means, nothing like（一点也不）等表示程度的副词修辞，表示程度。这些修饰语一概置于 as … as 结构之前。例如：

The little girl speaks Chinese *almost as well as a native speaker*. 那小女孩讲汉语几乎与本地人一样流畅。

If Tonny had worked *just as hard as John*, he would have passed the examination. 如果托尼能像约翰那样努力学习，他该通过那考试了。

She can tell you a story *quite as funny as this*. 她能讲给你听一个与这个一样十分有趣的故事。

Mary's *every bit as beautiful as her sister*. 玛丽完全和她姐姐一样漂亮。

Tom is *nothing like so outstanding as she told me*. 汤姆一点也不像她说的那样杰出。

● 在"as + 形容词/副词的原级 + as"前加上表示倍数或分数的词加以修饰，表示"是…… 多少倍"、"是……的几分之几"的意思。英语倍数表示法常见的有以下 5 种：

* … times + 名词短语

This reservoir is *four times the size of that one*. 这个水库的面积是那个水库的 4 倍。

* … times + 形容词/副词比较级 + than

The irrigated area in this county is *five times bigger than* in 2012. 这个县的灌溉面积是 2012 年的 5 倍。

* … times + as … as …

Asia is four *times as large as* Europe. 亚洲（的面积）是欧洲的 4 倍。

* … times + what 引导的分句

The total value of the products they turn out this year is four *times what it was last year*. 他们今年的总产值是去年的 4 倍。

* 用…%（percent）

The output of cotton in 2012 was 400% *greater than* in 2000. 2012 年的棉花产量是 2000 年的 5 倍。

Note：用百分比表示净增数，而用 times 或 fold 均表示包括基数 100% 在内。例如，表示增加 4 倍，要用 five times 或 five-fold。

倍数、分数修饰语前可加上表示程度的修饰语 almost, nearly, exactly, just 等，以加强语气。

What a surprise! The little Robert could drink beer almost *twice as much as his father did*. 多么令人吃惊啊！那个小罗伯特喝的啤酒几乎是他父亲的两倍。

d. "as much … as …与 as many … as …"

在涉及数量时，我们可以用 as much … as …或 as many … as …表达，但在 much 或 many 后要加个相关名词。

She hasn't got *as much money as she wanted*. 她没有弄到她原想要弄到的那么多钱。

I need *as many reference books as possible*. 我需要尽量多弄些参考书。

e. as much … as …不同于 as much as； as many … as …不同于 as many as。as much … as …中的 much 是形容词，修饰不可数名词或物质名词，as much as 中的 much 是代词；同样，as many … as …中的 many 是形容词，修饰可数名词，"as many as"中的 many 也是代词。

You ate *as much as you could*. 你们放开肚子大吃了一顿。（或：You ate as much food as you could.）

We didn't catch *as many as we'd hoped*. 我们没有抓到预期得那么多。（或：We didn't catch as many fish as we'd hoped.）

f. as … as …结构中，如第二个 as 后跟的是人称代词，这人称代词用主格或宾格均可。

My brother is *as tall as I/me*. 我弟弟和我一样高。

His elder sister studies *as hard as he/him*. 他姐姐学习和他一样努力。

但在代词是句子的主语时，只能用主格形式。

My sister is *as tall as I am*. 我妹妹和我一样高。

● as … as …可以表示同一个人或物的比较，多表示不同性质，意义为"既……又……"。

Lili is *as kind as honest*. 丽丽既诚实又友善。

The problems are *as numerous as (they are) trivial*. 问题又多又烦琐。

● as … as …还可以用于表示两个人或物不同性质的比较，表示程度相等或相当，意义为"……而……"。

He is *as kind as his sister is honest*. 他妹妹很诚实，而他则很友善。

His wife was *as beautiful as he was handsome*. 他长得非常英俊，而他的妻子则长得非常漂亮。

● as … as any, as … as can be 和 as … as ever

as … as any 相当于 as … as ever lived，意义为"杰出的，不弱于"；as … as … can be 表示强调；as … as ever 相当于 as … as before，意义为"和以前一样"。

Mr. Zhang is *as great a mathematician as any/as ever lived*. 张先生是一位非常杰出的数学家。

John is *as wrong as wrong can be*. 约翰大错特错了。

Grace is *as green as green can be*. 格蕾丝是毫无经验的生手。

My trust in Lei is *as firm as ever/before*. 我对蕾的信任和以前一样坚定。

g. 原级比较中的替代和省略

● "as +形容词/副词 + as "结构中，后半部分 as 从句中有些成分常可被替代或省略。如果两个比较对象是属同类事物或具有同一属性的，那第二个 as 后可用 one, ones, that, those 等词替代前面 as 后的相关的单复数名词或名词词组。

This novel is *as interesting as the one (that) she wrote last year*. 这部小说与她去年写的那部一样有趣。

This picture is not *as beautiful as that one*. 这幅图片没有那幅（图片）漂亮。

The cottages in the suburbs are not quite *as expensive as the ones in the city*. 郊区的别墅不像城里的（别墅）那样贵。

● as … as 结构中，多数情况是第二个 as 后省略一些与第一个 as 后相同的词语。具体的省略情况大致有：

＊省略 as 从句中的部分谓语或整个谓语。

This room is not *as bright as that one (is)*. 这间房间没有那间敞亮。

Jane is not regarded *as beautiful as other girls (are)*. 大家都认为简没有其他女孩漂亮。

＊省略 as 从句中的主语和大部分谓语，此时只剩下状语，有时是宾语。这种 as 与后面的剩余部分也可叫无动词状语从句。

It is cold here *as in Harbin*. 这儿像哈尔滨一样冷。（只保留了地点状语。它的完整形式应是 as it is in Harbin. In Harbing 与 here 相对应。）

Lili respects him as much *as me*. 丽丽尊敬他像尊敬我一样。（只保留了宾语 me, as me 的完整形式是 as Lili respects me）

＊有时省去部分谓语。

Lei is working *as fast as she can*. 蕾正尽快地干着活。

* 在特定的语篇中可以省去后面的整个 as 从句。

—Is this French novel *as difficult as that one*? 这部法语小说是不是和那部一样难读？

—No, I don't think so. It is *not as difficult*. 不，我不这样认为。它并不那样难读。（句中 difficult 后的 as that one 被省去了。）

* 不同性质的比较不可省略。

My home town is *as beautiful as it is ancient*. 我的家乡不但美丽而且古老。

This shirt is *as expensive as it is beautiful*. 这件衬衫价格很贵，但很漂亮。

两个不同成分比较时，不可省略，但可替代

Grace likes dancing *as much as she does her husband*. 格蕾丝如爱自己的丈夫一样爱跳舞。

The furniture in South is *as good as that of other regions in the country*. 南方的家具和这个国家其他地区的家具一样精美。

* 省去 as … as 中的第一个 as。

He's (*as*) *hard as snails*. 他冷酷无情。

His elder sister studies (*as*) *hard as he does*. 他姐姐学习和他一样努力。

B. 比较级等级比较

此结构是表示"比……更"的意思。

The price of gold on the world market has been rising *higher each year*. 国际市场上的黄金价格每年都在上涨。

We had *less* rain this winter *than* last year. 今年冬天降雨比去年少。

Jane runs *faster than* her elder sister. 简比她姐姐跑得快。

There are *more students* in this room *than* in that room. 这个教室的学生比那个教室的多。

a. 比较等级的否定

比较级的否定有两种形式：一种是"not + as/so + 形容词/副词原级 + as"，此较常见；还有一种是"less + 形容词/副词原级 + than"。

She is *not as/so hardworking as John*. 她没有约翰用功。

Robert *doesn't* speak Russian *as fluently as Mary does*. 罗伯特说俄语没玛丽说得流利。

Tom's car is *less expensive than Zhang Ling's*. 汤姆的汽车没有张林的贵。

b. 比较级比较中的一些问题

比较级比较中有好多问题需要说明，如在何种情况下可以不用 than，什么时候又可变 than 成 to，在什么时候可用原级表示比较级等。

● 形容词比较级中，在下列情况下，形容词比较级不带 than。

* 在表语结构中。

Her mother is *better* now. 她母亲好多了。

It was *colder* yesterday. 昨天天气寒冷些了。

The apples will get *redder* in the fall. 苹果在秋天会变得更红。

* 当与名词或 one 连用时。

He wants a *longer* pencil. 他想要一支较长的铅笔。

Give me a *thinner* book to read. 给我本薄一点的书看。

Bring me a *smaller* one. 给我带个小一点的来。

* 在英语中，有些句子的"比较"上的表达是不言而喻的，它们不再需要用 than 引出相比的对象。

You have made the house *bigger*. 你们把房子扩建了。

We must keep our work *cleaner*. 我们的作业应该保持得整洁些。

Mark wants the work done *better*. 马克要求把这工作做得更好些。

在英语中，有一些只能作定语的形容词比较级词，它们后面就不再需要用 than。这些词有：inner（内部的），outer（外部的），upper（上面的），former（在前的），latter（后面的），utter（完全的），elder（年龄较大的）等。因为它们本身就是含有比较意思的比较级词，所以都没有比较级和最高级形式。

The novel reveals the *inner* world of a staunch revolutionary fighter. 小说展示了一个坚强的革命战士的内心世界。

Man has started the journey to *outer* space. 人类已经开始到外空间旅行了。

Mary was happy in the *latter* years of her life. 玛丽幸福地度过了晚年。

With father away the house is in *utter* confusion. 由于父亲不在家，家里变得极度混乱。

Note：在 lesser 用作 little 的比较级时只能作前置定语，因此就不能和 than 连用。

Of the two actors, he is *lesser* known. 两个演员中，他名气小一点。

She doesn't waste time on these *lesser* matters. 她没有把时间浪费在这些小事情上。

- than 变 to 的一些情况

在某些形容词本身有比较意思时，它们后面不能再用 than，而要改用 to 来表达比较的意思。这些词主要有：anterior（前面的），former（在前的），inferior（下等的），junior（年少的），senior（年长的），superior（较高的），posterior（以后的）等。

My room is *superior to* yours.（= My room is better than yours.）我的房间比你的那个好。

Her mother is *junior to* me.（= Her mother is younger than I/me.）她的母亲比我年轻。

- 用原级表示比较级

Mr Zhang is twenty minutes late.（= Mr. Zhang has come twenty minutes later than he should have come.）张先生迟到二十分钟。

- 用最高级表示比较级

The Yellow River is *the second longest* river in China. 黄河是中国第二长河流。

Lili is *the fattest* girl but one in her class. 丽丽是她班上第二胖女生。

- 比较级比较的修饰语

与上面说到的原级比较结构 as … as 前可有修饰语，也可没有修饰语。比较级比较前可用"数词＋名词"以表示确切的度量，也可用 a great deal, a little, far, a lot, much, slightly, still 等加以修饰，以表示所比较的程度。

He is *six years older* than Mary.（= He is older than Mary by six years.）他比玛丽大六岁。

"How are you, boy?"said Mr. Crimwing. "小孩子，你身体好吗？"格林威先生说。

"*A great deal better*, thank you, sir," replied Oliver. "好多了，谢谢你，先生，"奥列佛尔回答。

I think that economics is *a little more* complicated than political science. 我认为经济学比政治学复杂些。

This hall is *slightly smaller* than that one. 这个厅比那个厅小些。

- 用表示倍数或分数的词置于比较级比较前表示确切比较

Rice output this year is *twenty percent higher than* last year. 今年的水稻产量高于去年20%。

The ink in this bottle is *four-fifths more than* in that one. 这个瓶子里的墨水比那个瓶子里的墨水多了 4/5。

Kuwait oil wells yield nearly 500 *times more than the US wells*. 科威特油井产油几乎是美国油井产油的 500 倍。

Last year, Henry earned *three times more than his father*, who has a better position. 去年亨利赚的钱是他父亲的三倍，虽然父亲的职位更好。

- 比较级中的替代和省略

* 替代：比较级比较结构中的替代与 as … as 结构中的省略和替代基本一样。如果两相比之物是同类事物或同一属性，那 than 从句中和主句相同的名词性词组可用 one（单数），ones（复数），that（单数或不可数），those（复数）等替代。如果 than 从句中的代词与介词搭配，要用 that 和 those 替代，不可用 the one 和

ones。助动词 do 可替代与主句中相同的谓语动词。

The courses she is taking this term are more difficult than *the ones* last term. 她这学期学的课程比上学期的难些。

This shirt is better than *the one* I bought the day before yesterday. 这件衬衫比我前天买的那件要好。

The flowers in his garden are less beautiful than *those* in our garden. 他花园里的花没有我们花园里的漂亮。

The cover of this book is more beautiful than *that* of most other books. 这本书的封面比大多数书的封面好看。

She works harder than her elder brother *does*. 她工作比她哥哥努力。

* 省略：与 as … as 结构中的省略也基本一样。than 从句中的省略大致有下列几种：

省略 than 从句中的主语

The intelligence ability of an athlete is usually far greater than *would be expected*. 运动员的智力通常要比预想得高得多。

省略 than 从句中的部分谓语或整个谓语

My wife can type faster than *I can*. 我妻子打字比我快。

Tonny is more friendly than *the other boys in his class*. 马克比班上其他男孩更为友好。

省略 than 从句中的主谓语或整个 than 从句

It is colder in Beijing than *in Shanghai*. 北京比上海寒冷些。

Does Robert feel better now（than *he did before*）？罗伯特现在感到好些了吗？

● more than 不表示比较的情况

* "more than +形容词"表示"不只是"、"不仅是"、"非常,最"。

Lei is *more than pretty*. 蕾岂止美丽！

We're *more than happy* to hear of your escape. 听说你逃出去的消息,我们岂止开心！

The old Tom is *more than talkative*. 那老人何止是健谈啊！

* more than 置于名词词组前表示"多一些",than 后没有比较从句。

More than sixty students went to the cinema last night. 昨晚六十多名学生去看电影。

Mr. Wang died *more than* ten years ago. 王先生十多年前就过世了。

It is *more than* seventy miles to Suzhou. 到苏州城有七十多英里路。

* "more than +带 can 的从句"表示否定。

That kind of work is *more than you can do*. 那样的工作你做不了。

Her behavior is *more than I can stand*. 她的行为我无法忍受。

* "more +形容词 +than +形容词"的意思是"与其说……不如说……"。

Xiaoli is *more excited than happy*. 与其说小丽快乐,不如说她兴奋。

The little boy is *more stupid than honest*. 与其说那个小男孩老实,不如说他愚笨。

You are *more a friend than a teacher*. 你是老师,更是朋友。

One of the blind men said,"The elephant is *more like a snake than a tree*." 其中一个瞎子说："与其说大象像棵树,倒不如说更像一条蛇。"

* "no more +形容词（名词词组）+than …"是"与……一样不"、"和……都不"的意思。

He is *no more fit to be a general manager than a boy would be*. 正如一个小男孩不宜当总经理一样,他同样不宜当总经理。

A whale is *no more a fish than a horse*. 正如马不是鱼一样,鲸也不是鱼。

● 双重比较

"the more … the more" 结构又称"双重比较"和"成比例比较"。

* "the more … the more"结构是由两个形容词或副词的比较级用 and 连接起来组成,表示动作的进一步加快、情况变得更复杂等。

Life in the modern society is becoming *more and more complex*. 现代社会的生活变得越来越复杂。
Because the little girl was afraid, she walked *faster and faster*. 因为小女孩害怕，便跑得越来越快。
The line of people waiting for buying mooncakes is becoming *longer and longer*. 等待买月饼的队伍越来越长。

* "the more … the more …"结构表示成比例递增或递减，两者相互制约，通常前面表示条件，后面表示结果。当然，这里的两个 the 都是副词。有好多"the more … the more …"结构已经成为固定用语，但更多的是以完整形式表达完整意思。

The sooner, the better. 越快越好。
The more, the better. 越多越好。
The more, the merrier. 人越多越热闹。
The earlier the little boy gets up, the better it is. 那个小男孩起得越早越好。
The more I practise, the more experience I will gain. 我实践得越多，我经验就越丰富。

C. 最高级比较

The Sun Hill is *the highest* hill in this area. 太阳山是这个区域最高的山。
Chen Ling studies (*the*) *hardest* in our class. 陈林在我们班学习最努力。
但英语中也有不用-est 或 most，而用其他词语表达最高级方式。

a. 用原级或比较级表示最高级

● 有否定意思的词与 so … as 搭配表示最高级，在这种结构中，其主语往往是否定词。

Nothing is *so difficult as* this. (= This is the most difficult thing in the world.) 这事情最难了。
No novel is *so interesting as* Mark's *The Lonely Village*. (= Mark's novel, *The Lonely Village* is the most interesting novel in our country.) 没有一部小说比麦克的小说《偏僻的村庄》更有趣了。
None is *so blind as* those that won't see. (Proverb) 不愿看的人最瞎。

● 有些比较级的否定结构（如：can't/couldn't + 比较级）可以表示最高级，意思是"最/再……不过，不可能更……"。

Nothing better. 那最好不过了。
I *can't agree more*. 我完全同意。（我再同意不过了。）
The weather *couldn't be worse*. 天气再坏不过了。
That could give her *no greater pleasure*. 那使她再高兴不过了。
I have *never seen a prettier sight*. 我从没看过比这更美的景象了。

b. 用肯定式的比较级、原级或其他形式表示最高级

● 用"比较级 + than any other + 名词"表示最高级

Nanjing is *larger than any other city* in Jiangsu. 南京是江苏省最大的城市。
John is *abler and more active than anyone else*. 约翰是我所知的人中最能干、最有活力的人。
Jane's handwriting is *better than anyone else's* in her class. 简的书法是班里最好的。
Mark is *taller than anyone else* in her class. 马克是班里最高的人。

● 用"as + 原级 + as ever"表示最高级

Mike was *as brave a man as ever* lived in the country. 迈克是这个国家无与伦比的勇士。
Tonny is *as great a philosopher as ever* breathed. 托尼是最伟大的哲学家。

● 用"more + 形容词 + than the + 同一形容词构成的名词"表示最高级

The painting is *more valuable than the valuables*. 这幅画价值连城。
She is *more Chinese than the Chinese*. 她是地地道道的中国人。

● 用"单数名词 + of + 同一名词复数"表示最高级

Grain is *the treasure of treasures*. 粮食是最为宝贵的东西。
Confucius is *the teacher of teachers*. 孔子是万师之表。

● 用"more than 结构"结构表示最高级

She is *more than thirsty*. 她十分口渴。(more than + 形容词)

This *more than satisfied her*. 这使她十二分的满意。(more than + 动词)

● 用"nice/good/fine/rare/lovely/bright + and + 另一形容词"表示最高级。在这一结构中,第一个形容词起副词作用,相当于 very,quite,rarely,thoroughly,对第二个形容词加以强调。

The room is *nice and warm*. (= very warm)这房间很暖和。

The tea is *good and strong*. (= quite strong)这茶很浓。

The tree is *fine and tall*. 这棵树很高。

He was *rare and hungry* after a whole day's work. 他工作一整天后感到很饿。

c. 有时,最高级形容词不表示比较。英语中最高级形容词不表示对比,而是表示加强语气,含有"非常"、"十分"、"在很大程度上"的意思。

We'll do it with *greatest* pleasure. 我们将十分愉快地干这件事。

The little girl spoke *in the softest of* voice. 那个小女孩以很柔和的声音说话。

You all know that water for a battery must be in *the purest* possible condition. 你们都知道供电池用的水必须是非常纯净的水。

We would be *most* (= very much) pleased to see you. 我们非常高兴见你。

d. 关于 most 这个词

It is a *most* important matter. 这是一件非常重要的事情。

We got to know *most* well-known people in the town. 我们终于认识了这城市里的绝大多数知名人士。

We got to know *the most* well-known people in the town. 我们终于认了这个城市最有名的人物。

显然,上面例句 1 中的 a most 是 very 的意思,most 在句中不重读;例句 2 中的 most 是个形容词,意思是"大多数,大部分",作此义时其前没定冠词;例句 3 中的 the most 当然是形容词最高级形式。

② 广义比较句

这种句型就是不用形容词、副词的比较形式来表达比较等级意思的句子。

A. 广义比较等级句的表达形式

广义比较等级句的表达形式众多,常见的有:用"形容词 + to"表示比较级;用动词表示比较级;用短语动词表示比较等级;用 the same,equally,enough 等表示原级;用"too + 原级"、"for 短语"表示比较等级;本身就含最高级含义的形容词表示最高级;其他表示最高级意义的情况等。

a. "形容词 + to"表示比较等级

常见的"形容词 + to"表示比较等级的短语有:posterior to（比……迟）, anterior to（比……早）, prior to（先于……）, previous to（比……早）, superior to（比……优;胜过……）, inferior to（不如……）, senior to（比……大）等。

I got there *anterior to* her arrival. 我比她早到那里。

Tonny came *posterior to* my arrival. 托尼来得比我迟。

The event took place *prior to* that one. 这件事比那件事早发生。

Mike died *previous to* his wife's death. 迈克比他妻子早逝世。

Their company is incomparably *superior to* our firm. 他们的公司比我们的公司具有无比的优越性。

His father is only nineteen years *senior to* him. 他父亲仅比他大十九岁。

Henry said he was *inferior to* others in many respects. 亨利说他在很多方面不如人家。

b. 用"动词"表示比较等级

有一些动词及其句型可以表示比较级的意思,如 exceed(大于),excel(优于,胜过他人的),surpass(胜过,超越)。

Beijng *exceeds* Nanjing in size and population. 北京在人口和面积方面大于南京。

Mary's computer vastly *excels* mine in performance. 玛丽的电脑在性能上远远超过我的。

Mike *surpasses* me in strength. 迈克的力气比我大。

c. 用短语动词表示比较等级

有些短语动词就表示比较意义,如 prefer to(宁要……不要……;比较喜欢……而不喜欢……),contrast with[将……与……对比(相比较)]。

Lili *prefers* walking *to* cycling. 丽丽宁可步行,也不骑自行车。

I like both tea and coffee, but I *prefer* tea *to* coffee. 我对茶和咖啡都喜欢,但相比之下更喜欢茶。

d. 用 the same,equally,enough 等表示原级比较

No one's fingers are *equally long*. 没有一个人的手指是一样长的。

It's *clear enough*. (= It's clear as is necessary.) 讲/说得够清楚了。

e. 用"too + 原级"、"原级 + for 短语"表示比较等级

The string is *too short*. (= The string is shorter than necessary.) 这根线太短了。

These boys are tall *for their ages*. 就年龄而言,这些男孩算是高了。

B. 广义比较级中表示最高级的情况

a. 用像 last, supreme, top, ultimate, far 等本身就有最高级意义的词表示最高级

● last 这个词是没有比较等级的形容词,其意思中有"最新的;最时髦的;最低的;最坏的;最不可能的"。

John is the *last* man to steal. 约翰极不可能偷东西。

Robert was the *last* person to arrive. 罗伯特是最后到达的人。

● supreme 是表示"职位最高的;最大限度的;最优的,卓著的"的意思,无比较等级。

He has achieved one of this century's *supreme* achievements. 他已经取得了本世纪巨大的成就之一。

George is the *supreme* man here. 乔治是这里职位最高的人。

● top 作形容词作"第一的;最好的;最高的"解时没有比较等级。

Fred is my *top* man. 费来德是我的领导。

Tonny is the *top* player in their team. 托尼是他们队最优秀的运动员。

George lives on the *top* floor. 乔治住在顶层。

● 当 ultimate 意思是"最大的;极好的"时,它也是个没有比较等级的形容词。例如:

The sun is the *ultimate* store of power. 太阳是最大的能量贮备库。

This is the *ultimate* style in hats. 这是帽子的最佳式样。

C. 广义比较级中其他情况表示最高级的形式

其他情况表示最高级的情况大致有:用 no, nothing 之类的词表示最高级,用习惯用语表示最高级。

a. 用 no,或 nothing 之类的词表示最高级

用 nothing 或 no 之类的词表示最高级时,这些词可能处于主语位置,也可能处于谓语的位置,也可作主语的定语,还可能作谓语部分的定语。

Nothing ancient or modern seems to come near it. 古今一切,似乎没有一件事可与这个相比。(nothing 作句子主语)

No one is to be compared with John for resourcefulness. 没有一个人比得上约翰的足智多谋。(no 作定语,修饰主语 one)

George has *no equal* in playing chess in the old town. 在那古镇上,乔治下棋没有敌手。(no 作名词宾语 equal 的定语)

b. 用 any, anything, not, no, nothing 等与同等比较 as ... as 相搭配表示最高级

We haven't seen *any* place *as fascinating as* this. (= This is the most fascinating place.) 我们从未见过如此迷人的地方。

Nobody has helped her with her English *as greatly as* Tonny did. 还没人像托尼那样在英语上如此大地帮助过她。

Nothing surprised him *so much as* the death of his best friend. 没有什么像他的好朋友死讯那样令他如此吃惊的了。

c. 用习惯用语表示最高级

英语里,有些习惯用语本身就是表示最高级的,如:second to none(首屈一指;独一无二;比谁都好), all in all(一切的一切;最心爱的东西;最心爱的人),first class(第一流)等。

As a portrait painter, he is *second to none.* 作为肖像画家,他是首屈一指的。

If his cold is still bad, tell him to try this medicine—it's *second to none.* 如果他感冒还不好转,告诉他试试这个药——它比什么药都好。

My interest in sailing was my *all in all.* 对航海感兴趣就我来说是至关重要的。

We are *all in all* to each other. 我们彼此相亲相爱。

My wife is *all in all* to me. 我的妻子是我最心爱的人。

The violinist was quite good, and he was *in the first.* 这位小提琴家相当高明,他是第一流的。

(9) 条件状语从句

① 真实条件和表示法

A. 祈使句 + and + 陈述句

Persevere, and we will succeed. (= If we persevere, we will succeed.) 我们坚持就会成功。

Make haste, and we will be in time for the meeting. (= If we make haste, we will be in time for the meeting.) 我们快点就能按时与会。

Show me the man you honour, and I will know what kind of a man you are. (= If you show me the man you honour, I will know what kind of a man you are.) 把你尊敬的人告诉我,我就知道你是什么样的人。

Let's give you some help, and you will be able to improve in your studies. (= If we give you some help, you will be able to improve in your studies.) 我们帮助你一下,你会在学习上有所提高。

第二个分句通常用情态动词 will 表示将来,但也可以用一般现在时。

Give him an inch and he will take a mile. 得寸进尺。

Arrive late once more and you're fired. 再迟到一次,你就会被解雇。

连词 and 可以省去。

Do it at once, (and) you will never regret. 不马上做,你们就会后悔。

B. 陈述句或疑问句 + and + 陈述句

但第一个分句须含祈使意义。

You have only to see her and you will find her interesting. 你只要见到她,你就会发现她很有趣。

Jane only has to think a little bit, and she will see the reason plainly. 简只要稍微想一下就会清楚地明白这个道理。

Why don't you come this evening and we'll have a chat together? (= Come this evening and we'll have a chat together.) 你怎么不今晚来和我们一起聊一聊呢?

C. 名词短语 + and + 陈述句

名词短语常常是分句的省略形式,杨元兴先生称之为无动词分句。

One step further and you are lost. (=If you take one step further, you are lost.) 再向前一步,你就完了。
One more effort and we will succeed. (=If we make one more effort, we will succeed.) 再努一把力,我们就会成功。
One more such blunder and you are done for. (=If you make one more blunder, you'll be done for.) 再出一次这种错,你就完蛋了。
Another half hour and all doors and windows would be locked. (=If another half hour should pass, all doors and windows would be locked.) 再过半小时,所有的门窗都要锁上了。

D. or (else) 和 otherwise 等于 if not

a. 祈使句+陈述句

Don't move, or we'll shoot. (=If you move, we'll shoot.) 不许动,否则我们就开枪。
Persevere, or you will fail. (=If you do not persevere, you will fail.) 坚持下去,不然你们会失败。
Hurry up, or else you'll be late for the meeting. 快点,不然你开会要迟到了。
Dress warmly, or else you'll catch cold. 穿暖和点,不然你会感冒。
Put on your raincoat, otherwise you will get wet. 穿上雨衣,不然你会被淋湿。

由上述例句可见,否定的祈使句可变成肯定条件句,再加上主句;肯定的祈使句可变成否定的条件句,再加上主句。下面两句单独用 else 连接的句子也属此情况,不过这种表达不多见。

Be quick, else you'll be late. 快点,不然你要迟到。
Take this medicine; else you will be sick. 把这药吃了,不然你会生病。

or else 后的分句可以省去,表示威胁。

Do what I say—or else! 照我说的做,否则!
You wash it properly, or else! 你好好把它洗干净,否则!

b. 陈述句+陈述句

Now we must go or we shall be late for the birthday party. 现在我们必须走,不然参加生日宴会我们要迟到了。
You must start at once, or else you shall miss the last bus. 你必须立即出发,不然就赶不上末班公共汽车了。
He must go there quickly or else he will not be back in time. 他得快点到那里去,不然就不能按时回来。
Faith must have adequate evidence, else it is mere superstition. 信仰必须有充分的根据,否则就完全是迷信。

E. 关联连词 the … the …

第一个分句含有条件意义,the 后接比较级形容词或副词,其 the 当然是副词;第二个分句表示结果,其 the 是连接词。整个句子意思是"(如果)越……,(就)越……"。

The more you learn, the more you know. (=If you practise more, you will know more.) 学习得越多,懂得越多。
The harder we study, the greater progress we will make. (=If we study harder, we will make greater progress.) 我们越用功,进步就越大。

有时,可以把表示结果的分句放在前面,表示条件的分句放在后面,但第一个"the+形容词或副词"不能放在句首。

You dance the better, the more you practise. (=The more you practise, the better you sing.) 越练就跳得越好。
This stone gets the harder, the longer it is exposed to the weather. (=The longer this stone is exposed to the weather, the harder it gets.) 这石头暴露的时间越久,就变得越硬。

F. 无连词的并列短语表示真实条件

无连词并列短语中所要表示的条件包含在前一部分,这种结构多见于谚语。

Out of sight, out of mind. (=If someone is out of sight, he will soon pass out of mind.) 眼不见,心不念。
Love me, love my dog. (=If you love me, love my dog.) 爱屋及乌。
Grasp all, lose all. (=If you try to grasp all, you will lose all.) 贪多必失。

First come, first served. (= If one comes first, he will be served first.) 先来先招待。

Easy come, easy go. (= If money comes easily, it will go easily.) 来得容易去得快。

从上述句中可见,例句1是无动词复合句,省略的条件从句中保留了表语,主句中保留了状语;例句2、3、4 也分别可以扩充成主从复合句。

G. 非谓语动词及其短语表示真实条件

a. -ed 分词及其短语表示真实条件,可以由连词 if 和 unless 引导,实际上是从句的省略形式。

United we stand, *divided we fall*. (= If we are united we stand, if we are divided we fall.) 我们团结则存,分裂则亡。

Water, *given enough time* (= so long as it is given enough time), will dissolve almost any substance. 只要有足够的时间,水几乎可以溶解任何物质。

She will come *if asked*. (= if she is asked.) 如果请她,她会来。

The crops will grow more quickly *if watered regularly* (= if it is watered regularly). 如果按时浇水,这些庄稼会长得更快。

Unless compelled to stay in by bad weather (= Unless I am compelled to stay in by bad weather), I go for a walk every day. 除非天气不好被迫待在家里,我每天都要散步。

Unless told otherwise (= Unless you are told otherwise), be here every night. 除非另外告诉你,否则每天晚上都到这里来。

Note: -ed 分词独立结构也可以表示条件。

All things considered (= If all things are considered), Rose's paper is of greater value than yours. 如果全面考虑,罗斯的论文比你的论文更有价值。

b. 在-ing 分词短语表示条件时,可以由连词 if, once, unless 引导。

Turning to the left (= If we turn to the left), we will find the post office. 向左转,我们就会看见邮局。

Looking out of the window (= If I look out of the window), I can have a full view of the city. 如果朝窗外看,我可以看见全城的景象。

If coming by car (= If you come by car), take the A10 and turn off at the A414. 如果你开车来,走 A10 号公路,在 A414 处转弯。

Once having made a promise (= Once Mr. Yang has made a promise), he should keep it. 杨先生一旦许下诺言,就应该遵守。

Unless receiving visitors (= Unless they receive visitors), patients must observe normal hospital rules. 除非有人来访,否则病人必须遵守医院正常的规定。

Note: 像-ed 分词独立结构一样,现在分词独立结构也可以表示条件。

Conciliation failing (= If conciliation fails), force remains; but *force failing* (= if force fails), no further hope of conciliation is left. 和解失败,还可以靠武力;但武力失败,就不会有和解的希望了。

c. 不定式短语也可表示条件,但不常见。

One would be a fool *not to take the opportunity*. 如果不抓住机会,他就是傻瓜。

Mike will apologize *if (it is) only to avoid bad feeling*. 如果是为了避免引起不满,迈克会道歉。

To survive (= If we are to survive), we must have food. 要生存,我们就得有食物。

d. 介词短语表示真实条件

介词短语也可以表示条件,这种情况,杨元兴先生称之为无动词条件从句。

Without food (= If I do not have food), I cannot survive. 没有食物,我就不能生存。

In the event of rain (= If it rains), his birthday party will be held indoors. 如果下雨,他的生日宴会将在室内举行。

In case of his not being there (= If he is not there), ask his brother to help you. 如果他不在那里,你就叫他

弟弟帮助你。

介词短语可以由连词 if, once 等引导,这种结构实际上是从句的省略形式。

If (*it is*) out of the question, please tell me. 如不可能,请告诉我。

Once (*you are*) over the pass, we will see the town below you. 翻过那个山口,我们就会看见下面的城镇。

e. 名词短语表示真实条件

Your refusal to come might give offence. 你如果拒绝来就会得罪人。

His tendency to arrive late often can result in his being fired. 他如果经常迟到就会被开除。

H. 其他结构表示真实条件

连词 if 引导的形容词短语等可以表示条件,它们通常是无动词省略句;还有定语从句也可表示真实条件。

a. "if + 形容词短语、代词短语、副词短语、介词短语等"也可以表示条件指示。

Come if (*it is*) possible. 来吧,如果可能的话。

If anyone (*knows*), she knows. 如果有人知道,那就是她了。

Go to bed. *If not* (= *If you don't go to bed*), I'll tell mother. 去睡觉。你不去,我就告诉妈妈。

If (*she is*) still alive, Grace must be at least ninety years old. 如果(她)还活着,格蕾斯至少九十岁了。

There are few people nowadays, if (*there are*) any, who remember Robert. 现在记得罗伯特的人,如果有的话,也不多了。

The rumour may be true; *if so* (= if the rumour is true), he will be in trouble with the government. 流言可能属实;要是那样,政府要惩罚他。

Xiaowei went to the countryside to serve the farmers. *If not for that*, he wouldn't have gone. 小魏到乡下去为农民服务。如不为此,他是不会去的。

b. 定语从句表示真实条件:有时定语从句也含有条件意义。

He *that would eat the fruit* must climb the tree. (= If anyone would eat the fruit ...) 想吃果子就得爬树。

Anyone who comes here is welcome. (= Anyone is welcome if he comes here.) 到这里来的人都受欢迎。

c. where ... there ... 这种结构表示"如果……则,若……则"。

Where bees are, there is honey. 哪儿有蜜蜂哪儿就有蜜。

Where there is no fire, there is no smoke. 无火不冒烟。(无风不起浪)

Where there is a will, there is a way. 有志者事竟成。

② 非真实条件的表示法

A. if 从句表示非真实条件

用 if 表示假设的非真实的条件,从句谓语动词用虚拟语气。此部分详见本书"虚拟语气"部分。

另外,含有非真实条件的句子常常用来表示建议和请求,使人听起来更带试探性,更加不肯定,因而语气显得更加委婉。

Would it be all right *if we came round at about ten*? 我们十点左右来,好吗?

It would be nice *if you helped me a little with the homework*. 如果你帮我做点家庭作业,那就好了。

She should be grateful *if Tom would reply as soon as possible*. 如汤姆能尽快答复,她将十分感激。(如蒙早复,则甚感激。)

一般来说,通常与现在事实相反的条件产生与现在事实相反的结果,与过去事实相反的条件产生与过去事实相反的结果。但有时也不一定,这需要根据条件与结果具体时间关系而选用动词的适当形式,这也是传统语法上讲的"错综时间条件句"(Conditional Sentences of Mixed Time)。

If Ruth knew any foreign language, we would have sent him abroad. 鲁斯要是懂外语,我们早派他到国外去了。

If I had followed the doctor's advice, I would be much better now. 我要是听从了医生的劝告,我现在就好多了。

If you were in better health, I would have allowed you to join them in the work. 你要是身体好一些,我早就让你和他们一道工作了。

If you hadn't got everything ready by now, you should be having a terrible time tomorrow. 要是现在一切还没准备好,明天你们就糟了。

If I hadn't been working hard in the past few years, things wouldn't be going so smoothly. 要是过去几年我没有努力工作,现在一切不会进行得这样顺利。

这种错综条件句还是少模仿为妙。一般情况下还是按正规句法表达为好。

B. 其他连词引导的从句表示非真实条件

if only, unless, suppose/supposing (that), but (that), only (that) 等从属连词引导从句都可用来表示非真实条件。

a. if only 通常单独使用,谓语动词用虚拟语气一般式表示与现在或将来事实相反的愿望,用虚拟语气完成体表示与过去事实相反的愿望。if only 有时也可分开成 if ... only。

If only she were still alive. 要是她还活着就好了。

If only he didn't drive so fast. 要是他开车不那样快就好了。

If only she had gone by taxi. 要是她坐出租汽车去就好了。

If I had *only* known. 要是我早知道就好了。

b. 偶尔,unless 也引导非真实条件状语从句。

I shouldn't dream of going *unless he wanted me*. 我不会想去,除非他要我去。

I wouldn't be saying this *unless I were sure of the facts*. 要是我不相信这些事实,我就不会说这话了。

c. suppose/supposing (that) 引出的从句中谓语动词通常用虚拟语气一般式,表示假设现在或将来事实相反的非真实条件;主句是疑问句时,有时可以省去。

Suppose / Supposing your parents knew how you're behaving here, what would they think? 要是你的父母亲知道你在这里的表现,他们会怎么想呢?

Suppose / Supposing (that) I were left alone on a desert island, what is the first thing I would do? 要是我一个人被留在荒岛上,我第一件事会做什么?

Suppose your father saw you, what would he say? 要是你父亲看见你,他会说什么呢?

But *supposing* Ruth remained unconvinced? 但是,假如还有鲁斯一个人不信服(怎么办)呢?

从句谓语动词偶尔也可以用虚拟语气完成体,表示假设的和过去事实相反的非真实条件。

Supposing the boy had gone out of his mind, what was the cause of it? 假如那个男孩已经疯了,那原因是什么呢?

C. 否定连词(组) but for, but (that), only (that) 和 except (that)

这种连词(组)引出的从句谓语动词虽用陈述语气形式,却包含着非真实条件,所以主句谓语动词一般用虚拟语气形式,也有不用虚拟语气的。but for (= if it were not for, 接名词短语) 和 but that 意义为"要不是"; only that 相当于 were it not that, 意义为"如果不是"; except that 相当于 only that, 意义为"倘若不是,要不是"。

But for air and water, nothing could live. 没有空气和水,什么也活不了。

The sunset is charming, *only but it is near dusk* (= except that it is near dusk). 夕阳无限好,只是近黄昏。

He'd succeed, *only he's rather lazy* (= if he were not lazy ...). 他要是不懒就会成功了。

He would have written before *but he has been ill* (= if he had not been ill ...). 要不是他一直生病,他早就写信了。

Robert could not have believed it, *but that he saw it*. 要不是罗伯特亲眼看到,他是不会相信的。

But that he has a family (= If he didn't have a family), he would have left England long ago. 他要是没有家庭,他早就离开英国了。

She would go with you, *only that she is too busy* (= if I were not too busy). 要是她不太忙的话,她愿意和你一起去。

I would go *except it's too far* (= if it were not too far). 要不是太远,我愿意去。

I would go with you, *except that I have to work that day* (= if I didn't have to work that day). 要不是那天我得工作,我愿意和你一起去。

D．用 otherwise 引导的并列句表示非真实条件

在含 otherwise 的并列句中,当第二个分句用虚拟语气形式时,第一个分句虽然用的是陈述语气形式,但含有非真实条件。

She's getting old—*otherwise she would keep him.* (= If I were not getting old, I would keep him.) 我老了,不然我会留住他。

The young man had intellect, *otherwise I should have scorned him.* (= If he hadn't had intellect, I should have scorned him.) 那年轻男子有非凡的才智,不然我会看不起他。

E．用介词短语表示非真实条件

a．介词短语也可以表示非真实条件。

What would I do *with a million dollars* (= if I had a million dollars)? 如果我有 100 万美元,我怎么办?

I could not have succeeded *without your help* (= if it had not been for your help). 要是没有你的帮助,我不会成功的。

But for Gordon (= If it hadn't been for Gordon), they should have lost the match. 要是没有戈登,他们早就输掉这场比赛了。

We might have done even better *under more favourable conditions* (= if conditions were more favourable). 要是条件更有利,我们会干得还要好。

b．不定式短语、-ed 分词短语和-ing 分词短语也可以用来表示真实条件。

• 不定式短语表示非真实条件。

To look at her (= If we were to look at her), we could hardly help laughing. 我们要是看一看她,就不能不笑。

To hear him speak English (= If one were to hear him speak English), one would take him for an Englishman. 听他说英语,你会以为他是英国人呢。

It would be easier for us *to do it this way* (= if we were to do it this way). 我们这样做会容易一些。

• -ed 分词短语表示非真实条件时,可以用连词 if 引导。

Left to itself (= If it had been left to itself), the country would long have achieved its unity. 要是没有外国干涉,这个国家早就统一了。

Born in better times (= If he had been born in better times), he would have done credit to the profession of letters. 他要是生得逢时,他早就为文坛增添光彩了。

If asked to comment (= If I were asked to comment), I should insist that I have nothing to say. 要是有人叫我发表看法,我会坚持说我没什么说的。

• -ing 分词短语可用于表示非真实条件,但所见不多。

Happening in war time (= If it were to happen in war time), this would amount to disaster. 要是发生在战时,这会酿成大祸。

Other things being equal (= If other things were equal), she would buy the black dress rather than the white one. 如果其他方面一样,她就买那件黑色的衣服,不买那件白色的。

③ 推测条件句

推测条件句就是推测可能实现的条件。推测条件句通常由连词 if 引导的从句表示。

不管从句的主语是什么，谓语动词一律用"should + 动词不定式"表示，在正式文体中可以省去 should，用动词原形表示。而主句谓语动词常用陈述语气或祈使语气，如条件实现的可能性很小时，也可用虚拟语气表示。

If it should rain, you had better stay indoors. 要是下雨，你们最好待在室内。

If I should see her, what will/would I do? 我要是见到她，我怎么办？

If you should meet Rose, ask her to come here. 如果你碰到罗丝，叫她到这里来一下。

If the rumour (*should*) *be true*, everything is possible. 要是传闻属实，任何事情都可能发生。

If she (*should*) *be ready to help us*, let her come forward. 如有人帮助我们，就站出来吧。

If night (*should*) *fall before they get out of the swamp*, they are lost. 要是天黑他们没有走出沼泽地，他们就要迷路。

A. 从句谓语动词一般用"情态动词 should ＋一般体动词"不定式表示对将来情况的推测。

这种推测可以用进行式动词不定式替代，还可以用完成体不定式，表示对已发生了的情况的推测，但这并不常见。

If you should be passing, come and see me. 要是你路过，一定来看我。

If Tonny should have called at the club on his way home, he'll have been given the parcel I left there for him. 要是托尼回家时到俱乐部去过的话，他们可能把我留在那里的包裹给他了。

B. 在正式文体中，从句也可以不用连词 if 引导而用倒装语序，而把 should 置于从句之首。

Should we be free tomorrow, we will come. 要是我明天有空，我就来。

Should I see your father, I'll tell him you are quite well. 要是我见到你父亲，我会告诉他你很好。

Should she change your mind, no one would blame her. 她要是改变主意，没有人会责怪她。

④ 间接条件句

间接条件句(Indirect Conditional Sentences)就是指与结果无关的条件句。间接条件句总是由连词 if 引导的从句表示。根据它们在句中的作用可以分为三种。

A. 表示礼貌、客气等

If you want to eat, there are some food on the table. 如果你想吃点东西，桌子上有。

Mary is far too considerate, *if I may say so*. 玛丽考虑太周到了，如果我可以这样说的话。

Chomsky's view cannot be reconciled with Piaget's, *if I understand both correctly*. 乔姆斯基的观点和皮亚杰的观点是不可调和的，如果我对他们两人的观点理解正确的话。

情态动词 will 可以用于这种从句。

If you will come this way, I'll take you to the teacher's office. (= Please come this way, and I'll take you to the manager's office.) 请走这里，我带你到经理室去。

B. 表示愤怒、讽刺等

If you ask me, (I will tell you) she's a fool. 要是你问我，(我会说)她是个傻瓜。

The war was started by the other side, *if we remember our history lessons*. 这场战争是由另一方挑起的，如果我们还记得我们学过的历史课的话。

Einstein's theory of gravitation is based on a mathematical concept, *if you've not forgotten already*. 爱因斯坦的万有引力理论是以数学概念为基础的，如果你没有忘记的话。

C. 表示强调的情态动词 will 可以用于这种从句

If drugs will (= can) cure your mother, this drug should do the job. (= This drug will certainly cure your mother.) 如果用药能治好你母亲，这种药就行。

If sugar will (=can) dissolve in a hot liquid, *this chemical will do so too.* (= This chemical will certainly dissolve in a hot liquid.) 如果糖能溶于热液体,这种化学制品也能。

D. 表示间接或直接地提高出建议、请求、提问或解释某种情况

If Ruth wanst to borrow a shoe brush, there's one in the bathroom. 如果鲁斯想借鞋刷,浴室里有一把。(表示间接提议)

If you're going my way, I need a lift back. 如果你和我走同条路,我可以搭你的车走吗? (表示间接提出请求)

If we like watching football, the Shanghai Football Team will be playing Hong Kong this afternoon. 如果我们想看足球赛,今天下午有上海队与香港队的比赛。(表示解释说明)

⑤ 修辞条件句

修辞条件句(Rhetorical Conditional Sentence)是借用条件句的形式来表示有力的论断。修辞条件句总是由连词 if 引导的从句表示。根据它们在句中的作用可以分为两种。

A. 主从句表达的同是事实或均不是事实

从句是事实,主句就是事实,从句不是事实,主句就不是事实;反之亦然。

If they're Irish, I'm the Pope. (= As I'm obviously not the Pope, they're certainly not Irish). 如果他们是爱尔兰人,我就是教皇了。

If I believe that, I'll believe anything. (= You certainly can't believe that). 如果我连那种事都相信,任何事情我都可以相信了。

If he doesn't get first prize, he's no son of yours (= he certainly will get first prize). 要是他得不到一等奖,他就不是你的儿子。

B. if a day / man … 中的 if 不表示条件

在 if a day, if a man, if a yard, if a penny, if an inch, if an ounce 等类似结构中, if 不表示条件,而是对年龄、重量、身高、价值、数量等进行强调,意义为"一定,至少,无论如何"。

He's ninety *if he's a day.* (= He's certainly ninety.) 他一定有九十岁了。

The painting will cost 1,000 pounds *if a penny.* (= Ths painting will cost at least 1,000 pounds.) 这幅画至少卖到1000英镑。

The army is 100,000 *if a man.* (= The army is at any rate over 100,000.) 这支部队人数起码超过10000人。

这种用法的 if 也可以引导从句,放在主句之后。

The package weighed ten pounds *if it weighed an ounce.* (= The package certainly weighed ten pounds.) 这包裹一定有十磅重。

The painting must be worth a thousand dollars *if it's worth a cent.* (= The painting must certainly be worth a thousand dollars.) 这幅画一定能值1000美元。

Mark earns 5,000 *yuan* per month *if he earns a penny.* 马克一个月的确能挣5000元人民币。

第26章 否定句

26.1 否定句概述

含有否定词或否定意义的句子称为否定句。英语中的否定结构形式多样,表达复杂,有部分否定、全部否定、近似全部否定与部分否定、双重否定等。我们把这些否定归纳为两大类,即词汇类否定和结构类否定。

26.2 词汇类否定句

词汇类否定句是通过词汇手段对句子意思给予否定。这些词汇可以是名词、形容词、连词、动词和一些固定词组、介词(短语)、副词短语等。这一类含否定意义的词或词组、结构等也可叫"含蓄否定"。

(1) 用名词表示否定

英语中常用一些带有否定含义的名词来表示否定。这些名词常见的有:failure, absence, lack, negation, shortage, refusal, ignorance, Greek to/all Greek to 等。

All our efforts ended in *failure*. 我们的一切努力都以失败告终。
During my *absence* from school, they learned a new lesson. 当我不在学校的时候,他们学了一篇新课文。
In many countries there is a *shortage* of building wood. 许多国家都缺少建筑木材。
Latin is *Greek to* her. 她对拉丁文一无所知。
Jim can't buy a new car because of *lack* of money. 因为没有钱,吉姆买不起新轿车。
We are in complete *ignorance* of his plans. 我们对他的计划一无所知。
The matter is *all Greek to* me. 我对那事一无所知。

(2) 用连词表示否定

常见的带否定含义的连词有:unless, rather than 等。
We shall go *unless* it rains. 如果不下雨我们就去。
He is a businessman *rather than* an engineer. 他是实业家,不是工程师。

(3) 用带否定词缀的词表示否定

由否定前缀 ab-, dis-, il-, ill-, im-, in-, ir-, mis-, non-, un-等和否定后缀-less, -free 构成的词都表示否定意思。

It is *abnormal* for her to walk in her sleep. 她有梦游症,这是不正常的。
What he said was *illogical*. 他说的话不合逻辑。
Bacteria are *invisible* to the naked eye. 细菌是肉眼看不见的。
The book is *useless*. 这本书没有用处。
Do you know this sea is *ice-free*. 你是否知道这个海没有流冰?

(4) 用形容词词组表示否定

英语中有一些形容词跟某些词合起来组成词组表示否定的意思。这些含否定意义的形容词组有：far from, clear of/from, free of/from, short of, devoid of, absent (from), alien to, foreign to, ignorant of, reluctant to, blind to, far and few between(很少) 等。

I was very *far from* getting what I wanted. 我远远没有得到我想要得到的东西。

Rose is now *clear of/from* suspicion. 罗丝现在不受怀疑了。

These tickets are *free of* charge. 这些票是免费的。

Those children seem to be quite *devoid of* any sense right or wrong. 那些孩子似乎根本不懂得事情的对与错。

I must stop a bit, I'm *short of* breath. 我喘不过气了,得歇一歇。

What his plans are I am quite *ignorant of*. 我一点也不知道他的计划是什么。

He is *reluctant to* leave his hometown. 他不愿离开家乡。

Holidays are *far and few between*. 假日很少。

(5) 用固定词组表示否定

一些包含否定含义的固定词组或固定搭配常用在句中表示否定。

She is *the last* woman I'll talk to. (= I'll never talk to her.) 我绝不与那个女人说话。

This version is *anything but* faithful to the original. (= It is not faithful to the original.) 这个译本一点也不忠实于原文。

That box is *too small to hold* all these things. (= That box is so small that it can't hold all these things.) 那盒子太小,装不下所有这些东西。

(6) 用介词(短语)表示否定

英语中有些介词也有否定含义,如：above, beneath, beyond, instead of, from, except, but, but for, past, without, in vain, in the dark, at a loss 等。这些介词中只有 without 是显性否定,其余都是隐性否定。

① above: 表示隐性否定时,介词 above 的意思是"超出……的范围"、"品质上超脱于(卑劣或不足称道)那些东西"。

A true gentleman is *above* envy, jealousy or vindictiveness. 一个真正有教养的人是没有妒忌、猜忌或报复心的。

I think he is *above* writing such an essay. 我想他写不出这样的论文。

His heroism was *above* all praise. 他的英雄行为是赞美不完的。

在口语里,上句的否定形式常作为一种间接肯定法(litotes)。

He is *not above* telling a lie, if it will serve his purpose. 如果说谎能为其所为,他就不惜说谎。

② before：在口语中,介词 before 表示隐性否定时意为"与其……宁可；宁愿……而不……"。

I'd choose sherry *before* port, any way. 不管怎么着,我宁愿要雪利酒,也不要葡萄酒。

The soldier has chosen death *before* dishonor. 那位战士宁死而不受辱。

③ beneath: 介词 beneath 表示隐性否定时的意思是"不值得"。

This kind of thing is *beneath* attention. 这类事情不值得关注。

Such a fellow as that is *beneath* my notice. 那种家伙我不屑一顾。

④ beyond: 介词 beyond 是"范围、限度、水平、能力超出；多于；为……所不能及"的意思。

We do think that it is *beyond* her power to fulfill the task within three days. 我们的确认为要她在三天内完成任务是力所不及的。

It was a case *far beyond* the physician's skill. 这病远非这位医生的医术所能治疗的。

⑤ but 和 except: 作介词用的 but 和 except 作"除……之外"时，含否定意思。

We go to work every day *except* Saturday and Sunday. 我们除了星期六和星期天之外天天上班。

All the students attended the meeting *except* you. 除了你，所有的学生都参加了会议。

They're all wrong *but* me. 除我以外，他们都错了。

Everyone is ready *except* Tom. 除汤姆之外，每个人都准备好了。

⑥ instead of: 这短语虽然表示"代替"，但也隐含否定之意。

I should be at school *instead of* lying here in bed. 我应该去上学，而不应该躺在床上。

⑦ past: 介词 past 意为"(能力、程度、范围等)超过"之意，也含否定意思。

He said some of her poems were *past* comprehension. 他说她的某些诗作无法理解。

Her uncle injured his left leg, and the pain was almost *past* bearing. 她的叔叔左腿受了伤，那疼痛简直无法忍受。

⑧ at fault, at a loss: 介词 at fault 表示"出错"，at a loss 表示"不知所措"。

Her memory is *at fault*. 她想不起来了。

I found myself *at a loss* for words of consolation. 我简直想不出安慰的话来。

⑨ within: 介词 within 是"不超出时间、范围"的意思。

How can they finish building the hall *within* half a year? 他们怎么能在半年不到的时间内造好那个礼堂呢？

The farm is *within* five miles from here. 那农场离这里不到五英里。

⑩ out of, out of place: out of 表示"不再处于某种状态，不在……里面"，out of place 表示"不适当"。

You'd better stay *out of* that affair. 你最好不要去管那件事。

His statement was entirely *out of place* on such an occasion. 在这种场合，他说的话是完全不适当的。

(7) 用动词(短语)表示否定

用带否定含义的动词(如 escape, fail, decline, defy, doubt, lack, miss, negate, refuse, reject, wonder)和动词短语(如 shut one's eyes to, turn a deaf ear to, keep ... dark, refrain from 等)表示否定很常见。

Her name *escapes* me. 我不记得她的名字了。

She *failed* to pass (= didn't pass) the examination. 她没能通过考试。

Please *refrain from* smoking in public places. 请勿在公共场所吸烟。

Please *keep* the news *dark*. 请不要把这个消息说出去。

Note: 有些词语如 ... either, ... neither, ... not even ... 等不能和含蓄否定的谓语动词连用，而要和谓语的否定结构搭配。

误：If one doesn't have a great aim in life, he lacks the motive to work hard, either.

正：If one doesn't have a great aim in life, he doesn't have the motive to work hard, *either*. 要是一个人没有伟大的生活目标，他也就没有勤奋工作的动力。

误：I doubt the story, not even in the least.

正: I don't believe the story, *not even* in the least. 我不相信这个故事,甚至一点也不相信。

(8) 用带否定含义的 more than ... can 结构表示否定

这种句子表示"不能"或"不可能",语气比较委婉。

That's *more than I can do*. (= I can't do all that. / It's impossible for me to do that.) 我做不了那件事。

He has *more books than he can read*. (= He can't read all his books. / It's impossible for him to read all his books.) 他有读不完的书。/他读不完他所有的书。

(9) 用"All ... +含否定意义的词"表示否定

All the students failed in the exam. 所有的学生考试都失败了。
All the misprintings escaped his attention. 所有的印刷错误他都没有注意。

(10) 用副词短语表示否定

常见的副词短语有:much less/still less/let alone, by no means, in no way, no longer, no more, not ... at all, not ... in the least。

Youth lost will return *no more*. 青春不再。
She is *not* worried *in the least*. 她一点也不担心。
She is *by no means* selfish. 她绝不自私。

26.3 结构类否定句

结构类否定句就是指用否定意义的副词 not, no, little, hardly, never, seldom, rarely 置于句子的某些不同的位置上,使句子的意思变成否定。我们把结构类否定句分为一般否定句和特殊否定句两大类。这些否定句中的结构复杂,形式多样。

(1) 一般否定句

一般否定句(General Negative Sentence)是指否定词出现在谓语动词部分,即否定谓语动词。这是一种最常见的英语结构否定句。这种结构的否定句一般可以分三种情况:

① 对谓语动词 be 进行否定

这种结构通常是"主语+be+not+表语"。
They were not teachers. 他们以前不是教师。
We are not workers. 我们(都)不是工人。

对于 be 动词的否定说法有两种:一是 be 和主语连在一起如: I'm (You're, He's, She's) not a worker;二是 be 和 not 连在一起,说成 I ain't (you aren't, He isn't, She isn't) a worker。

Note:ain't 是非标准英语词,常用于方言里或未受教育的人间的交际。它不仅用来表示 am not, 还可表示 are not, is not, have not, has not,一般情况少用这些表达。

You *ain't* going. 你不去。
It *ain't* raining. 天不在下雨。
I *ain't* seen him. 我没有看见他。
He *ain't* got the time. 他没有时间。

但在美国好多地区,有文化的人也常用 ain't, ain't I (我不是吗?)几乎成了他们的口头禅。

② 否定 be 动词以外的其他谓语动词

这种否定结构是"主语+do (does)+not+谓语动词",也就是把 not 放在动词前面,not 之前再加助动词 do (does)。

They *did not* go there. 他们没去那里。

He *does not* smoke. 他不抽烟。

Do not anticipate trouble, or worry about what may never happen. Keep in the sunlight. 不要预设困难, 也不要担心也许永远不会发生的事。要看到事情的光明面。

Notes: A. 当 have 用作谓语表示"有"时, 其否定形式在英国英语中不需要助动词 do, 美语中则常与 do 连用。

〔英〕He *hasn't* a book in his hand.

〔美〕I *don't have* a book in my hand.

〔英〕She *hasn't* many friends here.

〔美〕She *doesn't have* many friends here.

B. 在古代作品里, 否定词 not 可以直接放在动词后面构成一般否定式。

By a name I *know not* how to tell thee who I am. (Romeo and Juliet. II ii.) 我不知道怎么跟你说我叫什么名字。

C. 如果谓语动词前有助动词或情态动词, not 就应放在它们的后面。

Mary *has not* read the novel. 玛丽没有看过那部小说。

He *cannot* (*can not*) do it. 他不会做这件事。(cannot 是英国写法, can not 是美国写法)

如果谓语动词前有几个助动词或情态动词, not 应放在第一个助动词或情态动词后面。

We *have not* been doing homework. 我们一直没有做作业。

She *must not* be waiting for me. 她肯定不在等我。

(2) 特殊否定句

特殊否定句是指对充当主语、宾语、表语或状语的词和短语进行否定, 即否定谓语动词以外的其他句子成分, 其结构是"not + 主语 + 谓语动词 + 其他句子成分"或"(主语 +) 谓语动词 + (间接宾语) + not + 其他句子成分"。注意, 要把 not 放在所否定的成分之前。

Not a word came from her lips. 她一句话也没有说。(否定主语)

Not to grasp firmly is *not to grasp at all*. 抓而不紧等于不抓。(否定主语和表语)

We have decided *not to go there again*. 我们决定再也不去那里了。(否定作宾语的动词不定式)

She warned her son *not to touch it*. 她告诫她儿子不要去碰它。(否定宾语补足语)

Rose lived *not far off*. 罗丝住得不远。(否定状语)

Not knowing what to say, I kept silent. 不知道该讲些什么, 所以我保持沉默。(否定状语)

A man of words and *not of deeds* is like a garden full of weeds. 光说话不办事的人犹如光长野草的花园。(否定介词短语)

My wage is *not* 1,500 *yuan* a month. 我的工资每月不到1500元。(否定数词)

{ —Can you come? 你能来吗?
  —I'm afraid *not*. (= I'm afraid that I can't come.) 恐怕不能。(否定从句)

26.4 否定范围

"否定范围"(Scope of Negation)是指句子中得到否定的部分。否定一般要用否定词, 带否定词缀或隐含否定的词才可表达否定的概念。我们可以从数量、程度等方面对否定范围进行分析、研究。否定范围通常有三种情况:全部否定、近似全部否定和部分否定。

(1) 全部否定

全部否定(Complete Negation)是完全彻底地否认一个事物的存在或其真实性。全部否定的概念可以用下列几种形式来表示：

① 用否定词

这些否定词有：no, not, nothing, nobody, none, nowhere, never, neither, nor, or 等。

No words can describe the scene. 这景色非言语所能形容。

He is *no* teacher. 他谈不上是教师。

Note：no 放在 be 和名词表语或其他形容词之间，意为"绝不是"，表示强烈的否定。这种否定也称作"绝对否定"。例如，She is not a teacher. 只是一种客观叙述，表明"她不是教师，而是从事其他职业的人。"而 She is no teacher. 却表示说话人鲜明的主观感情，具有非常强烈的否定意味，也就是说"她不配当教师"或"她根本不够资格当教师"。

The task is *no* easy one. 这绝不是一件容易的工作。

Victory would *not* be so far off. 胜利不是那么遥远了。

He had *nothing* to do all day (long). 他整天无事可做。

Nobody knows about it. 没有人知道这件事。

None of them are/is here. 他们没有一个在这儿。(none 可用作单数，也可用作复数)

She had *nowhere* to go. 她没有地方可去。

He *never* spoke unless necessary. 除非有必要，否则他从不讲话。

Neither is a worker. 两个人都不是工人。(通常 neither 作主语时，谓语动词用单数，口语中也可用复数的)

Neither you *nor* I could do it. 你和我都不能做这件事。

Mary does *not* go to office on Saturdays or Sundays. 玛丽星期六和星期天都不去上班。

按照英语的表达习惯，当句中谓语动词有 not，其后用 or 时，表示两者都否定。or 也可以改用 nor，如果并列第一项后有逗号，或多项并列，都用 nor。因此，上句可改成 Mary does not go to office on Saturdays, nor on Sundays.

② 用"not + 不定代词或不定副词"

这些否定词有：any, anyone, anything, anywhere 等。

I have *not* got *any* money with me. 我身上没有带钱。

He did *not* know *anyone* (*anybody*) in that city. 他在那个城市不认识任何人。（更口语化。）

He did *not* say *anything*. 他什么话也没有说。

They *did* not go *anywhere* yesterday. 他们昨天什么地方也没有去。

Note：汉语可以说"任何人都不……"，但英语中 any, anybody, anything 等不定代词总是跟在否定词后面，也不能作否定句的主语。不能说：Anybody cannot do it。要说：Nobody can do it. （没有人能做这件事）。

在俚语中，"not + half" 表示否定。

I do *not* believe *half* of it. 我对此半点儿也不相信。

(2) 近似全部否定

近似全部否定是指大体上否定一个事物的存在或真实性，常用 almost, nearly, next to, practically 等加上否定词 no, not, nothing 等来表示近似全部否定的概念。

Almost no one believed him. 几乎没有一个人相信他。

The speech said *next to nothing*. 这个演讲近乎言之无物。

有些词,像 hardly (= almost not), barely (= almost not), scarcely (= almost not), seldom (= almost never), rarely (= almost never), few (= almost no), little (= almost no, nothing)等,为最常用的表示近似全部否定(准否定)的语言表达手段。

There's *hardly* any coal left. 几乎没有剩下什么煤了。

He had *barely* time to catch the train. 他差一点没赶上火车。

We *scarcely* know him. 我们不大认识他。

This kind of plant is *rarely* found in this area. 在这个地区几乎找不到这类植物。

Very few people knew it. 几乎没有人(极少人)知道这件事。

Little remains to be done. 几乎没有什么可做的。

像 little 之类的半否定词后面可跟"or + 全否定词"以加强语气。

We know *little or nothing* about it. 我们几乎一点不知道这件事。

He *seldom or never* goes to see a film. 他很少甚至不去看电影。

(3) 部分否定

部分否定(Partial Negation)是局部地或在一定程度上否定一个事物的存在或真实性。它有四种常见的结构:

① 用含不定量意义的代词与 not 搭配

用 all, everyone, everything 等与否定词 not 搭配。

All that glitters is *not* gold. (= Not all that glitters is gold.) 闪光的未必都是金子。

Everyone in society does *not* work for money. (= Not everyone in society works for money.) 并不是社会所有的人都为金钱而工作。

Everything in our country is *not* perfect. (= Not everything in our country is perfect.) 在我国并非一切都十全十美。

Note:有些句子的否定范围要根据上下文来确定。虽然其否定结构形式像是"部分否定",但实际意义是"全部否定",带有 not even 的强调含义。

All the money in the world will *not* make you happy then. 纵使全世界的钱都给你也不会使你幸福。

② 用"限定词 + 名词"与 not 搭配

用 "all, both, every, many, much, some 等 + 名词" 与 not 搭配。

All his words are *not* credible. 他的话不完全可靠。

Both (*the*) *windows* are *not* open. 两扇窗子不是都开着。

There are *not many books* on the shelf. 书架上没有许多书。

There isn't *much food* in the house. 家里食物不多了。

Some young people don't like pop music. 有些青年不喜欢通俗音乐。

③ 用频度或程度副词与 not 搭配

用 always, often, fully, wholly, altogether, entirely 等与 not 搭配。

Don't always rely on your parents. 不要老是依赖父母。

She doesn't *often* go there in winter. 她冬天不常去那里。

She didn't *fully* understand me (= what I said). 她不完全懂我的话。

I *don't wholly* agree with him. 我不完全同意他。

Her work was *not entirely* a failure. 她的工作并不是完全失败。

④ 用 and 连接的同等成分与 not 搭配

这时,句中的 and 有 but 的意思。

He can *not* sing *and* dance. 他不会唱歌,但会跳舞。(不要错译成:他不会唱歌和跳舞。)

This film is *not* interesting *and* instructive. 这部电影没有趣味,但有教育意义。(不要错译成:这部电影没有趣味和教育意义。)

(4) 双重否定

我们都知道,否定是对肯定而言,肯定又是对否定而言。有时,一个句子里会出现两个否定,叫双重否定(Double Negation)。双重否定的常见句型有下面几种:

① 否定词 + 否定词

I *never* helped *nobody*. 我常常帮助别人。

I *can't not* obey. 我不能不服从。

No one has *nothing* to offer to society. 每个人对社会都不无贡献。

It was *not* for *nothing* that he spent three years studying the subject. 他花了三年时间研究这题目并非毫无收获。

Note:有时一个复合的两个分句都是否定句,其含义或相当于上述的"双重否定"结构,或只是一般否定陈述,要根据上下文加以区别。

It's *not* that I do *not* wish her well. 我并不是不希望她好。(双重否定)

I *don't* know why he *isn't* there. 我不知道他为什么不在那里。(一般否定陈述)

② 否定词 + 含否定意义的词

I was *not unprepared*. 我不是没有准备。

He is *not ignorant*. 他不是不知道。

Nothing is *impossible* to a willing heart. 世上无难事,只怕有心人。

The period of waiting was *not limitless*. 等候的时间不是无限的。

③ not(no) + without 短语

No one is *without* his faults. 人谁无过。

We can *not* see *without* eyes. 我们没有眼睛就看不见东西。

There is *no* gains *without* pains. 不劳则无获。(这个句型常用缩略形式:No gains without pains; No pains, no gains.)

④ there be + no + 主语 + but 从句

There is no man but has his faults. (= There is no man who does not have his faults.) 没有不犯错误的人(人谁无过)。

There is no rule but has exception. 没有无例外的规则。

There is no child but knows him. 每个小孩子都认识他。

Note:but 在此为关系代词,相当于是 that/who … not。

在早期英语中,有一种形式的双重否定,其表达的意义不是肯定,而是否定。办法是或删去一种否定,或将其中一个否定词语改为非断定词语。

I *don't never* go swimming in September.

→ I *never* go swimming in September. 我从不在 9 月份游泳。

Jane *doesn't* want *none* of that cake.

→ Jane *doesn't* want *any* of that cake. 约翰不想要那种蛋糕了。

⑤ 否定词 + so/too + 形容词/副词 + but 从句，否定词 + such a + 名词 + but 从句

No task is so difficult but we can finish it. 任务尽管再困难，我们总可以完成。
She is not such a fool but she can tell it. 她还会笨得连这个也不知道。

⑥ 否定词 … so/as … as

None are *so* blind *as* those who won't see. 瞎莫过于视而不见。
Nothing is *so* precious *as* time. 没有任何东西比光阴更可贵。

⑦ 否定词 + 表示否定意义的副词

You can *not/never/hardly/scarcely* be careful enough. (= You can not be sufficiently careful. = You can not take enough care.) 你越仔细越好。
One can *not* be *too* faithful *to* one's duties. 对自己的职责越忠实越好。

26.5 多余否定（赘言否定）

有时句中的否定结构并不表示否定意义，而是表示委婉的肯定。
I'm wondering if we *cannot* have another chance. 我不知道我们是否还有一次机会。
I am writing to ask for your help in seeing if the provisions of the agreement *cannot* be implemented. 特函请惠予关照协议条款可否在今后几周内实施。

26.6 含蓄否定

结构上是明显的肯定，但含义却是否定的，这被称为"含蓄否定"（Implicit Negation）。这种含蓄否定有以下几种情况：

(1) 用带否定含义的虚拟句和条件句表示

I wish I could go with you. (= I'm afraid I can't go with you.) 我多么希望我能和你一起去/但愿我能和你一起去。
I would discuss with you in more detail, but that I have something urgent to attend to. (= As I have something urgent to attend to, I can't discuss with you in more detail.) 要不是我有急事要去处理，我会和你更详细地商讨的。

(2) 用带否定含义的肯定句来表示

此多用于口语，常带有感情色彩。
God knows what has become of him. (= No one knows what has become of him.) 上帝知道他变成了啥样子。

(3) 用带否定含义的修辞性疑问句和感叹句来表示

Who would have thought of it? (= No one would have thought of it.) 谁还会想到它呢？
Would you do better if you were in my place? (= It would be impossible for you to do better if you were in my place.) 如果你处在我的地位你能干得更好吗？
Much I care! (= I don't care at all.) 我真是好管闲事。
If ever I hear the like! 我还听这一套！
I'll be damned if I'll go. (= I refuse to go. / I won't go.) 我要是去就是混账王八蛋。

26.7　如何加强否定的语气

（1）用"not + 最微量的词（组）"加强

I *don't* care *a bit*. 我一点也不在乎。
There is *not a jot of truth* in the story. 这个故事一点真实性也没有。
It's *not* worth *a farthing*. 它一文不值。
I *haven't* got *the slightest idea*. 我一点也不知道。
It *doesn't* matter *in the least*. 这一点关系也没有。

（2）用"It is not … that"句型加强

It is not he who laughs first that laughs best. 笑得最好的并不是笑得最早的。
It was not in the zoo that she met your sister yesterday. 她昨天不是在动物园碰到你妹妹的。

（3）用"not + 最大范围的词（组）"加强

No man on earth would ever believe it. 没有任何人会相信它。
No trouble in the world, I assure you. 我向你担保，一点问题也没有。
It makes *no difference at all*. 一点区别也没有。
Nothing in the world would please him more. 没有什么东西更能使他高兴。

（4）用"否定词 + 副词或副词（组）"加强

It *simply* will *not* do. 根本不行。
I *cannot possibly* allow it. 我绝对不允许。
He is *certainly not* qualified for teaching English. 他教英语肯定不够格。

（5）用"否定词 + whatever/whatsoever"加强

I *cannot* see anyone *whatever*. 我一个人也没看见。
There can be *no* doubt *whatever* about it. 对此事不容有怀疑。
No one whatever would believe it. 谁也不会相信。
You have *no reason whatsoever* to talk like that. 你毫无理由这样说话。

（6）用含否定意思的成语加强

His answer is *by no means* satisfactory. 他的答复一点也不令人满意。
He doesn't know algebra and geometry, *not to mention* calculus. 他连数学和几何都不懂，更不用说微积分了。
I will *in no wise* give up study. 我绝不放弃学习。

（7）用倒装句型加强否定

用倒装句型来加强语气是英语中常用的强调手法之一。当 no，not，never，seldom，little，hardly，rarely 等否定词或带有这些词的词组放在句首时，句子引起倒装，起到强调否定的作用。
Never shall I forget him. 我永远不会忘记他。（比较：I shall never forget him.）
Hardly could I recognize her. 我几乎认不出她来。（比较：I could hardly recognize her.）

Little do I know about him. 我对他几乎一无所知。（比较：I know little about him.）
Rarely did I see her. 我极少见她。（比较：I rarely saw her.）
Seldom do we meet each other. 我们很少见面。（比较：We seldom meet each other.）
Not for the life of me could I understand what they were talking about. 我无论如何也听不懂他们在谈什么。
（比较：I could not for the life of me understand what they were talking about.）

（8）用重复否定词语加强否定

用重复否定词语的方法加强语气，是指在一个否定词或否定句后，再加上一个或几个含有否定含义的词、词组或者句子，表示强调。

I'll *never* agree to this plan, *never*. 我绝不会同意这个计划，绝不。
There are *no* students in the classroom. None at all. 这教室里没学生，一个也没有。
"*No*, *no*, *no*," said the man quickly. 这男人连声快速地说："不，不，不。"
He does *not* go out for holidays, *not* even in summer. 他从不出去度假，甚至夏天也不出去。

26.8 两种转移否定

转移否定(Transferred Negation)主要指将语义上属于从句或谓语动词后的不定式的否定转移至主句或前面。

（1）主句中表示看法的动词的否定，其否定意义要转移到后面的宾语从句

如主句中的谓语动词是 anticipate, believe, calculate, expect, fancy, feel, guess, figure, imagine, presume, reckon, suppose, surmise（推测，猜测），think 等时，句子的否定实际上在后面的宾语从句上，即构成转移否定句型，表示"认为……不……"、"觉得……不……"之类的意思。口语中常用"转移否定"来否定动词后面的判断。当主句中主语为第一人称代词时，用"don't + 表示判断或看法的动词"。

I *don't think* (that) he is wrong. 我认为他没有错。
I *don't believe* he can fix the bike. 我认为他修不好这辆自行车。
I *don't suppose* it's the rush hour yet. 我想现在还不是交通拥挤的时间。
We *don't expect* he needs help. 我们想他不需要帮助。
She *doesn't feel* I can stand it much longer. 她觉得我不能再忍受下去了。
They *don't suppose* anyone will object to the plan. 他们想不会有谁反对这个计划。

下面的句子否定的不是宾语从句，而是动词不定式。在这种结构中，转移否定可以与特指否定转换。
He *didn't* expect to win.（转移否定）
= He expected *not* to win.（特指否定）他想不会赢。

（2）主句中的否定词 not 否定后边的状语

① 否定主句后的原因状语或原因状语从句

当主句是否定式谓语，后接表示原因的 because 从句或短语时，主从结构之间如无逗号分开，否定的重点很可能不是主句的谓语动词，而是 because 从句或表示原因的介词短语。这种句型通常可以转换成特指否定结构。

He *didn't* leave college because he was tired of learning.（= He left college not because he was tired of learning.）他退学并非因为他厌倦学习。
She *doesn't* teach because teaching is easy for her.（= She teaches not because teaching is easy for her.）她当

老师并非因为教学对她来说容易。

The machine does *not* stop in account of the shortage of oil. (= The machine stops not on account of the shortage of oil.) 机器并非因缺油而停转。

② **否定其他状语**

在一般否定句中，有时否定词虽然出现在谓语动词部分，但不是否定谓语动词本身，而是否定动词后面的状语。

She didn't go to school by bike. (= She went to school, but not by bike.) 她不是骑自行车上学。

I *don't* come here to hear your grievances. (= I come here not to hear your grievances.) 我不是到这里来听你发牢骚的。

③ **下述两种情况不用"转移否定"**

A. 某些表示判断或看法的动词不用"转移否定"

这些动词是 assume, fear, presume, surmise 等，它们在主句里面的否定只限于动词本身，不转移到后面的宾语从句。试比较：

I don't assume (that) he will came. 我不相信他会来。

I assume (that) he won't come. 我相信他不会来。

B. 有时限于固定的结构，如固定词组或固定含义，否定词只能用在从句中

误：I don't think that she can help laughing.

正：I think that she can't help laughing. 我想她会忍不住笑的。

误：I don't bet that he will repeat the story until he is compelled.

正：I bet that he won't repeat the story until he is compelled. 我确信，除非被迫他是不会复述这个故事的。

第 27 章 句子的省略

27.1 句子的省略概述

句子的省略,就是指省去句子中的某些词语,使表达趋于简单、明了。不管口头,还是书面,人们都喜欢用简洁的言语传递信息、表达感情。省略的作用除了节省笔墨和时间外,还能突出新信息,并使上下文的联系更紧密。节约词语的方法很多,如用省略(Ellipsis)、替代(Substitution),有时也用无动词句(Verbless Sentence)的表达形式来实现;而单词句和短语句中绝大多数句子也是省略句。省略应不引起误解,也就是说省略后的句子不能产生歧义,不然就不能省略。更具体地说,省略的原则有两个:被省略的词语必须要在上下文中找到或可以从语境中推断出来,或者可以根据分析语法结构后判断出来;在恢复被省略的词语后,句子结构必须要规范。

27.2 省略的类型

省略句的类型有语篇省略、语境省略和结构省略三种。语篇省略是指以上下文为依据的省略形式,也就是说被省略的词语是在上文出现过的;语境省略是以语言环境为依据的省略,也就是说,被省略的词语可以从语言环境中看出来;结构省略是指以语法结构为依据的省略,也就是说,按照语法结构来说,在一定情况下,限定词、连词、关系词、介词等可以省略。

(1) 语篇省略

His son is a teacher and his daughter (is) a doctor. 他的儿子是教师,他的女儿是医生。
Tom works in a factory and his brother (works) on a farm. 汤姆在工厂工作,他弟弟在农场工作。
I can (speak English), and Bob certainly can speak English. 我能说英语,鲍勃当然也能讲英语。
Jane washed (the shirts), Mary ironed (the shirts), and Alice folded the shirts. 简洗衬衣,玛丽熨衬衣,艾丽丝叠衬衣。
She will drive to (London), but (she will) fly back from London. 她将开车到伦敦,但乘飞机回来。
He was a friend to (the party leader), and (he was) a supporter of the party leader. 他是那个党的领导人的朋友,也是他的支持者。
从上述例句可见,例句1、2的省略在上文中出现过,例句3、4的省略词语在后面出现,例句5、6的被省略词语交错出现在上文和下文中。

(2) 语境省略

下面这些句子属语境省略,被省掉的词语很容易加进去。
(I) Thank you for your gift. (我)谢谢你的礼物。
(Do you) Want coffee or tea? (你)要咖啡还是茶?
(It) Serves you right. 你活该。

(3) 结构省略

It is impossible (that) they will finish the work within a week. 他们在一周内完成这工作不可能的。
I hope (that) you won't do that again. 我希望你不要再那样做了。
That's the university (which) we visited yesterday. 那就是我们昨天参观的那所大学。
Tom left (at) about four o'clock this morning. 汤姆今天早晨大约4点钟就走了。

27.3　省略在具体句中的体现

(1) 简单句中的省略情况

① 在口语中出现时

在口语中，不管是回答别人的问话，还是在接着别人说话时做出的回答，都会出现这种省略情况。

{ —How are you getting on with your work? 你的工作进行得如何？
　—*Pretty well*. 还不差。

{ —Where are you going? 你上哪儿去了？
　—*To the library*. 到图书馆去。

{ —Are you tired? 你累吗？
　—*Not very*. 不太累。

{ —The film was very touching. 这部电影很动人。
　—*Yes, and very instructive too*. 是的，而且很有教育意义。

{ —I have finished writing an article about English Syntax. 我已写好了一篇关于英语句法方面的文章。
　—*Really*? 真的？

{ —Mike won't come to the party tonight. 麦克今晚不来参加晚会了。
　—*Why*? 为什么？

② 向人提出要求或问题时

在向人提出要求或提出问题时，用简单句多，而且用省略句很常见。

Anybody in? (= Is there anybody in?) 里面有人吗？

{ —Mary, right? 玛丽，对吗？
　—*Wrong*. 错。

{ —Had your lunch? (= Have you had your lunch?) (你)吃过中饭了吗？
　—*Why not*? 为什么没吃呢？

③ 陈述自己的意见时

在陈述自己的意见的时候，基本上都要用省略的陈述句。

(I, We) Hope to go there with you. 希望与你一起去那里。
(I am) Glad to meet you. 见到你很高兴。
(It is a) Nice day again. 又是个好天气。

④ 在祈使句、命令句、感叹句中

很多命令句和感叹句是省略句，而其中又有很多是无动词句。

(You) Come here. (你)过来。
A good idea! (= It is a good idea!) 好主意！

Hats off! (= You put your hats off!)脱帽!

How interesting! (= How interesting it is!)多么有趣啊!

(I'm old.) You (are) old? (You are) Not a bit of it! (我老了。)你老了?(你)一点也不老!

上面例句2、3、4、5是无动词句,例句1不是,因come是保留下来的谓语动词。

⑤ 在"表示提议的句子"中

表示提议的how about, what about 也是典型的省略句,也叫无动词特殊疑问句。

How (do you think) about going out for a walk? 出去散散步怎么样?

What (do you think) about the election? (你认为)这次选举怎么样?

(2) 并列句中的省略情况

省略在并列句中出现得很多。在并列句中,有两个或更多的分句含有相同的词语时,无论在句中作什么成分,为了避免重复,往往只保留一处而把其余的那些省去。

① 被省略部分的位置

A. 多数情况省略后面的

通常保留前面分句中的词语而把后面的省去。

They left for Nanjing yesterday and we shall (leave for Nanjing) tomorrow. 他们昨天去了南京,而我们明天去。

I can't see you today, but I can (see you) tomorrow. 我今天不能见你,但我明天可以。

B. 省略前面的

有时,也可以保留后面分句中的词语而把前面的省去。

Mike might have been (writing letters), and Peter certainly was, writing compositions. 麦克也许在写信,彼得肯定在写作文。

Jim is (playing for the school), and George may be, playing for the school. 吉姆在为这所学校打球,乔治也许也要为这所学校打球。

C. 交错省略

They can (pay the full fee) and (they) should pay the full fee, but (they) won't (pay the full fee). 他们能够而且应该付全费,但他们却不(付全费)。

D. 并列复合句中的省略

Mr. White didn't see who spoke to her, but (he saw) who took her away. 怀特先生没有看见谁跟她说话,但他看见谁把她带走了。

We tried to help him when he was in trouble, but (we tried) in vain (to help him). 他有困难时,我们曾设法帮助他,但没有用。

② 并列句中的省略内容

A. 省去主语

这样的情况是把并列句变为含有并列谓语的简单句。

Rose may see you tomorrow or (she) may phone you later in the day. 罗丝或许明天来看你,或许今天晚些时候给你打个电话。

Her brother didn't like it, yet (he) said nothing. 她弟弟不喜欢那东西,但他什么也没有说。

Agues come on horseback, but (agues) go away on foot. 病来如山倒,病去如抽丝。

B. 省去表语

She seemed angry, and her husband certainly was (angry). 她好像生气了,她丈夫肯定生气了。

She looked (tired), and (she) indeed was, tired. 她看来(疲倦了),也确实疲倦了。

He was at Oxford, but his brother wasn't (at Oxford). 他在牛津大学读书,但他弟弟没有。

You were (my teacher), are (my teacher), and (you) will still be my teacher. 你以前是,现在是,将来仍然是我的老师。

C. 省去整个谓语

No one can do it but she (can do it). 没有人能干这种活,但她会。(除她之外没有人能干这种活)

Are you going or (is) Henley (going)? 你去还是翰里去?

They are all wrong but Peter (is not wrong). 他们都错了,但彼得没有错。(除彼得之外他们都错了)

但有时省去谓语可以把并列句变为含有并列主语的简单句。

Is Mary or (is) John going? 是玛丽还是约翰去?

D. 省去连系动词和表语

John was the winner in 1970 and Bob (was the winner) in 1971. 约翰是1970年的获胜者,鲍勃是1971年的获胜者。

The administration seems obstinate in our school and the teachers (seem obstinate) in your school. 我们学校当局似乎很固执,你们学校的老师似乎也固执。

有时还可以连同主语一起省去。

It's cold in December in England, but (it's cold) in July in New Zealand. 英国12月很冷,而新西兰7月很冷。

E. 省去谓语动词及其短语,保留情态动词或助动词

John needn't stay here, but George must (stay here). 约翰不必留在这里,但乔治必须留在这里。

I can't do it, nor can he (do it), nor can anybody (do it). 这事我不会做,他也不会,任何人都不会做。

He likes cheese, but his family doesn't (like cheese). 他喜欢奶酪,但他家里人不喜欢。

He has got the right answer but I haven't (got the right answer). 他找到了正确答案,但我还没有。

Peter might have been writing letters, and John certainly was (writing letters). 彼得也许在写信,约翰肯定在写信。

F. 省去助动词、情态动词和半助动词

They were having a meeting and we (were) watching TV. 他们在开会,我们在看电视。

John must clear the shed and Peter (must) read the book. 约翰必须打扫车库,彼得必须看书。

Mary will be playing the guitar and John (will be) preparing the supper. 玛丽将要弹吉他,约翰将要做晚饭。

下面是一小节关于读书的名言,其中省去的全是 are:

Some books are to be tasted, others (are) to be swallowed, and some few (are) to be chewed and digested; that is, some books (are) to be read only in parts; others (are) to be read, but not curiously; and some few (are) to be read wholly, and with diligence and attention. 书有可浅尝者,有可吞食者,少数则须咀嚼消化。换言之,有只需读其部分者,有只需大体涉猎而不必细读者,少数则须全读,读时须全神贯注,孜孜不倦。

G. 省去谓语动词而保留宾语或其补足语

a. 保留宾语

Peter likes Mary, but Paul (likes) Joan. 彼得喜欢玛丽,保尔喜欢琼。

John has written a poem and Bob (has written) a short story. 约翰写了一首诗,鲍勃写了一个小故事。

Yesterday John was given a railway set, and Sue (was given) a doll. 昨天约翰得到了一套铁路玩具,苏得到了一个洋娃娃。

Bob will interview some candidates this morning and (Bob will interview) Peter this afternoon. 鲍勃今天上午将会见一些候选人,下午将会见彼得。

b. 有时只保留宾语补足语

Histories make men wise; poets, (make men) witty; the mathematics, (makes men) subtle; natural philosophy, (makes men) deep; moral, (makes men) grave; logic and rhetoric, (makes men) able to contend. 读史使人明智,读诗使人聪慧,数学使人精细,自然科学使人深思,伦理学使人庄重,逻辑学和修辞学使人善辩。

H. 省去谓语动词(和宾语),保留状语

Truth speaks too low, hypocrisy (speaks) too loud. 真理的声音太低,伪善的声音太高。

Mary's brother is going to Paris and Mary (is going) to Rome. 玛丽哥哥到巴黎,她到罗马。

She will cook the meals today and her sister (will cook the meals) tomorrow. 她今天做饭,她妹妹明天做饭。

I. 省去主语和谓语的主要部分

a. 只保留宾语

Now she says this, now (she says) that. 她一会儿说这,一会儿说那。

I speak German pretty well and (I speak) a little French. 我德语说得好,也会说一点法语。

She has promised John a book, (she has promised) Bill a watch and (she has promised) Mary a doll. 她答应给约翰一本书,给比尔一只手表,给玛丽一个洋娃娃。

We are not afraid of hardships, nor (are we afraid of) death. 我们一不怕苦,二不怕死。

A short essay cannot aim at completeness, still less (can it aim at) exhaustiveness. 一篇短短的文章不能要求面面俱到,更不用说详尽无遗了。

b. 只保留状语

She came at last and thank goodness, (she came) all smiles. 她终于来了,而且,谢天谢地,还满面笑容。

Mary is flying to Madrid tonight and (Paul is flying) to Athens next week. 玛丽今晚飞往马德里,保尔下周飞往雅典。

He walked along cheerfully, sometimes (he walked) at full speed, sometimes (he walked) slowly. 他兴高采烈地走着,时而健步如飞,时而慢慢腾腾。

c. 有时只保留情态动词和助动词

He can (demand repayment) and (he) will demand repayment. 他可以而且会要求偿还。

They could (have saved more), and (they) should have saved more. 他们可以而且应该节省更多一些。

The document could have (been signed), and (the document) should have been signed. 这文件可以而且应该签字。

They can pay the full fee, and (they) certainly should (pay the full fee), but (they) probably won't (pay the full fee). 他们能够付全费,他们也应该这样做,但他们大概不会。

J. 省去(介词)宾语

He likes (smoking), and I hate, smoking. 他喜欢抽烟,我讨厌抽烟。

My father planned (all these houses) and my brother built all these houses. 我父亲规划而我哥建造了所有这些房子。

John crawled under (the fence), but Bill climbed over, the fence. 约翰从栅栏底下爬过去,比尔从栅栏上面翻过去。

K. 省去主语和(介词)宾语,把并列句变成含有并列谓语动词的简单句

Mark leads (us), (he) educates (us) and (he) stimulates us. 马克领导我们,教育我们,鼓励我们。

Li Ming walked up (the hill) and (he) ran down the hill. 李明向山上走去,然后跑下山来。

He may be above forty, but (he may) not (be) below (forty). 他的年纪可能在40岁以上,不会在40岁以下。

L. 省去状语或状语从句

Peter works (in London), and Bob lives in London. 彼得在伦敦工作,鲍勃在伦敦居住。

John spoke (rudely), and Jim answered rudely. 约翰说话粗鲁,吉姆回答也粗鲁。
I shall certainly object if they show the slides again, and you should object too (if they show the slides again). 如果他们再放幻灯片,我要反对,你也应该反对。

M. 省去名词短语的中心词

I prefer Dutch cheese and Mary prefers Danish (cheese). 我喜欢荷兰的奶酪,玛丽喜欢丹麦的奶酪。
He wore the blue shirt, but the white (shirt) suits him better. 他穿了那件蓝衬衣,但这件白衬衣更适合他。
Last year the number of middle schools in the town increased from twenty to twenty-five, (the number) of primary schools (increased) from forty to fifty. 去年,这个城镇的中学从 20 所增加到 25 所,小学从 40 所增加到 50 所。

N. 省去定语

Some of uranium atoms weigh 234 units, some (of uranium atoms weigh) 235 units, and some (of uranium atoms weigh) 238 units. 铀原子有的重 234 单位,有的重 235 单位,有的重 238 单位。
In 1988, the output of steel in this region amounted to 20 percent of the whole country, (the output) of coal (in this region amounts to) 25 percent (of the whole country). 1988 年,这个地区的钢产量占全国的 20%,煤产量占 25%。

Q. 主语、动词(谓语)、宾语一起省

一般情况下,在回答问题和并列句的第二分句中,主语、动词(谓语)和宾语可以同时省掉,而只留下副词、副词短语、动词不定式短语、过去分词或介词短语。

{—Do you like Lu Xun? 你喜欢鲁迅的文章吗?
—Greatly. (=I like Lu Xun greatly.) 非常喜欢。

{—Will you take a walk with us after supper? 你晚饭后愿不愿跟我们一起去散步?
—Not today. (=I shall not take a walk with you today.) 今天不去。

Bob wanted to pay for the tickets but not for the dinner. (=… but Bob did not want to pay for the dinner) 巴勃想要付票钱,但不想付饭钱。
很清楚,上面例句 3 是并列句中的第二分句省掉了主语、动词(谓语)和宾语(to pay),结果整个句子已成了一个简单句,but not for the dinner 仅是个状语而已。

③ 省去第一分句中的主谓语

这样以后就成了"名词短语+and+陈述句"句型;这里的名词短语是无动词分句的省略形式。
(We make) One more effort and we shall succeed. 再加一把劲,我们就会成功。
(Walk) One more step and you will fail. 再往前走一步,你就会摔下去。
A few minutes (had passed) and he lay asleep. 几分钟(过后)他就睡着了。

(3) 复合句中省略情况

为避免重复,在复合句中也可以省去能从上下文看出的词语。当然复合句中的省略有时出现在主句中,有时出现在从句中。

① 主句中的省略

A. 在答语中可以省去整个主句而保留从句

{—Where is my coat? 我的外衣在哪里?
—(It's) Where you left it. 在你原来放的地方。

{—When shall we begin? 我们什么时候开始?
—(You may begin) Whenever you like. 随便你们。

{―What shall we do? 我们做什么?
―(You can do) What you like. 随便你们。

{―Will you come? 你来吗?
―(I will come) If I have time. 有时间我就来。

B. 在口语中，主语是第一人称特别是 I 时，常常省去；如果谓语动词是 be，那连同 be 一起省去

(I) Don't know when it happened. （我）不知道事情什么时候发生的。

(I) Hope you'll like it. （我）希望你喜欢(它)。

(I'm) Sorry I've given you so much trouble. 对不起，(我)给你带来了这么多麻烦。

{―Will this do? 这行吗?
―(I'm) Afraid (it will) not (do). 恐怕不行。

C. 口语中的形式主语常和连系动词 be 一起省去

(It is) (A) Shame you can't stay for dinner. 很遗憾，你不能留下来吃饭。

(It is a) Pity (that) he can't swim. 可惜他不会游泳。

(It is) No wonder that he has succeeded. 难怪他成功了。

D. 在口语中，存在句的形式主语 there 常和谓语动词 be 一起省去

(Is there) Anything I can do for you? 我能为你效劳吗?

(Is there) Anything wrong with the car? 车子出什么毛病了?

(There is) No one but knows that. 没有人不知道那件事。

E. 在对话中，主句中与上文相同的部分常常省去

{―How are you getting along with your roommate? 你与你的室友相处得怎样?
―(I am) Not (getting along) so well as I expected. 没有我预料得好。

{―Does she have any books on physics? 她有物理方面的书吗?
―(She does) Not (have) any (books on physics) as I know. 据我所知，她没有。

{―Are you going to the party? 你要去参加聚会吗?
―(I'm) Not (going to the party) unless I'm invited. 不去，除非他们邀请我。

F. 从句在前、主句在后时，也可以省去主句中和从句相同的词语

If Mary will go, I will (go). 如果玛丽愿意去，我就去。

If he won't go, neither shall I (go). 如果他不愿意去，我也不去。

If she says she will come, she will (come). 如果她说要来，她会来的。

G. 关系副词引导的定语从句的先行项有时可以省去，省去后定语从句变成了宾语从句或表语从句

Let me know (the time) when you will come. 告诉我你什么时候来。

Do you know (the place) where they met? 你知道他们见面的地方吗?

That is (the reason) why we have succeeded. 那就是我们成功的原因。

H. 一些不及物动词、形容词和名词后的介词常和形式主语 it 一起省去，使介词宾语从句变成动词宾语从句、形容词宾语从句或同位语从句

We must see (to it) that the plan is carried out. 我们一定要设法实现这个计划。（变成动词宾语从句）

She was not aware (of it) that her daughter joined the army. 她不知道她女儿参军了。（变成形容词宾语从句）

There is no doubt (about it) that they will attend the meeting. 毫无疑问他们会参加会议。（变成同位语从句）

I. 省去整个主句

这种句子常是祝愿祈使句，表示和事实相反或不能实现的愿望。

a. 由(oh)that引导的句子：这种句子实际上省去了 I wish 或 how I wish。

(I wish) That I could go with you. 要是我能和你们一起去就好了。

(How I wish)That he were still alive! 要是他还活着就好了!
Oh (I wish) that he were here! 啊,要是他在这儿就好了!
Oh! (I wish) that I had but known! 啊! 要是我早知道就好了!
Note:上述情况中,如把连词 that 省去,需要用倒装语序。
Oh, were he only alive! (=Oh, I wish that he were only alive!) 啊,要是他还活着就好了。
Had I followed your advice! (=I wish that I had followed your advice!) 要是我听了你的话就好了!
b. 由 if (…) only 引导的句子:这种句子实际上省去了主句 how nice it would be 之类的句子。
Oh, (how nice it would be) if he could only come! 啊,要是他能够来该多好啊!
(How nice it would be) If only it would stop raining! 要是雨停了该多好啊!
(How nice it would be) If only he had seen me! 要是他看见我该多好啊!
(How nice it would be) If only he had arrived in time! 要是他按时到了该多好啊!
c. "oh+不定式短语"句子:这种句子实际上省去了 how I wish。
Oh, (how I wish) to be young again! 啊! 要是能再年轻就好了!
Oh, (how I wish) to be in England now that April's there! 啊,要是能回到现在已是4月的英国就好了!
d. 不定式感叹句:这种句子实际上省去了 I am astonished 或 it surprises me。
- to think + that 从句

(I am astonished) To think that you are so careless! 没想到你这样粗心大意!
(It surprises me) To think that all the money has been wasted! 没有想到所有的钱都被浪费掉了!
You people! (I am astonished) To think we have to support your kind with taxes! 你们这些人! 想想看,我们竟然得纳税养活你们这种人!
- "to think of + v-ing 分词短语"等句子

(I am astonished) To think of his having heard nothing of the news! 没想到他对这消息竟然一无所知!
(It surprises me) To think of your leaving us so soon! 没想到你们这么快就要离开我们!
(It surprises me) To think of all the money that he has! 没想到他有那么多钱!

② **名词从句中的省略**

A. 省去整个宾语从句

在答语中有时可以省去整个宾语从句。

{—Is she an engineer? 她是工程师吗?
 —I don't know (whether she is an engineer or not). 我不知道。

{—What did Mr. White say at the meeting? 怀特先生在会上说了什么?
 —I won't tell you (what Mr. White said at the meeting). 我不告诉你。

{—Where does he live? 他住在哪里?
 —He told me (where he lives), but I forget (where he lives). 他告诉过我,但我忘了。

B. 在宾语从句中保留 wh- 词

有时,由 wh- 词引导的宾语从句可以省去从句而只保留 wh- 词。
The yellow coat must be one of the boys', but I don't know whose (it is). 那黄衣服一定是那些男孩子中的一个的,但我不知道是谁的。
Mr White used my bike, but I don't know when (he used my bike). 怀特先生用过我的自行车,但我不知道是什么时候。
Please hand me one of those novels, I don't care which (you hand me). 请把那些小说中的一本递给我,无论哪本都行。
Bober has gone, no one knows where (he has gone). 鲍勃走了,没有人知道他上哪里去了。

They don't agree, but I wonder why (they don't agree). 他们不同意，我不知道为什么。

I'd like to help him, but we don't know how (we should help him). 我想帮助他，但我们不知道应该怎样帮助他。

C. 从句中省去与主句中相同词语

在宾语从句中可以省去与主句相同的部分的词语。

You may take whichever seat you like (to take). 你喜欢坐哪个座位就可以坐哪个座位。

You may give it to whomever you like (to give it to). 你喜欢把它给谁就给谁。

D. as 表语从句中可省去主语

as 引导的表语从句可以省去一些成分，通常是主语 what。

The chief reasons are as (what) follows. 主要理由如下。

His arguments are as (what) follows. 他的论点如下。

E. 从句中表示虚拟的 should 可省略

在名词性从句中，should 的省略主要用于虚拟语气句，从句中的谓语动词应该用"should + 动词原形"，但有时 should 可以省略，只用动词原形，其省略有以下四种情况：

a. 在谓语动词是 advise, insist, move, order, propose, suggest, urge 等表示"提议"、"建议"、"命令"、"要求"等意义的动词的宾语从句中 should 常被省去。

We *move* that the money *be used* for library books. 我们提议这笔钱用于图书馆购书。

I *suggest* that the work *be completed* by 12 o'clock. 我建议12点之前完成工作。

He *urged* that the library *be kept* open during the vacation. 他极力主张放假期间图书馆继续开放。

b. 当主语是 demand, advice, order, proposal, suggestion 等名词时，其后的表语从句中 should 常省去。

My *demand* is that you *finish* the work as quickly as possible. 我要求你尽快完成工作。

Their *proposal* is that the machine *be stopped* at once. 他们建议立即关闭这台机器。

c. 在 demand, advice, order, proposal, suggestion 等名词后的同位语从句中 should 常省去。

We gave the *order* that the test *be finished* before 6. 我们命令6点钟之前完成试验。

She made a *suggestion* that the new electronic instrument *be tested* at once. 她建议立刻检验这台新电子仪器。

d. 在 It is essential/(very) important/natural/necessary/proposed/suggested that ... 等表示意愿、主张、建议或命令的主语从句中 should 常省去。

It was *essential* that a change *be made* in the plan. 变更计划是必要的。

It is *very important* that an engineer *have* a wide knowledge of science and technology. 工程师要有广泛的科学技术知识是非常重要的。

It is *necessary* that he *learn* more from his master. 他要多向他的师傅学习是必要的。

③ 定语从句中的省略

关系词 as 引导的定语从句可以省去一些成分。

Such women as she (is) are rare. 她这样的人很少见。

He is as good a creature as (anyone) can be. 他是一个再好不过的人。

Rose gave the same answer as (she had given) before. 罗丝的回答和以前一样。

Robbie looked just the same as (he) ever did. 罗比看起来和往常一样。

④ 时间状语从句中的省略

A. 当从句的主语和主句的主语相同时

这时，从句里的主语可以连同动词 be(连系动词或助动词)一起省去。

When (we are) speaking English, we should pay attention to your intonation. 讲英语时,我们要注意语调。
While (I was) ready to help him, I wonder what he needed most. 我准备帮助他时却不知道他最需要的是什么。
Once (you are) combined with the masses, you will have inexhaustible strength. 一旦和群众结合,你就会有无穷的力量。

Note: 并非所有的状语从句都可以省略主语和 be 动词,由 after, because, before 等引导的状语从句一般要改写成介词短语等,用动名词代替 be 动词。

⎧ After he was killed, he was thrown away into the sea. 被害后他被扔进了大海。
⎨ After killed, he was thrown away into the sea. (误)
⎩ After being killed, he was thrown away into the sea. (正)

⎧ Because he was ill, he didn't attend the meeting. 由于生病,他没参加会议。
⎪ Because ill, he didn't attend the meeting. (误)
⎨ Because of being ill, he didn't attend the meeting. (正)
⎩ Being ill, he didn't attend the meeting. (正)

B. 从句的主语是具有指示意义代词 it 时
这时,可以和连系动词 be 一起省去。
We'll ask you to help us when (it is) necessary. 必要时我们要找你帮助。
I will certainly help you when (it is) possible. 可能的时候我一定会帮助你。

C. 主语是泛指的 we 或 you 时,也可以和动词 be 一起省去
It is safest, when (we are) in doubt, to remain silent. 拿不准的时候,什么也不说最保险。
A good way of learning English is to spend holidays in English-speaking countries, and while (you are) there, to stay if you can with an English family. 学英语的一个好办法是到说英语的国家去度假,在那儿,如果可能的话,就和一家说英语的人住在一起。

D. 主从句主谓语不同,从句中的主语与 be 也可省去
有时从句和主句的主语不同,在不引起误解的情况下,从句的主语和动词 be 也可以省去。
She told the children not to talk while (they were) eating. 她叫孩子们吃饭时不要讲话。
The teacher adviced the students to pay attention to grammar when (they are) speaking English. 老师叫学生说英语时要注意语法。

⑤ **地点状语从句中的省略**

A. 当从句和主句相同、谓语动词是 be 时
在从句的主语(指同主语)和主句的主语相同时,从句中的主语和连系动词或助动词一起省去。
Repairs will be made wherever (they are) necessary. 需要修理的地方都要修理。
The river is smooth where (it is) deep. 水深静流。

B. 当从句的主语是具有指示意义代词 it 时
此时可以和连系动词 be 一起省去。
Put in an article where (it is) necessary. 在必要的地方加上冠词。
Wherever (it was) possible we planted trees. 凡是能种树的地方我们都种了树。

⑥ **结果状语从句中的省略**
在口语中,以 so ... that, such ... that 引导的结果状语从句中的 that 可以省去。
I've been so busy these days (that) I could not even look after you. 这些天我忙得甚至都未能照看你。
Jane was so surprised she couldn't say a word. 简吃惊得一句话也说不出来。
It's such a good chance you mustn't miss it. 这样好的机会你一定不能错过。

⑦ since 引导的原因状语从句中的省略

由 since 引导的原因状语从句的主语和主句的主语相同时,可以连同动词 be(连系动词或助动词)一起省略。

Her nasty remarks are all the more insulting since (they are) intentional. 她那些恶毒的话,既然是有意的,就更有侮辱性。

Since (it is) agreed on by the majority, this plan will be carried out. 既然这个方案是多数人同意的,就一定要实行。

⑧ 条件状语从句中的省略

A. 当从句的主语和主句的主语相同时,可以连同动词 be(连系动词或助动词)一起省去。

If (you are) in doubt, don't hesitate to ask me. 如有怀疑就问我,不要客气。

I won't go unless (I am) invited. 我不去,除非请我。

The day, if (it is) well employed, is long enough for everything. 白天的时间如果利用得当,做什么事情都够了。

B. 当主句在前、从句在后时,常常省去从句谓语中与主句相同的部分。

She will tell him if you don't (tell him). 如果你不告诉他,她就告诉他。

I could do it if I would (do it). 要是我愿意的话,我做得到。

I'd like to go now if I may (go now). 如果可以的话,我想现在就走。

C. 有时从句在前、主句在后,也常常省去从句谓语中与主句相同的部分。

If I can (do it), I'll do it. 如果我做得来,我就做。

If they can (do that), they will do that. 如果他们能做那事,他们就做了。

D. 当从句的主语和主句的主语相同时,可以把主语和谓语的主要部分省去而保留状语。

We must go now, if (we) ever (go). 如果要去,我们现在就得走。

We shall meet on Saturday, if (we do) not (meet) on Friday. 我们如果星期五不见面,星期六将要见面。

E. 当从句的主语是具有指示意义代词 it 时,可以和连系动词 be 一起省去。

I'll drop in if (it is) possible. 如果可能的话,我顺便来一下。

I'll be there at four if (it is) necessary. 如有必要,我四点钟到那里。

F. 当从句是存在句时,常常把 there be 省去。

Errors, if (there are) any, should be corrected. 如果有错误,就应该改正。

Defects in the machine parts, if (there are) any, can be detected by this new-type instrument. 机器内部的缺陷,如果有的话,可以用这种新型仪器检查出来。

G. 在下面这些表示强调的习惯用法中,总是省去和主句相同的部分。

He measures eight feet, if an inch (= if he measures an inch). 他的确有 8 英尺高。

He is sixty, if a day (= if he is a day old). 他肯定有 60 岁了。

We have come three miles, if a yard (= if I have come a yard). 我们肯定走了 3 英里了。

H. 精练的谚语常常采用省略句的形式。

通常前面是省略形式的条件状语从句,后面是省略形式的主句。

Once bitten, twice shy. (= If one is bitten once, he will be shy twice.) 一朝被蛇咬,十年怕井绳。

(If one is) Sound in body, (he is) sound in mind. 身体强壮,精神健康。

(If you take) No pains, (you will make) no gains. 没有辛苦,就没有收获。

I. 在一定的语言环境中也可以把整个从句省去。

You might have stayed a few days longer (if you had wanted). (要是你愿意的话,)也许你能多住几天。

I wouldn't do that (if I were in your position). (要是我处在你的位置上,)我可不会那样做。

⑨ 目的状语从句中的省略

A. 在以 lest, for fear that 引导的目的状语从句中，情态动词 should 常被省略。

Every attention must be paid to her, lest she feel that she is inferior to any other friends. 一定要殷勤款待她，以免她感到自己的身份低于其他朋友。

These inquiries should be careful lest important data be overlooked. 要仔细进行调查，以免忽略了重要资料。

Let's hurry up for fear that we miss the meeting. 咱们快一点以免错过会议。

B. 以 for fear that, so that 引导的目的状语从句中可以省略 that。

Shut the window for fear (that) it may rain. 关上窗子以防下雨。

We all seemed afraid to say what was in our minds, for fear (that) it might start trouble. 我们似乎都害怕说出心里话，唯恐惹祸。

We read history so (that) we may repeat historical mistakes no longer. 我们研究历史，目的是不再重犯历史上的错误。

⑩ 让步状语从句中的省略

A. 由 though/although 引导的从句可以省略主语和谓语。

由 though 和 although 引导的让步状语从句中的主语和主句的主语相同时，可以连同动词 be(连系动词或助动词)一起省去。

Although (she is) still young, she is going very grey. 虽然她还年轻，但头发白了很多。

An ass is but an ass though (it is) laden with gold. 驴就是驴，即使驮的是金子。

Although (he was) seriously wounded, he flatly refused to quit the battle field. 他虽然身负重伤，却坚决不下火线。

B. 由 if 或 even if 引导的从句可以省去和主句相同的部分。

He seldom, if (he) ever (does), falls ill. 他几乎从不生病。

There are few, if (there are) any (mistakes), mistakes in the composition. 这篇文章几乎没有错误。

C. 由 -ever 的强调式 wh-词引导的从句也可以省去一些相同的部分。

Whatever the cause (may be), the result is certain. 无论原因是什么，结果是肯定的。

He always gets up early in the morning, whatever the weather (might be). 无论天气如何，他早上总是起得很早。

All countries, however small (they are), should enjoy equal rights. 所有国家，无论它们多么小，都应当享有平等的权利。

D. 由 no matter 加 wh-词引导的从句也可以省去一些成分。

You must return this book to me no matter when (you return it to us). 不管什么时候，你必须把这本书还给我。

Anyone, no matter who (he is), may point out our shortcomings. 无论什么人都可以指出我们的缺点。

E. 由 whether ... or 引导的从句也可以省去一些相同的部分。

His opinion, whether (it is) right or wrong, should be considered. 他的意见，不管对不对，都应该考虑。

This substance does not dissolve in water whether (it is) heated or not. 这种物质，无论加热与否，都不溶于水。

F. 在一定的语言环境中，甚至可以省去整个从句。

I couldn't go there (even if I wanted to go there). 我不能到那里去(即使我想去)。

We can't be too careful (no matter how careful we may be). 我们越细心越好(无论我们多么细心都不为过)。

⑪ 比较状语从句中的省略

比较状语从句通常是省略句,好多句子成分都可能在一定的语境下省去。

A. 省去主语

He is as diligent as (anyone) can be. 他勤奋极了。

Aren't you a little better than (you were) when I saw you last? 你现在不是比我上次看见你的时候好一点了吗?

You arrived earlier than (it was) usual/necessary (for you to arrive). 你到得比你平时(必须)到达的时间早些。

B. 省去谓语

John is taller than Tom (is). 约翰比汤姆高。

Facts speak louder than eloquence (does). 事实胜于雄辩。

She can tell you about it better than I can (tell you about it). 这事她能比我跟你说得更清楚。

C. 省去表语

It isn't as cold as it was (cold) yesterday. 今天没有昨天冷。

His son is more attentive in class now than he was (attentive) last year. 他儿子现在在课堂上比去年专心一些了。

D. 省去主语、谓语的一部分,有时可以保留谓语动词的一部分

She was more frightened than (she was) hurt. 她被吓得厉害,伤到没有受到。

His delight can be more easily conceived than (it can be) described. 他的快乐容易意会,难以言传。

有时可以保留表语。

Her son is as wise as (he is) brave. 她儿子既聪明又勇敢。

She is more thirsty than (she is) hungry. 她不是饿而是口渴。

E. 保留宾语

Her father speaks Russian better than (he speaks) French. 她父亲的俄语比法语说得好。

He is fond of work than (he is fond) of play. 他爱好工作胜过爱好玩耍。

F. 保留定语

Correct speech is less a matter of grammatical rules than (it is a matter) of clear thinking. 正确的讲话与其说是语法规则的问题,不如说是思路清楚的问题。

This is as a good chance to learn oral English as (it is a chance) to train our hearing. 这是学习口语的好机会,也是训练听力的好机会。

G. 保留状语

It is nearly as cold as (it was cold) yesterday. 今天差不多和昨天一样冷。

We can get there earlier by train than (we can get there) by boat. 我们坐火车比坐船能更早到达那里。

H. 有时可省去宾语

She got more than (what) she had asked for. 她得到的比她要求的还多。

I won't say more than (what) I know. 我不知道的事情我不会说。

I. 在一定的语环境中,也可以省去包括连词在内的整个比较状语从句

Does he feel better now (than he did before)? 他现在感觉好些了吗?

There can be no truer word (than that is). 这话再对不过了。

He is as strong as you, and works as hard (as you do). 他和你一样健壮,工作一样努力。

⑫ 方式状语从句中的省略

A．从句的主语和主句的主语相同时，可以连同动词 be（连系动词或助动词）一起省去。
He opened his mouth as if (he were) to speak. 他张开嘴，好像要说话似的。
Everything went off as (it was) planned. 一切都按计划进行。
B．as 引导的方式状语从句常常省去一些成分。
The nation rose as one man (would rise). 全国一致奋起。
You may spell the word as (you spell it) in French. 你可以按法语拼法拼写这个词。
You had better manage business as (you did) before. 你最好像以前那样经营这生意。
He remained, as he had been (a great lover of sport) in his youth, a great lover of sport. 他还像青年时代那样非常爱好运动。

⑬ **在用作状语的独立分词结构中的省略**
The meeting (being) over, the delegates walked out of the hall. 会议结束后，代表们走出大厅。
The work (having been) done, she left the office. 工作完成之后，她离开了办公室。

第 28 章　句子的替代

28.1　句子的替代概述

替代(Substitution)是用简单的词语代替比较复杂的词语或句子以避免重复的一种语法手段。其目的是为了节省笔墨,使上下文连接更紧密。我们常用替代这种手段,使句子更简明,朗读起来显得更爽朗、更有韵味。替代可以根据所替代的词语的不同而分为名词性替代、副词性替代、动词性替代和从句性替代四种。

28.2　替代与省略的区别

替代和省略不同,替代并不减少词语或句子成分,句子结构依然完整,替代和省略有时可以交替使用。

{ —Which book do you want? The black cover or the yellow cover? 你要哪本书? 黑封面的,还是黄封面的?
—Which book do you want? The black cover *one* or the yellow cover *one*? 你要哪本书? 黑封面的那本,还是黄封面的那本?

{ —How do you know Mary will attend the important meeting? 你怎么知道玛丽将参加那个重要会议?
—Rose told me (so). 罗丝告诉我(这事的)。

很明显,第一组例句中的第一句是省略句,而第二句是替代句,都用了替代词 one 替代前面出现的 book;第二组例句的答语中,不用 so 的,那就是省略句,用了 so 的,那就是替代句,这个 so 替代的是 Mary will attend the important meeting 这件事。

28.3　名词性替代

用替代词替代上下文中出现的名词或名词词组叫名词性替代(Sentence of Nominal Substitution)。名词性替代中所用的替代词有人称代词、物主代词、疑问代词、连接代词、指示代词、不定代词、数词等。

这些具体的词有:one/ones, it/them, so, these/those, the kind, the sort, the same, both, some, either, neither, none, many, whom, which, that, who, whose, but, as 等。

(1) 人称代词、物主代词、不定代词、数词等替代名词

{ —What's wrong with your new car? 你的新汽车怎么啦?
—It won't start. 它发不动了。(it = my new car)

This isn't my coat; mine is over there. 这不是我的外套,我的在那边。(mine = my coat)

My seat is next to that of our monitor. 我的座位在班长的旁边。(that = the seat)

Mao Zedong honoured Liu Hulan with *these* words: "A great life! A glorious death!" 毛泽东这样赞颂刘胡兰:"生的伟大,死的光荣!"(these = "A great life! A glorious death!")

She is kind-hearted, sincere and honest. *Those* are the most important qualities. 她善良、直率和诚实。这些是最重要的品质。(Those = kind-hearted, sincere and honest)

{—Can I have a cup of milk with sugar, please? 请给我一杯加糖的牛奶好吗?
—Give me the same, please. 也给我一杯同样的。(the same = a cup of milk with sugar)

Some equipment has been damaged, but none has been lost. 一些设备损坏了,但没有丢失的。(none = no equipment)

{—Have you any oranges? 你有橘子吗?
—Give me two/some. 给我两个/一些。(two/some = two/some oranges)

(2) 关于名词性替代的一些问题

① one 和 ones 的替代作用

one 和 ones 用来泛指上文提到的那类事物的某一个或某一些,它们在口语和书面语中很常见。

{—Is there a fountain-pen anywhere? 哪儿有自来水笔?
—Here is *one*. 这儿有一支。(one = a fountain-pen)

There are good books as well as bad *ones*. 既有好书,也有坏书。(ones = books)

We sent them a lot of big apples instead of small *ones*. 我们送了好多大苹果给他们,没送小苹果。(ones = apples)

Notes: A. 当名词词组中心词是不可数名词时,那就不可用 one 或 ones 来代替。如要避免重复,通常采用省略。

They prefer strong tea to weak (tea). 他们喜欢喝浓茶而不喜欢喝淡茶。

The old equipment works just as well as the new (equipment). 旧设备工作起来和新设备一样正常。

B. 有时,替代词 one/ones 和它们所替代的名词词组中心词的"数"可以不一致。

He prefers the large bottle to the small *ones*. 他喜欢这个大瓶子而不喜欢这些小瓶子。(ones = bottles)

We know her two elder children, but we don't know the youngest *one*. 我们认识她的两个大孩子,但我们不认识最小的那个孩子。(one = child)

② that 和 those 的替代作用

that/those 在表示对比的句子里常用来代替上文有 the 或其他限定词修饰的名词。这样的句子读起来韵味很足。

The garden of our house is larger than *that* of theirs. 我们房子的花园比他们房子的(花园)大。(that = garden)

The boys of Class One are stronger than *those* of Class Two. 一班的男学生比二班的男学生更强壮。(those = boys)

These machines are better than *those* we turned out last year. 这些机器比我们去年生产的(机器)好。(those = machines)

③ so 在某些动词后的替代作用

连系动词 be, appear, become, get, keep, prove 等后面的 so 用来替代前面或上文的名词。

He is a disgrace to his school, and to his family, and I have no doubt that he will prove *so* in aftertime to his country. 他是学校的耻辱、家族的耻辱,日后一定是国家的耻辱。(so = disgrace)

{—He is a rather naughty boy sometimes. 他有时是个很调皮的孩子。
—Yes, *so* he is. 是的,他确实是个调皮的孩子。(so = a rather naughty boy)

{—He has become a scientist. 他成了一名科学家。
—How did he turn *so*? 他是怎样成为科学家的呢?(so = a scientist)

④ it 和 them 的替代作用

我们经常看到用 it/them 来特指上文所提到的事物本身。

Tom lost his watch yesterday and he hasn't found it yet. 昨天汤姆把表丢了,至今没有找到。(it = his watch)

Mr. Black borrowed a book from me last month. Now it is time for him to return it. 上个月布拉克先生从我这儿借了一本书。他该把它还给我了。(it = the book)

Look, there are many children swimming in the pool. Do you know them? 看,有一群孩子在池塘里游泳。你认识他们吗?(them = many children swimming in the river)

⑤ kind 和 sort 的替代作用

kind 和 sort 通常用来替代不可数名词。

American food is not the same as the English *kind*. 美国的食品和英国的食品不一样。(kind = food)

Slang disappears quickly, especially the juvenile *sort*. 俚语很快地消失了,特别是儿童俚语。(sort = slang)

⑥ the same 的替代作用

the same 可以用作整个名词词组的替代词,通常指物,但它与它所替代的名词词组并非共指同一对象。

{—I'll have two poached eggs, please. 我要两个荷包蛋。
 —I'll have *the same*. 我也同样。(the same = two poached eggs)

{—I'd like a cup of coffee. 我要一杯咖啡。
 —I'd like *the same* with milk but without sugar. 我也要一杯咖啡,加牛奶但不加糖。(the same = a cup of coffee)

⑦ both, none, some, either, neither, many 的替代作用

Mr. Mao has two daughters; *both* live in Beijing. 毛先生有两个女儿,都住在北京。(both = two daughters)

Jim ordered the cement, but *none* has arrived. 吉姆订购了水泥,可是一点也没运到。(none = cement)

I have lived in Hong Kong and Macao, but I don't like *either*. 我在香港和澳门都住过,但我对这两个地方都不喜欢。(either = Hong Kong and Macao)

{—Did you see Rose and Mary? 你看到罗丝和玛丽了吗?
 —No, I saw *neither* of them. 没有,我哪一个也没看见。(neither = Tom and Mary)

Fifty people came—some stayed until the end but *many* left early. 来了 50 个人——有些人一直待到最后,但很多人先走了。(many = a large number of people)

⑧ 关系词的替代作用

在限制性定语从句中,关系代词替代前面的先行词,因此说关系词也起替代作用。

The lady *who* was talking with your father here yesterday is a painter. 昨天在这里与你父亲交谈的那位女士是位画家。(who = the lady)

I know the woman *whom* you mean. 我认识你所指的那个女人。(whom = the woman)

A child *whose* parents are dead is called an orphan. 失去父母的孩子叫孤儿。(whose = [a] child's)

The book *which* has been retranslated into many languages was written by my grandfather. (which = the book) 那本有多种译本的书是我爷爷写的。

The letter *that* I received from her yesterday is very important. 昨天我收到的她的那封来信很重要。(that = the letter)

There are very few *but* admire his talents. 很少有人不赞赏他的才干的。(but = who don't)

28.4 副词性替代

副词性替代(Adverbial Substitution)就是用一些副词来替代前面出现的状语。这是人们在日常会话

中,为避免重复,使句子简洁有力所常用的一种表达手段。

(1) 副词 here, there, then 可起替代作用

我们常用 here, there, then 等副词来替代表示地点和时间的副词词组。

① 替代时间

{ —Chen Zaixiang will graduate from Beijing Teachers' University next year. 陈在香将于明年从北京师范大学毕业。
  —How old is she *then*? 那时候她多大? (then = next year)

In 2015, the 53rd WTTC was held in Suzhou *then*. 2015 年,那时第 53 届世界乒乓球赛在苏州举行。(then = in 2015)

得说明一下的是,上面例句 2 中的 then 是替代了前面的 in 2015,当然是一个替代句;但这句又可说是一个左移了原句首时间状语 in 2015,而句末 then 是指代 in 2015 的指代副词(杨元兴,2007),这也是句名副其实的左移位句。

② 替代地点

{ —Could you tell me how to get to the Red-Star Cinema? 你能告诉我怎么去红星电影剧院吗?
  —Oh, sorry. I'm a stranger and I've never been *there*. 喔,对不起,我新来这儿,从没去过那儿。(there = the Red-Star Cinema)

We have got to the top of the hill at last. *Here* we will have a bird's-eye view of the whole city. 我们最后到达了山顶。在山顶上我们可以鸟瞰全城。(Here = At the top of the hill)

(2) 一些观点副词和语气副词起替代句子的作用

这些副词有 clearly, surely, frankly, truly 等,杨元兴先生称之为观点副词无动词句和语气副词无动词句。

Surely, I've met you before somewhere. 确信无疑,我以前在哪儿见到过你。(Surely = I'm sure that I've …)

Clearly, she is a wise woman. 显然,她是个精明的女人。(Clearly = It is clear to me that she is …)

Frankly, I'm not satisfied with what you had done. 坦率地说,我对你的作为不满意。(Frankly = If I can say frankly)

I don't think she is wrong, *truly*, what's your opinion? 我认为她不错。说实话,你的意见呢? (Truly = you tell me truly)

上述例句 1、2 中斜体词是观点副词,例句 3、4 中斜体词语气副词,它们分别替代了相关意思的句子或从句。

(3) 短语 like this/that, this/that way/for the reason 用作替代语

短语 this/that way, like this/that, for this/that reason 可以起替代作用,替代上文那些表示方式或原因的副词词组。like this/that 中, like 是介词; this/that way 前可看作省去了介词 by; for the reason 短语当然表示原因。

Always be frank and open to your colleagues. *That way* you will win their trust and confidence. 对同事总是要真诚坦率,这样你就会赢得他们的信任。(That way = By always being frank and open)

{ —His younger brother played computer games with great concentration. 他的弟弟聚精会神地玩电脑游戏。
  —I'm afraid he doesn't have his lessons *like that*. 恐怕他上课不会那样。(like that = with great concentration)

He cannot be charged with murder *for the reason* that he was not in town when the crime was committed. 他不

可能被指控为谋杀,原因是当谋杀案发生时他不在城里。(for the reason = he was not in town when the crime was committed)

(4) 副词 so 用作副词性替代

副词 so 有时也可以起替代状语的作用。

Her elder sister often dresses well, but sometimes she does not do *so*. 她姐姐经常穿得很好,但有时也穿得不好。(so = well)

He often behaved prudently, but he did not always behave *so*. 他有时表现很谨慎,但并不总是这样。(so = prudently)

(5) 在定语从句中一些关系副词对前面的先行词起指代作用

关系副词 when, since, before, after, that, where, why 等可以指代前面出现的地点状语、时间状语和原因状语。

He came last night *when* I was out. 他昨晚来时我出去了。(when 指代时间状语 last night)

Every hour *since* I came has been most enjoyable. 我来之后的每一个小时都是非常好玩的。(since 指代时间状语 every hour)

On the day *before* we left home there came a snowstorm. 在我们离家的前一天,下了一场暴风雪。(before 指代时间状语 on the day)

The year *after* she had finished college she spent abroad. 她大学毕业后的那年是在国外度过的。(after 指代时间状语 the year)

It happened on the day *that* I was born. 那件事是在我出生的那一天发生的。(that = when, 指代时间状语 on the day)

He fell from a tree. That's the reason *why* he was sent to the hospital. 他从树上掉了下来,这就是他被送往医院的原因。(why 指代前面的原因状语 He fell from a tree)

28.5 动词性替代

用动词替代动词词组或动词词组中心词这一语法现象叫作动词性替代(Verbal Substitution)。动词替代词常由 do 的一定形式担任,而作这种用法的 do 叫作"代动词"(Pro-Verb)。替代动词 do 用法有两种:一为替代动词词组,即整个谓语;二为替代动词词组中心词,即谓语动词。

(1) 替代动词 do 及其搭配的替代表达

替代动词 do 替代整个谓语时,形式要受主语人称和数的制约,并有现在时和过去时的形式变化。替代动词 do 也可以和助动词或情态动词以及 so, it, not 等搭配,构成各种复杂的动词词组,替代很多内容。

① do 替代谓语动词和动词词组的中心词

A. do 替代谓语动词

{ —She looks young. 她看上去年轻。
  —You *do* too. 你看上去也年轻。(do = look young)

{ —Does Mary know it? 玛丽知道这事吗?
  —Yes, she *does*. 是的,她知道这事。(does = knows it)

{ —Did you watch TV yesterday? 你昨天看电视吗?
  —Yes, I *did*. 是的,我昨天看了。(did = watched TV)

{—Will you prepare something for me? 你愿意为我准备些事吗？
—Yes, I *will*. 好，我愿意。（will = will prepare something for you）

{—Do you speak English? 你讲英语吗？
—Yes, I *do*. 我讲。（do = speak English）

{—Do you come every day? 你每天来吗？
—Yes, I *do*. 是的，我每天来。（do = come every day）

B. do 替代动词词组的中心词

替代动词 do 可替代动词词组中心词。do 作这种用法时通常都是实义动词。若是及物动词，后需跟宾语；也可与情态动词连用。这样的用法常见于比较结构句。

As we all know, the air holds the stone back less than it *does* the feather. 众所周知，空气对石头的阻力要比对羽毛的阻力小。（does = holds）

She plays the piano better than she *does* the guitar. 她钢琴比吉他弹得好。（does = plays）

His brother has never acted as he should have *done*. 他弟弟的表现一向不好。（done = acted）

I study modern history and do not *do* modern languages. 我研究现代历史，但不研究现代语言。（第二个 do = study）

② do so/it 的替代作用

A. do so 的替代作用及其非谓语形式

a. do so 的替代情况：替代动词 do 可以与 so 结合，构成复合替代动词 do so，它既可替代动宾谓语结构，又可替代动状谓语结构。

Mary can speak English fluently, but I am not sure whether her younger sister can *do so*. 玛丽英语说得很流利，但我不确定她的妹妹是否能这样。（do so = speak English fluently）（do so 替代动宾谓语结构）

I drink a lot. Does your elder brother *do so*? 我喝酒很多，你的哥哥也这样吗？（do so = drink a lot）（do so 替代动词谓语和状语结构）

He used to come late for class, but he no longer *does so*. 他过去上学常迟到，但是现在不再这样了。（does so = comes late for class）（does so 替代动词谓语和状语结构）

b. do so 的非谓语形式：do so 在句中可以采取非谓语形式。

"Yes, I think you'd better start earlier," said the man, and Jane was only too glad *to do so*. "我想你最好早些动身，"那人说道。而简也很愿意早点动身。（to do so = to start）

有时，do so 所替代的词语本身是非谓语动词。

I told him to come and see me the next day and he *did so*. 我告诉他第二天来看我，他真的来了。（did so = came and saw me）

B. do it 的替代作用及其中 it 的替代词

a. do it 的替代作用：替代动词 do 可与 it 结合，构成动词复合替代词组 do it，它可替代谓语动词和非谓语动词。

I can persuade him, but I do not want to *do it*. 我能说服他，但我不想这样做。（do it = persuade him）

If to die is good, I will *do it*. 如果死是件好事的话，我愿意去死。（do it = die）

Mary hopes to get the first prize, but can she *do it*? 玛丽希望得到头等奖，但她能得到吗？（do it = get the first prize）

The vase is broken. Who *did it*? 花瓶碎了。谁干的？（did it = broke the vase）

b. do it 中 it 的替代词：在 do it 这种替代中的 it 有时可用 that 或 this 代替，甚至可放在句首。

I asked her to type the letter for me this morning. She said she could *do that*. 我叫她今天早晨给我打这封信。她说她可以做到。

Do I love such a man? No, I never *do that*. 我爱这样一个男人吗？不，我从不爱。
Love my neighbours? *This* I will *do*. 爱我的邻居吗？我会爱的。

③ do so 与 do it 的关系

当 do so 用来替代动宾结构时，so 可用 it 替代，由 do so 变成 do it。

He got her home, but I don't know how he managed to *do it*. 他把她弄到家里，我不知道他是怎么弄的。（do it = get her home）

John is going to make the experiment and he wanted me to *do it*, too. 约翰要去做实验，他想叫我也去做实验。（do it = make the experiment）

Note：do so 和 do it 并非在任何情况下都可以取代的。从下面两句中可以看出它们之间的区别：

Jim is getting his house painted, and moreover, he wants me to *do it*. 吉姆正在油漆房子，并且要我也帮他油漆。（do it = paint his house）

Jim is getting his house painted, and moreover, he wants me to *do so*. 吉姆正在油漆房子，并且要我也把（我的）房子漆一下。（do so = get my house painted）

(2) "so + do + 主语" 与 "so + 主语 + do" 句型

① so + do + 主语

A. 如前面句子是肯定的，简略替代句就用 "so + do + 主语" 这种结构。如果后句中的主语与上文中的主语是不同的，且主谓词序颠倒。

Moths fly about at night. *So do bats*. 蛾在夜间飞行，蝙蝠也在夜间飞行。(So do bats. = Bats fly about at night, too.)

Robert likes English, *so does his younger sister*. 罗伯特喜欢英语，他妹妹也是的。

Li Na has finished her homework, *so have I*. 李娜做完作业了，我也做完了。

His mother graduated from Beijing University. *So did his father*. 他母亲毕业于北京大学。他父亲也是的。

B. 如果前面的句子是否定的，在简短反应或陈述同样的情况时，则要用 "neither/nor + 主语" 来表示。

{ —I don't like it. 我不喜欢它。
—*Neither/nor do I*. 我也不喜欢。

{ —Li Ping hasn't finished reading the book. 李平还没有看完那本书。
—*Neither/nor have I*. 我也没有。

② so + 主语 + do

这种替代结构中的主语与上文中的主语相同，用正常语序。对别人的话做出肯定的反应或同意前句主语所讲的情况时，常用这种结构。

{ —The students in Class 4 study very hard. 四班的学生们学习很用功。
—*So they do*. (= Certainly they study very hard.) 他们确实很用功。

{ —He is a good student. 他是个好学生。
—*So he is*. 他是的。

{ —He looks old. 他看起来苍老。
—*So he does*. (= He looks old indeed.) 确实是这样。

28.6 从句性替代

所谓从句性替代是指用某些词、短语替代名词性从句；用替代词替代名词性从句的现象叫作从句性替代 (Clausal Substitution)，含这种现象的句子叫从句性替代句 (Clausal Substitute Sentence)。其实，从句性替代中的 so，not，why not，if so/not 等均为无动词句。

(1) the same 替代一个名词性从句

替代语 the same 可以替代名词性从句，它也可以看作一个无动词句。

　　┌─—Jim thought it was possible. 吉姆认为这是可能的。
　　└─—Yes, I thought *the same*. 是的，我也认为这是可能的。(the same = that it was possible)

　　┌─—I lost my way in the galleries. 我在长廊迷了路。
　　└─—*The same* happened to me. 我也在长廊迷了路。(the same = I also lost my way in the galleries)

　　┌─—(I wish you a) Happy New Year. (祝你)新年快乐。
　　└─—The same to you. 也祝你新年快乐。(The same to you. = I wish a Happy New Year to you, too.)

(2) 从句性替代词 so 和 not 的用法

表示看法和意见的动词 believe, expect, fear, guess, hope, imagine, say, tell, think, suppose 和词组 be afraid 等后面 that 从句常用 so 或 not 替代。这种替代词 so 和 not 常用于答语中。在这种结构中，so 所替代的是肯定的陈述句，not 所替代的是否定的陈述句。so 在多数情况下置于句末，偶尔也有置于句首的。

① so 用来替代某些表示看法、意见的动词后的宾语时的位置

A. 置于句末

　　┌─—Do you think she will pass the examination tomorrow? 你认为她能明天通过考试吗？
　　└─—Yes, I think *so*. 是的，我认为她会的。(so = that she will come tomorrow)

　　┌─—Are you coming to the meeting? 你将参加会议吗？
　　└─—I suppose/hope *so*. 我希望参加会议。(so = that I am going to the meeting)

B. 置于句首

so 偶尔可以置于句首，这时能起到承上启下的作用，但 not 却不可以。这时，主谓倒装与否均可，但当主语是代词时就不倒装。

　　┌─—Oxford will win the boat race; at least, *so* all my Oxford friends say. 牛津将在划船比赛中获胜；起码我
　　│　 所有的牛津朋友都是这么说的。
　　└─—And *so* say most of the sports writers, too. 大多数的体育记者也是这么说的。(= So most of the sports writers say, too.)

　　┌─—They're leaving for Nanjing tomorrow, you know? 他们明天将动身去南京，你知道吗？
　　└─—*So* I heard. 我听说了。(这里，So I heard. 仍可被看成是 I heard so. 当然，so = that they're leaving for Nanjing that day)

② 从句性替代词 not 的用法和位置

替代词 not 的使用频率很高，范围很广。它在句中的位置总是在句末。有时，它还可以与情态副词搭配使用，组成一般疑问句的答语。

A. 置于句末

not 与 so 的位置一样，常用于句末。

　　┌─—Do you think she will come tomorrow? 你认为她明天会来吗？
　　└─—No, I think *not*. 不，我认为她不会来。(not = that she will not come tomorrow)

　　┌─—Is what he told you true? 他告诉你的事是真实的吗？
　　└─—No, I believe *not*. 不，我相信不是真实的。(not = that what he told me is not true)

B. not 与情态副词连用

not 可与情态副词 perhaps, possibly, probably, certainly, surely 等搭配，组成两个词的缩略。

{—Will they come? 他们来吗?
—*Perhaps not*. (= Perhaps they will not come.) 大概不会来。

{—Will you waste your time and money on that? 你愿意把时间和钱浪费在那个上面吗?
—*Certainly not*. (= Certainly I will not waste my time and money on that.) 当然不愿意。

③ 使用从句性替代词 so 与 not 的注意点

A. 有明显的肯定或否定时不用 so

因为 so 所表示的既不是肯定，也不是否定，它只是表示说话人的看法或想法的婉转说法，所以在有明显的肯定或有怀疑的答句中就不可用 so。

{—Are they going to visit the Great Wall this summer?
误：—I'm sure so.
正：—I'm sure they are. / I'm sure of it.（这是因为前面的 sure 是个意思很肯定的词，后面不可用 so）

{—There's going to be a meeting this afternoon.
误：—I know so.
正：—I know. / I know that.（这句中的 know 与上句中的 sure 一样，是表示肯定意思的词，其后不可用 so）

{—Rose will go to see her first teacher next week.
误：—I doubt so.
正：—I doubt if she will. / I doubt it.（答语中的 doubt 表示明显的怀疑，因此就不可用 so）

B. tell 后可用 so，而且有时可以省略

但 ask 和 know 后面不用 so。

Jack hasn't found a job yet. He told me so yesterday.（句中的 so = that he hasn't found a job yet）

{—Her sister asked me when I would go to visit Nanjing?
误：—Why did she ask so?
正：—Why did she ask that?

{—He has been to Shanghai.
—How do you know (that)?
—His brother told me (so).

C. 个别表示说话的动词 say 后可以用 so，不可用 not

正：He said so.
误：He said not.

D. 在非特殊人称代词 + say/seem/appear 时，后可用 so 或 not

当被替代的主语是非特殊人称代词，如 it, they 等时，so 和 not 都可以用在 say, seem, appear 等后面。

They say so/not. It says so/not.
It seems so/not. It appears so/not.

E. not 可以与 why 连用，但 so 极少与 why 连用

{—Chen Li didn't attend the important meeting. 陈丽没有参加那个重要会议。
—Why not? (= Why didn't she attend the important meeting?)
* Why so?（不能接受）

(3) if 后的 so/not 替代从句

so 可以用在从属连词 if 后面，替代内容与前面相同的从句，构成无动词条件从句。"从属连词 if + so/not" 常置于句中，可以被看成是一种插入语形式。这种无动词条件从句常被理解成 "if + so/not" 的前句是它的依据，而后句是 "if + so/not" 的结果。

We are told that he will come tonight, and if *so*, our meeting will be held tomorrow. 我们被告知他今晚要来，如果是这样，我们的会议明天可以举行。(if so 替代 if he comes tonight)

We are told that he won't come tonight, if *not*, there won't be any meeting tomorrow. 我们被告知他今晚不来，如果他不来，我们明天就没有会议了。(if not 替代 if he doesn't come tonight)

第 29 章　单词句和短语句

29.1　单词句和短语句概述

英语中有双元句(Two-Member Sentence)和单元句(One-Member Sentence)之说。凡含有主语和谓语两部分组成的句子称为双元句,只含一个词或一个成分的句子叫单元句。

Ouch! 哎哟!（表示疼痛）
Fire! Fire! 失火了! 失火了!
Help! Help! 救命! 救命!
An airplane! 飞机!
No parking! 不准泊车!
On foot. 步行(去的)。
Up the stairs! 上楼!

Happy birthday to you! 等句子就是单元句,或称单词句和短语句。这些单元句有些特别,它们在结构上讲是省略句,在形式上看是单词句和短语句。那么,什么叫单词句和短语句呢?杨元兴先生对单词句和短语句下的定义为:"一个单词或一个短语,其单词或短语的第一个词的首字母大写,后面有标点符号,并赋予一定的语调,表达一个完整意思的单词和短语。"著名语法学家 H. Sweet 说:"一个能充当句子的单词也能表达一个完整的意思,如 'Come!' (=I command you to come!)在这个单词句中,主语是不言而喻的,而谓语部分的 come 本身就可以构成一个句子。"对此, H. Sweet 称之为单元句,即单词句(One-Word Sentence),这是正确的。又如我们把短语 "happy birthday" 的 happy 中的 h 大写,在 birthday 后加上标点 "!",就成了一句祝贺句 "Happy birthday!"（祝生日快乐!）的句子。H. Sweet 把 "Come!" 与 "Happy birthday!" 不加以区别地统称为 "单元句" 是不严谨的,而杨元兴先生把像 "Happy birthday!" 之类两个词以上的单元句称之为短语句(Phrasal Sentence),这是完全正确的。

29.2　使用单词句和短语句的语境和好处

在日常社交和口语中,我们通常不使用完整的句子,这是因为在某种语境下不用完整的句子要比用完整的句子更能圆满地表达出我们的意思。反之,完整的表达法反而会将表意中某些至关重要的含义淹没掉。在语言交流中使用那些简短的句子,它们的意思反而更明白易懂。另外,因为单词句和短语句句型结构简单精练,读、写时又省时省力,所以不论在书面语还是在口语中,人们都喜欢用单词句和短语句。

有些单词句和短语句有它们自身的意思,如"Thanks.","Stand up.";另一些除了本义外还用来表示"同情"、"赞美"、"惊讶"等意思,如"Heavens!","Poor you!","Wonderful!"等。这些句型常用于对简单祈使句、感叹句、疑问句或其他句子的答语中。

29.3　单词句和短语句的分类

单词句和短语句有多少种呢?根据单词句和短语句的交际功能,我们拟把这些单词句和短语句分为七种类型,即称呼语、惊叹语、祈使语、问答语、问候告别语、感谢祝贺语、插入语。

(1) 称呼语

称呼语(Vocatives)是一种原始的单词句或短语句。它虽是单词或词组,但同情景和语调结合在一起,就可表达一种思想,以引起别人的注意。

Jim! Come (here)! 吉姆!过来!

这个称呼语,要是喊得声调高,元音拖长,那是叫吉姆到呼唤他的人那里去;要是元音短促,并带有生气声调,那就是责骂他了,意思是到"我"这边来,不要在那儿吵嚷。当然这个呼唤人或许是其长辈一类的人。

汉语中可以用呼语单独构成单词句,如"叔叔"、"李娜"、"老张"等。在这种情况下,英语往往用一个感叹号将称呼语和整个句子分开。句法上虽然可以把它们归入单词句和短语句一类,但是在语法上一般仍称为独立成分。

Hello! 喂!(用于电话中,以唤起对方的注意)

Ladies and gentlemen! I have brought two thousand coffins with me! 女士们!先生们!今天我已带来了两千口棺材。

这是一个交通安全演讲人引人入胜的开头语。听众自然要听他为什么要带两千口棺材来……

(2) 惊叹语

惊叹语(Exclamations)又叫感叹语,与称呼语一样,也是原始的单词句或短语句。它们是单词句和短语句中最常见的表达形式。惊叹词可以单独使用,构成单词句,也可以和感叹句、陈述句搭配,作独立成分用。单独使用时,书面语用感叹号(!),与陈述句或感叹句搭配时,则用逗号(,)与后面部分分开,在口语中用语调和停顿来表示。

Hurrah! 哇嗨!(表示快乐、欢迎)

Oh! 啊!(表示疼痛或惊讶)

Wonderful! 妙哉!(表示赞美)

同样,一些感叹短语也可以单独使用,实际上这些短语是一个带有定语的名词词组或是由 what 或 how 引导的感叹句省略主语和谓语所留下的短语。

Good ideas! 好主意!

Poor Bob! 可怜的鲍勃!

What a pity! 多可惜啊!

How interesting! 多么有趣啊!

(3) 祈使语

祈使语(Imperatives)是指一些祈使句式的单词句和短语句。它们由动词或动词和它的附加成分构成。祈使句一般以祈使式动词开头,没有主语,只有谓语部分,这些祈使句也是单词句和短语句中最常见的句型。

Go! 去!

Listen! 听!

Hurry up! 快点!

Stand up! 起立!

Turn off the light! 关灯!

有些祈使语甚至没有动词,剩下的只是状语部分,它们同样也是单词句或短语句。

Faster! 快点!

Away! 走开!

Off with your hat! 脱帽！

Just think of the cost! 想想那笔费用吧！

To think of his not knowing anything about it! 想想看，他对此事竟一无所知！

To think that all his efforts to help them had gone for nothing! 想想看，他尽一切努力帮助他们，但一事无成啊！

这些句子也可称作短语句，它们属于动词不定式类型的祈使句，用来表示感情。只是这种短语句有时在动词不定式后还带宾语从句。以 No 开头的禁止性短语也归为短语句。

No admittance! 禁止入内！

No help! 不许帮忙！

No spitting! 不准随地吐痰！

No talking! 不准说话！

No smoking! 禁止吸烟！

(4) 问答语

简练是任何一种语言发展的趋势，英语也不例外，尤其是口语。口语常不为规范语法的完整模式所压束，因此单词句和短语句在口语中出现的频率很高，特别是在有语境的问答语（Questions and Responses）中，即在回答别人的问题或是在接着别人说话时提出问题时，常采用单词句或短语句。

{ —Am I late? 我迟到了吗？
　—Yes (No). 是的（没有）。

{ —May I use your computer? 我能用你的电脑吗？
　—Certainly. 当然可以。

{ —Where has he been? 他去哪儿了？
　—To the library. 去图书馆了。

{ —Shall we go by plane or train? 我们坐飞机去还是坐火车去？
　—By plane. 坐飞机去。

{ —Chen Zaixiang has bought a TV set. 陈在香买了一台电视机。
　—When? 什么时候？

从上述例句可知，用来作问答语的单词句和短语句的表现形式很活跃，它们可以是肯定词 Yes，否定词 No，可以是副词 certainly, perhaps 等，可以是疑问词 when, whom, where，还可以是介词短语等。

此外，虽然表示命令和要求的祈使句一般不需要回答，但偶尔也用独特的答语作答，这些答语通常用词灵活、词语简短。它们大多也是单词句和短语句。

{ —Go there. 上那儿去。
　—All right. (Wait a moment.) 行（等一会）。

{ —Open the door, please. 请把门打开。
　—Why? 为什么？

{ —Hurry up. 快点。
　—Coming. 来了。

{ —Help yourself, please. 请随便吃。
　—Thank you. 谢谢。

(5) 问候告别语

问候告别语（Greetings and Farewells）经常由一些固定词组来表达。这些固定词组的问候告别语多数是单词句和短语句，其句尾用句号或感叹号。

Good afternoon! 下午好!
See you later!（So long!）再见!
Good night! 晚安!
Good-bye! Bye bye! 再见!
Cheerio! 干杯!（祝酒语）

(6) 感谢祝贺语

感谢祝贺语(Thanks and Congratulations)，跟问候告别语一样，也是一种被广泛应用的单词句或短语句，这些或许成了习惯用语。

Thanks! 谢谢!
Merry Christmas! 圣诞快乐!
Congratulations! 祝贺你!
Your health! 祝你健康!
A thousand thanks! 多谢!
Happy New Year to you! 祝你新年快乐!

(7) 插入语

插入语(Parenthesis)也属单词句和短语句，不过它是一种比较特殊的单词句和短语句，虽然它们比较少见，但有时还会碰到，如在描绘或叙述文章中，在日记、书信、随笔中，有时在有些名言中也会出现。

Now there came a little "flute" bit (of music)—very pretty!—a little chain of bright drops. 听! 有一丝长笛声般的音乐——非常优美!——就像一小串明亮的水珠落地。

Then we came to the ground. Marshes everywhere. No birds! No houses! Not a soul to be seen. 然后我们来到草地，到处是沼泽，没有飞鸟，没有树林，没有房屋，没有人烟!

有时在看到这些句型结构，虽从字面上看是一些较长的句子，但其中却有不少单词句或短语句。又如富兰克林的一句名言:The poor have little, beggars none, the rich too much, enough not one.（穷人入不敷出，乞丐一无所有，富人过犹不及，没有一个人刚好足够。）中，连续出现了三句栩栩如生的短语句，这三句揭露了社会不公，也剖析了人们的贪婪，这种表达效果是一般句子无法达到的。

29.4 单词句和短语句与省略的关系

省略句中有很多是单词句和短语句。在快速的口语谈话中，凡不需重复的词语都可以省去。因为在对话中，如果回答时用全文说出就显得啰唆、别扭。正如上面所说任何语言都在向"简洁"的方向发展着，而使用单词句和短语句是实现这一目标的有效手法之一。

—When will he leave? 他什么时候走?
—At 10:30 pm. (= He will leave at 10:30 pm.) 晚上10:30。

—She won't come. 她不会来了。
—Why? (= Why won't she come?) 为什么?

上述单词句和短语句也叫保留下了句子状语的无动词句(杨元兴,2012)。同样，在惊叹语、祈使语等句式中也常有省略现象。这些与上述例句一样，被省去的词语的意思根据语境可填进去。这些省略结构也往往以单词句和短语句的形式出现的。

What a capital idea! (= What a capital idea it is!) 好主意!
Splendid! (= That's splendid!) 太好了!
How beautiful! (= How beautiful these flowers are!) 多美啊!（这些花儿多美啊!）

Go out! (＝I command you to go out!) 滚出去!

也有一些习惯用语是因为省略了句子的主语而保留了谓语部分，或保留了主语，或保留了宾语，才变成单词句和短语句的。

Have lunch yet? (＝Have you had lunch yet?) 你吃过午饭了吗?
Thank you. (＝I thank you.) 谢谢你!
No smoking! (＝No smoking is allowed here.) 禁止吸烟!
Pardon. (＝I beg your pardon.) 请原谅!

虽然有些语法家认为以 No 开始的一些表示禁止意义的习惯句式不能算省略句。我们认为，这些句型被省略的部分是不言自明的，很容易被添加进去，因此把它们纳入省略句的范畴比较合适。

29.5　单词句和短语句的句法功能

因为绝大多数单词句和短语句是简单句的省略形式，所以我们很容易从上下文里确定被省去的内容，进而确定它们在原来句子结构中所处的位置以及充当何种语法成分。通过这样的分析，我们可以归纳出单词句和短语句可分别作主语(Subject)、谓语(Predicate)、表语(Predicative)、宾语(Object)、状语(Adverbial)、宾语补足语(Object Complement)、定语(Attribute)、独立成分(Independent Element)八种。

(1) 作主语

作主语的单词句和短语句常是简单句省去谓语部分而留下来的主语部分。这种单词句或短语句有时是问句的答语，有时是对上一句陈述句主语的追问，以进一步强调主语部分的信息。

{—Who is going to meet Professor Li? Your monitor? 谁去接李教授? 你们班长?
—Li Na. (＝Li Na is going to meet Professor Li.) 李娜。

{—Rose will be here tomorrow. 罗丝明天将来这里。
—Who? (＝Who will be here tomorrow?) 谁(明天将来这里)?

(2) 作谓语

单词句和短语句用作谓语有两种情况：常以祈使句的形式出现，这是因为祈使句常省去主语部分，只留下谓语部分；自然的谈话中留下的谓语部分。

Come! (＝You come!) (你)过来!
Stop talking! (＝You stop talking!) 停止讲话!
Listen to me! (＝You listen to me!) 听我说!
See you later. (＝I'll see you later.) 再见!
Serves him right. (＝It serves him right.) 他活该!
Doesn't matter. (＝It doesn't matter.) 没关系!

上面最后 3 个例句中，把非重读的主语省去，使句子更显简洁、明了。

(3) 作表语

一些简单句省去主语和连系动词后只剩下了表语，这些表语是单词句或短语句。这些单词句或短语句还是说明主语的内容或说明主语的特征的。现在，有些语法书把表语称为主语补足语。

Sorry. (＝I'm sorry.) 对不起。
Tired? (＝Are you tired?) 累吗?

{—What does he do? 他是干什么的?
—A novelist. (＝He is a novelist.) 小说家。

What a pity! (＝What a pity it is!) 多可惜啊!
Time for dinner. (＝It's time for dinner.) 晚饭时间到了。

(4) 作宾语

一些简单句经常同时省去主语和谓语部分,而只剩下宾语,有时是介词宾语。这些宾语也是单词句或短语句。这种情况大多出现在以 what 引导的感叹句、祈使句或要求提供宾语部分信息的答语中。

What a wonderful time! (＝What a wonderful time we had!) 玩得多高兴!
The salt, please. (＝Pass me the salt, please.) 请把盐递给我。
{ —What do you want to drink? 你想喝什么?
　—A cup of tea, please. 请来杯茶。
{ —Whom is he talking with now? 他在跟谁说话?
　—*Peter*. (＝He is talking with Peter now.) 彼得。

(5) 作宾语补足语

有些单词句和短语句作宾语补足语,这个补足语就是被保留下来的句子成分,不过还是给被省去的宾语在语义上进行补充说明的。而且,它们与宾语同样在逻辑上存在着主谓结构的关系。有时,这个宾语补足语还可能是被省去了的动词不定式的表语。

{ —Shall we paint the wall yellow or blue? 我们把墙刷成黄色还是蓝色好?
　—*Yellow*. (＝We'll paint the wall green.) 黄色好。
{ —What do you think of the performance? 演出怎么样?
　—*Capital*! (＝I think the performance to be capital!) 好极了!

(6) 作状语

作状语用的单词句和短语句大致有三种情况:① 祈使句中保留下的状语,这类单词句和短语句子常用来表示"邀请"、"命令"等意思;② 也有些疑问句同时省去主谓语,仅留下作状语的疑问副词或短语像这种情况更多地出现在对状语信息要求提供答复的特殊疑问句中;③ 表示让步的无动词句。这种无动词句也叫短语句,它们可以扩充为让步状语从句。

This way, please. (＝Come this way, please.) 请这边走。
{ —When will the meeting be held? 会议什么时候举行?
　—Tomorrow. (＝The meeting will be held tomorrow.) 明天。
Where to? (＝Where are you going to?) 去哪儿?
With whom? (＝With whom did her daughter go to school?) 她女儿以前跟谁一起上学?
{ —Where have you been? 你一直在哪儿?
　—At school. (＝I've been at school.) 在学校。
Sick or well, the pretty girl likes to listen to the music. 无论身体好坏,那个漂亮女孩总喜欢听音乐。(Sick or well ＝ Whether she is sick or well)
For years after retiring, *wet or fine*, Mr Chen gets up at six and has a run round the park. 退休后多少年来,不管天晴下雨,李先生总是六点起床,然后围着公园跑步。(wet or fine ＝ whether it is wet or fine)

(7) 作定语

单词句和短语句作定语时是修饰已被省去的主语或宾语的,并且它们经常以问句出现,表示听者没有听清楚或有怀疑,请求对方重复一下。

⎧—Bober's mother will attend the important meeting tonight. 今晚鲍勃的母亲将参加那个重要会议。
⎩—Whose? (= Whose mother will be here this afternoon?) 谁的？

⎧—I have three brothers. 我有三个弟弟。
⎩—How *many*? (= How many brothers do you have?) 几个？

⎧—He lost three gold watches. 他丢了三只金表。
⎩—Three? (= Did he lose three gold watches?) 三只？

(8) 作独立成分

如前面所述，单词句和短语句有时可以用作惊叹语、称呼语、插入语，并且可以与陈述句、感叹句等连用，充当独立成分。

Oh! How it hurts! 噢！疼极了！（惊叹语）

Alexandra! Can't you see he's just a tramp and he's after your money? 亚历山德拉，你看不出他只是一个流浪汉，在追求你的金钱吗？（称呼语）

Help arrived, *alas*! Too late. 援助终于到了，哎！太晚了。（插入语置句中）

You'll be able to get over the difficulty, *surely*! 你们的困难是能克服的，没问题！（插入语置于句末）

29.6 关于单词句、短语句的一些说明

事实上有一些单词句和短语句，从形式上看好像是单词句和短语句形式的省略句，但我们已无法也没必要增补其省略成分，实际上它们已成了习惯用语。像上面谈到过的"Help!"一句，我们不能只说被省略的词是 me。因为就凭一个 help 可以扩展为如"I want your help! Help me, please! I do need your help!"等，所以我们不能说它是省略了哪些词或是哪一些句子成分。

类似情况还有像"Good luck!"，"Hands up!"，"Hello!"，"Thanks."，"So long!"等表示"祝愿"、"问候"、"感谢"、"原谅"、"告别"、"命令"、"警告"、"惊叹"等的用语。它们所表示的意义可以为人们理解，然而从结构来说，很难确定它们缺少了哪些成分，用什么词来填补进去，所以这些词、语句不能算是省略了某些成分句单词句和短语句，它们经过长期使用，已发展成为约定俗成的习惯用语。在使用中不必追究其原先结构形式，更不须设法填补被省略的成分。

还有些不属于省略句的单词句或短语句，我们很难断定它们是主语、谓语，还是其他句子成分，如"Thanks"，"Cheerio"，"So long!"等。对于这些情况，我们可以不进行语法分析，因为了解它们的意思比了解它们的句法成分更有意义、更为重要。

第 30 章　主语与谓语的一致

英语中各种一致关系很多,但是,主谓一致(Subject-Verb Concord),即主语与谓语动词之间在人称和数上的一致,是英语中最重要的一致关系。总的说来,主语的单复数形式决定了谓语动词应采用的相应形式。但在实际使用中,有时会遇到各种各样主谓一致的其他情况,所以在处理它们之间的一致关系时,常常需要依据不同的原则,从不同的角度去分析和掌握它们之间的关系。

30.1　主语与谓语一致的原则

R. Quirk 等在 *A Comprehensive Grammar of the English Language* 中提出了主谓一致关系的三条基本原则:语法一致(Grammatical Agreement)、概念一致(Notional Agreement)和就近一致(Proximity Agreement)。

(1) 语法一致

主语为单数形式,谓语动词用单数形式;主语为复数形式,谓语动词也用复数形式。
The number of mistakes was surprising. 错误的数量很惊人。
Lei and Mary look healthy and strong. 蕾和玛丽看起来既健康又强壮。

(2) 概念一致

主语形式虽为单数,意义为复数,谓语动词要用复数形式。
John's family are having supper now. 约翰一家正在吃晚饭。
主语形式虽为复数而意义上却是单数,谓语动词要用单数形式。
Fifty dollars is too expensive for this dictionary. 这本词典 50 美元太贵了。

(3) 就近一致

这种一致就是谓语动词的单复数形式取决于最靠近它的词语。
Not only the teacher but also his students like playing football. 不仅老师喜欢踢足球,而且学生也喜欢踢足球。
Neither my gloves nor my hat goes with this dress. 我的手套和帽子都和这件衣服不相配。

30.2　主语与谓语一致的形式

主谓一致主要指名词作主语时的主谓一致、代词作主语时的主谓一致、数词及与数量相关的短语作主语时的主谓一致、并列主语的主谓一致、倒装句中的主谓一致以及动词不定式、动名词短语及从句作主语时的主谓一致。

(1) 不可数名词作主语时与谓语动词的一致

在 action, argument, advice, beauty, behaviour, cancer, conduct, childhood, friendship, fortune, history, happiness, honesty, information, justice, knowledge, kindness, laughter, magnificence,

progress, poverty, scenery, speech, traffic, work, will 等不可数名词作主语时,谓语动词用单数形式。
Robert's good behaviour deserves praise. 罗伯特的良好表现应该得到表扬。
There were a lot of people on the roads. 马路上行人众多。
Your information about Paris was out of date. 你提供的有关巴黎的信息已过时了。

(2) 主语为第三人称单数时与谓语动词的一致

主语为第三人称单数时,谓语动词一般现在时须用单数,be 的现在时用 is,过去时用 was。
Her answer differs from yours in every detail. 她的答案在细节上与你的不同。
We can't remember who this belongs to. 我们记不清这是谁的。
The car was making 60 miles an hour. 汽车以每小时 60 英里的速度运行。

(3) 助动词与主语在人称和数上的一致

当谓语动词由"助动词+主动词"构成时,只需助动词与主语的人称和数保持一致。
We are leaving tomorrow. 我们将于明天离开。
She is leaving tomorrow. 她将于明天离开。
Have you been to Suzhou? 你去过苏州吗?

(4) 表示"全体"、"部分"、"许多"、"多数"、"少数"、"无"、"种类"等不定数量的词语作主语时的主谓一致

① 主语为 all, any, enough, half, more, most, some 或由其所修饰时的主谓一致

这时,要根据意义一致的原则,谓语动词可用单数或复数形式。

A. 主语表示复数意义,谓语动词用复数形式。
All who have studied this question have come to the same conclusion. 所有研究过这个问题的人得出同样的结论。
All of us want to do the work better. 我们都想把工作做得更好。
She doesn't think any of her friends have seen me. 她想她的朋友都没有见过我。
Enough of the data have been collected. 已经搜集了足够的资料。
Half the oranges are bad. 有一半橘子是坏的。
Some of the arguments were founded on facts. 一些论点是以事实为依据的。
Some people were killed in the fire, but most were saved. 一些人在火灾中烧死,但绝大部分的人被救出来了。
Most of the students have already passed the examination. 绝大多数的学生已经通过该考试。

B. 主语表示单数意义或代表不可数名词,谓语动词用单数。
All of the pear was rotten. 整个梨都烂了。
Some of the work has been finished. 一些工作已完成了。
Half of the building was damaged in the flood. 在洪涝中半截楼被损坏了。
Most of the milk turned sour. 大部分牛奶变酸。

② 主语为 none 时的主谓一致

A. none 表示复数意义,谓语动词用复数形式。
None is/are frightened into submission by the threat of war. 没有(一个)人被战争的威胁吓倒。
None of these borrowings have affected the structure of our speech. 这些外来词一个也没有影响我们的语言结构。

B．表示单数意义或代表不可数名词，谓语动词用单数形式。

None is more qualified for the task than Tom. 执行这项任务，没有人比汤姆更合适的了。

There is none left. 全都没有了。

③ **主语为 both, few, a few, many, a good/great many, several 或由其所修饰时的主谓一致**

此时谓语动词用复数形式。

Both of his elder sisters are attending this university. 他的两个姐姐都在这所大学上学。

Few of your friends like him. 你的朋友中几乎无人喜欢他。

There are only a very few left. 只剩下很少几个。

Many of you have passed the examination. 你们中许多人已通过了这项考试。

Many hands make light work. 人多好办事。

A good many of us have no work. 我们中许多人没有工作。

Several of the pears are bad, and several more have worm holes. 有几个梨坏了，还有几个上面有虫眼。

Note：many is the 后跟单数名词，放在句首，意义为"多，很多"。

Many was the time we ate at that restaurant. 我们曾多次在那家餐馆吃过饭。

Many's the job she has left unfinished. 她还剩下许多工作没有完成。

④ **主语为 each, either, neither 或由 each, either, every, neither, no 所修饰时的主谓一致**

此时谓语动词用单数形式。

Three girls entered. Each was carrying a suitcase. 进来三个女孩，每人提着一个手提箱。

Each of the rooms is painted a different color. 每所房子都漆成不同的颜色。

Either of the plans is equally dangerous. 两个计划中无论哪一个都同样有危险。

Neither of them knows the truth. 他们谁也不知道真相。

Neither of us is happy about this situation. 我们俩对这局面都不满意。

No man is born wise. 聪明非天生。

Notes：A. neither 或 "either/neither of + 复数名词/代词"作主语时，谓语动词有时可用复数形式。

Jane doubts if either of them are coming. 简怀疑他们两人是否来。

Neither of the teachers are going to stay during the vacation. 假期里两个老师都不打算留下。

B. each, neither 位于主语后，作主语的同位语时，谓语的单复数由主语的数决定。

The girls each have an apple. 女孩每人有一只苹果。

You were each sentenced to one and a half years. 你们每个人被判一年半刑。

The two boys neither have a pear. 两个男孩均没有梨。

⑤ **主语为复合代词时的主谓一致**

Everyone who lives in the village has his own plot of land. 住在村子里的人都有自己的耕地。

Something has happened. 出事了。

Nothing is to be done. 没有什么要干的事。

Everyone praises the book. 人人都称赞这本书。

Everything goes well with Mark. 马克一切顺利。

Notes：A. 当 everybody, everyone, nobody, somebody, someone 作主语，其后带有反意疑问句时，反意疑问句中的谓语用复数形式。

Everybody disagrees, do they? 大家都反对，对不对？

Nobody is against it, aren't they? 对此无人反对，对不对？

Someone has been to Suzhou, haven't they? 有人已经去过苏州，对不对？

B. anyone/everyone 和 any one/every one 有区别。

any one/every one 多和 of 连用,而 anyone/everyone 则不能。
Any one of them may be chosen. 他们中任何人都有可能被选中。
Go to bed, every one of you. 你们所有的人都去睡觉。

⑥ 主语为 little, much 时的主谓一致

Quite a little of her spare time was spent in reading. 她用相当多的业余时间来看书。
Much has been done to improve conditions of work. 为改善工作条件,已做了很多努力。

⑦ 主语为"many a/more than one + 单数名词"和"one and a half + 名词复数"的主谓一致

此时,在意义上虽然是复数,但谓语动词用单数形式。
Many a comrade has sacrificed his life for the revolution. 许多同志为革命牺牲了自己的生命。
There is more than one answer to my question. 我的问题不止有一个答案。
One and a half pears is left on the table. 桌子上还剩下一个半梨。
A month and a half has passed. (= One and a half months has passed.) 一个半月已经过去了。

⑧ 主语为"the + 形容词/过去分词"或 the last, the remainder, the rest 名词的主谓一致

此时,谓语动词要根据意义一致的原则来决定其单复数形式。

A. 表示复数概念时,谓语动词用复数形式。

The young are full of vigour. 年轻人充满活力。
The unemployed lead a miserable life. 失业者过着悲惨的生活。
The rest/remainder of you are going on at once. 你们当中的其余人要马上继续前进。
The last of the apples are refrigerated. 最后一些苹果冷藏起来了。

B. 表示单数意义,谓语动词用单数形式。

The good in her overweighs the bad. 她身上的优点多于缺点。
The remainder/rest of the money was spent on furniture. 其余的钱都用来买了家具。
The rest needs no telling. 其余的就不必细说了。

⑨ 主语为 of 短语所修饰时的主谓一致

主语的意义由 of 后的内容决定,因为 of 前的词语只起限定作用,它们的谓语动词用单数还是复数,由 of 后边的成分决定,像这样的短语有 the majority of, a multitude of, multitudes of, a number of, large numbers of 等。

A. 谓语用复数。

The majority of his books are kept upstairs. 他的大部分书藏在楼上。
A vast number/Vast numbers of students are playing in the playground. 许多学生在操场上玩。

B. 谓语用单数。

有时 the majority of 后跟不可数名词或复数名词作主语,谓语动词也可用单数形式。
The vast majority of the students needs increased financial support. 大多数学生需要经济上增加援助。
The majority was in favor of the proposal. 多数人赞成这个建议。
The majority of the damage is easy to repair. 大多数的损坏易于修理好。

C. "a number of + 复数名词"后也接单数动词。

在某些语境中,"a number of + 复数名词"后也接单数动词(尤其在 there be 之后),这时说话人把整个短语当作一个整体来对待。
A number of books is missing from the library. 图书馆丢了许多书。
There was a large number of people over there. 那边有许多人。

D. "a couple of, dozens of, tens of, etc. + 不确切复数名词"时,谓语用复数。

像上面那些短语还有 scores of, hundreds of, thousands of, hundreds and thousands of, thousands upon thousands of, millions of 等。

There're a couple of letters on the table. 有两三封信在桌子上。

Scores of visitors come to China to visit the Great Wall. 许多游客来中国游览长城。

There are tens of reference books on this subject in the library. 图书馆里有关这个课程的参考书有几十本。

There were hundreds and hundreds of people in the park on Sundays. 星期天公园里有许多人。

E. "a brood of, a/this bunch of, a batch of, etc. +复数名词"时，谓语用复数，偶尔用单数。

那些表示"一簇"、"一队"、"一套"、"一排"、"一班"、"一群"、"一伙"等意义的短语有：a block of, a circle of, a class of, a cloud of, clouds of, a clump of, clumps of, a cluster of, clusters of, a colony of, a column of, a company of, a crop of, a crowd of, crowds of, a fleet of, a flock of, a gang of, a group of, a herd of, a host of, a line of, a lump of, a majority of, a pack of, a party of, a pile of, piles of, a rank of, ranks of, a row of, rows of, a school of, a series of, a swarm of, swarms of, a team of, a tribe of, a troop of 等。

a. 谓语动词用复数形式。

A flock of young girls were singing and dancing in the park yesterday. 昨天一群年轻姑娘在公园里唱歌跳舞。

A herd of problems have to be dealt with before we actually plunge into the project. 在动工之前我们还有许多问题需要解决。

The great lump of voters are still undecided. 大部分选民尚未拿定主意。

A bunch of keys are found in the car. 在车上发现了一串钥匙。

A pile of papers are waiting for Mike to correct. 一大堆试卷正等着迈克去改。

b. 谓语动词用单数形式。

Here comes a batch of recruits for the army. 这里来了一批新兵。

There is a pile of prints and letters on the table. 桌上放着许多印刷品和信件。

A fleet of ships is under orders to set sail. 一支船队正奉命起航。

There is a line of trees on either side of the river. 河的两岸都有一排树。

A flock of sheep was grazing in the field. 一群羊正在田里吃草。

c. 关于 a great/good deal of 后可否接复数名词。

a great/good deal of 后以前都说只接不可数名词，而在《牛津现代高级英汉双解词典》88年版的 P.299 的 deal 2 中出现了 have a great deal of friends 的说法。但其他词典均无此说，就是《牛津现代高级英汉双解词典》后来的版本也不见了这种说法。由此可见，a great/good deal 后可接复数名词的说法还没被广泛接受。而至今却还有人引用 a great/good deal of 后可接可数名词的不妥之说。

F. "a large amount of, a bit of, etc. +不可数名词"作主语时，谓语动词用单数。

像这样的短语还有：an abundance of, a good/great deal of, a large sum of, a great volume of, volumes of, a world of 等。

A large/great amount of water was spilt on the floor. 地板上洒了大量的水。

Vast amounts/A vast amount of heat is sent from the sun. 太阳释放出大量的热能。

There is a large amount of work for you to do. 有大量的工作需要你们做。

There's a world of truth in what she says. 她说的话很有道理。

Notes: a. an abundance of 后有时跟复数名词，但谓语动词仍用单数形式。

There was such an abundance of pears that year that many were left to rot under the trees. 那年梨丰收如此之多，许多都留在树下烂了。

b. the amount of 后有时也可接复数名词，但谓语动词仍用单数形式。

The amount of 5,000 dollars was lost in that trade. 在那宗生意上，损失总额达5000美元。

The amount of apples to be shipped is at least eight truckloads. 待装船的苹果总量至少有8卡车。

c. 但在当代英语中，amounts of 和 a large/great amount of 之后跟复数名词时，后接复数动词的情形也不乏其例，尤其在美国英语中。

A large/great amount of our investments are in property. 我们的大量资金投在房地产上。

large/great amounts of 后跟不可数名词时，谓语动词也可用复数形式。

Large amounts of money were spent on the building. 修这座建筑物花了大量的钱。

G. the bulk of（大部分），a flood of（大量的），a heap of（一堆），heaps of（许多的，大量的），loads of（许多的，大量的），a lot of, lots of, a mass of, a mountain of, a package of, a part/part of/the great part of, a percentage of, plenty of, a proportion of, a large quantity of, a sea of（许多的，大量的），scads of（许多的，大量的），a store of, a variety of,"分数、百分数＋of"后可跟复数可数名词或不可数名词，其谓语动词的形式由 of 后作主语的名词所表达的意义而定。

a. 后跟可数名词复数或某些集团名词，表示复数意义时，谓语动词用复数形式。

A variety of improvements are suggested at the meeting. 会上提出了许多种改进措施。

A great variety of toys were shown there. 那儿展出了各种各样的玩具。

Varieties of roses are grown here. 这儿种植各种玫瑰花。

There were scads of opportunities for all of you. 你们大家都有许多机会。

Four-fifths of the people present are against the plan. 出席的人有4/5反对这项计划。

A mass of students are entering the classroom. 大部分学生正在走进教室。

Note：在 there be 句型中，可根据就近原则，谓语动词用单数形式。

There was a mass of children in the garden. 花园里有许多孩子。

There was a flood of complaints about the bad language after the show. 演出结束后，人们对于表演中所用的恶劣语言提出了大量意见。

b. 后跟单数名词或不可数名词，表示单数意义时，谓语动词用单数形式。

There has been a large/small quantity of rain this spring. 今春雨下得很多/很少。

A small quantity of sugar was put in the boiled water. 开水里放了少量的糖。

A great deal of the furniture in the house is old-fashioned. 房子里的大部分家具是老式的。

There was a bank of snow in the way. 有一堆雪挡住了路。

Loads of milk has been distributed among the children. 在孩子们中分发了大量的牛奶。

Seventy-five percent of the surface of the earth is water. 地球表面的75%是水。

The great part of what Grace heard is only rumour. 格蕾丝听到的话大部分都只是谣言。

Notes：• 在当代英语中，a large quantity of 后面也可接可数名词，谓语动词也可用复数形式。

A large quantity of flowers have withered away in the garden. 花园里许多花都凋谢了。

• 有些 of 结构，of 前的部分是主要成分，其谓语动词一般根据语法一致原则，以 of 前词语的形式决定谓语动词的单复数形式。常用的这类短语有：a generation of, a kind of, a panel of, a pair of, a portion of, a set of, the amount of, the number of, the proportion of, the sum of, the variety of, the volume of 等。

A generation of people of a new type is growing up. 一代新人正在成长。

The number of books a man has read usually accounts for the man's knowledge and ability. 一个人读书的数量常常说明这个人的知识和能力。

A pair of gloves is a nice present. 一副手套是件好礼品。

The sum total of expenses for the trip was $800. 旅行的全部费用是800美元。

The variety of goods on display is surprising. 展出货物品种之多令人吃惊。

Note:"one+in（out of, of 等）+复数名词"作主语时,一般根据语法一致原则,谓语动词通常用单数形式,因为该结构的中心词是数词 one。

One out of twenty was badly damaged. 每二十个中就有一个受到严重损伤。

The check-ups on these 5,000 cars disclosed that one of four was defective. 通过对这 5000 辆汽车的检查,发现 1/4 的车有缺陷。

但在非正式文体中,有的遵循就近原则,谓语动词用复数形式。

One in ten suffer from bronchitis. 1/10 的人患有支气管炎。

One of the students were asked to answer the teacher's questions. 请一位学生回答该问题。

* 与 kind/sort/type/form of 连用的单复数名词作主语时,kind/sort/type 表示"种类"时,常采用"限定词（a,this,that 等）+kind/sort/type+of+名词"的结构,其后的名词不论是可数还是不可数,一般都不带冠词,谓语动词均采用单数形式。

This kind of wood splits easily. 这种木头容易劈开。

A kind/sort of new farm tool has been turned out. 一种新型的农具已经生产出来了。

This kind of apples is highly priced. 这种苹果价格很高。

This sort of men is dangerous. 这种男人很危险。

This type of wine is only made in France. 这种酒只产于法国。

Note:如果复数名词放在 kind/sort/type 之前,谓语动词则要用复数形式。

Things of a kind come together. 物以类聚。

Questions of this type compel the children to think. 这种类型的问题迫使孩子们去思考。

Oranges of this sort are highly priced. 这种橘子价格很高。

all/many/these/those/kinds/types/sorts/forms of 后跟复数名词（有时不可数名词）作主语时,谓语动词用复数形式。

Many kinds of apples grow in your garden. 你们花园里长着很多种苹果。

There are two types of rocks in this area. 该地区有两类岩石。

All forms of matter are composed of tiny particles. 各种形式的物质都是由微型颗粒组成的。

（5）"these/those kind/sort/type of+复数名词"作主语时,谓语动词用复数形式

Those kind of tests are good. 那种测验很好。

These sort of cars have their use. 这种汽车有它们的用处。

These sort of people are very difficult to get along with. 这样的人很难相处。

"what kind of+名词"作主语时,谓语动词形式由 kind 的单复数而定。

What kind of cherry tree flourishes best in this region? 该地区什么样的樱桃树生长最好?

What kinds of cherry tree flourish best in this region? 该地区哪些种类的樱桃树生长最好?

（6）what, which, who 作主语或作主语的定语时的主谓一致

当 what, which, who 作主语或作主语的定语时,其谓语动词要根据意义一致的原则,即由这些词所表达的意义或上下文来决定谓语动词的单复数形式。

① 表示单数意义,谓语动词用单数形式。

—Who was at the door? —The postman (was). 谁在门口?是邮递员。

What makes you think so? 是什么使你这样想的?

Which comes first, A or B? 谁先来的,A 还是 B?

② 表示复数意义,谓语动词用复数形式。

Which are our seats? 哪些是我们的位子?

Who have won Nobel Prizes for literature in the past ten years? 在最近的十年里,哪些人获得了诺贝尔文学奖?

(7) 以-s 结尾的名词作主语时与谓语动词的一致

① 表示学科的名词

acoustics(声学),athletics(体育课),classics(古典文学),economics(经济学),electronics(电子学),ethics(伦理学),gymnastics(健身术),linguistics(语言学),mathematics(数学),mechanics(力学),optics(光学),phonetics(语音学),physics(物理学),politics(政治学),statistics(统计学),therapeutics(治疗学),thermodynamics(热力学)等作主语时,谓语动词用单数形式。

Athletics/Linguistics is recommended for every student. 每一个学生都要上体育课/语言学。

Physics is not her strong point. 物理学不是她的特长。

Mathematics is a subject studied in nearly every school. 数学是几乎每所学校都要学的一门课程。

但是当上述名词表示其他意义时,谓语动词用单复数形式均可。

Politics sometimes has/have an unfortunate influence on character. 政治信仰有时会对人的性格产生不良影响。

Her mathematics are/is weak. 她的数学能力差。

The area of the room is 160 square feet, if my mathematics are/is correct. 如果我的计算正确的话,该房间的面积是160平方英尺。

② 表示游戏名称的名词

billiards(台球戏),bowls(滚木球戏),darts(投镖游戏),dominoes(多米诺骨牌),draughts(跳棋),fives(壁球),marbles(打弹子),ninepins(九柱球戏),skittles(九柱戏),rackets(拍球戏)等作主语时多用作单数,谓语动词用单数形式。

Billiards is my favorite recreation. 台球是我最喜爱的娱乐活动。

Is draughts a game for two? 跳棋是由两人玩吗?

cards 作主语时,谓语动词用复数形式。

Cards are played everywhere in China. 在中国,打牌到处可见。

③ 表示疾病的名词

AIDS(艾滋病),arthritis(关节炎),bronchitis(支气管炎),diabetes(糖尿病),measles(麻疹),mumps(腮腺炎),phlebitis(静脉炎),piles(痔疮),rabies(狂犬病),rickets(软骨病),shingles(带状疱疹,缠腰龙)等作主语时,被看作单数,谓语动词用单数形式。

Indeed, they say, AIDS is spread primarily by carriers who are not ill. 他们说艾滋病的确主要是由没有发病的病毒携带者传播的。

Rabies is spread only by the bite of an infected animal. 狂犬病只有被受感染的动物咬后才会传染。

Diabetes is a common disease. 糖尿病是一种常见病。

Generally measles occurs in children. 通常儿童易得麻疹。

但谓语有时也用作复数形式。

Rickets are/is caused by malnutrition. 软骨病是由于营养不良引起的。

Shingles are/is serious. How long has John had them/it? 带状疱疹很严重。约翰得这病多久了?

Mumps are/is fairly rare in adults. 腮腺炎在成年人中相当罕见。

④ 以-s 结尾,单复数同形的名词

barracks(营房),bellows(风箱),crossroads(路口),chassis(车架),Ladies(女厕所),headquarters(司令部),means(方法、手段),series(系列),species(种类),whereabouts(下落),works(工厂)等作主语时,谓语动词的单复数取决于名词在句中所表达的单复数意义。

A barracks was stormed by the enemy troops. 一所营房受到敌军部队的袭击。
Two barracks in the suburbs have been surrounded. 郊区的两所营房已被包围。
A headquarters was set up to direct the operation. 成立了一个总部来指挥作战。
Their headquarters are in Paris. 他们的总部在巴黎。
Every means has/All possible means have been tried. 每种方法/所有可能的方法都尝试过了。
There is only one means by which real success can be achieved, but there are many means by which we can make money. 取得真正成功的方法只有一个,但赚钱的门路却有很多。

⑤ **由两部分构成的表示工具名称的复数名词**

chopsticks(筷子),calipers(卡钳),compasses(圆规),forceps(钳子,镊子),glasses(眼镜),nail-shears(指甲剪),spectacles(眼镜),pincers(钳子),pliers(钳子),scales(天平),scissors(剪刀),tongs(钳子,夹子),tweezers(镊子),flares(喇叭裤),jeans(牛仔裤),pants(紧身长、短衬裤),pajamas(睡衣裤),shorts(短裤),suspenders(吊裤带),trousers(裤子),stockings(长筒袜)等作主语时,谓语动词用复数形式。

Forceps are medical instruments used for holding objects firmly. 镊子是用来夹牢物品的医学仪器。
The stockings were seconds and have some slight defects. 这长筒袜是次等的,因为稍有瑕疵。
The scales need readjusting. 这天平要重新校准。
My blue trousers have worn out. 我的蓝裤子穿破了。

如果上述名词前用 a pair of 来修饰时,句中的谓语动词要根据 pair 的单复数来决定。

This pair of scissors is made in Hangzhou. 这把剪刀是杭州产的。
Here are some new pairs of trousers. 这里有一些新裤子。

⑥ **某些以-s 结尾的名词(有的表示抽象意义)**

articles(货物),alms(救济钱物),archives(档案),arms(武器),clothes(衣服),contents(目录),eaves(屋檐),fireworks(烟火),funds(现金),goods,minutes(记录),morals(道德,品行),outskirts(郊区,郊外),remains(遗体),riches(钱财),shears(被剪下的东西),soapsuds(肥皂泡沫),stairs(楼梯),suburbs(郊区),thanks,wages,letters(文学),troops(军队),tropics(热带),writings(作品)等作主语时,谓语动词多用复数形式。

The minutes of the last meeting were read and confirmed. 上次会议记录宣读后被确认下来了。
Riches have wings. 钱财易散。
The goods/articles ordered last month have not arrived yet. 上个月订的货物还没有到。
The contents of this book are most fascinating. 该书的内容非常吸引人。

Notes:A. news 作主语时,谓语动词用单数。
No news is good news. 没有消息就是好消息。
Is there any news from the front? 有来自前线的消息吗?
B. wages 虽然用复数形式,但一般不与 many, few 或数词连用,但可以用 much, little, these, those 或物主限定词来修饰。
These/Their wages are too low. 这些/他们的工资太低了。
They don't receive much wages. 他们没得到优厚的工资。

⑦ **以-ings 结尾的名词**

doings(所需的东西),belongings(所有物,财产),bookings(订票),clippings(剪下物),diggings(开采物),earnings(收入,工资),filings(锉屑),findings(结论,研究结果),lodgings(出租房屋),savings(储蓄金),sightings(发现),surroundings(环境),sweepings(扫拢的垃圾),takings(收入),tidings(消息),winnings(赢得的钱物),workings(活动情况,工作原理)等作主语时,谓语动词通常用复数形式。

All my belongings are in this bag. 我所带的东西都在这个袋子里。

The sweepings of the godown have been disposed of. 仓库的垃圾已被清除掉了。
His savings are small. 他存的钱很少。
Takings do not cover expenses. 入不敷出。
Note：tidings(消息)作主语时，谓语动词可用复数，也可用单数。
Good tidings spread/spreads all over the land. 好消息传遍整个大地。
The tidings has come a little late. 这消息来得有点迟了。

⑧ 用作人名、地名、国家名称、组织名称、书名或报纸名称的复数名词

这些名词作主语时，一般用作单数，谓语动词用单数形式。
The United Nations was established in 1945. 联合国成立于1945年。
Mars is farther from the earth than the moon is. 火星离地球比月亮离地球远。
The Times usually speaks for the British government. 《泰晤士报》常常是英国政府的喉舌。
General Motors produces many different types of cars. 通用汽车公司生产多种不同类型的汽车。
Notes：A. Olympic Games 作主语时，谓语动词用复数形式。
Nowadays the Olympic Games are held in different countries in turn. 现今奥运会在不同的国家轮流举行。
B. 国家名称、组织机构名称等专有名词作主语时，有时也可用复数，特别是在英国英语中。
Our Planning Committee have considered your request. 我们的计划委员会已经考虑过你的请求。
The U. N. have debated the world trade. 联合国讨论了世界贸易问题。

⑨ 表示群岛、山脉、海峡、瀑布等地理名称，以-s结尾的名词作主语

此时通常用作复数，谓语动词用复数形式。
The West Indies, apart from the Bahamas, are commonly divided into two parts. 西印度群岛，除了巴哈马群岛外，通常分为两部分。
The Himalayas have a magnificent variety of plant and animal life. 喜马拉雅山脉有许多种类的动植物。
The Straits of Gibraltar have not lost their strategic importance. 直布罗陀海峡并未失去其战略上的重要性。
Note：在表示瀑布的名词之后，谓语动词用单复数均可。
Niagara Falls is a stupendous sight. 尼亚加拉瀑布是一种壮观的景象。
Niagara Falls are not as high as Victoria Falls. 尼亚加拉瀑布没有维多利亚瀑布高。

（8）集体名词作主语时与谓语动词的一致

集体名词一般只以单数形式出现，但是有些单数形式的集体名词常用作复数，有些常用作单数，有些有时作单数，有时作复数。因此，集体名词作主语时其谓语动词的用法可分为以下四种情况：

① 个体性集体名词

个体性集体名词(Distributive Collectives)是指由相同的个体成分组成的集体名词，如 clan(部族，宗派)，folk(人们)，kindred(亲属)，nobility(贵族)，people(人民)，cattle(家畜，牛)，poultry(家禽)，vermin(害虫)等。这类词作主语时，谓语动词一般用复数形式。
The nobility are the people who have titles: the dukes, earls, lords, etc. 贵族就是指那些有如公爵、伯爵、勋爵等头衔的人。
The Chinese people are brave and diligent. 中国人民勇敢勤劳。
These vermin do much harm to poultry. 这些害虫对家禽很有害。
另外，majority(多数人)，minority(少数人)也属于这一类词。它们作主语时，谓语动词通常用复数形式。
The majority were on John's side. 绝大多数人都支持约翰。
The nation wants peace, only a minority want the war to continue. 整个国家需要和平，只有少数人想让战争

继续下去。

② **概括性集体名词**

概括性集体名词(Generalizing Collectives)常用来概括从事相同行业或职业的人们,常见的有: artillery(炮兵), clergy(教士,神职人员), elite(社会名流,杰出人物,优秀分子), foot/infantry(步兵), gentry(绅士们), horse(骑兵), militia(民兵), police(警察), rank and file(士兵,民众,老百姓)等。这类词与定冠词the连用,一般属复数,作主语时,谓语动词也用复数形式。

The elite of the city were present at the reception for the governor. 本城知名人士都出席了州长欢迎会。

The police are on the track of the criminals. 警方正在追踪罪犯。

③ **种类性集体名词**

种类性集体名词(Class Collectives)表示某一类别东西的总称。

apparatus(器械), baggage(行李), clothing(衣服), crockery(陶器), cutlery(餐具), equipment(设备), foliage(叶子), footwear(鞋类), furniture(家具), jewellery(珠宝), luggage(行李), machinery(机械), merchandise(商品), millinery(女帽), poetry(诗), stationery(文具纸张), underwear(内衣), weaponry(武器)等。

这类词通常看作单数,作主语时,谓语动词也用单数。

There was some attractive furniture on show, but the prices were pretty steep. 一些漂亮的家具在展览,可是价钱相当高。

Much machinery needs oiling. 许多机器需要上油。

Poetry does not translate easily. 诗歌不容易翻译。

④ **团体性集体名词**

团体性集体名词(Group Collectives)可用作单数或复数。作为一个整体看待时,用单数;作为其中成员看待时,用复数。常见的这类词有: army(军队), association(协会), audience(听众,观众), band(乐队), board(委员会), brigade(队,组), choir(唱诗班), class(班), club(俱乐部), college(学会,社团), committee(委员会), company(队,连), congregation(宗教会议,全体教徒), council(委员会,理事会), couple(一对,夫妇), crew(乘务员,船员), crowd(人群), data(资料), enemy(敌人), family(家庭), firm(公司), gang(队,群), government(政府,内阁), group(群,组), jury(陪审团), majority(多数), management(董事会,资方), minority(少数), navy(海军,海军官兵), nobility(贵族阶层), opposition(反对党), orchestra(管弦乐队), party(党团体), public(公众), staff(全体人员), team(队), youth(青年人)等。

A. 看作一个整体,谓语动词用单数形式。

The committee consists of/is made up of seven members. 委员会由七名委员组成。

Some people say that today's youth has no sense of responsibility. 有人说现在的年轻人缺乏责任感。

B. 看作其中的成员,谓语动词用复数形式。

The committee agree to discuss the proposal at the next meeting. 委员们同意下次会议讨论该建议。

The youth of today are fond of dancing. 现在的年轻人都喜欢跳舞。

The class are taking notes in English. 这个班的同学在用英语做笔记。

(9) **表示时间、度量、价值、数量等名词复数和数词作主语时与谓语动词的一致**

① 根据意义一致的原则

把复数名词看作一个整体,谓语动词则用单数形式。

A hundred cents goes to a dollar. 100分等于一美元。

Thirty years is only a very short span in human history. 在人类历史上,三十年只不过是弹指一瞬间。
Seven days is quite enough for the return voyage. 来回旅程七天足够了。
One hundred dollars is more than she can pay. 100 美元非她所能承担。

② 根据语法一致的原则

把复数名词看作若干个个体,谓语动词则用复数形式。

There are three silver dollars in each of the stockings. 每只长袜中都有三枚一美元的银币。
The past two weeks have been the driest in the country's history. 过去的两个星期是该国历史上最干旱的。
Our last four years have been full of surprises. 我们过去的这四年充满了种种令人惊异之事。

③ "加、减、乘、除"算式中主谓的一致

A. 计算时,谓语动词多用单数形式。

Twenty plus six is twenty-six. 20 + 6 = 26
Sixteen minus five leaves eleven. 16 - 5 = 11
Seven times three is/makes twenty-one. 7 × 3 = 21
Fifty divided by five is ten. 50 ÷ 5 = 10
Three squared is nine. 3 的平方是 9。
Four cubed is sixty-four. 4 的立方是 64。

B. 两数相加并采用并列形式,或两数相乘时,谓语动词也可用复数形式。

Four and four make eight. 4 + 4 = 8。
Six times seven are forty-two. 6 × 7 = 42。

④ 数词作主语时的主谓一致

基数词作主语表示数目的大小并被看作整体时,谓语动词通常用单数形式。

Seventeen means ten and seven. 17 就是 10 加 7。
9999 is a large number. 9999 是个很大的数字。

但是当基数词表示的是两个或多个的人或事物时,谓语动词则用复数形式。

Fifty-eight were present at the meeting. 有 58 人出席了会议。
Twenty-eight were killed in the accident. 事故中有 28 人死亡。

⑤ 度量衡、货币单位等汉语音译名词作主语时的主谓一致

汉语音译(表示度量衡、币制等单位)的名词,如果看作一个整体,谓语动词用单数;否则,谓语动词则用复数。

Six jin of rice is equivalent to 3 kilo in the metric system. 6 斤米相当于公制 3 公斤。
Can you figure out how much is RMB 999.88 in American money? 你能算出人民币 999.88 元合多少美元吗?
Of this, about 9,000 mu were turned into rice paddy. 其中有 9000 亩改成了水稻田。

⑥ "数词 + 货币属格 + worth of + 复数名词"作主语时的主谓一致

由"数词 + 货币属格 + worth of + 名词(复数)的词组"作主语时,谓语动词的数应根据上下文表示的确切意义来判定。一般有两种情况:

A. 如果其中的名词(复数)是需要加以强调的,则谓语动词根据意义一致和就近原则,也用复数形式。

Nearly a million dollars' worth of famous paintings were damaged. 价值近百万美元的名画遭到了破坏。

B. 如果要突出价值,那么根据语法一致原则,谓语动词的数要和 worth 一致,用单数形式。

There is nearly a million dollars' worth of famous paintings on the wall. 那墙上陈列着的名画差不多要值一百万美元。

(10) there/here be 句型中的主谓一致

① 按就近原则

There is a variety of shops in the United States. 美国有各种各样的商店。

They had to stop here, because there was a heap of stones in the way. 他们只好停在这儿了,因为一堆石头挡住了去路。

Helen, come, here is a bag of candies for you. 海伦,来,这里有给你的一袋糖果。

在"there be + 并列主语"的句子中,谓语动词多数使用就近原则。

There comes a young lady and her two kids. 来了一位年轻太太和她的两个孩子。

There is his wife and family coming with him. 他的妻子和家人和他一起来。

There are some books, a pen and a pencil on the desk. 桌子上有一些书、一支钢笔和一支铅笔。

② 按意义一致原则

There are a pile of English grammar books on the desk. 桌子上有一大堆英语语法书。

There is still a lot of work to be done before the house is ready for occupation. 要使这房子完全准备好住人,还有大量的活要干。

There are a lot of students waiting outside. 外边有许多学生在等待。

Note:a lot of 后跟名词主语时,谓语动词的单复数形式通常由其后名词的单复数来决定。

There are a lot of skyscrapers in New York. 纽约有许多摩天大楼。

There is a lot of opportunity for investors in this part of the world. 在世界的这一地区,投资者有许多机会。

但是有的语法学家认为,在 there be 句型中,there 是形式主语,因此谓语应和 there 一致。因为 there 没有复数形式,所以谓语动词只能用单数形式。用 is 时,多用缩写形式。

There's lots of people in the lecture hall. 报告厅里有许多人。

There's many friends I would like to meet. 我想会见许多朋友。

(11) 并列主语的主谓一致

① 由 and 和 both 连接的并列主语与谓语动词的一致

A. 并列主语表示复数概念时,谓语动词用复数形式。

December and January are the coldest months. 12月和1月是最冷的月份。

Both bread and butter were sold out in that grocery. 那个食品杂货店里的面包和黄油都卖光了。

B. 并列主语表示同一个人、同一概念、同一事物时,谓语动词用单数形式。

The great scholar and poet is dead. 这位伟大的学者和诗人去世了。

His lawyer and former college friend was with him on his trip to Europe. 他的律师——也是他从前大学时代的朋友——同他一起去欧洲旅行了。

The Premier and Foreign Minister was present at the state banquet. 总理兼外长出席了国宴。

The singer and dancer is to attend our evening. 这位歌舞演员将参加我们的晚会。

C. 当两种和两种以上的物质混合成为一体作主语时,谓语动词用单数形式。

The smoke and gas fills the building. 满楼都是烟气。

Much mud and sand gathers to block the river, down which water and oil is flowing. 泥沙聚集堵塞河道,沿着该河,水带着油正在顺流而下。

Note:and 连接成对配套的单数可数名词作主语时,谓语动词用单数形式。常见的有:a cart and horse(一辆马车), a knife and fork(一副刀叉), a cup and saucer(一副杯碟), a hat and coat(一套衣帽), a table and chair(一套桌椅), a watch and chain(一块带链的挂表), a carriage and pair(一辆双马车), a coat and skirt(一套上装和裙子), salt and water(盐水), whisky and soda(苏打威士忌酒), the hammer and sickle(铁锤镰刀旗), a rod and line(一个有钓丝的钓竿)等。

The knife and fork has been washed. 刀叉已经洗好了。

A cart and horse was seen at the distance. 远远看见一辆马车。

D. 并列主语前分别用 each, every, many a, no 等修饰时,谓语动词用单数形式。

Each book and each paper was in proper place. 每本书、每张报纸都摆放得井井有条。

Many a worker and many a peasant has praised the play. 许多工人、农民都赞扬这个戏。

In our country every boy and every girl has the right to education. 在我国每个男童和女童都有权接受教育。

E. 一个单数不可数名词为几个并列的形容词所修饰时,可指一件事或几件事。这种名词作主语时,要根据意义一致的原则决定动词的单复数形式。

a. 表示复数概念,谓语动词用复数。

The German and English language have something in common. 德语和英语有些共同之处。

American and Dutch beer are both much lighter than British beer. 美国啤酒和荷兰啤酒比英国啤酒清淡。

b. 表示单数概念,谓语动词用单数。

Cool and fresh wind is blowing from the north. 从北方吹来凉爽清新的风。

Simple and plain living is a fine quality. 生活简朴是一种好品质。

F. 几个并列的形容词修饰一个可数名词时,谓语动词的单复数有以下三种情况:

a. 主语为复数名词时,谓语动词用复数形式。

Clever and dull students are treated alike. 聪明的学生和愚笨的学生受到同样的待遇。

b. 主语为单数名词时,谓语动词用单数形式。

A black and white kitten was found in the garden yesterday. 昨天在花园里发现了一只黑白色的小花猫。

The tenth and last chapter is written by Professor Lin. 第十章即最后一章由林教授撰写。

c. 由 and 连接两个带定冠词的名词修饰语或物主代词来修饰作主语的一个单数名词时,表示复数意义,谓语动词用复数形式。

The tenth and the last chapter are written by Professor Lin. 第十章和最后一章都是由林教授写的。

Her home and her office are on the third floor. 她的家和办公室均在三楼。

G. 并列的动词不定式短语或动名词短语作主语时,谓语动词通常用单数形式。

Early to bed and early to rise makes a man healthy, wealthy and wise. 早睡、早起使一个人富裕、聪明、身体好。

Drinking too much and smoking too much was responsible for his sudden and early death. 他突然早逝归咎于他酗酒贪烟。

但当并列的不定式短语或动名词短语作主语表示复数意义时,谓语动词用复数形式。

What to read and how to read are quite different things. 阅读的内容和阅读的方法是完全不同的事。

Hunting and fishing are very good sports. 打猎和钓鱼是很好的运动项目。

H. 带有并列动词的 what-从句作主语时,根据意义一致原则决定动词的数,如 what-从句表示复数意义,谓语动词用复数形式。

What I say and do are two different things. (=What I say is one thing and what I do is another thing.) 我说什么是一回事,我做什么又是另一回事。

what-从句表示单数意义,谓语动词用单数形式。

What I say and do is my own affair. (= That which I say and do …) 我说什么、做什么是我个人的事。

I. 并列从句作主语时,谓语动词用复数形式。

What I say and what I think are my own affair. (= What I say is my own affair and what I think is my own affair.) 我说什么和想什么都是我自己的事。

What he did and when he did it are the only things I want to know. 他做了些什么和什么时候做是我唯一想知道的事情。

J. 用 and 连接的名词所有格修饰主语时，主语可用复数形式，也可用单数形式，而谓语动词均用复数形式。
Jack's and Dick's room look to the south.（两个人各住一间，共两间）
Jack and Dick's room looks to the south.（两人共住一间）
Jack and Dick's rooms look to the south.（两人共住两间或两间以上）
Note：在此情况下，也有省去第二个短语的中心词的情况。
Her idea and John's are quite different. 她的想法跟约翰的想法完全不同。

（12）倒装句中的主谓一致

倒装句中主谓一致可分为三种情况：在倒装句中，主语为并列主语；一些副词、介词短语置于句首；"状语＋单数动词＋两个或两个以上单数名词"结构中主谓一致。

① 并列主语与谓语动词的一致

此时，谓语动词通常按就近原则处理。
In the distance was heard the applause of the people, the shouts and clapping of hands. 在远方听到了人们的喝彩、欢呼和拍手声。
Where is your mother and younger brothers? 你母亲和弟弟们在哪儿？

② 一些副词、介词短语置于句首及像 no sooner … than 之类的关联词等置于句首时的倒装句的主谓一致

表示地点的介词短语，一些含否定意义和方向性的副词，某些关联连词（no sooner … than, hardly … when），含有 no 的介词短语（on no account），频度、方式或程度状语 only, so 等置于句首时，也常采用主谓倒装的形式。这些倒装句中谓语动词的数一般遵循语法一致的原则，要与动词后面主语的数保持一致。
On the wall were famous paintings. 墙上是一些名画。
Near the eastern end of our country was the Pacific Ocean. 靠我国东面的是太平洋。
Hidden underground is a wealth of gold, silver, copper, lead and zinc. 地下埋藏了大量的金、银、铜、铅和锌。
On no account shall I meet him halfway. 我绝不向他妥协。
Hardly had he arrived at the station when the train began to leave. 他一到车站，火车就开动了。
Only then did I take pity on her. 只有在那时我才同情她。

③ "状语＋单数动词＋两个或两个以上单数名词"的倒装句的主谓一致

较多的情况是：单数动词后接两个或两个以上的单数名词。
On the right of each person is a table-napkin and a plate with a cup of tea on it. 每人右边有一块餐巾和一个盘子，盘里放着一杯茶。

（13）由 either … or, neither … nor 或 or 连接的并列主语与谓语动词的一致

由上述连词连接并列主语时，谓语动词通常根据就近原则，即动词的单复数形式以靠近它的名词或代词的单复数形式而定。
Either he or I am to attend the meeting. 不是他就是我去参加会议。
Neither money nor fame has influence on him. 名和利都不会影响他。
He or his assistants are to blame. 他或他的助手们应该受到责备。
Note：否定关联连词 neither … nor 虽然在意思上表示选择，但在不太正式的用法中，更多的是从概念考虑，由于含有"两者都不"的意思，因此用复数动词倒更显得自然。

Neither he nor his wife have arrived. 他妻子和他均没有来。
Neither money nor fame have influence on me. 名与利都不能影响我。
Neither father nor mother agree. 父母都不同意。

(14) 由 not only ... but also 连接的并列主语

此时,谓语动词通常遵循就近原则。由 not ... but 连接的并列主语,其中一个是肯定,一个是否定,其谓语动词须与肯定的主语在人称和数上保持一致。

Not you but I am to blame. 不是你而是我应该受到责备。
Not only the students but also their teacher goes to the exhibition. 不仅学生们而且他们的老师也去参观了展览会。

(15) 后跟介词短语的主语或其他连接词连接的并列结构的主语与谓语动词的一致

主语后跟介词 along with, in company with, together with, with, accompanied by, including, like, besides, but, except, in addition to, instead of, plus 等引导的短语或跟连接词 as well as, as much as, more than, no less than, rather than, let alone, not to mention 等连接的短语时,其谓语动词与这些短语前边的主语保持一致。

① 主语为复数时,谓语动词用复数。

All but the first mate were rescued. 除了大副之外,所有的人都得救了。
They except Mr. Smith have seen the film. 除史密斯先生外,他们都看过这部电影。
The parents, rather than their son, are responsible for the accident. 是父母,而不是他们的儿子,对事故负有责任。

② 主语为单数时,谓语动词用单数。

Tony, along with his parents, has moved to London. 托尼同他父母一起搬到了伦敦。
I as well as they am ready to help you. 不仅他们愿意帮助你,我也愿意帮助你。
Mr. Li, as much as his brothers, was responsible for the loss. 李先生和他兄弟们一样,要对损失负责。

Note:在口语中,由于上述词语与 and 意义相近,常根据意义一致原则,即使真正主语是单数,谓语动词也可用复数形式。

The captain together with half-a-dozen more were/was taken prisoners. 船长连同其他六人被关进牢里。
Mark as well as Mike were/was there. 马克和迈克都在那里。

主语后带有一个作解释用的同位语时,其谓语动词与前边的主语保持一致。

I, your teacher, am aware of the danger. 我,你们的老师,明白其危险。

(16) 从句作主语时与谓语动词的一致

从句作主语时,谓语动词通常用单数形式,特别是用 it 作形式主语时,动词总是用单数形式。

Whether this kind of chemicals is better has not been tried. 这种化肥是否好些还未试验。
When and where the meeting will take place has not been decided yet. 开会的时间和地点还未决定。
It is not yet settled whether Mary is going to London. 玛丽是否去伦敦还未定。

Note:当 what 从句作主语时,谓语动词多用单数形式,但在下列三种情况下,可用复数:

① 当 what 引导的主语从句的表语为复数时。

What was real to her were the details of her life. 对她来说真实的东西就是她生活中的琐事。

② 当 what 从句中的谓语动词和主语补足语均为复数时,主句中的谓语动词也可以用复数形式。

What appear to be large windows in the second storey are glass heat collectors. 在二层楼上看上去像是大窗

子的东西是玻璃集热器。

③ 当 what 从句是一个具有复数意义的并列结构时。

What she says and does do not agree. 她言行不一致。

⑰ 定语从句中主谓语的一致

在定语从句中,当关系代词在从句中作主语时,其谓语动词的人称和数要与其先行词保持一致。

It is a question that needs very careful consideration. 这是一个需要非常仔细考虑的问题。

Nothing in the world is difficult for one who sets his mind to it. 世上无难事,只怕有心人。

Note:"one of + 复数名词"结构后跟的定语从句中作主语的关系代词的先行词是 one 还是 of 后的复数名词,其谓语动词的单复数不同。

Robert is one of those people who have trouble making up their minds. 罗伯特是个那种难以拿定主意的人。

Grace is one of those persons who always think they are right. 格蕾丝是个那种总是认为自己正确的人。

但是,在非正式文体中,有时"one of + 复数名词"后的定语从句也用单数形式的谓语动词。

That is one of those remarks that are/is intended to start argument. 那是一句意欲引起争论的话。

在上述例句中,关系代词的先行词都是 of 后的复数名词,所以谓语动词都用复数形式。但是当 one 前带有 the 或 the only 时,关系代词的先行词是 one,而不是 of 后的复数名词,定语从句中的谓语动词需用单数形式。

This is the one of the books on the subject that has ever been written in French. 这是有关这个科目的书中唯一用法文写的一本书。

还应注意的是,当"one of which"这一结构在定语从句中作主语时,谓语动词一般与 one 一致,用单数形式。

There are different forms of energy, one of which is atomic energy. 有各种不同形式的能,其中之一是原子能。

(18) 动词不定式短语和动名词短语作主语时与谓语动词的一致

动词不定式(短语)和动名词(短语)作主语时,动词一律用单数形式。

To master science means to master laws of nature. 掌握科学意味着掌握自然法则。

Improving the production process is necessary. 改进生产工序是必要的。

(19) 在"It is + 被强调的主语 + that/who 从句"强调结构中

that/who 从句中谓语动词与被强调的主语在人称和数上保持一致。

It is Tom that makes such a noise. 是汤姆这样吵闹。

It is George who is wrong. 是乔治错了。

It is precisely the people who (that) create history. 正是人民创造了历史。

It is I who am responsible for the accident. 是我负责这起事故。

(20) 其他几种情况下的主谓一致

① 有些"the + -ed 分词"结构用来指具有某种特性的一类东西或抽象的概念,谓语动词一般用单数形式。

The known is less exciting than the unknown. 未知的比已知的更令人兴奋。

The unknown (= What is unknown) is usually feared. 人们通常对未知的事物感到忧虑。

② 指不止一种东西时,谓语动词有时也可用复数形式。

The unexpected always happen. 意想不到的事总是会发生。

③ 名词化的形容词表示一个抽象概念或某种特征时,谓语动词常用单数形式。

The beautiful exists in contrast with the ugly. 美的东西和丑的东西相比较而存在。

The new and progressive always trumps over the old and obsolete. 新的进步的事物总是要战胜旧的落后的事物。

④ 有些名词化的形容词既可表示类概念(指某类人),也可表示抽象的概念。表示类概念时,谓语动词用复数形式;表示抽象概念时,谓语动词用单数形式。试比较:

The old is sure to be replaced by the new. 旧的事物必然要被新生事物所代替。

The old are apt to catch cold. 老年人容易得感冒。

⑤ "the + 形容词的比较级/最高级"也可用作名词化的形容词。作主语时,根据含义选用单数或复数形式的谓语动词。

The more diligent of Class Three have passed the examination. 三班中比较努力的都考及格了。

The most important is that you have finished the task in spite of the difficulties. 最重要的是,尽管有困难,你们还是完成了任务。

⑥ 有时,名词化的形容词前面的定冠词 the 可以用物主限定词或其他限定词来代替。

Our injured were hidden among the masses. 我们的伤员藏在群众中间。

Thirty wounded were removed and twenty buried. 运走30个伤员,安葬了20个死者。

⑦ "the + 形容词"结构中,形容词可有副词或后置定语修饰。

The extremely/very wise can avoid such temptations. 大智者能避开这样的诱惑。

The old in spirit enjoy life. 精神上老年人能享受生活的乐趣。

⑧ "the + 形容词"被一个定语从句修饰时,从句中的谓语动词一般采用复数形式。

The injured who are losing hope need more help. 失去希望的伤者需要更多的帮助。

⑨ the former/the latter 用来替代前面出现过的名词/代词用作主语时,要根据它们所指代对象的数来决定谓语动词的数。

Of horses and sheep, the former are the more useful. 马和羊,前者更有用处。

⑩ "the + 表示民族的形容词"在特定的语言环境中(往往带定语),也可特指某个具体的成员,这时谓语动词要用单数。

The Swiss/The Dutch Tony came across in the street was very friendly. 托尼在街上碰到的那个瑞士人/荷兰人非常友好。

The Swiss/The Dutchman/is flying to Beijing. 那位瑞士人/荷兰人要乘飞机去北京。

⑪ 介词短语、副词和从句作主语时的主谓一致

非正式用法中,有时介词短语、副词和状语从句也可用作主语,这时谓语动词一般采用单数形式。

In the mornings is best for Mike. 早上对迈克最合适。

From here to New York is not very far. (= It's not very far from here to New York.) 从这里去纽约并不远。

Today's Lei's birthday. 今天是蕾的生日。

Because Grace wants to leave doesn't mean that I have to. 只因为格蕾丝想走并不意味着我也得走。